COACHING

Becoming a Successful Athletic Coach

Third Edition

WILLIAM F. STIER, JR.

**College at Brockport
State University of New York**

American Press
Boston, Massachusetts 02109
www.americanpresspublishers.com

COVER PHOTO CREDITS:

Photo #1: Courtesy of the University of Southern California (USC)

Photo #2: Courtesy of the National Association of Intercollegiate Athletics (NAIA)

Photo #3: Courtesy of the University of Nebraska at Omaha (Photo by Tim Fitzgerald)

Photo #4: Courtesy of Western Illinois University Visual Production Center

Photo #5: Courtesy of Western Illinois University Visual Production Center

Photo #6: Courtesy of Texas Tech University Sports Information

Photo #7: Courtesy of the College at Brockport, State University of New York
       (Photo by James Dusen)

DEDICATION

to my wife, Veronica Ann

and our loving family members

Missy Ann
Barbara Ann
Lori Ann
Reba Ann
Eryn
Mary JoAnn
Lucy Ann
Samantha Ann
Katie Lee
Joshua
Jessica Bree
Michael II
Jackson William
Dalton
Daphne
Dalhia JoAnn
Alycia
Mark
Michael
Patrick
Will III
Mic

for loving encouragement and continuing support.

ACKNOWLEDGMENTS

I wish to acknowledge the contributions which my wife, Veronica, and our extended family made to the completion of this book. To Veronica, who sacrificed much during the years it took to research and write this third edition and whose ever-present support and loving encouragement provided the motivation for its completion, I thank you from the bottom of my heart.

Appreciation is also given to the countless coaches, staff members and athletes with whom I have worked during my twenty-plus years as a coach and athletic director on the junior high, high school and collegiate/university levels. In particular, to Dr. Leo Kilfoy (St. Ambrose University), adviser, teacher/coach, role model, mentor and friend; and to Robert Davidshofer, (Cascade High School, Iowa), a most devoted friend and former assistant coach—I also dedicate this book.

I wish to express appreciation to my undergraduate and graduate students in my recent *Coaching Sports* classes and *Problems in Coaching* classes in which I field-tested portions of this manuscript during the years since the last edition. And, to all the institutions, sport teams, and organizations which shared the photographs that are included within this book, I thank you very much. Special mention should be given to several well-known coaches who served as role models for the author during the author's own coaching career, specifically, John Wooden of UCLA; Bear Bryant of Alabama; Pat Summit of the University of Tennessee, Joe Paterno of Penn State; and, Mike Krzyzewski of Duke University

And, finally, to Marci Taylor, editor at American Press, whose assistance and guidance throughout this project proved to be invaluable, much thanks and appreciation is due.

PREFACE

INTRODUCTION

This is the third edition of the popular book about coaching, the coaching of sports teams, which was originally titled *Successful Coaching: Strategies and Tactics*—and published in 1995. The third edition has some significant changes and improvements. These include the addition of numerous **new concepts** (for a total of 452). This third edition has updated and expanded information applicable for the current coaching scene. This information includes additional insights into the challenges facing coaches in today's ever changing and problematic environment in the 21st century. In addition, questions at the end of each chapter have been revamped where necessary to reflect current and relevant topics. And, finally, there are new research orientated questions at the end of each chapter which ask the reader to conduct surveys, interviews and conduct library research in an effort to find additional information, trends, and data on a variety of relevant sport and coaching topics.

The book was written from a very practical perspective to provide you, the would-be or current coach, with a realistic insight into the world of coaching amateur sports in the 21st century. The information, suggestions and recommendations presented are based on sound theoretical constructs coupled with the practical experience of the author who was a highly successful junior high, senior high and college coach and athletic director for almost 25 years. The information contained in this book is applicable at all levels of sport competition including youth sports, junior and senior high school teams, as well as the college or university level.

THE SCOPE OF THE BOOK

This book is written for current and future coaches irrespective of the sport or sports coached. This is not a "how to" book in coaching a *specific* sport such as basketball, field hockey, football, softball, or gymnastics, etc. Nor does it deal with the so-called Xs and Os of coaching a specific team or sport. Rather, the book has been written from a generic perspective, that is, the information presented is applicable for the coaching of *all* sports and at all amateur levels of competition.

THE BOOK'S OBJECTIVES

The objective of this book is to help the reader become knowledgeable in terms of what it takes to become a successful coach *and* to develop specific skills which will facilitate and significantly enhance one's competency level in coaching. In essence, this book has been written to help the reader become a more knowledgeable and skilled coach—a more effective, and efficient coach, one who understands the complexity of the varied and multiple tasks facing the modern day mentor.

Unique Features of the Book — Coaching Concepts

Presented throughout the book are 452 *Coaching Concepts*. These *Coaching Concepts* are general statements or principles that serve as guidelines for coaches in terms of very specific coaching situations. Each of these concepts or guidelines can serve as a potential focal point of decision making for the athletic coach.

These principles and guidelines can also aid the reader in developing a greater depth and breadth of knowledge relative to coaching a competitive sport. Succinctly presented, these principles involve sound coaching strategies and successful teaching tactics that are applicable for both the would-be and current mentors.

Additionally, at the end of each chapter there are two sets of questions for the reader to respond to. The first set of questions for each chapter are general questions that may be addressed from the reading of the chapter. The second set of questions for each chapter involves research questions that the reader must secure the answers to. The answers to these questions can be obtained through surveys, questioning individuals and library/WWW research efforts.

A Companion Book to be used with this Third Edition

A companion book titled: *Coaching: A Problem Solving Approach* (Second Edition), available from American Press, Boston, MA, and also written by the author, is recommended to be used in conjunction with the book you are now holding in your hands. The book *Coaching: A Problem Solving Approach* (Second Edition) introduces the reader to methods of preventing and resolving problems faced by coaches as well as a collection of 96 case studies [including questions for discussion and examination] dealing with modern day problems and pertinent challenges that face coaches in the amateur sports world. This problem-solving book enables the reader to "put into practice" some of the coaching theories, information, research and "book learning" to practical use through the examination of various problems presented through the case study approach.

The problems, presented through the 96 case studies in the *Problem Solving for Coaches* are listed below, divided into the following six categories.

CASE STUDIES INVOLVING ATHLETIC COACHES

CASE STUDIES INVOLVING ATHLETES

CONTENTS

Chapter 1

Introduction to Sports
and the Profession of Coaching

The night of the big game.

Coaching is a wonderful profession. It is exciting, rewarding and also challeng-ing. Coaching is an opportunity to help youngsters become not only better athletes, but better individuals and citizens of this great country of ours. The fact that you are thinking about becoming a coach is just great!!! The coaching profession presents many, many potential rewards for the coach and the coach's family. On the other hand, it can also provide not a few heartaches and challenges for those who find themselves being called *coach* as well as for members of their extended family and friends. This is true whether or not one is male or female or is involved as a full time or as a part-time coach. Likewise, it is true whether one is a head or an assistant coach, is coaching a youth sport team, a junior or senior high school team or a college or university squad.

As you read this book you will gain a better perspective of what coaching is all about. You will become aware of what it takes to become a successful coach at the various levels of amateur sport in this country. In reality, coaching is coaching. The major distinction coaches will find at different levels of competition is that they need to treat players differently because of the age, maturity and experience factors (Staffo, 1993). As you advance through this book you will be made aware of the need to make wise, appropriate and timely decisions—decisions that will facilitate your chances of becoming and remaining a successful coach.

A young man or woman typically begins to seriously think about becoming a coach sometime in high school or early in their collegiate career. The typical setting in which would-be coaches envision themselves coaching probably is in a junior or senior high school setting. This is not surprising because this is the level of competition which is most familiar to the future coach. However, there are other coaching opportunities the future coach should become aware of when examining the coaching profession and the job opportunities available therein. Many young people have only their athletic experience in youth sports and/or at the junior/senior high school levels upon which to base *their perceptions* of what it is like to be a coach. Sometimes their perceptions are accurate but in many instances they are not.

Future coaches must remember that they are viewing the coaching experience from their eyes, that is, from a rather narrow perspective, their own personal experience. This can be quite limited in many instances. Future coaches need to look beyond their own personal experiences in order to develop a realistic viewpoint of the world of sports and athletic coaching. Future coaches need to view sports and coaching not only from the eyes of the truly dedicated and highly motivated young athlete, but from the viewpoint of all types of athletes: those highly dedicated, motivated *and* skilled and those athletes who are not so highly dedicated, motivated and skilled.

It is important that young people who contemplate coaching on a full time or part-time basis become aware of all of the ramifications, the advantages and disadvantages of coaching as an assistant and as a head coach, at all levels of competition. In particular, it is essential that would-be coaches realize that not all of their future athletes will necessarily be as talented and conscientious as they themselves were (or think they were) as athletes.

At this point in your career, it would be advantageous to be able to specify exactly why you are considering becoming a coach. Before you read further in this book, take time to complete the two exercises at the end of this chapter which ask you to define those reasons that might motivate you to become a coach at some level and what qualities are necessary for a quality coach (A and K). Think about the reasons—at this point in time with your past experiences, current knowledge and present level of motivation, skills and competencies—that might indicate that becoming an athletic coach (full time, part-time, paid or volunteer) might be in your future.

A GLOBAL VIEW OF SPORTS

Everywhere one looks today one can find evidence that sports have indeed become big business in the United States, and the expansion and growth in popularity seemingly has no end in sight (Stier, 2006a). This is certainly true from the perspective of the attention that sports receive from the press (and the readers/viewers of the news media). One only has to note the amount of space devoted each day to the sports pages in the newspapers across this country,

Professional sports enjoy big time promotional activities.

as well as the innumerable radio broadcasts and televised contests, to come to the realization of the importance of competitive athletics and the big business of sports. One can also say that sports have become big business in terms of the large sums of money being made available to professional athletes and successful coaches of professional teams. Multi-million dollar contracts for professional athletes (and for some coaches) seem to be the norm today rather than the exception.

Elite College Coaches Join the Salary Arms Race

Even college coaches have gotten into the really big-money arena, both from their regular coaching salaries as well as from lucrative agreements with various corporations and sports related companies. An example of the large sums of money being showered upon the highly successful coaching elite at large Division l-A schools can be seen in the reported huge shoe and apparel contracts being signed with companies like Nike, Converse, Adidas, New Balance, and others. Although it has been common place for big-name coaches at Division I-A institutions (and a few coaches at other levels of competition, including high school) to sign lucrative shoe contracts with various sneaker companies since the late 1970s, in recent years we have seen such contracts reached seemingly gigantic proportions.

One early (1993) example of a big-time college coach negotiating a very lucrative contract, involving a major shoe contract, is Mike Krzyzewski, the well known basketball coach at Duke University. In the spring of 1993, the *Raleigh News and Observer* reported that Nike, the athletic-shoe manufacturer, and coach Krzyzewski, allegedly agreed to a multi-year shoe contract. The deal reportedly involved a $1-million dollar signing bonus and an estimated salary of $375,000 a year *for 15-years*, plus stock options in the Nike company (Reilly, 1993). Different figures were reported by the *Durham Herald-Sun* and included the $1-million dollar signing bonus and a $750,000 a year contract for seven years, *plus* a $75,000 annuity after the coach's retirement (Side-lines, 1993). The coaching elite, within the NCAA, Division I level, are indeed involved in the world of big money in addition to the world of high pressure, stringent demands, and often unreasonable expectations.

Prior to 1997, the National Collegiate Athletic Association (NCAA) has never actually regulated these types of contracts per se. At that time, however, a NCAA regulation was implemented that requires all such *outside employment* by NCAA Division I coaches to be approved annually, in writing, by the particular institution's president or CEO (1997-1998 NCAA Manual, 1997).

Typically, shoe and apparel contracts call for the coach to conduct clinics on behalf of the company, to advise the company on various products, and to use and endorse the company's products (as well as wear the company's apparel). In exchange, these companies often provide shoes and other apparel to the coach and the coach's team as well as pay the coach an outright sum over the length of the contract.

Big salaries for Division I coaches are not limited to so-called shoe contracts. Witness the case of Steve Spurrier and the University of Florida, which offered him (in 1997) a $12 million dollar a year contract to stay as football coach through the 2002 season. He left the University of Florida for the NFL and then onto the University of South Carolina. Another example of big bucks being earned by a coach at the elite NCAA Division I level can be seen at East Carolina University, where Steve Logan, the then 42-year-old head football coach was given a $1 million incentive in 1995 if he would remain with the university for a specific number of years. Specifically, he was to receive $500,000 if he stayed with the university for five years and another $500,000 if he remained a total of 10 years (Pirates Plan, 1995).

Coaching big-time football has proven to be a very lucrative career indeed for those select few who are very successful and who also occupy coaching positions at major football powers. Another example of an excellent pay package involved Bobby Bowden, head football coach at Florida State, who signed a contract in 1995 worth almost a million dollars (actually only $975,000) per year. This includes $150,000 from the university, $275,000 from radio and TV appearances, $225,000 from Nike Products, and $200,000 from various speeches and public appearances. The contract reportedly ran through at least the year 2000, and was subsequently renegotiated (Bowden will make, 1995). And, in 2006, the University of North Carolina hired Butch Davis as the head football coach with a seven-year contract worth $1.86 million annually. This ranked him 10th among all football coaches at the time and second in the ACC (Bell, 2006).

And take the case of coach Sabin. On January 5, 2007, (Tide's Saban returns, 2007) Nick Saban was introduced to the public as the new football coach for the Crimson Tide (University of Alabama) at a salary worth $32 million over an eight-year period.

Prior to leaving the NFL Miami Dolphins, where he was 15-17, he coached Southeastern Conference rival LSU to two SEC titles and a national championship in 2003. Before he left to coach Miami in the NFL, coach Saban signed in 2004 a seven-year deal with LSU for at least $2.3 million dollars the first year of the contract. This did not include other incentives which would have raised the annual payment to $3.4 million a year by 2010, had he stayed at LSU (Update, 2004). Even the Kansas University football coach, Mark Mangino, whose total 2005 compensation of $769,256 is not insignificant, *still ranked him dead last in his own conference (Big 12) among head football coaches* (KU football coach, 2006).

The Ohio State University pays both its football coach (Jim Tressel—a member of the $2 Million Club) and basketball coach (Thad Matta a member of the $1.5 Million Club) very well. In 2006 Coach Tressel earned $2.5 million while Thad Matta garnered $1.9 million in 2006 (OSU: The place where, 2006). For Jim Tressel this included a base salary of $450,000 in 2006-2007 and $600,000 in 2012-13. He also received $953,000 in 2006-2007 as public relations and apparel (Nike) compensation. In 2012-13 the PR and apparel compensation will be $1,525,000. The total projected compensation for remaining years of his contract is $17.4 million. Thad Matta's base salary in 2006-07 was $245,000; in 2011-12 it will be $390,000. His 2006-07 PR, apparel and camp compensation is $645,000 and in 2011-12 it is scheduled to be $950,000. The total compensation for the remaining six years of his contract is $9.2 million (Ohio State, 2006). Other examples of coaches who have hit the stratosphere in terms of annual salary and benefits include the University of Southern California's Pete Carroll who was reported to have earned slightly less than $3-million in 2006 while Charlie Weis (Notre Dame) garnered something between $2 and $3 million.

Basketball coaches have also joined the salary race. For example, Jim Boeheim, Syracuse University, earned a total of $838,276 (including $728,821 in base salary and $109,455 from contributions to an employee benefit plan and deferred compensation in 2004. This *does not include* other, so-called outside income, money from such sources as camps, his Nike shoe contract and other endorsements (Associated Press, 2004).

Other basketball coaches have also inked lucrative financial packages. Witness the signing of Steve Alford who inked a $975,000 compensation package which included a $210,000 salary at New Mexico in 2007 (Out with old, 2007). Coach Billy Gillispie left the state of Texas (Texas A & M) for Kentucky and signed a $1.9 million (guaranteed) annual contract that also included a potential $400, 000 in incentives for a possible annual income of some $2.3 million. In addition, his seven-year contract with Kentucky increases by $75,000 each year. And, the man he replaced, Tubby Smith, could earn an annual income of $3.1 million, which includes a $1.7 million guaranteed salary coupled with $1.4 more in additional incentives at the University of Minnesota (Coach salaries, 2007).

If one looks at the 2006 NCAA Elite Eight teams and the salaries of the head coaches one can see that six of the eight coaches were awarded significant raises, the average increase at the five public institutions averaged $332,000 each. In 2006, *USA Today* reported that the average basketball coach's annual salary of 58 of the 65 schools in the NCAA basketball tournament was almost $800,000. And, a survey of the NCAA D-1 Athletic Director's Association revealed that there were at least two dozen millionaire basketball coaches in 2006, while in 2001 there were only two.

Finally, the list below illustrates the annual pay (excluding bonuses) of the top 15 men's basketball coaches of the 65 schools that participated in the 2006 NCAA basketball tournament (FB coaches, 2007).

Top 15 Men's Basketball Coaches

	($ Million)
Rick Barnes, Texas	1.809
Tom Izzo, Michigan St.	1.795
Tom Crean, Marquette	1.688
Bill Self, Kansas	1.636
Jim Calhoun, UConn	1.500
Roy Williams, UNC	1.424
Lute Olson, Arizona	1.421
Billy Donovan, Florida	1.389
John Calipari, Memphis	1.327
Ben Howland, UCLA	1.312
Steve Alford, Iowa	1.270
Mike Krzyzewski, Duke	1.263
Billy Gillespie, Texas A&M	1.250
Bruce Pearl, Tennessee	1.124
Kelvin Sampson, Indiana	1.100

And, look at the reported *2007 coaching salaries of the highest paid basketball mentors in this country,* below (Coach salaries, 2007). In terms of profits for the basketball programs, the Department of Education (DOE) revealed that the average NCAA Division I men's basketball program made *a $1.7 million profit* during the 2005-06 academic year.

Men's Basketball Coaches Pay for 2007-08

Billy Gillispie, University of Kentucky
• Guaranteed: $2.3 million
• Incentives: up to $850,000

Tubby Smith, University of Minnesota
- Guaranteed: $1.75 million
- Incentives: $1.425 million

Rick Pitino, University of Louisville
- Guaranteed: $1.65 million
- Incentives: $575,000
- Retention bonus payable July 1: $1 million

Tom Izzo, Michigan State University
- Guaranteed: $1.61 million
- Incentives: about $100,000

Billy Donovan, University of Florida
- Guaranteed: $1.39 million
- Incentives: about $360,000
- Retention bonus payable in July: $300,000
- Note: Donovan was expected to renegotiate his contract following the 2007 national championship title

Bill Self, University of Kansas
- Guaranteed: about $1.15 million
- Incentives: $325,000

Bruce Pearl, University of Tennessee
- Guaranteed: $800,000
- Incentives: $72,000

To many, both inside and outside the coaching ranks, such sizable contracts or agreements between selected coaches and these corporations have become almost unconscionable. It is obvious that college coaching has become BIG BUSINESS (Staff and Wire Reports, 2004). Said C.M. Newton, former coach at Alabama and Vanderbilt, and an 11-year AD at the University of Kentucky: "I don't know the answer. You can't regulate it, and you wouldn't want to. You'd hope that people would prioritize it correctly, but we're a sports culture that puts a greater value on winning basketball games, sometimes, than we do on education" (FB coaches, 2007).

Woman Basketball Coaches Join the Salary Arms Race

Women who coach at the elite NCAA Division I level have also signed for bigger financial packages in recent years, although usually not at the level of their male counter parts. One coach who, in 1995, was successful in securing a comparable financial package was Patricia (Pat) Summitt, head women's coach at the University of Tennessee. Pat was given a contract extension in 1995 (through the 2000-2001 season) for an annual salary of $125,000 in base salary. With the signing of this contract she received the largest base salary of any University of Tennessee coach. Her total compensation was worth around $233,800 (Basketball, 1995).

And, in 1997 she received a raise to $390,000 a year with a new five-year contract. In 2007, the University of Michigan's women's basketball coach, Joanne McCallie, received a big salary boost, effective July 1st, to $500,000 annually (as part of a five-year contract), which with incentives, the total compensation could reach $643,000. Also, in 2007, the University of Texas hired women's coach Gail Goestenkors away from Duke with a huge annual compensation package of $1 million annually, which includes a base salary of $337,500 (Killian, 2007). Reportedly, Baylor University paid Kim Mulkey even more to become its head coach of women's basketball in 2007.

Sports are also big business from the perspective of the amount of money spent on sports and sports paraphernalia. The number of people who are active participants in *individual competitive and recreational sports* is growing at a rapid pace—witness the billions of dollars spent each year in such involvement and participation (Heliter, 1992).

Americans in general are great lovers of sports both as spectators and as participants. From the earliest times of organized sports in this country individuals, both the young and the not so young, have banded together in an effort to partake in and to view competitive physical activities. Actual participation in sports-related activities continues to play an important role in the lives of many people of all ages in this country, not just among the young. It is currently estimated that over 250 million Americans participate in at least one sports-related activity on a somewhat frequent or regular basis. This is a significant increase over what was estimated in 1990 (180 million) and as well as the 162.6 million participants that was reported in 1987 (Lincoln, 1992).

In terms of youths under the age of 18 participating in organized sports, over 50 million young people participated in some type of organized sports during 2008 (New National Coaching Report, 2008). Table 1.1 illustrates the changes in sport participation in terms of participation by individuals ages 7 and older according to the National Sporting Goods Association, Mt. Prospect IL. There was reported (11-4-08) that 2008-2009 saw some 7 million high school athletes participating in interscholastic sports nationwide (New Study-Based Handbook. 2008).

Table 1.1: 2006 versus 2001 Ranked by Percentage Change Participation more than once (in millions) seven (7) years of age and older. Ranking is by percent change

Sport	2006	2001	Percent Change
Total U.S.	263.1	251.0	4.8%
Football (tackle)	11.9	8.2	45.0%
Weight Lifting	32.9	23.9	37.6%
Hockey (ice)	2.6	2.2	18.2%
Wrestling	3.8	3.5	8.5%
Swimming	56.5	54.8	3.1%
Soccer	14.0	13.9	1.0%
Baseball	14.6	14.9	-1.5%
Basketball	26.7	28.1	-4.9%
Tennis	10.4	10.9	-5.1%
Softball	12.4	13.2	-5.8%
Volleyball	11.1	12.0	-8.0%
Golf	24.4	26.6	-8.3%

Obtained from: National Sporting Goods Association, Mt. Prospect, Illinois (2006)

Table 1.2 shows a ten-year history of sports participation (by individuals seven years of age or older) as revealed by the National Sporting Goods Association.

Table 1.2: Ten-Year History of Selected Sports Participation
Participated more than once (in millions)
by individuals seven (7) years of age and older

Sport	2006	2004	2002	2000	1998	1996
Baseball	14.6	15.9	15.6	15.6	15.9	14.8
Basketball	26.7	27.8	28.9	27.1	29.4	31.8
Football (tackle)	11.9	8.6	7.8	7.5	7.4	9.0
Golf	24.4	24.5	27.1	26.4	27.5	23.1
Hockey (ice)	2.6	2.4	2.1	1.9	2.1	2.1
Running/Jogging	28.8	26.7	24.7	22.8	22.5	22.2
Soccer	14.0	13.3	13.7	12.9	13.2	13.9
Softball	12.4	12.5	13.6	14.0	15.6	19.9
Swimming	56.5	53.4	53.1	60.7	58.2	60.2
Tennis	10.4	9.6	11.0	10.0	11.2	11.5
Volleyball	11.1	11.8	11.5	12.3	14.8	18.5
Wrestling	3.8	na	na	na	na	na

Obtained from: National Sporting Goods Association, Mt. Prospect, Illinois (2006)

Youth Sports Participation

It is estimated that youth sports provide opportunities for some 25 million youngsters, both boys and girls, to participate in a competitive athletic environment under the watchful eyes of almost 3.5 million coaches and administrators *outside of a school setting* (Stier, 2006a). More than 54% of youngsters in the United States participated in organized sports at the turn of the century. Obviously the youth sport movement is extensive in the United States. Youth sports can involve young people as early as 8 years of age and as old as 16 or 17. These youngsters are typically coached by *volunteers* from the local community, sometimes parents and frequently just interested adults. These coaches become involved in sports for any number of reasons, some more legitimate than others.

One example of a youth sport program is baseball's Little League. The organization was founded in 1939 by Mr. Carl Stotz (Little League, September 19, 1992). The game is played in six innings and on a smaller field in an effort to accommodate the younger players. Little League Baseball competition was initiated upon the concepts of fair play, participation, sportsmanship, teamwork and cooperation. With teams in some 60± countries sponsoring competition for 2.5 million players under the supervision of over 750,000 volunteers, Little League Baseball has become one of the largest and most successful youth sport programs in the world.

Table 1.3 depicts the growth of youth sport participation in this the United States between the years 1997 and 2006.

Table 1.3: 2006 Youth Participation [more than once (in thousands] in Selected Sports by individuals seven (7) years of age and older—Comparisons of 2006 Participation to participation in 1997

	Year	Total	Change vs 1997	Total 7-11	Change vs 1997	Total 12-17	Change vs 1997
Total U.S.	1997	240,325		19,466		23,071	
Total U.S.	2006	263,138	9.5%	19,472	0.0%	25,261	9.5%
Sport							
Baseball							
Baseball	1997	14,146		4,739		3,678	
Baseball	2006	14,646	3.5%	3,691	-22.1%	3,910	6.3%
Basketball							
Basketball	1997	30,660		6,837		7,880	
Basketball	2006	26,735	-12.8%	5,427	-20.6%	7,218	-8.4%

Football (Tackle)							
Football (Tackle)	1997	8,219		1,841		2,983	
Football (Tackle)	2006	11,888	44.6%	2,199	19.5%	4,149	39.1%
Ice Hockey							
Ice Hockey	1997	1,925		304		406	
Ice Hockey	2006	2,559	32.9%	430	41.3%	335	-17.5%
Soccer							
Soccer	1997	13,651		5,624		4,109	
Soccer	2006	14,024	2.7%	4,796	-14.7%	4,095	-0.3%
Softball							
Softball	1997	16,339		2,385		3,431	
Softball	2006	12,442	-23.9%	2,339	-1.9%	2,824	-17.7%
Tennis							
Tennis	1997	11,106		1,022		1,766	
Tennis	2006	10,356	-6.8%	787	-23.0%	2,216	25.5%
Volleyball							
Volleyball	1997	17,836		1,801		4,869	
Volleyball	2006	11,062	-38.0%	1,095	-39.2%	3,971	-18.4%

SOURCE: National Sporting Goods Association, Mt. Prospect Illinois 60056 (2007)

High School Sports Participation

On the high school level, almost one of every two students participated, on an annual basis during 1991 and continuing in 2006, in interscholastic sports (Olson, 1992; NSGA research reports, 2007). The all-time high (prior to 2007) in interscholastic sports participation was in excess of 6,450,482 during the 1977-1978 academic year. The number of boys and girls partaking of high school sports six years later, during 1983-84, declined to just over 5 million (Hiestand, 1992). During 1986-1987 slightly more than 5.2 million boys and girls played on interscholastic athletic teams (High School, 1987). Three years later, in 1990-1991, the figure increased to 5,298,671 million athletes. This number increased slightly during the next school year (1991-1992) to a total of 5,370,654 male and female participants in high school competitive sports teams (Still Popular, 1992). This is an increase of some 71,983 from the previous year. This number included 3,429,853 boys and 1,940,801 girls. These figures represented the highest participation by boys since 1980-1981 and the second highest ever for girls (Participation, 1992).

For 2002 the National Federation of State High School Associations revealed that more than 6.8 million high school students played school sports (this is 55.4% of all secondary school students) (Glenn, 2003). These athletes were coached by some one-half million high school coaches (Brylinski, 2002).

A national study (2006-07 High School Athletics Participation Survey), conducted by the National Federation of State High School Associations (NFHS), and reported in 2007, revealed high school sports participation increased significantly over the past year. In fact, there was an increase of some 183,006 students participating in high school athletics during the 2006-2007 academic year over the previous year (Retrieved 9-10-08, NSGA Research Newsletter, www.nsga.org).

The study indicated that the total number of high school students involved in school sports in 2006-2007 totaled 7,342,910 youngsters. It is interesting to note that there has been an increase in participation in high school sports for 18 straight years. The increase for 2006-2007 proved to be greatest single year increase since the 1995-1996 academic year, when there was a whopping increase of 225,168 youngsters over the previous school year. Participation by boys (4,321,103) in 2006-2007 was the highest since 1977-1978 when the figure was 4,367,442.

It is important to note that the participation by girls was more than three million (3,021,807), the first time that this number was reached (Retrieved 9-10-08, NSGA Research Newsletter, www.nsga.org). However, Sylwester (2004) revealed that athletic involvement of high school girls in state sponsored sports had reached a plateau in 2003-04, In fact, less than 34% of secondary school girls took part in state-sponsored sports over the previous six years.

In terms of specific sports, football continued to be the most popular interscholastic sport in 1992 with some 912,845 participants. During 2006-2007 football continued to have the greatest number of participants with some 1,104,548 participants. During that same year, the number of participants in boys' high school sports included: basketball (556,269), outdoor track and field (544,180), baseball (477,430), soccer (377,999), wrestling (257,246), cross country (216,085), golf (159,747), tennis (56,944), and swimming and diving (1-6,738), 156,944), and swimming and diving (106,738).

In 1991, Basketball was the second most popular sport that year for boys and the most popular sport for girls. However, soccer had an increase for both boys and for girls. Boys' participation in soccer almost doubled from 132,000 to 236,082 in the 13 years between 1979 and 1991. During the same time period, girls' participation increased almost six fold from 23,479 to a total of 135,302. In fact, soccer for boys surpassed wrestling as the fifth most popular sport at the high school level. For girls, soccer was the 6th most popular sport at the secondary school level (Participation, 1992).

In 1991, the five states with the greatest number of participants in high school sports were Texas (479,750), California (461,794), New York (291,591), Ohio (274,224) and Michigan (262,453) (Still Popular, 1992). In 2006, the top ten states in terms of the rankings included: Texas 763,967, California (735,497), New York (350,349), Illinois (334,358), Michigan (321,400), Ohio (315,473), Pennsylvania (276,911), New Jersey (247,332), Florida (230,312) and Minnesota (220,241).

There are many recognized benefits and advantages of high school athletic participation. Some of these include better academic grades, coursework selection, homework accomplished, educational aspirations, parental and occupational aspirations, college enrollment and highest educational level achievement as well as enhanced identify with the school and school related activities (Ishee, 2004).

The thrill of competition.

OPPORTUNITIES FOR PARTICIPATION IN COLLEGE SPORTS

Todd Holcomb wrote an interesting column on 5-19-07 which appeared in the Atlanta Journal-Constitution which is herein summarized. Many people would anticipate that 360,000 is a large number, a really BIG number. This 360,000 represents the number of student-athletes participating in NCAA sports. However, the NCAA actually revealed that total number of participating athletes as of May 2008 was 402,000. If you consider (and add) an additional several thousand athletes from NAIA schools, plus junior and community colleges as well as Christian colleges, etc. the total number of college athletes is closer to 450,000.

Although 450,000 seems like a staggering number, and many parents might be led to believe that this means that it might be easier to actually become a college athlete—they would be wrong in such an assumption. In reality, it is not easy to become a college athlete. In reality, although the odds vary by sport, by gender and by division, no sport at any level is easy. It's just that some sports are *really* hard to make and some are just regular hard.

Following are some various probabilities associated making the jump from high school sports to college sports for many of the men's and women's sports. These stats use participation statistics from the NCAA, the NAIA and the National Federation of State High School Associations, comparing the number of high school participants in a given sport compared to participants in college programs (this does not reflect the number of scholarships available):

Men's Sports	Women's Sports
Lacrosse, 8-1	Lacrosse, 8-1
Swimming, 13-1	Soccer, 13-1
Baseball, 14-1	Swimming, 13-1
Soccer, 15-1	Gymnastics, 14-1
Football, 16-1	Golf, 14-1
Golf, 17-1	Tennis, 18-1
Tennis, 18-1	Softball, 19-1
Track and field, 24-1	Track and field, 21-1
Basketball, 27-1	Volleyball, 23-1
Wrestling, 37-1	Basketball, 25-1

Note: 8-1 means there are eight high school athletes for every one-college athlete in this sport. Method: Participation rates in high school to participation at four-year colleges. Sources: NCAA, NAIA, National Federation of State High School Associations.

The Clips Research Department (College Athletic Clips) researched the website of the National Federation of State High School Associations and uncovered the following facts and statistics concerning participation at high schools across the US in the 2005-2006 academic year:

- Total US high school athletics participation: 7,159,904 (boys-4,210,000; girls-2,950,000).

- Football: 1,072,948 (including 1534 girls).

- Most of the 1million plus difference between boys and girls participation is accounted for by football.

- Basketball (boys' and girls'): 999,264.

- Outdoor track (boys' and girls'): 973,185.

- Soccer (boys' and girls'): 680,490.

From these figures, one can surmise that as many as 1,790,000 high school senior athletes (7.159 million total HS athletes divided by 4) were potentially competing for the 100,000 openings created in college sports as college seniors moved on (400,000 total athletes divided by 4).

With only 100,000 spots for 1,790,000 potential candidates it is easy to see that these are indeed challenges odds facing high school athletes who desire to continue their athletic participation, especially on scholarship status in so-called flagship sports. This does not mean that it is impossible, merely that it is indeed a challenge facing most young athletes, male and female.

Collegiate Sports Participation

Certainly at the major colleges and universities, sports are viewed as big business. Altogether, there are more than 3,400 two and four-year colleges and universities in this country. Most of these schools offer competitive intercollegiate athletic opportunities for their full time students. There were over 500,000 college and university students participating in competitive athletics at the college and university level during the 2008-2009 academic year. And, the number continues to expand for both men and women. The total amount of money involved with college athletics at all levels in this country seems staggering to most people.

Intensity is one of the keys to successful coaching.

Let's just look at the financial picture involving the sports of football and basketball at the NCAA, Division I level. The ten most successful big-time college sports programs (income wise) routinely have athletic revenues in excess of $70 million dollars (http://www.collegeathleticsclips.com/s/375/index.aspx?sid=375&gid=1&pgid=15&cid=292&newsid=822 retrieved 3-6-07). In terms of the sport of football, there are 18 so-called major bowl games. These major bowls pay out millions of dollars to participating teams. And, in the sport of basketball, in 1991 the National Collegiate Athletic Association (NCAA) negotiated a $1-billion (that is billion, not million) seven-year television contract or package (extending through 1998) with the Columbia Broadcasting Service (CBS) to televise future Division I basketball tournaments. This agreement also gave CBS the rights to televise 15 other NCAA championships during this same time period (Woods, 1993). However, in 2008, the NCAA was in negotiation with CBS for an astounding 6-billion, 11-year media contract (http://www.msnbc.msn.com/id/23924037/ retrieved 3-15-08). In terms of overall athletic budgets one is speaking of $80 million and above for the top Division

I institutions. Table 1.4 shows the total revenues of these top athletic revenue producing athletic programs.

Table 1.4: Total Revenues in 2006-2007 (in millions of dollars)

The Ohio State	$109.4
University of Florida	107.8
University of Texas	105.0
University of Tennessee	95.4
University of Michigan	89.1
University of Notre Dame	83.6
University of Wisconsin	82.6
University of Alabama	81.9
Auburn University	81.7
University of Iowa	80.2

Big Money to Be Earned at the NCAA Final Four

FINAL FOUR

A trip to the NCAA Final Four in basketball is worth millions to the participating schools. Universities' athletic coffers are enriched from television money to the tune of millions of dollars. In the Final Four basketball men's competition, each of the teams earns multi-millions of dollars each. *However, each of the 64 men's teams that qualified for the Division I playoffs were rewarded with more than $300,000 merely for the feat of being selected by the NCAA to participate in the tournament.* Today, basketball at the NCAA, Division I level is truly big time, big time both financially and big time news-wise.

In terms of total income, the NCAA receives millions of dollars in gross revenues as a direct result of the Final Four tournament. However, this was not always the case. The birth of the big-time basketball business on the college level had a far more humble beginning. It started during 1939 when the National Association of Basketball Coaches (NABC) initiated an eight-team, unofficial basketball championship to compete with the then year-old National Invitational Tournament (NIT). Initially, it was not very profitable. In fact, the turnout was so meager that the NABC relinquished control of the tournament and the NCAA assumed responsibility for it thereafter. The financial growth of this tournament was rather modest throughout the next few decades. Even some thirty-five years ago, 1972 to be exact, the Final Four grossed a mere $2-million dollars or so. However, between 1972 and the present time the growth and financial bonanza have been phenomenal to say the least.

Thus, today, the NCAA Final Four extravaganza and the major football bowls are prime examples of the big business impact of amateur, competitive sports. With this kind of money involved in just these two flagship sports at the Division I level, it is easy to assume, and correctly so, that the world of athletic competition at this level is indeed a (big) business with all of the risks, perils as well as the potential rewards and problems that would exist in the business world.

Financial Endowments at the College Level

In an effort to deal with the tremendous costs of fielding intercollegiate sports, some institutions have started to solicit funds for the creation of endowments for coaching chairs and/or scholarships for athletes. Don Winston, senior associate director of athletics at the University of Southern California, initiated in 1985 an endowment program, by position, for the USC football team. Funds were solicited for an endowment, the interest from which went to pay for the athletic scholarships, by specific positions, that is, quarterback, punter, tackle, tight end, fullback, etc. By 1993, the University had successfully funded 38 of the then permissible 85 football scholarships through such position endowments (Donald Winston, personal communication, August 22, 1997).

Stanford University, one of the leaders in athletic endowments, had a total athletic endowment of some 56 million dollars in the fall of 1993. From this amount, the athletic department was able to realize some $3-million to $3.5-million dollars each year to pay for 120 full scholarships for athletes (Susan Simoni Burk, personal communication, August 24, 1993). Stanford also has the head baseball and the head football coaching positions (salary) endowed.

A Yale University graduate, Joel E. Smilow, donated $1-million to endow his alma mater's head football coaching position. Smilow is president of Playtex, Inc. Cornell University established an endowment for its head football coaching position in 1982. The head football coaching position was also endowed at the University of Texas ($1M donation, 1984). Today, there are many Division I athletic programs that have followed these school into the endowment race.

Even Division III institutions have become involved in establishing endowments for their athletic programs. For example, the University of Rochester (New York) had a $1-million dollar gift pledged in 1984 from a former student athlete to help perpetually fund (endow) the head football coaching position. The interest from this endowment was to be used to provide needed funds for other football related expenses on an annual basis (Bilovsky, 1984; Jeff Vennell, personal communication, August 19, 1997).

POSSESSING A REALISTIC VIEW [OR PERSPECTIVE] OF SPORTS

Baron Pierre de Coubertin, founder of the modern Olympic Games, is credited with an excellent statement regarding amateur sport competition that remains appropriate to this day for youth, scholastic and college sports. This statement is the Olympic Creed, which follows.

> "The most important thing in the Olympic Games is not to win but to take part, just ask the most important thing in life is not the triumph but the struggle. The main issue in life is not the victory but the fight. The essential thing is not to have conquered but to have fought well."

One of the implications of the above statement is that sports continue to permeate our society. Simply put, sports are big. They are important in our society. One of the first sections of any newspaper read in the morning is arguably the sports page. To many people this seems natural and logical since the world of sports is taken quite seriously, both by participants and spectators. This includes all levels of competition from youth sports through high school and the college levels and, of course, the professional ranks.

Outside Pressures

The aggrandized importance placed upon successful sport participation and competition by many in our society—*by athletes, by parents, by the general public, by the media, by advertisers, by school administrators, and by coaches themselves*—creates challenges and problems, as well as opportunities, for the coaching practitioner. This is true whether or not the individual is a part-time or full time coach. It is also true whether one receives remuneration for coaching or volunteers one's time and services. Successful (winning) sports programs, such as football, can create great pressures that emanate from sport fanatics within the community, the school, and among athletes, parents and even the coaches themselves, for continued success on the proverbial playing field. For example, the Berwick, Pennsylvania football team, the Bulldogs in the 1990s, attracted more than 10,000 fans at every home football game. However, the population of Berwick is a mere 10,976. Nevertheless, this fervent support of the football team at this high school might be easily explained by the fact that at one time the Bulldogs had won 232 times and 14 championships in the previous 23 years (Football factory, 1994).

There indeed can be significant pressures and stresses placed upon an individual who assumes the role and extensive responsibilities of a coach, regardless of the level of competition. The tasks involved in coaching athletes are sufficiently complicated, challenging and difficult in and by themselves. When exacerbated by outside influences, the coaching process can become that much more Herculean and burdensome.

The competent coach needs to be fully aware of these challenges and problems inherent in the coaching process. Additionally, would-be coaches must be capable of meeting these challenges and problems in an acceptable and timely fashion. That is the purpose of this book, that is, to provide the would-be coach as well as the current coach with an accurate insight into the world of coaching at the amateur level of sport and to provide sufficient information and data with which to make informed and insightful decisions. For, in the final analysis, it is this ability to make informed decisions, decisions that are appropriate, timely and effective, that differentiates the successful coach from the unsuccessful coach or the outright charlatan or impostor.

CHALLENGING QUESTIONS FACING SPORTS TODAY

Being actively involved in sport and athletic competition, it is important to understand and to be capable of delineating the purposes of sport and the potential value of sport participation. Coaches should be capable of answering such questions as:

1. Why should there be opportunities for amateur sport participation and competition in our schools?
2. How does one justify youth sports?
3. Are sports worth the money they cost?
4. Does society in general and the local community in particular benefit from the existence of sports?
5. Are there real values and tangible benefits (immediate or long range) inherent for those involved with sports in a competitive environment? What are they?
6. Is there any guarantee that these values or benefits can be realized by the participants or society? Why or why not?
7. How can one take advantage of these values and benefits supposedly inherent in sport participation and athletic competition?
8. What are the downside risks, if any, in providing sport competition at various levels—both in and outside of the school setting?
9. Are sports in schools suppose to meet the need for entertainment for students and members of the community?
10. What are the qualities of a successful coach?

GOALS OF THE ATHLETIC PROGRAM IN SCHOOLS

Sports within a school setting should be an integral part of and contribute to the educational mission of the school. Ideally, school athletic programs should not exist primarily for the singular purpose of winning games, that is, providing the school and the community with a winning team or athletic program. In fact, winning, in and of itself, is only a secondary by-product to the overriding primary purpose of the athletic program, that is, the education of the participants through the vehicle of competitive athletics.

It really shouldn't matter if there are large, capacity crowds present at an athletic contest. Rather, what takes place within the athletic experience, on the court or field or in the pool, in terms of the individual student-athlete, is what really is important when all is said and done.

However, in the real world, it does indeed make a difference whether or not a particular athletic contest has a substantial crowd to some people, to the parents, some segments of the community, some administrators, the athletes and the coaching staff. Yes, "sports can ignite school spirit and serve as a glue for communities" (Roberts, 1991, p. 8-C). However, the presence or absence of a crowd, in and of itself, is a peripheral factor in the larger academic and athletic scheme of things within the scholastic sports scene.

COACHING CONCEPT #1:   **The focus of athletics should remain on the participants.**

It is important for coaches, parents and the general public to remember that the primary focus of the athletic experience should remain on the athletes themselves. In reality, the sports experience that is provided is for them, the individual athletes. When this fails to happen and the emphasis shifts to the all too common win-win syndrome or the focus moves to an outside booster faction or entity—coaches all too frequently find themselves on very thin ice and in an untenable position, a position over which they have no control. Coaches need to be alert to the dangers of positioning themselves where they can be unduly influenced or manipulated by negative or destructive outside forces.

NEGATIVE OR DOWNSIDE ASPECTS OF SPORT PARTICIPATION

Athletic participation does not guarantee the development of moral values for athletes. Sports of and by themselves are neutral. However, sports and the activities and events associated with the athletic scene have the potential to be betrayed, misused and abused—and even perverted. Being involved in sports can negatively affect behavior just as it can affect behavior in a positive fashion. There is no guarantee that athletic participation will result in the development of moral values for the athletes. Numerous examples are evident at all levels of amateur sports where individuals have succumbed to temptation resulting in the corruption and perversion of athletes, coaches, school administrators, public officials, fans (fanatics), and segments of the general public. Witness the infamous scandals associated with Southern Methodist University, Auburn University, Clemson University, Tulane University, Tulsa University and even Little League Baseball (27 Institutions, 1993; Little League Scandal, 1992). Secondary schools are not immune either. Witness the situation in 2007 at Canandaigua, New York. In the high school in that community the head wrestling coach was removed from his coaching position (while keeping his teaching post at the middle school level) after the police charged him with two counts of second degree harassment, one count of disorderly conduct and one count of endangering the welfare of a student (former wrestler)—stemming from three separate incidents during the school year (Goodman, 2007).

The world of sport has the potential to bring into being all sorts of improper, inappropriate and corrupt behavior on behalf of those who are associated with sports and those who crave such association. Some athletes cheat, lie and exhibit the worse type of unethical, dishonest and despicable behavior. Some coaches cheat, lie and exhibit the worse type of unethical, dishonest and despicable behavior. Some sports administrators cheat, lie and exhibit the worse type of unethical, dishonest and despicable behavior. And, some boosters and supporters cheat, lie and exhibit the worse type of unethical, dishonest and despicable behavior.

For example, on July 5, 2000, a parent, Thomas Junta (6'2" and 275 pounds), was charged with physically beating another parent (5' 11", 175-pound Michael Costin) *to death* following an ice hockey practice (Hockey dispute, 2000). In Swiftwater, Pennsylvania, police had to stop a brawl in October of 1999 after some 50 parents and players were involved in a physical confrontation at a football game for 11-13 year old youngsters. And, following a hockey game involving 11 to 12 year olds in Staten Island, New York, a parent (Matteo Picca) struck his son's coach (Lou Aiani) in the face with two hockey sticks. In April 1999, in Sacramento, California, a manager of a little League game who was coaching his own son beat up the manager of the opposing team. In Eastlake, Ohio, a father of a youngster playing soccer struck (punched) a 14-year old youngster who had contested the ball with the assailant's own 14-year old son (both youngsters were ejected). And, in Hollywood, Florida, July 12, 2000, a youth baseball coach broke the umpire's jaw following a hit to the face during a Police Athletic League contest for secondary school athletes (Out of control, 2000).

Or, take the case of the father (Dentist—Dr. Stephen Cito) of a high school football player who altered his son's headgears by filing down (sharpening) the buckle thereby injuring five of the opposing young athletes, one being sent to the emergency room of the local hospital (Father claims, 1996; Kids, its just a game, 1996). Also, in New Mexico, a high school football player (Gilbert Jefferson) struck a referee (Allen Bainter) and knocked him unconscious. This happened after Jefferson was kicked out of the game by the official (Foul Play, 1996; Piling on, 1996). And, both parents of a high school basketball player were accused of swinging at the official because the mother indicated: "I wanted to go down and tell the ref how I thought he did, that it was probably one of the most poorly officiated games I've ever seen" (Parents attack ref, 1998, p. 3-C).

Jon Saraceno, of the USA TODAY, cites numerous examples of lack of sportsmanship and violence that is prevalent in sports in our society. He cites the situation in which:

> " . . . a 10-year old boy is allegedly given $2 to throw a baseball at a batter. A father races out of the stands and slugs a 15-year-old soccer player in the mouths. Sheriff Deputies escort hockey referees to their cars after the officials are threatened by fans. A football coach lands in the hospital after arguing with another coach. A soccer mom accosts a teenage referee. A father sues the coach of his son's baseball team for—are you sitting down—not winning enough games" (Saraceno, 2002, p. 3-C).

Is it any wonder that some athletes fail to learn much of anything that is positive from their sport involvement? Or, that the causes of some of the problems are parents and the athletes themselves?

The general public has been somewhat divided on the value, if any, of competitive amateur sports and sports participation. A national survey of sports fans indicated that they felt that sport participation, even on the high school level, is *overemphasized* and *distracts from studies* (42% of the respondents), *causes too much adulation* to be placed on athletes (36%) and that *too many injuries* (22%) result from sport participation (Jegels, 1991). Many people, in and out of schools and sports, feel that there has been a trend for sports in general, not just sports at the interscholastic level, to be overemphasized. In fact, Eskenazi (1989) wrote a scathing critique on the increasingly commercialized aspects of high school sports—which is as appropriate today as it was twenty years ago—in which he pointed out:

"High school athletics have become the latest entree on the American sports menu, served up to help satisfy the voracious appetite of the fan. As a result, scholastic athletes are on the verge of becoming as important to the billion-dollar sports industry as their brothers and sisters—and just as vulnerable to big-time exploitation ... the fans' interest is more than equaled by that of three other forces: college and pro coaches hungry to see potential recruits, television companies craving more sports programming, and advertisers seeking new ways to reach the teen-age market (Eskenazi, 1989, p. 1).

However, the author believes that the negative consequences of sport and sport competition are but a small part of the total picture of sports in our society. The negative aspects associated with amateur sports, while they exist, represent only a small minority of individuals. For the vast majority of athletes, coaches and administrators, as well as fans and boosters, sport involvement becomes a wholesome, beneficial and educational experience, one that assists the individual, male or female, to become a better member and contributor to the society in which that person lives.

THE VALUE OF SPORT PARTICIPATION IN SCHOOLS

As stated earlier, sports have the potential for affecting individual athletes in both a positive as well as a negative fashion. Since positive outcomes do not come automatically, coaches and school administrators must consciously work to insure that positive consequences emanate from the athletic experience for the individual student-athlete. Whether or not participation has such a positive or negative consequence is dependent upon a number of factors. These include, but are not limited to, the quality of the coaching; the influence of the parents; the circumstances and expectations surrounding the sport experience itself; and not the least important, the individual characteristics, aptitudes, abilities and prior experiences of the youngsters themselves, figure 1.1.

Homecoming with the traditional athletic contests can be an exciting time for the entire college/university campus. President John Halstead and his wife, Kathy, participate in the homecoming parade, The College at Brockport, New York.

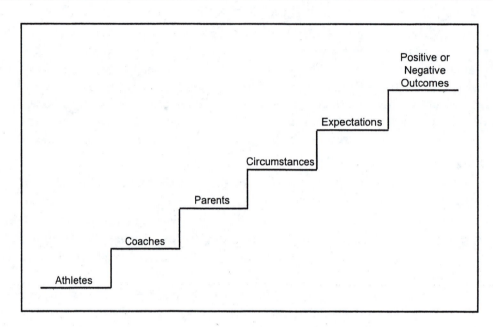

FIGURE 1.1—Factors Affecting the Athletic Experience.

JUSTIFICATION OF SPORTS IN SCHOOLS

Sports can be a valuable learning experience for young people. The challenge facing coaches and educators is to be sure that they provide experiences that are indeed constructive and positive in nature. In those instances in which sports exist within a school setting, it is essential that the athletic activities be educationally sound and thus provide positive learning experiences for the students. For in reality, *sports in schools can only be justified as long as they contribute to the overall mission of the educational institution that sponsors the athletic program.*

If any sports fail to respect the educational dimensions of our schools, or fail to be operated as an integral part of or become incompatible with the established educational mission, then there is absolutely no justification for supporting or sponsoring these sports under the umbrella or auspices of schools.

Sports are frequently said to mirror society. In fact, sports are a microcosm of society and, as such, participation exposes the athlete to the same pressures, challenges, problems and opportunities found in our society. As a result, sports participation provides athletes with what Riggenback (1991, p. 8-C) refers to as "sample life experiences on which to practice their developing skills." Providing meaningful and worthwhile sports programs can help individual students develop the skills necessary to become contributing citizens in our society. Athletic teams and programs, if properly administered, can serve as significant educational resources for our schools.

In fact, Joel E. Smilow, president of Playtex, Inc., said: ". . . it is my belief that football is an integral part of the very broad objective of attracting, educating and motivating persons with the potential to become tomorrow's leaders, irrespective of the field of endeavor they choose to pursue" (*The NCAA News*, 1989, p. 4).

A Lou Harris Survey in the early 1990s on High School Athletes found that both African-American and white high school athletes indicated that they believed sports participation helped athletes (themselves and others) in significant ways. For example, 65% of African-American and 45% of white secondary school athletes indicated that playing sports helps a great deal in avoiding drugs. Sixty percent of the African-American athletes and 32% of the white athletes revealed that sport participation helps in avoiding alcohol. And 44% of the African-American and 32% of the white respondents indicated that their sport involvement helped them become better citizens (Brady, 1993).

Richard Lapchick, the then director of Northeastern University's Center for the Study of Sport in Society said, in response to the findings of this survey, that:

> "Many African-American high school student-athletes while still carrying the unrealistic belief that they can be the newest rising star, now clearly understand playing sports is a vehicle that can deliver educational, social and life-skill benefits that will help make them productive members of society" (Brady, 1993, p. 2-C).

SPECIFIC POSITIVE OUTCOMES OF SPORT PARTICIPATION

There are many positive consequences or outcomes that are frequently attributed to amateur athletic participation. For example, individual and team sports are said to help teach individuals of all ages, male and female, very important and helpful lessons in terms of leadership and followship, decision-making, dedication, team work, and the ability to sacrifice. Individuals who partake of competitive sports are given opportunities to develop capabilities for budgeting time, establishing priorities, allocating resources and creating short and long-range goals (Stier, 1992).

Riggenback (1992) feels that athletes should become involved in sports in order to experience success, to actually accomplish something. This may be defined in any number of ways for different people at different levels. Participation in sports has shown that women's career paths have been facilitated through their involvement in sports. Specifically, in a national poll conducted by MassMutual Financial Group and the OppenheimerFunds, 82% of the female executives surveyed indicated that they had participated in organized sports and 81% agreed that such participation had "helped them function better on a team. In addition, 69% said sports had helped them develop leadership skills that helped their processional success, and 68% said it had helped them cope with failure" (Poll says, 2002, p. 1-E). Responding to this survey, Janet Wyse, a manager at OppenheimerFunds made the following statement: "There are lessons to be learned on a softball diamond or basketball court that are unavailable in a business school lecture hall" (Poll says, 2002, p. 1-E).

In a similar national study reported in 1999 by David Brennan who reported the results of a national survey sent to randomly selected high-level professionals. The findings revealed that 88.5% of the respondents felt that their involvement in competitive sports had significant carry-over value in their business careers. Specific findings indicated that sports competition resulted in the participants being mentally tougher. One of the respondents, New Jersey Governor Christine Todd, said: "Sports, both competitive and non-competitive, teach discipline, focus and the need to be able to think fast to meet changing needs" (p. 1). Those who took part in this national study included governors, college presidents and CEO's of Fortune 500 companies and 63.5%these participants revealed that their sports participation had had a definite impact on their careers and 94% felt that the impact of such involvement on their life was positive. Dr. Peterk Likins, president of the University of Arizona, and a former college wrestler, has this say: "As a university president and former professor of engineering, I have often said that I learned how to be a professor in the classroom, but I learned how to be a president on the wrestling mat" (p. 2).

Some of the achievements that may be possible through athletic participation include being able to:

1. Increase the physical and mental mastery of some aspect of the sport
2. Set a goal and to work toward it
3. Coordinate one's own efforts with those of one's teammates
4. Achieve and maintain the flexibility needed to respond to ever-changing situations
5. Make quick and appropriate alterations in plans, strategies and tactics

It is interesting to note that the realization of any of the above five objectives is not necessarily dependent upon actual winning of athletic contests. These objectives or accomplishments can be achieved through the participatory process itself regardless of whether or not the team emerges victorious on the scoreboard.

Sport participation has traditionally been credited with the potential for building character, pride and preparing participants for later life in our society. This is said to be accomplished by exposing the athletes to multiple challenges and adversity and the resulting pressures and stresses in an effort to teach them to adjust, to accommodate and to overcome such hindrances and hurdles—all the while keeping their sights on worthwhile objectives and goals. It may also be accomplished by placing athletes in situations in which they are able to experience successes and achievements in sports competition while accepting such prosperity and the resulting praise with appropriate humility and humbleness, figure 1.2.

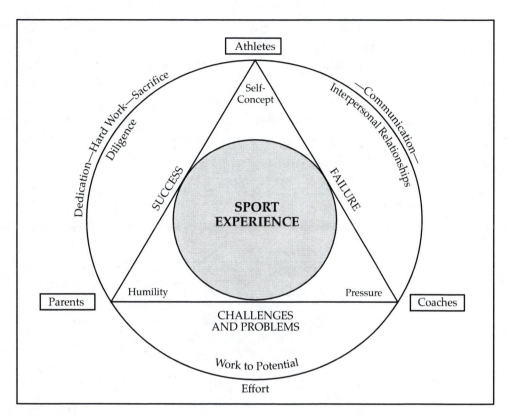

FIGURE 1.2—The Values of the Sport Experience.

Additionally, proponents of competitive athletics also claim that sports can have a positive impact upon the participants' academic self-concept in the classroom and, as a result, sports have the potential for helping to reduce the dropout rate among athletes. A recent survey (Athletic Notes, 1990) revealed that 61% of high school athletes, particularly black athletes, felt that their participation in sports had helped them in becoming better students in school. On the other hand, 36% of those athletes polled indicated that their participation in competitive high school sports did not make them better students. When the African American athletes were examined as a sub-group of all of the student-athletes surveyed in this study, it was found that almost 8 out of 10 of these student-athletes (79%) felt that their involvement in competitive sports provided them with very real academic benefits in the classroom.

Further, athletes can develop meaningful social skills through their dealings with others, including students (both teammates and non-teammates) as well as adults, in group settings and on an individual, one-on-one basis. Sociologists and political scientists have also postulated that participation also helps stem involvement in gangs and has the potential of reducing drug abuse and misuse.

Sports in many countries are thought to have significant benefits for society in addition to the individual participants. For example, the Prime Minister of the then newly independent Caribbean island nation of St. Kitts-Nevis indicated to the author, some 25-years ago, that the expanding sports program for the young people of that country was a planned, deliberate effort to solve potential social ills within the nation by keeping the young people involved in a wholesome, beneficial, interesting and time consuming activity (Dr. Kennedy Simmonds, personal communication, July 18, 1984).

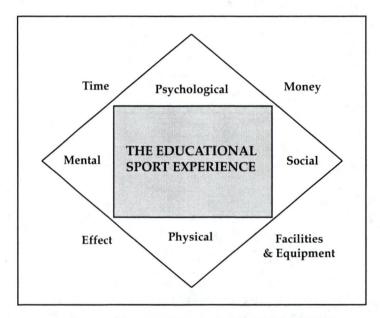

FIGURE 1.3—Input & Output of Athletic Competition.

The community leaders and sports organizers and administrators of that country had made a conscious value judgment and decision that the benefits that would accrue both to the individual participants (physically, socially, psychologically, mentally) and to the society of the newly formed island nation would be substantial, and in fact, would be well worth the cost in dollars and effort, figure 1.3.

The Dumb Jock Myth

Several studies have shown that participation in interscholastic sports does indeed increase academic performance and achievement. One nationwide study conducted by the Women's Sports Foundation revealed that participation in interscholastic sports can have a positive effect in terms of academic achievement, leadership aspirations, and social involvement. Another study titled *Minorities in sports: The effect of varsity sports participation on the social, educational and career mobility of minority students*, found that girls in high school, who comprised 37% of all varsity athletes nationwide, benefit as much from sports participation as boys and much in the same fashion. Hispanic females in rural areas and suburban white females who participated in competitive school sports had higher academic performance than non-participants. They were also more likely to earn the coveted college degree than similar females who were non-athletes (Study shows, 1990).

The so-called dumb jock myth is just that, a fiction, an unsubstantiated belief when applied to all females as well as all males who are involved in competitive athletics. Another study conducted by the Women's Sports Foundation also revealed that there was no evidence that participation in athletics hindered a student obtaining good grades. And, those female students who were on high school athletic teams were less likely to interrupt their high school education and drop out of school. The report concluded that females "stayed in school because they enjoyed sports . . . the friendships and popularity it fostered" (Study challenges, 1990. p. 16).

Additional Advantages of Sport Participation

A 1991 survey of 340 sports fans revealed that the biggest advantage of high school sports (82% of the respondents) was perceived to be in teaching the values of hard work and teamwork. Other advantages of sport participation at the interscholastic level included the opportunity for good physical fitness training and an improvement in overall school spirit (Jegels, 1991).

A study of students conducted in the state of Minnesota revealed that of those students who had dropped out of high school, some 94% had not been involved in any school activities such as athletics, student government, National Honor Society, music, scouts, journalism, etc. Also, those who participated in activity programs, including athletics, tended to have higher grade-point averages, better attendance records, lower dropout rates, and fewer discipline problems than students in general (Day-to-Day, August 19, 1989).

Top-level executives at Fortune 500 companies were questioned about the value they place upon extra-curricular type activity programs, including sports, in high schools. These successful business people responded to the survey by revealing how their participation in such activity programs, including interscholastic athletics, helped to pave the way for successful professional careers. The survey, published in 1989 by *USA Today,* revealed that almost all (95%) of the successful executives surveyed had participated in high school sports. Other activities in which the executives were involved included student government (54%), National Honor Society (43%), music (37%), scouting (35%), and journalism (18%). Michael Wright, CEO of Super Valu Stores, Inc., headquartered in Minneapolis, indicated that his participation in high school athletics *was a major factor in the formation of his personality and character.* He also revealed that the things he learned and the skills he developed as a result of his involvement in sports were significant in training and preparing him for his eventual success as a lawyer and business person (Day-to-Day, August 19, 1989).

Jack Kemp, former secretary of the U.S. Department of Housing and Urban Development, Vice-presidential candidate (1997), and a NFL quarterback for 13 seasons, indicated that his participation in sports, at both the amateur and professional levels, taught him that nothing great happens without both inspiration and perspiration. In football, he revealed that everything a quarterback does involves cost-benefit decisions, risk-reward ratios and marginal analysis. Every decision made as a quarterback was also both quantifiable and measurable. For example, the quarterback has a specific number of seconds to call the play, three seconds to release the ball and the play is either successful or is not, the team either moves down the field or does not advance the ball. Kemp claims that sport participation taught him additional lessons such as the need for loyalty as well as the necessity for both determination and audacity. He further acknowledged that athletic competition instilled in him the recognition that one succeeds in athletic competition as a member of the team, one family, one unit. As a result there is never room for racism, anti-Semitism or prejudice to be present within the successful athletic team or program (Kemp, 1992).

In summary, amateur athletes at all levels have the right to expect that through their participation in sports they will be able, commensurate with their abilities, potential, and expended efforts, to experience positive benefits including the development and/or enhancement of specific skills and competencies (Stier, 2006b). Some of these potential benefits include, but are not limited to, the following:

1. Attributes, such as strength, agility, flexibility, balance, cardio-respiratory [aerobic and anaerobic capacity], endurance, power, balance, reaction time, jumping ability, speed, etc.
2. The acquisition of specific sport knowledge
3. Physical growth and development
4. Awareness of and knowledge relating to the physical body
5. Knowledge of conditioning methods
6. The ability to compete and to cooperate
7. Emotional maturity and stability
8. A positive self-image
9. Respect for self and others
10. Better judgment
11. Enhanced leadership abilities
12. Increased maturity and growth
13. Willingness to sacrifice and be unselfish

14.   Willingness to postpone immediate gratification
15.   Willingness to share
16.   Capacity to work to one's potential or near potential
17.   Willingness to learn and achieve
18.   Ability to get along with others
19.   Ability to serve as a good example
20.   Willingness to follow directions and to obey rules and regulations
21.   Capacity to accept responsibility
22.   Ability to listen, to communicate
23.   Greater confidence
24.   Ability to develop pride
25.   Ability to recognize one's limitations and react accordingly
26.   Capacity for trustworthiness
27.   Ability to be loyal
28.   Ability to make a commitment
29.   Ability to be patient
30.   Ability to train diligently
31.   Ability to deal with success and failure
32.   Ability to set goals and priorities
33.   Possesses humility
34.   Ability to handle adversity, challenges
35.   Ability to deal with pressure and deadlines
36.   Ability to handle multiple tasks
37.   Capacity for empathy
38.   Exhibits sportsmanship—fair play
39.   Development of character
40.   Decisiveness
41.   Dedicated
42.   Accepts criticism
43.   Excellent work ethic
44.   Increased fitness and better health
45.   Coordination
46.   Development of general and sport specific skills
47.   Others . . .

SCHOOLS ARE DIFFERENT TODAY
THAN THEY WERE IN THE NOT-TOO DISTANT PAST

Coaches should realize that the schools where they are going to coach are indeed much different than schools were when they were students. Life, pressures, challenges and opportunities in school today are far different than just a generation before. During WW II public schools were faced with such student problems as the chewing of gum, running in the hallways, cutting in line, violating dress codes, talking in class. Today the problems and challenges facing youngsters in middle and secondary schools are many and varied, and much more serious. Today, concern with or fear of drug abuse and misuse, alcohol abuse, drop-out, AIDS, suicide, rape, teen pregnancy, child abuse, single parent families, robbery, assault, battery, violence, guns/knives, etc., are more the norm than the unusual. Coaches must understand the environment that their athletes, both male and female, must exist within while at school as well as outside of school.

COACHING CONCEPT #2:   **Coaches must understand the environment that their athletes, both male and female, must exist within while at school as well as outside of school.**

Coaches should also realize that a great number of youngster come from single parent families. This is especially true for African American children. In 1993, one-third of the 11 million African American children lived with a never-married parent; compared with just 4% of Hispanic white children, reported the Census Bureau from a study it conducted. African American children are three times more likely to live in poverty as white children (46% versus 16%). Sixty-four percent of African American children, in 1994, had an absent parent and 12% lived with a grandparent (For many black kids, 1994). The tendency for a significant number of our young people to live without their fathers being an integral part of their family life has lead to the coining of the term, *Fatherless America*. In fact, David Blankenhorn wrote in his famous book (1995) titled *Fatherless America* that 40% of young people in 1995 sleep in homes in which their fathers do not live (Whitmire, 1995). In the 21st century the situation has not improved significantly; in fact it has worsened in many cities.

The emergence of crime and the willingness of the young to commit crime is a serious and growing matter. "Between 1995 and 2010, the number of 15- to 19-year old males will rise by 30 percent. And the demographics of this group, based on the born out of wedlock and/or raised in poverty, offers little reassurance" (Whitmire, 1995, 11-A). In the same article, Mark Moore, a professor of criminal justice at Harvard, said the following: "If poor parenting, low income, a difficult adjustment, to school and low birth weight are indicators of future trouble, whether it be crime or drugs or school failure, we've got a lot of trouble headed our way" (Whitmire, 1995, 11-A).

WHY YOUNGSTERS PARTICIPATE IN SPORTS

There have been several studies conducted to determine the reasons why youngsters at various ages desire to participate in athletic competition. The motivation to become involved in sports is different among young people at all ages. At the youth sports level, Sheryl Mahler (1992), a mother of four sons and wife of Rick Mahler who pitched 13 years in major leagues, indicated that coaches all too frequently forget to lead off with fun. Youngsters will always play to win because it is in their very nature to be competitive, to strive to achieve. This is not necessarily a negative factor. It is just a fact. As a result of this reality coaches need to remain sensitive to what young children need at the youth sport level. That is, to have fun, to experience enjoyment, all the while they are learning and playing the competitive sport or game.

A study of 10,000 boys and 1,900 girls, grades 7 through 12 (ages 10-18), was conducted by Martha E. Ewing and Vern Seefeldt of the Youth Sports Institute of Michigan State University in 1987 and the initial results were reported in 1988 (American Youth, 1990). The most publicized and perhaps pursued objective (winning) of competitive sports is, in reality, a rather poor motivating factor for the majority of junior and senior high school students. The investigation revealed that the ten most important reasons why athletes played their best sport were:

1. To have fun
2. To improve skills
3. To stay in shape
4. To do something they are good at
5. For the excitement of competition
6. To get exercise
7. To play as part of a team
8. For the challenge of competition
9. To learn new skills
10. To win

Both boys and girls agreed on their number one reason for playing sports. Both sexes ranked having fun (enjoying themselves) as the major reason they became involved in their favorite sports. And, conversely, the lack of fun or enjoyment is the second most significant reason (see below) for dropping out of a particular sport activity.

Defining the Term "Fun"

In light of the fact that enjoyment or having fun is so important to young people in respect to their sport participation, especially youth sport and interscholastic involvement, it is important to come to agreement as to what is meant by the terms. Steven J. Danish (American Youth, 1990, p. 6) has defined fun in sports as "the quest for the balance between challenge and skill." If athletes find that there is an adequate balance between the challenge and the skill level, then the experience will be enjoyable, will be fun, figure 1.4. Athletes experience the greatest enjoyment and satisfaction when they establish their own personal challenges and can assess their own individual performances in light of these challenges. Similarly, intrinsic rewards and challenges in competitive sports are better than extrinsic since they emanate from the individuals themselves, instead of being focused on whether the contest is won or lost.

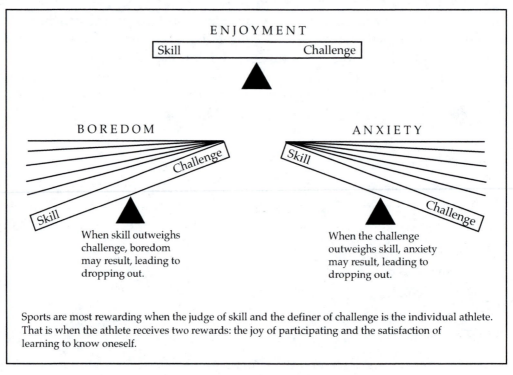

**FIGURE 1.4—Fun in Sports: A Balance between Skill and Challenge
by Dr. Steven J. Danish (American Youth, 1990) .**
[Reprinted with permission of the Sporting Goods Manufacturers Association, SGMA]

Athletes also participate because of social pressure, because their parents want them to do so, and because it is a chance to gain recognition and status (Sabock, 1991). In fact, 25% of those youngsters in the study by Ewing and Seefeldt felt that "they 'had to' be in sports because of outside pressure. They were more interested . . . in being with friends and making new friends" (American Youth, 1990, p. 5). Additionally, youngsters become involved in competitive sports because of their own egos (important person or big shot on campus), because such activity is frequently a way to keep up with their peers and because such involvement is frequently a way to impress the opposite sex (Stier, 1986).

WHY YOUNGSTERS DON'T PARTICIPATE IN SPORTS

In the same national study some 2,700 boys and 3,100 girls (ages 10-19, grades 7-12) responded to a survey and revealed some of the reasons *why they dropped out of playing a specific sport* (American Youth, 1990, p. 5). The researchers concluded that youngsters dropped out because of two principle reasons. First, the athletes were no longer interested in the sport activity. And, second, the experience was no longer fun. The highest dropout rate occurred at the early ages of 10 and 11. Those athletes who had dropped out indicated that they might get involved once again in sports if there were changes in (1) coaching, (2) the athletic schedules and (3) the organizational structure of the sports programs. This study revealed that sports participation, and the apparent desire to participate, declines steadily through the teen years (Ewing & Seefeldt, 1990). A significant number of young athletes become reluctant participants due to the pressure they experienced from outside sources, including parents and friends (Athletic Footwear Council, 1989; Ewing & Seefeldt, 1990).

The Youth Sports Institute reported that 59% of parents with youngsters in sports programs believe that their own children would prefer to play on a losing team than sit on the bench of a winning team. *In fact, around 90 percent of the youngsters actually selected playing for the losing squad if this provided them with a chance to actually play on a regular basis.* The Youth Sports Institute also reported that a survey of parents of youth sport participants revealed that 75% of the parents believe that adults get too involved and lose sight of the youth sports program's purpose and objectives (Coping with, 1988).

Danish (American Youth, 1990, p. 6) indicates that athletes tend to drop out of sport competition when they believe that the challenge posed by the sport experience far exceeds their own capabilities, skills and competencies. Similarly, athletes tend to leave the competitive sport scene when their individual skills far exceed the challenge of the competition and boredom sets in as a result (see figure 1.4).

Boys and girls who had dropped out of sport participation differed somewhat in terms of important changes they would suggest be made in competitive sports before they would ever consider to become involved once again. The 6 most important changes needed in competitive sports as viewed by former athletes (both boys and girls) who had dropped out of youth and/or high school sports (ages 12-18) are listed in Figure 1.5 (American Youth, 1990, p. 5).

The Six Most Important Changes I Would Make To Get Involved Again
In a Sport I Dropped (I would play again, if . . .)

BOYS	GIRLS
1. Practices were more fun	1. Practices were more fun
2. I could play more	2. There was no conflict with studies
3. Coaches understood players	3. Coaches understood players
4. There was no conflict with studies	4. There was no conflict with social life
5. Coaches were better teachers	5. I could play more
6. There was no conflict with social life	6. Coaches were better teachers

FIGURE 1.5—(from American Youth, 1990)
[reprinted with permission of the Sporting Goods Manufacturers Association, SGMA]

Why Girls Quit Athletic Teams

Stewart and Taylor (2000) revealed in a national study of female athletes why girls play and why they quit athletic teams/competition. Girls listed fun or having fun as the biggest reason for being involved in competitive sports. Conversely, the main reason for quitting sports was injury (26%) followed by time conflicts (18%) and coaching issues (16%). Girls described their favorite coaches as "fun, nice, listening to and understanding players, encouraging to individuals, knowledgeable, and pushing the team to do its best" (Sherman, 2002, p. 2).

Competition for the Athletes' Time

As students get older, that is, as they reach the high school level, there are many things, other than athletics, that compete for their time and attention. Specifically, there are many opportunities for involvement in activities other than sports which young people in high school find enjoyable, satisfying and rewarding. Also, times and society have changed in recent years. High school students no longer need be athletes to have high esteem among their peers or to be the so-called *big-shot on cam-*

pus. It is increasingly difficult to be an athlete and juggle all the things that are facing youngsters today. The pressures, peer and otherwise, are extreme and varied.

In addition, in the past (prior to 1950) only 5% of youngsters held jobs during the school year. By 1980, working during the school year had become the so-called norm for the vast number of high school students. By 1998, half of the 10 million youngsters between the ages of 15 and 17 worked regularly during the school year (Too many hours, 1998). And, in the early decades of the 21st century the need for young people to secure either discretionary (entertainment or personal) or necessary funding for a variety of needs is increasing and competing with the time necessary for athletic competition.

Today, it is easier to drive mom's or dad's car and go to the beach than it is to participate in competitive sports. Also, the drug scene is all too real in *many of the schools in this country*. Social activities have become a greater challenge and distraction among students, especially relationships with the opposite sex. There are many more activities and distractions vying for the would-be student-athlete's time and effort than in past years. And, all too frequently, these alternative activities, attractive as they may be, replace sports as the activity of choice by young people. In fact, the study conducted by Ewing & Seefeldt (American Youth, 1990) revealed that among 18-year students, watching television was the highest rated activity (chosen by 87% of the students). Just hanging out with one's friends was cited by 81% of these same students as the favorite activity of choice.

The Coach Seen as the Problem by Youngsters

In a survey of 34,000 students, aged 10-18, the young people cited two major problems with athletic participation as they saw it. *First,* too much time was demanded of the athletes. *Second,* students felt that there were too many unqualified coaches holding important coaching positions. Normally these types of criticisms are leveled toward non-school sports where there tend to be more novice coaches overall or coaches with little if any experience serving as head coaches. This faultfinding of coaches at the high school level might be a symptom that the hiring of high school coaches leaves much to be desired and that the qualifications of significant numbers of these coaches might be suspect (Coping with, 1988).

If there are problems with the coaching scene, at any level, much—although not all—of the responsibility and the blame can be placed at the feet of coaches. It falls upon the coach, who has the person-to-person contact with individual athletes, to create an educational and enjoyable athletic experience for those youngsters who choose to participate in competitive, amateur athletics. Thus, it behooves you—as a current or future coach—to do the very best job possible in providing a meaningful educational and enjoyable experience for your athletes. They deserve no less.

MILESTONES IN GENDER EQUITY
AND DISCRIMINATION IN SPORTS

COACHING CONCEPT #3:   Title IX has had a significant impact upon women, as sport competitors and as sport coaches.

With the enactment of Title IX of the Educational Amendments of 1972 (the Education Amendments to the Civil Rights Act of 1964), signed on June 23, 1972, the role of women in competitive sports was changed forever. This is true for women as competitors and as coaches. Title IX prohibits sex discrimination in educational institutions that receives any type of federal funds (Stier, 2008). The law specifically states: "No person in the United States shall, on the basis of sex, be excluded from participation in, be denied the benefits of, or be subjected to discrimination under any program or activity receiving Federal financial assistance" (Title IX, 44 Fed. Reg. at 71413).

Title IX and Gender Equity

COACHING CONCEPT #4:   Title IX affects every school that receives Federal financial assistance.

The law, as initially interpreted, had a direct effect on the sports program in every junior high, senior high, and college or university in this country that received any type of federal assistance whatsoever. Today, some proponents of gender equity have taken the position that the definitive definition of gender equity is *when either the men's or women's sports program would be pleased to accept as its own the overall program of the other gender* (Herwig, 1993a; Herwig, 1993b).

Competitive Sport Opportunities for Women Prior to Title IX

To better grasp the enormous impact that Title IX initially had on women's athletics, both in high schools and colleges during the past 30+ years, one must understand the status of women's sports prior to the law's passage. Prior to the mid-1970s, opportunities for athletic competition for girls on the secondary level were far behind the opportunities available for boys in most schools in this country. At the collegiate level the situation was similarly dismal. Although there were some exceptions, for the most part girls and women were treated as second-class citizens in terms of sport participation opportunities.

Historically, girls and women were neither encouraged to participate in competitive sports nor were they financially supported to the degree that the boys and men were at either the high school or collegiate levels. Even when sports programs and activities were made available for girls and women, the amount of financial and other types of support provided fell far, far short of what was provided for boys and men in similar situations.

Prior to the law coming into effect, opportunities for competitive athletic experience for girls and women were minimal at best. At the collegiate level, participation was hampered because of the small number of high school graduates coming to college with prior competitive sport experience. Although schools offered some intercollegiate sports for women, the number of sports were fewer than those provided for men, and the resources (financial and otherwise) supporting the women's sports were far, far inferior to what was available to men's sports.

Previously, girls in high school and women in college were not given their just due either in terms of opportunities for competitive sports or support, financial or otherwise, for adequate sports programs. The reasons were many and varied but the consequence was the same: Sexual discrimination was pervasive in our schools throughout the country insofar as sports were concerned.

Changes Brought about by Title IX that Affect Coaches

A key element of Title IX is that by 1978 all educational institutions receiving federal aid must be practicing nondiscrimination on the basis of sex in all of the institution's programs and practices. One natural consequence was the expected expansion of sport opportunities for women, especially in the area of sport participation as competitors and as coaches. For example, in the state of Indiana, the number of female participants involved in interscholastic sports recognized by that state's High School Athletic Association increased from 27,000 in 1972 to over 50,000 by 1992.

Similar gains have been seen on the national level. In 1972, some 300,000 girls participated in organized competitive sports at the secondary level compared to over 1.8 million just 20 years later (Sawyer, 1992). By the 1994-1995 school year, the number of girls participating in organized competitive sports at the secondary level was at an all-time high. In fact, 2,240,461 girls were participating during that year (Girls' participation, 1996). At the turn of the century the number of female athletes, at all levels of amateur sport, has never been higher, and the trend should clearly continue.

At the collegiate level the average number of women's sports offered by schools increased from 5.61 per school in 1977 to 7.24 in 1990 (Berg, 1990). During the 1994-1995 academic year there were over 105,532 women participating in organized competitive sports at the collegiate level (Girls' participation, 1996). Today, that number continues to in increase. An interesting result of recent court rulings has been the inclusion of booster club funds in the Title IX equation. This means that the money generated from the efforts of a booster club must be shared or distributed equally and appropriately with both male and female teams, even if the booster club was organized around or for a single gender (Berry, 2001).

However, even the passage of Title IX did not result in total equality, then or today. In fact, the schools of this country were brought kicking and screaming into some resemblance of compliance as a result of Title IX, but certainly not total compliance.

Grove City versus Bell

The teeth were temporarily taken out of Title IX insofar as sports were concerned when the United States Supreme Court ruled, on February 28, 1984, that *specific programs*, not an institution, must receive federal funds in order to fall under the auspices of Title IX. This suit *(Grove City College v. Bell,* 465 U.S. 555, 79 L. Ed. 516, 104 S. Ct. 1211 [1984]) was a result of Grove City College of Pennsylvania challenging the tenets of Title IX. Thus, because practically no athletic department at the time was receiving federal funds directly, the athletic programs were deemed to not under the purview of Title IX legislation. Unfortunately, many of the lawsuits that had been filed under Title IX and were in the process of being litigated became moot with the *Grove City versus Bell* ruling.

A Temporary Setback

However, this temporary setback to Title IX legislation for equality in sports for girls and women did not curtail the existing opportunities for sport participation (especially as competitors) for girls and women. It was like attempting to close the barn door after the horse ran out. The tremendous growth experienced by women's sports in the 1970s and early 1980s could not be reversed. In fact, opportunities continued to increase, and continues to this day.

The Civil Rights Restoration Act

The teeth were put back into Title IX by the Civil Rights Restoration Act of 1987, which was passed by Congress on March 22, 1988 over then-President Reagan's veto. This law restored institution-wide coverage of Title IX, effectively nullifying the Grove City versus Bell ruling. Almost immediately after the passage of this act several law suits were filed or filed again under Title IX. For example, on June 13, 1988, Temple University settled a Title IX lawsuit just three weeks after going to trial. The lawsuit, originally filed in 1980, prior to the Grove City case, charged the school with systematic sex discrimination by its athletic department. As a result of the agreement, Temple University agreed to add two women's sports and to raise its women's athletic participation rate from 34 percent to 43 percent.

Punitive Damages under Title IX

On February 26, 1992, the Supreme Court made a most important legal decision relating to Title IX. The decision *(Franklin* v. *Gwinnet County Public Schools,* 117 L. Ed. 2d 208 [1992]) resulted from a suit filed by a secondary school student in the state of Georgia who accused a teacher, who was also a coach, of sexual harassment. The Supreme Court ruled in the Gwinnet County case that individuals who file (and win) under Title IX are eligible for *monetary damages in addition to having their griev-ances redressed.* This decision of the court significantly raised the penalty for non-compliance with this law at schools and colleges that receive federal aid by making athletic departments liable for punitive damages if found to be in violation of Title IX (Mauro, 1992).

COACHING CONCEPT #5:   **The Franklin v. Gwinnet County Public Schools decision provided for monetary damages in addition to having grievances redressed.**

Prior to the *Franklin* v. *Gwinnet County Public Schools* decision, if schools were found guilt of noncompliance, they were, in effect, slapped on the wrist and told to get in compliance. There was not a great risk in failing to comply with the letter and the intent of the Title IX legislation prior to the then latest decision by the Supreme Court (Supreme court rules, 1992). Subsequently, however, there was more motiva-tion for adhering to the Title IX regulations, and that motivation was fear of mone-tary damages being awarded. The matter of monetary damages also served as a mo-tivating factor on behalf of potential plaintiffs and attorneys. Now, lawyers would be able to secure potentially greater financial awards for their plaintiffs (and for themselves) as a result of favorable Title IX verdicts than in the past.

On February 27, 1992, the United States Office of Civil Rights rendered a decision in which it found that Brooklyn College (a Division I NCAA institution at that time) was in violation of 10 of the 13 areas that comprise Title IX compliance. This investigation resulted from a complaint filed some 14 months earlier (December 1990) by athletes and staff at that institution. As a result of this ruling, the school agreed to remedy the discrimination but, shortly after, elected to eliminate all col-legiate competitive sports and disbanded the entire athletic department for the next year.

On March 11, 1992, the NCAA released its long-awaited Gender Equity Survey. The national study revealed that after some 20 years of Title IX, college men still receive twice as many athletic scholarships as women at NCAA institutions. Additionally, while women make up 50 percent of the NCAA institutions in terms of full-time undergraduate population, they receive only 20 percent of athletic budgets and a measly 18 percent of the recruiting budget. Discrimination, overt or covert, still existed, the report clearly revealed.

Three Criteria for Determining Compliance with Title IX

Sports for women are more popular than ever.

Today, there are three generally accepted criteria by which compliance may be determined in terms of competitive athletics. The three-pronged test emanated from the United States Office for Civil Rights (OCR) and should be utilized to determine whether gender equity exists in competitive athletics in any given school or institution. Meeting any of these criteria would be prima facie evidence of compliance with Title IX, thus meeting the benchmark for gender equity in the competitive sports arena (Frankel, 1992; New Mexico, 2000; Internet Surveys, 2005; Weight, 2006, Stier, 2008).

These benchmark tests or criteria include: (1) providing opportunities for competitive sport participation for women and for men that are substantially proportionate to their respective rates of enrollment within the school, (2) showing a history and continuing practice of expanding opportunities for the underrepresented sex, and (3) actually proving that the organization has truly accommodated (fully and effectively) the interests and abilities of the underrepresented sex (Lederman, 1995; Bickford, 2001; Stier, 2008). The proportionality concept is an important one in that *it means that the gender ratio of the student body should be a benchmark for participation opportunities for athletes* (Herwig, 1993a).

Syracuse University Was the First Institution to Use the Safe-Harbor Defense in Meeting Title IX

Syracuse University, on June 12, 1996, received a summary judgment from a district court on the unequal-benefits and unequal-scholarship claims that were brought against the school by seven members of the school's club lacrosse team and the club softball team. Syracuse was the first institution in this country that successfully used the safe-harbor defense that evokes the claim that the school showed a history and continuing practice of expanding sport opportunities for women (Barr, 1999).

Using Internet-based Surveys

In attempting to satisfy the third prong, the U.S. Department of Education (DOE) attempted to clarify its position as how schools might show that the institutions were indeed satisfying the interests and abilities of the underrepresented sex. This was done when the Department of Education issued a clarification relative to Title IX on March 17, 2005. The clarification introduced a set of guidelines on how schools might actually measure student interest *which included the use of internet-based (e-mail) surveys of the existing student body* (Internet surveys, 2005). This internet-based survey technique (mass e-mailing) has generated a great deal of controversy but at present (2008-2009) the survey method still is an approved method of gauging interest and abilities of the underrepresented sex (Waldron, 2006).

COACHING CONCEPT #6: **Internet-based (e-mail) surveys may be utilized to determine (measure) student interest in school in athletic competition.**

There were nine general areas or components identified in 1996 that should have been examined in the athletic arena in terms of determining whether a school or department is in compliance with Title IX: (1) effective accommodation of student interests and abilities, (2) provision of equipment and supplies, (3) scheduling of games and practice times, (4) travel and per diem allowances, (5) opportunity to receive coaching and adequate compensation of coaches, (6) provision of a locker room, practice, and competitive facilities, (7) provision of medical and training facilities and services, (8) publicity, and (9) provision of support services (Paling, 1996).

In 2003, Moore cited the following 11 components within the Office of Civil Rights' document *Athletics Investigator's Manual* as the elements of an athletic program that should be addressed, in addition to the three prongs previously cited in this chapter.

1. Equipment and supplies
2. Scheduling of games and practice
3. Travel and per diem allowance
4. Access to experienced and quality coaches
5. Facilities

6. Medical and training facilities
7. Publicity
8. Recruiting resources
9. Academic tutoring services
10. Support services
11. Housing and dining facilities

The Elementary and Secondary Education Act

Title IX gained even more teeth when, on October 5, 1994, Congress passed and President Clinton, on October 20, 1994, signed, the Elementary and Secondary Education Act (more commonly known as *Improving America's Schools Act*). This law included the *Equity in Athletics disclosure amendment* that now required colleges to disclose information on their intercollegiate athletics programs relating to gender equity, starting October 1, 1996.

> "Similar to the Student Right-To-Know Act, which requires colleges to release information and publicize graduation rates of their students participating in their intercollegiate athletic programs, the Elementary and Secondary Education Act mandated institutions that take part in the federal student-aid programs and have intercollegiate athletics to provide an annual report containing specifics about opportunities and benefits provided to male and female student-athletes." (Gender equity, 1995, p. 7).

The reports are to contain, among other data, the following information:
1. Number of students by sex
2. Number of participants by sex
3. Total operating expenses for intercollegiate athletes
4. Gender of all head and assistant coaches
5. Amount of money spent on athletically related student aid
6. Recruiting expenses
7. Coaches' salaries for all men's and women's teams (varsity and subvarsity)

The result of this 1994 law has been even greater scrutiny on the spending for both men's and women's athletic programs at the collegiate level. High school students seeking an appropriate collegiate setting to become involved as a student and as an athlete now have much more data on which to base the important decision as to where they should go to college.

REFERENCES

Associated Press. (2004, November 17). *Democrat and Chronicle*, p. D-1.

Athletic footwear council studies young sports 'dropouts.' (1989, August). *National Athletic Director*, pp. 40-41.

Athletic notes. (1990, November 28). *The Chronicle of Higher Education. XXXVII*(13), p. A38.

American youth and sports participation—A study of 10,000 students and their feelings about sports. (1990, December). Athletic Footwear Association/Sporting Goods Manufacturers Association, Florida: North Palm Beach, pp 1-8.

Barr, C. A. (1999, October). Still afloat. Athletic Business, 23(10), 26-28.

Basketball. (1995, May 2). *USA Today*, p. 7-C.

Bell, R. (2006, December 3). Soaring pay for coaches stirs criticism. www.gotriad.com/apps/pbcs.dll/article?AID=/20061203/NEWSREC0101/61202016/-1/GTCOM0200

Berg, R. (Ed.). (1990, October). Women in sports—Reluctant role model. *Athletic Business, 14*(10), 15.

Berry, L. (2001). Balancing booster budgets. *Athletic Management, XIII*(2), 31-33, 35, 36.

Bickford, B. (2001). Ensuring equity. *Training & Conditioning, XI* (3), 23-27

Bilovsky, F. (1984, December 20). UR scores an endowment. *Democrat and Chronicle*, p. l-D.

Blake, N. (1997, June 10). Stallings' successor agrees to five-year deal at Alabama. *USA Today*, p. 13-C.

Bowden will make nearly $1 M per year. (1995, November 17). *USA Today*, p. 4-D.

Brady, E. (1993, November 8). Survey: Sports foster social unity. *USA Today*, p. 2-C.

Brennan, D. (1999, June 14). Survey shows participation has major impact on many successful careers. *News Release*, pp. 4.

Brylinski, J. (2002, October). National standards for athletic coaches (Report No. ED-2002-02). Washington, DC: ERIC Clearinghouse on Teaching and Teacher Education.

Coach salaries: from the stratosphere to the ionosphere. (2007, April 18). http://www.collegeathleticsclips.com/s/375/index.aspx?sid=375&gid=1&pgid=15&cid=292&newsid=890

Coaches pay tops at SU. (1996, November 27). *Democrat and Chronicle*, p. 3-D.

Coping with the coaching shortage. (1988, October). *Athletic Business,* pp. 20-22, 24.

Day-to-Day facts about co-curricular activities—High school activities: Keeping students in schools. (1989, August 19). Minnesota State High School League publication.

Eskenazi, G. (1989, March 5). Arena of big-time athletics is showcasing a younger act. *The New York Times,* pp. 1, as quoted in Sage, G. H., (1990). High school and college sports in the United States, *JOPERD/CAHPERD, 61*(2), 59, 61, 63.

Father claims he filed helmet strap. (1996, October 23). *USA Today,* p. 3-C.

FB coaches not the only ones making $ . . . (2007, March 21). http://www.collegeathleticsclips.com/s/375/index.aspx?sid=375&gid=1&pgid=15&cid=292&newsid=849

Football factory. (1994, September/October). *Modern Management, 37*(5), 59.

Foul play. (1996, November 4). *USA Today,* p 3-C.

For many black kids, a single parent life. (1994, September 15). *USA Today,* p. 3-A.

Frankel, E. (1992, November). Charging ahead. *Athletic Management, IV*(6), *14-19.*

Gender equity disclosure act signed into law. (1995, December/January). *Athletic Management, Vll*(I), 7.

Girls' participation in sports at an all time high. (1996, Summer). *GWS News, 23*(4), 6.

Goodman, J. (2007, February 1). Canandaigua wrestling coach charged, suspended. *Democrat and Chronicle,* P 3-B.

Herwig, C. (1993a, May 19). True equity, gender ratio top report. *USA Today,* p. 1-C.

Herwig, C. (1993b, May 19). Gender task force has more work to do. *USA Today,* p. 8-C.

Hiestand, M. (1992, October 15). *USA Today,* p. 10-C.

Heliter, M. (1992). *The dream job—Sports publicity, promotion and public relations.* Ohio: Athens, University Sports Press.

High school sports participation continues to show increase. (1987, October 19). *The NCAA News,* p. 7.

Hockey dispute ends with man's death. (2000, July 10). *USA Today,* p. 1-C.

Internet surveys okayed. (2005 June/July). *Athletic Management, XVII*(4), 4.

Ishee, J. H. (2004). Benefits of high school athletic participation. *Journal of Physical education, Recreation and Dance, 75*(7), 10.

Jegels, H., Jr. (1991, July 30). Pros, cons of high school sports, *USA Today,* p. 8-C.

Killian, D. (2007, April 6). Longhorns make new coach millionaire. USA Today, p. 1-B.

Kemp, J. (1992, September 17). Values learned on field. *Democrat and Chronicle*, p. 12-C.

Kids, it's just a game. (1996, November 25). *Sports Illustrated, 85*(22), 24-25.

KU football coach Mark Mangino's 2005 compensation totaled $769,256, but that's dead last in the Big 12. (2006, August 26). http://www.collegeathleticsclips.com/s/375/index.aspx?sid=375&gid=1&pgid=15&cid=292&newsid=485

Lederman, D. (1995, November 3). Murky clarification. *Chronicle of Higher Education, XLII*(10), A-51, A-52.

Lincoln, S. M. (1992). Sports injury risk management & the keys to safety. Coalition of Americans to protect sports (CAPS). *Journal of Physical Education, Recreation and Dance, 63*(7), 40-42, 63.

Little League scandal fashioned by win-at-all-costs organizers. (1992, September 19). *Democrat and Chronicle,* Rochester, New York, p. 3-D.

McCallie gets big salary boost. (2007, March 29). http://www.collegeathletics clips.com/s/375/index.aspx?sid=375&gid=1&pgid=15&cid=292&newsid=878

Mahler, S. (1992, April 14). The joy of victory is why sports exist. *USA Today*, p. 9-C.

Mauro, T. (1992, February 27). Sex bias law applied to schools. *USA Today*, p. 1-A.

Miller, G. (2003). National Federation of State High School Associations. *2002-2003 participation survey*. Indianapolis, Indiana.

Moore, B. (2003). Have a seat. *Athletic Management, XV*(3), 21

New Mexico conducts study. (2000). *Athletic Management, XII*(6, 9, 10.

New National Coaching Report. (2008, Fall). *NASPE News*. Issue 79, pp 1, 9.

New Study-Based Handbook Promotes Student Athlete Success In PA. (2008, 10-31-08). Retrieved, 11-4-08, http://www.medicalnewstoday.com/articles/127650.php

NSGA research reports. Retrieved 9-10-07: www.nsga.org.

1997-1998 NCAA Manual (1997, March). Kansas: Overland Park. National Collegiate Athletic Association.

Ohio State—Where bigger is often better. (2006, September 26). *College Athletic Clips,* http://www.collegeathleticsclips.com/s/375/index.aspx?sid=375&gid=1&pgid=15&cid=292&newsid=552

Olson, J. R. (1992, December). Easy money. *Athletic Business, 16*(12), 45-48.

Out of Control. (2000, July 24). *Sports Illustrated, 87-(93)*4, 87-95.

Out with old, in with new costs UNM $3.4 million. (2007, April 14) http:// www.collegeathleticsclips.com/s/375/index.aspx?sid=375&gid=1&pgid=15&cid =292&newsid=902\

$1M donation for athletics program. (1984, December 20). *Daily Sentinel,* New York, Rome, p. l-B.

OSU: The place where big is good. (2007, March 6). http://www.collegeathletics clips.com/s/375/index.aspx?sid=375&gid=1&pgid=15&cid=292&newsid=822

Paling, D. (1996, June-July). High school's Title IX story. *Athletic Management, VllI*(4), 22-24, 27.

Parents attack ref. (1998, December 11). *USA Today,* p. 3-C.

Participation in interscholastic athletics still rising. (1992, October 12). *The NCAA News,* Vol. 29, # 35, p, 8.

Piling on. (1996, November 13). *USA Today,* p. 1-C.

Pirates' Plan. (1995, October 26). *USA Today,* p. 2-C.

Poll says sport helps women's career paths. (2002, March 3). *Democrat and Chronicle,* p. 1-E.

Reilly, R. (1993, April 26). That's shoe business. *Sports Illustrated, 78*(16), 76.

Riggenback, J. (1991, July 30). Academics, not games, is a tool for life. *USA Today,* p. 8-C.

Riggenback, J. (1992, April 14). The joy of victory is why sports exist. *USA Today,* p. 9-C.

Roberts, J. E. (1993, February). Taking a stand. *Scholastic Coach, 62*(7), 5, 6. Reprinted from the March 1992 issue of the *Michigan H.S. Athletic Association Bulletin.*

Sabock, R. (1991). Coaching—A realistic perspective (4th ed.). San Diego, California: Collegiate Press.

Saraceno, J. (2002, March 6). Parents can be bad at being good sports. *USA Today,* p. 3-C.

Sawyer, T. H. (1992). Title IX: Some positive changes have occurred. *Journal of Physical Education, Recreation and Dance, 63*(3), 14.

Sherman. N. (2002). Why female athletes quit: Implications for coach education. *Journal for physical education, recreation and dance, 73*(2), 8.

Side-lines. (1993, April 21). *The Chronicle of Higher Education, XXXIX*(33), p. A-39.

Staff and Wire Reports. (2004, February 17). Knights, Big 12 coaches agree: College sports are big business, USA Today, p. 6-C.

Staffo, D. F. (1993, August). Alabama head coach—Gene Stallings. *Scholastic Coach,* pp. 50—52, 54, 56.

Stewart., C., & Taylor, J. (2000). Why female athletes quit: Implications for coach education. *The Physical Educator, 57*(4), 170-177.

Stier, Jr., W. F. (1986, March). Competencies in amateur/youth coaching. *Resources in Education.* (ERIC Document Reproduction Service No. Ed 263-060).

Stier, Jr., W. F. (1986, Spring). Needed skills and competencies of coaches involved in youth sports. *Proceedings of the United States Olympic Academy IX—June 26-30, 1985.* New York: State University of New York, College at Plattsburgh, pp. 57-64.

Stier, Jr., W.F. (1989, January). Making the case for youth sports. *The East-erner—Journal of the Eastern District Association of the American Alliance for Health, Physical Education, Recreation and Dance, 13*(1), 4.

Stier, Jr., W.F. (1992, Spring). The TRIAD assisting, advising, and assessment model: One institution's attempt to support the student-athlete. *Academic Athletic Journal.* ISN 0897-165X, pp. 34-42.

Stier, W.F., Jr. (2006a). Understanding sport management—From a global perspective. *Proceedings: 4th Congreso Regional Latinoamericano de la ICHPER•SD,* [4th Regional Congress in Latin America of the International Council for Health, Physical Education, Recreation-Sport and Dance], Venezuela: San Carlos.

Stier, W. F., Jr. (2006b, September 14). The importance of sustained growth and expansion in physical education among developing countries. Presentation made at the *Jamaica Physical Education Association and the Pre-Inaugural International Council of Health, Physical Education, Recreation, Sport and Dance Caribbean Meeting,* Kingston, Jamaica.

Stier, Jr., W. F. (2008). Sport Management: *The Business of Sport.* Boston, MA: American Press.

Still popular. (1992, October 7). *USA Today,* p. l-C.

Study challenges student-athlete stereotype. (1990, August). *Athletic Director, 7*(8), 16.

Study shows school sports to be a positive influence. (1990). *Update,* p. 5.

Supreme court rules that victims of intentional sex bias can sue colleges for punitive damages under Title IX. (1992, March 4). *Chronicle of Higher Education, XXXVlll*(26), p. A39.

Sylwester, M. (2004, September 1). Growth of girls taking part in sports levels out. *USA Today,* p. 14-C.

The NCAA News, (1989, December 18). p. 4.

Tide's Saban retruns to college roots. (2007, January 5). *USA Today*, http://www.usatoday.com/sports/college/football/sec/2007-01-04-saban-roots_x.htm

Too many hours at jobs jeopardizes high schooler's success, says expert. (1998, November 8), p. 16-A.

27 institutions under NCAA sanctions. (1993, January 13). *The NCAA News, XXXXIX*(19), 35

UCLA's Lavin gains players' attention with discipline. (1997, February 18). *USA Today*, pp. 1-C, 2-C.

UMass coach gets $1.4M for 4 years. (1996, October 21). *USA Today*, p. 17-C.

Update. (2004. February 20), LSU's Saban signs seven-year deal. *USA Today*, p. 2-C.

Waldron, J.J. (2006, April). Web-based surveys undermine Title IX. *Journal of Physical Education, Recreation and Dance,* 77(4), 4-6.

Weight, E.A. (2006). The pursuit of true legitimacy—Division I-A Title IX compliance after the additional clarification of prong three. *SMART Journal, III*(1), 42-54.

Whitmire, R. (1995, January 29). U.S. must make room for daddy. *Democrat and Chronicle*, p. 10-A.

Woods, B. (1993, April 12). The final four-tune. *Sports Illustrated*. Special Advertising Section, *78*(14), 4.

Name: _____

Student ID #:_____

EXERCISES FOR CHAPTER 1

A. Explain the reasons why you are thinking about becoming a coach. List the advantages that you see in the coaching profession for you as an individual coach.

_____

_____

_____

_____

_____

_____

_____

_____

B. Why should there be opportunities for amateur sport participation and competition in our schools?

_____

_____

_____

_____

_____

_____

_____

_____

C.   How does one justify youth sports?

_____

_____

_____

_____

_____

_____

D.   Are youth sports or interscholastic sports worth the money they cost? Justify your position.

_____

_____

_____

_____

_____

_____

_____

E.   Does society in general and the local community in particular benefit from the existence of sports? If so, in what way?

_____

_____

_____

_____

_____

_____

_____

F.   What are the real values and tangible benefits, (immediate, intermediate or long range) inherent for those involved with sports in a competitive environment?

_____

_____

_____

_____

_____

_____

G.   Is there any guarantee that these values or benefits can be realized by the participants or society? Discuss.

_____

_____

_____

_____

_____

_____

H.   How can one take advantage of these values and benefits supposedly inherent in sport participation and athletic competition?

_____

_____

_____

_____

_____

_____

_____

I. What are the downside risks, if any, in providing sport competition at various levels—both in and outside of the school setting?

_____

_____

_____

_____

_____

_____

J. Are sports in schools suppose to meet the need for entertainment for students and members of the community? Explain your position.

_____

_____

_____

_____

_____

_____

K. What are the qualities of a successful coach?

_____

_____

_____

_____

_____

_____

L.   What can be done to change the so-called dumb jock image that may be prevalent in many schools and communities?

M.   What are the implications resulting from the study (Athletic Notes, 1990) that revealed that more African-American athletes than white athletes thought that competitive athletic experience provided them with actual benefits in the academic classroom?

_____

_____

_____

_____

_____

_____

_____

RESEARCH QUESTIONS FOR CHAPTER 1

1. Survey a sport team, (a youth sport team, a junior high team, or a senior high team) and seek to find out why the athletes currently participate. Provide the answers below:

   _____

   _____

   _____

   _____

   _____

2. Canvas current college athletes and solicit reasons why they continue to participate in athletics at the collegiate level? Summarize the responses.

   _____

   _____

   _____

   _____

   _____

3. Survey coaches at different levels of competition and solicit opinions on why youngsters do or do not participate on sports teams. Provide a summary of your findings below.

   _____

   _____

   _____

   _____

   _____

   _____

4. Survey college athletes [preferably at different playing levels—Division I, II and III] and determine how difficult it was for them to earn a spot on the college team and ask them to relate their experience(s) in seeking a college team and playing spot.

_____

_____

_____

_____

_____

_____

5. Survey athletes on a team to determine what they *like* and *dislike* about their participation on the team.

_____

_____

_____

_____

_____

_____

Chapter 2

Developing a Realistic Perspective of Coaching

Basketball at its best in Louisville, Kentucky, Home of the University of Louisville.

COACHING—BOTH A SCIENCE AND AN ART

Coaching a sport has long been viewed as being both an art and a science. It is an art in that the actual delivery and implementation of the teaching techniques, the strategies and the tactics of any sport can be significantly affected and enhanced through the creative and innovative utilization and application of these principles and knowledge. It is this creative resourcefulness of coaches that can have a significant impact upon the learning processes of student-athletes and the development of physical and mental skills associated with the mastery of a competitive sport. Ingenious adaptations and use of teaching principles, strategies and knowledge to meet one's individual and very specific circumstances, needs or particular situation is indicative of the art of coaching.

59

Coaching is also a science in that there are fundamental, scientific ***principles*** and a body of knowledge underlying and supporting the tasks involved in coaching any sport at any level—youth sports, junior and senior high school, college and university as well as at the professional ranks. *These foundational principles hold true and are applicable regardless of the setting in which coaches or athletes find themselves.* It is the job of the future coach to begin to become familiar with the basic knowledge of coaching and understand the fundamental principles involved in making appropriate coaching decisions.

Coaching Concepts are strategically placed throughout this book. These concepts are ***principles*** which serve as guidelines for coaching decisions, both on and off the practice and game field. Additionally, these concepts or principles provide insight into the body of knowledge associated with and supporting the world of amateur sport coaching and competition.

COACHING CONCEPT #7:   **Don't be discouraged by hard work—coaching, done right, is challenging, is hard work and is demanding.**

VOLUNTEER COACHES VERSUS PAID COACHES

Coaches have long been recognized as one of the largest volunteer groups in this country. Yet, almost 40% of volunteer coaches leave their coaching positions each and every year. The turnover rate among volunteer coaches at all levels is phenomenal to say the least. It has been estimated that only about 1 in 6 coaches at any level are actually paid for their coaching efforts.

Even for these individuals who are paid for coaching sports, coaching usually makes up only a portion of their total responsibilities. In fact, 90% of those who do receive money for coaching are paid for only part-time involvement in coaching (SportScan, 1988, p. 1). For example, coaches might be employed on a full time basis by the sponsoring organization (such as a school) but they are usually assigned teaching tasks and/or given administrative duties in addition to their coaching responsibilities. Or, a person who holds a full time job in a business may be paid to coach an athletic team on a part-time basis.

The actual number of coaches who actually *earn their living* exclusively from the coaching of sports is exceedingly small. In educational settings, usually only those colleges and universities participating at the NCAA Division I or II levels of competition have the capability or luxury of hiring individuals whose only responsibilities involve coaching and the recruitment of student-athletes. And, not all coaches even at these elite levels of competition are hired exclusively as coaches. Of course, semi-professional and professional sports teams hire individuals whose sole responsibilities are those associated with the coaching and the winning of games. However, the major focus of this book centers on the so-called amateur level of sport competition.

CHALLENGES OF BECOMING A COACH

Those who are contemplating on of becoming a coach should have at least a rudimentary or fundamental understanding of the many challenges and problems facing coaches in the pursuit of quality sports programs. Both high school and college coaching (and sometimes youth sport coaching) has been and remains today a *pressure cooker* environment.

It is also necessary to be aware of numerous opportunities, advantages and positive consequences awaiting those who engage in the coaching profession. And, of course, in order to make informed decisions within the sport arena, one must be in possession of appropriate and accurate facts and data and have sufficient experience upon which to base such decisions.

Coaching can be hard, difficult and to some, not worth the effort. It can also be quite enjoyable and very worthwhile. It can be demanding, cruel and unforgiving. It can also be flattering, supportive and highly rewarding. Coaching can be a great experience, a great life or it can be a miserable existence, for both the coach as well as for the coach's spouse and children, if any. It is up to the individual person to make the decision whether or not to become a coach and/or to continue to remain a coach based upon that individual person's character, philosophy, personality, experience, expectations, goals, priorities, patience, abilities and potential for learning.

DEVELOPING A PHILOSOPHY OF COACHING

What exactly is a coaching philosophy? One's philosophy is a result of a person's values and beliefs. A philosophy can be described as a way of looking at one's own situation, one's own world (and the greater world in which one exists), one's own coaching job, one's own athletes (Jones, Wells, Peters, Johnson, 1982). Webster's New Collegiate Dictionary (1973, p. 861) provides several definitions of philosophy. Two such definitions include *an analysis of the grounds of and concepts expressing fundamental beliefs* and *most general beliefs, concepts, and attitudes of an individual or group.*

A person's philosophy is also a reflection of one's personality, experiences, environment(s) and one's skills and competencies. The way a coach acts and behaves in specific situations is affected by and is a reflection of one's personal and professional philosophies. Likewise, one's philosophy is formed by one's experience, by one's education, by one's knowledge and by the sum total of all that affects and touches the individual person.

An example of one coach's philosophy can be seen in the statement by Ms. Chris Weller, the former coach of the women's basketball team at the University of Maryland, College Park, who said: "Our philosophy is to learn how to be as successful as we can be, to be happy, to learn how to work together, to have integrity in what we do—not talk about it but do it" (Becker, 1992, 1-C). Coaches are frequently in an enviable position of being able to help athletes face the real world by placing them in situations where the athletes, individually and collectively, have to compete and to cooperate, to overcome hurdles and challenges, to establish priorities, to sacrifice and to experience both success and failure, so that they are able to live in society as meaningful contributors to that society.

Another example of a NCAA Division I coach's philosophy can be seen in comments made by Rick Pitino, while coach Pitino was head coach at the University of Kentucky, when he stated: "I have been successful as a coach because I've been able to get people to do things they didn't think they were capable of doing" (Balog, 1997, p. 6-B). Coach Pitino also proposes 10 possible steps to success, as a coach as well as in the world of business (Balog, 1997, p. 6-B). These include:

1. Build self-esteem.
2. Set demanding goals.
3. Always be positive.
4. Establish good habits.
5. Master the art of good communication.
6. Learn from role models.
7. Thrive on pressure.
8. Be ferociously persistent.
9. Learn from adversity.
10. Survive success.

On the high school level, coach Morgan Wooten, the winningest basketball coach at the secondary level (in 1997) with a 38-year record of 1,095-163, expressed his coaching philosophy when he stated:

"To make winning the main focus is a stumbling block. It gets in the way of the bigger focus. It's similar to someone focusing on being happy. You can't focus on being happy. Happiness is a by-product of living a good life. In the same sense, winning and championships are by-products of deeper goals, of having the right kind of philosophy" (Morgan Wooten, 1997, p. 9).

Each of us possesses a philosophy of life—even if we do not take time to articulate it. Coaches possess a philosophy of education and a philosophy of coaching. Having a coaching philosophy really refers to what you, the coach, think about any number of things related to the coaching scene, the athletes, and the value of sports themselves. Coaches need to develop a philosophy, a perspective, a belief and an understanding in terms of any number of different factors and elements that go to make up the coaching experience and/or which affect the athletic environment. Possessing a philosophy of coaching aids the coach in establishing priorities in terms of what the coach feels is important in coaching and in terms of what the individual does as a coach (Stier, 1993). In short, one's philosophy also can provide direction to one's actions (Wuest & Bucher, 1991).

COACHING CONCEPT #8: **One must be able to articulate one's philosophy of life and one's philosophy of coaching.**

For example, what are your feelings about winning and losing? What do you think about the need to sacrifice in order to achieve, both for coaches and for athletes? What do you think about when selecting a team? Do you make cuts? If so, how are the cuts made and when are they made? What criteria should be used? Do you have a rationale in terms of how cuts are made? How do you notify those who fail to make the team as well as those who are successful? Why? What are your thoughts about discipline? Would you demand your athletes to be on time for practices? What do you think about athletes missing a class? What about missing a practice or being late for a practice or a game? Do you discipline using peer pressure? Why? Do you discipline by punishing athletes physically and/or psychologically? What about team rules? Do you have team rules? Why? Would you expect athletes to wear specific clothes to a home or away game? What about appropriate hair cuts? What are your thoughts on the athletes' behavior outside of school or away from practices and contests? What about prohibition of drinking or smoking? What are your feelings about rules regarding drug abuse/misuse by athletes? Who should make and enforce the team rules? What about punishment for infraction of rules? Are such penalties determined and announced in advance? Do you treat all athletes equally? What is your definition of treating athletes fairly and appropriately?

What are your specific expectations of your charges? Why? How are these expectations made known and to whom? Are there exceptions made? What about the importance of cheerleaders and cheering spectators? What are your thoughts about eligibility rules and academic standards? What is your leadership style? Why? How would you motivate your athletes? Why? How do you feel about winning and losing? Why? How do you handle a loss? Why? A victory? Why? How do you want your athletes to behave following a loss or a victory? Why? What is your philosophy about conditioning and training of athletes—during the season and during the off-season? Where do you stand on the subject of drug education? What are your thoughts about the hiring and use of athletic trainers? What priority do you place upon recruiting athletes? How do you feel about retention efforts for athletes? Do you put forth special effort to retain athletes in the program? What are they? How would you motivate your staff? Why? How does the booster club play a role in your athletic program? How will you deal with parents? Why? What about the athletic and school administrators? How do you relate to the news media? Would you want to be involved in fundraising, public relations and promotional activities? *In short, what are your feelings and ideas regarding every aspect of the sport you are coaching and towards sports in general?*

COACHING CONCEPT #9:   **One's philosophy of coaching is not stagnant— rather it evolves and is ever changing in light of experience and knowledge.**

Elite competition at the national level.

The answers to these and other similar questions depend, to a certain extent, upon your personal and professional philosophy, your training and education, your experiences (both positive and negative), and the athletic circumstances you find yourself in at any particular moment. *Remember, your coaching philosophy is not stagnant.* Rather, it is an evolving, ever changing series of beliefs, ideas and preferences about any and all aspects of life, that is, sports, people, goals, challenges and coaching, just to mention a few. A coach will act and make decisions based upon that person's philosophy, experience and the pertinent facts surrounding any given situation. Thus, a coach's philosophy is in a constant state of flux and will change, matures if you will, as the coach grows as a person and as a professional.

What is your philosophy of life? What is your philosophy about education? What is your current philosophy of coaching? Turn to the end of this chapter and complete the exercise assignment titled: *Defining One's Current Philosophy of Life, of Education, of Sports, and of Coaching.*

An Example of One Public School System Philosophy of Athletics (Competition)

Even schools and departments of athletics have publicized philosophy of sport or philosophy of competition which guide their sport programs and the actions of their coaches. One example of this philosophy of sport (competition) can been seen in Brockport Central Schools' (New York) athletic department which has differentiated that public school system's athletic philosophy according to modified, freshman, junior varsity and varsity levels. That school's philosophy statements are provided below.

Modified—*This program of competitive sports focuses on the fundamentals of the game, rules, training and basic skills. Emphasis is placed on basic skill development and maximum participation is desired. Participants will play approximately the same amount of time. All members of the team that participate the entire season will receive an equal award.*

Freshman—*This program is similar to the modified program in that basic skill development is stressed. The participant should become versed in the rules of the game. It is recognized that every effort will be made to play participants in all contests. All members of the team that participate the entire season will receive an equal award.*

Junior Varsity—*The junior varsity level of competition is the program where increased emphasis is placed upon team play, physical conditioning and refinement of basic skills. Winning at the junior varsity level is considered important and participants should be taught how to cope with losing and crowd influence during contests. Each individual will be given the opportunity to play during the season at the discretion of the coach. All members of the team that participate the entire season will receive an equal award.*

Varsity—*The varsity level of athletic competition is the culmination of the high school athletic program. Team play, sportsmanship, individual physical ability, motivation and mental attitude are very important aspects of competition at the varsity level. The team definitely plays to win the contest but varsity contestants should accept the fact that important lessons are to be learned from losing. It is recognized that not all participants play in every contest. All members of the team that participate the entire season will receive an equal award. Ability and attitude will be the determining factors in making the team at the varsity level.*

COACHING CONCEPT #10: **Schools and athletic departments also possess distinct philosophies of sport at various levels of competition.**

ETHICAL BEHAVIOR IN SPORT COMPETITION

Ethical behavior, like prejudice, is not inborn but yet is learned. Nor is ethical behavior merely a matter of black and white—there are many shades of gray in between. Ethical behavior means that the individual is doing what is right, what is correct, what is within the boundaries of acceptable behavior, both on the athletic playing field and off. It involves moral behavior on behalf of the individual, even if no one else is aware of the person's behavior.

Some coaches strive to instill ethical and moral behavior (passing along cultural values and ethical standards of excellence) among their athletes by means of the use of appropriate stories or sport narratives that target moral thinking. Athletes can learn much from stories and narratives, they can learn about values, beliefs, ideas, good and evil, honesty, integrity, right actions, and making correct and appropriate decisions. Such narratives can play an important role in moral education of athletes at all levels of competition (Hochstetler, 2006).

COACHING CONCEPT #11: If you have a question whether something is ethical or correct, ask yourself this question: Would you be comfortable in broadcasting your action(s) or decision(s) throughout your community for all to know?

Athletic competition can bring out the best as well as the worst in people. Athletic competition can teach youngsters about fair play as well as help corrupt these same individuals. Sports in and of themselves are neutral in terms of right or wrong. It is how the sports are organized and utilized that determine whether or not positive or negative consequences will result in respect to individuals' behavior.

The Chronicle of Higher Education, in 1989, listed all of the NCAA Division I-A schools which had been caught cheating and were cited by the NCAA for violations during the decade of the 80s. "Nearly half of the institutions in the National Collegiate Athletic Association's Division I-A have been censured, sanctioned, or put on probation by the N.C.A.A. at least once in this decade" (Lederman, 1989, p. A-35). Why the extensive cheating and violation of rules and regulations?

It is important that coaches present a good example. Being a role model is an important responsibility and should not be assumed in a light hearted manner. Coaches should lead by example in terms of following the intent and the letter of the law, that is, the rules and regulations governing fair play and the individual sports. Ethical behavior also involves acts of commission (doing something) as well as acts of omission (not doing something). Doing something that one should not do is the same as not doing something that one should be doing.

Ethics is intricately involved in personal and professional decision making. It involves making decisions regarding what is right, what is appropriate, and what is fair. Coaches and athletes should be held to the highest ethical standards because of the nature of their involvement in sports. Involvement in sports is supposed to teach the participants sportsmanship and high ethical behavior. To do otherwise is the worse type of hypocrisy.

Unacceptable Behavior by Coaches

One of the saddest stories in coaching in the modern era involved Woody Hayes at The Ohio State University in 1978. It happened during the 1978 Gator Bowl (Jacksonville, Florida) with the buckeyes losing (eventually by a score of 17-15) to Clemson University. A Clemson's player, Charlie Bauman, intercepted an Ohio State's pass and was tackled/knocked out of bounds in front of the buckeye bench. Coach Hayes reacted by punching Bauman, and had to be held back by his own players, all in front of a national television audience. Coach Hayes was 65 years of age and was in his 33rd season as a head coach. The very next day, he was fired. He ended his coaching career with 238 wins, 72 loses and 10 ties. At OSU his record was 205 victories, 61 defeats and 10 ties. He never coached football again.

COACHING CONCEPT #12: Don't sacrifice your career over a Snickers bar.

It is important for coaches to realize that one's actions or inactions can have a significant impact upon one's career. Coaches who exhibit questionable behavior in terms of ethics can indeed be placing their current coaching positions, if not their careers, in jeopardy. Coaches too frequently fall victims to the enticements of forbidden fruit (dishonesty, unethical behavior), even when the so-called benefits of such behavior or questionable decisions seem not to be of such great consequence. Too many coaches sacrifice their jobs and even their careers over a Snickers bar.

We continually are exposed, via the news media, to numerous examples of dishonesty, cheating and unethical behavior by coaches, athletic administrators, booster groups and athletes. Cheating has become of epidemic proportions at the college level, especially at the Division I level. Witness the fact that almost half of the NCAA Division I schools were cited for cheating during the decade of the 1980s.

Examples of Questionable Ethical Behavior

A recent controversy has erupted in sports concerning the prevalence at the secondary and collegiate level of trash talk, the use of profanity as well as taunting and baiting. Some high school associations and groups have officially outlawed trash talk and profanity. The NCAA has now forbidden taunting and baiting of opponents by athletes and coaches in actual competition. The rule states that "a player or coach may not use profanity, vulgarity, taunt, ridicule, obscene gestures, point a finger, or bait an opponent" (Family Values Resolution, 1992, p. 3-E).

Another example of questionable behavior by a coach was reported in the USA Today and it dealt with Jim Harrick, Jr., the assistant basketball coach (his father was the head coach at the time) at the University of Georgia and the way he conducted his *Coaching Principles and Strategies of Basketball* class in 2001. Some of the questions (within the 20-question test) are provided below (Harrick. Jr.'s test, 2004).

1. How many goals are on a basketball court?
2. How many players are allowed to play at one time on any one team in a regulation game?
3. In what league to (sic) the Georgia Bulldogs compete?
4. What is the name of the coliseum where the Georgia Bulldogs play?
5. How many halves are in a college basketball game?
6. How many quarters are in a high school basketball game?
7. How many points does a 3-point field goal account for in a Basketball Game?
8. What basic color are the uniforms the Georgia Bulldogs wear in home games?
9. What basic color are the uniforms the Georgia Bulldogs wear in away games?
10. How many minutes are played in a college basketball contest?
11. Diagram the 3-point line.
12. Diagram the half-court line.
13. How many fouls is a player allowed to have in a basketball game before fouling out in that game?

The NCAA concluded that in this college/university level course, coach Jim Harrick, Jr., "fraudulently awarded grades of A to three men's basketball student-athletes" who took Harrick's class in 2001. He was also accused of allowing them to miss both classes as well as tests. Every student in that class received a grade of A" (p. 1-B).

Even the high school level of competition is not immune from unethical or illegal behavior by coaches and/or athletes. Witness the situation some years ago at East

Rochester (New York) high school (and reported in Rochester's Democrat and Chronicle newspaper). In this situation, the varsity wrestling coach was censored by Section 5 and one of the coach's wrestlers (who competed under an assumed name at an earlier wresting competition/tournament) was stripped of his chance at a state championship.

> **COACHING CONCEPT #13:** **Sportsmanship must be of the utmost importance for coaches and their athletes—it reflects the character of the participants and the value placed upon the competitive experience**

Sportsmanship: An Integral Element in Coaching and Sports

Sportsmanship has received greater emphasis by schools, coaches, parents, and sport organizations in recent years. Witness the *National Sportsmanship Day* (every March 6th) proclaimed by the Institute for International Sport at the University of Rhode Island. The *National Sportsmanship Day* was first proclaimed in 1990. (Mihoces, 2001). Today, the *National Sportsmanship Day* is held throughout the country on the first Tuesday of each March (Pitoniak, 2004).

Some years ago the board of trustees in Scarsdale, New York passed a *code of conduct* that sought to regulate improper behavior among fans (especially parents). In fact, it forbad such actions

Sportsmanship is a mark of a champion.

as "taunting, yelling, nasty things, booing opposing teams and generally misbehaving at games" (played on the village athletic fields) (No Bronx cheers, 1999, p. C-1.).

Enhancing Ethical Behavior by Coaches

Some schools seek to enhance the likelihood of ethical behavior of coaches by asking the coaches to create a personal and a coaching philosophy statement. "Creating a personal philosophy statement allows coaches to think about what is important to them, put those thoughts into writing, and communicate them" (Docheff, 2005, p. 21). After this is accomplished, when coaches are faced with ethical dilemmas they have their own ethical statements to guide them in making appropriate and timely decisions.

One Conference's Effort to Combat Inappropriate Game Behavior by Coaches and Increase Sportsmanship

Chuck Mitrano, commissioner of the Empire conference (upstate New York) in NCAA Division III, devised a method and strategy to track bad conduct of players and coaches (Pitoniak, 2004). The result has been an increase in civil and good behavior. The plan instituted by Mitrano involves a method of measuring bad and inappropriate behavior on behalf of athletes and coaches during athletic contests. The plan has the conference tracking examples of inappropriate or uncivil behavior in contests, keeping records/statistics of such behavior and sharing the information with the presidents of the schools to which the athletes and/or coaches represent.

Specifically, the plan: ". . . monitors unsportsmanlike conduct among its athletes and coaches by tracking the personal-conduct fouls they commit during each game and reporting the numbers to college officials" (Jacobson, 2004, p. A-37). The conference initiated the effort in the fall of 2002 when red cards were tracked in men's and women's soccer. Efforts were expanded in the fall of 2003 when all personal-conduct fouls were tracked for those sports that recognize them (basketball, soccer, field hockey, football, lacrosse, and volleyball).

The effort was expanded to 41 conferences and 430 NCAA Division III institutions in 2004-2005. The project was funded through an $11,000 grant from the NCAA. The initial findings revealed that most conduct fouls occurred in men's sports (Johnson, 2005). Among the Empire 8 colleges following the initiation of this program, Mitrano found a significant decrease in the number of instances of poor sportsmanship among the conference's athletes and coaches.

DIFFERENT VIEWPOINTS OF THE COACHING EXPERIENCE

Some coaches have expressed a sincere love for their profession and their job by likening it to experiencing Christmas almost every day of their lives. That is, they get up almost every morning just like they did as youngsters on Christmas day, all excited about what that day has in store for them. Coaching can be like that—for some individuals. Coaches are usually excited about their athletic responsibilities and the tasks and challenges that face them on any given day. Many coaches simply love to coach and feel that coaching is one of the few jobs they would do for free, if they were independently wealthy. This is because of the enjoyment and satisfaction they get from their coaching experience and from their dealings with the youngsters.

And some coaches go overboard with their never ending search for victories and success in sports. Witness former Texas Cowboy coach Jimmy Johnson who stated:

> "I know it's not a popular thing to say these days . . . . You're not supposed to say that you're obsessed with your job. But I am . . . . I am absolutely obsessed with winning football games for the Cowboys. . . . My nightmare is to sit at some three-hour dinner party between a couple of coaches' wives, making small talk." (King, 1993, p. 4).

Shortly after taking the Cowboys' job, Coach Johnson "divorced his wife because they grown apart and because he did not want family stuff getting in the way of the biggest job of his life. . . . He doesn't remember birthdays, not even his two sons', and doesn't do Christmas" (King, 1993, p. 4).

Johnson was also quoted as saying:

> "You program yourself to do whatever it takes to win . . . . You always remember you've trying to get your team in the best position to win. One reason I got the divorce is I didn't want to have to go to the social events you go to as a coach. I didn't want to have sit in the dinner parties and ask somebody's wife what [she] did, then say, 'Oh, that's nice.' I mean, GET ME OUT OF HERE! Everything I do, I mean everything, has to come first" (King, 1993, p. 6).

However, the apparent and single-mindedness and arrogance exhibited by former cowboys' coach Johnson can also be seen in the team's owner, Jerry Jones, who was quoted as saying:

> "There is no ego in my life. But, 15 (or) 20 years ago, I was wandering around Arkansas and Bill Clinton was (too). Who would have ever thought that one would go on power, prestige and fame. And the other would end up president of the United States" (As Gumbel learns, 1995, p. 2-C).

COACHING CONCEPT #14: **Coaches, who lose their enthusiasm for coaching, are unwilling to continue to make necessary sacrifices—exhibit the classic symptoms of coaching burnout.**

And yet, there are other coaches who have had their fill of the coaching scene. These individuals now express a begrudging attitude at all of the effort and time they have put into coaching over the years with so little to show for it from their current perspective. These are individuals who express the attitude of having paid their dues and express a burning desire to get out of the rat race of coaching. These are individuals for whom the coaching experience has become something of a burden to bear rather than something anxiously anticipated. Coaching has not only ceased to be fun and satisfying but has become something negative, has become painful and uncomfortable to experience. These coaches are exhibiting the classic symptoms of coaching burnout.

Who is right? Who possesses the more accurate picture of coaching? It all depends upon the individual coach as well as past and current experiences of the individual along with current perspectives and circumstances. No two coaches are alike. But, for many, coaching is indeed a young person's game. Look around you. Look at the coaches you know in youth sports, in interscholastic sports and at the college/university level. What percentage of these coaches are over age 50 or even 45 years of age and are still coaching or are coaching like they did when they started out in the profession, with the same enthusiasm, and even fanaticism (especially if their teams are not winning)?

> **COACHING CONCEPT #15: Coaches become more susceptible to burnout the longer they stay in the coaching profession.**

DROP-OUT AMONG COACHES AS THEY GET OLDER

Unfortunately, as coaches get older (mature, more experienced) they tend to leave the coaching profession. Why is this? Why is there a gradual, but nevertheless significant, decrease in the number of coaches who remain in coaching as they get older? The reasons may be many and varied. For some it is a matter of not winning enough. These are individuals who have been or are being judged by others and/or themselves as being unsuccessful, or worse yet, as failures. For others, they may simply lose interest.

For others it may be that their dream of coaching at a specific level or school never materializes, for any number of reasons. And, as a consequence, they simply drop out of the race for the elusive bigger, better position at a larger school or at a higher level of competition. For others it is a matter of burnout from the stresses and pressures of the job. Some individuals find as they mature that the time commitment becomes too much in light of new, higher, priorities. These individuals may develop other interests that compete for their time and effort. And, in other instances, individuals, both male and female, choose to leave coaching because the experience no longer satisfies them to such an extent that it is worth remaining as a coach with all of its accompanying challenges and problems. Many coaches, as they get older, find that the rewards and benefits emanating from coaching no longer offset or outweigh the sacrifices which must be made by coaches and the disadvantages which accompany coaching. For future mentors, it is important to be aware that if significant number of coaches did not leave the profession as they matured (as opposed to dying on the job) there would be few coaching vacancies for the younger, eager coaches-to-be to compete for and to secure.

> **COACHING CONCEPT #16:** Coaches need to evaluate the plusses and minuses associated with any coaching situation—in light of their own specific needs and situations.

PROS AND CONS OF COACHING

There are indeed many advantages to being an athletic coach, either a head coach or as an assistant coach, at all levels from the youth sports program, the interscholastic level, the college level or even in the semi-pro or professional ranks. However, there is also a downside to coaching—made up of significant challenges and risks which are evident in any coaching situation. It is up to the individual to be able to recognize and weigh the positive and negative aspects of any coaching situation. Then and only then should that person make a decision whether or not to become associated or remain involved as a coach in that particular situation and under those circumstances.

Many of the advantages associated with coaching are also reasons why individuals choose to be coaches in the first place and why they remain as a coach as long as they do. And, many of the disadvantages of coaching (at various levels) are also reasons why individuals either do not elect to enter the coaching profession or,

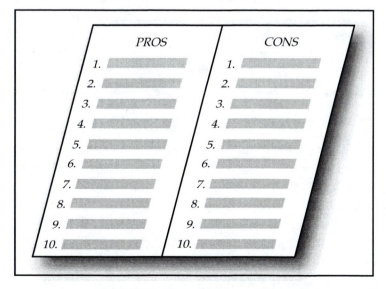

FIGURE 2.1—Pros and Cons of Coaching

after some years as coaches, choose to leave the profession. Before reading further, turn to the end of this chapter and complete the exercise titled: *Comparing the Disadvantages and Advantages of Being a Coach.*

POSITIVE ASPECTS ASSOCIATED WITH COACHING

Just as there are challenges and problems associated with the coaching of athletic teams, there are numerous advantages and positive aspects connected with being a coach at the amateur level. Not every coach views the coaching scene in the identical way. Some coaches view some aspects of coaching as very positive benefits connected with being a mentor. Other coaches view other aspects of the coaching scene as being very positive. Some of the more generally recognized positive aspects emanating from coaching are provided below.

Opportunities to Work with Young People

On the positive side of the ledger is the opportunity to work with young people, to have a role in their development and growth and to see the results of one's efforts, hopefully, in a positive vein. To be able to play a role in helping others can be a major reward for the coach. To see a boy or girl or young man or woman develop physically, mentally, psychologically, socially, morally and ethically is reward enough for all of the trials and tribulations which coaches endure in the performance of their duties.

COACHING CONCEPT #17: Coaches have great opportunities to have real and significant impact upon others, especially their athletes.

Opportunity to Make a Difference, to Influence Others

Coaches have a very important role to assume with their athletes. They have much to offer to their young charges. The potential influence or impact that coaches have upon their charges can be substantial. In fact, coaches at all levels probably have a greater impact and influence upon the behavior of the youngsters they coach than any other adult—other than the parents. And, in not a few instances, coaches can have more of an impact and be more of an influence than even an athlete's parents. "Research has shown that the coach plays a critical role in conducting a safe and educationally sound athletic program and that the coach is the single most important factor affecting the athletes" (Sisley & Wiese, 1987, p. 74).

The Excitement of the Chase

Additionally, the excitement of the contest can serve as a motivating factor and can be very gratifying to the coach. The ability to be in the center of action insofar as the athletic team is concerned is attractive to many coaches. Being well known and respected as a coach of considerable talent is a positive outcome of being successful. The activities and trappings associated with coaching can be exciting, exhilarating and rewarding.

Demonstration of Competence by the Coach

Being a coach places an individual in a situation in which the person is able to demonstrate specific competencies and skills in working with youngsters in a sporting environment. The competitive nature of sports provides a public platform or stage on which the skill and competency levels of both athletes and coaches are readily discerned by others. Being judged by others as successful and competent can be a highly motivating and satisfying experience.

Being Able to Coach Can Aid in Obtaining a Teaching Position

Being a qualified coach can greatly enhance the potential of securing a teaching position in a school system. This is because school systems are frequently in a desperate situation in terms of securing qualified coaches who are also able to teach within the system. Thus, would-be teachers, regardless of their teaching specialty, can increase their likelihood of being hired as a teacher on the elementary, junior high and high school levels if they are also able and willing to be a coach in at least one sport, and preferably two or more sports.

Opportunity for Travel

For some individuals coaching provides opportunities for travel. Travel opportunities involve team travel in competing with opposing teams. Travel is also involved in attending coaching clinics, conferences and workshops. For some coaches, travel opportunities might well be limited to one's own state. For others, travel will encompass many sections of the country. And, for still others, travel will mean extensive travel throughout the United States as well as extensive foreign opportunities.

Opportunity for Developing Personal Friendships, Relationships and a Special Kind of Camaraderie

Coaching can be a very close knit community. Those involved in the coaching profession are able to develop exceptional personal friendships and professional relationships with others that would not have been possible had it not been for their athletic involvement. Such involvements and relationships are not limited to other coaches or athletic people, although there is and always has been a special kind of camaraderie among those who belong to the so-called coaching profession.

Being a coach has the potential of opening many, many doors to other individuals, groups and organizations within the community, the state and the entire country. People in our society are fascinated with sports. They are fascinated with athletes. And, they are enamored with successful and high profile coaches. As a result coaches will find that they have many opportunities for developing numerous relationships and meaningful friendships with others.

Coaching is a Self-Motivating Activity or Involvement

Being involved in the sports scene as a coach is often a self-motivating experience. That is, being involved in sports is exciting in and of itself. Being a coach is exciting and motivating. One is able to take pride in one's accomplishments and in the accomplishments of one's players. It is fun. It is enjoyable. It is worth while doing for its own sake but it is nevertheless personally and professionally satisfying and therefore serves as a self-motivating activity.

Coaching Provides a Change of Pace for the Coach

Another advantage of coaching is that such an activity can prove to be a much needed and deserved change of pace for the mentor. Some coaches may teach math or English all day in the classroom. Their coaching activity after the normal school day is over provides a much needed respite from their regular teaching positions. And, since coaching a competitive sport is different than teaching a subject matter such as Business, Sociology or Biology within a classroom, such a change of pace is welcome indeed. Similarly, the part-time coach who holds a full time position in a corporation or business can find coaching an invigorating experience and refreshing change of pace after a day in a stuffy office or traveling on the road.

Opportunities for Career Advancement

Coaching may provide opportunities for further career advancement either in sports or in completely different areas. As stated earlier, coaching opens the doors for professional and personal relationships to be built with many other individuals, groups and organizations. As a result, it is frequently possible for coaches to advance their careers (outside of coaching) through these relationships that have been built as a result of their coaching involvement. However, the concept is a viable one at all levels. They are innumerable instances of successful individuals who started out in coaching only to find that their real career ladder took them out of coaching into another profession as a result of their success as coaches and the relationships they developed and nurtured while serving as coaches.

Vanderbilt University bowling coach talks with ESPN while his team celebrates the school's first ever NCAA team championship (2007).

Climbing the Ladder of Success as a Coach

There is another aspect of career advancement in sports. Specifically, those who are successful as assistant coaches often are able to move to head coaching positions. Those coaches who are successful at the junior high level or at the freshmen level are able to move up to the sophomore team or the junior varsity team and eventually to a varsity squad. And, individuals who experience success at small schools are often able to move as coaches to larger schools either on the high school level or the college level. Those coaches who are able to demonstrate competency at small colleges sometimes are able to move up the career ladder to larger colleges and then onto bigger universities. And, assistant coaches at big-time schools frequently are able to assume head coaching positions at Division I, II, III or NAIA institutions as a result of their successful experiences and affiliations at the Division I level of competition.

In other words, within the world of sports sponsored by educational institutions, there is a hierarchical structure in terms of organizational levels. For example, there are junior high schools, there are high schools, there are junior/community colleges, there are small four year colleges and universities as well as medium and very large colleges and universities. All of these offer opportunities for career advancement in terms of coaching. And, within each of these educational levels, are various coaching positions, again on a hierarchical basis, such as an assistant or a head coach on the freshman, junior varsity and varsity levels.

Opportunities for Significant Financial Rewards at the Higher Levels of Competition

In recent years, coaches at the higher levels of amateur sports have been receiving significant compensation packages, refer to chapter one. Although antidotal information has frequently pointed to the lack of adequate financial compensation for coaches, in reality, today, coaches—for the most part—receive fair compensation for the coaching jobs at schools and colleges. This is not to say that all coaches earn what the NCAA Division I football or basketball coaches receive, but rather that the compensation has improved over the past years and today the salary for coaches is fairly well received by those in the schools who coach.

Opportunity to Build Successful Sport Programs

The challenge of building a successful team in a sport can be a motivating factor for many people choosing to become a coach. The advantage of being one's own boss, being in control, being responsible for building and creating a successful team, is motivation enough for many young, would-be coaches.

Opportunity to Give Back Something to Sports

Almost all coaches have been athletes sometime in their youth. Many have expressed the opinion that one of the reasons why they became involved in the coaching profession was because of their desire to return something back to the sport world, to pay back part of what they had received as a result of their prior athletic experience. This desire to give back to sports is very real and is a valid reason, among others, for examining the possibility of becoming an athletic coach. On the other hand, many would-be coaches have expressed the conviction that they desired to be a coach so that they can do a *better* job of coaching than they had received as athletes.

COACHING CONCEPT #18:   **Coaches frequently don't know the effect they have had on others (e.g. athletes) until years later, if even then.**

It has often been said that coaches have the very real potential for significantly influencing many, many individuals in their roles as athletic coaches. This is especially true in terms of their athletes. However, for many coaches, it is not always clearly evident how considerable an effect one has had on one's athletes until years later, if even then. Much of the influence that coaches have on their young charges might not be clearly discernible at the time, or even in later years. However, the positive influence and impact that coaches do have on athletes can extend well beyond the immediate coaching scene. In fact, the sphere of influence that coaches can have on athletes can extend many years in the future and can have a significant and sometimes long range effect on the future behaviors and attitudes of their athletes.

Opportunity to Retain Some Association or Connection with Sports

As mentioned above, most coaches have been athletes themselves at some time in their lives. For many of these persons the experience had been very positive both in terms of the physical dimension and the non-physical dimension. As a result, these former athletes desire to retain some type of formal connection with the sports world and coaching provides one such avenue. These former athletes are still involved in the competition. They are still involved in the physical aspects of sports. They are able to continue to develop relationships with other like-minded, sports oriented individuals. In short, they can extend their happy marriage with sports by remaining involved in competitive sports as a coach, rather than as an athlete.

Involvement In Sports Keeps A Person Young in Mind and Body

Many coaches would swear on a stack of bibles that working with youngsters on a daily basis, in a sports setting, helps keep them young, both in mind and body. This close association with young people helps coaches remain active physically and mentally. Being a coach of youngsters is a demanding responsibility and one that forces coaches to retain the intensity, the attitudes, as well as the physical and mental vigor that are commonly associated with young people.

NEGATIVE ASPECTS ASSOCIATED WITH COACHING

Every potential coach must face reality and recognize that there are some factors that make coaching less than desirable; some things associated with coaching and sports that are a burden, a challenge or a hindrance and which must be recognized, overcome or at least dealt with. Some of these factors might be insignificant to some while to others they can be most consequential. Some of these factors, but not all, are presented below.

The Time Factor

Coaching can be an all-consuming experience for the neophyte and the experienced coach alike. Coaches of most school sponsored sports will spend upwards of 35 hours each week (including weekends) during their season doing a wide variety of athletic tasks ranging from actual coaching in a contest, recruiting efforts, personally scouting opponents and viewing films or video tapes, planning, conducting and evaluating practice sessions, meeting with athletes, parents, school officials, media, and members of the community as well as dealing with a myriad of other mundane details and seemingly mountains of paper work. These hours are in addition to the coaches' other responsibilities associated with teaching in the classroom or other full time employment responsibilities.

COACHING CONCEPT #19: Keep a balance between your family life, your personal activities, and your professional obligations and responsibilities.

Most coaches will find themselves involved in their sport(s) performing a variety of coaching related tasks throughout the calendar year even though they might not find themselves actually coaching athletes all year long. Thus, different coaching activities take place during the so-called preseason, in-season, post-season as well as the out-of-season spans of time.

Coaches need to be aware that the time factor. How they manage this invaluable resource can become a critical factor in their overall success. How much time the coach is willing and able to spend in coaching related tasks in contrast to the time spent on other job responsibilities and the time spent with one's spouse and family can have a profound effect upon one's personal life (family) and one's professional life (Hill, 2005).

COACHING CONCEPT #20: It is imperative to have a supportive spouse and family—don't neglect the home front.

Time Commitments for the High School Teacher/Coach

A high school coach who is also a teacher may arrive at school at 7:15 a.m. and teach through 2:30 or 3:00 p.m. During this time span the coach/teacher might have responsibility for classes, supervision of study hall(s), and lunchroom duties. Practice can run from 3 or 3:30 p.m. until 5 or 5:30 p.m., and in some cases as late as 6 p.m. By the time the coach is free to leave the practice site it can easily be 7 p.m. At home there are athletic practices to develop and lesson plans to design. Also, on some evenings, there are games to attend, either home and away. And, of course, for many sports there is the need to scout opponents during the season. Add to this the time spent on weekends attending clinics and workshops, as well as working (if a varsity coach) with junior varsity and junior high (middle school) sports programs (coaches and athletes), and it is clearly evident that the coach, especially while in season, has little free time. In fact, for many coaches, coaching during the in-season time of their season can become almost a full time involvement.

In reality, the so-called negative factors related to the profession of coaching should really be considered as *challenges* rather than *pressures* or as *insurmountable problems*. Mannie (2005, p. 10) provides the following nine hints for coaches to consider in their attempts to combat the burnout syndrome.

1. Be sure and spend, each day, quality time with family members.
2. Obtain at least 7-8 hours of sleep each night.
3. Each day be sure and eat regularly and eat nourishing meals.
4. Consume food rich in fiber should be eaten each day.
5. Consume food low in cholesterol, saturated fat, and Trans fat each day.
6. Watch what you eat. Eat red meat in moderation, and if you eat red meat have it baked, grilled, or broiled rather than fried. Fish and poultry are good substitutes for red meat.
7. Keep the condiments to a minimum, especially when eating out.
8. Don't be sedentary. Be sure and get 30 minutes of exercise during at least three days each week, 52 weeks a year.
9. Make periodic visits to your physician and be sure to have all appropriate tests (e.g., prostrate exam, colonoscopy, mammogram, blood pressure, blood lipid profile, etc.).

Hardships on the Spouse and Family Members

If the coach is married, there may be times when coaching obligations and tasks create conflict with and hardships for one's spouse. Sometimes the spouse perceives that coaching takes precedence over the well-being of the family. This sometimes does happen in spite of the best of intentions. It is hard on the fabric of the family to have the coach away so much of the time and to operate under the pressure and stress that sometimes accompanies the coaching position.

It is difficult to reconcile spending so much time with other people's children while sometimes having to neglect one's own children. A coach once lamented to the author that, in reflection, he now regretted having spent all of those years coaching football. He felt terrible having spent his time with other youngsters in practice and games while missing his own son's games which were played on the same days as his own team was scheduled to play. Coaches would do well to make arrangements to spend the appropriate time (quality time) with one's family. Coaching is often perceived by the coach as one of the most important things in the world. However, coaching may not be viewed in the same way by the spouse and children of the coach, especially as the years go by and the children grow older.

Unreasonable, Impolite, Violent, and Unsafe/Dangerous Reactions and Actions of Parents, Fans and Athletes

"Parents are sometimes unprepared for the gamut of emotions they experience while watching their children compete. The many violent incidents of today demonstrate that parents' emotions run too high simply because they want their children to do well in every activity. Some parents believe that their children's failures are their own and that it somehow reflects back on them as the parent" (Cromartie, 2001, p. 5).

Following are some examples of inappropriate actions by fans, parents and athletes.

A dad who was unhappy that the coach of his son's Little League team took his son out of the game, threatened to kill the coach. The father was arrested, sentenced to 45 days in jail, to three years' probation, six months of anger management therapy, as well as told not to engage in arguments at sporting events (Little League Dad, 2001).

In Toronto, Canada, the court charged a father with assault after he grabbed the face mask of his own daughter and violently shook it at a youth hockey game (Dad cited, 2001).

COACHING CONCEPT #21:   Parents can be unreasonable at times both in their actions and their attitudes—it comes with the territory.

In Florida parents of youngsters who are to compete in youth sports are required to take a class (involving a 19-minute video) in proper behavior as fans/parents. They must also sign a code of behavior. Failure to do so, and their children cannot play. A similar situation developed in El Paso, Texas where a 2 1/2 hour course was designed for parents of young players. The course comes with a manual that is required reading by the parents (Youth sports, 2001).

Below is a summary of outrageous conduct in sport.

- In Greensboro, North Carolina, a mother of a soccer player was arrested and charged for striking a teenage referee after a game.

- A Cleveland, Ohio parent punched a 15-year old boy on the soccer field because the father felt that his son was being pushed around by the bigger athlete.

- A soccer mom attacked and struck the father of an opposing player and was taken to the police station and charged. She was released on her own recognizance.

- A police officer in a small community was accused of paying $10 to a player to deliberately throw and hit a batter on the opposing team.

- In July of 1999, a father of one youth hockey player killed the father of another player (he beat the man to death) following a game in Massachusetts. He was charged with manslaughter (It pays, 2000).

- In September of that same year, a New Jersey's soccer game ended in a tie after parents of the players got into a fist fight (It pays, 2000).

- In Florida, nearly 100 parents and coaches were involved in a brawl following a football game (It pays, 2000).

Racial and Sexual Discrimination

In spite of recent gains by women in the world of coaching by women (witness the million dollar contract for the women's basketball coach at the University of Texas), women have experienced and are continuing to experience both overt and covert discrimination within the coaching ranks. Similarly, minorities have and are still experiencing discrimination in the coaching ranks. Witness the relatively small percentage of minorities in head coaching positions at all levels. Similarly, the number of women who serve as head coaches or as senior level athletic administrators, again at all levels, falls far short of what would be expected if there were not discrimination and artificial roadblocks hindering more active involvement by women. It is interesting to note that women, legally, are not classified as minorities in this country but are viewed as being members of a protected class. Yet, the existence of the glass ceiling or glass walls insofar as coaching advancements by women and by minorities is without question. However, with increased enforcement of the existing laws of this country and a change in the attitudes of those individuals administering the athletic programs, it is only a matter of time before the existing hurdles become less of a hindrance to women and minorities desiring to advance through the coaching ranks. However, it will not be easy or immediate. Such hurdles do indeed still exist and prospective coaches need to be aware of them.

> **COACHING CONCEPT #22:** Women need to face the reality that there still exists discrimination and roadblocks in terms of career opportunities as coaches.

Numerous ongoing and related studies have been conducted by Acosta and Carpenter (1987; 1988a; 1988b; 1990; 1992, 1997, 2000, 2003 and 2006) into the reasons for disparity in job opportunities between men and women in sports. In fact, these researchers have been involved in a multi-year [29th year] longitudinal study that has revealed a trend involving an overall decrease in the number of women as head coaches and as senior administrators within athletic departments at the secondary level (Acosta and Carpenter, 1997; Acosta and Carpenter, 2006). The research shows that today more females play in amateur sports than in past years while at the same time fewer women coach and fewer women serve as athletic administrators (More Women, 2000; Acosta and Carpenter, 2006).

Acosta and Carpenter (unpublished paper, 2006) cite various reasons for the decline in women coaches at all levels of amateur school sports. These are presented below:

Primary Reasons for the Decline in Women Coaches

1. Success of the old boy's club network.
2. Lack of support systems for females.
3. Failure of the old girls club network.
4. Females burn-out and leave coaching and administrative positions sooner than males.
5. Failure of females to apply for coaching positions.

Secondary Reasons for the Decline in Women Coaches

1. Lack of qualified female administrators.
2. Lack of qualified female coaches.
3. Time constraints due to family obligations.
4. Unconscious/conscious discrimination in selecting and hiring coaches.

Other Reasons for the Decline in Women Coaches

1. Perception that a female's family obligation will keep the woman from doing a good job.
2. Females being unaware of potential and current job openings.

3. Higher qualifications are expected of female applicants.

4. Females are more likely to fulfill both coaching and teaching duties than males.

4. Those who hire are less likely are unwilling to hire females because of fear that females are more likely to be more homosexual than male applicants.

Another challenge which women have had to face and continue to face in many areas is the unequal pay earned in comparison with their male counterparts who hold similar jobs. Although this is changing in many schools and school systems, it is not uncommon to find the male head basketball coach earning significantly more than the female head basketball coach, especially at the college level (NCAA, Division I). Of course, this deplorable situation is not unique to sports.

There is a need for *both women and men* to be willing to address this seemingly perpetual challenge. A summary of the current challenges facing women seeking employment opportunities is summarized by Stier (1985, p. 16):

> "The bottom line remains. There exists too few qualified female athletic administrators and coaches, too few opportunities for women to gain access-even at the bottom rung of the athletic ladder-to the athletic administrative and coaching positions, and there exists too few advancement opportunities for the small number of women who are able to secure the limited posts which do become available. Things will not change until it is recognized by all constituencies that successful athletic programs must involve female and male administrators and coaches in meaningful capacities. There exists an obligation to create such opportunities *now.*"

Women suffrage was passed in 1920 in the United States; however, women still lag today significantly behind men in salaries (for comparable work). In fact, the average weekly salary for women clerical workers in this country in 1991 was $348.00 while for men it was much higher, $459. In terms of managerial positions, women averaged $527 in weekly earnings while men garnered a handsome $753 per week. In 1990 46% of the United States work force was women (Nussman, 1993).

Teacher/Coach Role Conflict

Frequently, those individuals who have a full time job teaching and also coach face the possibility of being caught in a role conflict. In 2008 the situation is still I need of improvement. The teacher/coach role conflict refers to the situation in which the role of a coach might interfere with one's role as a teacher. For example, a softball coach desires to have team members released from the last two periods of the school day so as to prepare for and travel to an away game. However, as a teacher, this same individual knows that having young athletes consistently miss the same classes numerous times during the spring is not a sound educational practice. What should the coach do? As a coach it seems imperative that these athletes be excused from classes and be able to participate in the athletic contest. As a teacher, would the coach be so willing to have students from one's own class being excused 3-4-5-6 or more times in the spring so as to play on a softball team?

COACHING CONCEPT #23: **Being a coach and a teacher makes a person a prime candidate for role conflict—one must be able to juggle both areas of responsibilities while neglecting neither.**

Another example of the teacher/coach conflict is the individual who is hired to teach full time in the high school and receives an extra stipend to coach one or two or even three sports. This person must establish priorities and balance the responsibilities and tasks involved in both teaching and in coaching, figure 2.2. In this situation the teacher/coach is expected to usually assume teaching and related responsibilities from 7:30 or 8 a.m. to 3 p.m. or so *and* then to conduct practices from 3:30 to 5:30 or 6 p.m. In this scenario the teacher/coach receives 95%, if not more, of the total salary package for teaching and less than 5% for coaching. However, in the real world of teaching and coaching, it is not unusual for the teacher/coach to spend an inordinate amount of time on the coaching responsibilities and very little time and effort (relatively speaking) on the teaching tasks.

FIGURE 2.2—Juggling the tasks of a coach with other job responsibilities.

The witticism that has been around for decades, and which unfortunately has more truth in it than many would care to admit, is that teachers/coaches receive 90-95% of their salary for teaching and 5-10% for coaching—but that 75% of their attention and effort is devoted to coaching while only 25% is apportioned to teaching.

Coaching—Teaching Burnout

Sometimes coaches just become plain burned out. This is possible when individuals become tired of coaching. They no longer see any real and tangible benefits from continuing as a coach. These coaches fail to see any benefits accruing to their family either. In fact, they frequently perceive nothing or almost nothing but negative consequences from their continued involvement in the coaching experience. As a result, motivation is diminished, if not lost. And, the effectiveness and efficiency of these coaches are adversely affected. In short, coaches become tired of coaching and coaching becomes a chore instead of a joy as it might have been in past years.

COACHING CONCEPT #24: Coaches should have 20-years of experience rather than one-year's experience twenty times—the latter is indicative of a coach who has burned out.

As a tragic result, individuals who become burned out fail to exhibit the enthusiasm and the dedication so necessary for successful coaches. Coaches who are burned out no longer do their job with the zeal, determination, excitement and diligence that they once exhibited. Nor are their coaching tasks accomplished in an adequate fashion and at an acceptable level of performance. The inevitable consequences are that the athletes are short changed, the program suffers accordingly, and the team as well as the total athletic program can be significantly diminished in terms of quality.

Lack of Monetary Rewards

If you enter the coaching profession seeking only excitement, glamour, publicity, big money and the advantages of a high profile position you will probably be bitterly disappointed. Only some of the coaches of the so-called flagship sports at the really big-time schools, and the coaches at the professional level, earn the truly big bucks. For example, in 2007 it was reported that at 58 of the 65 schools in the 2006 Division I tournament field the average salary was nearly $800,000. However, in the BCS conferences, the average head basketball coach made some $1.2 million in 2007, not counting benefits, incentives or perks. In addition, in that same year, there were reportedly at least 24 millionaire basketball coaches at the big-time, Division I level of competition, while in 2002 there were only two. The coaches of six of the 2007 NCAA tournament's Elite Eight teams were awarded new contracts/deals as a reward for their teams' successes. Their raises were not inconsequential. For example: at the five schools where raises were part of the public record, George Mason, LSU,

Memphis, Texas and UCLA, the head basketball coaches of the men's team averaged an increase of $332,000 each (Wieberg, 2007).

COACHING CONCEPT #25: **Coaching is not all glamour and glitter—there are innumerable mundane, simplistic, boring but otherwise very necessary tasks that must be performed.**

Routine Tasks Involved In Coaching

Many aspects of coaching are not glamorous but rather tedious and monotonous, if not downright boring. For example, the innumerable meetings; scheduling activities; planning and conducting practices; scheduling tryouts; selecting youngsters for the team, working and facing challenges from students and their parents; recruiting student-athletes; involvement in pre-season, in-season, post season and out-of-season planning;

The intensity of coaching and competition.

attendance at clinics and workshops; working with boosters, the media, teachers, administrators and the public—can all be taxing, challenging but also exhilarating. Although many of the routine tasks are customarily assigned to assistant coaches, when such positions are available, this is not always the case.

The Win-Win Syndrome

What about the ever-present concern with winning in sports? What about the pressure to win, at almost any cost, which seemingly permeates many coaching situations? Is there a legitimate concern about an overemphasis placed on winning? Or, is this *all a bit to do about nothing*?

On the one hand there are those who say that coaches should not be subjected to the extreme pressure of having to win, win, and win some more. These proponents cite the pressure to win as the source of many, if not most, of the resulting evils associated with competitive sports at every level of amateur sports. There are proponents who advocate that schools should de-emphasize the importance being placed on winning so that the real educational benefits and other values of the athletic experience can be more readily realized.

**COACHING CONCEPT #26: Competitive sports are just that, competitive—
that is why score is kept.**

However, there are others who take the position that we need to deal with reality. Competitive sports are always going to be associated with the dimensions of winning and losing. After all, that is why score is kept. Thus, when individuals are hired to coach, winning (i.e., the success factor) must be taken into consideration just as it is in any profession or job. For example, when an individual is hired as an insurance or real estate salesperson, or is hired by a corporation to assume responsibility for specific tasks, that person is held accountable in a very real way. Why should not the coach be held accountable?

**COACHING CONCEPT #27: In the real world, results are what count—not
merely effort.**

If an individual does not sell sufficient insurance or real estate or fails to perform other tasks as assigned, the individual will not remain in that position for very long. The so-called bottom line is that an individual is not retained in the real world just because the person is a nice individual who tries hard. Results are needed. The ultimate criteria by which each of us are judged in our society is indeed whether one can produce. In sales, selling is one of the primary objectives, the bottom line. In business, generating a financial profit is one of the primary objectives, the bottom line. In the world of competitive sports, in coaching, winning is one of the benchmarks differentiating the successful from the unsuccessful.

Others would take the position that one shouldn't equate coaching with the business world or with the selling of insurance or real estate. These individuals cite the rationale that the coaching scene (other than the pros) is significantly different from the so-called real world of business and that comparisons between the two are not valid. They would argue that the tremendous emphasis placed upon winning in athletics in our schools is inappropriate (even at Division I) and that the emphasis should be placed upon the educational *process* itself rather than the mere *outcome* as determined by the score between two combatants—whether they are made up of individuals or teams.

> **COACHING CONCEPT #28: If coaches can't stand the heat—they should get out of the kitchen *(Harry Truman)*.**

Outside Pressures

Successful athletes exhibit the ultimate effort.

Coaches are often subjected to a wide range of outside pressures from parents, alumni, fans and members of booster clubs. These so-called supporters frequently have the advantage of perfect 20-20 hindsight and not infrequently make their feelings known concerning the supposed competency of the coach. Although many coaches voice the opinion that they feel more pressure from themselves in terms of high expectations, it is nevertheless evident that outside pressures on coaches can be extreme and unrelenting at times.

Hopefully, with adequate support from enlightened athletic administrators, coaches should be able to handle such pressures and resultant stressors. Nevertheless, a negative factor associated with many coaching situations centers around the efforts by outsiders to control or at least influence the coaching process—outsiders who have no right to attempt to do so. However, as former President Harry Truman was fond of indicating, *if you can't stand the heat you had better get out of the old kitchen*. Coaches, if they can't handle such pressure should not serve as coaches in pressure-packed sport environments.

Necessity of Making Tough Decisions

Being a coach places an individual in a situation where numerous tough decisions must be made. These are important decisions that can significantly affect the lives of many other individuals, groups and organizations. In reality, almost every decision that a coach makes has the potential for impacting upon others, whether they be student-athletes, other coaches, fans, boosters, administrators, or family members. Of course, the greatest impact any coach will have is upon that coach's own athletes and the coach's family. This is due to the nature of sport and coaching. This is a tremendous responsibility. It can also be a significant burden for any coach to carry. Some coaches can readily accept such a responsibility while others find this an uncomfortable chore.

Problems and Disagreements with Administrators

It is inevitable that coaches will experience honest disagreements with athletic administrators and/or school administrators. However, when disagreements grow into problems that affect the coach's ability to perform on the job, then the situation is serious indeed. Being able to work with sport and school administrators in a constructive manner rather than being antagonistic can be challenging for some and almost impossible for others. A disadvantage of being a coach is that as a coach one is often at the mercy of school and sport administrators who have the ultimate authority to make decisions that affect a coach's program and therefore one's future.

> **COACHING CONCEPT #29:** **Coaches must be capable of taking the necessary and appropriate steps when confronted with challenges and problems.**

Coaches usually have four possible responses in light of challenges and problems associated with their jobs. First, coaches can always leave the position and seek greener pastures elsewhere. Of course, there is no guarantee that there are any so-called greener pastures elsewhere, or that even if there were, that the coach would be able to secure a position elsewhere. Second, coaches can accept the situation as it exists in their current employment picture, including the existing problems and challenges, and do nothing but continue to do their job the best way possible. The third option available to coaches is to attempt to change the problematic situation that does exists and which presents a problem or challenge to them. Of course, any attempt to change the status quo must be within the appropriate guidelines of the organization. All of these three avenues are professionally acceptable in terms of how coaches handle problems and make decisions in response to problems or challenges that they experience on the job.

> **COACHING CONCEPT #30:** **Never bad mouth others when confronted with problems, difficulties or challenges—to do so is unprofessional, unprincipled and unethical.**

There is a fourth possible course of action that coaches might choose to take when faced with problems in the work place. However, this type of action is highly unprofessional, unethical and amoral. That is, coaches can cry, groan and moan. They can criticize individuals (behind their backs), policies and the organization itself. They can back-bite others. They can blame others and attempt to place a negative light on the actions of others. And, they can execute end runs around administrators. Needless to say, such actions can quickly spell an end to an otherwise promising career. For, in the final analysis, who would want to hire, promote or retain such an unprincipled person.

Over-Burdened with Details, Paper Work and Administrative Tasks

Many coaches frequently lament that if all they had to do was to coach they would consider themselves in heaven. To the contrary, they find themselves involved, almost on a daily basis, with many different administrative details and responsibilities. To be a successful coach, one must perform many tasks that do not directly involve the coaching of athletes either on a team or individuals basis. On the amateur level, it is the coaches who are frequently saddled with the responsibility of performing many of these tasks. If all you want to do is to work with athletes during practice and to coach them during the actual contests, you may want to reexamination your thinking. Most coaching situations, other than at the NCAA Division I level, are not like that at all.

COACHING CONCEPT #31: **There is usually no such thing as tenure or a continuing contract for coaches—there is no free lunch for coaches.**

Lack of Job Security

The vast majority of coaches rarely enjoy any real job security *as coaches.* Of course, those coaches who also teach in a school (kindergarten through the college level) can frequently earn continuing contract or tenure (lifetime job security, with only a few exceptions) as a teacher. However, they but rarely—if ever—can secure tenure as a coach. Instead, schools have followed the practice of granting a variety of different types of employment contracts to individuals who assume coaching responsibilities.

First of all, one should be familiar with and understand the terms **tenure** and **continuing contract** as they relate to full time employment within a college or university or a public school system. *These are terms that relate exclusively to teaching positions.* They are usually not associated with coaching or administrative type positions. These terms denote contract conditions that specify that the individual who is employed as a tenured teacher or one who is working under a continuing contract has, almost literally, a lifetime contract to continue in that capacity within that school or school system.

For all intents and purposes it is very difficult and extremely time consuming to attempt to remove a person (teacher) with tenure or a continuing contract from employment as a teacher. Conditions under which it is possible for the educational institution to violate or pierce the shield of protection afforded by the tenure or continuing contract include:

1. The employee being insubordinate.
2. The employee being neglectful of one's professional responsibility.
3. The employee being proved to be incompetent (which is very difficult and time consuming to prove).
4. The employee is proven guilty of performing an act that is morally reprehensible (moral turpitude).
5. The employee is found guilty of criminal behavior (usually a felony).
6. The school system or college experiences a true and bonafide financial exigency and the teaching job or position is eliminated.

In almost all other instances the teacher is guaranteed a teaching job—for life—once tenure or a continuing contract has been earned. The basic justification for tenure and continuing contracts is to protect the academic freedom of the teacher and scholar. Such protection has been deemed necessary to shield teachers from capricious and arbitrary employment and personnel decisions. Typically, such unjust, inequitable and prejudicial decisions come from administrators and managers who are prejudiced, unscrupulous, and/or are unduly pressured or influenced by others. A lack of tenure or continuing contract, it is said, would seriously inhibit the ability of teachers to be free to teach the truth. A lack of such protection would place the teacher at the mercy and whim of others seeking inappropriate influence in the area of the classroom.

In many states such a lifetime contract can be earned in our public schools, kindergarten through high school, in as few as 3 or 4 years of full time service on a probationary basis. In some states the probationary service is less and in others it is more. On the college and university level the probationary period for teachers is usually 5, 6 or 7 years after which the teacher is either granted a lifetime teaching contract or is required to leave the institution at the end of the next academic year.

Thus, it can readily be seen why coaches are not granted tenure or continuing contract *as coaches*. Typically, coaches, even those who teach, never receive tenure or a continuing contract for their coaching responsibilities even though they may receive such a contract for their teaching duties. In this situation, the teacher/coach might lose the coaching job (for any number of reasons or for no reason whatsoever) but would nevertheless retain the teaching position because of the tenure or continuing contract appointment.

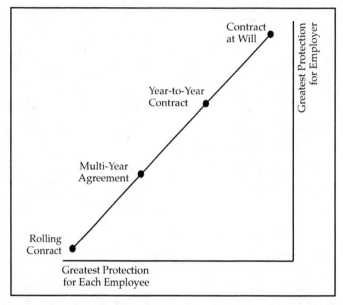

FIGURE 2.3—Common Employment Contracts for Coaches

Four of the more common types of employment agreements offered to coaches, both full time and part-time, include (1) rolling contracts, (2) multi-year contracts or arrangements, (3) year-to-year employment contracts, or worse yet, (4) employment at the whim of an administrator.

COACHING CONCEPT #32: Rolling and multi-year contracts provide much needed protection for the coach while simultaneously insuring that the sport program is not permanently stuck with a coach who no longer performs at an acceptable level.

   Rolling contracts typically call for a specified time period of employment, 3, 4 or 5 years. However, the length of time could be almost any number of years. In the case of the 4-year rolling contract, the coach is notified at the end of the first year of the contract whether one's performance has been satisfactory or not. If so, the contract would be renewed for yet another 4 *years*. If the performance is not satisfactory, the coach would not receive a new 4-year contract but would continue working in the second year of the original 4-year contract.

If a coach is at the end of the second year of the 4-year contract and the coach's performance is still not satisfactory, the employment of the coach is continued but the individual is then working under the third year of the original contract. However, if at the end of the second, third or even the final year of the current 4-year contract, the coach has corrected all of the perceived deficiencies, the administration would grant a *new 4-year contract to the coach.*

Multi-year contracts are related to rolling contracts but yet are significantly different. This type of contract simply means that the coach has a job for as long as the contract stipulates. The contract may be for 2, 3, 4, 5 years or longer. At the end of the contract period the coach either leaves the position since there is no longer any employment contract or the coach may be offered a new (and sometimes different) contract for future employment. Of course, the school and the coach might renegotiate the existing contract at any time. Thus, the coach might be given an extension to the existing contract at any time or the existing contract might be mutually declared null and void and replaced with another binding contract agreed to by both the coach and the school or employing entity.

This type of contract can also provide some protection for the coach from an arbitrary and capricious decision by administrators (or from undue pressure from boosters and outside constituencies) if it calls for the school to notify the coach annually as to the performance of the coach. The fact that the coach is notified prior to the end of each year whether or not the individual's performance is acceptable provides the coach with the opportunity to made adjustments and to correct the cited deficiencies. The fact that the administration is obligated to inform the coach prior to the conclusion of each year as to how the coach is being perceived in terms of overall and specific competencies can go a long way to avoid misunderstandings between the coach and the athletic administration.

The administration benefits from such a contract in that the athletic administration is able to formally, on an annual basis, evaluate and determine the competency of the coach. Hopefully, the coach, when informed of the administration's evaluations and perceptions of the coach's competency, will make any necessary corrections in behavior. Coaches are thus given an opportunity to correct deficiencies and to perform according to the standards and expectations stated in the annual evaluation. Another advantage accruing to the administration is that the athletic team is not saddled with an inferior coach for a protracted period of time. The greatest downside risk is that the sport entity must put up with the individual for the original period of time of the contract.

A **year-to-year contract** is one in which the coach has a specific 12-month contract and at the end (or near the end) of this contract the coach will either be notified that there will not be a new contract or the coach will be given a new 12 month contract. In this situation, the individual coach has the limited protection of the 12 month contract but nothing longer. Of course, such a contract could cover any number of months, 9, 10 or 11, for example.

The coach in this situation is always living near or at the edge in that the coach might not be employed again at the end of the annual contract. The coach is certainly at the mercy of the administration in this situation. In some states (New York, for example), a 12 month contract for coaches does not even require that a reason be given to the coach as to why the person is not being rehired. The contract language in many agreements is such that the coach is automatically not rehired unless the school formally notifies the coach in question that the individual is being rehired. The advantages of this type of contract obviously rests with the school or sport entity in that the administration can effectively terminate (not rehire) the coach after a specific number of months as an employee (coach) without any hassle. The only advantage for the coach with this type of contract is that there is at least a contract for a specific number of months—which is better than no contract at all.

The **contract at will** refers to a contract or agreement calling for the services of the coach who may be terminated at will by the sport or school administrator. That means that the coach could be fired at any time, for any reason or for no reason, by the administration. In this instance, all of the advantages are on the side of the administration. But, at least the coach has a job—for however long the school or sport organization wants the coach to have that job. But there is literally no job protection or security in this type of employment agreement.

Lack of Control by the Coach

The author's college coach advised him to never go into high school basketball coaching. The reason being that: "one day you will be sitting on the bench watching five 16-18 year-old youngsters running up and down the floor with your paycheck in their pockets" (Leo Kilfoy, personal communication, September 16, 1964). The moral of this little piece of advice centered upon the tenuous and precarious situations many coaches find themselves in terms of job security.

This can indeed be the case not only on the collegiate level but also, unfortunately, on the interscholastic level. In those situations where winning is of the utmost importance, coaches can indeed find themselves in a situation where their future, at least in terms of coaching, is dependent to a great degree on their ability to have their athletes emerge victorious on game day. To some coaches this is just part of the risk involved in the profession of coaching. To others, however, this type of pressure becomes untenable and unbearable not only to themselves but for their family as well.

> **COACHING CONCEPT #33: There are some things that are out of the control of the coach.**

A significant negative factor that every coach must face is that in any sport situation there are many things or factors over which the coach has *absolutely no control.* Additionally, there is a great deal over which the coach has *little, if any control.* And, there are some things that are just *difficult to control.* In reality what this means is that the coach can work as hard as possible in a specific area and still things can go wrong, disastrously wrong. For example, a coach might be very well versed in the area of conditioning. This coach might implement an excellent conditioning program for the athletes and sees to it that the program is adhered to religiously by the athletes. Nevertheless, members of the team—even star athletes—can be seriously injured and be lost to the team for extended periods of time.

COACHING CONCEPT #34: It may not be just, it may not be fair, it may not be right—but, whoever said life is just?

Is this the fault of the coach? No, of course not. Can the coach be blamed anyway by some? Of course. Coaches can't control all things affecting their team or program regardless of how hard they try. *Coaches need to face reality.* Some things will just happen that can prove disastrous to the team's chances for success in the win/loss column *in spite* of all that the coach tries to do or is able to do. Some additional factors that are sometimes out of the direct or total control of the coach, but nevertheless can still have an adverse effect upon the ultimate success or perception of success of the athletic team or program include:

1. Biases of news media
2. Poor grades—academic performance of athletes
3. Poor behavior in other classes and in the school environment; a general lack of respect in the school
4. Poor behavior out of the school setting itself
5. Other teams' strengths—caliber of opposing athletes
6. Natural skills and capabilities of one's athletes
7. Students not doing well in the sport (failure to achieve)
8. Students having personal problems at home which interfere with their performance
9. Student-athletes having other personal problems (besides problems at home) that interfere with their sports activities
10. Eligibility rules and academic standards of the school, conference and school
11. Influence of previously organized booster club(s)
12. Insufficient support or resources for the team such as facilities and equipment

13. Student-athletes looking disorganized in games, as if they were not coached

14. Competencies of officials

15. Competencies of superiors

16. Class attendance of athletes

17. Motivational level of athletes

18. Rehabilitative success of injured athletes

19. Players' reactions to officials and/or losing

20. Cheating or inappropriate actions by others

21. Competencies of opposing coaches

Yes, coaching can indeed be trying. Dealing with athletes as well as other individuals and the bureaucracy of education and sport organizations can be discouraging, if not downright exasperating at times. However, when all is said and done, coaching can be a very rewarding and pleasant experience. This is true regardless of whether the coach is male or female, the head coach or an assistant, a volunteer or a paid staff member. The determining factor is how the individual approaches and reacts to the tasks, the responsibilities and challenges of being a coach.

REFERENCES

Acosta, R.V. and Carpenter, L. (1987, April). Women in intercollegiate sport, 1977-86: A longitudinal study. Paper presented at the American Alliance for Health, Physical Education, Recreation and Dance National Convention, Las Vegas, NV.

Acosta, R.V. and Carpenter, L. (1988a). Perceived causes of the declining representation of women leaders in intercollegiate sports—1988 update. Unpublished Manuscript, Brooklyn College, Brooklyn, New York.

Acosta, R.V. and Carpenter, L. (1988b). Status of women in athletics: Changes and causes—Update. Unpublished manuscript, Brooklyn College, Brooklyn, New York.

Acosta, R.V. and Carpenter, L. (1990). Women in intercollegiate sports: A longitudinal study—Thirteen Year update 1977-1996. Unpublished Manuscript, Brooklyn College, Brooklyn, New York.

Acosta, R.V. and Carpenter, L. (1992). Job status: Reflections of immobility and resistance to job change among senior women athletic personnel, Unpublished manuscript, Brooklyn College, Brooklyn, New York.

Acosta, R.V. and Carpenter, L. (2006). A Longitudinal, National Study Twenty Nine Year Update 1977—2006, Unpublished manuscript, Brooklyn College, Brooklyn, New York. Also, retrieved February 7, 2006. http://www.collegeathleticsclips.com/article/519/study-women-in-intercollegiate-sport

As Gumbel learns, hard to be humble for Cowboys' Jones. (October 18, 1995). *USA Today*, p. 2-C.

Balog, K. (1997, March 31). Pitino keys in on how to make teams work. *USA Today*, p. 6-B.

Becker, D. (1992, January 29). Weller molds winner on, off court. *USA Today*, pp. l-C, 2-C.

Cromartie, F. (2001). Attitude in youth sport: Parent rage is killing kids. *Sport Supplement, 9(1), p. 5.*

Dad cited for shaking daughter's face mask. (2001, September 18). USA Today, p. 1-C.

Docheff, D. (2005, April/May). A little philosophy. *Athletic Management, pp. 21-22.*

Family Values Resolution. (1992, November 26). *Democrat and Chronicle*, Rochester, New York, p. 3-E.

Harrick Jr.'s test at Georgia a slam dunk. (2004, March 4). *USA Today*, p. 1-B.

Hill, D. (2005, August/September). Coaching with kids. *Athletic Management, XVI* (5), 24-26, 2831.

Hochstetler, D. R. (2006). Using narratives to enhance moral education in sport. *Journal of Physical Education, Recreation and Dance, 77*(4), 37-44.

It pays. (2000, December). *Athletic Business, 24*(12), 2000, 34-36.

Jacobson, J. (2004, May 1). Bad conduct, by the numbers. *The Chronicle of Higher Education*, pp. A37-A38.

Johnson, G. (2005, March 14). Empire 8 initiative becomes standard for tracking conduct. *NCAA News*, p. A-4.

King, P. (1993, August 6-8). I will not be a loser. *USA Weekend*, pp. 4-5.

Lederman, D. (1989, February 22, 1989). Nearly half the members in top division of NCAA cited for violations in this decade. *The Chronicle of Higher Education*, p.A-35.

Little League dad jailed. (2001, January 27). Democrat and Chronicle, p. 2-D.

Jones, B.J., Wells, L. J., Peters, R. E., & Johnson, D. J. (1982). *Guide to effective coaching—Principles & practice* (2nd ed.). Boston: Allyn and Bacon, Inc.

Kirk, S. (2006, May 5). Alabama football coach's entire package worth $10.7 million. *The Birmingham News, p. 1-C.*

Mannie, K. (2005, February). Tips from the trenches. *Coach and athletic director,* p. 10.

Mihoces, G. (2001, March 6). Sports scruples under scrutiny. *USA Today,* pp. 1- C, 2-C.

More women play, fewer coach. (2000, September). *Athletic Business,* 9(24), p. 26.

No Bronx cheers allowed in Scarsdale. (1999, May 31). *USA Today,* p. 1-C.

Nussman, K. (1993, August 26). Women's unfulfilled dream. *USA Today,* p. 9-A.

Pitoniak, S. (2004, March 2). NCAA eyes model study of unbecoming conduct. *USA Today,* p. 3-C

Sisley, B.L. & Wiese, D. M. (1987). Current status: Requirements for interscholastic coaches. *Journal of Physical Education, Recreation and Dance, 58*(2), 73-85.

SportScan—Coaching Careers Short & 2art Time. (1988, January/February). *American Coach,* Human Kinetics, Champaign, Illinois.

Stier, Jr., W. (1985). Letter to Editor. Catch-22 situation exists for women. *Journal of Physical Education, Recreation and Dance, 56*(9), 16.

Stier, Jr., W. F. (1993, March). *Education, Women and the Olympics.* (ERIC Document Reproduction Service No. ED 351300), pp. 12.

UCLA coach's pay is revealed. (1992, February 11). *USA Today,* p. 5-C.

Webster's new collegiate dictionary. (1973). Springfield, Massachusetts: G. & C. Merriam Company.

Morgan Wooten: Back in the trenches. (1997, January). *HKToday,* pp. 1-9.

Wieberg, S. (March 8, 2007). Success on the court translates to big money for coaches. *USA Today, p. 1-C.* Also, retrieve 3-9-2007: www.usatoday.com/sports/college/mensbasketball/2007-03-08-coaches-salary-cover_N.htm

Wuest, D.A. & Bucher, C.A. (1991). *Foundations of physical education and sport* (llth ed.). St. Louis, Missouri: Mosby Year Book.

Youth sports. (2001, June 10). Democrat and Chronicle, p. 2-D.

Name: _____

Student ID #: _____

EXERCISES FOR CHAPTER 2

A. Defining one's current philosophy of life, of education of sports and of coaching

1. *Philosophy of Life*—What are your thoughts about life itself? What is(are) the purpose(s) of life? What are your attitudes and feelings about life? What should life be like on this planet? In this country? At this point in time and in the immediate future (10-20 years hence)?

    ----

2. *Philosophy of Education*—What are your thoughts about education in general within this country? What are the purposes of our formal educational institutions? What are your attitudes and feelings about the formal educational processes in our society?

    ----

3. *Philosophy of Sports*—What are your thoughts about coaching and sports within the USA? What are the purposes of amateur sports? What are your ideas, attitudes and feelings about amateur sport in general?

----

4. *Philosophy of Coaching*—What are your ideas, attitudes and feelings about coaching? About athletes, parents, coaches, fans, boosters, school and sport administrators?

B. Defining one's career goals—Describe your career aspirations in terms of coaching. Where do you want to be in terms of coaching within five years? Within ten years? Within 15 years? Within 20 years? What do you see yourself doing within the coaching and sport arena during the next three decades?

C.   Coaching opportunities for male and female candidates—What are your opinions regarding the job opportunities that currently exist for female coaches in contrast to male coaches?

_____

_____

_____

_____

_____

D.   Comparing the Disadvantages and Advantages of Being a Coach—List below the disadvantages and advantages that you perceive to be associated with coaching as a full-time or part-time professional.

Disadvantages of Being a Coach	Advantages of Being a Coach

E.   Ethical Decisions in the Coaching of Sport

    1.   Should a basketball coach teach athletes to deliberately foul an opponent attempting to score via a lay-up the winning points in order to force the shooter to earn the points at the free throw line? Justify your answer.

----

    2.   Should the baseball coach teach the player running from first to second base to take out the shortstop who is attempting to execute the double play? Why?

----

    3.   Should the softball or baseball player streaking home on an infield hit deliberately run into and hit the catcher who is receiving the ball just as the base runner is about to reach home plate (with the intent to make the catcher drop the ball)? Elaborate on your comments?

----

4. Should the tennis server tell the judge (is the server ethically obligated) that the judge made an error in calling the serve *in* when the server knows that the serve was not *in* at all? Why or Why not?

----

5. Should the defensive player in basketball deliberately place his or her foot beneath an opponent's feet when the opponent is jumping up for a rebound so that the individual will land and sprain an ankle and be out of the game? Explain your answer in full.

----

6. Should a lineman in football deliberately hold an opponent knowing that the official will never see the infraction? Elaborate.

RESEARCH QUESTONS FOR CHAPTER 2

1. Interview both volunteer coaches and paid coaches at any level and determine the differences, if any, in terms of the duties, obligations, satisfactions and workload, etc., between the two types of coaches.

   ----

2. Ask an experienced secondary or college coach his/her philosophy of coaching and summarize the response(s).

   ----

3. Research (through the library or WWW) the current situation in which coaches and/or schools have been caught cheating and summarize the situation including punishment(s) and so-called justification for such cheating, if any.

   ----

4. Research at least three school systems salary schedule for varsity sports and summarize your findings.

_____

_____

_____

_____

_____

_____

5. Research via the library or WWW situations in which undue pressure is exerted against/upon secondary or modified (junior high) coaches and summarize your findings.

_____

_____

_____

_____

_____

_____

Chapter 3

Coaching Opportunities

The intensity of women sports.

COACHING OPPORTUNITIES AT DIFFERENT LEVELS

To have a better understanding of what it means to be a coach in the world of competitive sports, it is advisable to examine coaching from two different perspec-

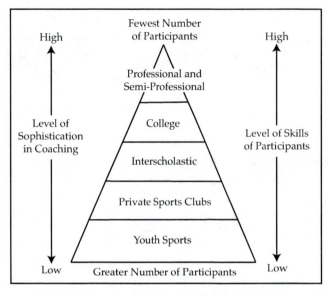

FIGURE 3.1—**Availability of Coaching Positions**

tives, that is, school sponsored athletic programs and non-school sports programs. When one looks at coaching in a school or educational setting one immediately thinks of the numerous junior high school, high school, junior college and college or university athletic programs. On the other hand, out-of-school coaching opportunities are available in numerous youth sports programs, recreational leagues as well as in private sports clubs, state organizations, and, finally, at the semi-professional and professional levels, figure 3.1.

COACHING YOUTH SPORTS

There are ample opportunities for individuals to serve as coaches in a variety of sports in any number of communities throughout the country. It is estimated that over 26 million youngsters (ages 6-16) are involved in out of school sports (Cary, 2004). Midget football, Vince Lombardi football, Pop Warner Football, youth swimming programs, Little League Baseball, Babe Ruth Baseball, PONY Baseball, American Legion Baseball, as well as youth ice hockey, basketball, soccer, lacrosse, and softball programs are just some examples of youth sports that are made available to youngsters in numerous hamlets, towns and cities throughout the United States.

The most popular sports [outside of school] for youngsters in this country are basketball, recreational bicycling, inline skating, recreational swimming, soccer, baseball, recreational walking, calisthenics, running/jogging, freshwater fishing, stretching, touch football, slow-pitch softball, court volleyball and skateboarding (By the numbers, 2001).

Some youth sports programs, such as Little League Baseball (2.5 million players in 50 states), Babe Ruth Baseball (945,000 players nationally) and Pop Warner Football (225,000 participants in 36 states), are organized on a national and even international level (Cary, 2004). Other programs, for example, Vince Lombardi Football, are organized on a regional and state-wide basis. And, still other youth sports programs are organized on a local or community wide basis (soccer, softball, ice hockey, etc.).

Beginnings of Formal Sport Competition at the Youth Level

Formal youth competition in football began in 1929 when a Philadelphia factory owner (wanting youngsters to stop breaking the windows of his plant) organized what became the Pop Warner youth football program (named after Temple University's famed football coach, Glenn Scobie Pop Warner). In 1934, in Williamsport, Pa., Carl Stotz, a worker in a sandpaper plant, organized what later because Little League baseball (Cary, 2004).

Competitive youth sport competition can also be organized under the umbrella of local park and recreation departments or can exist as free-standing sport organizations within any community. Almost every sport that is played at the high school level can also be offered on the youth sport level. Of course, local mores, customs and interest levels will dictate which sporting events are provided for boys and for girls at the youth sport level in different communities.

There has been concern expressed by professional educators and the general public about the lack of adequately trained and competent coaches, especially on the youth level. The dropout rate for young people, from youth sports to competition at a higher level, has been estimated to be 70% (Cary, 2004). Far too often it is the youngest, most vulnerable athletes, who find themselves coached by individuals who, although well-meaning, are also unprepared, poorly trained, and lacking in sufficient knowledge relating to youth and to the coaching of a sport. There are severe and very real risks facing young athletes at the hands of such ill-prepared and unskilled coaches. For example, participants in youth sports face both physical and psychological risks. Additionally, there is the question of potential legal liability in the event of negligence and resulting injury to the youngsters (A National Consensus, 1993).

Baseball is a popular sport from the youth level through the professional ranks.

Other problems associated with youth sports include the *little league syndrome* (overemphasis on winning, overly competitive programs), apparent mismatches between children's expectations and reality, poor examples by parents (attempting to live vicariously through their children), and the physical and psychological differences in terms of actual physical development of children. For example, the maturation process of a 12-year-old youngster may, on the one hand, be physically overdeveloped and similar to what a 16-year youth might be or, on the other hand, may be as underdeveloped as an 8-year old (Stier, 1986a).

The National Association for Sport and Physical Education (NASPE), an association of the American Alliance for Health, Physical Education, Recreation and Dance (AAHPERD), established some years ago a *Bill of Rights for Youth Athletes* (Thomas, 1984, p. 44). This list of ten statements is still appropriate today and provides guidance in terms of the type of current sport experience that should be provided on behalf of young athletes in this country, figure 3.2.

Bill of Rights for Youth Sports

1.   Right to the opportunity to participate in sports regardless of ability level

2.   Right to participate at a level that is commensurate with each child's developmental level

3.   Right to have qualified adult leadership

4.   Right to participate in safe and healthy environments

5.   Right of each child to share in the leadership and decision-making of their sport participation

6.   Right to play as a child and not as an adult

7.   Right to proper preparation for participation in the sport

8.   Right to an equal opportunity to strive for success

9.   Right to be treated with dignity by all involved

10. Right to have fun through sport

FIGURE 3.2—**Bill of Rights for Youth Sports** [Thomas, 1984, p. 44]

Of course, the success or failure of competitive youth sports is dependent upon the quality of adult leadership and supervision associated with the planning and implementation of the youth sport experience. Youth sports should be a wholesome, positive experience for all children who participate. The potential impact, both positive and negative, can be truly significant. It is up to the parents and the sport administrators to insure that the positive goals of youth sports are realized. There is a need to have coaches who possess a sound philosophy of teaching and coaching skills, who have knowledge of effective, safe and medically sound training methods, and skilled in sound delivery techniques. And, of course, there must be recognition that youth sports are not vehicles for ego trips for adults, either parents or coaches.

COACHING CONCEPT #35   **Winning should be the last objective in youth sports—keep the sport experience for the youngsters.**

National Youth Sports Coaches Association (NYSCA)
Code of Ethics

I hereby pledge to live up to my certification as a NYSCA Coach by following the NYSCA Coaches' *Code of Ethics*.

1. I will place the emotional and physical well-being of my players ahead of any personal desire to win.

2. I will remember to treat each player as an individual, remembering the large spread of emotional and physical development for the same age group.

3. I will do my very best to provide a safe play situation for my players.

4. I promise to review and practice the necessary first-aid principles needed to treat injuries of my players.

5. I will do my best to organize practices that are fun and challenging for all my players.

6. I will lead, by example, in demonstrating fair play and sportsmanship to all my players.

7. I will insure that I am knowledgeable in the rules of each sport that I coach, and that I will teach these rules to my players.

8. I will use those coaching techniques appropriate for each of the skills that I teach.

9. I will remember that I am a youth coach, and that the game is for children and not adults.

FIGURE 3.3—NYSCA Code of Ethics *[Engh, 1992, p. 44]*

Additionally, the NYSCA has been instrumental in establishing a national set of standards for youth sports, figure 3.4 (Engh, 1992, p. 45). These national standards of the NYSCA have been endorsed and supported by 82 national agencies and organizations. The actual list of 11 standards was created in 1988 when 43 of this country's experts in children's sports were brought together by the NYSCA in an effort to develop such a list of standards at this level of competition.

More recently, the National Youth Sport Coaches Association and Optimist International have collaborated in a joint effort to promote these standards nationwide. Specifically, both organizations initiated in the spring of 1993 a plan to identify and reward local groups and organizations that meet the criteria contained within the standards in sponsoring youth sport teams, leagues and competition. Additionally, both organizations will be involved in implementing a national education program for parents and for coaches.

High school and college athletes have a responsibility to help youngsters learn the fundamentals of a sport.

There are four stated goals of such an effort. These are (1) to encourage wholesome youth sports experience, (2) to actively discourage teams, leagues and competition organized along the line of the so-called professional sports mentality or model, (3) to eliminate or discourage overzealous parents who vicariously live out their sports frustrations through their children, and (4) to eliminate those coaches who continue to display the all too familiar win-win at all costs attitude and philosophy (Schmid, 1993, p. 15).

WHAT PARENTS THINK ABOUT YOUTH SPORT PROGRAMS

A national survey of parents was conducted several decades ago by the president of the *National Youth Sports Coaches Association* (Engh, 1988). The purpose of the study was to gather responses from parents in terms of youth sports. The findings of the study indicated that:

1. 60% think extra exercise such as running laps is acceptable discipline (even though coaching experts believe that such punishment is inappropriate).

2. 90% of parents feel that effort is or should be more important than outcome (winning or losing).

3. 95% think youth sports programs are very important to kids' development.

4. 23% think cutting kids from teams is *acceptable* while 77% believe that at this age level there should be no cuts.

5. 44% think all-star teams and awards are essential while 34% do not believe such are necessary [Engh (1988) indicated that all-star teams for children under 12 years of age undermine the team concept but nevertheless estimates that 95% of the youth leagues select all-stars].

6. 39% think basketball is the best sport for their children followed by baseball (36%) and soccer (15%).

7. 75% believe that football is the most dangerous youth sport.

8. 89% think parents play a key role in their child's success although 75% think adults really get too involved and all too frequently lose sight of the programs' purpose.

NYSCA National Standards for Youth Sports

1. **Proper Sports Environment**

    Parents must consider and carefully choose the proper sports environment for their child, including the appropriate age and development for participation, the type of sport, the rules of the sport, the age range of the participants, and the proper level of physical and emotional stress.

2. **Programs Based on the Well-Being of Children**

    Parents must select youth sports programs that are developed and organized to enhance the emotional, physical, social, and educational well-being of children.

3. **Drug-and Alcohol-Free Environment**

    Parents must encourage a drug- and alcohol-free environment for their children.

4. **Part of a Child's Life**

    Parents must recognize that youth sports are only a part of a child's life.

5. **Training**

    Parents must insist that coaches are trained and certified.

6. **Parents' Active Role**

    Parents must make a serious effort to take an active role in the youth sports experience of their child, providing positive support as a spectator, coach, league administrator, and/or caring parent.

7. **Positive Role Models**

    Parents must be positive role models, exhibiting sportsmanlike behavior at games, practices, and home, while also giving positive reinforcement to their child and support to their child's coaches.

8. **Parental Commitment**

   Parents must demonstrate their commitment to their child's youth sports experience by annually signing a parental code of ethics.

9. **Safe-Playing Situations**

   Parents must insist on safe playing facilities, healthful playing situations, and proper first-aid applications, should the need arise.

10. **Equal Play Opportunity**

    Parents, coaches, and league administrators must provide equal sports play opportunity for all youth regardless of race, creed, sex, economic status, or ability.

11. **Drug- and Alcohol-Free Adults**

    Parents must be drug- and alcohol-free at youth league sport events

FIGURE 3.4—NYSCA National Standards for Youth Sports

COACHING CONCEPT #36:   Coaches must be aware of safety issues—especially at the youth sport level.

Responsibilities of Youth Sport Coaches

There are specific obligations and responsibilities of coaches who work at the youth sport level. Specifically, they should be able to recognize unsafe practice and playing conditions and be capable of correcting such dangerous situations. They must emphasize the prevention of injuries as well as provide appropriate assistance and first aid when injuries do occur.

There is a national non-profit, educational and research organization—the National Youth Sports Foundation for the Prevention of Athletic Injuries, Inc., (NYSFPAI)—dedicated to the prevention of athletic injuries in youth. This entity serves as an educational resource and clearinghouse for information and provides data and advice to those interested in competitive youth sports, such as coaches, parents, athletes, and allied health professionals. The NYSFPAI also has established the month of April each year as national youth sports injury-prevention month and provides suggestions for different organizations to organize special events commemorating this theme annually.

COACHING CONCEPT #37:   Adjust rules, strategies and practice tactics to fit the abilities of the youth sport participants—youngsters are not miniature adults.

Coaches must also be capable and willing to adjust the rules of games, strategies and practice techniques to fit the capabilities, skill level, physical conditioning and maturation of the participants. Otherwise the needs of the youngsters are not being met. Similarly, coaches should be cognizant of the individual developmental level of *each youngster* and be able to match each student's readiness with appropriate techniques and tactics. Coaches need to remember that youngsters are indeed children, with the needs and abilities of young people; they are not miniature adults.

Thus, coaches need to be able to motivate students in an appropriate manner while maintaining a level of consistent performance. And, finally, they must be able to actually implement the teaching and practicing of skills in a manner befitting the capability and motivation of the individual youngster (A national consensus, 1993).

In short, youth sport coaches have tremendous responsibility for helping children experience the joy of learning physical skills by competing with peers who possess similar skills and experiences. Warren and Volpe (1991) have listed thirteen basic concepts outlining how to be a supportive coach. These concepts are listed in figure 3.5. When children are able to enjoy themselves, learn physical and social skills while experiencing the thrill and challenge of competition—the sports experience is successful.

When children at this level do not learn commensurate with their abilities and interests, when their enthusiasm is stifled, when they are burdened with feelings of inadequacy, when adults impinge upon the youngsters' ability to play and enjoy the sport, the athletic experience cannot be justified. In summary, when major potential benefits of competitive sports are not taken advantage of—there is a need for new leadership and/or for the elimination of that particular sport program.

How to Be a Supportive Coach

1. **Know your players as individuals.** Be sensitive to their needs in both sports and in their personal lives.

2. **Be patient.** Players get frustrated too. A tense atmosphere is not conducive to learning.

3. **Be fair.** Players depend on a coach to make decisions that are fair. A fair coach teaches fair play.

4. **Be consistent.** Do not give preferred treatment to the superstar. Discipline and team rules apply equally to all team members.

5. **Be available to your players.** Being a friend as well as a coach will earn trust and respect.

6. **Provide players with a mentor/role model in yourself.** Lead by example. What you say and what you do must be consistent.

7. **Listen to your players and let them have input into planning activities.** Take their criticism not as an attack, but as their wanting to play an active role.

8. **Never use a player to further your own interests.** Looking at a player as your ticket is not coaching. There is no place for a self-serving coach in any sport.

9. **Never break a player's self-confidence.** Always give specifics when making changes or giving constructive criticism.

10. **Know how to motivate your players.** Each individual has a unique motivating factor; find out what it is.

11. **Set realistic goals for your players as individuals and for the team as a whole.** Help athletes progress from potential to reality. Use short term and long term goal setting.

12. **Vary practice routines and make workouts fun.** Fun is the top motivating factor for participating in sports by most athletes. Make fun the number one priority at all your practices.

13. **Keep the team functioning as a TEAM.** This should happen naturally as a result of good coaching. Being aware of players' individual differences will help prevent personality conflicts. Demonstrating qualities such as fairness, patience, consistency, and leadership will lead to good moral among the team. Remember the team is a direct reflection of the coach.

FIGURE 3.5—How To Be A Supportive Coach [Warren and Volpe, 1991]

OTHER NON-SCHOOL COACHING OPPORTUNITIES

There are additional coaching opportunities, again outside of the traditional school setting, that can be assumed on either a paid or volunteer basis. For example, sports such as fencing, ice skating, gymnastics as well as various combative sports, such as judo, tae kwon do, karate, etc., frequently can be coached in so-called sports clubs. These teaching/coaching opportunities provide chances for individuals to become involved as a volunteer or paid coach either on a part-time or full time basis. The ages of these sport participants can range from as young as 6 or 7 years of age up to and including high school and even beyond. And, of course, there are numerous golf courses and tennis clubs where competent coaches can provide individual and small group instruction and coaching at different skill levels.

State Games

COACHING CONCEPT #38: State Games are in existence in many states and provide sport competition opportunities to individuals of all ages.

Additionally, more than 40 states, including New York, Texas, Pennsylvania, Illinois, Montana, Colorado, North Dakota, Wisconsin, Missouri, and Florida, conduct what is now referred to as State Games. The State Games concept was originated in 1976 within New York by Louis Wolfe, an attorney from Plattsburgh, New York. Mr. Wolfe envisioned annual competition among the best athletes (of all ages) within the state. Thus, the first State Games in the nation began on August 16, 1978 in New York. The state of Florida started its State Games (Sunshine State Games) two years later, in 1980. Pennsylvania initiated its Keystone States Games and Massachusetts began its Bay State Games two years later, in 1982. (Moriello, 1993; Cohen, 1977).

In 1999, in St. Louis, Missouri, a higher level of competition was inaugurated relative to the various State Games when on August 4th the inaugural State Games of America was held (State of the State Games, 1999). This athletic competition consisted of a four-day series of competition that brought "together more than 6,000 State Games champions from across the country to compete for even more medals in 15 different sports" (Conklin, 1999, p. 9.)

These various State Games provide numerous opportunities in which amateur sportsmen and sportswomen of all ages (from high school age athletes through the senior or master's level) can compete against their peers for individual and team championships and honors and distinctions, including ribbons and medals, etc. In the state of New York, the annual Empire State Games remains the nation's largest amateur sports festival in the nation. There are more than 7,000 athletes, coaches and officials involved in this annual sports festival which provides opportunities for competition in 28 sports (Moriello, 1993). It is estimated more than a million individuals have participated in such games in the United States as of 2009. The availability of such competition within various State Games provides numerous additional opportunities for volunteer coaches to be involved in both the team and individual competition.

COACHING IN JUNIOR AND SENIOR HIGH SCHOOLS —INTERSCHOLASTIC SPORTS

Sports at the junior or senior high school levels are referred to as interscholastic sports. There are approximately 25,000 high schools (private and public) in the United States and almost all offer some type of competitive sports against other like schools. Many schools provide competitive sport opportunities, at the freshman, sophomore, junior and varsity levels, enrolling as many as 20 to 25 teams, for boys and girls. Other schools offer more of a limited slate of competitive sports for their students. In some states, females play on selected male teams at the scholastic level. For example, Texas opened high school football, previously a sport played only by boys in the lone star state, to girls, beginning in the fall of 1993. At that time, the State Board of Education voted 9-3 to amend the University Interscholastic League rules which had forbade girls from playing previously (Texas allows girls, 1993). The fact is, however, that competitive sport at the interscholastic level involves a great many sports for both girls and boys. As a result there are numerous coaching opportunities for would-be coaches in these schools.

Competitive Opportunities at the State Level

In every state there are opportunities to compete for championships on either the state or regional/sectional levels. There are numerous opportunities for individuals to coach as an assistant or head coach in a variety of sports in a school setting in middle schools, junior high schools as well as the senior high school setting. At the high school level, between one-third and one-half of the high school teachers take advantage of opportunities to coach by coaching one or more sport teams (Life, 1988).

Coaching in Farm Systems Versus Independent Systems

In interscholastic athletic programs which employ the so-called farm system, varsity head coaches have the responsibility of also supervising all of the coaches who coach a particular sport at all levels below the varsity level. For example, the head varsity basketball coach in a high school that utilizes the farm system approach would have oversight over all of the basketball coaches at the junior varsity, sophomore, freshman teams in high school, as well as the junior high or middle school basketball programs. Such a head coach would have the responsibility of overseeing the type and style of play employed by the various coaches at the lower levels within that school system (Stier, 1989).

COACHING CONCEPT #39: There are coaching opportunities in farm systems as well as in independent systems within schools.

Coaching in the Farm System

For the non-varsity coach who works within such a formal farm system it is necessary to subordinate one's own philosophy and style to fit in the system dictated by the head coach. For example, the head varsity basketball coach in a high school might very well dictate that only man-to-man defense be played at the junior high or middle school level. Thus, the junior high basketball coach must adhere to this philosophy and implement this style of play.

Coaching in the Independent System

In those school systems where there is no formal farm system approach, each coach operates as an independent in terms of determining the style and philosophy of play. In other words, in the independent system or approach each head coach at each level (middle school, junior high, frosh, sophomore, junior varsity and varsity) has the responsibility for determining how one will coach and the style of play which the athletes will be required to learn and execute. There is no overriding master coach dictating how one will coach at the various sub-varsity levels.

Questions to Consider in Evaluating Possible Coaching Positions

The following five questions are of paramount importance when considering any coaching position.

1. Should the coaching hopeful apply for a position of assistant coach or head coach?

2. Is the job at a junior high or senior high school?

3. What level of competition is the job, that is, varsity level, junior varsity, sophomore, freshman, etc.?

4. Will the position be as a full time employee of the school or as a part-time, off-site coach who is employed full time elsewhere?

5. Is the coaching opportunity a paid or a volunteer position?

Two Competing National Coaching Organizations

There are two national organizations vying for memberships from high school coaches. First, there is the *National High School Athletic Coaches Association* (NHSACA) which was started on July 10, 1965 in Atlanta, Georgia. In the late 1960s the membership numbered about 5,000. However, in the late 1980s the membership has increased ten-fold to over 50,000 with 37 dual state associations. The NHSACA also publishes a national professional journal called *National Coach*. Scholastic coaches become a member of NHSACA simply by being a member of their state coaches association (Kimiecik, 1988). But many don't even realize that this benefit is automatic for them.

The second, competing, national coaching organization is called the *National Federation Interscholastic Coaches Association* (NFICA). This entity was initiated in New Orleans, in January 1981, when the National Council of the National Federation of State High School Associations voted to establish a national high school coaches association. In little more than a decade membership has ballooned to some 50,000 in late 1990s. The NFICA also has a professional publication, *National Federation News.*

High school athletics in this country are presently administered through state activities or athletic associations. The *National Federation of State High School Associations* (NFSHSA) is the national organization for these various state associations.

The National Federation rules committee has an NFICA voting member sitting on the committee and the president of the NFICA is an ex-officio member of the National Federation National Council. Since the National Federation establishes the rules and regulations for competitive interscholastic sports, coaches have an opportunity to become involved at the national level in various rules committees through membership in the NFICA. In some quarters, the NFICA is viewed as the NCAA of the high school sports world (Kimiecik, 1988).

It should also be noted that in addition to the *National Federation Interscholastic Coaches Association* (NFICA), the *National Federation of State High School Associations* (NFSHSA) also houses the *National Federation Interscholastic Officials Association* (NFIOA) and the *National Interscholastic Athletic Administrators Association* (NIAAA), the latter formed in 1977 (Gallon, 1989, p. 32).

The difference between NHSACA and the NFICA seems to be one of control and competition for membership. In some quarters, it has been felt that there has existed negative feelings and even animosity between these two competing national entities. The *National Federation Interscholastic Coaches Association* (NFICA) is an organization created by administrators for coaches. On the other hand, the *National High School Athletic Coaches Association* (NHSACA) was started as a coaches association formed by coaches for coaches. Two of the goals of the NHSACA are to support coaches in the field and to provide recognition to outstanding coaches. The NHSACA gives awards to deserving mentors annually.

Organization of Interscholastic Sports Competition

COACHING CONCEPT #40: Interscholastic sports are organized on a state level within this country through various states' athletic associations.

Sport competition at the junior and senior high levels within each state is organized and controlled by each state's athletic association. These state organizations establish and enforce rules, regulations and guidelines governing competitive school athletics at the junior and senior high levels. The rules and guidelines regulate such things as: eligibility, age of transfers, athletes, supervision, length of season, player conduct, officials, playing conditions, travel, awards, and health and safety of participants among others. On the national level, the *National Federation of State High School Athletic Associations* (NFSHSA) establishes rules and regulations for the conduct of sport competition on the interscholastic level in some sports, such as football and basketball.

There is limited intra-state competition among schools. In fact, there is no actual national championship competition per se in any sport on the high school level. However, *USA Today* does provide for a mythical national championship ranking (top 25 teams) on a weekly basis for the sports of basketball, football, soccer, baseball, and softball. And, at the conclusion of the respective seasons, the *USA Today* newspaper does identify a mythical national championship team in these sports.

Women's sports have come a long way since title IX (1972).

COLLEGIATE COACHING

There are over 1,600 independent (private) colleges and universities in this country with some 3 million students. Two-year institutions and colleges number over 1,200 institutions. Counting both independent and public institutions, there are more than 3,400 two and four year colleges and universities in this country. The vast majority of these schools offer some type of intercollegiate athletic programs. Some of the athletic programs at the college level are very extensive while other schools provide a more modest array of sports teams for women and for men. Many institutions offer both varsity and sub-varsity squads for specific teams. Collegiate teams compete within one or more of several national organizations which act as governing bodies for their member schools.

National Governing Bodies for Collegiate Sports

There are several national governing bodies that control amateur athletics on the college and university level in this country. Each of these governing bodies reflets a desire of the member institutions to join together for meaningful sport competition with other institutions with similar athletic philosophies, somewhat comparable resources, while operating under a codified set of rules and regulations. The commonality which brings a specific institution to join one or another national governing body will vary from school to school. In some instances, it may be a religious matter. For other schools, it may be a belief in non-scholarship competition at the college level. And, for still others, it may be the desire to be competitive at the highest level possible in terms of university athletics (Stier, 1987).

National Collegiate Athletic Association (NCAA)

Probably the most influential entity on the collegiate sports scene is the National Collegiate Athletic Association (NCAA). The NCAA can trace its origin from a 1905 meeting of 13 schools which met to attempt to implement football reforms. Later that same year the name Intercollegiate Athletic Association was created and in 1910 the organization's name was changed to the National Collegiate Athletic Association (NCAA). During the 2008-2009 academic year there were 1033 colleges and universities, an all time record, which held active membership in the NCAA. Some schools even hold dual membership in the NCAA and one or more national governing bodies such as the National Association of Intercollegiate Athletics (NAIA).

The breakdown of active membership by colleges and universities as of 9-1-08 is shown below, (NCAA website; www.ncaa.org).

Division I:	329
Division II:	282
Division III:	422
Total:	1033

Athletic competition in terms of national championships is provided in three distinct levels or divisions within the NCAA. These divisions and the number of schools belonging to each during the 2007-2008 academic year include: 329 in Division I, 282 in Division II, while the largest number of schools, 422 held membership in Division III, which is also the fastest growing division. For the 2008-2009 school year there was 429 NCAA Division III institutions (Retrieved 9-1-08 from http://www.ncaa.org/ on 9-1-08. In the future this number is anticipated to continue to grow. In fact, a recent article (Restructuring, 2007) had Division III growing to a very large number of 441, with anticipation that this number could reach 480 within the next 12 years (Retrieved 3-26-08, http://theithacan.org/am/ publish/sports/200803_Growing_pains.shtml. In 2008 the division had grown so large that there were serious discussions about breaking Division III into two separate divisions. However, a survey of members revealed that more than 60% of the Division III membership strongly supported the current structure with another 20% supporting the current structure. Thus, with over 80% of the Division III schools opposed to such a split it seems highly unlikely that this move will become a reality anytime in the near future (No Split. Now What? 2008).

During the 2008-2009 academic year more than 40,600 men and women participated in NCAA sponsored contests. NCAA athletes compete annually in some 88 national championship competitions in 23 sports (NCAA website; www.ncaa.org). The Division I and Division II categories of membership permit the awarding of athletic scholarships to student-athletes. However, the CAA Division III, initiated in 1973, is strictly a no-athletic scholarship division.

Division I member institutions have to offer a minimum number of sports for men and women with two team sports for each gender. In addition, there is a requirement that each playing season has to be represented by each gender as well and there are contest and participant minimums for each sport, as well as scheduling criteria. Other criteria that Division I schools must meet include minimum financial aid for their sports program as well as maximum financial aid awards for each sport that cannot be exceeded.

The NCAA further differentiates Division I by breaking down the membership in the sport of football into Football Bowl Subdivision (formerly Division I-A) or NCAA Football Championship Subdivision (formerly Division I-AA). Those schools classified as Football Bowl Subdivision schools (numbering 119 schools in 2008) typically have sophisticated, elaborate and diverse

Coaches must take a leadership role.

sports programs. These institutions also must satisfy minimum attendance requirements (i.e., average 15,000 people in actual or paid attendance per home game) over a [rolling] two-year time period. Those schools classified as NCAA Football Championship Subdivision teams (numbering 118 in 2007) are not required to satisfy any minimum attendance requirements. The remaining number of Division I institutions (92) do not offer football.

Current institutions that compete in the Football Bowl Subdivision (formerly Division I-A) consists of so-called big-time schools, institutions like Ohio State, Syracuse, University of Miami (Florida), Notre Dame, Southern California, and Penn State—which all vie for a national football championship in this specific Division. Those schools that compete for championships in the Football Championship Subdivision (formerly Division I-AA) are those schools that choose not to (or are unable to) meet the specific requirements for membership in Football Bowl Subdivision but yet desire to compete for a national championship in the sport of football, at a very high level or caliber of competition.

Membership in one of the specific divisions of the NCAA is a reflection of the competitiveness, availability of athletic scholarships and number of sports offered within the athletic program more than merely a matter of institutional size (student enrollment). The size of schools belonging to one of the various divisions of the NCAA range from the very small (under 2,500 students) liberal arts institutions at one end of the spectrum to the very large private or public institutions with 50,000, 60,000 and more students at the other end of the spectrum. Additionally, some very small institutions such as Fairfield University (3000 students), Holy Cross (2675 Students), Canisius College (3250 students), Colgate University (2800 students), St. Francis College [NY], (2100 students), Delaware State (3200 students), Lafayette College (2300 students), University of Maryland [Eastern Shore] (3600 students), Manhattan College (3600 students), St. Francis University of Pennsylvania (1400 students) and Wake Forest University (4000 students) all hold membership within NCAA Division I, although they have relatively small undergraduate enrollments (The 2007-2008 National Directory of Collegiate Athletics).

However, there are also very large colleges and universities that hold membership within Division III of the NCAA. Some of these schools include Hunter College (20,000 students), University of Wisconsin, Oshkosh (11,000), City College of New York (12,000 students), New York University (50,917 students), Buffalo State College (11,000), University of California [Santa Cruz] (14,500 students), University of Wisconsin at Eau Claire (10,500 students), University of California, San Diego (23,548 students), and the College of Staten Island (12,800 students) (The 2007-2008 National Directory of Collegiate Athletics).

Those who coach within NCAA Division I schools are usually assigned only coaching duties and are not involved in any significant fashion with the teaching of credit bearing classes. However, at NCAA Division II schools there are more coaches who are assigned limited teaching or other duties within the college or university setting. However, within Division II institutions there are still large numbers of coaches who are hired to coach the so-called "flagship or priority sports whose sole responsibility is the coaching (and recruiting) of an athletic team. It is not until one examines the NCAA Division III institutions that one will find the majority of those full time employees who have coaching duties also being assigned teaching duties and/or, in some instances, given administrative responsibilities (Steinbach, 2002). Of course, there are numerous part-time coaches involved at all levels of collegiate and university sports.

COACHING CONCEPT #41:   There are several national governing bodies or organizations overseeing and organizing collegiate sport competition.

National Association of Intercollegiate Athletics (NAIA)

The next largest governing body on the collegiate level is the National Association of Intercollegiate Athletics (NAIA). In 1937, James Naismith and others organized the National Association of Intercollegiate Basketball (NAIB) that would later be renamed the NAIA. The Association was structured around a men's college basketball tournament in Kansas City, which is now the longest continuous national collegiate tournament in any sport. Today, the NAIA services 288 members in the United States and Canada (2008-09) and offers equitable access and opportunities for young men and women to compete. Member schools represent 25 athletic conferences.

Approximately 45,000 student-athletes compete in 23 national championships in 13 sports under the banner of the NAIA during an academic year. There are 12 such national championships made available for men and 11 provided for women athletes

The NAIA currently provides for two divisions in the sport of basketball. In the NAIA, scholarships may be given to student-athletes both in Division I and Division II programs. The distinction between Division I and Division II schools is in the number of scholarship (based upon athletic ability) that can be provided to individual student-athletes. In all other sports within the NAIA, teams compete for national championships within a single division which allows institutions to award scholarships to participants if the sponsoring institutions so chooses. (Personal communication, Staci Schottman, 9-12-08). See www.naia.org.

National Junior College Athletic Association (NJCAA)

A third national governing body involves only two-year colleges and is called the National Junior College Athletic Association (NJCAA). Started in 1937 by a group of 13 junior colleges in the state of California, it held its first formal sports competition two years later. In 1941 the group became a national governing body. During the 2007-2008 academic year its membership totaled over 500 institutions. The NJCAA provides 47 national championships and 8 football bowl games in 17 sports for men and women in three distinct levels, Division I, Division II and Division III.

The NJCAA Division I is distinguished by allowing athletic scholarships to be given to student-athletes that include (1) tuition, (2) fees, (3) books, (4) room, (5) board, and (6) round-trip transportation from the athlete's home to the institution one time during the academic year. Those schools choosing to belong to the Division II of the NJCAA are allowed to provide student-athletes with tuition, fees and course-related books. And, Division III schools are those that provide no athletically related financial assistance or aid to student-athletes (NJCAA Office, personal communication, September 15, 2008). The official website of the NJCAA is www.njcaa.org

The National Christian College Athletic Association (NCCAA)

This national organization, incorporated in 1968 in Canton, Ohio, is comprised of a group of approximately 100 accredited Christian colleges and universities, including both liberal arts institutions and Bible colleges, throughout the United States of America and Canada. The NCCAA mission statement is:

1. The NCCAA is an association of Christ-centered collegiate institutions whose mission is to use athletic competition as an integral component of education, evangelism and encouragement.

2. We serve our members by setting association standards, developing communication resources, providing regional/national competition and partnering in outreach to our communities and the world.

3. We are committed to equipping student-athletes and coaches to make a positive impact for Christ.

The National Christian College Athletic Association provides athletic competition for both men and women. Competition is provided in two different divisions. Division I, four-year Christian liberal arts institutions; and Division II, four-year institutions that are designated Bible colleges or institutions that require every student enrolled to graduate with 20 hours of Bible. Division II institutions grants no athletic scholarships to student-athletes and do not grant any special financial aid or scholarships to student-athletes unless offered equally to other members of the student body. Twenty-two national championships for both divisions are provided in the sports of men's golf, men's and women's cross country, men's and women's soccer, women's volleyball, men's and women's basketball, baseball, men's and women's tennis, softball, men's and women's indoor track and field, and men's and women's track & field. Christian Service Projects are conducted during each championship experience. The web site of the National Christian College Athletic Association is www.thenccaa.org.

The National Small College Athletic Association (NSCAA) [no longer in existence]

Another national sport organization that existed for some years, but is now no longer a viable entity, was named the National Small College Athletic Association. The NSCAA got its start in 1966 when a group of coaches and athletic administrators banded together to provide national championships for very small schools. Initially, the name of the organization was the National Little College Athletic Association but was later changed to its name to the National Small College Athletic Association. Initially, this organization was an outgrowth of a desire to provide national championship opportunities for male athletes only in schools with a very limited enrollment (under 500 men). Later, national championships were expanded to include women teams. Prior to being dissolved in 2002, after 36 years in existence, national championships were sponsored for men and women in seven sports by the NSCAA for the member institutions of this national governing body. Today this organization is no longer in existence.

The United States Collegiate Athletic Association (USCAA)

In 2002 a new national organization for small two-year and four-year colleges was formed as a national entity offering competition for national championship status for its members. The national group's name was The United States Collegiate Athletic Association (USCAA). This group grew out of the demise of the National Small College Athletic Association (NSCAA). Members must have less than 1,500 students, although there have been exceptions to that requirement for institutions with so-called bare-bones athletic programs. In the sport of basketball, the NSCAA sponsors two divisions, one for schools offering financial aid to athletes and one for schools that do not [as well as for two year institutions and Bible colleges] (Very Small, 2002).

PROFESSIONAL COACHING OPPORTUNITIES

At the apex of the coaching profession within this country are the professional and semi-professional levels. As early as 1992 there were 83 different professional franchises in the USA (Lapchick, 1993) and numerous sports associations such as the Professional Golf Association (PGA) and the Ladies Professional Golf Association (LPGA). It is estimated that the LPGA had more than 200 employees. Professional teams exist in the sports of ice hockey, baseball, football, basketball, Lacrosse and soccer just to mention some of the more visible sports in the U.S.A.

Most coaches with these teams are typically salaried coaches but some teams also allow volunteers to be involved with the coaching and/or scouting staffs. Some of the professional and semi-professional sports organizations in the United States are provided below.

Number of Professional Leagues /Associations (Partial List)

American Basketball League (ABL) [women's professional basketball]
American Bicycle Association Bicycle Motocross (BMX)
American Hockey League (AHL)
Arena Football League (AFL)
Arena Football League
Beach Volleyball
Canadian Football League (CFL)
Continental Basketball League (CBA)
Global Basketball League
International League (baseball) (IL)
Ladies Professional Golfers Association (LPGA)
Major Indoor Lacrosse League (MILL)
Major League Baseball (MLB)
Major League Lacrosse
Major League Soccer (MLS)
National Association for Stock Car Auto Racing *(NASCAR)*
National Basketball Association (NBA)
National Bicycle League (BMX)
National Football League (NFL)
National Hockey League (NHL)
National Lacrosse League (NLL)
National professional paintball league (based in US) *(NPPL)*
National Professional Soccer League (NPSL)
Professional Bowlers Association
Professional Golfers Association (PGA)
United States Basketball League (USBL)
United States Bowling Congress
USA Cycling (multi discipline)
Women's Professional Football League
Women's National Basketball Association (WNBA)
World Football League (WFL)

The biggest challenge in becoming a coach in the professional ranks is initially breaking into the so-called inner sanctum according to Mauro Panaggio. Coach Panaggio, a highly successful basketball mentor at the NCAA Division III level, was able to successfully make the move to the Continental Basketball Association (CBA) where he is one of the most successful coaches at that level. Once an individual has secured a coaching position, any type of position, within a professional sports franchise, that individual is immediately on the inside (Mauro Panaggio, personal communication, April 12, 1995). But getting on the inside, that is the problem, that is the challenge. Once inside the inner circle of professional sports, it is very common to move from team to team within the sport. Although there is no typical, sure-fire route to becoming a coach at the professional level, there are two frequently followed paths to the big leagues that can be discerned.

COACHING CONCEPT #42: **Becoming a head coach depends upon being in the right place at the right time, with the right skills and right experiences, and knowing the right people.**

First, there are the former pro players who, upon retirement, secure assistant or specialty coaching positions in professional sports. These are individuals who have excelled in playing the sport or a specific position(s) and who are retained within the realm of professional sports for their knowledge and experience. Some of these individuals then work their way up through the ranks serving as specialty coaches and assistant coaches under a number of highly visible, successful head coaches, who in turn serve as mentors for these assistant coaches. After paying one's dues as an assistant coach, having demonstrated a high level of competency and loyalty, one is sometimes given the opportunity to become a head coach. But, there is never a guarantee that a head coaching position will become available and be offered to such an individual. The vast majority of coaches in the professional sports leagues have previously been professional athletes themselves. This is more prevalent in some sports and leagues than others. For example, baseball leads all professional leagues in having the greatest number of head coaches who had been professional athletes themselves.

A second avenue for coaches to become head coaches at the professional level, especially in football, is to become a highly successful and visible Division I college or university coach and to then make the jump from the university to the professional level. For example, Jimmy Johnson won two national football championships at the University of Miami (Florida). He then moved to the professional football team, the Dallas Cowboys where, after a few challenging and difficult seasons, his team subsequently won the 1993 and 1994 Super Bowls. In the sport of ice hockey, coach E. J. McGuire was the head ice hockey coach at Division III SUNY Brockport and then moved to assistant coaching positions in the NHL at both the Chicago Blackhawks and the Ottawa Senators. Dennis Green, the former Northwestern University and Stanford head football coach moved to the Minnesota Vikings in the fall of 1992. In the fall of 1991, coach Mike Krzyzewski, basketball coach at Duke University was reportedly sought by the Boston Celtics to become their head coach. This was after Duke's Blue Devils won the 1991 NCAA Division I basketball championship by defeating the University of Nevada, Las Vegas. However, in this instance, coach Krzyzewski declined the offer and elected to stay at Duke University where he won a second national championship the very next year.

However, not all highly touted and successful university coaches successfully make the adjustment from college to professional sports. For example, Lou Holtz moved from the NCAA, Division I level, at North Carolina State University, to the professional football league, the New York Jets, only to find out that he didn't like it at the professional level. He left after only a year and moved back to the college ranks where he subsequently coached and was very successful at the University of Arkansas, the University of Minnesota, Notre Dame University and the University of South Carolina. Ray Perkins, the former Alabama coach moved to the Tampa Bay Buccaneers and was released from that professional team and moved back to the college ranks at Arkansas State University. Other coaches who experienced great success at the big-time Division I levels but did not enjoy similar success at the professional level are Dick McPherson and Jerry Tarkanian. Dick McPherson, who won accolades as the head football coach at Syracuse University, assumed the head coaching post of the lowly New England Patriots in the fall of 1991, only to be summarily released only two years later. In basketball, Jerry Tarkanian went from UNLV to the San Antonio Spurs and lasted only 20 games while earning a 9-11 record before being fired and replaced by John Lucas. Coach Lucas was then serving as the head basketball coach of the Miami Tropics of the United States Basketball League (USBL). Lucas had also been a former standout basketball player himself and had played with the Spurs as well as several other professional teams. In June of 1994, John Lucas became head coach and general manager of the Philadelphia franchise.

The Value of Networking within Professional Sports

Yet another factor that cannot be discounted in terms of securing a professional coaching position is the network which exists within the professional ranks. It is indeed a matter of *who one knows* as well as *what one knows*. Without the *who* an individual will never be able to demonstrate the *what* in the professional ranks. A witticism that has been around the professional ranks for years goes something like this: *The hardest part of getting a head coaching job in the professional ranks is getting that first job. After the first job coaches are merely recycled from team to team—once a coach in the professional ranks, almost always a coach somewhere in professional sports.* Of course, there are always exceptions as cited above. However, the point is that once an individual lands a professional coaching position, it is subsequently much easier to be hired by other professional teams than it would be had the person possessed no previous professional coaching experience.

CHALLENGES FACING THE AMATEUR COACHING PROFESSION

The Problem of a Lack of Qualified Coaches

Today there is a severe shortage of qualified and experienced coaches for both youth sports and interscholastic sports. The problem has gotten so severe that the integrity of the sports programs themselves has been put at risk—and is at jeopardy in many cases. Individuals who are unqualified or under qualified are currently being allowed to coach our youth athletes as well as our junior and senior high athletes. There are people coaching today who are poorly trained or not trained at all. The result is that the coaching experience being provided for our young people is deficient, is wanting. And, as a result, those who are really paying the price for this inadequacy are the young athletes themselves.

Shortage of Youth Coaches

Most youth coaches are volunteers, a majority of whom are parents or relatives of the young participants. The major problems in terms of coaches at this level are insufficient numbers of *qualified* coaches (possessing the essential training and skills) and what is deemed to be an inappropriate priority placed on winning at the youth sport level by well-meaning adults.

Examples of Inappropriate Coaching Activities

Witness the disgraceful behavior of the team from the Philippines, the would-be Little League Baseball world championship team in the fall of 1992. In the first scandal of this nature surrounding Little League Baseball, the World Series championship was supposedly won by the team from the Philippines in the World Series competition held in August of 1992, in Williamsport, PA. (Hoffer, 1993).

However, the directors of the International Little League organization voted on Thursday, September 17, 1992, to strip the Philippine team of the title and instead awarded the championship title to the runner-up team from Long Beach, California. This was a case of pure and simple greed, overemphasis, selfishness, and egotistical behavior on behalf of the adult organizers associated with the Philippine program. The actual cheating and violations involved eight Philippine players, whose own teams had lost in their country's Little League tournament, being stacked on a single team. This was in clear violation of rules which prohibit such all-star teams. The

Philippine all-star athletes competed as a single squad in the world championship competition against teams which were not made up of all-star squads (Little league scandal, 1992).

COACHING CONCEPT #43: Youth sports should not be miniature professional sport experiences.

Other equally despicable examples abound in which adults attempt to make youth sports a miniature professional sport experience through ignorance of and/or disregard for the established and educationally sound policies and procedures designed to govern youth sports. For example, a midget football coach, when asked by parents why they could not bring water to their youngsters at the practice field, indicated that these athletes (grades 4, 5, 6 and 7) had to know what it was like to experience pain and discomfort in practice so that when things got tough and difficult in games they would know how to handle such adversity. Similarly, this same youth football coach required all of the youngsters to keep their helmets on their heads from the time they arrived at the practice or game until the activity was over (obviously, for the same inane reasons). And, another youth coach punished his football athletes by making them run (in full pack) a quarter mile from the practice site to an old oak tree down the road from the practice site whenever any of the youngsters misbehaved or failed to perform up to the coach's expectations. Inane

Shortage of Interscholastic Coaches

The coaching problem at the junior and high school levels is approaching the catastrophic level in that the recruitment and retention of qualified candidates has become one of the great challenges for athletic and central school administrators (Hill, 2002). There are essentially four problems, challenges or tasks facing schools and athletic administrators in terms of the employment scene of coaches. The first area of concern is the lack of full-time employment opportunities for coaches. The second challenge is to recruit and attract interested coaches. The third is to retain those qualified and successful individuals who have been hired as coaches. The fourth task is to insure that all individuals who are hired and retained are competent, knowledgeable and remain current in their field.

Dedication is a requirement for the successful athlete of any level.

The first problem relates to **employment opportunities** and the **attractiveness of the coaching jobs** which are available. The second revolves around the **hiring process.** The third challenge is concerned with **motivational and support processes.** And, the fourth problem involves or is concerned with an **educational or training process.** All four areas of concern [challenges or problems] must be addressed in an atmosphere of a severe shortage of qualified coaches combined with rather meager financial resources in support of both coaches and the actual athletic programs.

Reasons for the Shortage of Coaches

The expansion of sports at all levels in the past 40 years has been nothing short of phenomenal. This expansion of sports and teams has been accompanied by an equally impressive increase in the number of males and females participating in sports. The result has been a dramatic need for more coaches. Nowhere has this need been more evident than at the junior and senior high level although the effect has also been felt at the college and university level. As the number of sports and teams increase the demand for coaches continues to greatly outpace the actual number of individuals who are qualified to assume such positions of trust.

Also, more teachers are resigning their coaching duties while staying on as teachers. Thus, there is a reduction of available teaching slots for new coaches. Other factors include the time commitment and the lack of adequate remuneration (Coping, 1988).

Many people accusingly point to the passage of Title IX (1972) as *the cause* of the coaching shortage which has faced our schools for decades and which promises to haunt the education and coaching programs for many years to come. However, it is unfair to lay the blame for the problem which schools are experiencing in securing qualified coaches solely at the doorstep of Title IX. This is just not the case. Title IX and the resulting expansion of women's sports are but two contributing reasons for the ever present coaching shortage. The difficulty of securing and keeping qualified coaches existed well before the implementation of Title IX in 1974. The already existing problem was merely compounded by the passage of Title IX (Broderick, 1984).

The current and projected shortage of coaches on the interscholastic level may be attributed to four major factors. The first factor is a lack of qualified individuals, that is, an insufficient pool of candidates, willing and capable of assuming coaching duties under the employment conditions accompanying these jobs. Second, there has been an increase in the availability of teams, both male and female. Third, there has been a corresponding increase in sport participation by youngsters, both male and female. And fourth, even when qualified coaches are found it remains a challenge to retain them due to the fact that many of the coaching positions are only *part-time.* It is becoming increasingly difficult to require part-time coaches to undergo a stringent and extensive educational training program in order to be eligible to coach an athletic team that provides what is all too frequently merely a pittance in terms of monetary rewards.

Additional factors that contribute to the problem facing school and athletic administrators as they seek to secure *qualified* coaches include, but are not limited to, the following:

1. A decrease in the interest in coaching by individuals

2. An aging teacher/coach population

3. The retirement or withdrawal of older coaches (both teachers and non-teachers) from the profession

4. A greater number of *teachers* who currently coach but who are now tired of coaching and who are relinquishing their coaching duties

5. New teachers, especially physical educators, who don't wish to coach

6. Declining student enrollments in some schools with the result that additional full-time teachers (who might have been willing and qualified to coach) are not being hired

7. Fewer qualified young people entering the coaching profession

8. The amount of time (evening and weekend hours) required of coaches

9. The uncertainty of athletes' behavior

10. The perceived lack of support by administrators and the public

11. Unreasonable expectations of the coach held by others *and* the ever-present pressure to win-win

12. Outside forces and interference from fans, boosters and alumni

13. Inadequate pay or no pay at all

14. The lack of esteem or recognition given to coaches

15. Many coaching posts provide for only part-time involvement/employment

16. A lack of individuals who possess minimum coaching qualifications and experiences

17. The inability of coaches to control their own destiny in terms of the coaching situation

18. discrimination [conscious and unconscious] against women coaches in terms of (A) the hiring and promotion processes, (B) biases existing in the job setting itself, and (C) biases existing within the home environment, all of which results in fewer women seeking coaching positions or remaining in such positions

19. An increased interest in community sports and fitness thereby causing a greater interest (increase) in sport participation in schools

20. The rapid development of sports and increase of varsity *teams* for females

21. A general increase in the *number* of females as well as males participating in sports

22. An increase in the number of lower level teams for both females and males

23. A lack of acceptance and implementation of a national coaching education training program and/or certification process

24. A lack of job protection for coaches (both part-time and full time employees of schools)

Tenured Scholastic Teachers
Relinquishing Their Coaching Duties

Today, almost nationwide, the availability of potential interscholastic coaches who desire full-time employment in school systems far exceeds the availability of positions. This is especially true in light of the fact that there are usually more vacant coaching positions to be filled than there are full time teaching vacancies. In some schools where there are numerous coaching posts to be filled there may simultaneously be minimal full time teaching vacancies. In other schools where there are coaching vacancies, the teaching vacancies are in fact non-existent. A situation that exacerbates the already difficult problem of securing competent coaches is the fact that some teachers who also coach *resign* their coaching duties (but not their teaching responsibilities) *after* they earn tenure or are given a continuing contract. When this type of resignation from coaching happens, and it takes place all too frequently, schools are finding themselves behind the proverbial eight ball in terms of being able to secure a full time employee as a replacement to assume the coaching post. The reason is simple. There are simply no full time teaching posts available that a replacement coach/teacher could fill. The result is a part-time coach being hired. This individual, not being a full time employee of the school is all too often viewed negatively as a so-called rent-a-coach.

COACHING CONCEPT #44: Schools with only a coaching vacancy (i.e., no corresponding teaching opening to fill) are faced with hiring a rent-a-coach,

---

Thus the trend of schools to allow full time teachers, who also possess coaching duties in the school system, to resign from their coaching responsibilities while retaining their full time teaching jobs *has severe and very real negative consequences*. When individuals are hired as coaches *and as* teachers and subsequently give up their coaching responsibilities, the school is all too frequently left only with the option of hiring a **part-time coach,** someone from outside the school itself. This is because there are either (1) no teaching slots available for a new full time employee who might also be willing to coach, or (2) because there are no other full time teachers in that particular school or school system willing to take on the tasks of coaching the sport. Thus, as we enter the first quarter of the 21st century, there continues the alarming trend for ever increasing numbers of part-time, non-teachers being placed in positions of responsibility as head and assistant coaches in our junior and senior high schools. This has been a perennial problem and will continue unabated for the foreseeable future.

Some school districts have contract stipulations, regulations, and provisions governing hiring practices that require that when a teacher/coach is *removed* or *resigns* from coaching, that individual must also resign from teaching or be transferred to another school. In other districts and schools, regulations are somewhat different and although contract provisions may differentiate coaching responsibilities from teaching duties, these schools nevertheless require the nullification of the teaching portion of the contract when a coach/teacher is terminated (fired or removed) or resigns from a coaching post. In still other locales, a resignation or termination from a coaching position has absolutely no effect upon that person's full time teaching status.

A state official in Maine who requested not to be identified was quoted as saying:

> "In my state, it is not presently legal, but I think the answer to the problem is to have a coaching statute written such that a resignation in coaching means that the teaching as well as the coaching position is ended. At the present time we have people resigning from coaching after they receive tenure. Consequently, the school system must retain that person, but there is no teaching position for a new coach" (O'Brien, 1981, p. 25).

Advantages of Being a Full-Time Teacher and Coach

COACHING CONCEPT #45: The ideal (educational) situation is to have a coach who is employed full time as a teacher or administrator by the same district.

Usually school administrators attempt to appoint teachers within the school to coaching posts. The reason is that there are certain advantages from having full time teachers in the same school tending to the teaching and coaching responsibilities in that school. Some of these advantages are that these teachers/coaches are more familiar with the school atmosphere and regulations, they are a part of the educational family or staff at that school and therefore know and have close contact with other teachers within that school, they are able to have a closer presence and contact with their athletes during the school day and they can begin coaching immediately after school.

Coaches are teachers and motivators.

The Sad State of Affairs in the Hiring of Coaches

The need for interscholastic coaches greatly outnumbers those teachers employed by the schools who wish to coach. As a result, there is an ever-growing phenomenon, in terms of part-time coaches needed in our schools. In reaction to this phenomenon, various states have allowed junior and senior high schools to hire individuals as coaches who are not currently teaching in that particular district, but are not even certified as teachers. *In some states there are no licensing requirements for coaches at all.* This means that in these states, schools are permitted to hire individuals possessing little, if any, formal coaching training or experience. Many states permit individuals to coach with the bare minimum of what could be considered any type of real educational experience in the area of coaching (Sabock & Chandler-Garvin, 1986; Sisley & Wise, 1987; Partlow, 1992a). There has been a joke making the rounds of athletic directors for some time which goes something like this: *If you can walk while counting to 10 you could be hired as a coach by some schools, and they aren't too particular about one's ability to count.* This is a sad state of affairs which is indicative of what is happening in some parts of this country when it comes to the hiring of coaches.

Hiring Priorities

When the availability of qualified coaches have been exhausted in a particular school, administrators typically look outside that school but attempt to secure a teacher/coach elsewhere in the same school system. Thus, we have the situation in which an elementary or junior high school teacher travels to the high school in the same school system/district to assume coaching responsibilities once school is recessed for the day. However, not even this approach is frequently successful in securing the number of coaches needed. As a result the school administration is forced to look elsewhere.

In general, secondary school administrators attempt to secure coaches in light of the following descending order of priority (Stier, 1990):

1. Certified teachers who are competent coaches (via certification or education) who will teach and coach in the same school.

2. Certified teachers who are competent coaches (via certification or education) and will coach in the *same school system* where they teach, but not in the same building.

3. Certified teachers who are competent coaches (via certification or education) but *do not teach* in the same school system where they will coach.

4. Certified teachers who *do not currently teach* at all but yet can coach in a school system, having met minimal standards established by the state.

5. Individuals who *are not certified* as teachers but who can coach, having met minimal standards established by the state.

6. Individuals who *are not certified* as teachers, have little or no coaching training or experience, but nevertheless desire to coach either as a rent-a-coach (paid) or as a walk-on coach (volunteer).

Part-Time, Off-Site Coaches

Securing individuals who are not full time school employees to assume coaching responsibilities in the school, on a part-time basis, is certainly not the best alternative, but rather a necessary evil. The use of part-time coaches is a necessary consequence of the need to secure coaches when there are insufficient numbers of full-time positions for which individuals may apply. Those non-faculty individuals who come from off-site to coach part-time in a school are frequently referred to, in a somewhat derisive fashion, as **off-the- street coaches.** These so-called **off-the street** or **off-site coaches** are being utilized in our school systems as never before as either **rent-a-coaches** (those who are paid to coach) or as **walk-on-coaches** (individuals who volunteer their services).

There are both advantages and disadvantages (both for the school and for the coach) for the presence of volunteers as coaches at middle and secondary schools. Car done, (2000) provides a look at these advantages/disadvantages when the picture of volunteer coaches is examined by the perspectives of hiring, training, keeping, evaluating, and replacing volunteer coaches.

The part-time coaching situation is a consistent problem for both school adminis-trators and for would-be or wanna-be coaches. In many athletic situations there is simply no feasible way for specific coaching slots to be anything but part-time. In these situations, there are additional problems and challenges facing both the part-time coach and the school/athletic administration.

Part-time ". . . coaches may do an adequate job of teaching skills in the various athletic activities, but are deficient in the areas of supervision and do not emphasize commitment to excellence, self-discipline, sportsmanship, and loyalty. These values need more emphasis in working with our young people" (Sabock & Chandler-Garvin, 1986, p. 58). Part-time coaches are considered necessary burdens because without them, athletic programs would need to be curtailed and some teams would have to be eliminated. Part-time coaches are frequently accused of being unaware of school procedures or choose to ignore them. They are thought of as being out of the mainstream or loop of the school or educational setting in terms of dealing with such things as absences, suspensions, providing special assistance for athletes during the school day, understanding school rules and regulations and making referrals to ap-propriate offices. They are also unable to maintain close contact with their student-athletes during the regular course of the school day.

Challenges of Part-Time, Off-Site Coaches

Coaching on a part-time basis within an interscholastic or intercollegiate envi-ronment typically involves having a full time job elsewhere, thus necessitating trav-eling to the school following or before work in order to coach during one's so-called free time. The alternative is to be a full time teacher-coach who is hired as a full time employee within the school or school system in which one then is given coaching responsibilities, in addition to one's regular teaching, supervisory or administrative assignments. There may be advantages and disadvantages to being in either posi-tion, that is, a part-time or full time employee, depending upon each individual coach and one's specific circumstances and needs. The important point is to be aware of these advantages and disadvantages and to make an informed decision regarding one's coaching career.

There are numerous studies which purport to show that more and more coaches at the secondary level (scholastic coaches) are part-time, off-site coaches. Rog (1985) revealed that 60 percent of coaches in Maine high schools were non-certified teach-ers. According to Cohen (1992) some 30%-40% of all high school coaches are so-called **rent-a-coaches.** Sage (1990) estimates that the percentage of **rent-a-coaches** at the high school level is much higher, closer to fifty percent to sixty-six percent for the more than 190,000 athletic teams that are sponsored each year by high schools in this country (Life, 1988). It is estimated that 50% of coaches in California high schools are non-faculty coaches, off-the street coaches (Coping, 1988). Although the majority of walk-on-coaches (volunteers) are involved in the youth sports arena, there are significant numbers of volunteer coaches involved at the junior and senior high level as well as at the collegiate level.

Problems Associated With the Hiring of Part-Time Coaches

Broderick (1984) identified four major problems educational institutions are experiencing in using off-site coaches. These include: (1) a lack of knowledge of school procedures and eligibility requirements, (2) loyalty to local authority and policy are not the same as for on-campus coaches, (3) off-site coaches do not owe any particular allegiance to the school nor do they share the regular teacher/coaches' philosophical commitment to education, and (4) the rent-a-coach (walk-on) syndrome that currently plagues our schools (inappropriate priorities).

Problems with Some Part-Time Employment Agreements

COACHING CONCEPT #46: Being a part-time coach can be a precarious position on the secondary level—depending upon the union contract negotiated with the district.

Some part-time coaches are in a situation where they enjoy absolutely no job security at all as a result of a negotiated union contract covering all employees in that particular school system. In some states there are school districts that have negotiated union contracts stipulating that any full time teacher in the entire school district has hiring priority (preference) over any and all part-time candidates (those not possessing a full time teaching or other full time position) within the school district. What this means is that a part-time coach (head or assistant) may be hired to coach a team only when there are no interested candidates who are full time employees of the school or district. However, at the end of each season the employment contracts for all part-time coaches become null and void. As a result, a call goes out to all full time employees (including new hires) in that district asking if there is anyone who might be interested in assuming a particular coaching position. It has happened in some districts that a part-time, head coach with a championship team (made up of juniors and sophomores) is shown the door at the conclusion of the championship season because someone else (a full time employee in that district) has now decided to take the coaching post for the following year (perhaps because the entire starting lineup of players would be returning).

School districts and unions support this type of arrangement because of the inherent advantages that they see in having full time school employees being involved in the day-to-day coaching tasks and responsibilities. In these situations it is viewed as the better course of action to always have a full time employee as a coach rather than a part-time person who only coaches. Needless to say, not all districts subscribe to this philosophy and not all districts negotiate such employment contracts (nor implement them with equal vigor) giving such preference to full time employees.

Advantages for the Part-Time Coach

One must be careful lest one begins to think that there are absolutely no advantages in using part-time coaches in our school systems. This is simply not true. There are indeed some advantages in hiring coaches on a part-time basis. Some of the advantages for part-time, off-site coaches, include:

1. Coaches can provide for a different or fresh perspective.
2. Coaches can be highly motivated to be a coach due to the sacrifices they are willing to make.
3. Coaches are not tired and worn down by dealing with youngsters all day long.
4. The opportunity to attract otherwise highly qualified and highly motivated coaches who happen to be employed in a profession other than teaching.
5. Facilitate the hiring of coaches of a wide range of sports which might not be possible if all coaches would have to be full time employees.
6. To be able to secure the services of skilled, experienced and motivated individuals when no such personnel are available among full time teachers in the school/district.

The Hiring of Coaches with Questionable Credentials and Skills

Whether or not these **rent-a-coaches** or **walk-on-coaches** are qualified to serve as coaches is a matter of contention in many areas in this country. Sometimes coaches are hired regardless of whether or not they, in reality, possess minimum coaching competencies. As stated previously, some states have *no requirements* in order to be a coach and some states provide only *minimal requirements* which coaching hopefuls must satisfy. However, just being certified or meeting the *minimum* requirements (and the requirements are indeed minimal in some cases) established by a state or a school system does not automatically mean that the individual is, in fact, qualified and competent. In fact, this whole question of coaching competency has spawned much discussion within our profession (Partlow, 1992b; Engh, 1992; Seefeldt & Milligan, 1992; Johnson, 1992; Cvengros, 1992; Buckanavage, 1992; Broderick, 1984).

Of course, the question of coaching competency can also be raised about the full time physical education teacher or the English or history teacher who has been given the additional assignment of coaching in a school. How does one know whether or not these full time teachers of physical education, English or history are qualified to coach? Just because one has a degree in physical education certainly doesn't mean that the individual is the least bit qualified to coach an athletic sport (Stier, 1990).

COACHING CONCEPT #47: Just because a person is a physical education [teacher education] graduate—it doesn't mean the individual is qualified to coach an athletic team.

In the past, most physical educators have also been scholastic coaches in the schools. But as early as the 1960s, there was doubt expressed among the profession that physical education teachers, merely by virtue of being physical educators, were adequately prepared or possessed sufficient skills to be considered as qualified or competent coaches (Sisley and Wiese, 1987). This position is supported by Lopiano (1986) who echoed a similar judgment that just because one has a physical education degree (teaching) does not mean that the individual is automatically qualified or competent as an athletic coach.

For example, in New York State, anyone who is certified to teach physical education and who holds valid American Red Cross (ARC) first aid and Cardio Pulmonary Resuscitation (CPR) cards (and completes a child abuse class/course) is also certified as an athletic coach (New York State Regulations, July 1988; Guidelines, 1988). However, just because a person is a physical education graduate or possesses a New York teaching certificate in physical education doesn't mean that person is competent to be a coach (Stier, 1993). Grimsley (1987) indicated that it is questionable whether or not present professional preparation programs for physical education are actually producing qualified coaches. In fact, few physical education major programs today are specifically designed to prepare quality (first year, beginning, neophyte) coaches. Although coaching and physical education are certainly related areas with common bodies of knowledge, their applications are certainly different. As Cody (1987, p. 2) indicated over two decades ago: "Professionals are beginning to recognize that coaching athletic teams and teaching physical education are different experiences. Preparation for one is not necessarily preparation for the other."

Almost everyone who is knowledgeable in the coaching field recognizes that there is a definite need for training and more sophisticated education for those individuals seeking to become qualified and competent coaches at the youth, interscholastic and intercollegiate levels. What is needed is very specific training and educational programs to be put into place to insure that an adequate body of knowledge coupled with meaningful practical experiences, including practica and internships, are part of the total educational program to be provided for those coaching hopefuls—regardless of the sport or the level at which these would-be coaches intend to secure employment or volunteer their services.

REFERENCES

A national consensus on standards for coaches. (1993). *NASPE News*. Winter 1993. Issue 32, p. 3.

Broderick, R. (1984). Non-certified coaches. *Journal of Physical Education, Recreation and Dance, 55*(5), 38-39, 53.

Buckanavage, (1992). ACEP/NFICEP—Improving the quality of coaching in Pennsylvania. *Journal of Physical Education, Recreation and Dance, 63*(7), 60-63.

By the numbers. (2001, October/November). *Athletic Management, 13*(6), 29.

Cardone, D. (2000). For the love of it. *Athletic Management, 12*(6), 41-45.

Cody, C. C. (1987). Issue: A call for attention to coaching education. *NAPEHE Action Line, 10*(3), 1-2.

Cohen, A. (1992). Standard Time. *Athletic Business, 16*(12), 23-26, 28.

Cohen, A. (1997, May). Amateur athletics at its finest. *Athletic Business, 21*(5), 35-41

Coping with the coaching shortage. (1988). *Athletic Business*, XII, (10), 20-22, 24.

Cvengros, J. (1992). Michigan PACE—Educating Michigan's coaches. *Journal of Physical Education, Recreation and Dance, 63*(7), 58-59.

Engh, F. C. (1988, November 12). Kids and sports: The playing is the thing. *USA TODAY*, p. l-D.

Engh, F. (1992). National Youth Sports Coaches Association (NYSCA)—More than just a certification program. *Journal of Physical Education, Recreation and Dance, 63*(7), 43-45.

Farrell, C. (1993, January 13). Treat college sports like what they are—Big businesses. *USA Today*, p. 12-C.

Cary, P. (2004, June 7). Fixing kids' sports. *U.S. News & World Report*, pp. 44-49, 51, 53.

Conklin, A. (1999, August). State of the State Games, *Athletic Business, 23*(8), 9.

Gallon, A. J. (1989). *Coaching—Ideas and ideals.* (2nd ed.). Waveland Press, Inc., Illinois: Prospect Heights.

Grimsley, J. R. (1987, Spring). Coaching certification: Are we heading toward inferior coaches in nation's high schools? *Interscholastic Athletic Administration, 13*(3), 18-19.

Guidelines for coaching requirements, June 1988, *Regulations of the Commissioner of Education,* Appendix A, Section 135.4 (c (7) (i) (c). New York State Education Department, Division of Pupil Health and Fitness, Bureau of Physical Education, Albany, New York 12234.

Hill, D. (2002). Double Duty. *Athletic Management, 10*(6), 17-28, 30-31, 34-35.

Hoffer, R. (1993, January 18). Field of schemes. *Sports Illustrated, 78*(2), 57-67.

Johnson, D. (1992). Indiana PACE—A state's response to a coaching education crisis. *Journal of Physical Education, Recreation and Dance, 63*(7), 55-57.

Kimiecik, J. (1988, January/February). The politics of coaching—Two associations vying for coaches' allegiance. *American Coach.* Human Kinetics Publishers, Inc. Champaign, IL., pp. 1, 15.

Lapchick, R. (1993, January 8). Television Interview, Channel 13, Rochester, New York, (from: Northeastern University: North American Society for the Study of Sport).

Life as a teacher/coach. (1988, January/February). *American Coach.* Human Kinetics Publishers, Inc., Champaign, IL., p. 5

Little league scandal fashioned by win-at-all-costs organizers. (1992, September 19). *Democrat and Chronicle,* Rochester, New York, p. 3-D.

Locke, L. F. & Massengale, J.D. (1978). Role conflict in teacher/coaches. *Research Quarterly for Exercise and Sport, 49*(1), 162-174.

Lopiano, D. (1986). The certified coach: A central figure. *Journal of Physical Education, Recreation and Dance, 57*(3), 34-38.

Moriello, J. (1993, August 1). Wolfe's brainstorm became blueprint for a nation. *Democrat and Chronicle,* p. 12-E.

2007-2008 National Directory of Intercollegiate Athletics. (2008). Collegiate Directories, Inc., Cleveland, Ohio.

NCCAA Official Handbook. (1997, August). Marion, Indiana: National Christian College Athletic Association, p. 5.

News Fact File. (1990, May 9). *The NCAA News, 27* (19), p. 5.

New York State regulations of the commissioner of education sections 135.1, 135.2, 135.3, 135.5, effective July 1988. New York State Education Department, Division of Pupil Health and Fitness, Bureau of Physical Education, Albany, New York 12234.

No Split. Now What? (August/September, 2008). AthleticManagement.com., Volume 20, Number 5.

O'Brien, D. B. (ed.). (1981). Editor's afterwords—Legal alternatives. *Journal of Physical Education, Recreation and Dance, 52*(9), 25, 26.

Partlow, K. (1992a). *Interscholastic coaching: A national coaching certification survey* Champaign, Illinois: Human Kinetics-American Coaching Effectiveness Program.

Partlow, K. (1992b). American coaching effectiveness program (ACEP) Educating America's coaches. *Journal of Physical Education, Recreation and Dance, 63*(7), 36-39.

Restructuring Dividing D-III. (2007, August/September). *Athletic Management,* p. 9.

Rog, J. A. (1985). Maine coaches certification survey results. Unpublished manuscript submitted to *The Forum for the Future of Interscholastic Athletics in Maine* (FFIAM), reported in Houseworth, S. D., Davis, M. L. and Dobbs, R. D. (1990). A survey of coaching education program features. *Journal of Physical Education, Recreation and Dance, 61*(5), 26-30.

Sabock, R. J. and Chandler-Garvin, P. B. (1986). Coaching certification United States requirements. *Journal of Physical Education, Recreation and Dance, 57*(6), 57-59.

Sage, G.H. (1990, February), High school and college sports in the United States, *Journal of Physical Education, Recreation and Dance, 61*(2), 59, 61, 63.

Schmid, S. (Ed.). (1993, April). Industry briefings. *Athletic Business,* p. 15.

Seefeldt, V. & Milligan, M. J. (1992). Program for athletic coaches' education (PACE) —Educating America's public private school coaches. *Journal of Physical Education, Recreation and Dance, 63*(7), 46-49.

Sisley, B. L. (1985). Off the street coaches. *Journal of Physical Education, Recreation and Dance, 56*(9), 63-66.

Sisley, B. L. & Wiese, D. M. (1987). Current status: Requirements for interscholastic coaches. *Journal of Physical Education, Recreation and Dance, 58*(2), 73-85.

State of the State Games. (1999, August). *Athletic Business, 23*(8), 9.

Steinbach, P. (2002, September). The third word. Athletic Business, 2*(9), 46-50.*

Stier, Jr., W. F. (1985). Marketability and diversity within the physical education profession—The creation of the renaissance person. *New Jersey Journal of Health, Physical Education, Recreation and Dance—The Reporter, 59*(1), 10, 17.

Stier, Jr., W.F. (1986a). *Competencies of youth coaches.* Washington, D.C.: Research in Education (ERIC Document Reproduction Service No. ED 263-060).

Stier, W.F., Jr. (1986b, Spring). *Athletic Administration.* Athletic Administrators Expect Qualities, Competencies in Coaches. *Interscholastic Athletic Administration, 12*(3), 7, 9.

Stier, W.F., Jr., (1989, Spring). The pragmatic versus the philosophical approach to coaching sport—The assessment of the athletic experience by athletes. *Proceedings of the United States Olympic Academy XII—June 15-18, 1988.* Penn State University Park Campus, pp. 199-206.

Stier, Jr., W.F. (1990, March 15). Challenges facing the athletic coach and administrator coaching the elite athlete. Paper presented at the Escuela Nacional de Deportivos, México City, México, pp. 12.

Stier, Jr., W.F. (1993, March 25). *Physical education — Athletics: Articulation in colleges.* Paper presented at the national conference of the American Alliance for Health, Physical Education, Recreation and Dance, District of Columbia, pp. 8.

Texas allows girls to play boys football. (1993, February 13). *Democrat & Chronicle*, p. 5-D.

The NCAA. (1997). Overland Park, Kansas, pp. 24.

The 1994-1995 national directory of college athletics (men's edition). (1997). National Association of Collegiate Directors of Athletics Collegiate Directories. Ohio: Cleveland, pp. 448.

Thomas, J. R. (ed.). (1984). *Youth sports guide for coaches and parents.* Reston, Virginia, National Association for Sport and Physical Education and the Manufacturers Life Insurance Company, p. 44.

Warren, S. E., and Volpe, D. (1991). A collection of guidelines for youth sports participation. National Youth Sports Foundation for the Prevention of Athletic Injuries, Inc., MA: Needham, pp. 7.

Wieberg, S. (1992, September 29). NAIA takes risk with radical proposal. *USA Today*, p. 9-C.

Name: _____

Student ID #: _____

EXERCISES FOR CHAPTER 3

A.   What are some of the challenges and problems facing coaches at the youth sport level? At the interscholastic level? At the college level?

_____

_____

_____

_____

_____

B.   How would you, as a youth sport coach, attempt to adjust the rules of the sport, strategies and practice techniques to fit the capabilities, skill level and physical conditioning and maturity level of youngsters at this age level?

_____

_____

_____

_____

_____

C.   What are some of the significant differences (distinguishing factors) between the following national sport governing bodies?

NCAA (divisions I, II, III) _____

_____

_____

_____

_____

NJCAA _____

_____

_____

_____

NCCAA _____

_____

_____

_____

NAIA _____

_____

_____

_____

D.   If you wanted to hold a teaching <u>and</u> a coaching post in a college, at what level would you most likely find such employment? Why?

_____

_____

_____

_____

E.   Explain the basis for the evident lack of qualified coaches at the youth sport level and the interscholastic level?

_____

_____

_____

_____

_____

F. Why do interscholastic school administrators seek to employ individuals who can coach as well as teach at the same school or in the same district?

G. What are the advantages and disadvantages of being a part-time coach?

H. Make an argument for or against the statement that *just because one has a physical education degree or is certified to teach physical education, that individual is not necessarily qualified to coach a sport.*

I.   Plan and outline a strategy for the advancement of your career as a coach in junior high, senior high school, and/or at the college level.

_____

_____

_____

_____

_____

_____

_____

_____

_____

_____

_____

RESEARCH QUESTONS FOR CHAPTER 3

1.   Interview a youth sport coach and determine what qualities, training and experience the person possesses that might make the individual qualified to coach youngsters in a sports environment.

_____

_____

_____

_____

_____

_____

2. Interview a parent(s) of youth sport athletes and determine their opinions relative to the values and the negative aspects of youth sports for their child(ren).

    _____

    _____

    _____

    _____

    _____

    _____

3. Interview a parent(s) of youth sport athletes and determine their opinions relative to how they view the competency and skill level of the coaches of their child(ren).

    _____

    _____

    _____

    _____

    _____

    _____

4. Interview an athletic director who works at a high school which operates either a Farm System or an Independent System and determine the administrator's opinion as to the advantages and disadvantages of both types of systems and why that particular school operates under the system that it does.

    _____

    _____

    _____

    _____

    _____

5. Interview an area athletic director and determine the current status relative to securing head and assistant coaches in male and female sports at all levels of competition within the school. Additionally, find out what steps are taken to secure competent coaches for these teams.

Chapter 4

Standards and Educational Programs for Coaches

Head Coaches Earn Respect through Hard Work.

THE PROBLEM OF A LACK OF PROPER EDUCATION FOR COACHES

There is an old story (supposedly true) of four football coaches who were also teachers in a school in a small town in the mid-west who resigned their coaching posts but who remained as teachers. Since there were no other teaching vacancies in the school, the principal found it necessary to hire part-time coaches from the community. These new *rent-a-coaches* all had full time jobs elsewhere. They reportedly took the positions because they had been lifelong football fans (having watched numerous games on television and had even attended a few professional and Division

155

I games) and had envisioned themselves to be potential expert coaches. They had all played high school football. None of the four coaches had had any formal training or education in the area of coaching. Each practice day they would arrive at the school around 4 p.m. to conduct football practice. During the middle of the football season, three of the coaches arrived for a game slightly intoxicated. On Monday morning, the small town newspaper headlines blared across the front page of the sports section something like: "Football Coaches Intoxicated for Friday's Game—School Board to Meet Monday Evening to Decide Fate."

> **COACHING CONCEPT #48: One of the biggest problems facing sports today is the quality of coaching preparation programs.**

Naturally such an embarrassing and potentially dangerous episode has grave repercussions for the school, for the athletic program and for the coaching profession. However, these *rent-a-coaches* were no more coaches than four legs of a table. Nevertheless, their reprehensible and unprofessional behavior reflected negatively upon the school, the athletic staff at the school and the entire coaching profession. Yet, they were not true coaches, not truly competent coaches. They should not have been placed in the situation in which they would most likely fail and embarrass themselves, the athletes, the school, and the profession. Yet, they were hired and they did commit a grave, embarrassing error. Thus, this story, whether actually true or not, has significant implications for the coaching scene at all levels. Specifically, the story emphasizes the very real need to establish and enforce minimum standards for coaches. It also highlights the potential problems of a lack of rigorous standards for would-be athletic coaches. And, it points to the dangers of hiring unqualified individuals as coaches.

The Cry for Increased Standards for Coaches

Many parents as well as educational and sport leaders are calling for *increased standards* for coaching certification at the interscholastic level. There has long been dissatisfaction with the quality of athletic programs at the interscholastic level. This dissatisfaction or concern has been exacerbated in recent years by the failure of interscholastic sports to be clearly seen as an educational experience for the participating students (Stewart, 2006).

Much of the blame for the ills associated with junior high and high school sports has been placed at the feet of the administrators and coaches of such programs. Specifically, many point to the questionable tactics and strategies employed by interscholastic coaches and/or to their questionable training and education.

However, many sport authorities and parents feel that the fundamental [real] problem facing our junior and senior high schools today is a lack of warm bodies (qualified, motivated and interested) to assume the large number of coaching positions available in many of our sports programs across the country. The significant increase in the number of coaching positions in our junior and senior high schools is a result of expanded school athletic programs (Odenkirk, 1985). And, expanded sports programs in the 21st century are a result of increased interest in sport participation in general coupled with a dramatic increase in female participation in school based sports.

For a number of reasons, coaching certification has remained a rather low priority over the years in this country (Sabock and Chandler-Garvin, 1986). In fact, the process of coaching certification in interscholastic sports in our nation's schools has become less rigorous and more flexible (exceptions made even to minimal standards) today than in the 1950s and 1960s (Seefeldt, 1992). Various states, faced with the prospect of diminishing coaching prospects seeking coaching jobs at the interscholastic level, are reluctant to implement strident coaching requirements (Sisley & Wiese, 1987). In fact, just the opposite has happened. As the demand for more coaches has grown in the schools across the country, a great many states either reduced or simply maintained their minimal requirements for coaches in the public schools (Sisley 1985). And, of course, most states have minimal standards to begin with. In fact, the state of Pennsylvania was cited as one state that repealed, in 1984, its regulation that required certified coaches in the junior and senior high schools (Kelley and Brightwell, 1984).

Stier (2003) indicated that coaching certification is very important if the sports scene is to experience superior coaching by experienced, trained, competent, skilled and motivated mentors. Some entity must take the leadership role in the whole certification and/or accreditation process of coaching and coaching preparation programs. "The point is that some independent entity must assume responsibility of overseeing the accreditation process and determining the criteria that must be met and to become and remain a coach. In addition, there must be some 'teeth' in the minimum requirements that are established" (p. 10).

> **COACHING CONCEPT #49: Historically, there is a lack of substantial, consistent, agreed upon and implemented standards in the area of training of coaches.**

One of the problems associated with coaching certification is that approximately one out of every four head coaches of interscholastic teams (junior and senior high schools) possesses no professional preparation or formal training for such a task. In many cases, the only claim for any type of preparation is that the individual had previously participated on a high school, college or university athletic team (Grimsley, 1987). "It is unthinkable, unacceptable to allow a non-certified person to teach first grade based on the fact that the person had been through first grade at one time. And yet that is what we are doing when we employ non-certified persons to coach and assume they are qualified because they participated in sport at one time" (Sabock and Chandler-Garvin, 1986, p. 58). And Conn and Razar (1989) point out that it is indeed ironic that officials for scholastic athletic contests are required by their officiating association in each state to undergo a certification process in order to be allowed to officiate at games. However, no such certification process exists for all coaches who are involved in teaching the young athletes how to play an athletic sport.

LACK OF CONSENSUS ON COACHING COMPETENCIES AND STANDARDS

Coaching certification and training in this country at the national level is seemingly in a state of disarray, disagreement and confusion. At present there exists no national, centrally administered *credentialing* or *certifying* of youth sport coaches, interscholastic coaches or collegiate coaches in the United States, although there are several coaching education programs that are used in many states. Since 2000 there has been the National Council for Accreditation of Coaching Education (NCACE) which seeks to improve the quality of coaching preparation programs, see below.

In this country, there has long been a lack of a consensus among those who prepare and train coaches and among practitioners in the field as to what a qualified coach should be and what competencies the individual should possess (Sisley & Wiese, 1987; Cohen, 1992; Singer, 1992.). There is not even agreement in terms of the minimal qualifications or competencies for a coach as is evidenced by the differing minimal requirements established by various states. Although most professionals would agree that competent and knowledgeable coaches should be able to demonstrate some type of demonstrative skills and knowledge, exactly what those specific competencies should be remains open to interpretation (Cohen, 1992). Thus, even the subject of what should comprise the education and training of coaches has been in a state of flux. However, there have been recommendations regarding the need for some type of practicum or internship experience for would-be coaches for almost 40 years (Stier, 1970; 1984).

Two organizations which have worked together to make recommendations in terms of essential coaching competencies are the National Association for Girls and Women in Sports (NAGWS) and the National Association for Sport and Physical Education (NASPE). Both NAGWS and NASPE are associations of the American Alliance for Health, Physical Education, Recreation and Dance (AAHPERD). The

NAGWS/NASPE Joint Committee on Coaching Certification published a position paper titled *Coaching Certification* (1987) which included a list of these recommended coaching competencies. The competencies were grouped under the following categories:

1. Medical-legal aspects of coaching—sports medicine and first aid; legal liability

2. Human growth and developmental aspects of coaching—knowledge of human growth and development—related to health and safety—in the practical application for training and conditioning

3. Psycho-social aspects of coaching—motivation and sport psychology

4. Bio-physical aspects of coaching—application of the knowledge of anatomical, kinesiological and physiological principles provides a sound basis for maximizing performance and minimizing injury in athletic competition

5. Theoretical and technical aspects of coaching—organization, theory and techniques of coaching

6. Practicum in athletic coaching—practical laboratory experiences under a supervised practice in coaching

In the fall of 1992 the National Association for Sport and Physical Education (NASPE) began to seek support from various national sport governing bodies, the state high school athletic associations, various coaching associations, school administrators and boards of education as well as athletic directors in an effort to establish "a world-class coaching education system that will prepare coaches to be true professionals" (Cohen, 1992, December, p. 24).

In the winter of 1993 the National Association of Sport and Physical Education, headed by Dr. Judy Young, announced a major push toward developing a national consensus regarding *standards* for amateur coaches. This move toward consensus of coaching standards echoes the comments made by the then executive director of the USOC, Harvey Schiller, who earlier called for a "focus on the coach and the development of a national coaching system." One of the objectives calls for the establishment of various coaching categories from the beginning through the master levels (A National Consensus, 1993, p. 3). Dr. Young indicated that NASPE would be working with various related sports organizations and groups such as the USOC, National Governing Boards and the National Sports Federations in establishing suitable standards as well as developing appropriate educational systems for the preparation of qualified and competent coaches. Such education programs were envisioned to be both sport specific and generic in nature (Judy Young, personal communication, January 22, 1993).

COACHING CONCEPT #50: **The National Council for Accreditation of Coaching Education (NCACE) exists to improve the education/training of coaches through accreditation of schools preparing coaches.**

National Council for Accreditation of Coaching Education (NCACE)

In the summer of 2000, the National Council for Accreditation of Coaching Education (NCACE) held its initial national meeting (AAHPERD, 2007). Established in January of the previous year in Denver, Colorado, as the evaluating entity or body "of coaching education programs for single sport, multi-sport, distributors of coaching education and science/medical/educational coaching education-providing organizations" (Latest on NCACE, 2000, New NCACE Program, 2000; Coaching Education, 2004, p. 16).

The major objective of this body has been to help individuals who coach, at all levels of sport and sport competition, become better qualified and better prepared to be highly competent mentors for their charges. This is to be done by *assessing* coaching preparation programs and coaching certification programs, including those programs offered by colleges and universities. NCACE also created a resource publication titled: *Coaching Education: Guidelines for Coaching Education Programs* to provide assistance to those entities, groups and organizations offering coaching education programs and who want to prepare for program review by NCACE. The document provides an outline of steps to take to organize and develop the essential curricular elements which NCACE has identified as essential for coaching preparation programs (National Council, 2006).

"A quality, well-planned and implemented sport program, led by a trained coach, will enhance an athlete's skillful performance, physical fitness and health, establish positive attitudes, and improve life skills," said Judith C. Young, Ph.D., NCACE Executive Director. "Coaching education programs must develop the critical skills and knowledge to facilitate individual and team performance in sport in a safe, healthy, and ethical environment" (News release, 1-13-2003, AAHPERD, Reston, VA.). More information is available at the NCACE homepage at: www.aahperd.org/naspe/programs-ncace.html

NCACE also grants *accreditation* to educational programs that meet or exceed requirements established as essential to preparation of qualified and competent coaches at five different levels. NCACE facilitates coaching education programs in meeting the National Coaching Standards that were originally created in 1995 (*National Standards for Athletic Coaches*) following several years of study and work with consultants/experts. These standards have been the foundation of NCACE's mission to promote and improve quality coaching education for both practicing and prospective coaches.

In 2006, NASPE in cooperation with experts from national governing bodies of sport, the United States Olympic Committee, National Federation of State High School Associations, and the NASPE leadership reviewed, restructured and revised the 1995 standards for sport coaches in an effort to be more consistent with current sport research and best practice (personal communication Christine Bolger, 8-1-08). Hence, the new standards (***National Standards for Sport Coaches (NSSC), 2nd Edition***), as of 2006, were restructured into 8 domains (see below) and consisted of a total of 40 standards. By 2008 they have been endorsed by over 140 sport organizations. In addition to serving as guidelines for the preparation of future coaches, the standards can also: (personal communication, Christine Bolger of NASPE, 8-1-08):

1. Provide a definition for an accepted standard of professional practice
2. Help guide educational programs for coaches
3. Help educate the public about what coaches do
4. Serve as a basis for certification and/or accreditation programs

The following are the 8 domains that contain 40 standards that relate to coaching skills and knowledge: (personal communication Christine Bolger, 8-1-08; retrieved 9-1-08, http://www.aahperd.org/naspe/template.cfm?template=domainsStandards.html). See appendix A for additional information on the 8 domains and standards, including benchmarks.

Reaching for the spike.

1. Philosophy and ethics
2. Safety and injury prevention
3. Physical conditioning
4. Growth and Development
5. Teaching and communication
6. Sport skills and tactics
7. Organization and administration
8. Evaluation

STATE LICENSING AND CERTIFICATION EFFORTS

Since there are no national licensing or certification requirements for individuals involved in interscholastic coaching, any effort to establish any type of licensing or certification standards has been assumed by the individual states. There have been numerous efforts at identifying the state of affairs in terms of state licensing and certification efforts (Sabock & Chandler-Garvin, 1986; Noble & Sigle, 1980). In fact, at the turn of the century only 15 states had requirements for *formal coaching education* for all coaches (American Sports Education Program, 2001). However, the vast majority of states *have not required* specific coaching certification for their scholastic coaches. In fact, in 1987, only five states required coaching certification for coaches, either for all sports or only for a limited number of sports. Many states allow anyone to coach in junior or senior high schools if the individual merely possess a valid teaching certificate or a minimum of courses or classroom hours study aspects of coaching and/or first aid and CPR (Sisley & Wiese, 1987).

An investigation some years ago revealed that only 25 states (one-half) required all scholastic coaches to hold a valid teaching certificate. In fact, six states at that time required only head coaches to possess a teaching certificate. Two states required only coaches of so-called major sports to have a valid teaching certificate in order to be deemed qualified and competent to coach scholastic sports. And, 12 states had no such requirements in terms of a teaching certificate or any type of a coaching certificate for any scholastic coach. Only five states (Arkansas, Iowa, Minnesota, New York and Wyoming) required coaching certification for all or some of their scholastic coaches. The results of this study revealed that "the nation's interscholastic athletic programs may be at risk in light of the apparent lack of professional preparation of some coaches" (Sisley & Wiese, 1987, p. 77).

In addition to some states attempting to establish minimum certification requirements for scholastic coaches, there are numerous school districts in the United States which have taken it upon themselves to develop certification programs for those individuals who wish to coach in their districts. Some of these school districts included the Anaheim Union High School, Anaheim, California; Portland Public School District, Portland, Oregon; and the Seattle School District, Seattle, Washington (Coaching Certification, 1987).

In the fall of 2008 the National Coaching Report (New National Coaching Report) was released to the public. It ". . . provides a baseline of what is being done to train coaches at the youth and interscholastic sport levels" (p, 1). Information is available in terms of the 2008 requirements of each state and the District of Columbia as well as various sport organizations. The National Association of Sports and Physical Education (NASPE) has made the full report available (as of the fall 2008) at the following web site: www.naspeinfo.org/coachingreport.

Among the findings of the National Coaching Report (pages 1, 9) in terms of coaching education requirements for school based sports in 2008 are the following:

1. Eighty-four% of the states have some type of coaching education requirement (some have specific types of coaching related and/or conditioning type courses, some require first aid and/or CPR, while some states have a variety of different requirements).

2. Idaho has its coaching education requirements apply only to head varsity coaching positions.

3. Minnesota has its coaching education requirements apply only to paid coaches.

4. New Hampshire has its coaching education requirements apply only to first-time coaches.

5. Alabama has its coaching education requirements apply only to non-faculty coaches.

6. Fifteen states exempt would-be coaches who possess a teaching license/certificate (subject matter doesn't matter).

7. New York State exempts physical education teachers as the state equates teaching physical education the same as coaching.

8. Twenty-two% of the states recommend coaching education.

9. New Hampshire recommends that all volunteer coaches receive education/training in coaching sports.

10. The most frequently cited content areas of the coaching education efforts include:
    a. Fundamentals of coaching
    a. First aid
    b. CPR
    c. Sport rules (training)

New York State's Efforts to Educate and Certify Coaches

Presently (2008) New York State classifies potential school coaches into one of three categories [background]: (1) a certified physical education teacher; (2) a teacher certified in an area other than physical education, e.g. English, mathematics; or (3) a person who holds no certification as a teacher. Teachers of physical education are automatically certified to coach (http://www.emsc.nysed.gov/ciai/physed.html). All individuals who work as a coach of an interschool athletic team must hold valid first aid skills and knowledge certification (i.e., completion of an approved first aid and CPR courses) as well as pass a child abuse course/workshop (www.childabuseworkshop.com). By July 1, 2001, a law (Safe Schools Against Violence in Education Act) required new school district employees (both certified and non-certified) to undergo fingerprinting and clearance for employment.

Individuals who are not certified physical education teachers are required to complete the three course requirements established for coaching by the State Education Department [Philosophy, Principals, and Organization of Athletics in Education; Health Sciences Applied to Coaching; and The Theory and Techniques of Coaching—SPORT SPECIFIC] to obtain a professional [non-provisional] certificate to coach (retrieved 9-9-08, http://www.emsc.nysed.gov/ciai/pe/coaching.htm).

The New York State Education Department stipulated that by 2010 all instructors of the three required courses must re-apply to the State for approval (meeting the new criteria for instructors) in order to be able to teach the coaching courses. In 2008 the State developed an instructor evaluation survey to assist in the creation and development of new criteria for all instructors of the coaching courses for future school based coaches. The State planned that by 2010 the new standards and criteria would be in place for all instructors seeking to be certified as teachers of any of the three required course.

CONCERNS ABOUT HIRING UNQUALIFIED COACHES

> **COACHING CONCEPT #51: Select competent and certified coaches—don't shoot yourself in the foot by hiring unqualified coaches.**

Schools are rightly concerned about securing competent and qualified coaches for their sports (Bucher, 1987). There are some very real dangers when schools hire individuals to coach who do not possess the necessary skills and experiences, not the least of which is the very real likelihood of injuries resulting to the athletes in the coach's charge. Today, more and more schools are justly concerned about the potential for such physical harm to student-athletes and the subsequent liability exposure resulting from successful law suits. Schools need to be most careful in their screening and hiring efforts lest unqualified or incompetent coaches are hired. The presence of such coaches increases the potential for coaching negligence (Lopiano, 1986). One of the top priorities of coaches at the interscholastic level is the protection of the athletes. Coaches who lack adequate training in proper conditioning techniques, sports medicine and first aid techniques are perceived to be less capable of protecting their athletes' health and well-being (Steinbach, 2003).

WHAT SCHOOLS ARE LOOKING FOR IN HIRING A COACH

Coaches need to learn how to coach their specific sport(s). In some sports within the United States, coaches are able to qualify and earn various ratings in terms of sport coaching certification—at the national level. The sports of volleyball and soccer are but two examples. However, in most sports there is simply no recognized national certification of coaches in that particular sport.

Competencies Needed by Athletic Coaches

Coaches must develop skills in communication techniques, organization and administration and management, sport psychology, nutrition, sport physiology and conditioning, sport biomechanics as well as the prevention and treatment of sport injuries. Athletes of all ages need and deserve educated, skilled, motivated, and sensitive coaches who respect the student-athlete and understand the challenges and tribulations the individual athlete is experiencing regardless of age and skill level. To achieve these objectives, coaching hopefuls need to be introduced to the principles involved in the art and science of coaching combined with more in-depth exposure to sport science principles and sport specific information (Stier, 1986). In 2005, there was a push to make it a law in Massachusetts that would require coaches and athletes to learn sports psychology (Popke, 2005). Certification or education programs for coaches attempt to insure that would-be coaches are familiar with such areas as: (Bach, 2003)

1. The importance of developing a coaching philosophy
2. How to be an effective teacher and communicator
3. To keep expectations realistic
4. To be fair to all players
5. How to deal with unruly behavior
6. Important safety issues
7. Proper sportsmanship
8. The importance of a preseason parents meeting
9. How to deal with team problems
10. How to deal with problem parents

Recognized Strengths of Coaches

A state investigation revealed that scholastic coaches were deemed (by high school athletic directors) to be most competent and knowledgeable in the specifics (the Xs and Os) of the sport(s) they are currently coaching. These same athletic directors indicated that current coaches were deficient in the principles of psychology, physiology, preventing and recognizing injuries and the administration of their sport(s) (Houseworth, Davis and Dobbs, 1990). This same study revealed that coaches were most interested in attending clinics and workshops dealing with sport specifics and teaching skills—their strengths.

In a study of athletic administrators of college women sports programs, it was found that when specific undergraduate and graduate courses were ranked in terms of their importance for a head coaching candidate to be given a job offer—that the classes were broken down into two categories which the researchers coined context and perspective courses (history of sport, sociology of sport, philosophy of sport, etc.) and tools courses, such as use of computers, psychology of sport, organization and administration, sports medicine, coaching pedagogy, supervised coaching (internships), etc. In fact, the top five courses which the athletic directors of women sports at the college level ranked in terms of importance when it came to coaches getting a job were (Siegel & Newholf, 1992):

1. Supervised coaching
2. Psychology of sport
3. Organization and administration
4. Sports medicine
5. Coaching pedagogy

EDUCATIONAL OPPORTUNITIES FOR COACHES AND FUTURE COACHES

The training and education of would-be coaches and current coaches takes two forms; *pre-service* and *in-service* educational experiences. Coaches, like physicians and tax experts, are never through with their education and training. There is just too much that is changing in their field. Coaches must remain current. Once individuals are certified as a coach and have secured a coaching position, they cannot rest on their laurels. They must not become stagnant. As a result, coaches are faced with the lifelong task and challenge of studying, contemplating, evaluating, analyzing and synthesizing in an effort to continue to learn and remain at the cutting edge of their profession. In short, a coach is never through studying, learning and improving.

COACHING CONCEPT #52: Coaches must never stop learning on the job.

Pre-service Education Experiences

Pre-service education is a phrase which describes the education which takes place prior to the time when the individual actually engages in coaching an athletic team as a full fledged athletic coach. Typically, this takes place within the confines of a college or university if the future coach is a college student. However, if the would-be coach is not enrolled in a college or university, the pre-service education can consist of special courses, classes or workshops specifically arranged for future coaches to enroll in order to obtain the knowledge and to develop the necessary competencies for a beginning, inexperienced, first year coach.

In-service Training and Educational Opportunities

In-service training includes those educational experiences and opportunities made available to the coaches who are already on the job as caches. In this situation, the coach is currently engaged in coaching athletes in a competitive setting and is able to attend workshops, clinics, conventions as well as regular classes while engaged as a coach. These workshops, clinics and classes can be held on the school site or at other locations away from the school or school district.

Schools have an obligation to see to it that their coaches are given opportunities to keep up-to-date in terms of current coaching knowledge, techniques, strategies and methods. In fact, courts of law have ruled that schools and school districts have a definite responsibility and, in fact, a duty to provide "adequate, appropriate, and continuous in-service coaching programs" (Johnson, 1992, p. 56).

In-service educational opportunities can be broadly interpreted to also include access to materials as well as actual lecture type learning experiences. Thus, schools can assist in the in-service education of their coaches by providing the coaches with easy access to professional journals and sport publications. Some of the professional publications which might be of interest to coaches include, but are not limited to, the following:

Taking care of an injury during competition.

1. *Applied Research In Coaching and Athletics Annual*
2. *Athletic Administration*
3. *Athletic Journal (no longer being published)*
4. *Athletic Directory—The Coaches' Choice*
5. *Athletic Management*
6. *Basketball Clinic*
7. *Coach & Athlete (no longer being published)*
8. *Coaching Clinic*
9. *Coaching Sports*
10. *Coaching & Sport Science Journal*
11. *First Aider*
12. *International Council of Health, Physical Education•SD (ICHPER•SD) Journal of Research*
13. *International Journal of Physical Education*
14. *International Journal of Sport Communication*
15. *International Journal of Sport Nutrition*
16. *International Journal of Sport Managaement*
17. *International Journal of Sports Marketing and Sponsorship*
18. *International Journal of Sports Science & Coaching*
19. *International Journal of Volleyball Research*
20. *International Sports Studies Journal*
21. *Interscholastic Athletic Administration*
22. *The Journal of Coaching Education*
23. *Journal of the International Council of Health, Physical Education, Sport and Dance (ICHPER•SD)*
24. Journal of Issues in Intercollegiate Athletics
25. *Journal of the Legal Aspects of Sport and Physical Activity*
26. *Journal of the Quantitative Analysis of Sports*
27. *Journal of the Philosophy of Sport*
28. *Journal of Physical Education, Recreation and Dance*
29. *Journal of Quantitative Analysis in Sports*
30. *Journal of Sport Administration and Supervision*
31. *Journal of Sport Behavior*
32. *Journal of Sport and Exercise Psychology*
33. *The Journal of Sports Law & Contemporary Problems*
34. *Journal of Sport and Social Issues*

35. *Journal of Sport Behavior*
36. *Journal of Sport Business*
37. *Journal of Sport History*
38. *Journal of Sports Media*
39. *Journal of Sport Sciences*
40. *Journal of Sports Psychology*
41. *Journal of Sport and Social Issues*
42. *Journal of Strength and Conditioning Research*
43. *Journal for the Study of Sports and Athletes in Education*
44. *Journal of Teaching in Physical Education*
45. *Journal of Sport and Exercise Physiology*
46. *Journal of Sport Rehabilitation*
47. *The Journal for the Study of Sports And Athletes in Education*
48. *Journal of National Association for Academic Advisors for Athletics N4A*
49. *The Physical Educator*
50. *Recreational Sports Journal*
51. *Sociology of Sport Journal*
52. *Scholastic Coach*
53. *The Sport Coaching Journal*
54. *The Sport Journal*
55. *Sport Management and Related Topics (Smart)*
56. *Sport Management Education Journal*
57. *Sport Management International Journal*
58. *The Sport Psychologist*
59. *The Sport Supplement*
60. *Sports Marketing Quarterly*
61. *Strategies*
62. *Texas Coach*
63. *Training and Conditioning*
64. *Women in Sport and Physical Activity Journal*

PROBLEMS WITH CERTIFICATION AND INCREASED STANDARDS

There have been concerns expressed by some school administrators that with increased standards for coaching certification there may actually be a reduction in the number of qualified candidates who can be given a coaching position. There is always the potential for a reduction in the number of sports offered at the scholastic level if no qualified and competent coaches can be found and hired—certainly not an acceptable situation in most communities.

Another concern with increased standards is that there may be additional costs involved in attracting qualified individuals who have undergone specified training in order to meet the higher standards and be certified by the state or sponsoring organization. In other words, it may take additional monies to make it worth the coaches' time and effort. Of course, the end result would be increased costs for the scholastic sports programs—a fact that communities might find abhorrent.

COACHING CONCEPT #53: Some fear that increased standards for coaches may lead to fewer candidates desiring to become coaches.

Yet another problem with certification is that coaches are reluctant, once they meet minimum certification standards, to continue taking continuing education courses or participate in in-service education programs, other than the technical Xs and Os aspects of coaching.

Extending oneself to the maximum to excel.

Proponents of increasing the minimum qualifications of coaches and establishing certification of coaches argue that even if it does cost more, and they are not acknowledging the costs will be substantially greater, the end result will be worth it. Providing highly trained and quality coaches *is the first step* toward insuring that youngsters at the youth sport and interscholastic levels of competition are provided with a true and positive learning experience as a result of their athletic participation. After all, they point out; these young athletes are our future citizens. They deserve a quality athletic experience, one which is educationally sound and personally satisfying. If our society is unwilling to insist upon higher coaching standards and is reluctant to pay for appropriate training and certification programs for coaches then we—as a society—will pay dearly at a later date in lost opportunities to teach our youth meaningful lessons through the sport experience.

CONTENTS OF COLLEGE LEVEL EDUCATIONAL PROGRAMS FOR COACHES

Many colleges and universities teach a wide range of undergraduate and/or continuing education courses which they hope will help would-be coaches become somewhat knowledgeable and competent as first-year, beginning, neophyte coaches. It is presumed that these coaching candidates will continue, following their college career, in their efforts to develop additional coaching competencies. These classes usually fall under four broad categories:

1. Foundation courses—understanding sports and competitive athletics in general
2. Technical aspects of coaching—the Xs and Os of a sport
3. Organization and administrative aspects of sports and coaching
4. Practical aspects of coaching—practice coaching experiences similar to practice teaching for would-be teachers

TRAINING PROGRAMS AND COACHING STANDARDS FOR YOUTH AND INTERSCHOLASTIC SPORTS

Although there are no *national minimal standards* (required) currently established for coaches at any level, there are several national organizations and state groups involved in efforts to provide some type of educational and/or certification programs for would-be coaches. In some locales, youth sport organizers and promoters have adopted one or more of these coaching certification and educational programs as an integral component of the licensing or authorization process of coaches. As a consequence, these coaches participate in periodic (annual or biannual) workshops or coaching clinics designed to keep them up-to-date. Upon successful completion of the classes, courses, clinics, or workshops, the would-be coach is granted permission by the local youth sport organization to coach in that particular youth sport program. These programs provide the coaching hopeful with the basic skills in a number of essential areas including, but not limited to (Conn and Razar, 1989):

1. Sport fundamentals
2. Specific techniques and strategies (Xs and Os) of coaching a particular sport

3. Information relating to growth and development of youngsters in various age ranges.

4. Sport science

5. Sports psychology

6. Sport sociology

7. Legal liability

8. Conditioning

9. Nutrition

10. First aid

11. Sports medicine and injury prevention nutrition

12. Practice organization

COACHING CONCEPT #54: Professional preparation programs for coaches should provide an updated body of knowledge and enhance an awareness of appropriate coaching behavior

---

These training programs provide exposure to an updated body of knowledge and strive to enhance an awareness of appropriate coaching behavior. They also create a familiarity in terms of where to go to find out answers to questions which face the modern day coach. After all, a knowledgeable coach does not have to *know* all of the answers. However, an effective coach needs to recognize one's own limitations and be able to know where to find the appropriate answers.

EXISTING COACHING EDUCATION AND CERTIFICATION EFFORTS AND PROGRAMS

Institute for the Study of Youth Sports

One such organization is the *Institute for the Study of Youth Sports* currently located at Michigan State University. This is a non-profit, educational organization created to provide education programs for coaches. It is commonly referred to as the *Youth Sport Institute* or just the *Institute*. Started in 1978 by the Michigan state legislative, the *Institute* devoted its early years to working almost exclusively in the non-school athletic arena. The institute developed structured and comprehensive educational programs designed to train non-school coaches *(agency-sponsored sports coaches or programs)* involved in the youth sports of ice hockey, soccer, basketball, football, softball and baseball. However, in 1987 this organization expanded its efforts beyond youth sports when it introduced [initiated] its first educational program (PACE) at the interscholastic level, for coaches in junior and senior high schools (Seefeldt and Milligan, 1992).

Program for Athletic Coaching Education (PACE)

In 1987 the *Institute for the Study of Youth Sports* created PACE which is not a certification program. Rather it should be considered as an educational program. During the 1987-1988 academic year, the *Institute* began a special coaching course in the state of Michigan designed for non-faculty interscholastic coaches. This program for junior and senior high coaches was an extension or expansion of the coaches' educational program previously offered for so-called agency-sponsored sports coaches, including coaches of youth sports. The *Institute*, along with the Michigan High School Athletic Association (MHSAA) and the Michigan Interscholastic Athletic Administrators Association (MIAAA), cooperated during the spring and summer months of 1988 to create several significant modifications in the youth coaching course content, in an effort to meet the actual needs of junior and senior high coaches. The revised course has subsequently been restructured in light of the recommendations of the Joint Committee on Coaching Certification (Talking about, 1988). For the future, the Institute anticipates part of the dissemination process of PACE in the future will involve the use of teleconferences, video tapes and even videodisk systems.

Indiana's Center for Coaching Education (CCE) and PACE

Various states and city organizations as well as colleges and universities have availed themselves of the PACE coaching curriculum and courses. One such state which has endorsed the PACE curriculum and coaching program is Indiana. In November of 1988, the Center for Coaching Education (CCE) was established on the campus of Indiana State University for the purpose of coordinating efforts to improve youth sports programs in Indiana. Two years later, in 1990, the CCE and the Indiana High School Athletic Association teamed together and selected a single coaching education program for the entire state of Indiana. The program chosen was the Program for Athletic Coaching Education (PACE) which was created by the *Institute for the Study of Youth Sports*. The Indiana PACE program includes instruction in sport philosophy, sport science, sports medicine, sport management, legal liability, and sport-specific topics (Johnson, 1992).

National Youth Sports Coaches Association—NYSCA

Another national organization dealing with the training of youth sport coaches is the *National Youth Sports Coaches Association* (NYSCA). The NYSCA was started in 1981. Its headquarters is presently located in West Palm Beach, Florida.

The NYSCA has over 2,000 different chapters in all 50 states (Martinez, personal communication, August 3, 1993). The not-for-profit organization has sought to assist in the improvement of out-of-school sports for youth under the age of 16. The mission of the organization is to provide "better sports for children" (What We're All About, 1992, p. 2).

The organization seeks to improve the status of sports for youngsters through better education of coaches (Engh, 1988). Towards this end, NYSCA has been active in developing a *national training and educational program for volunteer coaches involved in youth sports.* The aim of this organization is not to prepare or educate coaches for the junior or senior school sports programs but rather to work with volunteer coaches at the youth level. At the present time, this educational program provides NYSCA certification as a youth coach to those individuals who successfully complete a three-year, three-level course of study (Curricular Requirements, 1992). By 1992, almost 450,000 men and women had completed the NYSCA certification. It is anticipated that by 2010, over 200,000 coaches will be completing the NYSCA certification annually. The NYSCA also provides member coaches with a half-million dollars legal liability insurance policy and also publishes an official newsletter, *Youth Sport Coach* (Engh, 1992).

Youth Sports Coalition of the National Association
for Sport and Physical Education

Another effort at providing guidelines for the conduct of youth sport athletic experiences was completed in 1986. It was at that time that the *Youth Sports Coalition of the National Association for Sport & Physical Education* (an association of the American Alliance for Health, Physical Education, Recreation and Dance, AAHPERD) and representatives from the *National Council of Youth Sports Directors* agreed upon the major content areas or themes which were recommended to be included in any beginning level youth sport coaching education program. The steering committee representing these two groups identified curricular objectives of youth sport coaches in terms of both (1) scientific bases of coaching and (2) techniques of coaching. Specifically, coaches of youth sports should develop competencies in the areas listed below—which in turn make possible very important outcomes for the individual athlete (Guidelines, 1986).

1. Medical-legal aspects of coaching:

   This coaching competency enables young athletes to be provided a safe and healthful environment in which to participate. The coach should have basic knowledge and skills in the prevention of athletic injuries, and basic knowledge of first aid.

2. Training and conditioning of athletes:

   This coaching competency enables athletes to receive appropriate physical conditioning for sports participation. The coach should use acceptable procedures in their training and conditioning programs.

3. Psychological aspects of coaching young people:

   This coaching competency enables a positive social and emotional environment to be created for youth athletes. The coach should recognize and understand the developmental nature of the young athlete's motivation for sport competition and adjust his/her expectations accordingly.

4. Knowledge of the growth, development and learning patterns of youngsters engaged in sports:

   This coaching competency enables athletes to have positive learning experiences. The coach should have a knowledge of basic learning principles and consider the current developmental level of the youngsters.

5. Sport specific coaching techniques:

   This coaching competency enables every young athlete to have an appropriate opportunity to participate regularly in a sport of his/her choosing. The coach should provide guidance for successful learning and performance of specific sport techniques, based on the maturity level or proficiency of the athlete.

In terms of specific techniques of coaching sports, this steering committee stipulated that coaches of youth sports should be knowledgeable in the techniques and varying styles of teaching/coaching the distinct physical activities associated with the sport that the individual has agreed to coach. This includes being able to (Guidelines, 1986):

1. Organize and conduct practice sessions throughout the season while providing maximal learning opportunities.

2. Recognize that youngsters, boys and girls, learn at different rates and be able to meet these individual differences by being flexible in one's teaching styles and methods.

3. be competent in selecting appropriate drills and learning experiences while being able to detect and analyze errors in performance.

4. be able to provide challenging but safe and successful experiences for young athletes by making appropriate modifications during practice.

5. Know and understand the key elements of sports principles and technical skills and the various teaching styles that can be used to introduce and refine them.

American Sport Education Program—ASEP

A dunk in basketball is aways a thrill for the crowd.

Yet another national organization dealing with the education of coaches is Human Kinetics Publishers in Champagne, Illinois. This company, a for profit, commercial enterprise, created the American Coaching Effectiveness Program (ACEP) in 1976. This program was the brainchild of Rainer Martens who was then a professor at the University of Illinois. He was also the founder and serves as the President of Human Kinetics, Champaign, Illinois. ACEP was originally developed with youth sport coaches in mind. However, in 1990, the ACEP concept expanded beyond attempting to provide educational experiences exclusively for youth sport coaches and sought to provide training programs for coaches at the interscholastic level.

In 1992, ACEP released the *Rookie Coaches Course* (K. Partlow, personal communication, August 5, 1993). As a result, "ACEP became the most popular and widely adopted coaching education program in the United States of America" (Partlow, 1992, p. 37). In fact, by 1992 ACEP was working with 41 Olympic national sport governing bodies, 32 states and more than 180 colleges and universities (Cohen, 1992, December).

In early 1994 the American Coaching Effectiveness Program (ACEP) was changed to the American Sport Education Program (ASEP) in recognition of its expanded mission (David McCann, personal communication, June 9, 1997). Currently, the ASEP educational program is broken down into a multi-level education program. The first level is the *volunteer level* and deals essentially with volunteer coaches in community *youth sports* programs. It is the second level, the *leader level* which has expanded beyond the youth sport area, and is for junior high or high school [interscholastic] coaches who have not had prior extensive coaching education. The third level, *master level, is* designed for those individuals who desire to pursue coaching as a profession rather than an avocation.

One of the goals of the original ACEP curriculum experts [organizers and planners] was to establish that coaching education in and of itself is far more than just presenting Xs and Os (Partlow, 1992). In May of 1990, the *National Federation of State High School Associations* (which was established in 1922) and ACEP got together and collaborated in the establishment of a special edition of the ACEP Leader (scholastic) Level curriculum. This distinct curriculum package is called the *National Federation Interscholastic Coaches Education Program* (NFICEP). "The NFICEP represents 50 state associations comprised of approximately 20,000 high schools representing over 200,000 coaches in the U.S." (Buckanavage, 1992, p. 61).

In the summer of 1997 the American Sport Education Program (ASEP) created two additional and new programs at the youth sport level. These were directly aimed to reach *parents* and *administrators* at the youth sport level of competition. One program is geared towards parents and is called **SportParent** while the second program is called **SportDirector**. **SportParent** is designed to assist "parents understand their roles and responsibilities, not only to their own child but also to their child's team, coach, and program. **SportDirector** helps youth sport administrators plan, program, and deliver quality programs" (ASEP's Volunteer Level, 1995, p. 10).

One state which has become involved in the ACEP/NFICEP program is the state of Pennsylvania. The Pennsylvania State Athletic Directors Association (PSADA) decided in 1989 to attempt to initiate some type of coaching education program for the coaches at the interscholastic level. This is the same state that only five years earlier, in 1984, repealed the state wide law requiring coaches to be certified (Kelley and Brightwell, 1984).

Thus, in 1990 the PSADA decided to utilize the ACEP coaching materials. Subsequently, this state organization utilized the special edition of the ACEP Leader Level curriculum cited above, the *National Federal Interscholastic Coaches Education Program* (NFICEP). This was because the National Federation of State High School Associations and ACEP joined together in the creation of the special edition. This program involves videotapes, textbooks, workbooks (Buckanavage, 1992). The PSADA endorsed the ACEP/NFICEP cooperative venture and began to recommend and promote this nationally recognized, multi-level program throughout the state of Pennsylvania.

A New Coaching Education Program on the Interscholastic Level

In January 2007, a new coaching education program was launched by the National Federation of State High School Associations (NFHS), called the Fundamentals of Coaching course. Previously, the NFHS and the American Sports Education Program (ASEP) cooperatively (in a partnership) trained thousands of coaches. However, now coaches can take the NFHS Fundamentals of Coaching course or the ASEP's Coaching Principles course, or both. Although both courses include material on communication, management and motivational aspects of coaching, the NFHS course includes so-called single-focus modules on such topics of hazing, sexual harassment avoidance and hydration (necessity of) (Popke, 2006).

COACHING CONCEPT #55: Although the National Federation does not mandate coaching education per se, some 37 states in 2006 had some sort of coaching education program in existence.

CANADIAN NATIONAL COACHING CERTIFICATION PROGRAM—CNCCP

In our neighbor to the north, Canada, there is the Canadian National Coaching Certification Program (CNCCP). The majority of coaches involved with the CNCCP will always be volunteers who work with youth sports, that is, youngsters 6-14 years of age. The CNCCP consists of five distinct levels and the objective is to train a competent coach in terms of both theory and technical components of coaching a specific sport. Both generic (theory) and sport specific coaching information is included within the various coaching components, in modules (Gowan, 1992).

Other Youth Sport Organizations—Local, State and Regional Levels

There are numerous other youth sport organizations, usually on the local and state level, which sponsor competitive opportunities for youngsters. Some of these organizations provide limited training or educational programs. Other organizations are not involved at all in the education of coaches, either for would-be coaches or for those already coaching. The major purpose for these organizations is to provide an organized and structured competitive setting for young boys and/or girls. Yet, in the majority of communities there are no minimal requirements of any kind for individuals to meet in order to coach and no clinics, workshops or educational programs provided for those who actually coach young boys and girls in the youth sport arena.

In fact, it has been estimated that less than 10% of youth coaches in this country have been effectively reached by any of the so-called national coaching educational or certification programs (Cohen, 1992). Today, the situation has not changed significantly. This is indeed a sad state of affairs for our sports programs and the youngsters who participate.

National High School Athletic Coaches Association—(NHSACA)

The National High School Athletic Coaches Association (NHSACA) had started work on the only so-called national certification program that adheres to the National Commission for Certifying Agencies (NCCA) guidelines. The NHSACA is attempting to secure mandatory certification of interscholastic coaches, *although this is yet far from reality today.* One of the difficulties that has faced this effort is the tendency "for schools and states to provide exemptions or exceptions to accommodate perceived shortages of coaches" (Seefeldt, 1992, p. 48). Nevertheless, in 2008 there is still no national certification program for coaches of interscholastic coaches that is widely accepted and adopted by a majority of the states in this country.

COACHING CONCEPT #56: There is still no national certification program for interscholastic coaches that is widely accepted and adopted by the majority of states in this country.

CURRENT STATE OF AFFAIRS OF COACHING EDUCATION AND CERTIFICATION

As can be seen from the above information, there have been a number of national organizations examining the possibility of either establishing coaching education programs or otherwise becoming involved with already existing programs. Organizations such as the Human Kinetics Publishers, the Youth Sports Institute, and the National Youth Sport Coaches Association, have been successful in developing *certification and/or education programs for coaches.* However, these programs have been focused, for the most part, more on youth sport programs *rather than at the advanced levels of coaching*, that is, the interscholastic or the college levels. This still is generally true even though more recent involvements of PACE and ASEP have been at the interscholastic level. As a result, there is still an absence of coaching education programs or courses that truly provide in-depth study for the education or preparation of highly skilled and competent coaches at either the advanced high school

Women's sports are truly competitive in nature and very popular throughout the country.

or college levels. Most of the coaching education programs that have been established in prior to the early 1990s have been geared to developing minimal coaching skills for part-time coaches at the youth or non-school level of competition.

On the other hand, level 3 of the Canadian National Coaching Program is recognized as including or dealing with the body of knowledge and experiences, both in depth and breadth, necessary for coaches employed at the higher levels of sport coaching (Siegel & Newholf, 1992).

Unfortunately, even as we have reached the 21st century, far too many coaches are still poorly prepared to be coaches at the youth sport level and the secondary level (junior and senior high schools). Additionally, far too many individuals are involved in the act of coaching not on a full time, professional basis. Rather, they do so as an additional professional responsibility (added on their full-time teaching duties in a school, for example) or as a volunteer (either in youth sports or in schools). The fact remains, there are far too many unprepared, insufficiently trained would-be coaches assuming the all important role of coaching our youth from the youth sport arena right on through and including the high school sports scene.

REFERENCES

A national consensus on standards for coaches. (1993). *NASPE News.* Winter 1993. Issue 32, p. 3.

AAHPERD. Retrieved, September 21, 2007, from http://www.aahperd.org/NASPE/pr_11603.html

American Sport Education Program. (2001). *Raising the standard: The 2000 national interscholastic coaching requirements report.* Champaign, Illinois: Human Kinetics.

ASEP's volunteer level. (1994, August), *HKToday*, Champaign, Illinois, p. 10.

Bach, G. (2003). What coaches should know. *Athletic Business, 27*(11), 70-72, 74, 76.

Berg, R. (2005, August). Coach's rules: How to become a top sports coach in 37 not-so-easy steps. *Athletic Business, 19*(8), 9.

Bucher, C. (1987). *Management of physical education and athletic programs.* St. Louis: Times Mirror/Mosby College Publishing.

Buckanavage, R. J. (1992), ACEP/NFICEP-Improving the quality of coaching in Pennsylvania. *Journal of Physical Education, Recreation and Dance, 63*(7), 60-63.

Coaching Certification. (1987). A position paper prepared by the joint committee on coaching certification of the national association for girls and women in sports and the national association for sport and physical education. Reston, VA: AAHPERD, pp. 1-6.

Coaching education: It takes a team effort. (2004, March/April). *UPDATE*, p. 16.

Cohen, A. (1992, December). Standard time. *Athletic Business, 16*(12), 23-26, 28.

Conn, J. & Razar, J. (1989). Certification of coaches—A legal and moral responsibility. *The Physical Educator, 46*(3), 161-165.

Curricular requirements for NYSCA certification. (1992). *National Youth Sport Coaches Association.* West Palm Beach, Florida.

Cvengros, J. (1992). Michigan PACE—Educating Michigan's coaches. *Journal of Physical Education, Recreation and Dance, 63*(7), 58-59.

Engh, F. (1988). Certifying quality coaches: An interview with Fred Engh. *Parks and Recreation, 23*(3), 42-44.

Engh, F. (1992). National youth sports coaches association (NYSCA)—More than just a certification program. *Journal of Physical Education, Recreation and Dance, 63*(7), 43-45.

Gowan, G.R. (1992). Canada's national coaching certification program (NCCP)—Past, present, & future. *Journal of Physical Education, Recreation and Dance, 63*(7), 50-54.

Grimsley, J. R. (1987, Spring). Coaching certification: Are we heading toward inferior coaches in the nation's high schools? *Interscholastic Athletic Administration, 13*(3), 18-19.

Guidelines for coaching education: Youth sports. (1986). Publication prepared by the Youth Sports Coalition of the National Association for Sport & Physical Education with Representatives from the National Council of Youth Sports Directors. Reston, VA: AAHPERD.

Guidelines for coaching requirements, June 1988, Regulations of the Commissioner of Education, New York, Appendix A, Section 135.4 (c (7) (i) (c),

Houseworth, S. D., Davis, M. L. and Dobbs, R. D. (1990). A survey of coaching education program features. *Journal of Physical Education, Recreation and Dance, 61*(5), 26-30.

Johnson, D. 1992). Indiana PACE-A state's response to a coaching education crisis. *Journal of Physical Education, Recreation and Dance, 63*(7), 55-57.

Kelley, E. J. & Brightwell, S. (1984). Should interscholastic coaches be certified? *Journal of Physical Education, Recreation, and Dance, 55*(3), 49-50.

Latest on NCACE. (2000, winter). *NASPENews,* p. 3.

National Council for Accreditation of Coaching Education. (2006). *Guidelines for accreditation of coaching education and instructions for the preparation of folios.* Manuscript. Reston, VA,

New National Coaching Report. (2008, Fall). *NASPE News.* Issue 79, pp 1, 9.

Lopiano, D. A. (1986, March). The certified coach: A central figure. *Journal of Physical Education, Recreation and Dance, 57*(3), 34-38.

New NCACE program designed to improve coaches for all athletes. (2000, September/October). *UPDATE,* p. 7.

Noble, L., & Sigle, G. (1980,). Minimum requirements for interscholastic coaches. *Journal of Physical Education, Recreation and Dance, 51*(9), 32-33.

Odenkirk, J. E. (1985). High school athletics and the shortage of qualified coaches: An enigma for the public schools. *The Physical Educator, 43*(2), 82-85.

Partlow, K. (1992). American coaching effectiveness program (ACEP)—Educating America's coaches. *Journal of Physical Education, Recreation and Dance, 63*(7), 36-39.

Popke, M. (2005, September). Attitude adjustment. *Athletic Business, 29*(9), 32, 34, 36.

Popke. M. (2006, December). Sideline schooling. *Athletic Business, 30*(12), 92-94.

Sabock, R. J., & Chandler-Garvin, P. B. (1986). Coaching certification United States requirements. *Journal of Physical Education, Recreation and Dance, 57*(6), 57-59.

Seefeldt, V.D. & Milligan, M.J. (1992). Program for athletic coaches' education (PACE)—Educating America's public & private school coaches. *Journal of Physical Education, Recreation and Dance, 63*(7), 46-49.

Seefeldt, V. (1992). Coaching certification: An essential step in reviving a faltering profession. *Journal of Physical Education, Recreation and Dance, 63*(5), 29-30.

Siegel, D. & Newholf, C. (1992). Setting the standards for coaching curriculums: What should it take to be a coach? *Journal of Physical Education, Recreation, and Dance, 63*(1), 60-63.

Singer, R. N. (1992, December 2). The place of football in higher education. Letter to the Editor. *The Chronicle of Higher Education, XXXIX*(15), p. B-4.

Sisley, B. (1985). Off-the-street coaches, methods for improving communication. *Journal of Physical Education, Recreation and Dance, 56*(9), 63-66.

Sisley, B., & Wiese, D. M. (1987). Current status: Requirements for interscholastic coaches. *Journal of Physical Education, Recreation and Dance, 58* (2), 73-85.

Steinbach, P. (2003, November). Emergency situation. *Athletic Business, 27*(11), 62-64, 66, 68.

Stewart, C. (2006). Coaching education online: The Montana model. *Journal of Physical Education, Recreation and Dance, 77*(4), 34-36.

Stier, Jr., W.F. (1970). The coaching intern. *Journal of Health, Physical Education, and Recreation, 41*(1), 27-29.

Stier, Jr., W.F. (1984). One university's answer to the professional preparation of athletic coaches. *Journal of Teaching in Physical Education.* 3(3), 13-16.

Stier, Jr., W.F. (1986). *Competencies in Amateur/Youth Coaching.* Brockport, New York: State University of New York. (ERIC Document Reproduction Service No. ED 263-060).

Stier, W.F., Jr. (2003). Issues: Should public schools require coaches to be certified? *Journal of Physical Education, Recreation, and Dance,* 74(5), 10.

Talking about PACE. (1988). Reston, VA: American Alliance for Health, Physical Education, Recreation and Dance.

What we're all about. (1992). *National Youth Sport Coaches Association.* West Palm Beach, Florida, pp. 1-9.

Who's coaching the coaches? (1996, May). *The Clipboard,* p.1.

Name: _____

Student ID #: _____

EXERCISES FOR CHAPTER 4

A. Why are there not national coaching standards for coaches at the youth sport level? At the junior and senior high level? At the college level?

    _____

    _____

    _____

    _____

    _____

B. What type of courses would you like to take at the present time to make you a better coach? Provide a rationale for your response.

    _____

    _____

    _____

    _____

    _____

C. What are your current strengths as a future or current coach? Why?

    _____

    _____

    _____

    _____

    _____

    _____

D.   What are your current weaknesses as a future or current coach?

_____

_____

_____

_____

_____

E.   What steps can you take now or in the immediate future to compensate for these weaknesses or deficiencies? Be specific and provide a reasonable timetable outlining your plans.

_____

_____

_____

_____

_____

F.   Read two coaching articles in different professional journals and *succinctly* summarize *(provide citations)* their contents below. State why you choose these two articles and identify how the reading of these articles might help you become a better coach in the future.

Article # 1: _____

_____

_____

_____

_____

_____

_____

_____

Article # 2: _____

_____

_____

_____

_____

_____

_____

_____

G. Describe the current state of affairs regarding the education and certification of coaches throughout the United States. Also, investigate the coaching certification requirements in your own state and briefly summarize the requirements, if any.

_____

_____

_____

_____

_____

_____

_____

RESEARCH QUESTONS FOR CHAPTER 4

1. Survey a current athletic coach (at any level) in terms of what formal pro-
    fessional preparation courses the individual had prior to becoming a coach.
    Also, inquire as to what subsequent coaching courses, workshops or clinics
    the individual has attended in recent years. Provide your assessment.

    ----

2. Interview a professor or director of a college coaching curricular program
    and determine whether that institution/department has sought or will seek
    accreditation from the National Council for Accreditation of Coaching
    Education (NCACE) and the reasons for that programs current status rela-
    tive to accreditation.

    ----

3. Visit an athletic director at a high school and determine how difficult it is to secure qualified individuals to coach sports at the school <u>and</u> what steps the AD goes to in order to obtain qualified coaches for male and female sports.

    _____

    _____

    _____

    _____

    _____

    _____

4. Interview a high school administrator and inquire as to whether the existing State standards (if any) are satisfactory in the administrator's opinion and determine the rationale of the person's opinion.

    _____

    _____

    _____

    _____

    _____

    _____

5. Interview a secondary school administrator (principal, superintendent or athletic director) and determine the types of in-service education programs the school provides for full and part-time coaches.

    _____

    _____

    _____

    _____

    _____

    _____

Chapter 5

Being a Successful Coach

Championships are won through team effort.

EVERYONE WANTS TO BE A WINNER

Every coach wants to be successful. No one enters the coaching profession, whether as a head or an assistant coach, as a paid coach or as a volunteer, not caring whether one succeeds or fails. Yet, there are successful coaches and there are unsuccessful coaches.

One such individual who coached at the highest levels (Notre Dame University) is Gerry Faust (Gerry Faust, 2001). Although coach Faust was a highly successful high school coach at Cincinnati's Moeller High School (174-17-2 over an 18 year period), at Notre Dame he was less than successful with a 30-26-1 record in 5 seasons. Following his stint at Notre Dame, coach Faust coached Akron University to a 43-53-3-record in nine seasons. Today, he is a successful motivational speaker and he credits his speaking popularity this way: "People listen to me because I'm not all about success . . . . They'll listen to someone who failed because most people fail at sometime in life" (p. 12).

Being Successful as a Coach Means More than Merely Winning

In today's society coaches are often expected to win but this is not all that modern day coaches are being judged on. In reality, they also are expected to meet the needs of their athletes, to have well-behaved athletes, to keep the parents happy, entertain the fans and boosters, keep the news media informed, satisfy the school administrators, and, in general, be all things to all people.

There are coaches who consistently demonstrate a high degree of knowledge and a thorough understanding of the intricacies of coaching and the needs of the individual athletes. There are coaches who are extremely effective, efficient and competent. And there are others who fall far short of the ideal and, in fact, frequently do not meet what is considered minimum competency levels as a coach of an amateur sports team.

What are the differences between the competent and successful coach and one who is not? Is it knowledge? Is it desire? Is it education or training? Is it luck? Is it experience? Is it the presence or absence of a mentor? Is it the ability to understand people? It is having superior athletes?

THE COACH WHO WAS AN ELITE ATHLETE

Many young people mistakenly believe that being a great athlete almost automatically insures that they will be highly successful coaches. Not true. In fact, being an elite athlete might even be a hindrance for some individuals. Although being an elite athlete might seem, at least on the surface, to give a real edge to the individual who becomes a coach because of the successful experience as an athlete, it is not necessarily true. Such experience might be an advantage in some instances. But, in others, it might prove to be an obstacle.

COACHING CONCEPT #57:   Being a great athlete doesn't insure success as a coach—in many instances it can be a hindrance.

The elite athlete is also the individual who is probably greatly motivated, very skilled and highly dedicated. To this type of individual the learning and mastery of physical skills associated with sports might come easily. Similarly, the dedication and motivation so necessary for success as an athlete might be second nature to the elite athlete turned coach.

Not true, however, for most athletes. Most athletes, including those who will be coached by the former elite sportsperson, will not necessarily be highly skilled, nor easily motivated or really very dedicated. Most athletes do not find learning of physical skills easy. And, there is a great difference between coaching the truly talented and skilled athlete and those individuals who are not at the elite level.

COACHING CONCEPT #58:   Patience is an essential ingredient in being a successful coach.

The former elite athlete who goes on to become a coach might not have many opportunities, if any, to coach athletes with similar skills and attitudes that the coach had possessed as an athlete. Many, if not most, of the coach's athletes will be average to good athletes. A few will be sub-par. However, few will be truly elite athletes. Coaches who were former elite athletes need to pay particular attention to developing empathy and an understanding of what it is like to be an average to above average athlete and not being capable of performing at the elite level. Having patience to teach and work with the unskilled, the unmotivated and the not-so-dedicated athlete is of paramount importance for the coach. This is doubly so for the coach who had been exceptionally successful as an athlete and who mastered one's sport with relative ease. Too many times the learning of skills or sport comes too easily to the elite athlete who then has great difficulty in attempting to teach these same skills, as a coach, to individuals less gifted mentally and/or physically.

Many former standout athletes have failed miserably in the coaching ranks, perhaps because they failed to be able to satisfactorily deal with those athletes who did not possess the attributes and abilities that they themselves possessed and had demonstrated so easily as athletes. Athletes are not clones of their coaches in terms of athletic ability, and skill or dedication.

FACTORS AFFECTING COACHING PERFORMANCE

Coaches constantly find themselves working with different people in different situations and under different circumstances. As a result, these coaches face differing challenges and problems which can affect their efficiency and effectiveness as coaches, both on and off the court or field. One of the greatest challenges facing coaches in schools (particularly in colleges, and specifically, in Division I, with flagship sports) is that the coach is far too often accountable for what players do and don't do even when the coach is not directly supervising the individual athlete (Pick Your Poison, 2001).

> **COACHING CONCEPT #59:**   **There is a movement toward extended, year-round (conduct of code) rules for athletes.**

This is even true at the secondary level and small college level at the present time. And, it is becoming more of a challenge for coaches as time goes on. There was a time when the coach was responsible for the actions and inactions of one's athletes only during the season in which the athlete was competing. In this type of situation the team rules (whatever they might be) would be in effect only during the season itself. Once the season was concluded, the individual athlete was not bound to follow the team rules for that sport. In later years, there has been a movement that the athletes had to adhere to the team rules during the entire school year—and in the same vein—the coach was to be held responsible for the actions and inactions of the athlete not only during the season in which the youngster competed but throughout the school year.

Thus, if the athlete misbehaved by causing a ruckus downtown the negative fallout that followed would be traced to the coach and, in a very real sense, the coach would be held accountable for the negative behavior of the youngster/athlete, even when not in season. Today, the pendulum has been swinging ever farther in that some schools where the coach is now judged (held accountable to some degree or other) for the behavior of one's athletes *even when school is not in session.*

For some schools—and the group seems to be increasing—students are being held to a higher standard by (". . . making their conduct rules apply year-round" (Orman, 2001, p. B-1). Thus, in these schools where rules have been *extended*, the athlete has to abide by the team's (or the athletic department's) rules and regulations 12 months of the year. In essence, some coaches are now being held accountable, at least to some extent, for the behavior of their athletes during the season, during the school year, and also during the time when school is not in session. Thus, individual coaches are now being evaluated/assessed, to a very real extent, in terms of the behavior of their athletes—during the season, during the school year, and throughout the calendar year. See appendix B for a sample of a school's *Extracurricular and Athletic Activities Code of Conduct.*

> **COACHING CONCEPT #60:**   **Coaches should be flexible.**

The only certainty in coaching is that nothing is certain. Times change. Schools change. Administrators change. Priorities change. Athletes change. Parents change. Media representatives change. Booster club memberships change. Coaches change. Expectations of coaches change. Resources change. Limitations fluctuate. Coaches must be able to roll with the punches, to be flexible and to react appropriately and in a suitable manner whatever the circumstances and challenges may be. There are three major factors that can have a significant effect upon the ultimate success or failure of a coach in any specific job, Figure 5.1.

Ultimate success in any specific coaching position can, to a great extent, be determined or is at least significantly affected by the following factors. First, the *job* (task) itself. Second, the *circumstances* or *setting* in which the *job* or task must be accomplished. And, third, the *personal and professional characteristics and qualities* of the individual serving as coach. These factors should be taken into account by any would-be coaching aspirant weighing the pros and cons of accepting a particular coaching position.

FIGURE 5.1—Factors Affecting Performance in Coaching

COACHING CONCEPT #61: Only worry about those things you can change—don't waste your energies on non-productive activities or projects.

Too many coaches become worry-warts. Too many coaches become obsessed and worry and fret about everything and everyone—all the time. As a result, they become frustrated and angry when they are unable to solve all of the perceived difficulties as well as the real problems. Experienced coaches learn that they should only worry about those things that they have a realistic chance of affecting or changing. If the school has a pass-to-play policy the coach should not (must not, shall not) continually worry, complain or whine about the existence of such a school policy. First of all, there is probably little if anything that can be done about it at the present time. Second, the coach's time and effort had better be concentrated on more productive actions. For example, the coach should work out a reasonable plan and program to insure that the athletes will do acceptable work within the classroom, that the youngsters have the appropriate support mechanisms and assistance necessary to be successful in the classroom.

COACHING CONCEPT #62: Know the difference between what can be changed and what can't be changed—and then take appropriate action.

It is O.K. to worry and fret *if* one can actually do something about it. It does no good for a coach to worry about the lack of a suitable facility if there isn't a snowball's chance in Hades of obtaining the use of a suitable facility in the immediate future. However, to worry about things completely out of one's control or influence is silly, ineffectual and potentially damaging to oneself and to one's program. Thus, it is imperative that coaches be able to determine what can be changed in their own employment situation and then to act accordingly.

The Job Itself

The type of job or position held by the coach is very important. Is the job on the junior high or senior high level? Is the coaching position at a junior college, small college or at a major university? Is the coaching position one of coaching youth sports? Is the position a head coaching position? Is it an assistant coaching position? Does the job involve a team or individual sport?

Is the job or task so formidable that it is impossible to be done? Is the expectation of the coach such that the job requires an individual who possesses very specific skills? And, will the coach who does not have those skills or competencies most likely fail?

A college competing at the NCAA Division I level that has a vacancy for the head coaching position in basketball would probably require that coaching candidates possess experience and demonstrated competency in the (1) recruitment aspect of the sport and in the area of (2) fundraising and promotion. These two expectations would be in addition to expected competency in the (3) technical skills of coaching strategies and techniques.

However, a head coaching position at a junior high school might not involve any activity in the area of external student recruitment (with scholarships and extensive eligibility rules) or in the area of fund-raising and promotions. Thus, the two jobs themselves are definitely different. Individuals who possess different skills and experiences are needed to be able to complete the tasks associated with each position.

The Setting or Circumstances of the Specific Situation

The setting, circumstances or the parameters surrounding any specific coaching position will have a significant impact upon whether or not coaches are successful. For example, what are the resources that are available to facilitate the coaching tasks? What are the objectives, goals or missions of the sport and the total athletic program where coaches are employed? What limitations (time, money, personnel, etc.) or restrictive policies are in place that might hamper a coach's effort to become successful? What has been the history in terms of successes and failures with athletic teams? How many teams are being supported or sponsored by the athletic or central administration? What are the expectations in terms of possessing winning records and what happens if such expectations are not met? How are individual sports viewed by the school administration, students and by the general public? Are some sports viewed as being more important or popular than others? Are the allocation and distribution of resources fair and equitable?

Coaching a Flagship or Top Tier Sport

All of the above statements can go a long way in determining the specific challenges facing a coach who accepts an athletic position. In some schools, some of the available competitive sports are designated as flagship sports or the sponsored teams are placed on a tiered system with teams on different tiers or levels receiving differentiated support and emphasis by the sponsoring school or organization.

COACHING CONCEPT #63: **Identify, recognize and understand the advantages and the risks associated with coaching a flagship or top tier sport.**

Those flagship sports or sports designated as being on the highest tier are the most heavily supported and emphasized. These sports are the cream of the crop and are the heaviest promoted and most popular. Those so-called non-flagship athletic

"Game coaching" is as important as "practaice coaching" if not more so.

teams or teams identified on a lower tier or level will receive fewer resources and are emphasized less. Naturally, the expectation for success is highest with the flagship sports since more resources are provided and a greater emphasis is associated with them. Thus, coaches would do well to recognize the circumstances affecting the team(s) that they coach since these circumstances or the setting in which they coach can have a definite impact upon their successes as coaches. The concept is simple, but yet very important. The circumstances and the setting are different for those teams identified as a flagship or top tiered sport when compared with those teams relegated to a lower level in terms of priorities, allocation of resources and expectations of success within the total athletic organization.

Dealing With the Pressures of Coaching

Some coaching jobs are more risky than others. Some coaching positions have more and varied types of pressure than others. And, some coaching posts also provide for greater and more diversified rewards and benefits than others. However, in general, there are and will always be significant pressures that every coach must work under. *Pressure just comes with the territory*, period!!! To assume otherwise would be foolish and unrealistic.

Coaches who also teach at the interscholastic level must accept the fact that they face pressure from both the academic and the athletic dimensions of their jobs. No other teacher in the high school (or middle school for that matter) is under such close scrutiny by both the school administrators and the community as is the teacher/coach.

COACHING CONCEPT #64:   Pressure comes with the territory—coaches need to adjust to and adapt to various types of pressures associated with the job.

The typical instructor in a high school, such as the history, English, or mathematics teacher, does not have to put up with the constant and critical evaluation by the public and the school community as does a head coach. The history teacher doesn't have the whole school as well as members of the community evaluating the teacher's effectiveness and teaching abilities every Friday night or Saturday afternoon. But that is exactly what happens with coaches. The English teacher doesn't have to have one's students compete against students in another school every week in order to determine the competency level of the students or the teacher. But that is exactly what happens with coaches.

Every time the coach's athletes take the field or the court, their coach is being evaluated by a whole range of groups and individuals. Many of these persons have no real understanding or appreciation of what it takes to be a successful coach of a competitive sport—but yet believe that they are very knowledgeable, if not experts in their own right. Yes, indeed, there are some severe pressures that coaches must be able to adjust to if they are to survive over the long haul as coaches. But, perhaps, the worst pressure comes from the coach. Coaches can be their own worst enemy in terms of pressure placed upon themselves.

COACHING CONCEPT #65: **Coaches can please some of the people all of the time, can please all of the people some of the time, but cannot please all the people all of the time.**

The above COACHING CONCEPT paraphrases the statement attributed to Abraham Lincoln and points out that coaches must recognize that they cannot possibly please all of their publics or constituencies, all of the time. To attempt to do so is foolish and quite impossible. Most of the time, it is difficult enough to just please a majority of the many groups and individuals comprising the sport publics and constituencies. The concept is clear—coaches are often in the precarious position of being asked to please everyone—a whole host of publics and constituencies. This is just not possible. This is part of the reason why coaches experience so much pressure and stress in their chosen profession.

A witticism that has been around coaching circles for many years that deals with just this concept was superbly presented by Sabock (1984, p. 49). The story involves an elderly man, a youngster and a donkey traveling along a roadway. The story goes something like this. The elderly man, the youngster and the donkey were walking and a group of spectators remarked that it seemed foolish for both people to walk when they had a donkey that could be ridden. So, the youngster hopped onto the donkey and the elderly individual walked alongside. Soon other people saw the trio and bitterly complained that the old man was walking while the youngster was taking it easy riding the animal. So, they switched. The youngster walked and the man rode.

It did not take long for others to view the scene and lodge a complaint about how selfish the man was in riding, thereby forcing the poor youngster to walk. In reaction to this criticism both the man and youngster both hopped on the donkey and rode a few blocks. Of course, as one would now expect, other spectators soon complained about how cruel and inhuman it was for the poor donkey to have to bear the burden of both the man and the youngster.

Undaunted, both riders proceeded to dismount and, as they were approaching a large crevasse or abyss over which a narrow wooden plank bridge stretched, both the youngster and the man attempted to carry the donkey on their shoulders. However, half-way across the wooden bridge the donkey became frightened and started to kick and buck to such an extent that neither could hold onto the animal. As a result, the donkey fell over the edge and down into the 1000-foot crevasse to its death. The morale of this story is that if one attempts to please everyone—one is likely to lose one's *ass*.

COACHING CONCEPT #66:   **Don't habitually cry wolf in terms of forecasting the team's future—but don't be overly optimistic either.**

Coaches need to walk the middle of the proverbial *road* when placed in a situation of providing a glimpse or a forecast into the team's future. On the one hand, coaches need to guard against being overly optimistic in terms of making predictions about the future successes of their teams. No one wants to be in a situation in which a team performs in an inferior fashion when just the opposite is expected or advertised. On the other hand, no coach wants to have a reputation as a crybaby, always moaning about what a tough year or season it is going to be.

Coaches need to take a moderate stance. They need to walk in the middle of the road while leaning towards the conservative side. Be honest in the assessment of your team's prospects and the prospects of your athletes. But, this doesn't mean that you have to broadcast the most optimistic prediction from the rooftops. It is better to err on the conservative side than to be caught in a situation in which your team is expected to perform far better than they in fact actually do.

The Story of the Four Envelopes

Coaches need to recognize that they typically only have a certain number of opportunities to be successful. Or, to put it another way, coaches are all too often typically only given a certain number of times for them to really make big mistakes or errors—before beginning to skate on thin ice. There is a long standing comic story about the Four Envelopes (author unknown) that illustrates the point that in many situations coaches are only given a certain number of chances to succeed—before they are held accountable for what they achieved or failed to achieve. The actual joke goes something like this: A new coach arrived at the school following the firing of the previous mentor. Upon arriving at his new desk, he found a note from the former coach as well as four sealed envelopes, numbered one through four.

The note welcomed him as the new mentor and wished him well. In addition, the note indicated that should the new coach ever encounter problems or challenges in the new job, the coach should open envelope #1. If a second problem developed then the second envelope should be opened, and so on, until all four envelopes have been opened.

Well, it was not long before the new coach ran into a big problem that looked as if it could not be solved. Opening the first envelope, the note said: "Blame your predecessor." So, the coach did so and everyone accepted that and forgave the new coach for the problem. Shortly thereafter, another problem arose and the coach was all too happy to open envelope #2 and read: "Blame the fact that you are new to the job." And everyone in the school accepted that as a reasonable excuse.

The third problem followed quickly on the heels of the second and envelope #3 read: "Blame your assistant(s)." And, again, this excuse was readily and easily seen as logical by all involved in the problematic situation. And, finally, facing the fourth (and biggest) problem thus far, the coach ran to the office, opened the desk drawer with envelope #4, opened it, and read: "Prepare four envelopes."

COACHING CONCEPT #67:   One is only forgiven for mistakes or errors a limited number of times before being forced to *face the music*.

The moral of this story is that coaches only get a limited number of chances, a limited number of excuses (the old adage, *three strikes and you are out*, might be appropriate here) before one is held accountable for one's actions or inactions. There is a point in time when one must face the music when one is judged by one's performance based upon the schools and the administration's expectations.

The Characteristics and Qualities of the Individual Coach

The third factor that can determine the success or failure of a coach is the competency or skill level of the individual coach. There are specific characteristics and qualities that enhance the likelihood of the individual becoming a more successful coach. There are meaningful experiences that will increase the likelihood of an individual being successful in the coaching arena. And there are specific skills and competencies required of successful coaches.

> **COACHING CONCEPT #68:   Never be overworked—but effort alone is not enough, quality performance is required.**

Coaches need to be willing to work hard. Coaches need to work hard to develop skills, competencies and knowledge. Of course, coaches need to put their efforts, in terms of their coaching competencies, skills and knowledge, where they will result in the greatest benefits in terms of realizing the stated objectives and goals of the sport program. One must not be overworked to the extent that the quality of one's efforts—overall—are compromised or made to suffer.

Generally speaking, coaches who are more knowledgeable, more skilled, more experienced and more dedicated (motivated) experience greater success over the long haul than those who are less knowledgeable, less skilled, less experienced and less dedicated. Of course, the factor of luck certainly does enter into the coaching scene. But, generally speaking, those coaches who are highly skilled through formal training and/or experience—both in terms of dealing with people and with the Xs and the Os of the sport—are more successful than those individuals who do not possess such qualities and skills.

> **COACHING CONCEPT #69:   Coaches who are more knowledgeable, more skilled, more experienced and more dedicated (motivated) experience greater success over the long haul than those who are less gifted.**

The concept remains, being successful as a coach is determined by the qualities of the individual, the type and scope of the job the individual accepts and those circumstances or the setting in which the individual is involved as a coach. Thus, being the right person, in the right spot, at the right time, with the right skills and having the right (proper) resources gives the person an edge in terms of being successful—maybe.

ADDITIONAL CONSIDERATIONS IN BEING A SUCCESSFUL COACH

There are further considerations that must be examined in detail when considering the competency level of coaches, diagram 5.2. The first of these are the *processes* that one must go through in terms of coaching athletes and working within the athletic arena. The second involves the specific categories of *skills and competencies* needed by all coaches regardless of the level at which they are involved—whether or not they are head coaches or assistant coaches. And, the third involves the numerous and general *obligations or responsibilities* that befall coaches on a day-to-day basis in sport coaching.

Coaches who are competent in terms of the processes involved in coaching, who possess the needed specific skills and are able to perform these skills at a high level, and who are capable of completing their explicit obligations and meeting their coaching responsibilities in full, will find that they are indeed successful in coaching.

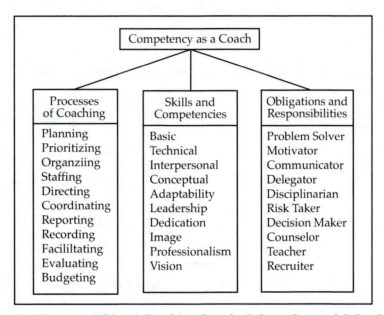

FIGURE 5.2—Additional Considerations in Being a Successful Coach

PROCESSES OF COACHING

There are certain processes that coaches are usually involved in—at least to a certain extent—during the pre-season, in-season, post season and out-of-season time that they devote to their sport. This is usually true regardless of the level of competition.

Coaches, by the very nature of their job, assume many of the responsibilities of administrators or managers in their role as athletic mentors. As such, coaches are being held responsible today as never before for demonstrating a high level of familiarity and competency in the processes presented below.

In 1937, two scholars (Gulick and Urwick, 1937) identified seven essential ingredients or processes for managers (leaders). These processes are (1) planning, (2) organizing, (3) staffing, (4) directing, (5) coordinating, (6) reporting, and (7) budgeting. These processes or ingredients became known by the acronym POSDCoRB. Stier (1994) provided three additional processes of (1) recording, (2) facilitating, and (3) evaluating. The author now adds yet one additional process, that of prioritizing, thus creating the acronym PPOSDCoRRFEB. In the sports arena, coaches, if they are to be consistently effective and successful must feel comfortable being actively involved in the processes of planning, prioritizing, organizing, staffing, directing, coordinating, reporting, recording, facilitating, evaluating and budgeting. For all of these processes are part of the life of a coach whether the team one coaches is a youth team, a junior or senior high school team, a college or university team or even a professional sports team.

Planning

Planning is an essential activity for coaches. Coaches, through planning, are able to determine what they are going to do *in the future*. It is the opposite of flying by the seat of one's pants. It is a structured process and involves recognizing what can be done, when it can be done, how it can be done, where it should be accomplished and by whom. Planning involves determining the foreseeability of any given situation, action or inaction. Planning also involves the ability to anticipate specific outcomes well in advance. Some of the areas in which planning is essential include determining—in advance—scouting assignments, components of practice sessions, conditioning programs, game strategies, team rules and regulations, risk management strategies, emergency first aid care, equipment purchasing, travel arrangements, etc.

Prioritizing

In an effort not to waste valuable effort and time, it is necessary for effective coaches to be able to prioritize those tasks that must be completed. Prioritizing simply means doing first things first, doing things that are more important first. Thus, those tasks that are essential or most important are tackled before the less important or non-essential tasks are performed. Failure to prioritize one's efforts finds the allocation of one's time, effort and other resources being directed aimlessly rather than on those objectives that will result in positive consequences.

COACHING CONCEPT #70:　**Coaches must be willing to make sacrifices—but that doesn't mean selling the kids, giving away the dog and completely giving up one's personal life.**

Making sacrifices seems to be synonymous with being a coach. Yes, coaches do make many sacrifices in order to be involved in sports as a coach. However, becoming a coach does not mean having to give up a normal life of a human being. Yet, that is exactly the image that some coaches project. For some coaches it is all coaching and everything else comes in a distant last.

In contrast to what some coaches might have you believe (see chapter two and the comments made by Jimmy Johnson, head coach of the 1993 Super Bowl Champions, the Dallas Cowboys), one does not have to give up everything to be successful in coaching. Then coach Johnson was quoted as saying: "Everything I do—I mean everything—winning has to come first" (King, 1993, p. 5). This one-sided approach to life/coaching is narrow indeed and is not recommended for those involved in coaching amateur sports at the youth, middle school, high school, college or university levels. One must indeed have a life—outside of coaching.

COACHING CONCEPT #71: **Coaches need to have a life outside of coaching—and so do their spouses and children.**

While there are coaches who demonstrate a similar work ethic and coaching philosophy as coach Johnson, it is not necessary to subscribe to this style of life/coaching in order to be successful. One can work hard without having to sacrifice every other facet of one's life. The secret to having a balanced existence as a human being, as a coach, is to concentrate on those things that are really important (to prioritize), that really have an impact upon the success of the individual athlete, upon the success of the team as a whole, and upon the coach as the leader of the team. In doing so, you will be able to have time to spend on other important aspects of your personal life, with your family and loved ones and your friends.

Coaching an be a family affair—author's five young children with the 1979-1980, nationally ranked, Cardinal Stritch College basketball team (24 wins and 6 losses).

Organizing

Coaches who are organized are able to get more done in less time than those coaches who are not organized or who are disorganized. An organized coach is capable of bringing together various elements within the athletic arena into a coherent whole. Proper organization facilitates the tasks which coaches must deal with every day. Being organized means that the coach is aware of the available resources and is capable of allocating the resources where they are needed most.

COACHING CONCEPT #72:   **Coaches not only have to be organized—they need to look organized.**

Organization is important for the coach as well as for the team and players who operate under the auspices of the coach. The players, individually and as a group (team), must be organized in terms of what they do, as individuals and as a team. And, they must be perceived to be organized by others. If athletes are organized and recognized as being organized by others—this bodes well for the coach who is recognized as the leader of the team and responsible for the behavior of the athletes and the team as a whole.

Staffing

Coaching is a people business (see chapter 6). Head coaches are intimately involved (in addition to their players) with assistant coaches, as well as with volunteers who might be involved in any number of areas related to the team. Being able to attract, screen, secure and retain qualified assistants and/or volunteers is an important part of the overall responsibilities of a coach.

Having quality people on staff (paid or volunteer basis) is a mark of a good manager. It is the responsibility of the coach to demonstrate a high level of skill in recognizing talent and potential both in terms of athletes and in staff (both paid and volunteer). Ideally, the staff associated with a head coach should be of such quality that they would be highly sought after by other coaches, athletic programs and schools. The same can be said of one's athletes.

Conversely, no head coach would want to be saddled with staff no other coach or athletic program would want. And, no coach would want to have athletes on the team no other coach would want to coach.

COACHING CONCEPT #73:   **One mark of a quality coach is the ability to identify, attract and retain quality personnel as well as players.**

Directing

Directing refers to the process by which coaches make others aware of what they, as coaches, would like to take place. Coaches must be capable of providing direction for individual athletes and for the team as a whole. Additionally, they are frequently involved in giving direction—in terms of behavior and tasks to be performed—to other individuals such as other coaches, athletes and volunteers.

Coordinating

Coaches need to coordinate tasks, things and people in their quest for success on the proverbial playing field. Many things must be accomplished at the same time with limited resources. As a result, coaches are like jugglers who are required to keep a large number of different balls (tasks, responsibilities) in the air without dropping any of them—all the while keeping an eye on the audience.

Coaches who teach and coach must coordinate their teaching tasks and their coaching responsibilities. Part-time coaches have to be able to coordinate their full time job responsibilities with their coaching responsibilities which comprise only a small portion of their daily routine, yet are extremely important both to the coach and the players and their families.

Reporting

Being a coach involves keeping others, individuals and groups, abreast of what the coach has done, is currently doing, and will be involved with in the future. Reporting is a form of communicating. It can be accomplished formally and/or informally. That which is reported can deal with facts, information, opinions and intentions. Reporting and accountability go hand in hand. Coaches report, in a variety of different methods and mediums, verbal and nonverbal, to athletic and central administrators as well as to athletes, news media representatives and to booster clubs.

Recording

An essential process that coaches must be adept in performing is the keeping of accurate and timely records. Coaches need to keep a chronicle of what takes place during their practices. Accidents and resulting activities must be recorded and filed. Financial records need to be maintained and reconciled. Adequate records provide a historical snapshot of what took place on a specific date, at a specific time and at an exact location. They can be most helpful in enabling the coach (and others) to evaluate what has taken place in the past so as to make necessary adjustments and decisions for the future.

> **COACHING CONCEPT #74:**   **Keeping a variety of accurate and useful records pertaining to one's coaching efforts is a mark of a quality coach.**

Coaches should maintain a variety of records during the preseason, in-season, post season and out-of-season time periods. These records can include, but not be limited to the following:

1. Inventory status
2. Budgetary situation
3. Number of athletes trying out for the team
4. Number of athletes making the team
5. Number of athletes who quit the team
6. Number of athletes removed (kicked off) the team
7. Number of athletes injured so severely they could no longer participate
8. Number of athletes remaining on the team
9. Number (anticipated) of athletes returning next season (by school year, position)
10. Athletes who lettered during the past season
11. Facility recommendations
12. Practice schedules (daily)
13. Accident reports (number of accidents and type of accidents/injuries)
14. Scouting reports
15. Attendance at clinics, workshops
16. Disciplinary actions
17. Team meetings
18. Parental meetings
19. Individual records in games
20. Game statistics—team and individual
21. Team records and statistics
22. Achievements and honors for team (conference, State)
23. Achievements and honors for coaching staff
24. Summary thoughts of the coach about the past season
25. Future thoughts of the coach for next year season
26. Others . . .

These records, facts and statistics can be most helpful to the coach when attempting to complete the so-called year-end report to the athletic director (and eventually, to the AD's superiors). This report is a recollection and compilation of important facts and data that provides, at a glimpse, an accurate snapshot of the season and is compiled at the end of the season or school year. It can also include conclusions, opinions, recommendations and future plans and/or expectations from the head coach to the athletic director. The report can also include anything else that the school's administrators might request.

Facilitating

A process in which every coach is involved is that of facilitating, that is, being in the so-called *help* or *assist mode* when dealing with others. The individual being assisted could be an athlete, a parent, a reporter, a spouse, a student, another coach or a booster club member, just to mention a few. To facilitate is to abet others in accomplishing their specific objective(s) or goal(s). Coaches are frequently called upon to serve in this capacity. It means assuming an unselfish role in carrying out one's responsibility as a coach.

Evaluating

Coaches need to be skillful in evaluating their own efforts and effectiveness, that is, a realistic and honest self-evaluation. And, it is important that the coach understand the evaluation process when it is applied to oneself (implemented by an athletic administrator) (Stier, 2005). Cardone (2006) indicated that the evaluation of coaches is a constant, on-going process, a fact that all mentors should remain cognizant of.

Additionally, coaches must be willing and able to evaluate (based on both objective and subjective criteria) their cohorts, their assistants and associates. And, of course, a most important process that all coaches must be involved in is the evaluation of their own players and potential players. This evaluation of student-athletes includes not only the physical attributes and playing abilities but also the so-called intangible qualities of an athlete, such as motivation, desire, ability to sacrifice, and the willingness to work hard. It includes the ability to select appropriate youngsters to become members of one's team. It also includes the ability to pick starters for a contest and when to substitute specific players into contests, at appropriate times.

Budgeting

Coaches can be involved in the budgeting process in a number of different ways. The budgeting process not only includes the planning for income and expenditures but also the accounting of money spent and collected. As a result coaches are involved, at least to some degree, in the construction of a team's budget as well as in the selection, ordering and upkeep of the squad's uniforms and equipment. Additionally, travel arrangements need to be made and followed as well as a whole host of other activities which have an effect upon the budgetary process and the budget itself.

A key concept to keep in mind is that all financial aspects associated with a team fall under the responsibility of the coach and that there are numerous decisions to be made by a coach which have an impact on the budget. Problems with any part of the budgetary process connected with the team can have tragic consequences for the coach who is expected to be able to manage money wisely and appropriately.

COACHING SKILLS AND COMPETENCIES

The nature of the beast—competitive sports—makes coaching challenging, exciting as well as perilous and somewhat unique in our society. Being successful as a coach necessitates that an individual possess a number of specific competencies or skills in order to be able to perform the variety of specific tasks under varying and trying circumstances.

COACHING CONCEPT #75:   **Coaching is not easy, if it were, anyone could do it successfully.**

There are numerous skills and competencies needed for those who would be successful coaches. These skills are varied and many are sophisticated in nature. However, in a very real sense, one should be pleased that the act of coaching is difficult, is challenging and is not for the faint of heart, or the unskilled or incompetent. Rather, one should be thankful that coaching requires highly trained, experienced and dedicated individuals assuming the responsibilities and challenges of coaching young people. If it was easy, if it required no sophisticated competencies—then any dummy could do it. And, that is certainly not the case. Coaching young people is hard. It is challenging. It is time consuming. It is formidable. *That is why the profession demands someone like you*, someone who will work to develop and enhance those skills, competencies and experiences needed to be successful coaches.

Coaching without All of the Tools

Coaches too frequently complain that they need additional assets, tools or resources (material and/or human) in order to be sucessful. However, coaches need to remember that almost anyone could be successful if one had all the tools, all the supplies, all the facilities, all the athletes, all the resources that one could ask for. In reality, this just never happens. Instead, coaches must approach their coaching tasks knowing that they will not possess all of the tools or assets that they probably would wish to have—but they must endeavor to do their best and must strive for success in spite of these so-called limitations and shortages.

COACHING CONCEPT #76:   **The mark of a great coach is one who can be successful in spite of not having all of the assets, resources and tools that one might wish for.**

The Renaissance Coach

Being a coach today means more than merely being knowledgeable in the Xs and Os of a particular sport. In fact, coaches today need to be renaissance individuals (Stier, 1986). Renaissance coaches are those individuals who are *experts* in at least one area of their primary sport(s) and preferably two. They also need to be very knowledgeable in a whole range of other areas related to their sport to boot. For example, an individual coach might be an expert in a particular type of defense or in conditioning. However, this same coach also needs to be knowledgeable in many other areas of coaching such as offense, eligibility rules, sports psychology, motivational techniques, injury prevention, communication, etc.

In yet another respect, renaissance coaches are those individuals who are experts in the coaching of a particular sport (or sports) and yet are knowledgeable in a wide range of other areas such as politics, music, art, literature, history, science, etc. In other words, coaches of today and tomorrow need to exist within the real world, within our society, and must be able to represent themselves as well-rounded individuals who are bright, articulate, intelligent, educated, and refined. This is because these same coaches need to be able to work with and relate to a wide range of other people, groups, cliques and organizations in the process of fulfilling their coaching responsibilities (Stier, 1992).

COACHING CONCEPT #77:   **Being knowledgeable, being competent, doesn't mean knowing all the answers—it does mean knowing where to go to get the answers.**

It is impossible to be knowledgeable in all areas of coaching. It is impossible to be an expert in every facet of coaching just one sport. However, it is frequently possible to find out answers to many puzzling questions and solutions to perplexing problems if one is capable of discerning how to attack the problem, how to approach the question, and where to go to seek possible solutions. A wise coach recognizes one's limitations but also recognizes that there are sources of information and help—individuals, organizations, professional literature, etc.,—from which the coach might obtain assistance in resolving challenges and solving problems.

COACHING CONCEPT #78:   **Don't be too proud to admit that you need assistance—it is better to be pragmatic and get the job done than stubborn and fail.**

Right on the mark—aiming for excellence.

Too frequently coaches feel that they have all the answers. These foolish mentors believe that they do not need help from anyone. After all, they are the coaches and they must know the answers, must know how to solve problems. It is better to swallow one's false pride, admit the need to seek assistance elsewhere, and then to do so. The task at hand is to be able to solve the problem, to overcome the hurdle, to get the job done rather than to fail while attempting to do it all by oneself, all the while hindered by one's pride.

CATEGORIES OF COMPETENCIES

Although there are literally hundred's of very specific skills which coaches should be able to perform in the course of their duties, all skills and competencies of successful coaches may be grouped for convenience under ten broad categories. Katz (1955) earlier identified technical, interpersonal and conceptual skills as being desirable attributes of administrators. Stier (1994) identified the additional categories of basic skills, dedication skills, and image skills as being necessary for coaches as well as managers of sport. Add to these the essential skills of adaptability, leadership, professionalism and vision and it becomes readily apparent that the job of a coach requires a person to be a well rounded, talented, able and conscientious professional.

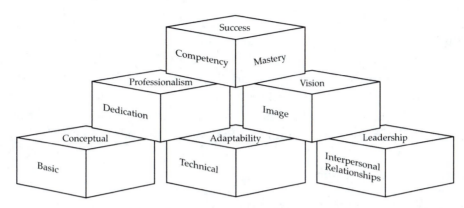

FIGURE 5.3—Ten Essential Coaching Skills

Mastery of skills and competencies within these ten categories is essential for competent coaches at all levels of sport competition. Possessing the numerous skills or competencies included within each of these broad categories will go a long way in enabling the individual coach to experience success as a mentor.

Basic Competencies

The basic skills which all coaches should possess are those same competencies which any educated individual in a civilized society should have. For example, coaches should be able to speak clearly, think logically, write intelligently, listen attentively, and read extensively. Coaches are also expected to be able to comprehend, analyze, synthesize and interpret accurately and in a timely fashion what they hear, observe, and experience.

Technical Competencies

In today's modern society, coaches need to possess competencies in terms of the mechanical aspects of teaching and coaching. For example, coaches must be comfortable and skilled in using the modern technology available to coaches such as computers, audio-visual aids, video tape machines, cameras, weight training equipment and supplies, printing and copy machines, and faxes, etc.

COACHING CONCEPT #79:   Mastery of the Xs and Os of a sport is viewed by many as the easiest facet of any coach's job.

A second area of technical competency involves the so-called Xs and Os of a sport. Coaches need to be knowledgeable in the strategies, the tactics and the techniques associated with the sport(s) they coach. For many coaches, this facet is the most interesting and the easiest in which to become highly competent.

However, one should not assume that technical competencies are limited to merely mastering the Xs and Os of a sport. Not true. Technical competencies are not limited to the mastery of the Xs and Os of any sport. Also included within this category is the technical knowledge and know how in the area of conditioning and training as well as injury prevention and first aid, just to name a few.

Interpersonal Competencies

Since coaching is a people profession, it is absolutely essential that the coach be able to work with a wide range of individuals and groups in a meaningful and productive manner. Interpersonal relationships are essential if a coach is to be successful. Stier (1986) reveals that more coaches fail as coaches because of their inability to work with other people (athletes and non-athletes), that is, for a lack of interpersonal skills, than for any other single reason (deficiency).

Today, coaches face players who are much more complex and certainly less pliable than they were in the days of the so-called coaching tyrants (and giants) (Reed, 1992). Thus, in the 90s and beyond the greatest challenge in coaching is in the dealing with athletes, being able to meet their needs, motivating them and reinforcing their efforts rather than mastering the technical aspects, the Xs and the Os, of the sport scene.

Conceptual Competencies

Coaches need to have a proper perspective. By this is meant that coaches must be able to have an accurate picture of the needs of the total athletic program and not merely be concerned with their own specific sport. Coaches will naturally look out for their own sport or sports. However, wise and experienced coaches will also demonstrate conceptual skills by being aware of the overall picture, being cognizant of the role and needs of the total sports program and then acting accordingly. Coaches must not operate as if they have blinders on and cannot see anything other than their own sport(s). Coaches need to broaden their horizons beyond their own sport and become an integral part of the total athletic program and become a team member along with all other coaches and the athletic administration.

Coaches who work in a school setting need to be willing to broaden their horizons even further—beyond the athletic dimension—and to become actively involved with other aspects of life—academic and social—within the school. This means going to the school play or to the art show. This means chaperoning a school dance or other event or volunteering to take tickets at a school function. It means being involved in other aspects of the school besides sports.

Adaptability Competencies

Since coaching is so unpredictable, just as athletic contests can be, coaches must be able and willing to adapt to changing situations. In other words, coaches need to roll with the punch(es). Individuals who are incapable of adjusting to changing situations in their workplace frequently find themselves out of the workplace and looking for another job.

An example of change which can take place in a school setting is when a new principal or superintendent is hired. Whenever a new administrator comes on board, there is always the possibility that priorities and emphases as well as allocation of resources can change. As a result, coaches who do not adapt, who cannot bend, who cannot accommodate the change, whatever it might be, are in for a potentially difficult and trying time.

Leadership Competencies

Coaches must be leaders. They are held in high esteem by the very nature of their position. Coaches need to be excellent motivators of others. Others must have confidence in their coaching ability. Coach must be capable of leading and directing others towards objectives and goals. One mark of leadership is the ability to get other people to do things and to get things accomplished. Coaches who are true leaders are those who lead by example as well as by direction. Coach Krzyzewski (Selinsky, 2001) is credited with pointing out that coaches must be leaders—and as leaders they must be skilled in team-building and in motivating others.

Dedication Competencies

Individuals who would become coaches must be highly dedicated to the multitudinous tasks which will face them in their job. Dedication simply means being able and willing to do whatever it takes in terms of time, effort and sacrifice to get the job done. It also refers to the spouse (and children) of the coach. This is because the coach's spouse must also be supportive, understanding and sympathetic to the tasks and challenges facing the coach. Being dedicated does not mean placing the coaching job ahead of one's family and neglecting the family. However, it does mean that one is committed to spending the time and expending the effort and the energy required to get the task(s) completed on a timely basis and at an acceptable quality level. Being dedicated doesn't mean just working long hours. But, it does mean working smart hours. Thus, *quality work, quality time on task* becomes much more important than just time spent (aimlessly) on task.

> **COACHING CONCEPT #80:** Coaches must be dedicated and this involves being determined and persistent in working toward reasonable and reachable objectives and goals.

Related to being dedicated are two additional traits that are also important. Specifically, *persistence* and *determination*. One must be persistent in one's efforts to perform those tasks necessary for the completion of one's work and areas of responsibility. And, one must be determined to perform one's job, one's tasks, in an effective and efficient manner. The following paragraph speaks to this concept.

Press On (author unknown)

"Nothing in the world can take the place of persistence. Talent will not; nothing is more common than unsuccessful men with talent. Genius will not; unrewarded genius is almost a proverb. Education will not; the world is full of educated derelicts. Persistence and determination alone are omnipotent."

Image Competencies

Coaches need to look and act the part of competent, qualified professionals. This means that coaches need to dress professionally. This means coaches need to communicate in a skillful fashion and as confident professionals. This means that the mannerisms of coaches must be appropriate. However, coaches must be concerned not only with style or the so-called fluff but also with substance. That is, the actual behavior of coaches and the appearance of their behavior must *be beyond reproach* and their competency must in fact be at a high level and viewed as such by others. Coaches serve as role models to athletes (especially the very young) and others. Thus, coaches need to practice what they preach in terms of drug abuse or misuse, use of alcohol, smoking, non-abusive behavior including honesty and ethical decision, gossip, language, nutrition and exercise.

Being interviewed prior to the big game.

Coaches need to present an image that will reinforce the perception and the concept that they are competent, experienced, educated professionals. This doesn't mean that coach must make a fashion statement every time they step out in public. However, it does mean that the coach must realize that they are in the public's eye and they are being judged by everything they do and don't do; by everything they say and don't say; and by the physical image they present not only while they are performing their jobs but also when they are not being coaches.

Professional Competencies

Professionalism is the watch-word. One mark of a true professional is the willingness and ability to keep current in one's field. Professionals are constantly cognizant of the need for in-service training and further education. Coaches, also, must realize that the art and science of coaching sports are undergoing constant change and the world of sport itself is in a state of flux. Coaches cannot remain competent for long without taking time and making the effort to remain on the so-called cutting edge of the coaching knowledge. This means that coaches need to participate in periodic coaching workshops, conferences and clinics. Coaches need to remain up-to-date in terms of the latest techniques, strategies and knowledge applicable to their sport and in sports in general. Coaches need to read the latest coaching and sport books, journals, magazines and newspapers. One would not expect a lawyer, an accountant, a dentist or a physician, upon leaving their university, to never again attend an educational conference or workshop or read an educational journal or book. If so, would you want that person to defend you in a lawsuit, prepare your taxes, fill a tooth or remove an appendix? Well, athletes and their parents deserve coaches who are as professional and who remain at the cutting edge of competency in their sport(s) as much as you deserve a competent, updated physician or attorney to tend to your needs.

Vision Competencies

Since coaching and sports are constantly changing, it is imperative that coaches have skills in terms of vision. This means that superior coaches possess a vision of what individuals, a team or a sport can be in the future. Coaches need to anticipate, to have a vision and to have foresight of what might come to pass so that they can prepare the way, if not lead the way. These are the coaches who do not merely rely on others to help them develop new skills or to improve skills already at hand. Rather, these are individuals who have the vision, the foresight, to see what might be possible in the future and to work towards that goal—ahead of the pack of other coaches.

GENERAL OBLIGATIONS AND RESPONSIBILITIES OF COACHES

Are there general responsibilities that reflect the type and range of activities and challenges that coaches find themselves facing? Are there specific tasks that coaches are required to assume because they are essential to their job? And, is there a body of knowledge which all coaches should be familiar with in order to become well-schooled and at least minimally competent within the profession of coaching? Are there different coaching styles commonly in vogue? *The answers to all four questions above are in the affirmative.* Coaches need to realize the following:

1. There are indeed *general responsibilities* which reflect the scope of coaches' jobs

2. There are *specific tasks* which every coach, regardless of the level they are coaching, must be prepared to do

3. There is a *definite body of knowledge* which coaches—regardless of their sport—must master in order to be proficient and skilled in coaching

4. There are *distinct and identifiable coaching styles*

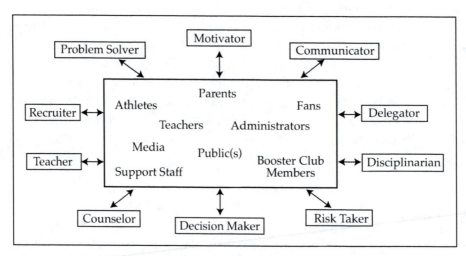

FIGURE 5.4—Ten Major Responsibilities or Tasks Facing the Coach

The information below will provide the reader with a better understanding of those general responsibilities as well as specific tasks that individuals must face in their role as coaches. Above all, coaches are *risk takers.* For the very nature of competitive sports in today's society forces coaches to take calculated risks in their efforts to be effective problem solvers, motivators and managers of human behavior, communicators, delegators, disciplinarians, risk takers, decision makers, counselors, teachers, and recruiters, figure 5.4.

The Coach as a Problem Solver

One of the major tasks facing the athletic coach in our society is that of a problem solver. Would-be coaches should take a positive problem-solving approach to the challenge of coaching competitive sports. However, an important aspect of problem solving centers on preventing problems from occurring in the first place. It sometimes seems as if that is all the coach does, that is, addressing problems or potential problems.

COACHING CONCEPT #81:   **Have an open mind—have empathy and be willing to attempt to understand the opinions and positions of others.**

There are problems with people. There are problems with athletes. There are problems to solve in terms of competitors' strategies and tactics. There are problems with parents. There are problems with administrators. There are problems with booster clubs. There are problems with the media. There are problems with alumni. There are problems with one's own staff (and their spouses). There are also problems with things. For example, there are problems dealing with equipment, supplies, facilities, injuries, travel, eligibility rules, budgets, available resources, fund-raising, etc. It is how the would-be or wanna-be coach handles the real and potential problems which will, for the most part, determine how successful the individual will be in the coaching profession. The objective is to have an open mind and be understanding of others.

COACHING CONCEPT #82:   **Coaches need to attempt to anticipate the worst case scenario and then plan to prevent such from taking place.**

The objective is to always plan for the worse case scenario, that is, to plan as if the worse possible situation might take place. Look into the proverbial crystal ball and anticipate what can go wrong. Remember Murphy's Law—*whatever can go wrong, will go wrong, at the worse possible moment.* If a problem nevertheless presents itself, the task becomes one of solving the problem with as little negative fallout as possible. If one is able to change adversity to an advantage, so much the better. When a problem is not able to be anticipated and/or prevented, efforts at damage control must be exerted so that the problem itself and the resulting fallout does not mushroom into a truly damaging situation either for the coaches or for the athletic program. And, of course, the final component of problem solving is not to allow a problem to reappear. A problem doesn't become a mistake unless one allows it to remain, to be repeated, or the damaging consequences become severe. Therefore, anticipation, prevention, reaction and damage control are key elements in any coach's repertoire involving problem solving.

Types and Sources of Problems

A coach faces problems every day. Some problems are small and petty. Some problems are somewhat significant but not earth shattering. Other problems are major and can indeed be of great consequence, both professionally and personally. Some problems involve people while others center upon inanimate objects or processes. Some problems are within the control of the coach while others are completely out of the individual coach's control.

As a result, the coach is sometimes, if not frequently, in an unenviable position of not always being in direct control of one's own destiny. Rather, the coach's success is frequently intertwined and even ultimately dependent upon other people, including athletes, fellow coaches, administrators as well as individuals, groups and organizations extraneous to the school or athletic entity itself.

Face reality, a coach must be able to anticipate, react to and solve problems, a myriad of problems in one's everyday existence. Thus, the would-be coach must be able to deal with a variety of problems in an effective and efficient fashion. In addition to being able to recognize that there will be problems in the everyday coaching process, the successful coach must understand the types of problems which will inevitably crop up on a regular basis. Finally, a coach should possess a personality which will stand-up to the seemingly incessant onslaught of these problems. It is essential, that the coach—male or female, young or old, inexperienced or a veteran—not experience unacceptable stress, and as a result suffer real harm and eventual burnout as a coach.

COACHING CONCEPT #83:   Coaches should not wear their hearts on their sleeves—but view problems as opportunities.

In short, the coach must be able to handle stress in a positive manner when dealing with a multitude of potential and real problems and challenges. A successful coach is one who is able to prevent, whenever feasible, problems from occurring. However, many times it is not possible to foresee and prevent problems. When it is not possible to prevent a problem(s), the coach must react in a positive vein, by dealing with the difficulty in a decisive, professional and timely fashion. Coaches should not take things personally when faced with problems or difficulties. To do so, distracts their attention away from the immediate task at hand.

COACHING CONCEPT #84:   If there were not problems and challenges there
would be no need for someone with your abilities
and skills

You, the future athletic coach, should view problems as opportunities. For, in the final analysis, if there were not significant problems associated with coaching there would be no need for an individual as dedicated, trained, experienced, and highly skilled as you will be as a member of this noble profession.

The Coach as a Motivator and Manager of Human Behavior

COACHING CONCEPT #85:   A can-do, enthusiastic, confident attitude is often
contagious and can do wonders towards
motivating others to action.

Coaches are constantly involved, perhaps immersed might be a better word, in the management of human behavior. Notice the key word is *management,* not *manipulation.* Coaches must not be involved in manipulation since this is viewed as a negative process. Rather, they should be earnest professional practitioners in managing the behavior of people. Whose behavior? Of course, the first category which comes to mind is that of the athletes themselves. However, there are other individuals and groups or organizations which the competent coach must be skilled in dealing with, i.e., influencing, motivating and managing in the positive sense of the word. In this respect motivational and persuasive skills are key elements in developing the capability of managing and influencing the thinking (convictions, beliefs, attitudes, opinions) and the behavior of others. Similarly, the ability to solicit cooperation and to negotiate win-win situations is highly desirable.

COACHING CONCEPT #86:   Be willing to cooperate with others—as well as to
compromise and to negotiate.

The Coach as a Communicator

Since coaching is a people game it is absolutely essential that coaches be excellent communicators. Coaches need to be themselves and not attempt to wear a mask or be someone they are not. Honesty, especially with athletes, is an important element in communication because youngsters can see right through someone who is at-tempting to bluff or to play a specific role. Coaches must be especially cognizant of the other person's non-verbal communication cues in addition to the more obvious verbal communication efforts.

Communication between the coach and athletes is imperative.

Most outstanding communicators have two things in common. Specifically, they are all passionate about the communication process themselves. They are also passionate on the topic/subject about which they are communicating. "No matter how many other things are tugging at them, great communicators are committed to sharing ideas in ways that make sense and that their listeners will care about," according to Kathleen Hessert, president of Sports Media Challenge (Ulrich, 2007, p. 32).

COACHING CONCEPT #87: When communicating take time to listen and observe.

It is important for coaches to learn to *listen* as well as to *speak* when attempting to communicate. After all, it does take two to communicate, a sender and a receiver. Coaches, because of their position, frequently fall into the trap of doing all of the talking and not enough listening. Coaches can easily assume the role of the controller and begin to dictate to others. Naturally, this is self-destructive. Take time to stop and listen to the other person and attempt to really understand what that individual is attempting to convey. Take time to walk in the other person's shoes, to view things from the other individual's perspective.

The Coach as a Delegator

Coaches cannot nor should they do everything themselves. No matter how dedicated, efficient or effective coaches might be, there are not enough hours in a day for coaches to do everything themselves that must be done. As a result coaches, at all levels, must learn to delegate tasks to others. For some, this may be distasteful or a very real challenge as they feel that no one can do a job or task as well as they can. However, it is important that coaches become comfortable in delegating specific tasks to others.

To whom can coaches delegate? They can delegate to students, other coaches, fellow teachers, volunteers, parents, student-athletes, booster club members, spouses, etc. There are five essential components to the act of delegation that coaches must remain cognizant of if they are to be effective and efficient delegators. When delegating coaches should:

1. Delegate only those tasks or jobs that are appropriate (head coaches would not delegate the task of picking squad members to the booster club).

2. Be sure that the person to whom the task is given is capable (a coach would not delegate to a freshman in high school the task of determining what the varsity team's training rules should be).

3. Make available necessary resources (one would not delegate the task of transporting a team to an away game without providing necessary transportation vehicles).

4. Grant the authority necessary to accomplish the task (one would not give the job of submitting next year's budget request to an individual without granting that person the official authority to do so).

5. Check on the person's progress—but don't interfere (the worse thing a coach could do is to assign a task and then still interfere with the person's attempt to do that task—yet the coach needs to know that the job is being carried out in a satisfactory fashion).

COACHING CONCEPT #88: One cannot delegate total responsibility.

An important concept of delegation is that no one can totally delegate responsibility for a task. If a coach delegates to an assistant the task of ordering needed equipment or supplies and the assistant makes an error resulting in the items not being on hand when needed, who is responsible? Can the head coach tell the athletic director that: "It is not my fault, I gave (delegated) the responsibility (task) of ordering those items to my assistant. It is the assistant's fault."

No, the responsibility remains with the head coach even though the task was given or delegated to the assistant. The principle remains, one cannot *totally* delegate the responsibility for a task even though the task itself might have been delegated. Thus, the coach who delegates tasks or jobs remains ultimately responsible for the consequences. This is why it is imperative that the coach delegate in a careful and discriminatory manner. *To delegate is important for a coach. To delegate carefully and effectively is imperative for a coach.*

The Coach as a Disciplinarian

COACHING CONCEPT #89   Be fair, be firm, be consistent when dealing with athletes.

There is a popular notion that coaches must treat all of their athletes equally, all alike. In reality, coaches do not necessarily need to treat their charges alike or equally. Rather, they need to treat their players fairly and appropriately. There is a significant difference. All athletes are individuals, that is, no two players are exactly alike. Each athlete has different backgrounds as well as different current circumstances that affect each of their lives. Thus, it is essential that coaches be willing to take these individual differences, backgrounds and circumstances into consideration in their decisions and in their dealings with their young athletes. Thus, coaches need to be fair, need to be firm, and need to be consistent in their relationships not only with athletes but in all of their dealings with others. But this doesn't mean that every athlete is treated in an identical or even equal fashion.

COACHING CONCEPT #90:   Be demanding of excellence—high expectations breed excellence while low expectations breeds mediocrity.

Fairness, firmness, consistency, and high expectations are four key components to being a successful disciplinarian. As stated above, treating athletes fairly, of course, does not necessarily mean treating everyone equally. Coaches need to recognize individual needs and be able to administer justice with wisdom and understanding and in a swift and fair manner. Yes, firmness is essential. However, being able to take individual differences and extenuating circumstances into consideration, when making decisions, dispensing justice and administering discipline, is equally important. And, finally, good discipline means appropriate and sensible expectations, involving fair and intelligent rules and regulations. Student-athletes need to understand what is expected of them and that there will be consequences for failure to meet those expectations. Coaches have a phrase for the dispensing of appropriate, just and effective discipline for their athletes—it is referred to as tough love—meaning that although disciplining athletes can be an unpleasant task, such is necessary and is done because of the fact that the coach cares so much for the individual athlete in question.

The Coach as a Risk Taker

> **COACHING CONCEPT #91:** Coaches are risk takers—do not be afraid to take calculated risks.

If nothing else, coaches are risk takers. The key, however, is to take calculated risks. Recklessness is not advised. Coaches bare their souls and their coaching/teaching efforts each time their charges take the field or court for all to see. Coaches assume risks in almost every decision they make because they are being held accountable for those decisions by others. And it becomes worse when many of those individuals evaluating the decisions of coaches have the advantage of 20-20 hindsight, that is, they assess coaches' decisions or non-decisions after they see the consequences of those decisions or non-decisions.

But coaches take risks not only in terms of decisions relating to their athletes, such as who will start, how long each athlete plays, who will be a substitute, and who will make the team, etc. They also take risks when choosing strategies, techniques and tactics they use in practice and in game situations. And they take risks in just being coaches because the nature of coaching is such that there is little job security in the coaching position itself. Even high school or small college teachers with tenure or a continuing teaching contract who also coach usually have no job guarantee or significant job protection when it comes to their coaching responsibilities.

The Coach as a Decision Maker

Coaches are required to make a hundred athletic or coaching decisions each day, if not more. During practices and game situations they must make decisions quickly. There are innumerable other decisions which must be made away from the playing or practice site. While many of these decisions are minor in nature, there are others which are indeed significant and far reaching. Coaches must feel comfortable in accepting this responsibility. They also must be willing and able to make decisions—based on subjective and/or objective criteria—in a decisive and confident manner.

Accompanying the territory of decision making is the ability to handle pressure and criticism (some just and some unjust) from those who might disagree with the coach for any number of reasons (some rational and some irrational). Handling the pressures of the job and being able to deal with criticism is just part of the job for coaches.

COACHING CONCEPT #92:   In dealing with criticism coaches need to be like a duck in the rain—let it roll off your back.

When making decisions it is imperative that decisions are appropriate, fair, just, and consistent and are based on facts whenever possible. Although people do not have to agree with every coach's decision, it is hoped that they would recognize that the decision making process itself was appropriate and fair even if the resulting decision itself is unpopular.

Coaches must determine which decisions to make themselves and which can be made by other individuals, including the student-athletes. How much decision making power should the coach share with others, especially athletes? Naturally, this depends upon the personalities of coaches, the maturity of the athletes, the history of the team, the expectations of the school and athletic administrations, and other circumstances which exist at the time. Some of the first and very important decisions which coaches must make—decisions which have great impact on the image of the coach and on the atmosphere permeating the team—relate to how practices are to be conducted. For example, decisions need to be made in terms of the following:

1.   What is to be done in the practice?
2.   When it is to be done?
3.   How it will be accomplished?
4.   Who is to do it?
5.   Where will it be done?
6.   Under what conditions will each task be accomplished?
7.   At what performance level will the task be done?

COACHING CONCEPT #93:   There are a thousand ways to skin a cat.

Are all of these decisions the exclusive purview of coaches? Or, will some coaches allow input or even allow decisions to be made in some instances by the athletes themselves? In some situations, coaches feel very comfortable in making all of these decisions themselves. In this way, the coaches retain complete control over all aspects of the coaching scene. However, in other situations there are coaches who are not the least bit ill at ease in giving more responsibility to their athletes in terms of making recommendations or even making decisions in areas that previously had been the exclusive domain of coaches. Again, there is no one way, no single correct way to go about coaching a team. Or, to put it another way, there are a thousand ways to skin a cat. There are many different methods and tactics which can be utilized to reach the same objective, that is, for the student-athletes to participate and achieve at a level that approximates their potential or near potential.

Other areas where decisions must be made are in the area of discipline and in terms of enforcing rules and regulations governing any number of different areas such as attendance, punctuality, academic achievements, eligibility, behavior problems, etc. In order to be able to make intelligent decisions, it is necessary to obtain and examine the facts in light of the specific situation or extenuating circumstances. Once the needed information, the facts of the case, are available the coach can then assess the situation, make a judgment based on experience, knowledge as well as existing policies and procedures, and render the decision. *It is important to recognize the appropriateness of decisions based on both subjective and objective judgment.*

Coaches should exercise this decision making ability while being cool, calm and collected. To the contrary, making rash decisions or making decisions while in the so-called crisis mode is a recipe for disaster. To prevent problems, one must be able to think, to examine various facts and to anticipate possible consequences of one's actions and inaction. This should be accomplished without undue pressure or stress to make one decision over another (see chapter 12, Problem Solving Strategies for Coaches).

COACHING CONCEPT #94: **Coaches should, generally speaking, make important decisions while being cool, calm and collected.**

Subjective Rational for Decisions

Since coaches are called upon every day of their lives to make numerous decisions, many of them on the spur of the moment, many such decisions are subjective in nature, at least in part. Coaches frequently use subjective judgment in arriving at who will start a game. They are frequently subjective in their interpretations and enforcement of team rules and in making substitutions in game situations. In reality, coaches don't have to always have a definitive, easily justifiable reason (based on cold, hard facts or data) for doing something. Coaches make decisions and act in a certain fashion because of experience, because of intuition, because of a hunch or feeling or because of a desire to experiment, just to name a few reasons. An example of a subjective judgment can be seen when a coach decides, after viewing athletes perform in practice, on the basis of that coach's opinions or feelings (which are based upon experience) that a particular athlete is more competitive than another and/or fits better with the other starters on the team. As a result, the coach may give this player a starting berth.

In the realities of life coaches are able, for the most part, to come to conclusions and render decisions based upon both objective and subjective judgment. However, coaches need not be apologetic about using subjective judgment in making decisions. That is why the individual has been hired in the first place, that is, to make decisions based on that person's knowledge, skills and experience. Even in interpreting facts and hard data, the coach is always faced with interpreting the information in light of one's experience, one's education, one philosophy, etc.

Objective Rational for Decisions

In some instances, coaches will make decisions based on very specific, objective data. For example, if a coach enforces a rule that any player who is five minutes late for practice cannot play in the next game—it is rather easy to look at one's watch and see if the student-athlete is actually five minutes late. If so, the objective data, the number of minutes the student athlete has been late, will enable the coach to render a decision that is wholly objective. However, if this coach wanted to take into consideration any extenuating circumstances which might have existed in terms of *why* the athlete was late, the coach is then placed in a position of making a subjective judgment.

In making objective decisions, coaches need to rely on hard data and facts when attempting to make evaluations and arrive at reasonable conclusions. For example, the swimming coach who times each of the athletes as they swim a specific distance and then uses that data, that information, to determine those athletes who will actually compete in an upcoming meet.

The Use of both Subjective and Objective Judgment

However, things are rarely, if ever, as black and white as some people might prefer. Rather, there is a great deal of gray area in which coaches must operate. Thus, it should be no surprise that experience plays such an important role in the decision making process and that most decisions involve both subjective and objective judgment.

For example, in the sport of wrestling, there are some coaches who utilize so-called wrestle-offs to determine who will start the next match. A wrestle-off is where two teammates competing for a starting spot on the team will wrestle against each other in a practice session. The victor in this practice match thus earns the right to start for the team at that weight division at the next match. In this situation, the objective data would be the fact that one athlete defeats another in the practice competition. Thus, the winner, based upon this objective criterion, starts.

However, there are other wrestling coaches who would never use such a criterion to make such an important decision. First, these coaches feel that such wrestle-offs are not really conducive to producing the best competitor for the actual wrestling match. There are too many 2 o'clock wonders or practice marvels who can do well in a practice session but who choke in actual competition. Coach Don Murray, one of the winningest NCAA Division III wrestling coaches in the country, with 5 national championships and 4 second place teams in the past 25 years at the College at Brockport, State University of New York, downplays the use of such practice competitions in deciding who starts. He cites the rationale that the head coach is obligated to use subjective judgment, based upon knowledge, experience, and training in arriving at such an important decision. One should never place such blind faith in such an objective criteria. (Don Murray, personal communication, September 8, 2007). After all, most basketball coaches would be hesitant to make a decision as to who will start an important upcoming game on the basis of which players shot the best field goal percentage during the previous week's practices and scrimmages. Instead, these coaches would want to maintain the right to make such a decision based upon their own subjective judgment, upon their own feelings, their own experience, their own observations.

The Coach as a Counselor

Today more than ever before, coaches are expected to be counselors to their charges as well as to other coaches. However, coaches serve as counselors to students not only in terms of athletics per se but also, in many instances; they find themselves counseling student-athletes in the personal domain as well. In this respect, coaches would do well to remember that they serve as a role model and as a substitute parent to many students. As such, they are an authority figure to youngsters and serve as a source of trust, security and confidence to others.

Coaches must remain alert to insure that their charges who need guidance and counseling actually receive meaningful assistance and timely support. Above all, however, the relationship between individual coaches and individual athletes must remain on a professional level. Coaches must pay strict attention to their actions and how their actions are perceived by others. It is of paramount importance that coaches not step over the bounds of propriety (or be perceived to do so) when it comes to dealing with others, especially athletes and students. This is especially important when the coach happens to coach athletes of the opposite sex.

The Coach as a Teacher

COACHING CONCEPT #95:   Coaches are role models—coaches need to be careful in their actions on and off the court or field.

First and foremost, coaches are teachers. What an awesome responsibility and tremendous opportunity it is to be a teacher. Coaches can teach in a *deliberate manner*. They can deliberately plan for what they intend to teach and for what they intend their athletes to learn. Coaches can also *accidentally teach* things (by chance). This means that others, including athletes, can learn from coaches a variety of important concepts and values in an accidental manner, by chance, without coaches deliberately attempting to convey such teachings. And, coaches are capable of teaching their charges in an *incidental manner*. That is, some information and knowledge are disseminated or taught as a minor consequence of or a result of some other teaching activity or effort. As a role model, coaches teach by what they do and do not do as well as by being what and who they are. This teaching by example is a great responsibility for all coaches. Much of that which is learned through accidental or incidental teaching is accomplished through role modeling and by example—both on and off the job.

COACHING CONCEPT #96: **Student-athletes need to be treated as individuals—with dignity, respect and appropriate expectations.**

It is a significant responsibility for coaches to be teachers of the young. Coaches must strive to be at the cutting edge in terms of teaching and evaluation techniques. They must develop competencies in motivating students to learn. Coaches must recognize that all students have differing needs, different capabilities and different potential. Coaches must treat athletes as human beings, with dignity, understanding, empathy and intelligence. They must know how to present material and skills to be learned so that students may attempt to master the material at their own individual rate of learning. They also must be competent in recognizing when students are making errors and be able to correct errors while at the same time reinforcing correct behavior and performance.

Teaching for Competency in the Psychomotor, Affective and Cognitive Domains

Youngsters who participate in competitive sports are given opportunities to learn many things of value in several different dimensions: intellectual, emotional, psychological and, of course, physical. They are able to best develop and mature physically, emotionally and psychologically in a nurturing and positive environment. It is the responsibility of the coach to provide such a learning environment.

Youngsters improve in terms of their physical conditioning and ability to train. They master higher levels of physical skills. They gain self-confidence, develop skills both in time management and in the setting of priorities. They learn to deal effectively with people. They gain access to a wealth of facts and information. They increase their knowledge base and intellectual awareness. They expand their understanding of strategies and tactics. They increase competency in safety matters. In short, athletes learn, they mature, and they expand their intellectual, social, psychological and physical capacities. And, they have opportunities to accomplish all this while being able to enjoy themselves. It is the coach's responsibility to recognize these potentials of each individual player and to take steps to help the athlete improve as a person and as an athlete.

The Three Domains of Learning

When attempting to work with athletes, to teach and coach these young people, coaches should think in terms of the three domains of learning; that is, the cognitive domain, the affective domain and the psychomotor domain. As knowledgeable, experienced and trained professionals, coaches are expected to deal with the development of motor/physical skills as well as the fitness level of their charges (*psychomotor* aspects). Coaches are also expected to help their athletes learn about the social dimensions, perspectives, attitudes, values, and interests of competitive sports (*affective* domain). This includes the ability of athletes to deal with others on both an individual basis and in group settings (Gensemer, 1985). And finally, coaches who are true teachers are also involved in helping athletes develop intellectually, gaining knowledge and information and being capable of using this knowledge in various settings and in different circumstances (*cognitive* domain). Thus the cognitive aspect of coaching deals with the development of knowledge, the ability to think and evaluate, interpret, analyze and synthesize information in order to interpret the information or knowledge gained by the individual (Barrow & Brown, 1988). Figure 5.5 illustrates the interrelationships between the cognitive, affective and psychomotor domains (Wuest and Bucher, 1991).

Of course, the younger the athlete is, the greater the opportunity for influence being exerted by the coach. The older the athlete the more difficult it is, though not impossible, for the coach to have significant influence over that person's behavior. This is why coaches of youth sports must be especially careful of their behavior on and off the playing field or court as their extremely young players are very susceptible to being influenced and affected by the attitudes, opinions and behavior of coaches.

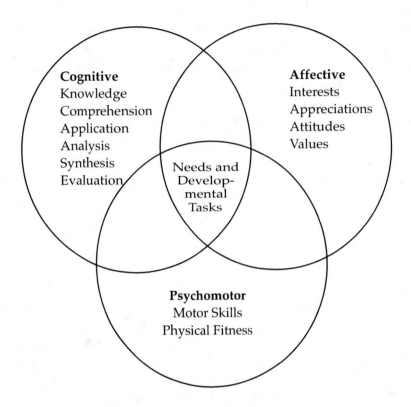

**FIGURE 5.5—Interdependence of Cognitive, Affective, and Psychomotor
Domains and their relationship to needs and developmental tasks.**
*[adapted from Wuest, D. A. & Bucher, C. A. (1991). Foundations of Physical Education and Sport.
St. Louis: Mosby Year Book, p. 65.]*

The Coach as a Recruiter

COACHING CONCEPT #97:   **The recruitment of athletes, at every level, is an
integral part of the coaching responsibility.**

Every coach is a recruiter. Let's repeat that statement. *Every coach is a recruiter.*
That is correct. Recruitment of athletes, at every level, is an integral part of the
coaching responsibility. Whether the coach is at the college or university level or is a
mentor in high school, junior high or is a coach of a youth sport team—that individual who is called *coach* has as a major responsibility the recruitment (and retention)
of athletes.

SPECIFIC TASKS AND OBLIGATIONS OF COACHES

There are numerous specific and distinct tasks that face all coaches. These are responsibilities that require a combination of skill and experience. While some of these tasks are rather mundane, others are more time consuming and sophisticated in nature. Some tasks involve dealing with people, that is, individuals, small groups and organizations. Other tasks involve not people but things.

COACHING CONCEPT #98: There are some specific tasks and responsibilities that are required of almost every coach—whether the coach is at a small high school or at a large university.

Some of the specific tasks that confront most coaches involved in an academic setting are provided below. Although this list is by no means conclusive, it does provide an insight into the broad range of activities and obligations confronting both inexperienced and experienced coaches in an academic environment. Even coaches of youth sports—outside of the school setting—face many of these challenges and responsibilities.

1. Creating a team or sport handbook or playbook
2. Determining the eligibility of athletes
3. Creating a Code of Conduct
4. Selecting team members
5. Preventing injuries and reacting to accidents/injuries
6. Academic advising—use of support services
7. Planning practices
8. Conducting inventory of equipment and supplies
9. Caring for (cleaning/upkeeping) equipment and supplies
10. Purchasing of equipment and supplies
11. Monitoring of study hall—for athletes
12. Implementing special game day activities
13. Planning transportation
14. Filming—video taping
15. Utilizing audio-visual aids in the teaching of skills, in team preparation and in scouting
16. Selecting team managers

17. having student-athletes excused from class (due to practices/games)
18. Selecting, training and evaluating assistant coaches and support staff
19. Working with spouses and children of other coaches
20. Selecting team captains
21. Establishing and enforcing team rules and regulations
22. Selecting and implementing appropriate punishment for rules infractions
23. Planning for home event management
24. Insuring proper crowd control
25. Recruiting potential students for one's own team
26. Assisting high school athletes select an appropriate college or university
27. Developing a farm system for one's own team
28. Implementing time management techniques
29. Establishing and implementing substance abuse policies and programs
30. Establishing an athletic hall of fame
31. Creating newsletters
32. Establishing athletic awards
33. Dealing with a variety of other constituencies—in and out of the school setting
34. Planning and implementing strength and conditioning programs
35. Evaluating opponent's capabilities—as individuals and as a team
36. Speaking before various publics and constituencies
37. Generating additional funds and other resources.
38. Involvement with community groups and booster clubs
39. Assisting and organizing promotional activities
40. Establishing plans for pre-season, in-season, post season and out-of-season
41. Scouting opponents (teams and individuals
42. Other . . .

AREAS OF KNOWLEDGE APPLICABLE TO THE COACH

There are also specific areas of knowledge that are extremely important for coaches to be familiar with—if they are to be current in terms of their total responsibilities and are to be capable in the teaching of their sport to athletes. The *total body of knowledge* supporting the coaching of sports is immense and continues to expand every day, both in scope and in depth. Would-be coaches, as well as those currently holding coaching positions, need to make concerted efforts to be at least minimally competent in each of the categories listed below.

1. Legal liability—accident reduction/prevention
2. First aid and CPR
3. Sport psychology and motivation
4. Sociological aspects of sport
5. Conditioning and weight training
6. Growth and development of youngsters—biological aspects of coaching
7. Business aspects of sport including—purchasing and budgeting
8. Public relations and fund-raising
9. Ethics of sport
10. Eligibility rules
11. College student recruitment rules (NCAA/NAIA, etc.)
12. Teaching physical skills
13. How athletes learn
14. Planning practices
15. Xs and Os of coaching specific sports
16. Time and stress management
17. Legal aspects of sport; laws affecting sports
18. Recognizing talent

Athletes must respect coaches.

IDENTIFIABLE COACHING STYLES

> **COACHING CONCEPT #99: In coaching—be yourself.**

An individual's coaching style is determined by one's experience, training and personality. There is a real need to be oneself as a coach. Athletes as well as others can see through a charade put on by a coach. Coaches need to be comfortable in their coaching tasks and therefore need to establish a style that fits their personalities, their experiences, and their temperaments.

> **COACHING CONCEPT #100: There is more than one way to coach—no single coaching style is equally effective for every coach.**

There is no one, single coaching style which guarantees success. In fact, there is no guarantee for coaching success, period. In fact, just the contrary. There are ample examples of highly successful coaches with very different or distinct and even conflicting coaching styles—both in practices and in actual competition. For example, witness the differences in the coaching styles of former coaches like Bobby Knight (Indiana and Texas Tech), Dean Smith (North Carolina), Johnny Wooden (UCLA), Ed Heithcoth (Michigan State), and Al McQuire (Marquette). All five coaches have won NCAA national basketball championships in the NCAA Division I. Yet, none of these coaches are identical clones of one another. In some instances, they can be said to be quite different in their coaching styles as well as the way their teams play the sport. The point is that there are indeed many ways for a coach to be successful and many different styles of coaching.

Both the personality and previous experience of coaches have great influence upon the way they coach and treat athletes. There is no right or wrong coaching style per se. Would-be coaches need to act in a manner that they feel comfortable with and which is effective for them while being fair, just, and appropriate for their athletes, at the youngster's current level of competition.

A variety of coaching styles have been identified over the years. The six styles delineated below include: (1) the authoritarian or autocratic coach, (2) the dictator, (3) the benevolent dictator, (4) the humanistic coach, (5) the democratic coach, and (6) the Laissez-faire or permissive mentor. Doubtless, there are other styles or variations.

The Authoritarian or Autocratic Coach

In this style, the coach is absolutely the ultimate decision maker. The coach literally is the final authority in terms of how everything is to be conducted and implemented. Autocratic coaches are task oriented and tend to exert control over things and people. Many coaches fall under this category in some of their relationships with athletes as well as non-athletes.

The Dictator

Coaches who are dictators also seek to control the coaching situations. However, dictators are frequently arbitrary and capricious in their actions while also demonstrating a task orientation type of philosophy. The statement *my way or the highway* adequately represents their feelings regarding their treatment of not only athletes but others who are associated or connected with their athletic program.

The Benevolent Dictator

The benevolent dictator is the coach who feels that he or she knows what is best for others and therefore must, in a benevolent or parental fashion, be in a position of deciding what is most appropriate for these individuals. The benevolent dictator does not act out of spite or malevolence. Rather, this coach acts as a kindly patriarch or matriarch for one's children in order that the youngsters' needs are met. But, it is the benevolent dictator who nevertheless makes the decisions and sets the tone for the sports program and all that takes place in practices and contests.

The Humanistic Coach

This type of coach has empathy with others, especially with players. This coach deals with athletes as individuals, as human beings, with understanding and compassion. This coach is not standoffish or unreasonable in one's expectations of others. Rather, this individual understands others as human beings and acknowledges the existence of strengths and weaknesses of individuals. Similarly, the humanistic coach is one who acknowledges that he or she is also human, capable of making mistakes or misjudgments just as any other person.

The Democratic Coach

Being a democratic coach does not mean that all decisions are made by majority rule. Far from it. Nevertheless, those coaches who tend to be democratic in their relationships with their players are exemplified by a tendency to solicit and accept input, suggestions and ideas from others, including athletes, in some of the areas relating to the coaching scene. However, the final decisions (as well as the responsibility) still rest with the coach. In a democratic coaching atmosphere, many decisions may be arrived at through consensus or as a result of ideas proposed by others. Additionally, these coaches frequently give their charges many possible options and allow them to choose one or more alternatives.

Laissez-faire or Permissive Coaching Style

This style of coaching is noted for a rather free-wheeling atmosphere where there is little structure. Some people criticize this style as being a lazy person's way of coaching. Others feel that such an atmosphere facilitates the athletes' growth and development in terms of responsibility and decision-making. The laissez-faire is noted for few parameters being established in terms of how things should be accomplished or implemented. In fact, a very loose atmosphere marks this type of coaching style where athletes have a great deal of unrestricted freedom in terms of their actions and decision making both on and off the floor or field.

COACHING CONCEPT #101: Coaches operate within several styles—depending upon the situation and circumstances.

However, in the real world of competitive sports it would probably be inappropriate to attempt to classify coaches exclusively in any one single category. In fact, coaches tend to exhibit the characteristics of several, if not most, of these styles as they go about performing different coaching tasks and interact with different individuals and groups at times during the season (Gallon, 1989).

Some coaches, for example, may become a dictator when it comes to the style of play that their athletes will engage in during competition. On the other hand, they may be very democratic when it comes to such matters as pre-season conditioning activities as long as the athletes end up on a specific date being in shape and capable of demonstrating their conditioning on the field or court. These same coaches might be rather laissez-faire when it comes to the type of team or behavioral rules as long as the athletes don't embarrass themselves, the coaches and the school. Thus, it is easy to see how an individual coach might not conveniently fall into one or even two of the distinct categories listed above. Each coach is also an individual person with individual traits, different experiences and preferences. That is what makes one coach different from another.

REFERENCES

Barrow, H. M. & Brown, J. P. (1988). *Man and movement: Principles of physical education*. Philadelphia: Lea & Febiger.

Cardone, D. (2006, August). Exceeds expectations. *Athletic Management, 14*(8), 57-61.

Gallon, A. J. (1989). *Coaching ideas & ideals* (2nd. ed.). Prospect Heights, Illinois: Waveland Press, Inc.

Gensemer, R. E. (1985). *Physical education: Perspectives, inquiry, applications*. Philadelphia: Saunders.

Gerry Faust, Notre Dame coach. (2001, February 21). *Sports Illustrated* p. 12.

Gulick, L. & Urwick, L. (Eds.). (1937). Papers on the science of administration. New York: Institute of Public Administration.

King, P. (1993, August 6-8). I will NOT be a loser. *USA Weekend,* pp. 4-6.

Katz, R. (1955). Skills of an effective administrator. *Harvard Business Review, 33*(1), 34-35.

Maisel, I. (2001, January 15). Pick your poison. *Sports Illustrated,* p. 21.

Orman, D. (2001, December 4). Extended rules for athletes. *Democrat and Chronicle* B-1

Reed, W. F. (1992, November, 30). Youth must be heard. *Sports Illustrated,* p. 86.

Sabock, R. J. (1985). *The Coach* (3rd ed.). Champaign, IL: Human Kinetics. p. 38.

Selinsky, D. (2001, February/March). The coach difference. *Success,* pp. 28-33.

Stier, Jr., W. F. (1986, Spring). Athletic administration: Athletic administrators expect qualities, Competencies in coaches. *Interscholastic Athletic Administration,* pp. 7-10.

Stier, Jr., W. F. (1992). Understanding fundraising in sport: The conceptual approach. *Sport Marketing Quarterly, I*(l), 41-46.

Stier, Jr., W. F. (1994). *Successful sport fund-raising.* Dubuque, Iowa: Wm. C. Brown & Benchmark.

Stier, W. F., Jr. (2005, November 1). *Physical Education and Sport in North, Central and South America—Trends, Problems and Solutions.* Presentation made at the United Nations' International Conference for Sport and Education in Bangkok, Thailand.

Ulrich, L. (2007, August/September). Your turn to talk. *Athletic Management, XIX*(5), 30-38.

Wuest, D. A. & Bucher, C. A. (1991). *Foundations of Physical Education and Sport.* St. Louis: Mosby Year Book.

Name: _____

Student ID #: _____

EXERCISES FOR CHAPTER 5

A. In your opinion, what are some of characteristics of a winning or successful coach at the youth sport level? At the junior or senior high school level? At the college level?

B. Discuss the statement: " . . . being a superior athlete can help or can hinder one's efforts to be a successful coach."

C.   Discuss the statement: "The only certainty in coaching is that nothing is certain."

   _____

   _____

   _____

   _____

   _____

   _____

   _____

   _____

   _____

D.   Of the different *processes of coaching* (PPOSDCoRRFEB)—which do you anticipate will be the most challenging or most important for you as a coach? Why? What steps do you anticipate you can take to develop competencies in these processes?

   _____

   _____

   _____

   _____

   _____

   _____

   _____

   _____

   _____

   _____

   _____

E. Of the ten essential coaching skills, interpersonal competencies have been described as an absolute essential ingredient in the coach's arsenal. Explain why this may be true.

F. When do problems in coaching become challenges or opportunities for the individual coach or coaches? Provide examples.

G.   Coaches are expected to make decisions based on both subjective and objective data or information. Provide examples of such decision making opportunities in the sport(s) in which you intend to coach.

H.   Discuss the statement: "All coaches usually fall within a single classification or category in terms of coaching style."

I.   What is your opinion regarding the concept that *coaches should not cry wolf* when they communicate with others? Elaborate your philosophy in this regard.

RESEARCH QUESTONS FOR CHAPTER 5

1. Ask a current coach to classify himself or herself in terms of *coaching styles or coaching philosophy*. Seek to determine why the coach believes he or she falls under a specific or single category.

   ----

2. Interview current coaches and seek to determine what pressures they face in their roles as coaches and what steps they attempt to use in meeting these pressures.

   ----

3. Interview a high school varsity coach and find out what the coach feels are the differences between a competent and successful coach and one who is not.

   ----

4. Through the interview process, find out from a varsity high school coach the person's opinion regarding the movement toward extended, year-round (conduct code) rules for athletes.

    _____

    _____

    _____

    _____

    _____

    _____

5. Visit with a high school athletic director or varsity coach and determine what type, if any, of year end report is expected from the individual varsity coaches and what happens within the school system to the year end reports from each of the varsity coaches. That is, what *comprises* the year-end report and how are the different reports *used* by the coach, the AD and the school administration?

    _____

    _____

    _____

    _____

    _____

    _____

Chapter 6

Coaching is a People Business

NCAA Division III athletic programs have sophisticated facilities.

THE SECRETS OF COACHING

COACHING CONCEPT #102: There is no secret formula in coaching.

Many would-be coaches are of the opinion that one of the so-called secrets to becoming a successful coach rests in solving or mastering some mysterious offensive or surreptitious defensive techniques, tactics or strategies. These individuals are of the notion that discovering the answer to the mystery surrounding the so-called technical aspects of coaching, the Xs and Os of coaching strategies, would enable them to be able to produce winning teams on a consistent basis.

Nothing could be farther from the truth. The belief that successful coaches are in possession of some type of secret technical knowledge or strategy is just a fallacy, a piece of coaching folklore.

> **COACHING CONCEPT #103: Working effectively with people is one of the keys to being a successful coach.**

If there is one factor or quality that is probably essential in terms of having a positive effect upon the competency level of a coach, *it is the ability to deal with and relate to a wide range of individuals.* Who are these individuals? They include athletes and non-athletes, youngsters and adults, knowledgeable sports people as well as individuals who have little, if any, knowledge of sports or of coaching. It is this ability to work with *people* that is frequently *the* determining factor between an individual being a highly successful mentor and an average coach (or worse).

Joe Gibbs, then coach of the NFL Redskins, is a firm believer in the importance of being able to deal with people. In 2004 he was quoted as saying: "Unless you're an accountant that has to deal with figures or maybe a chemist that has to deal with chemicals, dealing with people is everything, and that's what any kind of team sport is all about" (Wood, 2004, p. 9-C.)

TECHNICAL VERSUS THE INTERPERSONAL ASPECTS OF COACHING

In reality, most coaches are pretty well schooled in terms of the technical aspects of coaching their sport(s). Usually coaches, even beginning coaches, are pretty well motivated in keeping up-to-date or current in the new approaches to the technical aspects of coaching their specific sport(s). One of the reasons for this is that this part of coaching is concrete in nature. Plus, many coaches have played the primary sport that they coach. Finally, most coaches are fascinated with the Xs & Os of coaching and find this aspect of their job both interesting and fulfilling.

As a result most coaches are avid readers of the numerous professional magazines and journals that examine the tactics and strategies (Xs and Os) of coaching specific sports and which are available in most libraries. These same individuals also frequently attend coaching clinics and workshops which are conducted throughout the United States in an effort to hear highly visible college and high school coaches share their success stories (as well as failures) and advocate their own coaching styles, tactics and strategies.

However, it is the ability to work with other people—in and outside the actual coaching arena—that determines the eventual success of the team and the coach. This is because the assistant or the head coach, whether of a youth sport team, a high school squad or a college team, does not operate in a vacuum. Coaches must be skillful in working with their athletes as well as other individuals in the performance of their coaching tasks and in carrying out other athletic responsibilities. A coach can possess great technical knowledge in terms of the Xs and Os of a sport, that is, the strategies involved in a sport, and yet still not be successful. Failure can be the result of deficiencies in people-skills. That is, inadequacy in working with players, parents, other school people, members of the public, etc., can doom an otherwise skilled coach who is very competent in the technical aspects of the sport.

COACHING CONCEPT #104: Don't keep secrets—be open in what you do.

One of the worse things a coach can be accused of doing is keeping secrets, that is, not being open or honest in what one does. No, this does not refer to being secretive in terms of the strategies and tactics to be used on the playing field or court. Rather, this refers to being open and honest in one's dealings with others—athletes, parents, members of the public, school and sport administrators, etc.

It is important that others—individuals and groups—have a fair understanding and interpretation of what you are doing and why you are doing it. Be prepared to explain your rationale for action, whenever possible and appropriate. Athletes should know where they stand in your eyes. There should never be great surprises in respect to your decisions in dealing with others. The absence of openness might be perceived as being devious and dishonest by others, a reputation that is certainly not desirable as a coach.

An old coaching story that emphasizes the importance of being open in what one does has a naked person walking down the street with only a band-aid on the individual's shoulder. As expected, a large crowd gathered gawking at this individual. However, they were all paying attention to the band-aid and wondering what was under it. The moral of this anecdote is that people are usually most concerned, interested, curious and critical with that which is hidden or secretive. Thus it is far better to be open about what one has done or is currently doing and be willing to provide reasons or rationale for one's actions and decisions. To be otherwise is to invite criticism and to be viewed as reticent, overly reserved and devious. If one has nothing to hide, why act like one does?

COACHING CONCEPT #105: Look at yourself through the eyes of others (outsiders) to get a realistic and honest perspective of who you are and your worth.

Coaches need to be sensitive to the impact and influence they have on others, both in the athletic program and within the general public. Take time to consider how others might view you and your actions. How are you viewed as a coach by athletes, parents, booster club members, the athletic director, the school administration, etc.?

How are your actions and decisions accepted and interpreted by others? How are you valued by others?

This does not imply that coaches need to constantly second guess their every move or decision as a coach. What it does mean is that you, as a coach, need to be cognizant that others form opinions and make decisions based upon their perceptions and understandings of what you do as well as what you fail to do. Thus, it is important to consider how others—in and out of the school/sport setting—view you and interpret your performance as a coach and as a caring individual.

COACHING CONCEPT #106: Never get into a fight with a skunk.

Being a coach, by the very nature of the job, places one in many situations in which disagreements might arise and confrontations result. It is a wise coach who recognizes the difference between normal disagreements on the one hand and inappropriate and unprofessional confrontations on the other. There are some individuals (and groups) who just enjoy being argumentative and hostile with others. There is usually no way for the coach to remain unscathed in this type of confrontation, argument or disagreement.

Coaches need to be wary of being drawn into such negative, antagonistic and detrimental confrontations with the so-called skunks as this usually leads to disaster. Thus, it behooves the coach to recognize these types of individuals and groups (the skunks) and to realize that it does absolutely no good to attempt to be drawn into arguments, fights or confrontations with them.

COACHING CONCEPT #107: Working hard doesn't guarantee success—one needs to work smart.

UNDERSTANDING THE WORK ETHIC IN COACHING

Another fallacy of coaching involves the work ethic. Some coaches believe that if they work hard and long hours they are bound to be successful. They mistakenly equate hard work with guaranteed success. These coaches have an attitude that they will simply out work their opponents and therefore will be rewarded with success. Granted, coaches are known for working hard and long at becoming competent teachers and coaches of their sport(s). However, there is a real danger in equating hard work and effort with competency and being a successful coach. There is a little matter of actual competency and doing the right things at the right time—not to mention having talented, elite athletes who perform well under pressure.

A mark of a successful coach is one who does *not only work hard but also works smart.* This simply means that coaches need to recognize that it is not how long one works or how much effort one puts into the challenge of coaching that determines success. Rather, success is a result of what the coach actually accomplishes and not how hard one works. Young coaches frequently complain about how hard they work, how many hours each day they put in on the job. And yet, they wonder why they are not as successful as other coaches, especially those coaches who seemingly do not spend the time or expend the effort with their own programs.

Coaching and Working on Task

The answer to this apparent dilemma or contradiction is that *some coaches can obtain significant results with less obvious labor because of the effectiveness and efficiency of their efforts.* Also, successful coaches are able to prioritize tasks and do those things that will bring tangible results. Other less effective coaches seem to drown in a sea of wasteful exertion because they do not work smart (on task) and have not determined those activities and efforts that **are truly effective** and worthwhile in comparison to those activities that are ineffectual, or even worse, downright wasteful.

> **COACHING CONCEPT #108: Working 24-hours a day doesn't guarantee success—if anything, such compulsion frequently leads to athletic and personal problems, including burnout.**

Many would-be coaches, as well as current coaches at all levels, have the mistaken impression (or act as if they believe) that the harder one works the more successful the person will naturally become. Not so. It is not merely a matter of how hard one works. Rather, it is the **quality** of one's efforts that really matters. It is how *effective* and *efficient* one works rather than how *long* or how *hard* one works.

This can be seen in the situation where a young basketball coach (Jimmy Smith) approaches the athletic director to complain that no one seems to give him much respect or appreciation for all of the hard work that he (Jimmy Smith) does in coaching basketball. In fact, coach Smith felt that he was one of the best and hardest working coaches on the staff since he proudly stated that he arrived at school before 7 A.M. almost on a daily basis. In fact, coach Smith claimed that he rarely left for home until well past 11 in the evening since he was so busily involved in recruitment efforts.

It became clear that the basketball coach compared himself with the baseball coach (Ralph Jones) and bemoaned the fact that everyone on staff, in the school and even in the community, seemingly worshipped the very ground that coach Jones walked on—even though coach Jones was rarely seen on campus and practically never stayed late in the evening working on recruiting, etc.

Effort versus Results—Quantity versus Quality

Coach Smith was nearly devastated when he was informed by his athletic director that credit was not to be given for mere effort. Rather, results are what counted. The fact that it seemingly took the basketball coach 16 hours each day to perform the duties he perceived as being necessary is immaterial in terms of being viewed as a competent coach. It was pointed out that merely working hard or merely spending the time (hours, days, weeks, and months) on various tasks is not the conclusive factor in determining the competency of a coach. In fact, spending so much effort, spending an inordinate amount of time attempting to reach objectives or goals might be seen as a lack of competency, might be assessed as a waste of time, and might be viewed as a lack of organization and an inability to plan and prioritize.

The athletic director attempted to help the basketball coach, as politely and gently as she could, by pointing out that it is not the quantity of work but rather the quality of the results of such work that is important. The fact that the baseball coach did not have to spend 16 hours, 12 hours, or even 10 hours a day performing those tasks necessary for the baseball team to be successful is a testament to that coach's *quality* of work, skillfulness in managing time and in establishing priorities.

Far too often coaches feel that more is better when it comes to effort or work within the coaching arena. However, just the opposite may be true. Coaches need to be effective mentors and teachers, and this includes the ability to achieve objectives in a reasonable amount of time and with a judicious amount of effort. Again, this concept involves not only the work and effort of the coaching staff but holds true for the athletes in practices as well.

Stressors, Pressures and Burnout

> **COACHING CONCEPT #109: Recognize the signs and symptoms of burnout—and take precautionary actions.**

Coaching burnout is the result of stress, stress that is not dealt with by the individual coach in an acceptable fashion. "Stress is an emotionally disruptive or upsetting condition occurring in response to adverse external influences. It is capable of affecting physical health by prompting an increased heart rate, a rise in blood pressure, muscular tension, irritability, or depression"(Cain, 2007, p. 52).

Such stress can result from the inability of coaches to get done all that seemingly needs to get done. Such stress can also result from dual role conflict, such as being a teacher and also a coach. However, all coaches experience stress. It is part of the job. It comes with the territory. Some stress and pressure can be a positive thing. However, too much stress or the inability to adequately handle stress can have a very negative effect upon the coach and the coach's performance. How individual coaches react to and cope with stress and the symptoms of stress will determine how successful they are in avoiding the classical burnout symptoms that are all too common with coaches, at all levels.

A pilot study involving high school and college coaches conducted in 2005 (Taking the job) revealed an extremely high average heart rate while on the sidelines (120 beats per minutes). That rate is twice the high as an average person at rest (60-70 beats per minute) and approaching what firefighters experience (140 beats per minute) when entering a burning structure. Stress and pressure—and the perception of stress and pressure—can cause physical reactions on the coach, reactions that are not good for the health and wellbeing of the individual coach.

Possible Symptoms of Extreme Stress and Burnout

Frequently, coaches who are victims of burnout feel physically and mentally exhausted, experience a feeling of helplessness in one's personal and professional life, are unmotivated, view themselves as being less than competent or as actual failures, and resign themselves to feeling that things will not or cannot be better or improve.

Some additional specific symptoms that coaches might experience as a result of too much stress include: (1) waking up tired, even after getting what should be sufficient sleep, (2) arguing or being combative with family, friends or staff members, (3) seemingly being afflicted with many tiny illnesses all the time (headaches, colds, backaches or stomach problems), (4) having difficulty concentrating on the tasks at hand, (5) being tired or listless during the day, (6) possessing poor eating habits or loss of appetite, (7) always complaining, being overly critical, or voicing negative comments about others, (8) blaming others for one's own deficiencies or difficulties, (9) ineffective in time management, and (10) not being able to accomplish assigned tasks and responsibilities of the job. Naturally, there are other symptoms of burnout and extreme stress. Similarly, just because a person experiences one or more of these symptoms does not necessarily mean that the individual is unduly stressed out or is experiencing burnout on the job (Stier, 1987).

However, it is wise to pay attention to how one reacts to one's coaching job and to the pressures and stressors associated with the competitive position. Coaches need to be prepared to recognize the negative symptoms of stress if they are to avoid the serious catastrophic consequences of being burned out. And, it is necessary to take steps to prevent such stressors and pressures from having too negative an effect upon your professional life, your personal life and your physical and mental well being.

Coping Strategies in Overcoming or Combating
Stress and Pressure on the Job

> **COACHING CONCEPT #110: Concentrate on the present and the future—not on the past.**

The key to dealing with the debilitating effects of stress is to recognize the stressful situation one is in and focus on the present and the future rather than on the past (one cannot change the past). Burnout and the symptoms of burnout should be aggressively addressed on both the social (personal) and the professional levels. Strategies for reducing the negative effects or consequences of stress, that is, burnout, typically revolve around making changes (establishing different priorities) in terms of how one views one's life and what one does at (1) work, (2) at home, (3) in recreational pursuits (hobbies) and (4) in social involvements.

> **COACHING CONCEPT #111: Assume a proactive stance in dealing with the negative consequences of stress and burnout.**

It takes work and effort to successfully combat the stressors and pressures associated with coaching in a competitive setting. This means that coaches should assume a *proactive stance* in combating stress. One way this can be accomplished is by taking classes, attending clinics or enrolling in workshops that teach time management skills as well as relaxation or mental training skills.

Some other successful strategies of combating stress and pressure associated with coaching include (1) eating right, that is, consuming the appropriate amounts of salt, calcium, meat, carbohydrates, fats, alcohol and caffeine, (2) stop being a workaholic (learn time management and set realistic goals and priorities), (3) participate in an appropriate exercise regimen, (4) take positive steps to rekindle one's enthusiasm by developing new areas of interests outside of sports (a relaxing and enjoyable hobby), (5) take advantage of family, friends and colleagues as support mechanisms by scheduling personal time with others, (6) eliminate use of tobacco products, (7) assume new or different responsibilities within the world of sports, (8) recognize and take pride in one's accomplishments—(and those of one's athletes) in and outside of sports, (9) rethink the reasons why you entered the coaching profession in the first place, and (10) learn to take one day at a time while enjoying being alive in this wonderful world (Stier, 1988).

COACHING CONCEPT #112: There are many factors that affect coaching competency.

Determining when One Should Continue to Coach or to Leave the Profession

Manos (2001, p. 72) provided some criteria to use when coaches are weighing the options between quitting the profession or to remain as a coach. Toward this end, it is suggested that one should consider hanging up one's shoes when the following factors come into play:

1. Practices become really tedious.
2. Actual competition is no longer satisfying, fun.
3. The sport is no longer challenging.
4. You do not look forward to working with the team.
5. You are anxious to leave practice each day.
6. You are physically and/or mentally exhausted each day.
7. All of your athletic/coaching goals have been reached.
8. You have no real athletic/coaching goals.
9. The technical aspects, especially the Xs and Os, are a chore and not a challenge.
10. You no longer enjoy discussion strategies and tactics with fellow coaches.
11. You no longer desire to improve your skills and competencies.
12. The problems (boosters, athletes, parents, administrators) associated with coaches are a real drain mentally.
13. If there are other goals or challenges that take priority over coaching.
14. You become overly frustrated with everyday problems.
15. Stress and pressure become so pervasive that your mental and physical health suffers.
16. You overreact to problems or challenges.
17. You find yourself leaving conflicts unresolved.
18. You cannot accept losing or losses.
19. You feel that the time, effort, sacrifice and problems are not worth the coaching experience.

On the other hand, Manos (p. 23) suggests the follow factors might convey the feeling that one should remain as a coach (retire or take a break from coaching), for example, when:

1. Coaching is still an exciting experience.
2. Coaching is still a gratifying, fun or satisfying experience.
3. You find your friendships and colleagues satisfying and rewarding.
4. You still enjoy the challenge of coaching.
5. You still enjoy the challenge of competition.
6. You look forward to practices and working with athletes.
7. You look forward to games and contests.
8. Coaching serves as a vehicle for professional growth.
9. The financial compensation is adequate.
10. You receive satisfaction and fulfillment from your relationships with athletes, parents, boosters, administrators, etc.

BEING SUCCESSFUL AS A COACH

The thrill of victory.

Being a successful coach is the result of a combination of many things, including luck, being in the right place at the right time, possessing adequate and accurate technical knowledge of the sport being coached, making correct and timely decisions, being willing to take calculated risks, having the capacity to relate to and understand the needs and motivational triggers (hot-buttons) of one's own athletes, as well as being able to work with and influence the behavior and opinions of other individuals and groups.

Being Evaluated as a Coach

All coaches are evaluated. They are evaluated by their players. They are evaluated by parents. They are evaluated by fans and boosters. They are evaluated by members of the community. And, they are evaluated by school authorities, including the athletic director, and the AD's superiors. Of course, it is the assessment by the athletic director and school authorities that really count, although what others think about the coach should not be dismissed out of hand. This is because the opinions and feelings of others (influential community members, fans, boosters, parents, athletes, etc.) can often have a significant influence (impact) upon school administrators and board members and their opinions of the coach.

It is important that coaches (assistant coaches and head coaches alike) understand fully how they will be evaluated as coaches and what criteria and procedures are to be used in the evaluation process. There are numerous formal evaluation instruments that schools utilize to assist in the evaluation process of coaches—head coaches, assistant coaches, coaches who are employed full time by the school district or college/university, as well as part-time coaches. See appendix C for samples of several types of evaluation forms that represent a sample of instruments used in the assessment process of coaches.

COACHING CONCEPT #113: Evaluation of coaches is an on-going process, a continuous assessment that continues through the school year.

These assessment instruments are often used in conjunction with personal observations, feedback from athletes as well as non-athletes, won/loss records, recruiting efforts, coaching behaviors, academic status of athletes, behavior of athletes, and self-evaluation data, etc.

Listed below is a partial list of criteria used by many athletic directors and school administrator to evaluate/assess the skill, competencies and achievements of those working as coaches.

1. The number of students who try out for your team
2. The number of athletes who stay on your team
3. The number of athletes who flunk out (become ineligible)
4. The number of athletes quit the team
5. The sportsmanship of athletes
6. The sportsmanship of coaches
7. The achievements of your athletes (on and off the proverbial playing field)
8. The number of complaints about the coach (from athletes, parents, others)
9. How well the coach cares about one's athletes, even if a youngster can no longer play
10. How well the coach cares about and treats *all* of one's athletes, *not just the starters*
11. Whether the coach makes significant mistakes in critical decisions
12. Whether the athletes make significant mistakes in critical decisions
13. Whether the athletes look like they are coached

14. Whether the coach *looks* and *acts* like a professional coach/teacher
15. The number (and type) of injuries on your team
16. How one conducts the athletic banquet
17. The extent to which one's athletes are in excellent condition
18. Whether the coach stays at the cutting edge in terms of knowledge, skills, etc
19. How much student-athletes actually improve
20. Physical conditioning of athletes

Pressures and Perceptions of Pressures on Coaches

In a study of Texas high schools it was found that principals reported the frequency of coaches' firings/dismissals based on a variety of reasons. The researchers also found in their survey of coaches' perceptions of why coaches were dismissed/fired were in general agreement with the actual reasons as stated by the principals. The study found that coaches were removed from their coaching duties based on the following: losing (47%), poor relations (13.2%), school board/administrative direction or decision (8.8%), failed duties (6.4%), poor student relations (5.2%), or, misconduct or sexual misconduct (4.9%). Poor teaching was the reason for being fired that was cited the least by principals. The study also revealed that over two-thirds (67.2%) of the high schools fired a coach during the previous year. Firings were more common among larger high schools (Miller, Lutz, Shim, Fredenburg and Miller, 2005).

There has been an interesting series of studies (conducted over period of some 40 years) of high school athletic programs (surveying principals) looking into why coaches have been fired or dismissed and the number/percentages of coaches that have been fired (Lackey, 1977; Lackey, 86; Lackey, 94, Scantling & Lackey, 2005). The 1977 study found 44.8% of the school studied had fired or dismissed a coach during the time that the principal had served at the school. The major reasons for the firings were: poor relationships with athletes and students (23%); improper personal habits of coaches (21%); not winning (16%); poor public relations (15%); poor classroom teaching (13%). All other reasons accounted for the remaining 12% (Scantly and Lackey, 2005).

A decade later, coaches had been fired or dismissed at 25% of the schools (Lackey, 1986). The reasons for the dismissals include: poor won-loss records (32%); lack of technical coaching skills (31%); human relationship problems (16%); and improper conduct of the coach (12%). An interesting aspect of this study was that the researcher asked the principals to rate how much pressure existed on coaches at the school. The findings revealed that pressure was great at 8% of the schools; was somewhat great at 27% of the schools; moderate at 46% of the schools; little at 13%; and, no pressure at the remaining 2% of the schools surveyed (Scantly and Lackey, 2005).

Fast forward to the 1994 study (Lackey) and this investigation found that coaches were fired at 38% of the schools surveyed. The coaches were dismissed for the following reasons: poor coach-player relationships (19%); inability to motivate players (16%); poor public relations (14%); improper conduct by the coach (13%); inadequate social relationships with parents and patrons (10%); failure to win (9.5%); and other reasons (18.5%) (Scantly and Lackey, 2005).

The 2005 study published by Scantly and Lackey revealed that coaches were dismissed at 56.4% of the schools surveyed. In terms of why coaches were fired, the principals provided the following reasons, in rank order: poor coach-player relationships; lack of coaching skills; improper conduct of the coach; not winning enough; and (tie) poor public relations and inability to motivate players (Scantly and Lackey, 2005).

DEVELOPING POSITIVE WORKING RELATIONSHIPS

> **COACHING CONCEPT #114: No person is an island—coaches need to work with other people in the daily conduct of their business.**

Coaches, by the very nature of the tasks and challenges facing them as coaches, must be able to work harmoniously with others. Just as John Donne (1623) wrote that *no man is an island entire of itself, every man is a piece of the continent, a part of the main* so too must coaches realize that they cannot operate outside of the mainstream of society. Coaches do not exist in a vacuum. They do not operate in isolation. They are not really self sufficient. They must not be perceived as acting as a so-called *Lone Ranger*. Rather, they must work with and are dependent upon other individuals, groups (large and small) and organizations if they are to be truly effective in their job. Who are these people with whom the coach must work?

Coaches need to treat others (including those in the community) in a professional and positive fashion. A concept that is prevalent in the business world dealing with *customers* also has implications for coaches. The concept goes like this: for every 100 customers who are mistreated, only 5 complain. However, 66 of these unhappy customers will never patronize that business again; and, they also complain to an average of 10 other individuals about their negative treatment. Coaches should substitute the words fan or community member or parent for the word customer in the above example. The moral is simple; treat everyone in a just and professional manner lest others feel (correctly or incorrectly) injured and put upon.

COACHING CONCEPT #115: Don't create adversarial relationships with others—you may have to work with them in the future.

There is a wide range of possible individuals and groups that can have an effect upon or can exert influence upon a coach. Wise and experienced coaches make an effort to develop positive working relationships with each of these groups and/or individuals. One is rather foolish to limit the potential benefits by taking a stand-offish posture or distant position when it comes to working with these groups and individuals. And, one truly invites disaster (quite literally) when a confrontational or adversarial stance is taken in working with others. This is because the coach must still work with these same individuals or groups tomorrow and the day after tomorrow and the following day. To quote an old sage, *don't cut off your nose to spite your face*. Yet, that is exactly what coaches do when they become confrontational in their relationships.

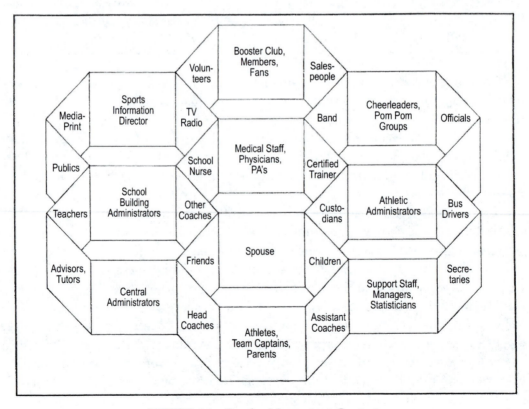

FIGURE 6.1—Coaches' Important Contacts

There are some coaches who indicate that there isn't time to devote or spend *(waste)* with these constituencies, co-workers or peers. They further exert that whatever time is available must be spent on the really important activities such as actual coaching tasks. This is hogwash and the coach who takes this stance is indeed foolish. One must realize that the really important and immediate task at hand, in fact, the imperative objective, *is the development of a sound working relationship with others, starting with one's own players*. The ultimate objective, the creation of a successful athletic program or team, is dependent upon first having positive relationships with those constituencies involved in or associated with the coaching process. A partial list of categories of individuals with whom coaches might find themselves working in their capacity as a coach is depicted in figure 6.1. A more definitive listing is provided below.

Athletes	Team Captains
Parents	Student Managers & Statisticians
Athletic Administrators	Sports Information Director
Building or School Administrators	Media Representatives
Central Administrators	Other Coaches in School
Support Staff	Other Coaches at Other Schools
Plant Management Staff—	Teachers in One's Own School
Grounds keepers	Academic Advisers & Tutors
Custodians	Cheerleading and Pom-Pom Groups
Secretaries	& Advisers
Bus drivers	Band & Musical/Band Director
Medical Staff	Officials
Team Physician or PA	College Coaches
School Nurse	Fans, Booster Clubs and Community
Sports Medicine Trainer (NATA)	People
Physical Therapist	Salespeople
One's Own Head Coach	One's Own Spouse and Children
One's Own Assistant Coach(es) &	Business Owners
Family Members	Sponsors and Advertisers

ESSENTIALS OF A SUCCESSFUL ATHLETIC PROGRAM

There are five essential components or ingredients of any good sports program whether the level of competition is at the junior high level, the high school level or the collegiate level. These components are (1) motivated and skilled athletes, (2) qualified and competent coaches combined with skilled teachers in the classrooms, (3) interested and supportive parents, (4) knowledgeable and helpful athletic and

Team sports require cooperation, sacrifice and unselfishness.

central administrators, and (5) loyal and informed community supporters, fans and boosters.

These five components may be likened to five legs propping up a large table, figure 6.2. All five ingredients are necessary in order to have a truly successful program (represented by the table top) which meets the needs of the athletes as well as other constituencies associated in some capacity with the athletic program. If any of these five ingredients are missing or fail to provide adequate support—the table top begins to tip and eventually falls (the program fails).

The table top itself represents specific programmatic aspects or facets of the total athletic program. These programmatic areas number six and include: (l) the academic program (classes) in the school, (2) the sports medicine support services, (3) the actual athletic practices and games, (4) the support or counseling help available for the student-athletes in terms of class work, drug education, personal and family problems, etc., (5) the recruitment and retention efforts exerted on behalf of student-athletes, and (6) the promotions, public relations and fundraising activities undertaken on behalf of the sport program.

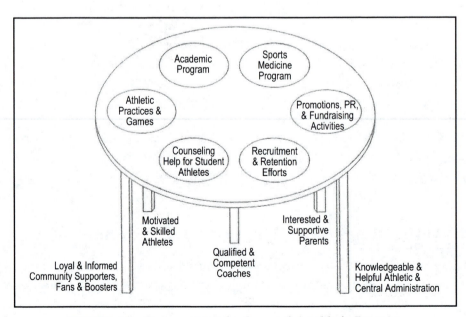

FIGURE 6.2—Components of a Successful Athletic Program with Essential Supporting Resources

If the above five support components or ingredients are effective and efficient in providing quality assistance and support on behalf of the six general programmatic areas within the school, there is a good chance that the total athletic and academic experiences of the student-athletes will be positive. However, it takes the effort, the work and dedication on behalf of the athletes themselves, their parents, coaches and teachers, administrators and community people—all working together—to provide a meaningful and satisfying sports experience. Through the efforts of these individuals and groups, worthwhile programmatic facets of the total athletic program will be possible. As a result, there will be a quality athletic program and the athletes will benefit from their experiences with the total program.

WORKING WITH ATHLETES

> **COACHING CONCEPT #116: The most important interpersonal relationship for a coach is that with the athletes**

Coaching effectiveness essentially depends upon the ability of the coach to relate to, work with and motivate one's own players. Coaches must remember that they are to coach athletes and not a specific athletic sport (Coakley, 1990). There is a subtle but nevertheless a very real distinction when it comes to being a competent and skilled coach. Successful coaches help their athletes to perform at the highest level that they are capable of performing—in actual competition. To accomplish this necessitates that the coach be capable of determining the needs of each individual athlete on the team. Then, the coach should attempt to meet these needs, if appropriate and possible.

If coaches are able to successfully motivate their athletes and have them reach their potential or near potential, it becomes almost immaterial as to the type of offense or defense that may actually be implemented. If athletes are performing at the level at which they are capable, it becomes almost inconsequential which specific strategies or tactics are employed by a coach. Teams have won championships in every sport using a variety of offensive and defensive tactics and varying strategies. What is important is how well the individual athletes are performing their skills both individually and as a member of the team.

> **COACHING CONCEPT #117: In chalk talk, whoever has the chalk last, usually wins—in real life, whoever has the best players, usually wins.**

One has to have the talent to win. A story about a big-time football coach will help illustrate this point. At a large coaching clinic, a highly successful coach displayed two films of athletic teams running the identical offensive play. The first film showed the athletes executing the play off tackle and the fullback was seen breaking through the opening created by the offensive linemen for a 23-yard gain. The speaker diagrammed on the blackboard the details of the blocking scheme and the running pattern. He emphasized how the play was designed to work. And, he showed again the successful film with the runner gaining 23 yards.

Then, the coach ran a second film which showed a different offensive team executing the identical football play against a different defensive squad. In this film, however, the fullback—instead of gaining 23 yards—was thrown for a 6-yard loss. What was the difference? The same offensive play was used by both teams. The same defensive alignment was used by the two defensive teams. The only difference was the quality of the players, the talent of those athletes on the field. In the second film, the offensive team was composed of athletes who did not possess the skills, the talents and the attributes that the offensive athletes in the first film possessed. As a result, the running play was a miserable failure as shown in the second film. Why? Because the determining factor was not the offensive play itself. The play involved a well thought out attack and strategy. *The athletes themselves were the determining factor.*

COACHING CONCEPT #118: Confidence in the coach and in the coach's strategies and tactics is essential if the players are to excel.

Coaches need to be able to gain the confidence of their athletes and develop a positive relationship, one that facilitates the motivational process needed in the coaching arena. *Being a successful coach today requires that the individual be part father and mother-figure, part psychologist, part promoter, part counselor, part motivator, part fortune teller, part administrator—and it doesn't hurt one little bit if one can walk on water.*

Athletes Serve As Public Relations Conduits

Another reason why coaches need to relate to athletes is because these youngsters are the prime source of first-hand information about the coach and the athletic program. Athletes talk and confide to their parents, their friends and other people in the community. Athletes' friends talk to their own parents and to other people in the community. And their friends talk to other people in the community. The image of the coach, to a certain extent, depends upon what athletes communicate to their own parents. And it is the parents who in turn are excellent and effective conduits of information, opinions, biases and prejudices to an even wider circle of individuals within the community, figure 6.3.

> **COACHING CONCEPT #119: Keep one's ego in check and emotions under control—never allow one's emotions to cloud one's judgment.**

It does not take long at all for a specific image or reputation of a coach, whether accurate or not, to spread throughout a community. And, the source of many of these impressions, these images, these reputations, are the individual athletes on the team. For who better is in a position to know the coach than the athletes? Who spends so much time with the coach in practice and game situations? Who is in the best position to speak from personal experience and to be viewed as an important source of accurate and timely information about what the coach does and does not do (and the reasons therefore)? This doesn't mean that the perceptions held by the athletes are accurate. It only means that athletes are viewed as a prime source of information about the coach and the team and that they are usually not reluctant to share their opinions and convictions.

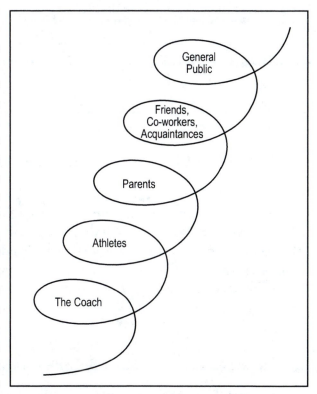

FIGURE 6.3—The Spiral of Information about the Coach

> **COACHING CONCEPT #120: In coaching—perceptions frequently are as important as reality.**

Coaches need to remain cognizant that perceptions are as important as reality. If the athletes believe that something is true about the coach, then for those athletes it is true. Thus, coaches need to be sure that the images or the perceptions of their behaviors are accurate. If athletes feel that the coach doesn't care about them as individuals and are only using them to win games for the coach, this perception (hopefully erroneous) should be addressed early and be corrected. If the perception persists, the negative atmosphere that will surely follow can significantly disrupt the relationship between the coach and the athletes. Consequently, it is important for coaches to closely monitor not only how they act but how their actions are viewed, accepted and perceived by others, especially by their own athletes. For in reality, coaches are held responsible (liable) for their athletes' perceptions.

COACHING CONCEPT #121: Athletes have many opportunities to make judgments of their coaches—consequently, coaches need to be excellent role models.

HOW ATHLETES PERCEIVE COACHES

The way coaches behave, in practices, in game situations and out among the general public, has a significant impact on how they are viewed by their own athletes. The fact that coaches spend so much time with athletes on a daily basis, throughout the sport season as well as out-of-season, means that athletes have many opportunities to see their coaches during the best of times as well as during the worst of times. As a result, coaches need to exercise caution in terms of the image or message(s) that they project, consciously and unconsciously, as a result of their behavior on and off the playing field or court.

Positive Characteristics and Behavioral Activities of Coaches

Stewart (1993, p. 24) defined coaching behaviors into three distinct categories. First, cognitive behaviors, those actions that demonstrate knowledge in terms of teaching, communication and development skills. Second, affective behaviors, those actions dealing with feelings such as caring, praise, love, humiliation as well as favoritism and motivation. And, third, physical behaviors, those actions or activities that:

> ". . . could be quantified or documented with 'hard' examples such as stressing winning above everything, showing up late or unprepared for practice, stressing doing your best, using player input and being available for the player on and off the field."

Using these three broad categories, Stewart (1993) surveyed 87 students in an introductory college class in coaching and asked them to identify those actions or behaviors of coaches which characterizes their favorite and least favorite coaches. Both positive and negative behaviors were obtained for the three categories of cognitive behaviors, affective behaviors, and physical behaviors.

COACHING CONCEPT #122: Athletes have very definite ideas and opinions as to the qualities and characteristics of a competent coach.

These previous athletes identified their favorite (most effective) coaches as individuals who had knowledge of the rules and the sport, could communicate that knowledge to their charges, and who demonstrated a real concern to help the individual athlete improve. Additionally, these coaches were identified as being demanding but also incorporated fun in their practices and workouts. Ineffective coaches failed to exhibit the above characteristics and also demonstrated a decided lack of communication skills with their players.

It was interesting to note in the Steward (1993) study that there were more descriptors in the affective domain than the other two. In this category, the favorite coaches were those who were good motivators, were honest and forthright in their dealings with the players, demonstrated confidence and pride in the athletes, as individuals and as a group. Negative coaches, on the contrary, were viewed as lacking enthusiasm, not being consistent in their actions and in the treatment of others, having no self control themselves, and, in general, lacking respect for others and not caring much about others. These ineffective coaches were characterized in terms of being egotistical, inconsistent, impersonal and biased regarding their athletes while practicing humiliation towards others, including athletes.

In terms of the physical behaviors of coaches, those coaches viewed as positive stressed individual and team improvement without involving extreme criticism, humiliation or belittling. These coaches tended to work one-on one with their athletes and employed little screaming or yelling at the athletes. Contrary, the negatively viewed coaches were supporters of the concept that winning is all important and is the ultimate objective. These coaches also demanded respect without earning same, abused some athletes on the team, ran up scores over hapless opponents, and finally, motivated via fear and degradation in practices and contests.

A comprehensive listing of the positive coaching behaviors as viewed by former athletes and presented by Stewart (1993, p. 28) is provided below:

1. Is a good teacher
2. Teaches every player (individual attention), every aspect of the game

3. Teaches sportsmanship and respect for opponents
4. Stresses the total student athlete
5. Knows the sport
6. Sets weekly goals (reasonable) for the team
7. Uses good training techniques
8. Stresses fundamentals first, winning second
9. Is a good motivator
10. Establishes trust
11. Cares about players, both on and off the field
12. Is patient, supportive and interested in players as individuals
13. Lets athletes know where they stand (feedback) and why
14. Is upbeat and encouraging
15. Knows how it feels to have a bad performance
16. Is understanding and honest
17. Builds confidence in athletes
18. Cares for the development of the total person/athlete
19. Creates pride in players and builds confidence among athletes
20. Is enthusiastic
21. Is proud of players regardless of whether the team wins
22. Shows and earns respect
23. Is fair and consistent in dealing with athletes, especially in the areas of who starts and plays and in disciplinary matters
24. Listens to players
25. Stresses individual and team improvement
26. Allows athletes to make some decisions
27. Does not dwell on an individual's or the team's mistakes

Conversely, a summary of the specific negative coaching behaviors identified by these former athletes includes (Stewart, 1993, p. 28):

1. Infrequently praises athletes
2. Does not consistently enforce rules and shows favoritism (not fair)
3. Is a poor listener (poor communicator)
4. Does not spend time with unskilled players
5. Does not provide positive reinforcement (poor motivator)
6. Humiliates and ridicules athletes
7. Is impersonal, uncaring and self-centered

8. Stresses winning at all costs
9. Is egotistical and disrespectful of athletes
10. Does not demonstrate good sportsmanship
11. Does not take responsibility when things go wrong
12. Is too dominant, too critical, exhibits a bad temper (expresses anger), and doesn't care about the athletes (selfish)
13. Is intolerable of opinions or questions from athletes
14. Demands respect without earning it
15. Is uninformed and not knowledgeable about the sport itself

Anshel (1990) cited numerous negative coaching patterns or behaviors which coincided with some of the negative behaviors identified by Stewart (1993), including:

1. Failure to treat players as individuals
2. Ineffective communication
3. Inability to explain coaching strategies and decisions to athletes
4. Inability or unwillingness to justify role status of non-starters
5. Failure to utilize assistant coaches in an appropriate manner
6. becoming angry at athletes and acting out the anger

COACHING CONCEPT #123: Athletes are very emotional and biased about their involvement in sports.

From the above discussion and lists, it is clear that athletes do indeed make decisions (form perceptions, opinions and create attitudes) regarding the professional competency level as well as the personal qualities or characteristics of their coaches. These perceptions and attitudes are based upon their own personal relationships with these coaches, both in practices and games, as well as from their dealings with their coaches outside of the actual coaching dimension. These perceptions can also be reinforced or diminished through interaction and communication with other athletes and individuals within the community itself.

And, these athletes can also perpetuate and disseminate their own perceptions and feelings by sharing same with others, including other athletes, students, news media, parents, and innumerable individuals within the school itself and in the community. Thus, it certainly behooves the coach to demonstrate positive coaching behaviors, those that will reinforce the instructional efforts of the coach when dealing with their athletes, both on and off the court. Each student-athlete must be treated individually in a fair and consistent manner. This is so the athlete is able to build and maintain self-respect and a positive self-image while at the same time experiencing the opportunity to increase one's knowledge and skill in the sport being practiced. Failure to do so places the individual coach in jeopardy of being perceived as exhibiting negative coaching behaviors, behaviors that will serve as significant deterrents to a successful athletic experience for both the athletes and the individual coach.

WORKING WITH PARENTS

Just as it is imperative that the coach possess a good working relationship with athletes, it is paramount that coaches are skilled in working with the parents of athletes (Cardone, 2001). Towards this end, it is suggested that the parents of the individual athletes be involved and kept informed of those aspects of the coaching scene involving their offspring. This means that there should be opportunities for parents to be involved in the program. Parents need to be made aware of the program's objectives. They should know what is expected of the athletes and themselves. And, they should understand in general terms why things are done the way they are done with the athletic program and team.

Sabock (1991) indicates that parents often subscribe to the so-called *every concept*. This means that some parents are so possessive of their children as athletes that they act as if they desire or expect that their youngster will not only play in *every* game, but will start *every* game, play *every* minute and will score *every* point.

COACHING CONCEPT #124: Familiarity breeds confidence—get to know the parents of your athletes.

Another reason why it is important to have a working relationship with parents and feel comfortable in communicating with them is that it is sometimes more difficult for these same parents to develop hostility towards the coach if they have had contact and meaningful communication with the mentor. Coaches are frequently criticized for any number of things (actions and inactions). Many times such criticism is unwarranted and unjustified. However, if there is no communication, no personal relationship or prior experience with the coach, the parents have no basis on which to form an opinion or to make a decision other than what they hear from others (rumor, hearsay, etc.).

COACHING CONCEPT #125: It is more difficult (although not impossible) to be stabbed in the back by an individual if that person knows you well.

Thus, it just makes good sense to have good working relationships and open communication lines with parents. Parents can be strong allies as well as terrible adversaries. Parents of athletes can have a significant impact on how others in the community view the coach. Parents, most of whom are tax payers and active members of the local community, have many opportunities to influence the thinking of others regarding the competency of the coach (both in and out of the school setting).

There is another very important reason to develop positive relationships with parents and to help them, as parents, understand what the athletic experience is all about. The reason is that these parents can provide assistance and support to the coach who works with their youngsters. If parents are knowledgeable and supportive of what the coach is trying to do, there may be less of a challenge in dealing with their youngsters.

Developing relationships with parents requires some work and effort on the part of the coaching staff. But, it is effort well spent in terms of fruitful benefits accruing to the coach and the team. Positive relationships need to be established between the coach and the players and the parents, figure 6.4. It is essential that parents, athletes and coaches possess a harmonious working relationship if the coaching environment is to be enhanced. The chances for a productive and meaningful athletic experience (for all concerned) are greatly improved if the parents, the athletes and the coaching staff all work together, feel comfortable communicating with each other, and understand the rationale for which decisions are made.

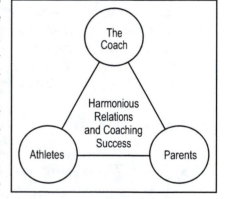

FIGURE 6.4—The Triumvirate
of Coaching Success

Strategies to Establish Good Relations with Parents

There are many strategies available to coaches in establishing good communication avenues with parents. Remember, one of the major objectives of any coach is to develop meaningful relationships with the parents of those athletes on one's team. Another major objective is to create an educational opportunity in which parents are able to learn more about the coach, about the coach's philosophy and style, and about the team and the sports program. This sharing of information and knowledge can be accomplished through deliberate, planned efforts or can be accomplished as a result of incidental or accidental contacts with parents. Any effort that will facilitate the realization of these two objectives is worth considering. A partial list of some effective tactics or strategies in developing positive relations with parents and educating the parents is provided below.

1. Meeting parents—on an individual basis
2. Scheduling a pre-season mass meeting with parents of athletes
3. Creating team newsletters for parents and team
4. Periodically making a personal phone call to parents or taking time to speak to parents when the opportunity presents itself
5. Conducting periodic open forums for parents, athletes and fans
6. Scheduling the end-of-year athletic banquet for the team

Meeting Parents—on an Individual Basis

Coaches would do well to take the time to personally meet the parents of their athletes in a one-on-one situation. This might mean scheduling a meeting at school or even visiting the parents in their home for 20-30 minutes. During this visit the coach's expectations of the parents of the athlete could be discussed as well as overall goals and objectives of the athletic team. Similarly, the coach could use this opportunity to share any special information regarding any number of things, such as coaching style and tactics, emphasis being placed on school work and general behavior of all team members. The coach could also share with the parents the tentative role as a member of the team that the coach sees at that point in time regarding their son or daughter.

Scheduling a Pre-season Mass Meeting with Parents of Athletes

Other coaches have scheduled a meeting of all parents (with or without their youngsters being present). Frequently this is a pre-season meeting held at the school. At this meeting, some of the same information cited above could be shared in terms of what is expected by the coach of the athletes and the parents. An explanation of team rules and regulations can be given and clarified. And, there can be a sharing of coaching strategies and tactics, etc., with the parents. A real effort should be made by the coach to get to know the parents and vise versa.

Parents need to feel comfortable that their children are in good hands and that their youngsters will be given a fair shot at participating on the team. The opportunity for questions and answers from the parents can be time well spent. Also, giving parents the coach's home phone number with the invitation to call whenever there is a concern or question can prevent much misunderstanding and can help create an atmosphere of openness and fairness.

COACHING CONCEPT #126: The ultimate decision making authority for both team selection and individual playing time rests with the coach.

This does not mean that the coach is inviting parents to call up each week and question or complain why Johnny or Mary did not play in the previous game. Nothing of the sort is implied. In fact, coaches should use these face-to-face meetings (on an individual basis or in a group setting) to specifically deal with that type of potential confrontational situation by sharing the coach's philosophy or feelings regarding the type of questions that would be appropriate and those deemed inappropriate. Some coaches believe that they never want to be asked by a parent why a youngster is not getting more playing time. Other coaches feel that they will discuss this topic in general terms with a parent(s) but only on a non-game day and in the privacy of the coach's office. Still other coaches feel quite comfortable in responding to that type of question at almost any time it is brought up by a parent.

COACHING CONCEPT #127: Coaches should let parents and others know their philosophies and their expectations.

The point is that coaches should convey their preferences and expectations in any number of ways with parents. These meetings must involve two-way communication, however. Parents intensely dislike being lectured to with no opportunity to share information or feelings with the coach. Such meetings can also enable coaches to listen to the parents' thoughts, concerns and expectations. Since communication is a two-way street, it is imperative that coaches listen and actually hear the message that the parents are attempting to convey. Providing written handouts to the parents can be especially helpful in providing crystal-clear documentation that can be referred to by the parents (and athletes) throughout the season.

A Success Story Involving a Pre-season Meeting Between Parents, Athletes and Coaches

Inviting athletes along with their parents for an individual family meeting or for a general team meeting at school can create very positive results. For example, a woman who coached the varsity boys' volleyball team at a rather large high school scheduled a mass meeting early in the season at the school. The parents and their youngsters were invited to attend the 45-60 minute gathering. Light refreshments were served and for the first 10-15 minutes all those in attendance had an opportunity to informally visit with one another. The head coach and her assistant wisely spent this time circulating around the room introducing themselves to those parents whom they did not already know and reacquainting themselves with those parents they already knew.

The formal portion of the meeting began with the head coach welcoming everyone and stressing how important it was for the athletes and the program to have the visible support and backing of the parents. She went on to explain her coaching philosophy and the value of sport participation for her charges. She was very specific in terms of her expectations of the athletes in terms of punctuality, academic progress in school, general behavior on and off the court, commitment, team work, etc. The parents were informed of the team rules and the range of possible penalties for specific violations. And, information was distributed regarding the drug education program which the athletes would be involved in during the season.

The assistant coach was also formally introduced to the group and was given an opportunity to share information regarding her role and responsibilities as an assistant coach. Parents were asked by both coaches for their continued support, especially in the area of team rules. And, the parents were encouraged to ask questions during the meeting as well as anytime during the season.

COACHING CONCEPT #128: Too many cooks can spoil the pot—one does not coach by committee.

The head coach also pointed out that selecting the initial team, determining which athletes were to play at what point in time, as well as what position the athletes were to play, were strictly decisions to be made by the coaches. The adage *too many cooks spoil the pot* was cited to make the point that there are some areas in which only the head coach can be the decision maker. The coach spoke in general terms of the qualities she looked for in selecting players as well as in making substitutions during a game. It was emphasized that a coach frequently must make substitution decisions based upon both subjective and objective decisions in light of the experience of the coach. Finally, the coach reminded parents that the coaches see the players during two to three hours of intense practice each day and it is only the coaches who see how the athletes react during practice and under pressure, on a daily basis. Thus, it falls solely upon the shoulders of the coaches to make these types of decisions.

Creating Team Newsletters for Parents and Team

Another method of maintaining a close communication link, although admittedly a one-way avenue, is to create a periodic team newsletter that is sent to parents. The tone and contents of the newsletter can set the stage for how the publication is accepted by the parents and how helpful it is to the coaching staff. It is imperative that it should not be a complaint or bitch sheet. It should not publicize or mention negative aspects at all. Rather, the content should be upbeat and should emphasize the positive aspects of the team and the team members, both players and coaches. The publication can also provide insight into upcoming opponents as well as general information about the sport itself at all levels.

The real purpose of the newsletter is to keep the parents (and the athletes) informed and even entertained. Parents often have a need to feel a certain professional and personal familiarity with the coaches. Parents should possess an idea of what the coaching staff is attempting to do and what they are all about—both personally and professionally. With computers and any number of suitable software packages available today, coaches have a wide range of possible choices to select from in their efforts to create such a professional looking newsletter.

Periodically Making a Personal Phone Call to a Parent or Taking Time to Speak to a Parent When the Opportunity Presents Itself

There are many opportune times during a season or during the calendar year when it might be advantageous for a coach to simply pick up the phone and initiate a chat with selected parents. The topic of conversation might be almost anything. It could relate to the team or to the parent's youngster or just be about a general sport or non-sport topic. The purpose of the effort is to develop and foster a positive personal and professional relationship between the parent(s) and the coach.

COACHING CONCEPT #129: Strike when the iron is hot when it comes to communicating with and fostering relationships with parents.

Similarly, coaches should not shy away from opportunities to physically walk up to a parent(s) and begin a friendly conversation. These opportunities might present themselves both on and off the athletic grounds. For example, coaches might run into parents in the grocery store, in a department store, or in a specialty shop. Additionally, coaches might take advantage of the opportunity to visit with and strike up a conversation with parents when the latter are at a game, at a booster function, at a school play or art exhibit, or at any other school sponsored function, regardless of whether or not the actual activity is sports related.

Conducting Periodic Open Forums for Parents, Athletes and Fans

Planning for and publicizing so-called *Open Forums* can go a long way in helping to establish communication channels with parents and with other constituencies. What exactly are *Open Forums?* These are meetings that are scheduled periodically, monthly or bimonthly for example, throughout the season or the calendar year. At these well-advertised meetings parents, athletes and fans can come together to listen to the head coach (and assistants) and ask questions. The coach can use these opportunities to provide insight into the current status (potential bragging opportunities) of the team, the coach's perspective of the season and the team, information about upcoming opponents and challenges, and the general state of affairs in that particular sport at that particular level as well as at other levels of competition.

These meetings can last anywhere from 30 to 90 minutes and should be informal. They can be held in a classroom or gymnasium. Or, the gatherings can be held in a restaurant setting or even in the home of the coach. Regardless of where the *Open Forums* are held, the major objectives remain the same. That is, an opportunity for people in the community to get to know the coach and for the coach to become familiar with them through the medium of the *Open Forum.*

End-of-Year Athletic Banquet for the Team

The traditional athletic banquet that takes place at the conclusion of a team's season is an excellent opportunity for the coach to augment the communication efforts between the coach and parents as well as to highlight the past season happenings and next year goals (Mano, 2002). The culminating team banquet is an opportune moment to recognize and thank the numerous individuals who helped make the just concluded season the success that it was. Even if the team was not successful in garnering more wins than losses there are innumerable opportunities for a coach to cite successes with the team and with individuals in areas other than the final won/loss record. It is imperative that the coach be cognizant of and takes time to mention both small and great accomplishments and achievements of individuals and of the team itself. And, coaches need to take time to publicly thank and give recognition to those individuals who played a special role in helping the team (especially the unsung heroes whose work is behind the scenes and is frequently not seen or appreciated).

The team banquet is also an occasion for the coach to be seen in a slightly different light by players and by others. The atmosphere can be relaxed and casual with everyone having an enjoyable time. This team banquet or gathering is the capstone for the season and as such it should be a rewarding experience for everyone and a source of pride to those who were a part of the team and who supported the program. It should also be a beginning for the next year's season, and as such, emphasis should be placed on creating a positive environment for off-season work and commitment. The future starts here.

Everyone associated with the team, athletes and non-athletes, parents, supporters, teachers, administrators, etc., should all be made to feel that they have had and continue to have an important role to play in the happenings associated with the team. Most of all, the players and their parents, should be made to feel that they indeed played a significant and productive role with the team.

WORKING WITH ATHLETIC AND SCHOOL ADMINISTRATORS

Coaches must have a positive relationship with their athletic directors. The key to this relation is communication, interaction and trust (Berkwitz, 2006). Sharing with one's boss your goals for the sport is a step in the right direction. So too is making the athletic director aware of what is happening with your sport, your team—your needs, your plans, etc. And, being aware of the goals and objectives of the boss is equally important if one is to be an integral part of the AD's *team*.

COACHING CONCEPT #130: Never surprise your athletic director—always keep your boss informed of your intended actions in controversial situations.

Kicking a person off a team has the potential for being a very controversial situation. In such situations, it would behoove the coach to keep the athletic director and other appropriate administrators apprised of the situation. In short, sometimes it is smart to run through your intended plan of action with your athletic director to be sure that there are no hidden agendas or problems lurking in the background of which you are unaware. Naturally, the coach must adhere to the established policies and procedures dealing with the removal of a current athlete from a team.

If there is a potential problem with removing a current member of the team from the squad, it is better to be forewarned by the athletic director ahead of time than to find out about it after the coach had told the athlete to leave. If you inform your athletic director of your intentions and receive the go-ahead—should you end up sitting on the *end of the proverbial limb*—your athletic director will be sitting right there alongside you. It is easier to survive controversies when you have the full backing and support of your athletic director.

COACHING CONCEPT #131: Find out what your boss wants—then do it.

It is important that coaches understand exactly what is expected of them by their superiors, both athletic administrators and school administrators. If the athletic director has specific expectations of a coach, it would be foolhardy indeed for the coach to fail to find out the expectations much less to actually disregard them. If the athletic or school administration expects that athletes will perform satisfactorily in the classroom and graduate on time, the coach had better become actively involved and very supportive of the academic progress of the players. If the expectation is that the athletes will behave like gentlemen and ladies, the coach had better work to insure that the youngsters indeed exhibit such behaviors. The priorities of the administration, one's bosses, had better become the priorities of the coach if friction is to be prevented. And, friction with one's superiors is the last thing a coach needs.

COACHING CONCEPT #132: Never disagree in public with established policies, procedures and practices—adhere to the company line.

Coaches demand respect and agreement in terms of their players. There can only be one coach. Similarly, coaches need to adhere, especially publicly, with the stated policies, procedures and practices of the sport and the academic administration and hierarchy. It is perfectly permissible to disagree in private with one's boss or the administration, as long as it is astutely done. However, this disagreement must not leave the confines or the privacy of the administrators' offices. Coaches must be very careful lest they share any professional disagreements that they have with others, especially administrators, with outside individuals or groups. Loyalty is very important and coaches must adhere to the established or stated company line.

As pointed out in Chapter 2, there are three professionally accepted options open to that individual if a coach strenuously disagrees with a policy, practice or decision. First, the coach can actually leave the position and take a job elsewhere. In essence, the coach vacates the unacceptable or uncomfortable environment. Second, the coach might choose to accept the decision of one's superiors even though not agreeing with the decision. This happens all the time to every employee in every type of organization. Third, the coach can stay in the position and work within the system, within the confines and restrictions of the organization and administrative structure, to change those policies, practices and decisions. This effort requires both time and political savvy on behalf of the coach. The fourth option involves unprofessional activity on behalf of the coach. That is, the coach stays and back bites, complains, criticizes and undermines the efforts of the administration in those areas in which the coach does not agree.

The Importance of the Chain of Command

The *chain of command* concept gained initial acceptance within the military arena. However, a *chain of command* actually has a vital role in most organizations. It is indeed "essential for effective management, accountability, and a strong means of operation" (Hoch, 2005, p. 12). In the absence of the so-called *chain of command* the school would find parents or athletes or boosters or fans merely heading straight to the top of the organization. In a school system, this might involve the principal, or in some cases the superintendent or board members. In the case of a college or university, this might involve a dean, vice president or president.

For coaches, the *chain of command* means that the assistant coach should not bypass one's head coach and (secretly) go directly to the athletic director or principal. To do so will be to effectively *back stab* or to *cut off the knees* of one's boss, the head coach. Similarly, if the head coach jumps over the athletic director and goes directly (without the knowledge of the AD) to the superintendent, one has effectively has violated the *chain of command*. This type of behavior is unacceptable, unprofessional and a breach of high ethical standards.

COACHING CONCEPT #133: Never jump the chain of command—be completely loyal.

Those who coach in a school setting must develop sound working relationships with administrators, both athletic administrators *(athletic directors, associate and assistant athletic directors)* and school administrators *(high school level: principals, assistant principals and superintendents; college level: deans, vice presidents, presidents)*. These are the individuals who have significant impact upon coaches' professional lives. Administrators, including school administrators, central administrators *(office of the superintendent or office of the president)* and athletic administrators all make numerous decisions that have a direct as well as indirect effect upon coaches, their athletes and the sport program. The absence of positive working relationships and excellent communication channels between coaches and administrators can literally place coaches between a rock and a hard place.

COACHING CONCEPT #134: Keep administrators abreast of your activities and achievements—don't be afraid to toot your own horn.

Thus, it is important that these administrators know what their coaches are attempting to accomplish as coaches. Similarly, it is important that administrators are kept up-to-date in terms of what coaches are doing in respect to their teams and athletes. This is because these administrators are then in a much better position to make intelligent decisions in those areas that are so vital to the sport scene in their schools. Coaches should keep their administrators up-to-date and current via written and verbal means as well as by actions on and off the playing and practice fields.

Coaches should attempt to make sure that administrators know what (goals, objectives) they as coaches are attempting to accomplish, how (means, methods) they are going about it, and the reasons (why, justification) for these goals and objectives. And, most important, coaches need to professionally but assertively make known their individual and team achievements and accomplishments to administrators on a consistent basis. There is a thin line between being an overbearing braggart on the one hand and being professionally assertive on the other when it comes to informing administrators (bosses) of one's activities and making the administrators aware of one's competency level and achievements as a coach. Successful coaches with longevity have learned to master this all important interpersonal skill. Those coaches who have not learned to master this competency frequently find themselves being former coaches.

COACHING CONCEPT #135: The athletic director is the most important school administrator for the individual head coach.

The most important school administrator, insofar as the head coach is concerned, is the athletic director (AD). This is simply because of the number and the importance of all of the decisions that an athletic director makes on a day-to-day basis. It is the athletic director, on the high school level, who evaluates the individual head coach and who provides recommendations to school administrators, including the principal, and in some instances, to the superintendent of schools. On the college level, it is the athletic director who makes personnel recommendations to a dean, a vice president, or even the president of the institution.

COACHING CONCEPT #136: Coaches must develop positive and professional relationships with the school's support staff and other professional personnel.

SCHOOL'S SUPPORT STAFF AND PROFESSIONAL STAFF

Coaches must work almost on a daily basis with support staff within a school. These individuals include custodians, bus drivers and secretaries. It also includes the school nurse, the team physician, the physician assistant (PA), the band director, the cheerleader adviser, etc. In short, coaches, due to the very nature of their job, would do well to take the time to develop positive working relationships with all such support and professional personnel.

Custodians, Grounds keepers, and Bus Drivers

It has often been said that having a positive and productive working relationship with custodians and grounds keepers is absolutely critical to the success of a coach, both on the high school and college levels. While this might be a slight exaggeration, many coaches believe that the most important support staff person in a school for a coach is indeed the custodian or grounds keeper. This is because of the fact that coaches are dependent upon the assistance of custodians and grounds keepers in the upkeep and preparation of the facilities that are essential for both practices and contests.

COACHING CONCEPT #137: **The custodian usually plays a major role in helping a coach manage day-to-day facility and equipment challenges.**

Experienced coaches cite the general principle that custodians and grounds keepers are not only in a position to help the individual coach on a daily basis (often going well beyond their actual job descriptions) but, and more importantly, these support personnel, by the nature of their jobs, are in a position to hinder or sabotage a coach more than any other support staff. For example, how many coaches have not forgotten to do something like request the bleachers be set out (or in) for a certain date? How many coaches have never needed a custodian to go beyond the call of duty (job description) to help the coach solve a problem? How many custodians are in a position to have direct, yet informal, contact with athletic and school administrators not to mention central administrators? Thus, it behooves coaches to go out of their way to develop a positive relationship with those members of the custodial and grounds staff. The same case can be made for bus drivers or other support staff.

One hand does wash another. When coaches are willing to go the so-called extra mile in working with custodial staff, the custodians are more likely to reciprocate, thus resulting in a much smoother operation for the sport, for the coach and for the athletes themselves. One key to this mutually supportive relationship is the ability for coaches to treat custodians with respect and professional courtesy while recognizing them (formally and informally; privately and publicly) for their all important work and contributions to the team. People like to be appreciated and coaches who express sincere appreciation are using a powerful motivating tool.

COACHING CONCEPT #138: **The secretary is also a most important professional support staff member for coaches.**

Secretarial Staff

Special mention should be made regarding the secretarial staff. In some high schools as well as many colleges there may be a separate secretary for the athletic department. However, in others, the athletic department may share a secretary with another department or office. In any case, the head coach of a specific sport usually does not enjoy the privilege of having the exclusive use of a private secretary except in the very large sports programs on the college level.

Thus, it is important that coaches develop a professional relationship with the athletic department's secretarial staff. Ditto in the case where the secretary in another department is assigned to do selected tasks for a coach. This is because of the invaluable assistance and service that a secretary can provide to any coach. Conversely, a secretary is almost always in a position to hinder and frustrate, deliberately or incidentally, the wishes of a coach. It is the rare coach who does not need the assistance of the secretary to cut through the red tape or to correct the errors within a letter or to suggest a better or faster way of accomplishing something within the bureaucracy of the educational institution or system.

Coaches also need to be sensitive to the fact that a secretary cannot always drop what is currently being worked on to immediately tackle a coach's task—no matter how important or urgent the coach may think it might be. Just as with the custodial staff explained above, showing sincere consideration, courtesy, and appreciation for the work of the secretary are key ingredients in developing a sound, professional working relationship with this all important support staff person.

Working with the Team Physician, Physician Assistant, School Nurse, Sports Medicine Trainers and Physical Therapists

Coaches just cannot get away from having a constant, on-going, professional relationship with members of the *medical team*, whether the individual is the school nurse, the team physician, physician assistants (PA), a certified sports medicine trainer (NATA), or a physical therapist. The facts of life are such that some athletes, at any level, will indeed become injured and will need medical attention. It is necessary that coaches understand their role and the roles of members of the medical team when athletes are injured.

COACHING CONCEPT #139: Take advantage of physicians and other medical personnel who are trained and experienced in sports medicine.

It is important for coaches to recognize that there are physicians who are trained and knowledgeable in the area of sports injuries. On the other hand, there are physicians who do not have such training and understanding. As a result it behooves the coach to take advantage of those physicians who are knowledgeable and experienced in treating sports related injuries and illnesses. This is because physicians trained in sports medicine are frequently able to get the athletes back on their feet and ready for competition very quickly while still safeguarding the health and well-being of the athletes.

Both the role of the coach and the role of medical professionals should be clearly delineated and articulated by the administrators overseeing the sports program. Frequently such written policies, practices and procedures are provided in the departmental handbook of an athletic program. When one considers the health and physical welfare of the athletes, it is the responsibility of coaches to take advantage of the specialized knowledge of the members of the medical team associated with any sports program. Of course, all coaches should have a valid American Red Cross First Aid card and the CPR card and be competent to render first aid in the event of an emergency or injury. Coaches must also be knowledgeable (and feel comfortable in seeking the services of knowledgeable individuals) in the area of prevention of injuries and accidents to their athletes.

In looking at the area of potential accidents, injuries and illnesses with athletes, coaches need to be knowledgeable and competent in terms of (1) preventing injuries and accidents to their athletes, (2) recognizing the nature of the injuries to athletes and rendering, when appropriate, immediate and temporary care until the arrival of the appropriate medical personnel, (3) following the recommendations of the medical personnel as to when the injured athlete may return to practice and/or competition, and (4) working and cooperating with the trained medical staff (nurse, physician, certified trainer, physician assistant, physical therapist) in any rehabilitation activities prescribed for the injured athletes by the medical personnel.

In May of 2007 the National Athletic Trainers' Association and the NCAA released the findings of a national study (covering the previous 16 years) on college injuries in 15 different sports. The study revealed that the sports with the highest rate of injuries included: football, wrestling, and men's soccer. The lowest rates included: softball, women's volleyball, and baseball. There were four key findings as revealed in the report which included: (Sports Medicine, 2007).

1. Injuries to the lower extremities accounted for more than half of college athletes.

2. Injuries during preseason occurred two to three times more than injuries during in-season.

3. Injury rate during competition was higher than during practices.

4. There was an increase in the rates of concussions and ACL injuries during the 16 years which were covered by the study (although better identification and reporting efforts might have skewed the data regarding concussions and ACL injuries).

COACHING CONCEPT #140: It is the responsibility of trained medical personnel—not the coach—to determine when injured or sick athletes can return to practice and competition.

One of the perennial concerns facing coaches today when an athlete is seriously ill or injured is how long the athlete will be lost to the team. Typically, schools follow a policy that states whenever an athlete misses a practice or a game due to illness or injury (or when the athlete sustains a serious injury such as loss of consciousness even for a few seconds) that athlete must be seen by a trained medical personnel (physician, nurse, physician assistant or certified trainer) before that athlete is given the green light to play again. The decision of when such an athlete can return to practice or actual competition *must be left up to the medical personnel, never the coach.* This policy is implemented to protect the athlete from being pressured or allowed to return too soon following an injury or illness, thereby exacerbating the situation still further. Just as the coach would be outraged should an athletic trainer attempt to usurp the duties and responsibilities of the coach by attempting to make coaching or strategy decisions for the players, the coach must not attempt to perform the duties rightfully allocated to the trainer. The coaching should be left up to the coach and the medical decisions should be left up to the appropriate medical team member, that is, physician, physician assistant, nurse, physical therapist or certified trainer.

The reason that a coach should not make the decision whether or not such an injured or ill athlete should return to competition or practice is that the coach has a vested interest in getting the youngster back as soon as possible. Additionally, the coach usually does not have the appropriate medical training necessary to make such a decision. Let's face it; there is extreme pressure on the coach to get athletes back for practice and competition as soon as possible after an injury or serious illness. This is especially true when the youngster is a star athlete whose presence is viewed as necessary for victories on the playing field or court.

Functions of an Athletic Trainer

The athletic trainer, in those sports settings where the coach is fortunate enough to have direct access to a certified trainer, has the responsibility of preventing injuries which includes program organization and administration of the sports medicine office; recognizing and evaluating injuries on the spot for those athletes who are hurt; injury management (working with other medical personnel) and treatment of the youngster; injury rehabilitation until the player is capable of returning to competition fully recovered; and, providing education and counseling to both athletes and members of the coaching staff.

WORKING WITH OTHER COACHES, TEACHERS, AND COMMUNITY MEMBERS BUILDING RELATIONSHIPS

Coaches must be able to deal with and work with several other groups within a school setting. If you are a head coach with assistants, then you must be able to work with them. If you are an assistant coach, you must be capable of dealing with your own head coach. Whether or not you are an assistant or a head coach, whether you are a teacher in the school or work outside the school setting, there is a need to be able to work with teachers in the educational institution. Similarly, you must have a good relationship and develop a mutual respect, as a member of the total educational *team*, with other coaches within your own school. Finally, there are those coaches from opposing schools with whom you will have both a competitive relationship as well as a professional, cooperative, and even collegial relationship.

Working with One's Own Head Coach

> **COACHING CONCEPT #141: Always be loyal as an assistant coach—loyalty is the basic expectation of an assistant coach.**

Assistant coaches have been called, next to United States Marine recruits at Parris Island (South Carolina), the *lowest form of life on planet earth* (Stier, 1992). This is because as assistants they are at the beck and call of the head coach and are expected to perform all of those duties assigned to them by the head coach. Frequently, such duties include those that no one else wants to do. Sometimes, the tasks are those mundane, unglamorous, tedious assignments that are given to the new kid on the block. Nevertheless, the assistant coach must be willing to perform these and other tasks in an effort to demonstrate competency to the head coach so that other, more interesting and important responsibilities might be assumed in the future.

The two major traits that the assistant coach should demonstrate is that of (1) complete loyalty to the head coach and the (2) ability to increase one's mastery of the game under the tutelage of the head coach. It is essential that the assistant coach is completely loyal to the head coach. Should an assistant coach professionally disagree with the head coach on some matter, it is naturally acceptable for this to be discussed with the head coach, in private. However, when the head coach has made a decision it is the responsibility of the assistant coach, regardless of whether or not the assistant coach agrees, to *totally support* the position of the head coach. To do otherwise would be unprofessional and disloyal.

COACHING CONCEPT #142: There is no such thing as a free lunch—assistant coaches must be willing to pay dues.

An assistant coach should have the ability to increase one's mastery of coaching skills and competencies. With added experience and exposure to the head coach, the assistant should be in a position to continually increase one's coaching abilities. As a result, assistant coaches who demonstrate that they are able to perform specific tasks are usually given additional tasks, with greater responsibilities. Thus, assistant coaches are able to increase their sphere of competencies as well as the level of their coaching skills. However, assistant coaches must be able to demonstrate that they can do the tasks that have been delegated to them before they can expect to be given more important tasks and more sophisticated responsibilities by their head coaches.

In short, assistant coaches need to be humble in their role as assistants (don't be a *know it all*); they must be willing to accept delegated tasks without grumbling; and, they must be competent in performing all delegated responsibilities so that they will continue to be given ever increasing responsibilities as a member of the coaching team.

Working with One's Own Assistant Coach(es)

COACHING CONCEPT #143: Head coaches have an obligation to recruit, train, evaluate, reward and motivate assistant coaches.

Head coaches have the responsibility to recruit qualified assistant coaches. However, the responsibility of the head coach does not end when the assistant coach is on board. There is a continuing responsibility on behalf of the head coach to motivate, train, educate and evaluate the assistant coach so that the assistant not only performs satisfactory but will also improve as an assistant coach. Head coaches assume a very important role in respect to their assistants, that of teachers and mentors. Successful and highly competent assistant coaches can be a real boon to the head coach. It is up to the head coach to see to it that each assistant's potential is realized. This can be an awesome responsibility.

COACHING CONCEPT #144: Loyalty is a two way street.

Loyalty is an essential ingredient in any relationship between two human beings. This is especially important with head coaches and assistant coaches. The relationship between the head coach and assistants is a special kind of relationship which can either significantly enhance the coaching experience or can severely hinder the effectiveness of the coaching scene. In exchange for loyalty, dedication and hard work on behalf of assistants, the head coach must assume responsibility for helping the assistants gain additional knowledge and experience. Assistant coaches should blossom under the careful tutelage of the head coach. Loyalty is a two-way street. Assistants should be loyal to the head coach and should provide significant support to the coaching efforts for the team. On the other hand, head coaches should be loyal to their assistants and need to provide significant support to the assistants by educating them further in the finer parts of coaching and providing opportunities for the assistants to expand their areas of expertise and gain meaningful experience.

An Exemplary Example of Professionalism by a Head Coach

Bear Bryant of Alabama fame was known as one of the toughest competitors in college football. However, he also was capable of showing great respect and love for former assistant coaches, his protégés. An extraordinary display of sportsmanship and professionalism was seen in 1969, when Gene Stallings, a former player and assistant to coach Bryant, beat his mentor in the 1969 Cotton Bowl 20-16. After the game, "Bear Bryant rushed to the middle of the field, grabbed his old player, and lifted him up in the air for the world to see" (Masin, 1993, p. 10). Although winning was very important to the Bear, so too was sportsmanship, loyalty and professionalism.

COACHING CONCEPT #145: Head coaches should secure assistant coaches who compliment their strengths as well as support their weaknesses and compensate for their deficiencies.

Good assistants are worth their weight in gold in the eyes of a knowledgeable head coach. In selecting assistant coaches, a head coach should attempt to choose competent and dedicated individuals who are highly motivated and willing to work hard and continue to learn. Additionally, a head coach should look for assistants who possess skills and competencies which will not only compliment the head coach's strengths but will also compensate for any weaknesses or deficiencies which the head coach might possess.

For example, if the head coach is not particularly strong in terms of conditioning and physical training aspects of the sport, but is exceptionally strong in strategies, tactics and motivational side of coaching, the assistant coach(es) should be expert(s) in the areas of conditioning and training. Or, if the head coach is an expert in a specific style of play (man-to-man defense in basketball, for example), but is weak in terms of zone defensive tactics, the head coach had better select an assistant(s) who is (are) very knowledgeable in zone type defenses (and how to beat them).

As a head coach with an assistant or assistants, you have a significant responsibility. You are professionally *obligated* to help each of your assistants, in exchange for their loyalty and their competent assistance and service, grow professionally as coaches. You are the teacher and mentor for your assistants. It is your responsibility to fairly and honestly distribute work, tasks, and responsibilities to your assistants in accordance with their abilities, interests and potential for further professional growth.

COACHING CONCEPT #146: Head coaches should provide to assistant coaches opportunities for growth and professional experience as a reward (motivation) for competency and as partial compensation.

COACHING CONCEPT #147: Head coaches must have empathy with their assistants' spouses and other family members.

Effective head coaches also recognize the importance of not neglecting the spouses and other family members of assistant coaches. Head coaches must insure that the assistants and their families are treated and accepted as part of the sport family. Head coaches must be willing to show appreciation and understanding of the many and varied sacrifices that spouses and children of assistant coaches must make. Enabling the family members of assistant coaches to feel a part of the athletic program is essential.

The assistants must also be made to feel of value. They must know that they are an important component in the overall success of the sport team. They

Appropriate and timely strategy sessions can win games.

must be given opportunities to experience success and failure (without being guil-lotined on the spot). And they must be given the opportunity to develop ever-greater skills and competencies in all aspects of coaching the sport.

> **COACHING CONCEPT #148: Head coaches are mentors to their assistants.**

Being a mentor to one's assistants means more than merely helping them grow professionally in terms of their own skill as coaches—it does indeed include this. However, the responsibility of a head coach goes beyond this and includes helping the individual assistant coach advance to the next level of coaching. This means helping the assistant coach get a new position, perhaps at a different school or different school system. This might mean providing positive recommendations on the individual's behalf in support of the person's candidacy for another job and actively campaigning on behalf of the assistant.

This might also mean advancing an assistant coach, for example, from the freshman level to the junior varsity level. Or, this might mean promoting the freshman coach to the position of junior varsity head coach. In short, the head coach owes it to each assistant to be an advocate for that individual when the assistant desires to move up within the coaching ranks. Naturally, this assumes that the assistant coach is competent, is loyal, and is ready to assume a different coaching role with greater responsibilities and scope.

> **COACHING CONCEPT #149: One of the best compliments a head coach could receive is for an assistant to move on to an even better job.**

A wise and experienced head coach is noted for indicating to new assistants that if the assistants work hard, are loyal, are competent, are able to develop higher level coaching skills, and can play an integral part in the total sport program as assistants—they will be given (in light of their abilities and interests) ever increasing opportunities to develop and improve their coaching skills and to demonstrate their competencies. And, when these assistants are ready to move on in their careers to greener pastures, the head coach will do all that is possible to see to it that they will get the best coaching jobs possible. The head coach does this by being an active advocate (providing recommendations and leads for coaching positions) for an assistant who is ready to advance to the next level in coaching, whatever that next level might happen to be.

> **COACHING CONCEPT #150: One hand washes another when it comes to relationships between head coaches and their assistants.**

Talk about motivation! No wonder potential assistant coaches flock to serve under this head coach. However, the professional relationship is a two-way street between the head coach and the assistant coach. In this type of situation, one hand does wash another.

> **COACHING CONCEPT #151: Head coaches should visibly demonstrate their appreciation for all of the work their assistants contribute to the overall program.**

It is one thing to tell assistant coaches how much you, as the head coach, appreciate their efforts and sacrifices. It is another to actually show appreciation in a demonstrative fashion. One example of a head coach providing a meaningful and significant *thank you* to his assistants revolves around the story of a head football coach who was invited to deliver a major speech at a national coaching clinic. After giving the presentation, the head coach went to the motel where his assistants were staying and called a brief meeting. When all of the assistants gathered around, he gave each of them an equal share of the money he received for his speaking at the clinic. And, he told them that the team would not have been successful that season and he would not have been invited to speak at the clinic had it not been for their extraordinary contributions to the program. He closed the meeting by thanking the coaches and suggesting that they spend the money on their families since they, too, sacrificed much during the season.

Working with Team Captains

The topic of team captains can sometimes be controversial. Whether or not coaches should use captains is an individual matter for each coach. There may be advantages and disadvantages for the coach and for the team depending upon any number of factors that can only be determined by the individual head coach. Since many sports require that a captain be designated before the start of an athletic contest, many coaches are faced with the challenge of how to select captains, what to do with them, when to select them, and what should their duties be as captains.

The head football coach at Traverse City, Michigan, decided to do something with the selection process of his captains. Specifically, the coaching staff was tired of captains being chosen based on popularity. So, the staff instituted a process where candidates who wanted to be captains were interviewed in a formal interview process by members of the coaching staff. The candidates for captain donned suits and ties and were interviewed in a formal setting (Captains, 2003).

Other schools have instituted formal training seminars for captains on leadership. Many State associations as well as the NFHS have implemented such seminar training programs to provide guidance, education and meaningful experience for all captains in a school (Cardone, 2004).

Exactly what are, or should be, the roles of the team captain or captains? Is the selection of captains merely a popularity contest? Should they be selected by

Big time sports require big time facilities.

the team members or by the coaching staff before the season? Should captains be selected following the end of the season by their peers in recognition of their leadership and achievements during the season? Should captains be selected by the coach on a weekly basis as an indication of their superior contributions to the team during the previous week?

COACHING CONCEPT #152: Responsibilities of captains must be clearly delineated and understood by coaches, captains and the remaining team members.

In some instances, coaches have found that captains are more trouble than they are worth. If the role of the captain or captains is not clearly delineated, there can be many problems for the coach, for the captain(s) and for the team. All too frequently, the pressure placed on captains can be immense and can cause problems for the captains as well as for their teammates if the expectations are not clearly spelled out by the coaching staff. Should the captains serve as an actual liaison between the team members and the coaches? What exactly does the term liaison mean? How do the athletes interpret it?

Are captains merely conduits through which messages can be relayed from coach to team members? Or, are captains expected to relay their interpretations of messages, attitudes and feelings from the team members to the coaches? What power, if any, does a captain have on a day-to-day basis with other athletes? Can power go to the head of a youngster who is designated as captain for the season? Can captains change from the start of the season to its conclusion?

Designated Captains for the Week or Multiple Captains

COACHING CONCEPT #153: Choose captains carefully—athletes can frequently change in terms of their behavior, their attitudes and in their dedication.

Student-athletes can change in terms of their behavior and dedication during the season. They frequently change in behavior and attitude from month to month and from week to week. Some change daily in terms of their dedication and contributions to the team and the sport program. More and more coaches are leaning towards restricting the duties or responsibilities of captains. A number of coaches also are selecting different captains weekly throughout the season on the basis of which athlete performed at an exceptional or extraordinary level (on and off the field or court) during the previous week. Essentially, these weekly captains have as their sole responsibility to be the designated captain for the next competition.

In this manner, there are more opportunities for numerous athletes to be able to be captains during the year. Coaches can also appoint multiple captains for a specific game or contest. Those athletes who become *captain for a day* are also not placed under any significant pressure to serve as a formal leader with one's peers throughout the long season. And, the coach can reward and motivate individual athletes by designating them as captains for the game either just prior to the game or on the day before the contest itself.

Other coaches, wary of difficulties and challenges of having youngsters carry the burden of being captains for the entire season; allow the team to select an honorary captain or captains after the conclusion of the season. This is in addition to having different athletes serving as designated game captains during the season. In this way, the captain (or captains) can be recognized for their outstanding contributions over the length of the season to the team *after the fact*.

Working with Student Managers and Statisticians

COACHING CONCEPT #154: Coaches need to carefully select, motivate, train, and publicly reward student managers and statisticians.

Perhaps the greatest unsung heroes of any sports program are the student managers and statisticians who work so diligently in support of the team, the coach and the individual players. It is a foolish coach who does not expend extra effort in soliciting, training, evaluating and motivating quality managers and statisticians. Managers are typically called upon to do a myriad of tasks—tasks that are often mundane, boring and unappreciated. Managers often become jacks of all trades in their efforts to help the coaching staff and the team.

Student managers can be given responsibility for insuring that proper athletic and medical equipment and supplies are available for practices and games, making sure that water is available for the athletes during games, helping the coaching staff keep track of time during practices, taking care of uniforms and practice gear, maintaining inventory of supplies and equipment, keeping a variety of records for the staff, among others.

Student Managers and Statisticians Are Neither Maids Nor Servants

It is the job of the coaching staff to insure that student managers, who volunteer their time and efforts, are treated in an appropriate, professional manner. These managers should receive sufficient motivation and reinforcement in addition to appropriate training so that they can take pride in their contributions to the overall team efforts. The players must be instructed in terms of how to treat and work with the team manager(s). It is important to stress that the student managers are an integral part of the team itself. They are not slaves or maids for the athletes or coaches. For example, no one is above picking up one's own towel and uniform, not even star athletes (or coaches). The managers are there to help the coaching staff and the athletes in a variety of different and difficult tasks. However, student managers must never be abused or misused.

At the college level the statisticians are usually provided by the Sports Information Office. However, for those coaches who find themselves without the services of a trained pool of competent statisticians provided by the sports information director's (SID) office it can be a monumental chore to obtain students or other volunteers to keep accurate stats. Yet, sports cannot be properly conducted without accurate and timely records and statistics of team and individual achievements and performances. Hence, it is imperative that the services of skilled statisticians be secured and retained throughout the season.

Working with the Sports Information Director (SID)

In those college or university athletic programs that enjoy the presence of a professional sports information director (SID), it is imperative that the coach develop a close professional relationship built on trust and a willingness to cooperate with the SID. The SID is responsible for all public relations, publicity and statistics for the athletic programs, including individual teams and staff members. The SID is also responsible for press releases, media guides, tip sheets, statistics, etc. In some programs, the SID also has responsibility for promotions and some fundraising activities. However, in the larger colleges and universities these latter two areas frequently fall under the office of an assistant or associate athletic director (for development).

In some smaller colleges, there may not be an official SID working within the athletic department. Instead, many such institutions assign some of the typical responsibilities of a sports information director to an employee working in the office of public relations or some other related department. At the high school level and in youth sports, there are usually no SIDs, period. At these levels it is usually the responsibility of the coaching staff to assume the role and duties of the so-called SID. The construction and dissemination of press releases, media guides, tip sheets, statistics, game scores, etc., to the various media is a time consuming and challenging job. To be a coach, having responsibilities for these areas in addition to coaching duties, without significant assistance, can be a real burden. Yet at the interscholastic and youth sports levels, coaches find themselves writing press releases and providing statistics and other types of communication to area news media and to their own fans, supporters, parents and boosters.

Working with News Media Representatives

Coaches must be skilled in dealing with the news media.

Whether or not a coach enjoys the support of having a sports information director, it is nevertheless important to work with representatives of the news media (Hoch, 2001). On the high school level where many coaches are their own SIDs, it is imperative that they find out what information is needed by the various media reporters and announcers. "When communicating key messages to the media, one must understand the manner in which the media function" (Pedersen, Miloch & Cothran, 2006, p. 12). Naturally this will vary depending on whether the news media is radio, television or some form of print publication (daily, weekly, suburban, penny-saver, or local, state or national, etc.).

Once coaches find out what information the media representatives need in order for the media representatives to do their jobs, it is the responsibility of coaches to see that the media people get what they want. This might mean that only certain statistics following games are needed. This might mean that the statistics and game information is to be presented in a specific format to make the media person's job that much easier. This might mean that the coach (or manager or other volunteer) is to only call the scores in during a specific time period.

In short, find out what each of the media outlets in your area needs and wants and then get it to them, on time, accurately, and in the correct format. Remember that in today's media world "statistics alone don't usually impress a sports reporter unless they compare with the all-time greats at a state or national level" (Brewer, 2005, p. 50).

COACHING CONCEPT #155: Good, interesting stories sell newspapers and magazines, not mere numbers or statistics

---

When writing one's own news release, use the traditional inverted pyramid style (Stier, 1994). That is, include the most important information in the first few lines or paragraphs. Additional lines or paragraphs should add to the story or supplement the main points. The reason for the inverted pyramid style is that should the story be too long for the paper or the radio or television spot, the announcer or reporter can easily edit the news release by simply lopping off the extra paragraphs or lines by starting at the bottom and working backwards.

COACHING CONCEPT #156: Be aware of the foot-in-mouth syndrome when dealing with the media.

There is always the very real danger of putting the proverbial foot in one's mouth when dealing with the media, especially when one is being interviewed. Coaches must be very careful what they say and how they say it when being interviewed by representatives of the news media. A *good rule to follow is to think before speaking.* That may not sound very original but that doesn't mean it is not an important concept. Also, keep your responses short and to the point. Don't drag out your responses. Don't allow the reporter to put words in your mouth. If the reporter asks you (a common ploy) if what you said or meant was *so and so*—if the reporter's statement does not exactly reflect what you said or what you meant, it is up to you to say so—and be assertive in doing so.

An example of a coach putting a foot in one's mouth might be Bobby Knight, former coach at Indiana University, when he was being interviewed by Connie Chung on April 25, 1988 during an NBC-TV special. Coach Knight made an insensitive remark dealing with rape (indicating that if rape was inevitable, one might as well relax and enjoy it) that drew much national criticism in the following days, weeks and months. Think of how others might interpret what you say and speak accordingly.

Working with Other Coaches within the School

Every coach in a school setting, whether a head coach or an assistant coach, must be capable of working with other coaches who coach other sports in that school. There is always the possibility of internal jealousies and bickering existing when competitive, driven, energetic coaches work and compete together. The potential for confrontational or adversarial relationships among coaches is exacerbated when there is internal competition within the school for resources such as money, equipment, supplies, facilities, support, fans, publicity, recognition, etc.

COACHING CONCEPT #157: Coaches within a school must work with their peers, and be seen to operate in a cooperative manner rather than a confrontational mode.

It is important for an individual coach to be able to get along with fellow coaches within one's own school. This is frequently difficult. It is always challenging. Yet, coaches need to relate in a positive way with their fellow coaches who are similarly competitive, highly motivated, energetic and goal oriented. They need to operate and be seen to operate in a cooperative mode rather than a confrontational manner. One of the worst raps an individual coach can get is to be unresponsive and uncooperative with one's fellow coaches within one's own school or institution.

As a result it is imperative that one goes out of one's way to help other coaches and to facilitate coaches in the performance of their tasks. A coach who is, or is perceived as, an obstructionist or an egomaniac serves no useful purpose at all and can only significantly hinder and frequently jeopardize one's own position as a coach in the school.

A Generous Coach Helps Others

A wrestling coach at a medium size university overheard the gymnastic coach complain about having forgotten the tape for the mats to be placed under the apparatus for that afternoon's gymnastics competition. The wrestling coach had a meet himself the very next day. However, upon hearing that the gymnastic coach was in a very serious predicament, through his own forgetfulness, with no available mat tape, this wrestling coach volunteered to help out. The wrestling coach had the tape taken off of the wrestling mats which he had already set up for the next day's competition and given to the gymnastic coach for use in the meet to start some four hours later.

The wrestling coach then proceeded to track down additional mat tape from colleagues at a nearby university in time for his wrestling tournament the next day. Why did the wrestling coach go out of his way to help a fellow coach? Was it out of the goodness of his heart? Was he just naturally generous? Did he feel sorry for the gymnastics coach who had made an error and misplaced the mat tape? Was the wrestling coach helpful and generous because he himself might need assistance sometime in the future and wanted to be sure that other coaches in the department might be willing to help him?

Maybe all of the above reasons played a part in the wrestling coach's decision to go out of his way to lend assistance to a fellow coach. Certainly other coaches and the athletic director became aware of the wrestling coach's generosity and professionalism. This was because the wrestling coach did not keep his action a secret—he discreetly made sure that other people became aware of what he had done.

One important point here is that the act of kindness, of assistance, was performed. Another important concept to remember is that the wrestling coach made sure that others became aware (in an appropriate fashion) of his extraordinary efforts to help solve a fellow coach's problem. Politically speaking, it was important for the wrestling coach that others became aware of the fact that he was a team player and was willing to go out of his way to help another coach.

There is more to this story, however. You would think that the gymnastics coach would have been so thankful of the assistance from the wrestling coach that he would have expressed sincere thanks and appreciation to the coach and would have indeed helped spread the word regarding the generosity and kindness of the wrestling coach. However, this was not the case. In fact, the gymnastics coach *never* thanked the wrestling coach. Instead the gymnastics coach literally grabbed the mat tape from the wrestling coach and acted as if the gymnastics team deserved to receive the mat tape from the wrestling team even though it was the gymnastics coach who had forgotten his own tape. Even after the gymnastics meet the gymnastics coach never thanked the wrestling coach. In fact, the gymnastics coach never mentioned the incident again.

Did this behavior become common knowledge among other coaches and athletic administrators? Did this behavior and attitude by the gymnastics coach help create a negative reputation for the gymnastics coach? The answer to both questions is *yes*. Within a week almost every athletic staff member knew what had happened. Doubtless, every athletic staff member had an opportunity to form an opinion regarding the actions of both the wrestling coach and the gymnastics coach. One does not have to be a rocket scientist to anticipate that other coaches did not go out of their way to help that gymnastic coach in the future.

Working with Coaches at Other Schools

Coaches must be aware of the importance of developing a positive, professional relationship (mutual respect) with coaches at other schools, including those coaches with whom they compete in athletic competition. Granted that opposing coaches are competitors but this does not mean that a wholesome, cordial, respectful and professional relationship cannot exist between competing coaches. The coaching fraternity is a close knit, loosely organized group of individuals. Coaches need to be treated with respect. Coaches who run up the score against opposing teams quickly earn a specific type of reputation within the coaching ranks. Coaches who are egomaniacs, stuffed shirts, and who are uncooperative with their peers at other schools soon find themselves correctly identified as prima donnas and are treated as such by the coaching fraternity.

Working with Teachers within the School

Every coach in a school setting will be placed in a situation in which it is absolutely necessary to work with teachers. Selected teachers have daily contact with one's athletes. It is often necessary or advisable for coaches to remain in close professional contact with these teachers for any number of reasons. Coaches need to remain aware of the academic progress or lack thereof—of their athletes. Coaches need to become immediately aware of any problems individual athletes are experiencing in individual classes. Coaches need to communicate to teachers an honest concern about the academic progress of their athletes and can accomplish this by remaining in close professional contact with individual teachers. Coaches, especially those in the fall and spring seasons (coaches of soccer, field hockey, baseball, softball, track, etc.), frequently are in a position of requesting that their athletes receive permission to be absent from class (or leave early) due to scheduling of home or away contests.

In many academic settings, coaches follow the practice that (and some schools have the policy of requiring) the names of student-athletes be submitted to their teachers at the start of the season identifying these students as athletes. This is done for several reasons. First, teachers are made aware which students are athletes and—if the school policies permit—these students might be excused from some classes in order to attend an away or home contest. Second, teachers are sometimes asked to notify the coaching staff in terms of the athletes' academic progress on a periodic basis. Third, teachers have a ready access to someone (the coaching staff) to communicate with should the student-athletes experience academic or non-academic problems in their classes.

The key concept is to view the teachers as colleagues and collaborators in the total educational experience of the student-athletes. Teachers must know that coaches recognize that the academic scene takes precedence over the athletic endeavors.

Of course, coaches need to be careful lest they are viewed by individual teachers (or athletes) as interfering with the individual teachers' classroom authority. No coach wants to be viewed as attempting to unduly or inappropriately influence a teacher's action regarding the granting of a grade for a student-athlete. Likewise, coaches should not be perceived as requesting unreasonable special treatment for student-athletes.

COACHING CONCEPT #158: Be a team player within the school setting—don't be a prima donna.

However, this does not mean that athletes should not be given *appropriate special treatment*. There can be inappropriate as well as appropriate special treatment for student-athletes. Student-athletes do represent their educational institutions by participating in co-curricular or extra-curricular activities called *athletics*. These student-athletes frequently, and justly so, receive special treatment allowing them to successfully meet their obligations in the classroom and on the playing field due to the nature of their athletic involvement. Such appropriate special treatment might include early registration for classes, special make-up tests, periodic notification by teachers of the athletes' academic progress to individual coaches, permission to miss a specific number of classes (with appropriate make-up assignments required) in order to participate in various contests, establishment of special study halls for athletes, provision for special academic help or tutoring for selected athletes, etc.

Frequently, there are school policies that determine when and if a student-athlete may obtain permission to be excused for a class due to athletic participation. Coaches need to be cognizant of such policies and accompanying procedures and follow these rules closely. The worse case scenario is for coaches to be perceived by teachers (and administrators) as uncaring in terms of the academic welfare of their student-athletes and/or manipulative with teachers in attempting to secure inappropriate special treatments for their charges. No coach should attempt to pressure a teacher to give a student-athlete an unearned grade or other privilege that is not permitted by the school policies and practices. On the other hand, just because a student is an athlete should not mean that the student-athlete should experience hardships or roadblocks that would preclude being involved in both the academic and athletic scenes within the school.

COACHING CONCEPT #159: Athletes should not be discriminated for or against because of their sports participation.

In short, student-athletes can be treated differently than the general student body, that is, they can receive permissions, privileges and special support because of their involvement in sports. This is entirely appropriate and is part of the educational mission of the school. On the other hand, there is a fine line that coaches and student-athletes must walk lest one is perceived to abuse this privilege. However, pressure for illegal or inappropriate special treatment of athletes (pressuring teachers to change grades or to use different criteria in grading an athlete's academic work, etc.) is never acceptable.

COACHING CONCEPT #160: Be a part of the school life and environment—support and attend non-athletic activities within the school.

Coaches should be seen by others within the school (students, faculty, administration) as being supportive of all aspects of the school. This means that coaches should attend and be seen at various non-athletic events and activities within the school setting. Attending theater presentations, science fairs, dances and art shows indicates that the coach is part of the school community and is not only concerned with sports.

Working with Academic Advisers and Tutors

In some schools, especially at the college and university level, academic advisers are made available exclusively for the student-athletes. Other institutions have their athletes advised by the general academic advisers who work with all students within a department or program. And, in some instances, especially on the high school level, individual teachers or guidance counselors serve as academic advisers to all students, including student-athletes. In other schools, special advisers are utilized to supervise the overall academic and social progress of the student-athletes and to advise and counsel the student-athletes in academic, athletic and personal matters. And, in other settings, advisers are available to help individual athletes in terms of tutoring the players in those academic subjects in which they may be experiencing difficulties.

Proper Utilization of Academic Advisers and Tutors

In any school setting, the academic progress of the student-athlete should take precedence over all other activities and involvements. Coaches would do well to work closely with the academic advisers (and tutors, if any). Tutors can be formally designated and approved by the institution or can be informally associated with the athletic department and with the coaching staff. Tutors are given the assignment of teaching, on an individual basis, selected athletes in specific academic areas. Tutors might be helpful teachers, students or even people from the community who merely volunteer their services to help out a particular student-athlete in a specific subject area. The task remains the same, that is, to help the student-athlete learn the material in a given class or course.

Both advisers and tutors share the responsibility of assisting athletes in their academic endeavors. They must not do the work for (or on behalf of) the student-athlete. Advisers and tutors also help the coaching staff understand the academic status and progress of the individual athlete. Tutors, when available, have the responsibility of working, on a daily basis, with individual students in helping them grasp and comprehend the academic subject in which they are enrolled.

> **COACHING CONCEPT #161: The primary objective, the overriding goal, of the student-athlete is to be successful in the classroom—athletic competency is a secondary but worthwhile objective.**

Coaches commonly espouse the philosophy that the top priority of a student-athlete while in school is in the academic domain. If coaches really believe in this position, then it behooves them to work closely with and support the efforts of academic advisers and tutors. This can be accomplished by reinforcing their efforts to have athletes excel in the classroom, by insisting that athletes do well academically, and cooperate with the advisors and tutors, in order for the athlete to be eligible to compete or even practice.

For example, coaches can require their athletes to attend study halls established by the advisors or tutors or else forfeit playing and practice time. Great care must be taken lest coaches be tempted to exert undue and inappropriate influence on the advisers and tutors on behalf of a star athlete. Such actions are not only counter-productive but can be very destructive to the all important relationship between the academic dimension and the athletic dimension.

Working with Cheerleaders, Pom-Pom Groups and Advisers

Many sports teams have cheerleaders (or pom-pom groups) associated with them. The appropriate use of such groups can be quite effective in the promotion of the sport team itself as well as providing excellent competitive, social and educational opportunities for those student members (male and female) of the cheerleading team or the pom-pom squad. Coaches as well as advisers to the cheeleaders and pom-pom groups need to closely cooperate with one another. There needs to be a clear understanding of the responsibilities and duties of the cheerleaders and members of the pom-pom group during the athletic contests. In some programs, cheerleaders are not allowed or are at least discouraged from traveling with the

Cheerleaders can be an integral part of an athletic team (program).

athletes on the same bus. This is because some coaches believe that they would be a distraction to the athletes either prior to or following the contest. In other programs, cheerleaders are welcomed to travel with the teams. Regardless of the specific policy or practice, it is important to have prior knowledge of a policy or practice that affects both the athletic team and the support groups such as the cheerleading squad and/or the pom-pom group.

Coaches would do well to provide positive and public reinforcement (expression of appreciation) to these student cheerleaders and pom-pom participants. Similarly, making their advisers aware of how much they and their students are appreciated by the coaches and the athletes will go a long way to insure a positive working relationship with the cheerleaders, their parents and advisers.

Cheerleading as a Flagship Sport or Activity

Cheerleading should not always be thought of as a mere appendage of a major varsity sport such as football or basketball. A growing phenomenon in cheerleading circles—at both the secondary and the college level—is the availability of competition at the national level with national titles at stake and with the availability of academic college scholarships for highly skilled and elite performers in cheerleading. Ansberry (1993, March 26, p. A-1) states that "cheerleading has become a one-way ticket from small towns to the big time and to a degree of sophistication . . . all 16 University of Kentucky cheerleaders get scholarships, and nearly every Southern university courts the best high-school cheerleaders." In fact, in one county in the state of Kentucky, the cheerleading squad has garnered six national championships between 1981 and 1993, while the high school's football team suffered through a winless 11-game schedule in 1990.

Thus, sport coaches need to understand the emerging role of the cheerleading squad as the 21st century approaches. In more and more schools "cheerleading is not seen exclusively as a popularity contest for . . . airheads whose talent was measured in decibels and spunk, cheerleading has become a rigorous activity-half gymnastics and half dance-that requires long hours of hard work" (Ansberry, 1993, March 26, p. A-4). For some coaches, cheerleaders might be welcomed partners while for others, cheerleaders might be perceived as unwelcomed competition, both for fans' loyalty and for scarce resources (financial and facilities).

Working with the Band and the Musical/Band Director

Just as cheerleading or pom-pom groups are closely affiliated with some sports, there are teams that traditionally are associated with a variety of musical groups, including marching bands. Football is one prime example of a sport that is associated with a marching band concept. Musical ensembles and small bands often play at basketball games. Music, of course, can be provided at a variety of sporting events. Music can be heard at gymnastics meets, swimming meets and wrestling matches, as well as many other sports.

Whenever student musicians are involved with an athletic team, coaches need to cooperate with these students and their advisers or directors. The goal is to have a positive working relationship so that the objectives of both the athletic team and the musical group can be realized simultaneously. And, of course, it doesn't hurt one little bit if the coaching staff and the athletes are genuinely appreciative of the effort and the quality music produced by these student musicians.

Working with Officials

Perhaps there is no non-school group of individuals who are more important to coaches in terms of developing a professional relationship than officials. Coaches must be respectful of officials at all times, especially during games. The day when a coach, at any level, can continually bait, antagonize, and abuse an official is long gone. Coaches need to recognize the fact that officials have a job to do and that the job is indeed a challenging one. Disagreeing with calls made by officials is not only unprofessional but bush-league to say the least, regardless of the poor examples sometimes displayed by some Division I coaches.

It has been suggested for many years that all sport coaches should be required to pass the official's certification test in the sport(s) that they coach as well as in one additional sport. Thus, these coaches would at least be knowledgeable in the rules of the sports that they coach. And they would also able to

Coaches must respect officials and insist that athletes do likewise.

work in their off season as an official of another sport, at least in the early stage of their careers, to find out exactly what it is like to be an official.

Far too many coaches (and the situation is not limited to young, inexperienced coaches) are simply ignorant of the rules and regulations of their own sport(s). As a result, they frequently attempt to argue with an official over a rule that they themselves do not know or have misinterpreted. Or, coaches complain about the accuracy of the call itself by an official.

COACHING CONCEPT #162: Officials never cost a team an earned victory—it is the failure of the coach and the athletes to adjust to the game that determines whether or not victory is earned.

When coaches behave inappropriately and unprofessionally by berating and arguing with officials during contests, they are embarrassing themselves, their teams and their institutions in public. They are also delivering a very specific message to their athletes. That is, these coaches are telling athletes that officials can determine whether or not the team will win or lose the game. This is simply an inappropriate message. First of all, it is incorrect. Officials do not cost a team a victory. There has never been an athletic contest that has been played on this planet that has not had serious errors on the playing field by both athletes and coaches. Thus, even if officials do make mistakes, and being human they do, it is not the infrequent misjudgment or error by the official that causes a team to lose. Rather, it is the other errors by the athletes and the coaches that make the deciding difference. Coaches must learn to accept responsibility. They should not blame officials.

COACHING CONCEPT #163: Athletes and coaches must learn to adjust to the style of officials and to act and play accordingly.

To look at it in any other light would give the erroneous message that athletes cannot control their own destiny in a given competitive setting. In truth, athletes and coaches have their destiny almost completely in their hands when they compete in any athletic contest. Coaches would do well to instruct their players to play the game as they were taught and to forget the complaining about so-called questionable calls or non-calls by the officials. Instead, athletes (and their coaches) should learn to adjust to the officiating style just as they would be expected to adjust to their opponents' different and varying styles. Their opponents must also adjust to how officials are calling a particular game. It is this failure to adjust, the inability to react in an appropriate fashion by coaches *and* athletes, which causes the greatest problems for themselves.

COACHING CONCEPT #164: Don't use inferior officiating as an excuse or justification for losing.

Perhaps the major reason why coaches and athletes fall into the trap of complaining about officials is that they mistakenly believe that claims of incompetent officiating serves as an excuse should they lose a contest. Far too often this so-called excuse becomes an all too convenient crutch, and as such, becomes a justification for not winning. Besides, coaches and athletes who complain about officiating merely convey the image of being crybabies, which they are.

Working with College Coaches Seeking Recruits (if a High School Coach)

High school coaches, sooner or later, will come into contact with college coaches who are in the process of recruiting potential athletes for their own college or university programs. College and university coaches are always attempting to locate quality high school student-athletes whom they might recruit to their own team following the athletes' high school graduation.

It is imperative that the high school coach be conversant with the recruiting scene at the college level. That is, the high school coach should have a pretty good idea of the basic rules and regulations pertaining to the NCAA and the NAIA national organizations (as well as the NJCAA) regarding what is permissible in the recruitment of high school athletes by universities and colleges. For example, many parents (and even some secondary coaches) are surprised when they learn that NCAA institutions cannot award a guaranteed 4-year athletic scholarship. Many parents and secondary coaches are confused about the NCAA Proposition 48 legislation that regulates minimum academic standards for freshmen athletes who receive athletic financial assistance at NCAA Division I and II schools.

High school coaches must be aware of what is in the best interest of their athletes. This is a very complicated, but yet extremely important, area that all coaches in high school must become familiar with in their role as mentors, counselors and advisers. High school coaches have an obligation to become reasonably knowledgeable and competent in the world of college student-athlete recruitment. These coaches should be able to paint an accurate picture—of expectations, pros and cons—of the recruitment scene for their athletes and the parents of their athletes. These coaches should be able to give sound and appropriate advice to their athletes and the parents while at the same time walking the proverbial tightrope between ignoring the student-athlete on the one hand and attempting to control the athlete's every move on the other.

As a college or junior college coach, it is equally important to be able to work successfully with high school coaches. College coaches work hard to develop a good rapport with their high

Great facilities only enhance the athletic experience.

school counterparts. For it is at the secondary level that the majority of athletes are recruited for the four-year colleges and universities. For junior college coaches, almost all recruits come from the high school level. As a result, it is the high school coach who can either be of significant assistance or a tremendous liability in your recruitment efforts. Being honest in one's dealings with prospective athletes, their parents and their high school coaches can go a long way to developing credibility among secondary school people, credibility that is so desperately needed if one is to experience significant success in the recruiting wars.

WORKING WITH FANS, WITH THE COMMUNITY, AND WITH BOOSTER CLUBS

COACHING CONCEPT #165: Fans are always emotional, usually prejudiced and sometimes rabid about their team(s) and their perceptions of their own knowledge of sports.

Coaches all too frequently view their jobs as merely working with athletes on the field, on the court or in the pool. Not true. Coaches have a responsibility to also develop competency in working with people and organizations within the community, with fans, and booster clubs or athletic support groups (ASG). Coaches do not operate in isolation. Coaches live in a fishbowl. Everything they do, as well as what they do not do, both in and out of school, is subject to scrutiny by others in the community, by fans and by booster club members.

Although many coaches would like to feel that their coaching careers are dependent strictly on what they do during practices and in games, nothing could be further from the truth. Individuals and groups in the community in which the coach works and lives can have a powerful impact on the career of a coach. The sooner that coaches recognize the need to identify important role players within the community (called centers of influence—COI), the better. The sooner that coaches realize that they must appropriately deal with members of booster clubs, parents, influential community members, etc., the better.

The following two examples provided by Smith (2005) may be extreme but they nevertheless reveal the type of outside pressures and power that parents, community members and school board members have in the world of sports and coaching.

Example # 1: McQueen High School, Reno, Nevada, literally placed an athlete on the varsity baseball team after the youngster was cut during tryouts. This surprising action took place even after the board and the AD admitted that the tryouts were conducted correctly. In fact, the AD and board had supervised the tryouts for the baseball team. The result: the youngster was put on the team by the board even though cut by the head coach.

Example #2: Center High School, Antelope, California, a school board member whose son was not selected as the team's starting quarterback retaliated by getting a fellow board member to also vote not to renew the head coach's contract. This act of retaliation resulted in the resignation (in protest) by the athletic director, the entire football staff and eight other athletic coaches at the school.

Coaches need to become part of the community. They need to contribute and be recognized as contributors to the community. They should take an active part in the booster club or the athletic support group should one exist in their school. They should pay attention to the needs of the sport fans, alumni, and various influential individuals and groups within the community and attempt to meet

Mascots play an important role in providing excitement for the fans.

these needs. It is the rare coach who can completely ignore these important constituencies. This is especially important when the team's won-loss record is less than sterling. In many instances where a team might have faltered during a season or two, the coach can still retain the support of the administration and the outside constituencies if the coach had earlier taken time and expended the effort to cultivate these constituencies and groups by developing a positive working relationship and by creating good communication between the coach and others.

The concept is that *coaches should make an honest effort to become an integral part of the community in which they coach and live.* They need to belong to local churches, to service clubs, and be actively involved in youth groups. They need to be seen as a regular human being living and working within the community. In fact, some schools or school districts even have a requirement that coaches who also are teachers must live within the school district in which they teach. Others do not. The point, however, is that coaches must become an integral part of the community, especially if they are full time employees of the school or school district.

> **COACHING CONCEPT #166: Be sure that the perceptions that people have of you and your program are accurate—take time to educate fans and the general public.**

As stated earlier, the perceptions that people hold are sometimes as important as reality. If people in the community, if booster club members, if fans, all feel that the coach is not knowledgeable, is not very dedicated and lacks coaching skills, the coach is in jeopardy. Conversely, if the coach is viewed as a qualified, dedicated and skilled mentor by those in the community, among fans and booster club members—the coach is indeed in an enviable position of having such important support from these outside constituencies.

Working with Salespersons

Dealing with salespeople can often be a very trying experience as well as very rewarding and helpful. Coaches are always busy and sometimes resent being interrupted by sporting goods salespersons unless it is the coach who has initiated the contact. Nevertheless, coaches will have to learn to deal with salespeople in a polite and professional manner. Salespersons do not deliberately attempt to interrupt a coach's busy schedule. Letting salespersons know when you can be contacted by phone or in person, and when you cannot, will go a long way to solve the problem of being interrupted. One should always be civil and polite regardless of the circumstances. Salespersons can be of significant assistance when it comes time to selecting and ordering proper equipment and supplies and receiving same on time. They can also be of immeasurable assistance in an emergency in which the coach is in desperate straits because of missing supplies or broken equipment.

DEVELOPING A POSITIVE RELATIONSHIP WITH ONE'S OWN SPOUSE AND CHILDREN (IF ANY)

> **COACHING CONCEPT #167: Build a sound foundation at home before worrying about things at school or with the team.**

The social life of a coach can be severely limited. Similarly, the personal life of a coach is often severely and negatively affected by being a coach—at any level. As a result, one of the major challenges facing coaches is how they can balance their work commitment and their personal commitments to family and friends. Spouses and children of coaches frequently feel isolated and neglected by coaches who feel compelled to devote what might be seen by their family as extraordinary, unnecessary and unfair amount of time away from the family working on coaching tasks.

Spouses of coaches can feel anxious, frustrated, depressed, lonely, and angry if they do not understand the challenges and time commitment facing coaches, head and assistant coaches (paid as well as volunteer coaches). It is up to the coaching spouse to make the effort and to take the time to assist one's partner (and children, if any) to adjust to and accept the normal difficulties and challenges facing all coaches' family members.

One must face reality, the time commitment is frequently great for coaches of most sports. The time spent in practices, travel to and from contests, actual games themselves, planning time, out-of-season conditioning efforts, etc., are all necessary and yet take valuable hours away from the coach's family and friends. This challenge needs to be reconciled by both the coach and the coach's family.

For women who desire to coach, the problem of time commitment is further exacerbated because of the traditional role of women in our society and in the family unit. For example, women who are married and also coach are sometimes expected by their spouses to continue in the traditional role of wife, mother, house cleaner, cook and bottle washer. In short, these women face the sometimes insurmountable problem of being expected to perform all of the traditional roles imposed upon women in the olden days in addition to shouldering the extensive responsibilities and time commitment of coaching a sport.

All these tasks are sometimes expected of women without any real assistance in terms of home responsibilities. As a result, many women just cannot do both. Nor should they be expected to. They cannot do an adequate job of coaching and then be expected to come home and also do all of the housework, all of the cooking, the raising of the children, the buying of the groceries, the washing of the dishes, etc., etc., etc.

Where is the husband in all of this? Where are the other family members? Where can women go and to whom can they turn in an effort to solicit assistance in the home so that they will have adequate time to spend in coaching a sport? Women have enough handicaps to overcome in breaking down the discriminatory hiring and promotional practices without having to also be faced with such challenges at home.

REFERENCES

Ansberry, C. (1993, March 26). For some girls, cheerleading offers a leg up in life. *The Wall Street Journal, CCXXI*(59), A-l; A-4.

Anshel, M. M. (1990). *Sport psychology: From theory to practice.* Scottsdale, Arizona: Goruch Scarisbrick, Publishers.

Berkowitz, K. (2006). Same team. *Training and Conditioning, XVI*(3), 33-34, 36-38.

Brewer, J. (2005, June/July). Getting the word out. *Athletic Management, XVII*(4), 49, 50, 52-54.

Cain, B. (2007, August). What, me worry? *Athletic Management, XIX*(5), 51-52, 54-56.

Captains with resumes. (2003, April/May). *Athletic Management, XVII*(3), 4.

Cardone, D. (2001). Parent talk. *Athletic Management, XIII*(5). 41-45.

Cardone, D. (2004). Captains in training. *Athletic Management, XVI*(3), 33-34, 36,-37.

Coakley, J. J. (1990). *Sport in society*. St. Louis, Missouri: Times Mirror-Mosby College Publishers.

Donne, J. (1623). Devotions upon emergent occasions. Meditation # 17.

Hoch, D. (2001, August/September); Signs of the time. *Athletic Management, XIII*(5), 47, 48, 50, 51, 53.

Hoch, D. (2005, February). *Coach and Athletic Director, 6*(98), 12-13.

Lackey, D. (1977). Why do high school coaches quit? *Journal of Physical Education and Recreation, 48*(4), 22-23.

Lackey, D. (1986). The high school coach, a pressure position. *Journal of physical Education, Recreation and Dance, 57*(3), 28-32.

Lackey, D. (1994). High school coaching—Still a "pressure cooker" profession. *Journal of physical Education, Recreation and Dance, 65*(6), 68-71.

Mano, K. (2002, April/May). A trophy and a smile. *Athletic Management, XIV*(3), 24-26.

Masin, H. L. (1993, August). Here below—Bear baiting. *Scholastic Coach*, p. 10.

Miller, G., Lutz, R., Shim, J., Fredenburg, K., and Miller, J. (2005). Dismissals and perceptions of pressure in coaching in Texas high schools. *Journal of Physical Education, Recreation and Dance, 76*(1), 29-33.

Manos, K. (2001, October/November). Sailing away. *Athletic Management, 13*(6), 22-23.

Pedersen, P., Miloch, K., & Cothran, D. (2006).s Increasing program exposure through enhanced media relations. *Journal of Physical Education, Recreation and Dance, 77*(7), 10-12, 52.

Sabock, R. J. (1991). *Coaching—A realistic perspective* (4th ed.). San Diego, California: Collegiate Press.

Scantling, E. and Lackey, D. (2005). Coaches under pressure: Four decades of studies. *Journal of physical Education, Recreation and Dance, 76*(1), 25-28.

Smith, L. (2005, August/September). Getting on board. *Athletic Management, XVII*(5), 39-43.

Sports Medicine Sweet Sixteen. (2007, August). *Athletic Management, XIX*(5), 15.

Stewart, C. (1993). "The way you were, or the way you wished you were," *Coaching behaviors: 50*(1), 23-30.

Stier, Jr., W. F. (1987, Spring). *The A, B, Cs, of administration.* Presentation made at the national convention of the American Alliance for Health, Physical Education, Recreation and Dance (AAHPERD), Las Vegas, Nevada, pp 11.

Stier, Jr., W.F. (1988, Spring). *Challenges facing women coaches and administrators in higher education in the United States today: Survival tactics for the female athletic coach.* Presentation made at the national convention of the American Alliance for health, Physical Education, Recreation and Dance (AAHPERD), Kansas City, Missouri, pp. 13

Stier, Jr., W.F. (1992, April 14). *The role of Olympism in education.* Presentation made at the National Convention of the American Alliance for Health, Physical Education, Recreation and Dance (AAHPERD), Indianapolis, Indiana, pp. 9.

Stier, Jr., W.F. (1994). *Successful sport fund-raising.* Dubuque, Iowa: Wm. C. Brown & Benchmark.

Taking the job to heart. (2005, June/July). *Athletic Management, XVII*(4), 16.

Wood, S. (2004, April 15). 'Skins' Gibbs has fun with 'total life change'. *USA Today,* p. 9-C.

Name: _____

Student ID #:_____

EXERCISES FOR CHAPTER 6

A. Describe why coaches cannot operate in a vacuum as coaches.

B. What are some of the major pitfalls facing coaches in dealing with individuals or groups [specify the group or individuals]?

C. How can an assistant coach go about establishing a positive relationship with the head coach?

D.   What are some of the symptoms of burnout for a coach and what can a coach do to prevent or react to being burned out.

E.   Provide examples of ways that a coach might be able to make parents and others know of the coach's philosophy and expectations. Be specific in your examples and provide a rationale for your comments.

F.   What suggestions might you make to your fiancée in an effort to educate your future spouse as to what life might be like married to a coach?

G. How do you view the relationship between coaches and officials? Explain how you, as a coach, would attempt to work with officials. Why?

H. What steps might be taken to solve or prevent problems between coaches or teams and the faculty within the school?

I. Explain how coaches can serve as role models by specifying things that they can do in real life that will help them become positive role models.

J. How would you justify the need to spend the necessary time and effort working or coaching with the need for a coach to have personal time to spend with one's family?

RESEARCH QUESTONS FOR CHAPTER 6

1. Interview female and male coaches about their problems and challenges in becoming a coach and remaining a coach. Compare the responses between male and female coaches.

    ----

2. Go to the library and research the topic of the lack of female coaches at the college and high school levels. What are the reasons you feel are at the root of this apparent shortage of female coaches?

    ----

3. Survey and interview faculty and school administrators and solicit their ideas and perspectives pertaining to problems that are created by athletics (sports themselves, athletes, coaches) within the school.

    ----

4. Ask a high school athletic director how varsity and sub-varsity coaches are evaluated. Solicit information as to the criteria, method and timing of such evaluation efforts.

    ----

5. Find out from a varsity high school coach (of a flagship sport) how the school *schedules* end-of-season banquets and the rationale behind this practice, that is, how the banquets [if there is more than one] are structured and organized. In addition, determine the varsity coach's opinion as to the effectiveness and efficiency of the coach's own banquet and what steps the coach takes to make it a meaningful experience for athletes and parents alike.

Chapter 7

Coaching Successful Teams

Successful coaches are excellent role models.

COACHING CONCEPT #168: Winning teams are made up of highly skilled athletes coached by highly competent coaches.

FOURTEEN ELEMENTS OF A WINNING TEAM

Coaches seemingly are always on the search for that certain something that might give them and their athletes an edge over their opponents. These coaches want to know whether or not there are significant differences between teams that consistently

319

win and those that do not. Are there distinctive and distinguishing characteristics of winning and losing teams that can be identified? If so, what are those identifiable factors that distinguish the successful and winning teams from those teams that are not, and are coaches able to use this knowledge to help them as coaches?

In reality, there are several factors that do in fact have a very real effect on a team's ability to emerge victorious in competition. And, coaches can indeed use this knowledge to enhance their own coaching competency and improve their team's chances of success. In fact, there are 14 major factors that distinguish consistently winning teams from those teams that consistently lose the battle of the scoreboard. These factors or attributes include:

1. Better skilled athletes

2. Better teaching and coaching of the sport skills in practice

3. Better team and player selection

4. Suitable and wise placement of players within the team

5. More effective recruitment and retention of athletes by the coach

6. Better game coaching—superior bench coaching

7. Better conditioned athletes

8. Fewer injuries among players

9. Highly and better motivated athletes

10. Greater confidence exhibited by athletes

11. Fewer mistakes than the opponents

12. Superior support mechanisms, programs and systems

13. Evidence of superior support in terms of facilities, equipment, supplies, and staff personnel

14. Competing against weaker opponents

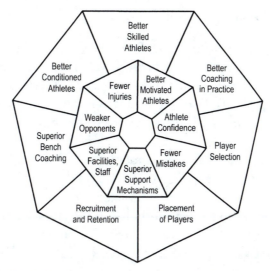

FIGURE 7.1—Factors to Consider in Building a Team

Better Skilled Athlete

Winning teams consistently have better athletes. Yes, there are exceptions in particular contests and sports where an obviously more talented group of athletes are beaten by a team comprised of less talented players. The same can be said of individuals in the individual sports. However, over the long run, the better athletes—all other things being equal—will prevail. The old coaching adage is still true and applicable; *you have to have the horses (talented, dedicated, motivated players) to be a consistent winner.* High School basketball teams made up of 4'10" athletes do not win state championships regardless of how nice the youngsters are or how hard they try or how long they practice.

Better Teaching and Coaching of Sport Skills in Practice

Regardless of the talent level of individual athletes, the ability of the coach to actually teach these individuals the sport skills is critical. Even elite athletes can benefit from the skilled teaching and coaching of sport skills. Average athletes improve their skills and become above average in their skill level. Above average athletes can improve sufficiently to become good or great athletes. And great athletes, with excellent teaching and coaching assistance in practice, can reach elite level in the performance of their skills. Teams and individuals enjoying the benefits of highly skilled teaching and coaching during practices will develop and demonstrate improved skills and thus enjoy a decided advantage over those who do not experience superior coaching experiences.

Better Team and Player Selection

Winning teams have coaches who have excellent judgment when it comes to making superior decisions in terms of selecting athletes to make up the team. Being able to recognize present and future talent in youngsters is a highly prized attribute of coaches. This is an ability that can be learned and enhanced through experience and by consciously working with other coaches who have already developed a high level of skill in recognizing talent.

There are four characteristics or elements that coaches frequently seek in their players. These characteristics include: (1) heart, (2) courage/guts, (3) brains, and (4) physical ability. There are many such characteristics of individuals that help to create a superior athlete. Other characteristics mentioned by many coaches as being thought of as being essential for individuals to become superior athletes include: (1) being motivated, (2) possessing certain specific skills, (3) having specific physical attributes, (4) being mature, and (5) having decision making ability. See chapter nine for information on desirable characteristics as suggested by the author.

Suitable and Wise Placement of Players in Suitable Roles

Not only is the aptitude (capacity) to recognize talent important but the ability to realize how these individual athletes might be utilized to the team's and the individual's greatest benefit is equally, if not more, important. Coaches who are skilled in appropriately placing athletes in specific roles or positions within a team enjoy success to a greater degree than those coaches who lack such skills. Some athletes are more effective when placed in specific positions on the team. And, other athletes become more effective when asked to assume specific roles.

Being able to recognize whether an athlete will be able to reach his or her near potential playing as a starting guard or a reserve forward on a basketball team is an important skill on behalf of a coach. Similarly, being able to recognize whether a student should be placed in a leadership role of being a captain or co-captain is equally significant. And, deciding whether an athlete should play second base or left field can be a crucial decision for both the individual athlete and for the team as a whole.

More Effective Recruitment and Retention of Athletes

On the college and university level, coaches have long been expected to be competent recruiters of talented athletes. However, even coaches on the youth sport level and the secondary level must be concerned with student recruitment. Youth sport coaches must scout and solicit potential athletes in the community and get them interested in trying out for the squad. Junior and senior high coaches must be especially adept at identifying potential athletes roaming the school's hallways who are not currently participating in their sport and encouraging them to become involved in the sport.

In today's world of amateur sport, these coaches cannot just sit idly by and expect to have talented youngsters drop in their lap. Rather, these coaches need to recruit youngsters to their sport(s)—individuals who hopefully will develop into highly skilled and coachable performers. And, those coaches who are successful in not only attracting youngsters to their sport but who are equally adept at retaining these athletes will enjoy greater success in competition than those coaches who are constantly faced with dropouts from their team. Successful recruitment and successful retention are both keys to successful teams.

Better Game Coaching—Superior Bench Coaching

Superior teams are noted for coaches who are superior decision makers in competition, in the heat of the battle. Likewise, outstanding individual athletic performers usually are associated with coaches who are excellent decision makers in actual competition, in the heat of battle. Coaches assume the role of a general overseeing the conflict of competition, directing resources and making decisions. Coaches need to demonstrate excellent leadership and split second decision-making in many areas, both in practices and in games. Making timely and appropriate decisions in competition, on the spur of the moment, separates the great coach from the average coach. The result is that bench coaching plays a significant role in a team's and an individual's consistent success on the field, on the court, or in the pool.

Bench or game coaching refers to making decisions in terms of substituting players in competition. It also refers to the coach's ability to select the best and most appropriate group of student-athletes to compete and play together as a unit anytime within a specific game situation. And it refers to the competence of a coach in employing and changing tactics and strategies against a team that is also employing specific counter stratagem and maneuvers throughout the contest.

Better Conditioned Athletes

An integral part of any team's success is the conditioning of the individual athletes on the team. Those teams and individuals who are in better physical condition than their opponents possess a real advantage which can be translated into victories. Physical endurance and conditioning are significant factors in competitive sports. Better conditioned teams and individuals outlast inferior conditioned opponents. Additionally, individuals possessing a superior level of physical conditioning are able to execute physical skills *at a higher level for a longer period of time* than opponents lacking such a high level of conditioning.

Fewer Injuries among Players

One of the things that can negatively affect an otherwise successful team is the injury factor. Injuries seemingly are *the* curse of competitive athletes. Injuries can knock athletes out of competition and practices for significant amounts of time. Not only are these talented athletes unable to compete and/or practice but their absence often disturbs the equilibrium of the team by forcing players to assume different roles with different teammates. And, the time and effort required for rehabilitation and regaining of conditioning and previous skill level can be most troublesome and time consuming. Injuries can often be traced to a lack of physical conditioning and/or poor choice of physical activities (exercises, drills, etc.).

Coaches of girls and women have noted that females are more likely to suffer anterior cruciate ligament (ACL) injuries than their male counterparts. In fact, women suffer this dreaded injury five times more frequently than men. The ACL is one of the major ligaments within the knee capsule. These ligaments also help in the stabilization of the knee while providing a connection from the front of the tibia to the back of the femur.

> **COACHING CONCEPT #169: Injury prevention activities (especially during the off-season and preseason time span) are the key to reducing major injuries during the season.**

Today, coaches of women should pay particular attention to the prevention of such injuries. Many orthopedic surgeons, athletic trainers, as well as biomechanists, believe that biomechanical factors are possibly one of the best methods of preventing ACL injuries among women. As a result, coaches would do well to consider altering their preseason conditioning programs as well as the conditioning work that takes place in the off-season. Some of the elements of the prevention practices include teaching the women the positions that are most likely to result in ACL injuries and how to avoid such situations. As a result, many coaches subscribe to various jumping and balance exercises (ACL Experts, 2000).

Teams and individuals with infrequent or inconsequential injuries to key players possess significant leverage over those teams that do experience such injuries. Although some injuries can be considered unpreventable (acts of God), there are other instances where accidents and their occurrence fall under the category of being preventable. Coaches are able to prevent or minimize the severity of many, although not all, injuries or accidents. This can be accomplished through proper conditioning, the teaching of appropriate physical skills and tactics, and following normal safety precautions during both practices and games.

Highly and Better-Motivated Athletes

Highly motivated athletes are formidable opponents. Individuals who are able to be self motivated, or who can be effectively motivated by coaches, possess advantages over individuals who are not as highly motivated. Part of being motivated is being willing to sacrifice and to work at performing at a high level. Athletes who are eager to not only play the sport in actual competition, but who are enthusiastic about practice and preparing themselves to be highly skilled and competitive, will emerge victorious against opponents who lack such resolve.

Greater Confidence Exhibited by Athletes

Teams and individuals who are successful in competition exhibit superior confidence. This confidence can exist in three areas. First, the ability to have confidence in oneself and one's own abilities. Second, confidence in the ability, competency, knowledge base and experience of the coach. And third, confidence in what the individual athlete(s) and the team are asked to do. Successful teams, those which consistently win, exhibit such confidence both in terms of the team itself and in terms of the individual athletes.

An athlete receiving the best of medical care by a trained (certifed) athletic trainer.

COACHING CONCEPT #170: Consistent winning teams reduce the number of significant mistakes while still taking calculated risks in competition.

Fewer Mistakes than Opponents

The old coaching axiom that the team that makes the fewest mistakes is usually the winner is true. And this factor does not only pertain to a sport like football. Comparable teams and individuals who make fewer mistakes than their opponents will usually emerge victorious, period. Competitors need to be instilled with the ***ability to prevent costly mistakes at critical times*** while not forsaking the willingness and capacity to assume reasonable and appropriate risks. One of the keys to being successful in competitive sports is to take calculated risks while still keeping serious mistakes (turnovers, faults, violations, for example) to a minimum. The key is simply not to beat oneself—make the opponents do it.

COACHING CONCEPT #171: Successful winning teams are focused teams—teams and individuals who struggle lack the ability to remain focused.

Superior Support Mechanisms, Programs and Systems

Individual athletes and teams who have superior support programs from the administrators and organizers possess an advantage over those competitors who lack such mechanisms, systems or programs. This advantage can easily transfer into victories on the court or field. Such mechanisms might involve academic support programs such as the availability of special tutors and/or mandatory study halls for athletes as well as special academic advisors, etc. Other examples might include drug education programs, peer and professional counseling efforts, time management seminars, and career guidance assistance.

These efforts by the sport organizers and/or by school administrators tend to provide significant support and assistance to the individual athletes. As a result, these youngsters are then able to better focus their efforts and concentration on their sports activities without being distracted by negative or detrimental factors. The ability of individual athletes and teams to remain focused on their athletic pursuits without undue distractions is a decided advantage when it comes to being successful in competitive sports. Being provided with adequate and timely support programs and assistance facilitates the ability to remain focused.

State of the art facilities can be a great boom for the athletic teams and individual performers.

Evidence of Superior Support in Terms of Facilities, Equipment, Supplies, and Staff Personnel

Athletes who have access to high quality facilities, equipment, and supplies as well as skilled support personnel usually have an edge in their competitiveness and their readiness for competition. These assets can be significant because they can facilitate the individual athlete's development and mastery of a sport. These substantive advantages include tangible items such as quality weight rooms, sports medicine facilities, competitive facilities, specific equipment and appropriate supplies. These benefits also include medical support staff such as the team physician, the physician assistant, the NATA athletic trainer and strength/conditioning instructor or coach.

Competing Against Weaker Opponents

By definition, the team which wins over an opposing squad is one that has competed against an opponent who was not as successful or skillful (therefore inferior) as the victorious squad, at least on that particular day and time. However, the deliberate scheduling of weaker opponents can have a truly significant effect upon a team's overall won/loss record. This deliberate scheduling of inferior opponents (commonly referred to as bunnies) is called *padding one's schedule*. It is more frequent in those situations where teams and coaches are able to have a voice in who they will play—in contrast to being locked into a conference schedule, for example.

Don't ever let anyone kid you. Scheduling appropriate opponents (bunnies) can go a long way toward making possible a winning season in terms of won/loss records. Many teams pad their early season schedule with antagonists who are not expected to provide exactly overwhelming opposition. Just look at many of the successful basketball teams, especially on the NCAA Division I level, and examine the true difficulty of their overall competition. Basketball teams at Georgetown University and at Marquette University had at one time earned reputations in some quarters of scheduling a number of so-called bunnies, especially during the early part of their seasons. Thus, they were almost insured that a significant number of victories would be added to the win column for a particular season. On the other hand, there are basketball teams like the University of Louisville that are known for not scheduling so-called bunnies in the early part of their seasons. These teams attempt to play the very toughest of opponents throughout their schedule while letting the chips (in terms of wins and losses) fall where they will.

This doesn't mean that all coaches should attempt to schedule all the weakest opponents that they can to their schedule. However, wise and prudent scheduling of opponents (adversaries that are comparable in terms of skill level and winning tradition) can result in a better chance for an acceptable won/loss record (however that term is defined).

One of the problems in scheduling opponents, especially when it comes to the sport of football, is that scheduling of opponents is frequently done many, many years in advance. Some scheduling, especially on the college level, is done 5 to 10 years and more, in advance. Thus, teams that are scheduled in 2010 to play each other in the year 2020 might find themselves totally mismatched in terms of the two teams' overall skill level a decade later. In this instance, a team is caught playing a totally mismatched (weaker) opponent with the end result almost a certain *win* for the record book.

DEVELOPING AN INDIVIDUAL COACHING STYLE

COACHING CONCEPT #172: Emulate, but don't try to be a carbon copy of other coaches, even coaching icons—be yourself.

Coaches need to develop their own individual coaching and teaching philosophies and styles. Coaches should be careful lest they attempt too closely to exactly imitate coaches whom they admire or coaches who had coached them. One of the problems of attempting to mimic other coaches is that each person's personality and experiences are unique to that specific person. Also, no two coaching situations are ever identical.

Hence, coaches need to be themselves. They cannot be other people. Today, athletes are street wise and can spot a faker a mile away. And, nothing destroys the credibility of a coach faster than not being honest and upfront in one's dealings with others, especially athletes. It is one thing to attempt to imitate and mimic another coach in every way and another to merely use a quality coach as an example or model. Many coaches admire a specific quality of an outstanding coach and attempt to demonstrate that quality in light of one's own personality and circumstances. However, to attempt to be that person, to exactly imitate and to become a carbon copy in terms of another coach's style and action is not wise, expedient, or advisable. In short, it does not work. Be yourself.

Intensity of competition.

There was only one Johnny Wooden in men's basketball. There was only one Paul Bear Bryant in football. There was only one Jody Conradt in women's basketball. There was only one Knute Rockne in football. There was only one Bela Karolyi in gymnastics. Each successful coach has individual qualities that other coaches might do well to adopt, but one should not seek to imitate another coach in each and every respect.

COACHING CONCEPT #173: Learn from the mistakes and successes of others—you won't live long enough to make them all yourself.

Coaches' decisions and actions are a reflection of their personal and professional philosophies. And, one's philosophy is colored by one's beliefs, personality, experiences, attitudes and opinions. Coaches should be themselves, be honest and forthright in all that they do and with whom they work. They should not attempt to be what they are not, nor should they become a carbon copy of someone else. However, this does not preclude learning from the mistakes and successes of other individuals, for in reality one doesn't live long enough to make all of the mistakes oneself. It is imperative to learn from others—from their successes as well as their failures.

COACHING CONCEPT #174: Be cautious in coaching like you were coached.

LEARNING FROM ONE'S PREVIOUS COACHES

Beginning coaches frequently attempt to coach like they were coached when they were athletes. Sometimes they attempt to mimic the coaching style of their former mentors. Or, they merely wish to utilize many of the same tactics, strategies and techniques of those who had coached them when they were young. This can result both in positive as well as negative consequences. If these would-be coaches were coached by well-trained, experienced, highly skilled and knowledgeable teachers, these would-be coaches might indeed be in a position to learn in a positive sense from their experiences as an athlete. However, if their previous coaches were not up to-date in what they employed in the teaching and coaching of the sport, if they were not highly skilled, these would-be coaches might well be emulating inferior, out-of-date and/or dangerous coaching tactics and strategies.

Another example will suffice to point out the potential folly of merely copying coaching tactics used by a previous coach. If an individual would attempt to coach in 2010 as that person was coached in 1990, it is entirely possible that that person's coach in 1990 might have coached like he or she was coached in 1970. And, in turn, that coach in 1970 might have used techniques and tactics copied from that person's coach way back in 1950. And, that coach in 1950 might well have copied the same tactics and strategies from a coach who had coached that person way, way back in 1930.

> **COACHING CONCEPT #175: Never do things just because that is the way that it was done before—have a valid rationale for coaching the way that you do.**

So, to take this example to the ridicules extreme, a coach in the year 2010 might be employing a coaching or conditioning tactic, a teaching technique, a disciplinary strategy or a motivating scheme that received its initial baptism of fire in 1930—and might or might not be defensible in terms of modern coaching knowledge in the present time. Thus, it is imperative that the modern day coach be capable of determining the reason(s) why any specific coaching tactic, technique or strategy is being employed. If the sole justification for doing something is *because that is the way we have always done it*—it is time to reexamine one's decision making processes and one's judgment.

An Unacceptable Coaching Tactic

An example of a common coaching tactic used in practices today but which lacks any real justification is that of punishing athletes by making them run laps or suicide drills. Today, the enlightened coach knows that one should not punish athletes in an abusive fashion by making them run laps or sprint the stairs or execute traditional suicide drills. By doing so the coach is making youngsters use that which comprises the very essence of an athlete's capability—the athlete's body—in a negative fashion with potentially damaging consequences, both physical and psychological.

Yet, there are literally thousands of coaches today who continue to punish athletes via physical means, such as by making young men and women run suicide drills until near exhaustion. Coaches also punish athletes psychologically through mind games and humiliation in front of peers. Why? The answer seems to be because it has always been done that way, because that is the way they were coached. Now this is not to say that suicide drills cannot be used as a conditioning technique. They can be used. It is the punishment factor that is being called into question, that is, the physical punishment and psychological punishment of athletes.

When suicide drills are used, it is important that they are utilized in a *constructive, positive manner rather than part of a punishment exercise.* For example, suicide and related drills can be an integral and successful part of an overall conditioning program. However, coaches need to explain their rationale behind the drills and how these drills are expected to increase the players' endurance, quickness, strength and stamina, etc. Additionally, coaches are able to kill two birds with one stone in using such suicide drills by having athletes (in sports such as soccer or basketball) run the patterns while dribbling or passing the ball, for example. Thus, physical conditioning and skill enhancement can be worked on simultaneously by the athletes, in a constructive fashion.

Additional Unacceptable Past Coaching Practices

There are other questionable or improper coaching practices that have taken place in the past. Ten such examples are enumerated below. The modern day coach needs to be on the guard against these and other improper coaching practices.

1. In the past, coaches did not allow athletes to have access to water during practices as well as athletic contests. Today, we now know that is an unacceptable practice.

2. In the past, football players were taught to spear and hit with their helmet as a first point of contact with an opponent. Now we know spearing is dangerous and is strictly forbidden by the rules.

3. In the sport of basketball, coaches have taught their players to utilize a baseline or sideline drill in which a defensive player had to stay motionless while taking a charge from a dribbler, who in turn had been assigned the task of dribbling directly to the basket through the defensive player. We now know this to be an unsafe and hazardous act (Hazelrigg, 1983).

4. Previously, in the sport of wrestling, athletes were sometimes pitted in practice against others who might be 2-3 weight classes apart. Coaches did this to teach the smaller wrestler a lesson as part of a disciplinary action. Today, we know this to be unacceptable, and potentially dangerous and legally negligent.

5. In basketball, players have been instructed in the past to step under an opponent's foot of the opponent who is jumping for a rebound in an attempt to cause the opponent to sprain an ankle when coming down on the extended foot. This is not only an example of unethical conduct by the coach (and player), but is obviously physically dangerous as well.

6. Instructing one's own player to start a fight with an opponent's star athlete in the hope of having both players ejected from the contest is a coaching tactic that is recognized as being totally unacceptable. However, many current day coaches can remember when such instructions were given to their teams in years past.

7. Use of potentially harmful, if not downright dangerous, warm-ups and stretching exercises in various training programs for sports. Such so-called leftover exercises that are now recognized as potentially harmful for athletes include the yoga plow, neck circles (performed too quickly), bridging (wrestling), standing toe touch, straight-leg sit-ups, full squats, hurdler's stretch, back hyper extensions and hip twists (Warning, 1989).

8. Some of the language used by coaches in the past would be totally unacceptable in today's society. Not only were vulgarisms sometimes accepted or

tolerated, but even racially derogatory words were commonly uttered without challenge in some coaching quarters. However, today such behavior is not only inappropriate but is not being tolerated. Witness the case of Keith Dambrot, the former basketball coach at Central Michigan University, a NCAA Division I institution. Mr. Dambrot was discharged in the spring of 1993 following a statement that he allegedly made in front of his players. He reportedly said: "I wish I had more niggers on this team" (Athletics Notes, 1993, April 21; Sidelines, 1993). Even making a public apology for his poor choice of the word "nigger" and promising never to use the term again was not sufficient to save his job.

9. Even verbal aggression towards athletes and/or severe reprimanding of athletes by coaches is coming under closer and closer scrutiny in today's athletic circles. In the spring of 1993 the women's basketball coach at the University of California at Los Angeles (UCLA) resigned following a student's complaint of verbal abuse and the university's decision to review the program. Ms. Billie Moore, head coach for the previous 16 years, who had lead the team to national prominence and who also coached the 1976 U.S. Olympic team to a silver medal finish, was quoted as saying: "the coaching profession has become less enjoyable." She also indicated that students today have a "different level of sensitivity . . . I don't know if you can push them as hard as you could 10 years ago" (Athletics Notes, 1993, April 28).

10. Abusive physical conduct by coaches against players, once prevalent among coaches, is now viewed as being totally unacceptable. The laying of hands on a player by a coach just cannot be done today. In the past the coach was the king or the law and had a great deal of latitude in terms of physical striking of athletes. Not so today. Today, physically hitting or slapping an athlete is likely to result in a lawsuit as well as almost immediate dismissal.

The examples provided above all speak to unacceptable or dangerous practices conducted and condoned by some coaches, for the most part, in the past. Today, enlightened coaches know better. Knowledgeable coaches don't punish athletes by making them use that which is to be used in a game. Competent coaches don't place their athletes in harm's way where the youngsters might become seriously injured.

THE ATHLETIC SCENE IS DIFFERENT TODAY

Another reason why it may not be advisable for you to attempt to coach just like you were coached is that the athletic scene today is different than it was in the past. In fact, the so-called competitive athletic experience is different today than only a decade or two ago. Sports have and are changing. The way that competitive sports are viewed by participants and spectators alike have changed in recent years. In short, sport participation, the athletic experience, as well as the atmosphere associated with and permeating competitive sports, are different today than just a generation ago.

REASONS BEHIND CHANGES IN COMPETITIVE SPORTS

There are many factors that support the notion that the coaching scene has significantly changed within the past 10 or 20 years. Eleven of the more important factors that have brought about significant changes for competitive sports, at all levels, include the following:

1. Today there are numerous attractive alternatives for the potential athletes.
2. Athletes are different today—they have different needs, aspirations and distractions and they act different today.
3. Athletes are coming to high schools and colleges with enhanced skill levels mastered earlier in their athletic or sport careers.
4. Presence of better nutrition practices and knowledge of nutrition.
5. Availability of better conditioning for athletes under the guidance of coaches including both physical training and the area of sport psychology.
6. Existence of better physicians, medical care and rehabilitation programs (NATA certified trainers, physical therapists and physician assistants).
7. Greater availability of better equipment and protective gear—although this sometimes creates a myth of indestructibility which can be a problem in itself.
8. Accessibility to better audio-visual aids by both coaching staffs and athletes.
9. An increase in and greater sophistication of workshops, clinics and camps as well as written materials that provide excellent in-service educational opportunities for coaches as well as for athletes of all ages.
10. Greater specialization by athletes in one sport—the two-sport or three-sport athlete is quickly becoming an endangered species.
11. Implementation of rule changes as well as advances in strategies, training techniques and coaching tactics.

COACHING CONCEPT #176: Be aware that there are any number of attractive alternatives vying for the time, effort and attention of athletes.

There Exists Numerous Attractive Alternatives for the Potential Athlete

For many would-be athletes competitive sports do not hold the same appeal or are as attractive as in the past. The magnetism of competitive sports for many youngsters might not be what it used to be. Today's athletes frequently view (and rightly so) the athletic experience as just one of many different opportunities in which they can enjoy themselves, gain prestige, and develop pride. There are many

other avenues through which would-be athletes can have any number of different physical, social, psychological and emotional needs met. As stated in Chapter 1, today more than ever before, there are many, many different and very attractive activities and experiences vying for the attention of potential athletes. In the so-called olden days, one sure way to become a big person on campus was to be an athlete. Today, with our society the way it is, there are many other ways—some involving a lot less effort and sacrifice on behalf of the young person—to achieve prominence in schools and among peers. In short, there are a multitude of other activities and experiences competing for youngsters' time, interest and effort. Coaches need to recognize this fact and be capable of dealing with the challenges which it presents.

Perfect form increases the likelihood of success.

Athletes Are Different Today—
They Have Different Needs and Act Different Today

Coaches need to understand that athletes, both physically and emotionally, are not carbon copies of their counterparts a generation ago. The coaching process itself has evolved into a different animal. By the time youngsters reach high school, many have had significant experiences (some successful and some not so successful) in dealing with coaches, fans, peers and the pressures of competition. Athletes today have different expectations than their predecessors did only a few years before. When the author was a young coach, it was common to have athletes do whatever any coach demanded or asked because the demand or request came from the coach. And, the coach knew best. The coach was the boss, the king. This was also true with parents. When youngsters complained to their parents about what the old coach did or did not do, the frequent reply was that the coach *knew best* and the youngster should shut up, buckle down and do what the coach said.

COACHING CONCEPT #177: Coaches no longer are viewed as being omnipotent, held in awe, or placed on a pedestal—either by parents or by athletes.

Parents and society, in general, have changed how they view athletics and the total athletic experience. In the past, the coach was held on a pedestal, respected and almost never questioned. A generation ago, little thought was paid to the so-called General Patton style, that is, the autocrat who screamed, ranted and demanded that things be done the coach's way. A quip in sports some 25 years ago had the coach yelling: "jump" and the scared athlete would jump up in the air, and midway up, would yell: "how high, sir?" Today, this type of attitude is going the way of the dinosaur. Parents use to tell their youngsters to keep quiet and to do whatever the coach demanded because the coach was the coach (and the coach was always right). Today, the coach is all too frequently looked at differently. Witness the frequent firing of coaches and the players' revolts on the college and high school levels in recent years.

Boycotts by Athletes

In year's past there have been numerous well-publicized instances of protests lodged by athletes against their coaches on the college level because of the coaches' actions or their performance. These rebellions involved athletes either walking out, threatening to walk out and/or demanding that their coaches be relieved of their duties. For example, in November of 1992, the football players at Morgan State University signed a petition seeking head coach Ricky Diggs' dismissal. He remained on the job. The football squad at the University of South Carolina was 0-5 for the season when players voted October 12, 1992 to ask head coach Sparky Woods to resign. He did not. In April of 1993, head basketball coach at the University of California, Lou Campanelli, was summarily fired from his position by the athletic director because of an allegedly abusive coaching style including abusive language towards the athletes. This followed complaints from some of the athletes.

Athletes' Boycotts at Division III

Player boycotts, rebellions and complaints are not the exclusive domain of big-time sports at the NCAA Division I level. For example, little Iowa Wesleyan (with less than 1000 total students) was the scene of a football players' strike coupled with a demand by the players for the ouster of first year football coach Charlie Moot. The players demanded the firing of the coach because the players perceived that they were being treated with disrespect by the coach. In this instance, the then president of the institution, Robert Prins, indicated that the coach would not be removed from his duties. He further revealed that any players wishing to transfer would be released to compete immediately (Colleges, 1993).

COACHING CONCEPT #178: Players are bolder than ever in expressing their dissatisfaction with what they perceive to be inadequate coaching—regardless of whether or not the perceptions are accurate.

During the latter part of the 20th century, the vast majority of the varsity ice hockey players at the State University of New York (Brockport), a NCAA Division III institution, complained about the coaching effectiveness of their head coach. The athletes specifically complained because the head coach had cut some players that the remaining athletes wanted on the team. In fact, these players announced that they would boycott the team until the coach was indeed fired—no ifs, ands or buts. In that situation, an exacting investigation was conducted by the athletic director who found absolutely no justification or substance to the players' complaints. The coach was retained and the players' resignations from the team were accepted by the athletic director. In point of fact, the very next year that same coach, with new players, had the most successful won/loss record in the history of that institution.

Athletes' Boycotts at the High School Level

However, player boycotts and threats of boycotts are real and have increased in recent years. Such boycotts and insurrections have also occurred on the high school level. Bob Starkey, boys' basketball coach at Loudoun County High School, who survived a players' move to oust him from coaching, feels that: "We'll probably see more of it. Everyone feels they have a right and a say in the way things are run. Coaching, as we once knew it, is changing. We're in an era of questioning, of dissent" (Tom, 1993, March 3, p. 1-C).

The problem is not limited to male athletes. Witness the situation with Traci Schneeweis who led the girls' basketball team at Robinson High School in Fairfax, Virginia, to the 1990 AAA state championship in the state of Virginia. She was later suspended on December 20, 1990 by her principal following complaints from some of her athletes and parents that the coach was verbally abusive. There are numerous examples each year when athletes are complaining about coaches, boycotting teams, and quitting sports.

> **COACHING CONCEPT #179: Coaches are being held to a higher level of standards in terms of coaching behavior and in terms of expected competency.**

Today, well into the 21st century, the trend is clear. How coaches treat athletes is coming under much closer scrutiny and coaches are being held to a higher standard of behavior in terms of how they treat their charges in practices and in games. And, this change in how coaches are perceived by athletes, parents, school administrators and members of the public extends also to other areas, such as legal liability.

When I Was an Athlete Syndrome

Another concern which current coaches need to be aware of is the *when I was an athlete* syndrome. This refers to the expectations (some reasonable and some not) that coaches have towards their players in light of their own prior experiences as athletes. In fact, athletes may never have been like some coaches perceive them to have been in the good old days. Coaches sometimes have an inflated or distorted image of what athletes (themselves and others) were like in the past. Too frequently coaches expect that their own athletes should behave or act just like they themselves acted (or, as they think they acted) when they were athletes. This can have tragic consequences. *Coaches need to distinguish reality from fantasy and act accordingly.*

Coaches, when they were athletes, might indeed have been very dedicated and focused on the sport and willing to make sacrifices for the team. These coaches might have been exceptional, highly skilled athletes. They might have been quick learners, capable of mastering physical skills with minimal effort, etc. However, the youngsters these coaches now coach might not have these same qualities and attributes. Today's coaches need to be able to adjust to situations in which not every youngster they coach will possess the motivation, the desire, the capacity or even the skill level that their coaches would expect.

Sometimes one of the greatest challenges facing coaches who had been outstanding athletes during their playing days is being able to work with athletes who are not at the same elite level as the coaches might have been. As a consequence, these coaches need to exhibit patience and develop an understanding of the challenges being faced by athletes who do not possess the same talent as their coaches did when they were the same age.

> **COACHING CONCEPT #180: Don't expect your athletes to care about your sport(s) as much as you do—most of them won't.**

Not only must coaches recognize that each athlete is an individual with different levels of emotional maturity, dedication, motivation, desire, and willingness to sacrifice, but they must recognize that today's athletes do not necessarily exhibit the same characteristics as previous athletes. Probably no one cares more about the team or sport than the coach. This is understandable. Coaches should not be discouraged by the fact that their athletes do not always place the sport or their own involvement at or near the top of their priority lists. Don't expect your charges to care about the team to the extent that you do—the vast majority of them won't, but that is o.k. It just makes it more challenging to be an effective coach. This danger of unrealistic expectations by coaches regarding what athletes should do and should not do is very real and must be guarded against.

And, let's face it, coaching today is generally recognized as more difficult than in the past because both the athletes and the world they live in are different today. Today, athletes live in a society which is very complicated and challenging. They are exposed to more and diverse pressures than ever before. As a result, today's coaches are facing greater and greater hurdles in the performance of their duties. Many coaches are of the opinion that some of the reasons coaching today is so difficult is that athletes:

1. Are deemed to be more selfish today and lack an understanding of the team concept
2. Have a tendency to act like prima donnas
3. Seem less dedicated and are easily discouraged
4. Are more difficult to motivate (they are easily distracted)
5. Have unrealistic expectations of their own abilities and of the athletic experience itself
6. Frequently are not willing to make a major commitment to sports
7. Frequently do not have self-improvement as a major goal
8. Desire immediate gratification instead of working for the future
9. Can obtain satisfaction and positive reinforcement through many activities other than athletic involvement
10. Prefer jobs (and the things that a job and money can purchase) over sports

Athletes Are Coming to High School and College with Enhanced Skill Levels Mastered Earlier in Their Athletic or Sport Careers

Athletes are starting their competitive sport careers at an earlier age than ever before. Witness the abundance of organized youth sports on the local, regional and national levels. As a result, many youngsters are arriving at the junior high school and senior high school levels with enhanced skills and understanding of the technical aspects of their sport.

Presence of Better Nutritional Practices and Knowledge of Nutrition

Kids are indeed bigger, taller, heavier and stronger today. Some of the reasons for this can be attributed to the presence of greater knowledge of nutrition and better health and nutritional practices. The fact that athletes enjoy better health and are capable of greater physical accomplishments enhances their competency level in competitive sports.

Successful athletes must be in the best of physical condition.

It doesn't take a genius to compare individual athletes of today with those of only a generation ago and discern the physical differences in terms of size and weight as well as physical ability. Athletes of today possess greater physical attributes than their counterparts only a few years ago.

Part of the reason for this physical growth in our young people is due to better nutrition among our citizens. Coaches, today, are under tremendous pressure to be knowledgeable and up-to-date in terms of their own knowledge of nutrition and especially relative to nutrition and its impact upon the athlete's competitive performance. Coaches need to be knowledgeable in the whole area of nutrition, but especially so in terms of myths, misconceptions and poor eating habits that seem to permeate our society. They need to teach their charges about proper nutrition through formal educational efforts as well as through being an excellent role model (teaching by example). This education can be through example, formal instruction as well as using so-called teachable moments (Anderson, 2004).

COACHING CONCEPT #181 **Coaches should strive to improve athletic competitive performance through proper nutrition and nutrition education.**

Availability of Better Conditioning for Athletes
under the Guidance of Coaches—Both in Terms
of Physical Training and in the Area of Sport Psychology

Sport psychology was not even a term commonly in use in athletics as recently as 35 years ago. Conditioning and training programs have significantly increased the capability and potential of present day athletes. This includes both physical conditioning programs as well as the mental aspect of training the athlete, that is, the involvement of sport psychology. Today, more and more coaches, at all levels, are recognizing the importance of the psychological dimension of sport conditioning, training and preparation. The result is a much improved and competitive athlete.

Existence of Better Physicians, Medical Care and Rehabilitation Programs
(NATA Certified Trainers, Physical Therapists and Physician Assistants)

Athletic trainers facilitate safe competition.

The medical breakthroughs just in the past decade or two have been phenomenal, to say the least. In the past when athletes were seriously injured, they were absent from the practices and games for a far greater amount of time than they are today. This is in large part thanks to the ever-increasing skill of sport physicians and advances in surgical techniques. One example is the arthroscopic surgery that is now routinely done on the knee and elbow. Twenty years ago this was not as commonly done as it is today. In addition to this type of advance, there is the matter of the increase in the number of qualified athletic trainers certified by the National Athletic Training Association (NATA). Finally, there have been significant advances in rehabilitation techniques carried out under the watchful eyes of either physical therapists or certified athletic trainers that have had a major impact on today's coaching environment.

Greater Availability of Better Equipment and Protective Gear—
Although Misuse of Protective Gear Sometimes Creates
a Myth of Indestructibility Which Can Be a Problem in Itself

The advances made in the past 20-years in the area of various conditioning and weight machines, for example, have had an unbelievable impact upon the capability of present day athletes. Players today are able to develop their physical attributes to a far greater extent through the use of the wide range of conditioning and training equipment. From free weights to nautilus to universal machines, the list of such conditioning devices is almost endless with more coming on the market every year.

The protective gear available to those athletes participating in all sports, but especially in the contact sports of football, hockey and lacrosse, has changed the way these sports are played forever. The availability of better, safer and more effective equipment enables the athletes to physically extend themselves more fully while decreasing the danger of a catastrophic injury or accident. However, the availability of safer and more effective protective gear has sometimes created a false sense of security or invincibility on behalf of the individual athlete. Nevertheless, such equipment and protective gear have significantly changed the way athletes practice and compete in sports.

Accessibility to Better Audio-Visual Aids and Mechanical Devices by Both Coaching Staffs and Athletes (Video Tape Machines, Caddy-Cams, Assessment and Testing Instruments, etc.)

The availability of high-tech mechanical and training devices, as well as audio-visual aids, have enabled the athlete and the coaching staffs to scientifically examine the challenges of preparing a superior trained athlete. Today, every team has ready access to the video camera and VCR/CD player. Individual athletes and whole teams are closely taped and scrutinized via the video camera in an effort to assess as well as to determine how to improve individual and team performance. There are many other examples of technical advances that have enabled coaches and athletes to scientifically study, assess and suggest ways for improving the physical performance of athletes.

An Increase in and Greater Sophistication of Workshops, Clinics and Camps as Well as Written Materials That Provide Excellent In-service Educational Opportunities for Coaches and Athletes

Without a means of disseminating and utilizing the new knowledge supporting the mastery of physical skills and conditioning in competitive sports—knowledge itself is useless. This is where the availability of workshops, clinics and camps come into play. These serve as in-service educational opportunities for coaches and would-be coaches to upgrade their coaching knowledge and skills. Coaches, like physicians and nurses, must remain at the cutting edge of their profession. The knowledge supporting the coaching of competitive sports is rapidly changing. It is the responsibility of the competent coach to insure that one remains competent by keeping up-to date with the latest training, motivational, conditioning and coaching techniques, strategies and tactics. This can be accomplished through professional reading and by attendance at appropriate workshops, clinics and camps. The existence of camps and clinics for athletes has also played a role in changing competitive sports.

Greater Specialization by Athletes in One Sport—the Two-Sport or Three-Sport Athlete is Quickly Becoming an Endangered Species

Sport specialization is exemplified by the student-athlete electing to concentrate on a specific sport, to the exclusion of other sports, on a year round basis. Such specialization, which is on the increase by athletes in high schools and colleges, is a two-way sword. On the one hand, such specialization can enable an athlete to increase one's skill level in a sport and also enhance the athletic performance of the team the athlete plays on (Watts, 2002). This is possible because the individual concentrates on one specific sport—all year round, year in and year out.

However, on the other hand, many educators and sports people are questioning the wisdom of such specialization, especially when it occurs at early ages. At what cost does the specialization extract from the individual athlete and from the total sports program? Can the athlete become burned out, physically and/or psychologically? The debate continues to rage on. It frequently becomes a case of *keeping up with the Joneses*. When a number of teams or athletes begin to specialize and are perceived to have an unfair advantage as a result over their opponents, there is a domino effect and pressure is felt for other teams and individuals to also specialize to catch up. However, as long as sport specialization continues, we will see higher levels of skills being developed in younger athletes.

Implementation of Rule Changes as Well as Advances in Strategies, Training Techniques, and Coaching Tactics

There are numerous examples of rule changes in many sports that have significantly affected the way sports are organized and played. For example, in basketball there has been the addition of the 3-point shot and the shot clock. There have also been advances in terms of strategies and coaching tactics. The wish-bone in football, the Fosbury Flop in track, and the match-up zone defense in basketball are but three examples.

There have also been new or adapted training techniques for competitive sports in general as well as sport specific conditioning programs. One example would be the use of plyometrics, a training concept that was brought to the United States from Europe by Fred Wilt, a former Olympic athlete who also coached the women's track program at Purdue University (Von Duvillard, Flynn, Jones & Vetro, 1990). Plyometrics has frequently been described as those activities that utilize speed as well as strength in an effort to create a significant explosive type of movement, reaction with increased power (Chu, 1983).

EXPLAINING THE *WHY* IN COACHING

> **COACHING CONCEPT #182. Explaining the *why* to athletes and parents enhances learning and facilitates relationships.**

Yes, coaching has changed. Today, things are different. Today, athletes are demanding and expect to know *why* certain things are being asked of them. Parents, as never before, want to know *why* coaches acted in a certain fashion or made a specific decision, especially when the decision affects their own children. It is especially important to explain the reasons for the team rules—both to athletes and, when appropriate, to their parents. Accountability is upon the coaching profession and individual coaches as never before. Today's coaches must not only have sound, defensible reasons for doing or not doing something but must be ready to express and defend their actions and inactions—not only to themselves but to others as well.

This can be a change for the good. Experience has shown that athletes learn physical skills better and perform at a higher level when they understand the rationale behind that which they are asked to do. Athletes are typically not always willing to blindly follow the directions shouted by coaches. As pointed out earlier, athletes don't immediately jump (and on the way up, ask: "how high coach?"), when coaches yell. Today, the situation is somewhat changed. Now, the athlete is more likely to ask: "why, coach?" However, coaches need not fret as this can be a positive development for two very important reasons. First, it makes the coach think twice lest one makes questionable or ludicrous decisions and/or expresses unreasonable expectations of one's teams and individual athletes. Second, it fosters a better understanding on behalf of the individual athlete in terms of making them more knowledgeable of the sound coaching and teaching rationale supporting the specific activity that the coach is espousing.

The more individual athletes understand in terms of the reasons behind why they and/or the team are asked or required to do something, the greater the likelihood that the athlete and the team will be successful in carrying out the course of action as dictated by the coaching staff. Of course, this is not implying that the coaching atmosphere is a democratic process where everyone votes on what strategies to employ. Nor does this imply that the coach must take time out to explain each and every decision (during a game or even a practice, for example) to the athletes, either individually or collectively. Common sense, however, does suggest that coaches attempt, when feasible and practical, to explain why they, as coaches, make the decisions they do. In conclusion, the explanation of why helps motivate the athlete and facilitates the learning process by helping the athlete and the coach possess a clear understanding of the rationale behind the coach's tactics and strategies.

REFERENCES

ACL experts look for consensus. (2000, December/January). *Athletic Management, XII*(1), 12, 14, 17 -20

Anderson, R. (2004, October/November). Up to speed. Athletic Management, XVI(6), 37-38, 40-43.

Athletics Notes. (1993, April 21). *The Chronicle of Higher Education, XXXIX*(33), p. A-40.

Athletics Notes. (1993, April 28). *The Chronicle of Higher Education, XXXIX*(34), p. A-36.

Chu, C. D. (1983). Plyometrics: The line between strength and speed. *National Strength and Conditioning Association Journal*, 5(4), 20-21.

Colleges. (1993, April 27). *USA Today*, p. 11-C.

Hazelrigg, G. (1983, January). Taking the charge—Tactics taught in basketball may lead to injury, liability. *The First Aider*, pp. 1, 21.

Sidelines. (1993, April 28). *The Chronicle of Higher Education. XXXXIX*(34), A-35.

Tom, D. (1993, March 5). Relationship faces new pressures. *USA Today*, p. l-C, 2-C.

Von Duvillard, S. V., Flynn, D., Jones, K. & Vetro, V. (1990, March). Plyometrics for speed & explosiveness. *Scholastic Coach*, pp. 80-81, 97.

Warning: Watch the warm-ups. (1989, Fall). *The First Aider*, p. 3.

Watts, J. (2002). Perspectives on sport specialization. *Journal of Physical Education, Recreation and Dance*, 73(8), 32-37.

Name: _____

Student ID #: _____

EXERCISES FOR CHAPTER 7

A.   Of the fourteen elements of a winning team, which, in your opinion, are the two or three most important elements in terms of having a successful, winning team? Why?

B.   Cite two coaches who have an excellent reputation as coaches and as human beings who might serve as excellent models of competent mentors and state the reasons for your choice.

C.   Explain the statement that *it is fine to have idols and heroes in terms of coaches but it would be foolish to attempt to become a clone of another coach.*

D. Cite some significant changes that have occurred in sports and society in the past 20-30 years and explain how these changes might have very real implications for you as a coach today.

E. How would you as a coach attempt to motivate would-be athletes to become athletes and keep their interests high in light of all of the other attractions vying for their time and effort?

F. What are the advantages and disadvantages of the increasing emphasis on greater specialization by current day athletes in one sport to the exclusion of other sports?

G. Which is more important, in your opinion, the ability to recruit or the ability to retain athletes who have made a team? Provide a clear rationale and justification for your answer.

RESEARCH QUESTONS FOR CHAPTER 7

1. Interview current athletes as well as individuals who were former athletes 20 years or more in the past and attempt to determine the differences between being an athlete in the past and presently? In what areas are there differences and how do these differences, if any, create challenges and problems for current-day coaches?

----

2. Ask a high school varsity sport of a flagship sport how the coach operates in terms of getting and keeping the coach's athletes in top condition. Be specific in outlining the conditioning efforts of the coach.

_____

_____

_____

_____

_____

_____

3. Interview a varsity coach who has coached for at least 20 years and find out what the coach thinks about the fact that *coaching today and being an athlete today happens to be different than in past years.*

_____

_____

_____

_____

_____

4. Interview a current varsity coach and solicit information relative to what the coach thinks about the area of nutrition and nutrition education for the athletes on the coach's team. Outline the tactics the coach takes to educate and inform athletes on proper nutrition practices.

_____

_____

_____

_____

_____

_____

5. Interview a varsity second coach in terms of how the coach attempts to reduce or eliminate injuries to the athletes and what the coach does following serious injuries to the athletes.

Chapter 8

Coaching Practices, Hints and Strategies

Water Polo—An Up and Coming Sport in Colleges and Universities.

GUARDING AGAINST OVEREMPHASIS ON WINNING

Coaches are constantly striving to be successful. In sports, one *sure sign of success* for many people is to have a winning team. However, not every coach can be successful to the extent that they can enjoy a winning program nearly every year (Stier, 1993). What happens when a team is not successful? That is, what are the consequences of a losing season? What happens when several seasons come and go and that elusive goal of *winning* is still not a reality?

Far too often in the above scenario, the coach is no longer the coach. This can take place at all levels including youth sports, interscholastic sports, and college sports. Removal of a coach for perceived incompetence is not the exclusive property of professional sports or major, big-time (NCAA Division I) university programs. It can happen anywhere.

How can coaches attempt to protect themselves from being vulnerable in a profession that places such emphasis upon success, winning, and being victorious in competition?

The first step is for the coach not to make the mistake of always talking about emerging victorious and having winning seasons. People quickly pick up on that kind of talk. Athletes begin to place winning at the top of their priority list. Parents tend to focus on the results of contests rather than upon the competition itself when coaches consistently refer to winning and emerging victorious over opponents. Even athletic administrators succumb to this type of temptation when the win-win syndrome is being constantly reinforced by the coach.

COACHING CONCEPT #183:   Coaches shouldn't always talk about winning or victories—instead, emphasize the importance of doing one's best.

What should be done if the coach is not to place so much emphasis upon winning? What is the alternative? The answer is simple. Instead of emphasizing the winning aspect of competition one should highlight the fact that the athletes, and the team as a whole, should perform up to their potential. Some years ago, the United States Army coined an excellent praise relating to motivation and goal setting, that is, *Be All That You Can Be.* That is a pretty good concept for coaches to remember and subscribe to in their coaching efforts.

Doing one's best should be one's motto—both from the standpoint of the coaches and from the team's perspective. That is what Johnny Wooden, famed former basketball coach of the UCLA Bruins, did. And he was a true winner, from every perspective, a gentleman coach whose teams were crowned national NCAA champions ten times during the 1960s and 1970s.

It has been reported that coach Wooden never used the word *win* in discussing goals and objectives with his players. Instead, he encouraged them to do their best, to be all that they could be, to work to their potential. If athletes concentrate and focus upon doing their best and are successful in competing at or near their peak level of performance—both individually and collectively as a team—the so-called winning should take care of itself.

COACHING CONCEPT #184: No person is truly indispensable—there is always someone who can take your place.

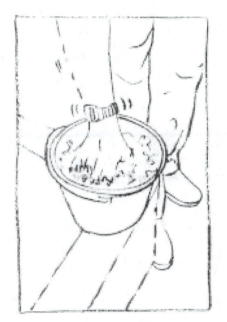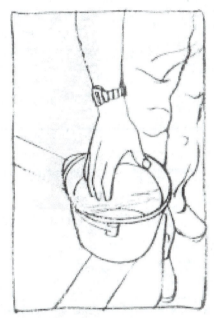

FIGURE 8.1—Being Indispensable

Far too often coaches, especially those successful coaches who have had significant accomplishments on and off the playing field, begin to think of themselves as indispensable to their athletic programs and to the sponsoring entities. However, this is just not true, figure 8.1. Coaches need to recognize that regardless of how successful they are or have been that there is always someone capable of following them and carrying on the so-called torch towards continued success in that sport setting.

THERE'S NO INDISPENSABLE PERSON

Sometime when you are feeling important,
Sometime, when your ego's in bloom,
Sometime, when you take it for granted,
That you are the best qualified person in the room,
Sometime, when you feel that your absence
Would leave an unfillable hole,
Just follow this simple instruction
And see how it humbles your soul.

Take a bucket and fill it with water,
Put your hand in it, up to your wrist,
Pull it out, and the hole that is remaining
Is a measure of how you will be missed.

You may splash all you please when you enter,
You can stir up the water galore,
But stop, and you will find in a minute,
That it looks quite the same as before.

The moral in this quaint little story
Is to do the best that you can
And be all that you can,
Be proud of yourself,
Take pride in what you accomplish,
but remember,

THERE'S NO INDISPENSABLE PERSON.

Anonymous

Behavioral Expectations of Successful Coaches

Coaches need to be cognizant of the fact that even with outstanding success, they are still going to be held to a specific level of behavior—both on and off the playing field. Sport history is replete with examples of highly successful and well thought of coaches who stepped over the line in their behavior, forcing the administration to take action which often resulted in the removal of the individual from coaching responsibilities.

Take, for example, the legendary Woody Hayes, former coach at The Ohio State University. With all of his success, with the history of being recognized as one of the greatest football coaches at the college or university level, he lost his job following the striking of a Clemson player during the 1978 Gator Bowl. Coach Hayes was removed from his coaching position and yet the football program continued to thrive and prosper under the tutorage of those who subsequently held the title of head football coach.

Of course, it doesn't always take something as drastic as slugging an athlete (one's own or an opponent's) to find out just how dispensable one really is in any given coaching situation. Arrogance and conceit on behalf of a coach can also be that individual's undoing. Coaches who think and act like they are special, who do not treat others with respect, who lack the social graces expected of any professional, and who believe that their success as a coach makes them untouchable or indispensable to the sports program—in all likelihood could be in for a rude awakening.

COACHING CONCEPT #185: Don't take yourself too seriously—keep a sense of humor.

Coaches should never take themselves too seriously. Although many coaches would like to think that the success of an athletic team or the progress of an individual athlete can be traced directly to their own hard work and competency, this may not be the case at all. While coaches can justly take some of the credit, a great deal of the credit should also go to the individual athlete or athletes, their parents, the athletic administrator, the school administration and a whole host of other individuals and organizations.

It is best for coaches to also possess a sense of humor in the conduct of their work and in the pursuit of their objectives and goals. Don't take yourself too seriously. For most people involved in the sport scene, the experience is a game, a contest, a means of recreation. Coaches are merely one cog in a very large wheel of sport and life. Taking oneself too seriously and lacking a sense of humor can result in creating an image of arrogance and conceit.

COACHING CONCEPT #186: Be humble—realize that you don't know all the questions, much less all the answers.

Being humble means more than being willing to give credit where credit is due. It also implies that the coach never stops learning in one's quest to become a highly skilled mentor. Coaches are always learning. They learn from their experiences (successes and failures). They also learn from books, from journals and magazines, from attendance at clinics and from workshops, conferences and conventions. Coaches are very similar to physicians in that they always need to keep up with the times, to remain current in the knowledge base of their sport(s).

Too frequently, coaches become cocky and begin to believe that they know it all. Experiencing too much success too early in one's career can have that effect upon some individuals. In reality, coaches never stop learning. Coaches should *never stop wanting to learn* and working towards that goal.

COACHING CONCEPT #187: **Don't become too satisfied with your own accomplishments—keep hungry for success and excellence.**

Just as athletes very rarely reach perfection in their role as sportsmen or sportswomen, coaches also rarely reach perfection in their performance as coaches. Being satisfied with one's performance or with one's past achievements can take the edge off the enthusiasm of the coach. It is important for coaches to retain that drive, that motivation, that desire for further improvement in one's performance. For only when a coach is hungry for additional goals, and is willing to continue to sacrifice and work diligently, will the coach be motivated to achieve and to continue to work hard, to work effectively and efficiently in the role of a coach.

COACHING CONCEPT #188: **Don't be absorbed with details and the search for perfection to that extent that one loses sight of the ultimate objectives.**

Coaches are frequently being admonished to pay attention to details. And this is sound advice. However, such advice must be balanced with the reality of the situation in which the coach and the athletes exist. One should not be so preoccupied with details that one loses sight of the overall goal(s) of the program. Not everything the coach or the athletes accomplish needs to be perfect. There is a difference between perfection and acceptable levels of performance by individuals, groups and teams. Coaches should not expect perfection either in themselves or in their charges. Rather, coaches need to come to a reasonable balance in terms of what to expect of themselves, their staff and their players.

COACHING CONCEPT #189: **Don't be so overly concerned with the so-called objective of winning that you forget about the process.**

Coaches are sometimes so pre-occupied with the objective of winning that they are neglectful of the actual process or processes involved in reaching that objective as well as many other important tasks and responsibilities associated with their athletic programs. Yes, winning is important. However, *how* one wins (or attempts to win) is as important, if not more so, in today's athletic programs at all levels of competition. Winning is not the only criterion by which the coach is being judged today. What the coach does on and off the athletic practice and game field is very important. Today, the significance of the end result is tempered by *how* a coach actually goes about performing one's jobs and responsibilities. For example, a coach who wins while physically abusing one's players, or who neglects the academic pursuits of the athletes, or who employs unethical or questionable strategies and tactics, will soon be looking for a new job regardless of the level of success experienced.

COACHING CONCEPT #190: Fame and honor are fleeting—coaches should remain gracious especially when they are successful.

An important lesson for all coaches to learn is that regardless of how successful they may be, regardless of the praise and approval heaped upon them, they must realize that in many instances, they are only as good as their last season, and in some cases, only as good as their last few games. Not only are they not indispensable but they can quickly become excess baggage and even a liability in a very short period of time.

Thus, coaches would do well to consider examining their behavior, especially when they are successful and have been for some time, to insure that their actions and inactions are indeed appropriate. It is imperative that coaches are not seen by others—both inside the coaching or educational organization as well as those in the community—as being offensive, abusive or impertinent. The mark of a great coach is one who is gracious, both in victory and defeat.

The reward for hard work and dedication—victory.

BEING VIEWED AS COMPETENT AND SUCCESSFUL BY OTHERS

It is important for coaches to be viewed as competent and knowledgeable by others, both individuals and groups, both in school and in the community. This is important throughout a coach's tenure at a particular school or with a specific team. This is especially important when a team is not enjoying the fruits of consistent victories on the playing field or court. There are several strategies coaches may employ to booster the image of their coaching competency in the eyes of others. Similarly, there are tactics that coaches can use to insure that their athletic squads are held in high esteem by others. Remember, a coach is judged by how the team performs and how individual players perform (on and off the sport playing field) as well as how the coach performs.

COACHING CONCEPT #191: Don't keep your superior(s) in the dark concerning your professional activities.

For example, coaches would do well to insure that their athletic directors and other school administrators are kept abreast of the coaches' professional accomplishments and professional activities. No, this does not mean that the individual coach becomes a braggart to the athletic director and others. Rather, it is suggested that the coach tactfully make administrators aware of the positive activities and achievements that might otherwise go unnoticed.

Casually mentioning that one attended a coaching workshop or clinic impresses upon others that the coach is making an effort to remain current in the field of coaching. Mentioning to others how one's scouting trip turned out gives a clear signal that the coach is putting forth the effort and actively pursuing professional activities that are expected of a competent coach. Of course, as already pointed out in an earlier chapter, effort alone is not sufficient. Nevertheless, it is important that individual coaches make a concerted effort to make others aware that they, as coaches, are spending the time, making the effort, and performing the tasks that competent, dedicated coaches are expected to do. Being seen doing one's tasks, performing one's job, assuming one's responsibility at an accepted level is all important.

Being involved in a summer camp or being invited to help a coach at another school are activities that can help increase the professional prestige and image of a coach in the eyes of others. Writing for a coaching publication is evidence of mastery of subject matter, in this case, the coaching of a sport. Similarly, speaking at clinics or workshops can enhance the image of the coach if the right people are aware of such professional contributions.

COACHING CONCEPT #192: Use the year-end team report to highlight the team's and the coach's achievements and accomplishments.

The final, year-end sport or team report is an excellent opportunity for a coach to professionally highlight one's achievements as well as the team's accomplishments for the administration. Coaches should use the creation of the written year-end report to carry a message to the athletic and school administration that the coaching staff is professional, productive and competent.

COACHING CONCEPT #193: **A coach's competency is judged in light of the performance of the team and players—both on and off the playing field.**

For many people, including parents, athletes, fans, the public, and even administrators, if the team wins, the coach must be highly skilled. If players are exceptional and demonstrate a high level of skill, it is sometimes perceived that the coach is an excellent mentor. Conversely, if a team loses, it is the coach's fault. If individual players perform poorly, it is because the coach lacked the ability to teach or adequately motivate the players. *Of course, this is not necessarily true.* Nevertheless, there are many people who judge the competency of a coach in just this fashion.

Thus, it behooves the coach to employ strategies and tactics that will place the coach in a favorable light in terms of evaluation and perception of the coach's competency as a coach and mentor. This means that the coach needs to be able to emphasize aspects of the sport and the competition other than the mere winning of a contest(s). Although these tactics and strategies can be used at any time, it is especially important to employ such strategies when coaches are facing a losing record with their teams.

COACHING CONCEPT #194: **Always know why your team is not winning—be able to point to extenuating circumstances affecting the success of the team.**

No, this does not mean that the coach is a cry baby and constantly offers a myriad of lame excuses for losing. But it does mean that if a coach and team are going to experience a lack of success on the playing field it behooves the coach to be able to rationally explain some of the reasons why this is taking place. For example, a coach could be playing a whole host of younger or inexperienced players. A high school coach who plays predominantly sophomores on the basketball team (if they are the best players available) will usually be granted some slack even in those settings where winning is highly prized by the various constituencies and publics and by the athletic administration.

Starting Young Players

Taking this line of thought one step further, coaches who are playing seniors and yet continue to lose on the court or field might want to reconsider their choice of whom to start and/or play. Instead of playing seniors on a team which continues to be defeated, it might be wise to at least consider playing sophomores and juniors, that is, those youngsters who will return to the school/team the following year with additional experience.

The author was faced with just such a situation as a new head basketball coach at a medium size high school in a basketball crazy community. Playing a senior laden team, the squad was experiencing a truly dismal season from a won/loss stand-point. Bringing up sophomores to play on the varsity squad and benching the seniors resulted in some severe criticism from some quarters—especially the parents of the seniors. However, the move at least gave the new head coach a reason for losing if indeed the team was to continue down that same path. The rationale was that if the team was going to experience disaster, then the team would do so with sophomores rather than with seniors. That is, the coach and the players were building for the fu-ture. The sophomores were going to be given valuable experience and would have two more years of playing time on the varsity squad.

The fact of the matter, in this particular case, is that the sophomores began to win as starters, and the team finished with an overall winning record, including a first-time ever trip to post season competition. This, in itself, certainly negated any long term criticism in that particular community and school for the coach's decision to start the sophomores instead of the seniors.

Presence of Injuries

Another factor that can be pointed out as a reason (not an excuse) for a team experiencing difficulty in competition is the presence of injuries. An injury to a key athlete is one of those things that sometimes, in spite of one's best efforts, just oc-curs, just happens. Sometimes, a team is left shorthanded and at a decided disad-vantage because of a single injury or multiple injuries. This fact needs to be recog-nized by the coach. And the coach must be subtle in making this fact known to the appropriate individuals and groups.

No coach wants to be seen as a chronic complainer bemoaning the presence of injuries and using them as *the* excuse as to why the team is not winning. However, used judiciously, such information can blunt much of the criticism that might other-wise be leveled at the coach of a losing team.

Bad Luck

And, of course, sometimes a team will simply end up on the *proverbial sharp end of the stick* because of bad, blind luck. Yes, luck, or fortune, whatever you want to call it. Perhaps the team has engaged in a hard fought battle and the outcome really was dependent upon a single act, perhaps near the end of the contest. For example, in football the final pass from the two-yard line falls incomplete with no time remaining—and the offensive team loses the hard fought, well played, and superbly executed contest. Perhaps the potential receiver could just have well caught the pass as not. The difference might just be that intangible, luck or fortune.

Superior Opponents—Giving Other Teams Their Just Due

> **COACHING CONCEPT #195: Sometimes teams and individuals lose because their opponents are superior—period.**

Another reason why a team loses is because their opponent is better. It can be as simple as that. Why does the reason for a team losing a contest have to be because one's own team did not play well? Or, because the youngsters did not try? Or, because some of the players were not in adequate condition? Or, because the athletes did not want it badly enough? Or, because the officials were terrible? Or, because of the lack of a home court advantage? Or, because the team made too many stupid and inexcusable mistakes? Or, because the team ran out of time?

How ridiculous coaches sound sometimes when they attempt to explain away a loss by their team. In reality, teams usually lose because they play against opponents who have superior skills and talent. Or, teams lose because coaches make significant mistakes and are out-coached—either on the playing field or prior to even showing up for the contest (on the practice field/court).

In reality, it is infrequent that the public is treated to such an honest and refreshing response from a coach following the team's defeat by hearing that the real reason for the loss is that the other team played very well and was simply a better team, period. It should not be disconcerting to point out that the other team (athletes and coaches) performed exceptionally well and that is why that team emerged victorious on that particular night.

Thus, there is nothing wrong, nothing embarrassing, about the coach admitting that one's team got beat by a better, a superior, a more talented opponent. Give the other team its due, period. It is better to be honest and to have a realistic perspective of why one's team was beaten than to attempt to make up reasons which only exacerbate a negative situation in terms how others look at the coach and the efforts expended by the youngsters.

Women sports involve strenuous and demanding competition.

HIGHLIGHTING SIGNIFICANT ACHIEVEMENTS BY ONE'S OWN ATHLETES

The concept is simple. Coaches need to be able to point to a number of significant accomplishments and achievements, their own and those of their athletes, during the course of a season (Stier, 1992). If a team is winning, that is, possesses a winning record, this fact alone may be all that is necessary to satisfy some people, both in and outside the school. When a team wins, people tend to notice. When a team wins, most people are happy most of the time. Coaches don't have to do a lot of bragging when their teams are winning. Coaches don't have to dwell on the obvious.

COACHING CONCEPT #196: **Coaches need to be able to point to significant accomplishments of their teams and individual athletes other than winning—especially if their teams are not winning.**

However, when a team is not winning, that is an entirely different situation. When a team is experiencing a losing record or fails to record victories over specific opponents, especially important rivals, coaches can sometimes become vulnerable. To counteract this precarious exposure, it is important to be able to point to significant team and individual athletes' accomplishments and achievements.

The point is that there must be something positive or significant about the team or individual athletes that others can take pride in as parents, as athletes, as fans, as administrators, as teachers, etc. It is important to remember that perceptions of a coach's competency are closely tied to how the athletes and the team is perceived. If positive things can be attributed to the team and individual athletes, the coach can also be viewed in a positive light.

What can be done to take some of the heat off of the coaching staff? What are some of the athletic and non-athletic accomplishments and activities that generate pride and a feeling of confidence in the skill level and competency of the coach? What are some team achievements (exploits) that will indicate that the coach is competent, even if the team is not currently experiencing a winning season? Listed below are several strategies that can be used to create or reinforce a positive image, impression, or reputation of the coaching staff as well as the individual athletes and the team as a whole.

1. Indicate by actions and words that you care about your players as individuals and not just as talented athletes who can help win games.

2. Become known as an excellent teacher of skills, especially fundamentals.

3. Emphasize the academic achievements of student-athletes.

4. Stress the importance of non-academic (social and personal) achievements of student-athletes.

5. Stress the high level of competition comprising the team's schedule.

6. Have athletes look clean cut, professional and neat.

7. Insure that athletes exhibit good sportsmanship.

8. Make a special effort to insure that your student-athletes behave in school and within the community.

Indicate by Actions and Words That You Care About Your Players as Individuals and Not Just as Talented Athletes Who Can Help Win Games

Far too often, coaches are thought to care only about those athletes who possess superior talent or physical attributes. These same coaches are often perceived to coddle and pamper the so-called star athletes. These coaches expend a significant amount of effort on such individuals. They lavish an extraordinary amount of time upon youngsters who are instrumental to a team's (and therefore the coach's) success. On the other hand, those athletes who are not of star quality, those with only average ability or less, are often seen as being neglected by some coaches or, at best, tolerated. And, all too often, there are coaches who seem to drop their interest and support of an athlete the moment the youngster is no longer in a position to play a key role in garnering much sought after victories, either by choice, circumstances or happenstance.

COACHING CONCEPT #197: **A mark of a good coach is one who cares about the athlete even when the youngster can no longer play for the team—it is easy to care about a 7' tall, sophomore basketball All-American.**

Athletes may become ineligible to compete on a team because of any number of reasons. They may have used up their eligibility. NCAA rules permit 8 semesters of competition within a 5-year span of time. Some state high school associations prohibit competition for those youngsters reaching their 18th birthday prior to the start of the sport season. Youngsters may encounter academic difficulties and become ineligible for competition or they may have misbehaved in some fashion and be declared ineligible for further practice or competition by the local sponsoring entity. Or, an athlete may have become injured and is prevented from further competition. Of course, youngsters have been known to quit a team because of any number of reasons. And, athletes have been dismissed from the team by the coach for failure to do something or because they did something they were not supposed to do.

How the coach treats the former athlete after the youngster is no longer a member of the team says a great deal about the coach. Let's face it. It is easy for a coach to show interest in and support for a so-called star athlete. It says a lot about a coach who continues to go out of the coach's way in an effort to help a student, a former athlete, who is not even a current member of the school team (for whatever reason).

Since the youngster is no longer in a position to help the coach earn a victory, the reason for the coach to continue to support, help and counsel the former athlete is certainly not a selfish one on behalf of the coach. Quite the contrary. Coaches who go out of their way to continue to help former athletes, even those who might have left the team under negative or controversial circumstances, are viewed as honest, unselfish and thoroughly professional individuals. These are the coaches who are seen as legitimately concerned about the welfare of an individual, a former athlete, and not influenced or motivated to action because the young person might be able to win a couple of games for the team (or for the coach). To be viewed as such a professional and caring mentor goes a long way to justify one's being retained in a coaching position.

Become Known as an Excellent Teacher of Skills, Especially Fundamentals

The key to being successful as a coach in competitive sports, if there is one, is to be a sound teacher of fundamentals and basic skills. Fundamentals and basic skills must be mastered by athletes. More advanced strategies and tactics can be introduced later when athletes and teams have developed and demonstrated command of the sport's basic skills and fundamentals.

Coaches need to be excellent teachers of basic skills and fundamentals. Too many coaches remain fascinated with the ultimate concept of winning, with advanced strategies, and sophisticated tactics to the almost exclusion of fundamentals. In reality, teams and individual athletes adequately schooled in the fundamentals of a sport have an excellent chance of ultimately achieving success by building on a sound foundation. The lack of fundamentals, on the other hand, frequently spells disaster in most competitive situations.

Steve Alford, former All-American basketball player at the University of Indiana and a former Olympian and professional player, was quoted as saying: "I had good teachers when I was 8 who taught me to shoot. Coaches care about wins and losses. Teachers care about skills" (Brady, 1993). *Coaches should be teachers.* They should be concerned that their charges actually learn fundamentals and master skills at an appropriate rate of progression.

COACHING CONCEPT #198: Be sure that athletes look like they were coached—stress fundamentals and emphasize the necessity of not making stupid mistakes.

Nothing undermines the confidence of a coach more than having athletes or teams commit stupid errors during a competition. In football, having repeated errors in snapping the ball is inexcusable. In basketball, there is no justification in having an abundance of turnovers, especially when the opponents are not even pressing. In volleyball, failing to get the ball over the net while serving only invites criticism and fault finding by others. In relay races, the frequent dropping of the baton is worthy of reproach.

While some may excuse, or are at least be understanding, when a team is beaten by a superior opponent, few will be so quick to forgive a coach of a team that consistently beats itself by committing what is viewed by some as preventable blunders or mistakes. The key is to insure that the athletes look like they were coached. If athletes and teams are to lose on the so-called playing field or court, they need to be beaten by superior opponents. They should never beat themselves by committing preventable goofs. To do so may signal to some that they were inadequately coached.

This is why some coaches of team sports subscribe to the conservative philosophy of coaching in terms of strategy and tactics. Woody Hayes, former football coach at The Ohio State University, when asked why he did not pass more frequently, reportedly replied that three things can result from passing in football, and two of them are bad (incomplete passes and interceptions).

COACHING CONCEPT #199: If one is to lose in sport competition—it is frequently better to have the score close than to lose by a big margin.

Some coaches stress the importance of always keeping the score close. These coaches believe that if they can keep the score close, their teams are never really out of contention. That is, such teams are always within striking distance of emerging from the contest as victors. A secondary benefit to this way of thinking, according to some, is that the team that is beaten by a small margin is looked upon more favorably by others (parents, fans, boosters, administrators, the public, etc.) than when a team is routed by a lopsided score. Of course, continued losses, even by close scores, can place coaches in jeopardy.

Emphasize the Academic Achievements of Student-Athletes

Always emphasize the academic accomplishments of your student-athletes. Every coach needs to point to some aspects of the program as successful. Therefore, highlight and publicize the academic achievements of individual athletes and the team itself. It is interesting to note that frequently the grade point average (GPA) of a majority of athletic teams in any given school is probably higher than the GPA of the total student body. This is because each athletic team is comprised of a relatively small group of people in comparison with the total student body. The student body encompasses *all* of the students in the school—those with low GPAs and those with high GPAs.

As a result, the odds are that your team's GPA will be higher than the grade point average of the total student body within the school. If this is the case, promote and highlight this fact. If only some of your athletes have high GPAs, then promote that fact. If some of your charges are on the student honor roll, publicize that fact. If your athletic department has a student-athlete honor roll—publicize the names of your athletes who earn this distinction. If an athlete earns Academic All-American honors, make people aware of this extraordinary achievement.

Think about initiating a so-called academic support program for your team or for individual athletes. This may consist of nothing more than a supervised study-hall several nights a week. It may include special tutoring for selected athletes by volunteer teachers or other students. Of course, as the coach, you should always emphasize the fact that academics come first before athletics. You might want to impose a minimum GPA average in order for athletes to practice or compete. You might insist that your athletes consistently attend class and be attentive while in class. If you do so, be sure and communicate (publicize and promote) this fact to parents, students, teachers, administrators and others.

COACHING CONCEPT #200: If a tree falls in a forest, does it make any noise if there is no one there to hear it fall?—the answer is NO!!!

It is important that coaches publicize their own good works, their accomplishments and achievements as well as their athletes' good deeds and exploits. An old coaching anecdote indicates that half of the benefit of any accomplishment is lost unless others become aware of it. Therefore, coaches need to make sure that positive accomplishments and good deeds are made public for many individuals and groups to learn about. *This is sound advice.*

If you, as a coach, really accept the notion that academics have priority for student-athletes, and as a result your actions consistently support this philosophy, you had better make sure that others know of your efforts and your support. This may take the form of your paying close attention to the academic status of your student-athletes. That is, by communicating with teachers of your athletes to determine the academic status and progress of the youngsters. This may also involve your suspending athletes from practice or games if they fail to exhibit appropriate behavior in the classroom or fail to meet certain academic standards. Of course, if this becomes necessary, be sure and let the teachers and administrators know of your actions so that your support of the academic integrity of the school becomes well known.

Stress the Importance of Non-Academic Achievements of Student-Athletes

Of course, there are many areas other than the academic arena that coaches can point to with pride in terms of the actions of their youngsters. In reality any achievements of athletes can be pointed to with pride by the coaching staff. At a minimum, coaches should be able to point with pride the fact that each of their athletes exhibits the three Cs of deportment, that is, *civility, citizenship and character*. These traits should be exhibited by athletes both on and off the proverbial playing field, court or pool.

Some of these activities can include involvement in drug education programs where high school athletes visit elementary schools and speak about the dangers of drugs. Or, college athletes can speak at various high schools and junior high schools—both to non-athletes and to athletes at these schools. Situations in which student-athletes are leaders in and outside of school should be highlighted and publicized. For example, the consequences of athletes successfully assuming leadership positions in student government can be far-reaching and positive in terms of the image of the

Sometimes a bunt can be as effective as "going for the fences."

athletic squad and the mentoring efforts of the coaches.

Having one's athletes volunteer their time to work with Boy Scout and Girl Scout groups or other worthy organizations (Special Olympics) in the community can go a long way to promote the positive image of the team, the coach and the school. Athletes conducting a car wash to benefit a local charity organization can create very positive impressions among the community in addition to providing a meaningful learning experience for the athletes themselves. Of course, as stated above, it is the responsibility of the coach to see that a wide range of constituencies and publics are made aware of such good deeds, involvements, and accomplishments.

Stress the High Level of Competition Comprising the Team's Schedule

> **COACHING CONCEPT #201:** No one likes an excuse maker—provide explanations rather than give excuses.

If your team has a strenuous schedule, stress this fact. However, do not emphasize the arduous schedule as an excuse, but rather as a matter of fact. Remember, no one likes an excuse maker. However, there are ways to use the presence of a truly tough schedule to one's advantage, even if the team's won/loss record leaves much to be desired.

Take pride in having a very competitive or arduous schedule, if that is what you are either blessed or cursed with as the coach. Share this reality in a positive manner with others—within and outside of the immediate athletic scene. Do so in a non-complaining but informative, factual fashion. Being recognized as going up against very competitive opponents might very well provide some measure of refuge from some of the unreasonable expectations and potential criticism by uninformed individuals and groups.

Have Athletes Look Clean Cut, Professional and Neat— Athletes Should Look Like Athletes

This doesn't mean that every athlete on the team must have a crew cut hair style. However, image is always important, especially the image of athletes. The image that the team and individual athletes project is very, very important in terms of how the coach is perceived by others, both in the school and in the community.

Should coaches consider dress codes for their athletes for both home and away games as well as while they are in school? Many coaches would say, "yes, absolutely." The type of dress code will depend upon the individual setting and circumstances that you, the coach, find yourself in at any given point in time. It is especially important to examine the type of dress codes that had been acceptable in the past in any given sport's program.

Some coaches expect a specific level of appearance (as well as behavior) by their charges at all times, while in school *and* out of school. Other coaches only have such expectations while the student-athletes are in school or going to and from an athletic contest. You as a coach must decide what you will expect and require of your charges in this area.

When athletes present a clean cut, professional, and neat image, they are projecting this representation not only for themselves but for the athletic program, for the team, and for their coach(es). They are indicating, by their adherence to the coach's wishes or expectations, that they are supporting the team standards, are subscribing to the established goals and objectives and are willing to be influenced by the coach.

Certainly there are restrictions (laws and school rules) regulating what coaches can and cannot do in terms of establishing and enforcing specific dress codes. Coaches cannot have unreasonable expectations (rules) regarding the image presented by their athletes. For example, dress codes that unreasonably restrict the length and style of the athlete's hair will not stand up in court. Likewise, the prohibition of beards for athletes is not acceptable in court unless there is a health or safety reason for such prohibition, such as in the sport of wrestling. And, the presence of earrings worn by male athletes outside of competition cannot be forbidden by the coach as a part of the (non-game) dress (behavior) code for the team.

However, it should not astound you to find that there are coaches who are able to instill enthusiasm in their charges, are able to motivate their athletes, are able to influence their players to such an extent that the players will eagerly (if not reluctantly) buy into the image philosophy and expectations of their coach. This ability to influence one's athletes is a highly desirable and prized skill, one that can be learned and improved upon with effort.

COACHING CONCEPT #202: **The image of one's athletes reflect directly on you as their coach—therefore insure that the image each athlete projects is indeed a positive one.**

Believe it or not, coaches are indeed judged by how their team members look and how they act—on and away from the playing field. Thus, coaches should spend the effort to educate the athletes in terms of how they should visually present themselves in terms of their image and their behavior in school and in the community.

It is also important that athletes demonstrate maturity and a certain level of sophistication *while competing* in an athletic contest. Losing one's composure or one's temper is not the image of a mature, competent, well-trained athlete. It is important to remember that the coach is often held accountable for the actions (and inactions) of individual athletes and for the team as a whole. Therefore, it is imperative that the coach be willing to communicate reasonable expectations regarding the image (*physical* image as well as *behavioral* image) of each athlete, individually and collectively—at all times.

Insure That Athletes Exhibit Good Sportsmanship

One of the traditional objectives of competitive sports is the teaching of good sportsmanship. Thus, it behooves the coach to insist that the athletes (and the coaching staff) do indeed demonstrate good sportsmanship at all times, but especially in the heat of battle, in the actual contests. "Both the NCAA and NFHS basketball rules committees have made curbing rough play a major point of emphasis for several years" (Read, 2003, p. 29). It is this rough play that is often the catalyst that leads to various types of poor sportsmanship behavior.

Crying over a bad call by an official, or being slapped with a technical foul or deliberately violating the letter or intent of a rule or regulation are certainly not examples of exhibiting good sportsmanship. In fact, criticism of officials by the athletes should never be tolerated. Courteous treatment of all officials will help create a positive image for the team. Athletes should never deserve to be hit with a technical foul (in the sport of basketball). In soccer, players must never receive a card for unsportsmanlike conduct. Hockey players should never earn a trip to the penalty box because of a deliberate attempt to injure an athlete.

In western New York, in the general area of Rochester, New York, Section 5 basketball has a code of conduct applicable for fans and participants at basketball contests. On page 54 of the Section 5 handbook is a section devoted to sportsmanship (Code of Sportsmanship) for spectators, athletes, and coaches. Included within this section are the following 8 rules or guidelines (Murphy, 2001).

1. Keep cheering positive. There should be no profanity or degrading language or gestures.

2. Avoid actions which offend visiting teams or individual players.

3. Show appreciation of good play by both teams.

4. Learn the rules of the game in order to be a better informed spectator.

5. Treat all visiting teams in a manner in which you would expect to be treated.

6. Understand and abide by the rules and regulations of the game.

7. Accept victory and defeat with grace and dignity.

8. Remember that the use, abuse and resulting negative influence of drugs, including alcohol and tobacco, is detrimental to the game and its participants.

The New York high school Section 5 officials also have specific recommendations or suggestions for players and for coaches. For players, the handbook indicates that players are to "demonstrate self-control and respect at all times, be they officials, spectators or other athletes" (Murphy, 2001, p. 9-A).

For coaches, the publication indicates that ". . . coaches are asked to promote good sportsmanship by setting a positive example while coaching the high school athletes. They should also respect the integrity and judgment of the sports officials" (Murphy, 2001, p. 1).

Good sportsmanship also extends to the visible relationship between the team members. Having the players be visibly supportive of one another, whether an individual is a starter or a substitute, is important not only for the players themselves but in terms of how the team is viewed by others. Chapter two has additional information about a college conference's effort at increasing the caliber of sportsmanship exhibited by coaches involved in all sports. In addition, the efforts of that conference commissioner have resulted in the NCAA adopting this plan to increase sportsmanship for all NCAA Division III institutions (Pitoniak, 2004; Johnson, 2005).

Make Special Efforts to Insure that Your Student-Athletes Behave in School and within the Community

It is very important that your student-athletes exhibit appropriate behavior *in school*. You, as their coach, are being judged, consciously or unconsciously, by their behavior in school. If some of your athletes misbehave in the academic setting, that is a reflection upon their team and their coach—you.

Ideally, your athletes should earn the reputation of being young gentlemen and young ladies within the school. Teachers and school administrators should be able to point to your athletes and indicate that their behavior is exemplary and is probably a direct result of their coach's competency and influence.

Conversely, any trouble or disturbance that your athletes get into within the school will have people thinking (if not actually verbalizing) something like: "there go those spoiled brats, those out-of-control athletes again—why can't their coach control these prima donnas."

COACHING CONCEPT #203: Coaches today are being held accountable for the actions of their individual athletes within the community.

The same concept holds true in terms of the behavior of individual athletes *within the community*. If an athlete is caught breaking the law, breaking and entering, drinking while under age, theft of a motor vehicle, or any number of greater or lesser violations of the law, the fact that this individual is an athlete reflects upon the competency and influence of the coach.

TEAM RULES FOR THE MODERN DAY ATHLETE: ESTABLISHING AND ENFORCING APPROPRIATE AND FAIR TEAM RULES

Coaches must be capable of developing meaningful relationships with their players in all aspects of the coaching scene. The ability to make wise, timely and appropriate decisions, especially when it comes to dealing with athletes, will to a great extent determine the level of success you will experience as a coach.

Part of the development of any meaningful relationship between athletes and coaches hinges upon how the coach and the coach's actions are perceived and accepted by the individual athletes. The expectations of a head coach is reflected in terms of rules and regulations governing both individual and team behavior. It is the responsibility of the head coach in each sport to determine what is acceptable and unacceptable behavior, on and off the playing field.

The rules and regulations that are established are important in and of themselves. However, the manner in which these rules are established is also important. And, how they are communicated, explained and justified to athletes as well as to others, individually and collectively, is equally important.

COACHING CONCEPT #204: Perceptions are as important as reality when viewed by athletes—rules and regulations must be viewed as appropriate by the athletes.

Coaches need to be sure that whatever rules are established are appropriate and justified—both in reality and in the eyes of the athletes. Similarly, coaches need to be sure to enforce rules and regulations in an appropriate, consistent and fair manner. And, finally, the punishment must fit the crime.

It is absolutely essential that athletes *believe* in the rules and regulations that are established. It is important for the athletes to understand that the rules are necessary and apropos for their team in that particular setting and the current circumstances. Involving the athletes in discussing, and even in recommending specific rules, is sometimes a wise strategic move on behalf of the head coach. Many coaches have found it expedient and useful to involve the athletes themselves in the process of establishing team rules and regulations as well as the consequences for violating said rules.

> **COACHING CONCEPT #205:** Don't push rules and regulations down the athletes' throats—athletes will more readily accept and support something if they truly believe in it.

The time when coaches can just say that: "I have a set of rules and you, the athletes, are going to have to do it my way (abide by my rules) or hit the highway" is long gone in most amateur coaching situations. Today, experienced coaches seek input from their athletes rather than attempt to assume the so-called dictator's role. In many instances, coaches who seek input from the athletes in terms of rules take the opportunity to have a frank dialogue with their charges at which time the athletes are educated regarding the pros and cons of establishing such rules. The necessity or advisability of rules in general as well as specific rules in particular can then be examined. Similarly, the issue of punishment or consequences can then be addressed both from the athletes' perspective and from the coaches' point of view.

> **COACHING CONCEPT #206:** Predetermine the behavioral expectations of team members—and communicate same with athletes, parents, and others.

It is sound practice for coaches to predetermine, when they are calm, cool and collected, the criteria by which their athletes will be judged in terms of proper behavior—both on and off the playing field. Similarly, it is important that these expectations be shared with the players, their parents, the athletic administration as well as others. The purpose of doing so is to enable everyone to understand exactly wat is expected of the athletes.

Of course, such expectations must be reasonable and appropriate. So too must be the consequences or the punishment levied against transgressors. However, it is not necessary for the actual punishment to be determined in advance for each and every single possible infraction of the rules or expectations.

Towards this end, coaches would do well to work very hard to explain the rationale behind a variety of possible rules. Athletes will buy into and accept the rules if these rules and regulations are shown as helping the team reach objectives which the athletes deem important. However, having the rules dictated to the team by the coach, imposed from the top without any input from or consideration for the athletes, is ill-advised.

> **COACHING CONCEPT #207:** Don't embarrass your athletes by hanging dirty laundry out for all to see.

Athletes deserve *not to be embarrassed* by their coaches. There will inevitably be instances in which there will be disagreements between athletes and coaches. These controversies or disagreements can either be serious or trivial. However, regardless of how serious or trivial they are, it is essential that the team's so-called dirty laundry is not held out for all in the school and/or community to see. Rather, such situations should be kept confidential—between the coach and the individual athlete(s) in question. It serves no purpose to disclose to outsiders the nature of any personnel problems or challenges with the team or individual athletes. Such disclosure merely embarrasses youngsters. And there is no good purpose in embarrassing one's own athletes. Many things will transpire within any team that should be kept within the team, within the sport family.

> **COACHING CONCEPT #208: When disciplining an individual athlete—neither the public nor the press deserves to know the details of disciplinary actions.**

Sports are inherent violent and the potential for injury is very real.

At the higher levels of competition, that is, at high schools and colleges, especially at those athletic programs which are of a highly competitive nature and are followed closely in the media by the general public, reporters will be hounding and pressuring coaches to divulge the nature of serious rule infractions or any disagreements between the athletes and the staff. Don't embarrass your athletes (or the school) by disclosing confidential matters to the public via the media. Just express the fact that such matters are between you, the coach, and the individual athlete, period. If the discipline involves having an athlete miss a contest, it will suffice merely to say that the individual athlete will not be playing in a specific game, in response to any inquiry from the press.

JUSTIFICATIONS FOR RULES AND REGULATIONS

> **COACHING CONCEPT #209: Have a really good reason for every rule and regulation you establish—don't have a rule just to have a rule.**

Coaches need to have a clear reason for establishing every single rule and regulation affecting their team. To have a rule just to have it is senseless, unwarranted and, all too frequently, counter productive in the long-run. It is important that a coach not establish a rule just because another coach has that same rule and that coach is very successful. Every coach is different. Every team is different. Every coaching situation is different. Coaches need to adapt to the situation in which they find themselves—and this includes the types of athletes they have—and make sound judgments in light of the existing circumstances of their present coaching positions.

One of the prime justifications for team and individual rules and regulations rests in the fact that they can provide guidance for the athletes in their behavior on and off the proverbial playing field. Rules and regulations provide benchmarks or standards governing both appropriate and inappropriate behavior. Rules are thought of as definitive expectations. They can often be a reflection of the team's and/or coaches' philosophy of sport, of competition. And, they can serve as a screening mechanism, thereby eliminating those would-be athletes who are insufficiently motivated and unable or unwilling to adhere to the established expectations. Finally, some teams have rules and regulations governing very specific behavior because such rules are dictated by the policies of the central administration or by the athletic administration.

Similarly, the consequences for violating rules, or the possibility of such consequences, can often serve as significant deterrents to unacceptable individual and team behavior. Coaches attempt, through rules and regulations, to prevent inappropriate and negative behavior by their athletes. It is the preventative aspects of behavior that is the crux of rules for athletic teams. Such consequences (punishments)—when applied consistently and fairly—are also an essential component or element of team discipline. For without appropriate and timely consequences (punishments) the mere existence of rules and regulations becomes mute and ineffectual and, in fact, they become meaningless and are a farce.

COACHING CONCEPT #210: **Preventing problems is easier than solving them once they have occurred—appropriate team rules can help in this regard.**

Being able to anticipate pitfalls is an important skill of any coach. Prevention is easier than attempting a cure. The instituting of team rules is one way to prevent problem areas from developing. This is because athletes know what is expected of them. They also know that they will be held accountable for their behavior—involving both actions and inactions—and will be punished for violating team rules and codes of conduct.

> **COACHING CONCEPT #211:** **Codes of Conduct should be up-to-date and cover appropriate behavior of fans, athletes and coaches.**

Codes of conduct should be an integral aspect of any athletic program or team. The code of conduct contains clear statements that guide the athletes, fans and coaches in terms of proper and appropriate behavior. Paling (2005, pp. 57-58) provides the following 7 rules for the creation of and utilization of effective codes of conduct.

1. Update the code periodically to match the current climate.
2. Make sure your code is in sync with the conference and/or State codes.
3. The code should be easily understood by coaches, players, parents and fans.
4. The code should provide for a range of penalties.
5. Consider loosening the attendance rules (in light of athletes' lifestyles).
6. Always allow for due process.
7. Be sure to adequately communicate the code to all appropriate audiences.

Many areas of coaching can serve as pitfalls or quicksand for would-be successful coaches. Thus, it behooves the coach to be watchful for these danger areas and to plan appropriately in terms of team rules or expectations of behavior. Being cognizant of potential problems or challenges is a wise and prudent survival tactic for coaches. Typical areas governed by team rules and regulations include, but are not limited to, the following:

1. General behavior and decorum in a contest or game as well as in practice
2. General behavior and decorum in the classroom
3. General behavior and decorum in the school, outside of the classroom setting
4. General behavior and decorum in the community
5. Academic progress
6. Drinking
7. Use of tobacco products
8. Abuse and misuse of drugs
9. Curfews and punctuality
10. Language
11. Dress and personal appearance
12. Handling equipment and supplies

13. Dating

14. Behavior during the off-season

15. Expectations in terms of conditioning

16. Following directions

17. Hazing

COACHING CONCEPT #212: **Coaches possess tremendous amounts of power over their athletes—use such power judiciously and wisely.**

Being a coach is about power: the power to make decisions, the power to influence others, the power to get things done, the power to help others, and the power to prevent injury. This is an awesome responsibility, one which must not be taken lightly but exercised with great care and discretion.

The power of the coach can be the result of being given the position itself, the title of coach. However, a coach can also derive power by virtue of what the coach is and does, both as a person and as an expert teacher in the sport. Knowledge is power. Expertise is power. Experience is power. Influence is power.

COACHING CONCEPT #213: **Athletes should be motivated to meet behavioral expectations through persuasiveness rather than coercion.**

It is imperative that coaches do not abuse or misuse the power that naturally accompanies individuals who assume the role of a coach of young people. Thus, coaches need to take very seriously the responsibility that goes with the power of the position.

They must prudently and discreetly use the power that they have as mentors less they become abusive. This is especially important when it comes to the establishment of rules and regulations and the administering of punishment.

Coaching Through Intimidation and Fear

The old adage that *one can get more accomplished with sugar than vinegar* is certainly appropriate in this area of the coaching scene. Coaches can get their athletes to do certain things through intimidation and coercion. Coaches can literally force their athletes to perform out of fear. However, this is the use of power in the true negative sense; it is the use or abuse of power at its worst. Almost any idiot coach can threaten athletes through fear and the possibility of severe punishment. It takes a skilled, competent and caring individual to influence or lead athletes towards a specific course of action through persuasive reasoning and appeal to logic or emotion.

ESTABLISHMENT OF RULES, STANDARDS OF BEHAVIOR AND CONSEQUENCES

COACHING CONCEPT #214: Never make a rule you can't enforce—or might not wish to enforce.

Coaches need to be very careful that they don't end up with rules or regulations which create more problems than they solve. Coaches should never have a rule or regulation that cannot reasonably be enforced, either because of legal entanglements or because it is unreasonable or inappropriate. Is it legal to require one's athletes to shave their heads in order to make the team? No! Is it reasonable to mandate that a youngster run 10 miles for being late (for the first time) a grand total of five seconds? No!

Similarly, a rule should never exist that the coach might not wish to enforce under some circumstances. A coach who states that "anyone who is late for the practice before a game day will not be able to play in the next contest" might well regret having made that utterance, especially when it is the star athlete, the All-State standout, who is 30 seconds late.

Don't make stupid rules that might force you, as the coach, to act in a way that does not serve the welfare of the team, the individual athlete, and yourself. *Think* before making pronouncements. *Think* of the implications of making rules and the consequences of enforcing them.

Competitive sports can often serve as a rallying point for many communities.

COACHING CONCEPT #215: Don't punish an offending athlete by also punishing the entire team.

Punishing an entire team for the offense of a single athlete can be viewed in two ways. For example, an athlete breaks a team rule such as being late. The coach has a rule that anyone who is late must run 15 laps around the facility—and that the rest of the team must accompany the offending athlete. This is an extreme example of peer pressure. In this instance, the coach anticipates that an athlete will think twice before violating a rule that will invoke punishment for the entire team—because of the peer pressure. And indeed, peer pressure can be severe in this type of situation. However, when an athlete does violate such a rule and the punishment is administered, the result can be unfair to other team members.

A second instance in which an entire team can be punished for the infraction(s) of an individual athlete is when the offending athlete, in this case the star of the team, is benched for a game or two because of a specific violation. If the upcoming game happens to be a big game or crucial to the success of the entire team (the final game of the state tournament, for example), not only is the offending athlete being punished (by not being allowed to compete) but all team members are similarly being punished by being placed in a competitive situation with the team being at less than full strength. Thus, coaches should be reluctant to specify a punishment such as benching athletes for a game or more for a minor transgression type offense. Benching an athlete can be a rather severe punishment for the offending athlete and for the team itself. Would not another type of punishment, other than being benched, be appropriate for some types of rule infractions? Of course.

Naturally, there are circumstances and situations that call for an athlete to be denied the privilege of competing on a team. However, exercise caution when assigning this particular punishment. Too many coaches rely on the threat of benching athletes to control their charges. However, when an athlete misbehaves, the coach is then faced with the prospect of administering the punishment. And, the punishment can hurt others who are innocent, including the coach.

COACHING CONCEPT #216: **If you are going to make a team rule, or specify the punishment for an infraction of a rule—then be consistent and treat all athletes similarly.**

Nothing destroys the credibility of a coach more than playing favorites. Treating some individuals on the team in a preferential manner is foolish. Doing so can be a threat to the harmony of the team, and in some instances, to the survival of the coach. This is especially true in terms of how coaches treat those individuals who violate rules. Treating star athletes differently—without any real justification (actual extenuating circumstances) is never warranted.

In the example provided above with the star athlete being late for practice, what should the coach do? Should the coach make an exception because the athlete happens to be the star and the team will most certainly lose without the services of this standout? Of course not. On the other hand, what would have happened if the person being late was one of the substitutes? Is there justification for treating the star in a different manner than the substitute in this type of situation? The answer is clearly, no.

COACHING CONCEPT #217: **Establishment of team rules vary among coaches depending upon their philosophy, their experience and their level of competition.**

Coaches vary greatly in their dealings in the whole area of rules governing student-athletes' behavior. Some coaches prefer to be very specific in terms of detailed rules. Some coaches have many rules covering almost every conceivable situation. Other coaches have few rules.

And, still other mentors prefer not to have rules as such at all (other than those that may be dictated by school policy). These individuals prefer to merely make their expectations of athletes' behavior known but choose to have no established rules as such specified. There is no definite answer that is appropriate for every coach in every situation at every level. You, as the coach, must decide how you will use and implement team rules.

PUNISHING ATHLETES WHO VIOLATE TEAM RULES

COACHING CONCEPT #218: **It is not necessary that punishment for every single serious, semi-serious or minor transgression be determined in advance— coaches should allow themselves some slack in light of extenuating circumstances.**

Many coaches believe that they need *some discretion* in terms of administering punishment for some types of infractions. Towards this end, these mentors *do not specify punishment* (in advance) for any rule transgression. The opposite view is taken by those coaches who elect to identify and *predetermine specific consequences for every breach of rules*. Other coaches provide specific consequences for *some* rule violations while providing *no specificity* at all in terms of punishment for other types of violations. And, some coaches have found that providing *a range of possible punishments or consequences* for misbehavior or rule contravention works best for them.

In some situations the athletic or school policy stipulates very explicit consequences for violations of specific rules. Typically, violations of *significant or serious rules* have predetermined consequences. For example, violations of drug abuse poli-

cies or academic eligibility regulations often bring specific, predetermined consequences, period.

Other rule violations, so-called minor infringements (such as being late for practice, missing curfew or failure to adhere to a dress code, missing a weight room
workout) might carry no predetermined punishment or consequences. In these instances the coach is able to make a decision in terms of a realistic and appropriate
response depending upon the situation.

**COACHING CONCEPT #219: When it comes to disciplining student-athletes—
the punishment should fit the crime.**

It is absolutely imperative to have the punishment fit the crime. Is it reasonable to
bench an athlete for five contests for merely being a few seconds late for practice? Is
this a reasonable punishment when there has been an ongoing blizzard taking place
outside? Is such a harsh consequence ever appropriate for what might seem, on the
surface, to be a minor infraction? Is this punishment a reasonable course of action for
a reasonable, caring coach? Does the punishment fit the crime?

Coaches can attempt to instill discipline in other ways than attempting to be a
hard nose in terms of their demands and expectations. Being a disciplinarian, being
tough, being a hard task master, does not mean being unreasonable or irrational in
one's decision making. One can be a disciplinarian, can be viewed as firm and strong
and yet can also be humanistic in the approach one takes in dealing with the athletes.

**COACHING CONCEPT #220: Never threaten student-athletes—coaches need
to walk silently and carry a big stick.**

There is a significant difference between giving advance warning as to consequences for improper behavior and threatening your athletes. Coaches should *never*
threaten their athletes with possible consequences—unless they are fully prepared to
follow-up on their threats. For example, the coach who yells at Mary (in front of the
team) that the next time Mary is late for practice she is going to sitting the bench for
a month is asking for trouble. What happens when Mary is three minutes late for
practice? Will the coach really bench Mary (especially if she is the star) for a whole
month? If not, what is the value of the threat? What does Mary think of the coach
after hearing such a boastful threat? What do the other team members think?

Coaches would do well to walk silently and carry a big stick. This means that
coaches should refrain from threatening, from yelling, from being overly boisterous;

all the while telling youngsters what will befall them if they step out of line. Rather, realistic expectations should be shared with one's charges and appropriate punishment should be administered swiftly, consistently, calmly, expediently and fairly. Too many coaches are big bags of wind. They seemingly are always yelling, always threatening, always admonishing and too frequently intimidating. Respect is not earned by the loudness of one's words or by the use of threats. Respect is gained by earning it, not by demanding it. Coaches earn respect by acting in a professional manner, by being fair, firm, and by treating their athletes with respect.

COACHING CONCEPT #221: Fool me once, shame on you—fool me twice, shame on me.

When it comes to making decisions regarding whether or not an athlete should be kept on a team following an infraction(s) of various rules or regulations, it is wise to think of the aphorism, *fool me once, shame on you—fool me twice, shame on me*. This statement emphasizes the importance of coaches taking a firm stand in terms of their expectations in the area of athletes' behavior, especially in light of established expectations, rules and regulations. There does come a time when the behavior of an athlete is such that the coach, for the good of the team as well as for the good of the transgressor, must remove the offending athlete from the athletic program.

COACHING CONCEPT #222: Don't go out of your way looking for violators of team rules the night before the state or national championship—you just might find them.

Young coaches frequently have the attitude that they are going to play the role of a police officer in terms of checking on their athletes to be sure that they are abiding by the established team rules. In some instances, this may be totally appropriate. In others, however, it might not.

There is the story of the college head basketball coach who had established a rule that any athlete caught out after curfew or frequenting a liquor establishment three days prior to any game would be suspended for two games. Well, the week of the post-season tournament rolled around, the coach decided that he would initiate unannounced checks on the athletes a couple of days before the quarterfinal tournament game.

So, the coach visited some of the local bars and—surprise—found two of his starters in one of the bars drinking a cola with friends (who were drinking alcohol beverages). Because of the curfew rule that had been established for the team earlier in the season, the coach was forced to bench both players. And, as a result, the squad was soundly beaten in the next tournament game.

Even though the two athletes had not been drinking any alcohol in the tavern, their mere frequenting the establishment was sufficient to kick in the predetermined punishment for violating the established rule. Since the team was in a single elimination post season tournament, there proved to be only one more game and these elite athletes missed it. And, the team and the offending athletes were punished for the transgression. All because of the extraordinary effort on behalf of the head coach.

Success in sports is often a matter of inches.

COACHING CONCEPT #223: Hindsight is twenty-twenty—the problem is that one can't change what has already happened.

In hindsight, perhaps the rule itself was not defensible or wise. Also, the decision to test the rule, to check on the athletes, might not have been the smartest move by that coach at that particular point in time.

Many coaches, even those who do have established rules and consequences, do not go out of their way to find violators (especially just before the **big game**) for fear that they just might be successful. In that event, they would be forced to administer the predetermined punishment. Coaches do not have to be police officers in respect to monitoring every action of their players. Common sense must prevail, for the good of the individual athlete, for the good of the team, and the good of the total athletic program.

COACHING CONCEPT #224: Never make a major disciplinary decision in anger or in haste—think of the consequences for the student-athlete, the parents, the program, and for yourself.

The old saying *haste makes waste* is certainly true in terms of coaches making snap decisions or who are quick in their judgment in terms of reacting to minor and major infractions of rules and regulations by athletes. Coaches need to be careful lest they react to a crisis in an inappropriate manner and, in fact, overreact. Saying something that one comes to regret later when one is calmer is an awkward situation to find oneself in—especially when it is a public embarrassment. Rather, coaches need to take their time to fully assess the ramifications of the situation and then take time to consider all alternatives before coming to a definitive decision and course of action.

COACHING CONCEPT #225: Never discipline a student alone, in a serious situation—have witnesses.

Coaches would be well advised to use caution when working with and advising students in the privacy of their offices. One of the reasons why offices and class-rooms within schools are built with glass windows or doors leading to the hallway is so that others may see what takes place within that room. All too often coaches (as well as teachers) are falsely accused of improper conduct with students in their offices. Coaches should use good judgment and not place themselves in a situation where they are alone with a student when that student is encountering a traumatic, discomforting or confrontational experience.

COACHING CONCEPT #226: Never take it personally when an athlete breaches established disciplinary rules or regulations or disregards the program's code of conduct.

Coaches shouldn't take it personally when they are confronted with a rebellious athlete. Don't become personally affronted when a youngster fails to adhere to the stated expectations in terms of behavior—on or off the proverbial playing field. Don't overreact to misbehavior. These things will happen from time to time even on good teams, with good youngsters coached by competent coaches. There are both proper and improper responses to each and every transgression by an athlete—it is important that coaches respond in an appropriate and professional fashion. Do not overreact.

Examples of improper responses include becoming personally angry, becoming personally insulted, being distracted on a personal basis rather than viewing the situation on a purely professional basis. Youngsters will indeed be youngsters. Young (as well as not so young) athletes will not always measure up in terms of what is ex-pected of them (by coaches, by parents, by teachers, by administrators, and by their peers). Rules will be broken or bent or skirted—coaches need to remember to respond in a professional, calm, appropriate, and fair manner. Coaches must never become angry to such an extent that their decision making ability is impaired or seriously affected.

COACHING CONCEPT #227: When making judgments regarding athletes—try to walk a mile in their shoes.

Coaches need to be understanding. They need to be compassionate. They need to comprehend where the athletes are coming from in terms of their history, culture, and environment, their abilities, the challenges and distractions facing these youngsters on a daily basis, their needs; and, in light of their goals and aspirations.

Placing oneself in the athlete's shoes is often enlightening and thought- provoking. Doing so helps the coach better understand the behavior of the individual athletes and enables the coach to make necessary adjustments for the benefit of the team and the athletic program. Interpersonal relationships between the coach and individual athletes can be greatly enhanced and facilitated by this approach.

COACHING CONCEPT #228: In dealing with problem athletes, don't be too proud to seek advice and counsel from those whom you respect.

It is always wise to solicit recommendations and input from others before coming to a final decision in terms of major disciplinary actions against student athletes. Confer and consult with other coaches, administrators, and others in order to obtain input which might be helpful in arriving at a decision. The objective is to come to an appropriate determination, to make a correct decision.

Many times coaches, especially inexperienced coaches, lack the maturity and the wherewithal to come to a proper conclusion in making decisions affecting athletes. Don't be too proud to seek advice elsewhere. Don't be so stubborn that you refuse assistance from others. Take advantage of the experience of others, both their successes and their failures. No one person has all the answers. It is still up to the coach to make the final determination, the final decision, in light of the information and advice obtained elsewhere.

REFERENCES

Brady, E. (1993, February 16). To hit your best shot, hit the gym. *USA Today.* p. 2-C.

Johnson, G. (2005, March 14). Empire 8 initiative becomes standard for tracking conduct. NCAA News, *p. A-4.*

Murphy, T. (2001, February 22). Keep your cheering positive. *Brockport Post,* p. 9-A.

Paling, D. (2005, February). Clear directions. *Athletic Management, XXXXVI*(2), 57-58.

Pitoniak, S. (2004, March 2). NCAA eyes model study of unbecoming conduct. USA Today, *p. 3-C*

Read, D. (2003). Clean up the court. *Athletic Management, XV*(3), 28-30, 32-34, 363-7.

Stier, Jr., W. F. (1992). The TRIAD assisting, advising and assessment model: One institution's attempt to support the student-athlete. *Academic Athletic Journal,* ISSN 0897-165X, pp. 34-43.

Stier, Jr., W. F. (1993). The ins and outs of evaluating coaches. *Athletic Management, V*(3), 34-37, 39.

Name: _____

Student ID #:_____

EXERCISES FOR CHAPTER 8

   A.   Explain how you, as a coach, might convey your competencies to:

      1. The Athletic Director

               _____

               _____

      2. Principal or President

               _____

               _____

      3. Booster Club Members

               _____

               _____

      4. Faculty

               _____

               _____

   B.   Why should coaches not talk about winning so much?

          _____

          _____

          _____

   C.   What strategies should you use in making sure your athletes perform as if they were properly coached?

          _____

          _____

          _____

D.   How would you handle a team's loss? Why?

_____

_____

_____

_____

E.   What would be your reactions to athletes being jovial immediately follow-ing a team loss?

_____

_____

_____

_____

F.   What are your beliefs regarding team rules? Be specific in terms of the types of rules and how they might be established and enforced. Justify your statements.

_____

_____

_____

_____

_____

_____

G.   Would you go out of your way to discover (check out) athletes to see if they are breaking rules? Why? Be specific in your response.

_____

_____

_____

_____

_____

RESEARCH QUESTONS FOR CHAPTER 8

1. Interview a varsity coach of a flagship sport and inquire as to the pressure the coach feels from the AD and school administration terms of winning and being successful as a coach. How much pressure does the coach place on himself/herself?

   ----

2. Ask a varsity coach how the coach keeps the athletic director aware of all of the good things that the coach does and is involved in as well as the team's and individual team members' achievements

   ----

   ----

3. Research the professional literature and summarize *factors* that help a coach learn why a particular team (and individual athletes) is not performing as well as expected.

   ----

4. Check with a varsity coach and determine what rules and regulations (and consequences for failing to adhere to such rules/regulations) the coach has for the team and the rationale for such rules.

----

5. Obtain a *code of conduct* for the athletic program from a high school athletic director and summarize its essential elements. For whom is the *code of conduct* written and why is it in existence?

Chapter 9

Major Challenges and Tasks Facing Coaches

Determination plus ability equals success.

FIVE MAJOR AREAS OF RESPONSIBILITY

There are five major responsibilities or tasks that face every coach regardless of the sport coached or the level of competition in which one finds oneself. Each of these areas deals with personnel, either directly or indirectly. If coaches are to be consistently successful, it becomes imperative that they be capable of meeting these challenges. In so doing, the coach will have a full arsenal with which to go into battle against opponents. Additionally, being capable of coping with these five major challenges facilitates the establishment of a true team concept among the players (substitutes as well as starters) and the coaching staff, a significant factor in the makeup of any successful athletic program.

In order to be consistently and significantly successful, coaches need to be competent in terms of (1) planning strategies, (2) recruitment (and retention) of athletes, (3) team selection (cuts and/or dismissals), (4) being a good *practice coach*, and (5) being a *good game* or *bench coach*, figure 9.1.

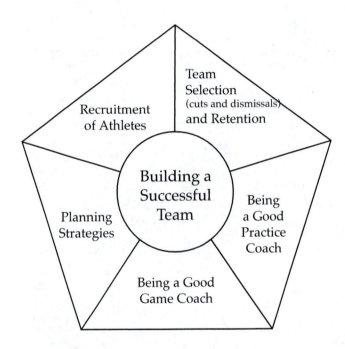

**FIGURE 9.1—Essential Player Personnel-Related
Tasks and Responsibilities**

PLANNING STRATEGIES

COACHING CONCEPT #229: Prepare, prepare, and prepare!

Coaches need to be able to develop plans and strategies for their coaching efforts—ahead of time. Coaches must not fly by the seat of their pants in terms of the decisions they make and the actions they take or do not take. The ability to pre-plan in terms of a coaching system, various strategies, tactics, and activities are essential for the would-be successful coach.

COACHING CONCEPT #230: Coaches need to have a reason for everything they do or do not do—they must not be perceived as flying by the seat of their pants.

Coaches must plan in terms of what they are going to do and in terms of what they would like to have happen—in every respect. This includes more than just what their athletes are going to do in terms of practices and games. There are a wide range of other decisions that must be planned for by the coach well in advance of the actual implementation of action. For example, the coach needs to decide how team members are to be selected, how to inform those who tried out for the team whether or not they have made the team, how uniforms are to be distributed and collected, which teams will be scouted, how the team is to travel to away games, what exactly the team rules are, how the team rules are to be determined and enforced, etc. The list could go on and on and on. Advance planning is necessary, absolutely essential. Advance planning helps to prevent disasters and makes good use of available resources and assets.

COACHING CONCEPT #231: Advance planning and proper organization helps to project to others a high level of competency on behalf of the coach and also increases the coach's effectiveness and efficiency.

Another advantage of advance planning is that the mere act of planning helps to project an aura or atmosphere of competency on behalf of the coach. Thus, there is a decided advantage to being viewed by one's superiors and by influential members of the community as a well organized, efficient and effective coach who excels in planning.

COACHING CONCEPT #232: Hindsight is 20-20—use the past as a tool in planning for the future.

Learn from the past, both successes and failures, those of others as well as your own. An important phase of the planning process is to take advantage of the past. That is, to repeat those things that have proven to be successful in the past and not repeat those activities or efforts that were not as successful as we would have liked. In short, we need to learn from our past and the past of others. There is an old maxim that individuals need to learn from their mistakes. All well and good. However, coaches are not going to live long enough to make all of the mistakes themselves. As a result, it is imperative that productive and successful coaches learn from the mistakes (and successes) of others. In this way, future decisions and endeavors will have the benefit of hindsight, of advanced planning which will hopefully result in more effective, efficient and successful efforts on behalf of the coach.

**COACHING CONCEPT #233: Coaches must be accomplished planners—
anticipate needs and problems in advance.**

Coaches must be able to plan ahead and anticipate what they must do and what must be accomplished by others. Successful coaches anticipate problems. They plan, plan and then plan some more. They plan their own future behavior. They plan the activities of their assistants. And, of course, they plan, well in advance, the activities in which their athletes will be engaged, both on and off the playing field.

**COACHING CONCEPT #234: Have contingency plans waiting in the
wings—and be ready, willing and able to use
them.**

This is not to say, however, that everything coaches do can be anticipated and planned for in advanced. That is simply not true. Coaches do need to deal with the unexpected. In fact, this is a highly prized characteristic or quality of successful, experienced mentors. Coaches do need to make quick (not snap) and timely decisions, based upon the best information available and in light of their own training, education, and experience as well as the circumstances in which they find themselves.

**COACHING CONCEPT #235: When you are hired, know in advance what is
expected of you and what is feasible or
possible—one doesn't win a basketball
championship with unskilled players.**

Coaches should attempt to minimize situations from occurring that they, as coaches, had neither anticipated nor planned lest they are perceived as operating via the crisis mode. If coaches are hired with the expectation that they should or will win the conference or state championship, they had better ascertain whether or not this is a realistic expectation—prior to accepting the job. This means making an evaluation as to what resources are available to reach the established objective, that is, winning a championship. Advance planning and assessing of the current circumstances surrounding the coaching situation can help the coach make appropriate decisions in this regard.

Productive coaches are those men and women who take the time to think ahead, to anticipate various happenings and consequences and to plan accordingly. *Planning should permeate every aspect of a coach's professional activity.* Coaches are always involved in planning, either in terms of actually planning for future activities (their own or others), implementing and carrying out a planned activity, or assessing just how well their plans and subsequent actions turned out, that is, whether or not they were successful in what they tried to do.

COACHING CONCEPT #236:   Those who fail to plan—in reality plan to fail.

PLANNING FOR THE ENTIRE CALENDAR YEAR

When planning, coaches should think of their coaching efforts in terms of four distinct time periods within any given calendar year. These four time periods can be conceptualized as (1) the *preseason*, (2) the *in-season* or *regular season*, (3) the *post season*, and (4) the *out-of-season* periods of time. During each of these time frames, coaches must be involved in planning, evaluating and implementing a variety of activities dealing with all aspects of the coaching scene.

Coaches need to plan in terms of *people* (athletes, parents, teachers, fans, etc.), in terms of *tangible objects* (equipment, supplies, etc.), in terms of *processes* (scheduling transportation, scheduling contests and officials, ordering budgetary items and services, etc.), and in terms of *coaching strategies* (type of offense and defense to employ, the style of play to be implemented, the type of conditioning to employ, etc.), figure 9.2.

The important concept that coaches need to remember is that coaching is not merely a two or three-month involvement, especially coaching sports in an educational institution. Today, more and more, coaching in a school setting means that head coaches are concerned with their sport throughout the 12-month calendar year. The same can be said of many assistant coaches. These coaches must be planning and/or implementing a part of an overall plan throughout the calendar year. Thus, breaking down the year into the four categories of *preseason, in-season, post season,* and *out-of-season* makes sense. Such an approach helps the coach budget one's time and assists in breaking down one's responsibilities throughout the whole year and completing the tasks in a timely fashion.

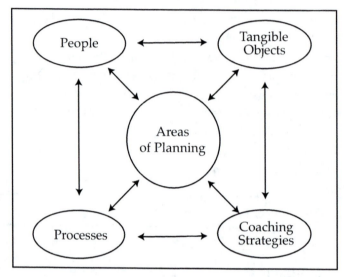

FIGURE 9.2—Areas where Planning is Essential

COACHING CONCEPT #237: Pay attention to details—for want of a saddle the horse was lost, for want of a horse the battle was lost, for want of the battle the war was lost.

During each of these four time segments, coaches will have to deal with a whole range of challenges, problems, and deadlines involving a wide variety of individuals. Provided in the next few pages are some key examples of the various types of tasks facing head coaches in each of these four time segments. Although every sport is somewhat different in terms of the specific tasks required of head coaches, there are great similarities between all sports in the type of planning and foresight required of successful coaches. For example, football coaches need to be concerned with the certification of football helmets following the conclusion of the season. The helmets must be recertified as safe for use by athletes prior to the start of the next season. Although not all sports have this exact same task to be faced, ice hockey, softball, baseball and lacrosse coaches have similar responsibilities in terms of their helmets.

Many sports require that the coach in charge (the head coach) check and insure that the team's equipment and supplies are safe for use in a subsequent season. For example, every coach who uses a weight room facility must check prior to its use by the team that the equipment is safe. Additionally, the gymnastics coach must have all of the apparatus recertified each year. That is, an expert must examine, certify and warrant that each piece of apparatus is safe to use before the athletes are permitted to work out on the equipment at the beginning of the following season. Similarly, soccer, lacrosse, softball and baseball coaches (just to mention a few) must also insure that their fields are safe following the down time from the end of one season to the beginning of the new season. This involves physically checking or inspecting the facilities, the physical grounds, to warrant that the playing field is safe and appropriate for use by the athletes. Naturally, such checks must also be done daily prior to the start of the next day's practice or game.

COACHING CONCEPT #238: **Don't change for change sake—however, don't be reluctant to make changes when appropriate and needed.**

Some of the general tasks which face all coaches, regardless of the specific sport in which they are involved, are presented below. Many of these tasks or responsibilities, while presented in a specific time frame (preseason, inseason, post season, or out-of-season); can be dealt with in more than just a single time segment. For example, planning for conditioning can take place throughout the year. However, this task is presented here as a responsibility to be addressed during the preseason time period.

The Pre-season Practice Time

Pre-season involves that period of time between the official start of practice for that specific sport and the date of the first regularly scheduled contest. This is the period of time during which the coach must teach the athletes all that they need to learn, at least at a minimum level of competency, prior to being thrown into actual competition against other teams or other individual athletes.

COACHING CONCEPT #239: **Would-be athletes, during tryouts, should strive to impress the coaching staff that they possess specific skills, competencies and abilities if they desire to make the team.**

In point of fact, during this preseason period of time there are six specific objectives that the coach and the players must reach. Specifically, this is a period of time when (1) the coaching staff selects those individuals who will make the team, (2) to keep the athletes in shape, and if need be, to increase the conditioning of the athletes, (3) teach athletes what they need to know to compete by the time of the first competition, (4) the coaching staff is able to get to know more about each individual member of the team, (5) each individual members of the team is able to learn more about each of the coaches; and, (6) the team members are given opportunities to learn more about each other.

This is an important period of time for both the coaches and the athletes. This is when the team selection process takes place, that is, when coaches select those players who will initially make the team. Or, phrased another way, this is when the coaches will decide who will make the team and who will not be acceptable candidates for the squad. This is the period of time when coaches use their experience, knowledge and intuition to start to conceptualize what comprises the starting unit. This is when new athletes to the team begin to formulate their initial, first-hand opinions of the coaches and of the team itself. It is during this time period when the foundation for the team chemistry is established.

COACHING CONCEPT #240: Coaches should not use the word *cut* during tryouts as one doesn't cut the youngsters who are not yet members of the team but are merely attempting to make the squad.

The use of words and phrases can have far reaching consequences. Witness the use of the words *cut* or *cuts* or the phrase *making cuts* when dealing with tryouts for athletic teams. When coaches use the phrase *making cuts* it implies that it is the coach who is making the action of cutting or removing the youngster from the squad or team. Parents mistakenly interpret (consciously or unconsciously) this phrase and the tryout process as one in which the coach acts (often in a capricious and arbitrary manner) in a negative way toward their son or daughter by removing or cutting the youngster from the team. Nothing could be further from reality.

What really happens is that the youngster attempts to demonstrate the skill, competency and abilities that will help the team. And, if the young person impresses the coach (or coaching staff) sufficiently the youngster is allowed to join the team. If not, the youngster is not invited to be a team member.

The wanna-be athlete is not *cut* from anything as the young person trying out for the squad was never a member of the team in the first place. By not using the phrase *making cuts* the coach reinforces the concept that it is the responsibility of the would-be athlete to make the team. Thus, if the student does not sufficiently impress the coach(es) then it is the student who bears the responsibility for not making the team. It is not the coach who removes or kicks the student out or off of anything.

It is critical that several things be accomplished during this pre-season time period. First, the athletes must be prepared mentally for the initial competitive experience that season. Second, the athletes must maintain or develop a suitable and acceptable level of physical fitness prior to engaging in actual athletic competition. And, third, the athletes must master, at least at a minimally acceptable level, the techniques, the strategies, the knowledge, and the physical skills required in that specific sport appropriate for the level of competition to be met.

An example of a high school's spring preseason meeting agenda which was given to coaches is provided below. The list of items to be covered by the athletic director and coaches in a group meeting was a result of the AD's planning expertise and experience. The list below was provided by the then athletic director (Doug Wescott) of Brockport High School (New York).

Preseason Items for Discussion with Coaches

1. Physical master sheet should be in the coach's possession—keep with you—valuable information. See Emergency Card—Keep in Medical Kit.
2. If cutting players—guidelines—communication—3/5 days. Managers, players. Criteria form to be used for all sports in which cuts will be made.
3. Accident reports—follow up with phone calls.
4. Medical Kit—Blood issues, inhaler, bee kit, etc. The coach is to return them to the student after the last game.
5. Salaries.
7. Officials' Vouchers—check, review and sign.
8. Team roster—update with secretary as soon as changes occur.
9, Practice/game schedules—update with secretary as changes occur.
10. Scholar Athlete Program.
11. Number of participants.
12. Operation Offense—Chemical DFA.
13. Equipment manager—all supplies and equipment request through the manager.
14. Leaving event with parent—Transportation Regulations—Use district form.
15. Sitting on the bus—location.
16. Trainer—times—use of.
17. Transfer students.
18. Selective Classification—through school nurse.
19. Academic eligibility—make sure you know the process, reminder: students who need extra help should be excused or allowed to come late to practice.

20. Controlling—blood borne diseases—rubber gloves—packets (Have you reviewed the video yet?).
21. Use of school keys—issuance.
22. Contest Reports—Dealing with the press—Gannett (Varsity to call in your scores).
23. Review of certification—whose responsibility.
24. Sportsmanship.
25. Food/party regulations—Health Department.
26. End of Season:
    a. Inventory returned to equipment manager.
    b. Awards (list) to secretary.
    c. Evaluation completed and meeting with Athletic Director.
27. Memo and Ballot.
28, Banquet.
29. Players and parent meeting mandatory for players and strongly suggested for parents (all levels). Items to be covered:
    d. Program Philosophy.
    e. Practice Requirements.
    f. Playing Time.
    g. Guidelines Specific to Your Sport/Program.
    h. Training Rules.
    i. Discipline.
    j. Parent Involvement.
    k. Game Day Expectations.
    l. Academic Eligibility.
    m. NCAA Requirements.
    n. Sportsmanship–use handout.
    o. Note: Please contact secretary with date, time, and location of your meeting. A Booster Club representative will attend your meeting to talk with parents regarding the Booster Club.

COACHING CONCEPT #241: **Encourage or require athletes to report to the first practice session in reasonable physical shape—better yet, in excellent physical shape.**

Many experienced and successful coaches expect, in fact require, that their athletes arrive for the first day of official practice in some resemblance of pretty good (or even excellent) physical conditioning and mental or psychological readiness. They do so in order that valuable time is not wasted during the pre-season weeks on beginning conditioning (physical, mental or psychological) activities which could just as easily have been achieved or accomplished prior to the athletes reporting for that first day of practice. These coaches feel that the pre-season time should be spent maintaining an already high level of physical and mental conditioning. This is because in many cases, the time available for pre-season activities is relatively short and time is of the essence. Similarly, these mentors have the attitude or belief that the pre-season period of time should be primarily devoted to teaching and developing the mental and physical skills of their charges as well as imparting the required knowledge, strategies and techniques necessary for success in a particular sport.

Fans serve an important role in amateur sports.

COACHING CONCEPT #242: There can be too much of a good thing— especially when it comes to practice time.

Practices should be planned so that there is sufficient time for the athletes to retain appropriate individual and team skills already learned, to maintain or increase conditioning, to learn new skills and knowledge, and to practice in game-like situations the skills, the knowledge, the strategies, and the tactics, necessary in actual competitive situations. Practices should not habitually be long, drawn out affairs. There is no definitive research that indicates that the longer the practices the better it is for the learning curve of the individual athlete or for the team as a whole. On the contrary, practices can be extended for too long a period of time. There can be practices organized in such a manner that instead of facilitating learning, instead of increasing the mastery of skills, and instead of promoting team cohesiveness—the opposite is achieved. During lengthened, drawn-out practices, learning can be hindered and athletes (as well as coaches) can become bored, frustrated and discouraged to the extent that meaningful learning during practice is not feasible or possible.

The point is simple. Keep practices to a reasonable length. Two hours or two-and-a-half hours for actual practice time is reasonable. Sometimes 90-minutes are sufficient. Keeping athletes in practice for three or four hours is foolhardy and not defensible. See chapter 10 for additional information about conducting meaningful and successful practice sessions.

The In-season (Regular Season) Period of Time

The *in-season* segment of time is often referred to as the so-called *regular season*. That is, that time between the first official competitive contest and the date of the last regularly scheduled contest (excluding post season competition). This is the time period when athletes, individually or as members of a team, will continue to develop and refine their competitive skills through practice *and* through actual competition against others in their effort to achieve a winning record, a successful season, a conference championship as well as individual and group recognition.

Coaches need to be wary that they not prejudge youngsters. Do not assume that athletes will remain as they once were. Not true. Athletes are capable of making significant strides in terms of their capabilities, their physical abilities, their mastery of skills and their comprehension of the intricacies of their game or sport. Coaches do themselves and the youngsters a great injustice if they categorize specific athletes as a certain type of person or athlete and fail to allow for the individual to improve (Stier, 1986)

COACHING CONCEPT #243: **Athletes will usually improve throughout the regular season because of hard work, experience, passage of time and the effectiveness of coaching.**

Coaches need to recognize that many athletes will mature physically, socially, psychologically and mentally during an academic or calendar year as well as during a sort season. These improvements can be as a direct or indirect result of experience, the passage of time as well as from hard work by the athlete and/or the effectiveness of the coach. As a result, some athletes may develop and improve into much improved competitors. And, coaches must recognize this potential for improvement. Coaches should expect that as time passes there will be improvements demonstrated by individual athletes and by the team itself.

The Post Season Period

The *post season* encompasses that period of time between the end of the regular season competition (the last regularly scheduled contest) in a particular sport and the last contest actually played that season. This assumes, of course, that the teams or individuals in question are invited to or otherwise qualify for this type of championship competition following the conclusion of the regularly scheduled season.

On the high school level, some sport competition is organized or structured so that teams are able to begin what is considered by many to be an entirely new season, the post season, following the conclusion of the regular in-season competition. It is during this time of post season competition that high schools are able to literally start anew in a given sport and work towards the ultimate goal, that is, a regional championship or the state championship in a particular sport. In some sports and in some states, involvement in the post season competition is not automatic. Rather, individual athletes as well as some sports teams have to actually qualify, on the basis of won/loss records during the in-season or regular season competition. In the case of individual athletes, they may be required to qualify for post season competition on the basis of actual achievements and accomplishments (distances, times, victories achieved during the regular season) in order to be invited (to qualify) for post season competition.

On the college and university level there are many opportunities (for individuals and for teams) for post season competition in a variety of sports due to the availability of many post season conference tournaments as well as regional post season competition. For example, almost all major (NCAA Division I) basketball conferences (with a few exceptions, have post season basketball tournaments. The winners of these post season tournaments, held after the conclusion of the regular or in-season competition is over, qualify for one of the highly sought after NCAA basketball tournament bids. Of course, the NCAA Division I basketball tournament also has wild card slots which are distributed to quality teams that have failed to win their post season conference tournament, failed to win the regular (in-season) conference championship or play as independents.

However, in some sections of the country there are still other structured post season competitive opportunities on the college level for both teams and for individual athletes. For example, in the east there is the Eastern Collegiate Athletic Conference, commonly referred to as the ECAC. The ECAC is a collection of 290 colleges and universities which compete against each other along divisional lines (NCAA Divisions I, II and III) (personal communication, 1997, August 21, 1997). Many of these colleges and universities hold membership in the ECAC as well as in other athletic conferences. The point, however, is that the ECAC regularly provides post season competitive opportunities in some sports for successful athletic teams, especially for those institutions which fail to garner one of the coveted bids to one of the NCAA post season competitions at the Division I, II or III level.

As a result, regardless of whether one finds oneself coaching in high school or on the college or university level, there is a very real possibility that you, as a coach, as well as your athletes, will have the opportunity to anticipate, to plan for and, hopefully, to actually take part in post season competition.

The Out-of-Season [Off Season] Months

The *out-of-season* segment of time is that time between the end of the last official contest in one's particular sport and the start of the official practice date for the subsequent sport season as authorized by the appropriate governing organization or body (conference, state or national sport governing entity). This is when the athletes are usually left on their own (although with strong suggestions or recommendations for specific activities by their coaches) to continue to work on the development of their physical skills, their conditioning and the mastery of their particular position or specialty. This is a challenge that coaches at all levels face (Read, 2001).

Coaches would do well to pay particular attention to this period of time because much of what has been accomplished by the athlete and the coaching staff may be lost or reduced if one is not careful. Coaches need to provide guidance and direction for the athletes in terms of what should be done (and what should not be done) during these out-of-season months. Off-season conditioning, weight training, skill practice time (individually and with others), as well as involvement in informal competitive contests all play a part in the out-of-season or off-season regimen.

Coaches need to be careful lest they violate any rules or regulations restricting any direct coaching activities during the off-season. However, successful coaches stress to their athletes the need to remain in reasonable physical shape during this time. Successful coaches emphasize to their charges the need to remain focused and self-motivated in terms of their sport. Successful coaches place emphasis on the importance of returning to the sport at the beginning of the next season in tip-top shape, with improved skills and eager to begin the quest for excellence during the subsequent season.

COACHING CONCEPT #244: **All work and no play makes Jack or Jill a dull person—allow for some down-time during the post season and out-of-season, both for athletes and for members of the coaching staff.**

However, successful and experienced coaches are equally aware of the importance of athletes experiencing some down-time, that is, time away from the rigors of practice and competition. Youngsters, at all ages, need time to distance themselves from the competitive sport environment. Then, when they return, some days, weeks or even months later, they are hopefully refreshed, eager and even anxious, and highly motivated to once again assume the role of a competitive athlete. Too much pressure to excel in competitive sports can result in an athlete becoming stale or, worse yet, burned out. There has to be a happy medium in terms of the amount of time and effort devoted to an athlete's primary sport(s) during the official off-season.

The same can be said of coaches. Since coaches are susceptible to burnout just as are youngsters, they need to be able to take valuable downtime away from their sport(s). Coaches need to periodically distance themselves from their sport(s), for the benefit of themselves, for the benefit of their families, and for the benefit of their athletes.

RECRUITMENT OF ATHLETES

> **COACHING CONCEPT #245:** **One cannot make a silk purse out of a sow's ear—neither can one make a star athlete out of someone who lacks the potential for excellence.**

The success of athletic teams (and therefore, coaches) is at least partially dependent upon the quality of the athletes attracted to the team or the sports program. Therefore it is very important that coaches are successful in attracting potential players to the team who are likely to be able to excel—with an ordinary amount of hard work and dedication—at that particular sport.

"Getting students to try out for your sport takes more than posting a sign on the locker room door" according to Keith Manos, former coach of two sports at Richmond Heights (Ohio) High School (2001, p. 15). Brittain (2006) cites the importance of (1) adequately publicity about the team and the try-out process, (2) keeping things positive (rewarding, enjoyable and satisfying, (3) communicating with students and their parents year around, and (4) good/quality coaching in the recruitment and retention of quality prospects and athletes to any sport team.

The recruitment process is just as important at the junior high level and high school level as it is in the college ranks. In fact, it is important at every level, including youth sports. Granted that the so-called recruitment process is decidedly different at the youth sport level than at the junior/senior high level. And, of course, recruiting of athletic talent at the college and university level is different again. One modern technique of recruiting that is seeing more and more use, especially at the college and university level, is the World Wide Web (the Internet) (Fielitz, 2000).

> **COACHING CONCEPT #246:** **The recruitment and retention of quality athletes are two essential tasks or challenges facing every coach at every level.**

The fact remains, recruiting (as well as retention) is an essential process for every coach. In fact, the recruiting and retaining efforts and skills of coaches will have as much to do with the eventual success or failure of individual coaches as any single area of coaching. There is an old coaching proverb that goes something like this: to be a *good coach* one should either be an excellent *recruiter* or an excellent *teacher/mentor* in that particular sport. To be a *great coach* one must be both an excellent recruiter and an excellent *teacher/mentor* of the sport.

Recruitment of quality athletes or individuals who have the potential to become quality athletes is a highly prized skill. And there have been many successful coaches, both at the secondary and the collegiate levels, who have remained very successful in the coaching profession, for a long period of time, due to their skill in attracting (and retaining) quality youngsters who possessed high levels of skills and/or who were able to improve upon their skill level.

Similarly, the masterful teaching of skills and knowledge to athletes is also a highly prized competency. And there have been many successful coaches, at both the secondary and the collegiate levels, who have enjoyed significant, long term success on the basis of their exceptional talent in teaching young men and women the skills and knowledge of a particular sport.

However, those truly great coaches, those extraordinary mentors, possessed exceptional skills in terms of both recruiting and teaching. In short, the great coaches are highly competent in both recruiting talented and quality would-be athletes and in teaching their charges how to improve upon their level of play, both in terms of physical skill and in terms of knowledge and understanding (strategies and tactics) of the sport or game.

COACHING CONCEPT #247: Recruitment is only half of the battle—retention is equally, if not more important, for eventual success, figure 9.3.

It rarely does the coach much good, over the long run, to recruit outstanding athletes or individuals with the potential for athletic excellence to a team if those same athletes do not remain committed to the sport program. In fact, recruitment of an individual to a team can be detrimental to the overall progress of the team if the individual does not stay with the squad. Rather, if the individual becomes disenchanted, becomes discouraged, becomes bored, becomes indifferent, becomes a burden—the coach (and the team) loses in more ways than one.

Recruitment and Retention—The Two Essential Components of Having Superior Athletes

For example, when an athlete leaves the squad, the team and the coach loses what could or should have been a definite asset to the team in the future, if not in the immediate present. However, there is another angle to this loss of an athlete from the team to which the individual was actively recruited. This is the fact that there has been precious time wasted and effort misspent with this particular athlete who leaves the team for whatever reasons—whether appropriate and justifiable or not. Most, if not all, of the time spent by the coaching staff in practice with this individual has been wasted. Most, if not all, of the time taken up by the now departed individual in game situations now seems wasted. And, the effort that went into recruiting the youngster is for naught. In fact, with the value of hindsight, the time spent on this now absent athlete could have better been spent on other athletes, those individuals who still remain with the team.

Thus, it behooves the coach to diligently work not only in the recruitment process but also in terms of retaining those quality athletes who become members of the squad. Without effective retention efforts, all the recruitment work can become useless.

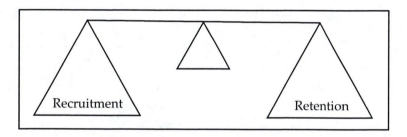

FIGURE 9.3—Recruitment and Retention— The Two Essential Components of Coaching

Recruiting at the Youth Sport Level

COACHING CONCEPT #248: Recruiting of athletic talent takes place at all levels—from the youth level, the secondary level and, of course, the college or university level.

At the youth sport level coaches, managers and league administrators are involved in making the competitive sport experience attractive enough to youngsters (and acceptable to their parents) so that the young, potential athletes will elect to try out for the team. Youth coaches need to provide an attractive experience for youngsters and must convince the young girls and boys that it is indeed fun to participate on the athletic team.

Even at the youth sport level, there is the familiar problem or challenge of retaining those youngsters who made the initial commitment to compete on a team. Hopefully, these same coaches, managers, league administrators and parents are also sufficiently knowledgeable and skilled in making the experience so interesting, challenging and enjoyable for these young boys and girls that the youngsters will remain with the team throughout the sport season and also be involved in other types of sport experiences for years to come.

Recruiting at the Junior/Senior High Level

Recruiting at the junior and senior high levels is somewhat different. For one thing, the potential athletes are older. Additionally, many have had previous competitive sport experience—some positive, some negative, and some neutral. There are also other attractive alternatives vying for the time, attention and effort of these young people. For example, members of the opposite sex come into play in terms of competition for the time of these youngsters, both boys and girls. At the high school level, there is the matter of vehicles, cars, trucks and motorcycles, since young girls and boys reach the age when they can obtain driver's licenses and have access to vehicles (or when their friends begin to drive).

And, finally, there is a matter of limited spots or places on the various teams at these levels. Whereas in some youth sports all who try out for the teams are guaranteed a spot on some team, and in many instances, are also guaranteed a minimum amount of playing time in each contest—this is not true in most junior high competitive sports programs and is certainly not the case at the high school level.

Thus, the junior and senior high coach is faced with the formidable challenge of recruiting those students who have the potential for athletic growth and development. At these levels the recruitment process is really somewhat different than the recruitment scene in colleges and universities. This is due to the fact that in the junior and senior high schools, the coaches are involved in attracting and recruiting students from the general school population to try out for their teams. Many coaches scrounge through the general school population, especially the physical education classes, in an effort to find young boys and girls who might have the talent, the potential and the interest in becoming interscholastic athletes. Similarly, potential standouts can be identified by coaches sometimes merely by virtue of their physical size and attributes. For example, how many junior high coaches have had their attention caught by a 6'5" youngster in 7th or 8th grade and attempted to interest the student in trying out for the basketball team or the football team?

With all of the distractions that face our students in junior and senior high schools, it is all the more necessary for coaches at these levels to be active in recruiting potential players for their teams. The time when most coaches could just sit back and wait for the onslaught of talented, interested and highly motivated youngsters to flock to their door begging to play their sport is long gone. Today, the recruitment ability of coaches even at this level is important.

COACHING CONCEPT #249: **There can be many reasons why an athlete quits a team—some are valid but others are not.**

Reasons behind an Athlete's Departure from a Team

Attrition of athletes might be due to four major reasons. First, youngsters may simply quit the squad. This is done for any number of reasons. For example, they lose interest. They also find new interests or avenues where they now prefer to spend their time and expend their efforts. Sometimes they are mad at the coach. Some have to work in order to gain money. Others have family problems and have to quit. While others quit because they feel they aren't getting sufficient playing time. The reasons go on and on.

Second, athletes can be lost to teams by being declared ineligible to compete. Such ineligibility might be due to failure to satisfy minimal academic standards, those standards established by local schools, by conferences as well as by the various state or national governing bodies. Other students lose some of their eligibility because of some other deficiencies in terms of residency requirements, age, or transferring from one school to another. Third, athletes can be lost to teams because they are actually dismissed from the team for behavioral problems or because they fail to abide by established rules and regulations. And, fourth, athletes can be lost from a team because of an accident, injury or some other factor out of the control of the individual athlete such as the family moving away to a different city.

Whatever the reason, whenever an individual athlete is lost to a team the consequences are generally negative for the athlete, for the team itself and for the sponsoring organization of the athletic team. For example, when an athlete prematurely leaves a team, the coach is faced with the reality that most if not all of the time and effort spent in practice and in game situations with this now departed individual was wasted in terms of that athlete not being able to make future contributions to the team. If the coach had spent the same amount of time and effort with another athlete who had remained with the program, that athlete might now be in a better position to be a significant contributor.

We have seen how coaches must be effective recruiters at all levels if they are to have sufficient numbers of athletes, athletes who possess the appropriate level of talent and skill. We have also seen

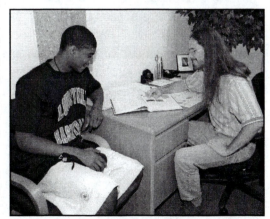

Academic advising for student-athletes is necessary in today's collegiate sports.

how a sports program can be damaged if the coach is successful in attracting and recruiting talented and high skilled athletes only to lose these same athletes from the team for whatever reason. Coaches must be competent when it comes to recruitment and retention.

*Helping High School Athletes Pursue
Further Participation at the College Level*

It is important that high school coaches be willing and able to assist and advise their charges in terms of the possibility of continuing their athletic participation beyond the high school years. A few high school coaches will be blessed with so-called blue chip athletes, those youngsters who will be highly sought by the elite of the big-time, Division I level universities and colleges.

Other coaches will have athletes who might qualify for full or partial athletic scholarships at Division II schools, NAIA institutions or at the junior college level. However, the majority of high school athletes are not scholarship prospects. There are many youngsters who just want to play, to compete at the collegiate level regardless of whether or not they receive any athletically-related financial aid.

COACHING CONCEPT #250:   High school coaches have an obligation to be knowledgeable about the collegiate recruitment process—and willing to advise and counsel athletes who desire to play in college.

The point, however, is that high school coaches have an obligation to be knowledgeable in the college recruiting scene for their athletes, whether the youngsters are capable of playing at the scholarship or non-scholarship levels. This requires an honest and earnest effort on behalf of secondary coaches to keep up-to-date with the ever changing recruitment scene for the high school graduate. And it necessitates coaches being willing to spend the time and effort counseling the individual athletes and their parents. An article that was published more than 35 years ago is as applicable today as the day it was written. The title of the article is *Everything the Athlete Always Wanted to Know about selecting a college—But was afraid to ask* and it appeared in the coaching publication, *Scholastic Coach* (Stier, 1974). This article lists many, many factors or characteristics of collegiate institutions, athletic teams and coaches that may have a significant and direct impact or influence upon the academic and athletic success/failure of the individual athlete (seeking a college education and an opportunity to continue one's athletic career).

Participation Opportunities at the College Level

Even for those talented athletes who are not Olympic caliber and who will never be professional caliber athletes, there are very real opportunities for sizable amounts (partial if not total) of financial assistance that they can receive towards their college costs *plus* the visibility of being recognized as an outstanding athlete playing at the elite or near elite levels of competition within the United States. Financial assistance for those athletes desiring to attend college can consist of outright academic awards, athletic related gifts of aid, work study (employment) opportunities, and school loans.

Recruiting at the College and University Level

College and university coaches must actively recruit off-campus in order to gain skilled athletes. Some coaches have athletic scholarships to offer recruits while others (schools belonging to NCAA Division III) have no such inducements. The college coach must be an excellent recruiter of talent. This is because no matter how good a person might be in terms of teaching sport skills; one still has to have the horses in order to compete with those opposing teams that do have superior athletes. And, on the collegiate level, all opposing coaches are hard at work recruiting talented athletes. If one is not a competent and successful recruiter, one cannot remain competitive for long.

COACHING CONCEPT #251: **At all levels of collegiate sports the recruitment process is important—within Division I, it is a matter of life and death for coaches.**

Nowhere is the recruiting game played with more seriousness and commitment than at the college/university level. Nowhere is the lack of recruitment so visible on the playing field than in college athletics. For the college or university coach, recruiting success is often a life and death struggle, professionally speaking. Those coaches who are successful in attracting quality student-athletes have a decided initial advantage over those teams which struggle with less talented athletes.

It is at the collegiate ranks that there is open competition (recruitment) on a national, if not international, scale for those athletes possessing exceptional athletic talent and physical prowess in competitive sports. Even within the NCAA Division III, where no athletic scholarships per se are permitted, the recruitment battles and efforts are almost every bit as intense as on the big-time, NCAA Division I level, at least for those who coach at this level. Recruitment is big business at the collegiate level of competition, period.

Unreasonable Expectations for Athletic Success at the Elite Levels

On the big time level (NCAA Division I), the benefits of being recruited in terms of the athletes can often include complete financial assistance for all of their direct college costs. Additionally, for a select few athletes who are the cream of the crop, there is the tantalizing prospect of professional careers in sport on the horizon, with the resulting mega-bucks. Never mind that only a very small percentage of athletes in high school ever make it as a Division I player. Or, that only an infinitesimal number of college athletes ever make it big on the professional level.

Many young athletes, and their parents alike, have an erroneous concept of the likelihood of playing sports beyond high school, especially at the elite level of competition. Similarly, they also fail to comprehend the brutal and competitive realities in terms of securing meaningful athletic scholarships from the so-called elite athletic schools. The harsh reality of real life is that the odds are 100 to 1 against a high school athlete ever playing in college and are 12,000 to 1 against playing in the pros (SportScan, 1988). The point is that a majority of high school athletic standouts believe or hope that they can be a successful college athlete and a large number of collegiate athletes have unrealistic aspirations of making it all the way to the professional ranks.

Unreasonable Expectations for Athletic Success in Professional Sports

The odds that any high school athlete will play a sport on the professional level are remote—about 10,000 to 1. As far as probabilities go, there's a better chance of, say, taking a coin, flipping it, and having it land on heads 13 times in a row" (Simons, 1997, p. 48). When examining the sport of basketball, a comparison of the number of participants at various levels is enlightening indeed. Over a decade ago it was found that there were approximately a quarter of a million high school basketball players. And, the number of NCAA Division I basketball players numbered only around 4,700. Additionally, in that same time period they were only around 60 new NBA athletes (NBA Stardom, 1998). Today, the odds are even more challenging.

Challenges of High School Athletes Playing in College

In the 21st century the number of college athletes exceeds 500,000 in any given year, the odds of a male or female high school athlete actually playing beyond graduation in a four-year college or university is not very high, especially in those sports that offer full scholarships. Although the odds do vary by gender, sport as well as division of competition, the fact is that it is difficult to make a college *team in any sport*, and in some cases it is extremely difficult.

Chances for High School Athletes to Compete in Athletics beyond High School

The NCAA web site (retrieved 9-11-08) reveals (figure 9.4) the estimated odds for high school athletes to compete on an athletic team following high school. The chart below depicts the probability for six flagship teams, men's and women's basketball, football, baseball, men's ice hockey and men's soccer.

Student-Athletes	Men's Basketball	Women's Basketball	Football	Baseball	Men's Ice Hockey	Men's Soccer
High School Student Athletes	546,335	452,929	1,071,775	470,671	36,263	358,935
High School Senior Student Athletes	156,096	129,408	306,221	134,477	10,361	102,553
NCAA Student Athletes	16,571	15,096	61,252	28,767	3,973	19,793
NCAA Freshman Roster Positions	4,735	4,313	17,501	8,219	1,135	5,655
NCAA Senior Student Athletes	3,682	3,355	13,612	6,393	883	4,398
NCAA Student Athletes Drafted	44	32	250	600	33	76
Percent High School to NCAA	3.0%	3.3%	5.7%	6.1%	11.0%	5.5%
Percent NCAA to Professional	1.2%	1.0%	1.8%	9.4%	3.7%	1.7%
Percent High School to Professional	0.03%	0.02%	0.08%	0.45%	0.32%	0.07%

Note: These percentages are based on estimated data and should be considered approximations of the actual percentages. Source: http://www.ncaa.org/wps/ncaa?ContentID=279

FIGURE 9.4: Estimated Probability of Competing in Athletics beyond the High School Interscholastic Level (2008).

Another way of looking at the chances of athletic participation at higher levels is provided in figure 9.5. The data provided in this figure are participation statistics gathered from the NCAA, the NAIA and the National Federation of State High School Associations. The statistics below compare the number of high school participants in a given sport compared to participants in college programs (this does not reflect the number of scholarships available) (Holcomb, 2007).

In another study, the College Athletic Clips' research department gathered the following statistics/inferences from the web site of the National Federation of State High School Associations. Specifically, during the 2005-2006 school year there were a total of 7,159,904 high school athletes. Of this number there were 4,210,000 boys

Men's Sports	Women's Sports
Lacrosse, 8-1	Lacrosse, 8-1
Swimming, 13-1	Soccer, 13-1
Baseball, 14-1	Swimming, 13-1
Soccer, 15-1	Gymnastics, 14-1
Football, 16-1	Golf, 14-1
Golf, 17-1	Tennis, 18-1
Tennis, 18-1	Softball, 19-1
Track and Field, 24-1	Track and Field, 21-1
Basketball, 27-1	Volleyball, 23-1
Wrestling, 3	Basketball, 25-1

**FIGURE 9.5—Comparison of Participation in Secondary Schools to those
at Four-Year Colleges and Universities
(Note: 8-1 = 8 high school athletes to every 1 college athlete)**

and 2,959,000 girls. If one divides the number of high school athletes (7,159,904) by 4 (years in high school) we find that approximately 1,790,000 seniors (soon to graduate) competing for approximately 100,000 openings on the college/university level. Parents and youngsters should be made aware of such lopsided odds (College Athletic Clips, 2007).

Unreasonable Expectations by Minority High School Athletes

The trend to have unreasonable expectations of one's future success in big-time college athletics, and even in the professional ranks, is especially prevalent among minority athletes in high school. This has become a source of significant concern for educators and athletic coaches alike, for such misconceptions can have disastrous consequences for the individual athlete, for the school systems and for society as a whole. "The problem of such unrealistic perceptions is that the avenue they may see are sports and here is the tragedy, these youngsters put all their eggs in one basket and that basket may have a big hole in the bottom and they will not reach their unrealistic goal" (Myers, 1991, p. 4-C).

**COACHING CONCEPT #252:   The odds of an athlete actually becoming a major
player at the collegiate and professional levels
are not great—too many youngsters have
unreasonable expectations.**

Coaches at all levels, but especially at the secondary level, have a responsibility and obligation to present a realistic picture to each of their athletes regarding that athlete's future in sports and out of sports. The objective is to paint a realistic perspective of the real world for one's athletes so that the youngsters can adequately prepare for the real world in which the individual must live for the rest of his or her life.

The Chronicle of Higher Education contained an article (Athletics Notes) on November 28, 1990 that indicated that secondary school athletes, particularly African-American athletes, had unrealistically high expectations about the possibility of their playing on athletic teams at the college level *as well as* in the professional leagues. In an earlier survey, a poll conducted by Louis Harris and Associates for Northeastern University's Center for the Study of Sport in Society, it was discovered *that all of the minority male football and basketball athletes* (currently playing at the secondary level) *surveyed indicated that they believed they would indeed go on to play athletics in college and further, some 32% of the respondents indicated that they would be able to successfully play at the professional level.*

The survey involved almost 2,000, 10th, 11th and 12th graders. Of this number, around 70% of the students either were currently playing varsity sports or had played sports sometime during their high school career. The study also revealed that 59% of all the African-American athletes questioned, regardless of sport, thought they could go on to play at the college level while some 43% indicated that they anticipated playing professional sports. However, only 39% of the white students polled indicated that they could play in college and only 16% has aspirations of participating within the professional ranks as successful athletes.

A 1993 study conducted by the Lou Harris Survey on High School Athletes found that 51% of African-American high school athletes and 18% of white high school athletes believed that they would beat the 10,000-to-l odds of making it in the professional ranks in some sport (Brady, 1993a). The same investigation revealed that 65% of the African-American athletes in secondary schools and 49% of the white high school athletes believe that they were actually going to beat the 100-to-l odds of playing athletic sports at the collegiate level. Richard Lapchick, the director of the Center for the Study of Sport in Society, indicated that such expectations are in reality, in most cases, mere fantasies. "And, when reality sets in, these same would-be athletes could be in for a significant emotional letdown" (Brady, 1993a, p, 2-C).

There have been various percentages presented in the literature in terms of the success rate of high school athletes at the elite college level and the professional level. In one report it was estimated that only about one percent of secondary athletes actually participate in varsity sports at the collegiate level and less than 1 in a 1,000 make it to the professional football or basketball teams (Athletics Notes, 1990). In fact, Brady (1993b) indicates that the odds of a high school athlete playing any professional sport are far less, that is, about 1 in 10,000. Sociologist Jay Coakley has calculated that 3% of college football players make the NFL and 2.6% of college basketball players make the NBA (Myers, 1991). Today, it is still as difficult if not more so than in the past.

Actual Success Rate of Black Athlete at the Professional Levels

There are some 30 million African-Americans in this country. Of this number, there are approximately 1,100 participating in the National Football League, (NFL), the National Basketball Association (NBA) or in major league baseball (MLB). In 1989, the NCAA revealed that 44% of African-American football and basketball players a predominantly white Division I schools and 36% at predominantly black schools expected to become pro athletes, compared to 20% of their non-black team-mates (Myers, 1991).

Sport	White	African-American	Hispanic
football	1/62,500	1/47,600	1/2,500,000
baseball	1/83,300	1/133,300	1/500,000
basketball	1/357,100	1/153,800	1/33,300,000
hockey	1/66,700	n/a	n/a
men's golf	1/312,500	1/12,500,000	1/33,300,000
women's golf	1/526,300	n/a	n/a
men's tennis	1/285,700	1/2,000,000	1/3,300,000
women's tennis	1/434,800	1/20,000,000	1/20,000,000

Note: no odds were given where there were no participants

FIGURE 9.6—Chances of Making it at the Professional Sport Level

The odds of white, African-American and Hispanic high school athletes actually making it at the professional level in eight of the professional sports is taken from Myers (1991, page 4-C) and is presented in figure 9.6.

Distribution of Scholarships at Division I Schools Among White and Black Athletes

During the 1990-1991 academic year, it was estimated that there were 13,600 African-American athletes receiving scholarship aid at Division I schools. Most of these scholarships went to athletes participating in revenue sports, that is, football and basketball. Although these athletes comprised only 4% of the general student body in Division I schools during 1990-1991, they received over 62% of the basketball scholarships and 50% of the football scholarships. However, in the sports of baseball, golf and men's swimming, the number of African-American athletes on scholarships was minimal (7.8%, 2.8% and 1.9% respectfully) (Myers, 1991).

Importance of Retention Efforts in the Recruitment Process at the College Level

However, as stated earlier, the recruitment process is only half the battle. Every year, the news media points out numerous talented university level athletes who quit a particular team and move on to another athletic program at

Pressure always exists in competitive sports, that is the nature of the activity.

a different institution. For whatever reason, student-athletes become dissatisfied with their present circumstances as athletes and desire to pursue their fortunes elsewhere. Many times, it is a case of the grass looking greener on the other side of the fence. However, this is not always an accurate assessment. Nevertheless, one of the major problems and challenges facing college and university coaches today is retaining those athletes in the program who had been recruited. The negative publicity and fallout from a disgruntled former athlete leaving the team can be damaging to the image of the team and of the coach.

COACHING CONCEPT #253: **It does no good to recruit the top athlete in the United States—if that athlete subsequently leaves, is kicked off the team or flunks out of school.**

Additionally, almost without exception, whenever an athlete leaves a team prematurely (other than the family moving away), it always seems to be the team's fault, or the coach's fault, or the school's fault, or the organization's fault. It rarely happens that the athlete takes responsibility for the separation. As a result, the departed athlete, and all too frequently the parents as well, frequently tell other people, friends, parents, previous teachers and coaches, etc., the reasons for the youngster's early departure from the athletic team, from their obviously biased and skewed perspective. The end result is that the coach, the team, the total sports program and even the school or sponsoring organization can receive a black eye. Such a tarnished image and reputation can be the result of negative information and opinions of a disgruntled former athlete (and parents).

> **COACHING CONCEPT #254:   When athletes prematurely depart from a team—it is never their fault, rather it is the fault of the coach, the program, the school, or sponsoring organization.**

And, of course, when an athlete leaves the athletic program prior to exhausting one's eligibility, it is always the fault of the coach, the school or the program. When a disgruntled athlete leaves the team, for whatever real reasons, it is frequently the coach or the program that is to blame. The athlete feels that the coach was too strict or too lenient; the school was too difficult or not challenging enough; the rules were too lax or restrictive; the athlete didn't get sufficient playing time; the athlete didn't get a fair shake; the coach played favorites; the other players were too stuck up; the school atmosphere was too boring or there were too many distractions; the dorm was too quiet or too noisy; the school was too close to home or too far away; the school was too confining or no one cared about students; the competition was too soft or too stiff, etc.

Whatever the reasons, real or perceived, behind the athletes' premature departure from the team, you can bet that most of the time the athletes will be blaming others rather than themselves. When such an athlete returns home and bad mouths the coach and/or the program back in the old high school, and shares the negative experience with previous high school coaches, teachers, guidance counselors, administrators, friends, and family members, there is a very good possibility that the college coach will be viewed in a negative light.

This is especially true if more than one athlete, over a period of years, returns to the same home area with the same critical message. Thus, it is very important that college coaches recruit athletes wisely and judiciously and recruit those student-athletes who are likely to experience success on the playing field, in the classroom and in the social setting of the institution and the community. And, it is equally important for the coach and support staff to do all that is possible to support those student-athletes as students and as athletes so that they will stay in the academic and athletic programs until they graduate and have exhausted their eligibility.

Just as former athletes spouting negative messages (sour grapes) can damage the reputation of a school and an athletic program, former student athletes who are successful graduates and who experience success within the athletic dimension of the college or university can do wonders in terms of positively selling the merits of the school and the sports team/program.

STRATEGIES FOR SELECTING TEAM MEMBERS

Team selection is an all important aspect of any coach's job. However, there are really three distinct aspects to this major responsibility. First, there is the process or task of actually selecting those individuals who will make the squad and those who will not be retained as team members. Second, there is the matter of how those candidates who fail to make the team are informed of this fact. And, the third perspective to the team selection concept revolves around what happens when it becomes necessary to remove a member of the team *from* the squad who had originally been selected to be a member by the coaching staff.

In short, coaches need to be skilled in choosing team members as well as fair and honest in cutting those candidates who are deemed not qualified or suitable for inclusion on the team. Additionally, coaches need to be skilled in recognizing when and if an individual athlete should be removed as a team member (Stier, 1986, Spring).

Team Selection (cuts and/or dismissals)

COACHING CONCEPT #255:   Head coaches have the *exclusive right* to determine who will make their team.

A basic, fundamental right of every head coach is to determine who will and who will not make the team. There will inevitably be pressures, some overt and others covert, placed on coaches when it comes to team selection. Sometimes pressures will come from parents. Sometimes pressure will be exerted from central administration or even the athletic administration. And, there is always the possibility of coercion being exerted from segments within the community, including the booster club or athletic support group.

Nevertheless, it is the coach who, as the resident expert in the sport (that is supposedly why the coach was hired in the first place), must assume the responsibility of making the final selection of the team. Coaches must not abdicate that right or responsibility.

Although the head coach has ultimate responsibility and authority for making the final decisions in terms of who will make the team and who will not, it is nevertheless important that the process of team selection be fair. It is also imperative that the *perception of the process* itself be judged fair and appropriate by others—by the would-be players, their parents, the administration, and the general public. Nothing hurts the credibility of the head coach more than a shaky team selection process. To be accused by individuals of being unfair and unjust, of playing favorites, of unethical behavior, of incompetence and ineptness—even if it is not true—is hardly desirable.

As a result, it is suggested that the team selection process be clearly explained and communicated to all concerned well in advance, figure 9.7. There is a trend today in athletic circles, especially at the levels below collegiate competition, to explain the team selection process and to have a process that is clearly understandable and defensible to others.

COACHING CONCEPT #256: The perception of the team selection process must be such that the process itself is fair, just, appropriate and defensible.

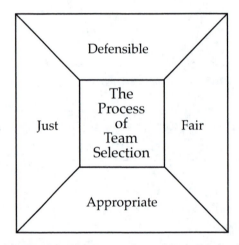

FIGURE 9.7—The Perception of Team Selection

COACHING CONCEPT #257: Coaches may utilize subjective and/or objective criteria in the selection of team members.

An important concept pointed out earlier in this text is that decisions can be made on the basis of both subjective and objective criteria. It is important for coaches to be cognizant of the fact that although both subjective and objective criteria may be used in the team selection process, subjective criteria may be used exclusively if that is the wish of the head coach. However, the author suggests that this not be done except in extenuating circumstances.

Coaches should use both objective and subjective criteria as part of their arsenal in determining who is qualified to make the team. Picking team members is a fairly difficult challenge and can have significant ramifications, both on the playing field and in the community, for the coach, the athletes, the parents and the program itself.

COACHING CNCEPT #258: In potentially ticklish or political situations in team selection—use some type of objective criteria.

One of the reasons why it is suggested that coaches **always** utilize some objective measurement when determining the makeup of the final squad is that they will have some hard data, some documentation to use in explaining to others (athletic director, the parents, the unsuccessful candidate) should it become necessary to do so. This is especially important in ticklish or political situations in which youngsters who do not make the team might have influential parents or supporters in the community. A second, and more important, reason to use some objective criteria or measurements is that the data and information can indeed be helpful to the coach in making such a decision.

Even though coaches are expected to rely upon their subjective judgment and experience (for they are the experts, that is why they were placed in that position) in making coaching decisions, it is also wise to have some documentation, some hard data, to substantiate, to support, the coaches' final decisions in terms of final team selection. Coaches who give as a reason "I just felt that Samantha Ann plays the sport better and deserved a spot on the team" make themselves vulnerable to criticism. This is true even though many coaches can and indeed do use their subjective judgments, their opinions, their feelings, their estimates as the sole means of picking some team members and eliminating others. Although some may just look at candidates actually playing the sport and feel comfortable in picking those who will comprise their squad, it is suggested, to be fair to each youngster and to provide the coach with as much information (and protection should a problem develop) as possible, that both objective and subjective criteria be used in the team selection process.

Today, most coaches usually utilize a combination of objective and subjective criteria in making an assessment of a youngster's ability to make the team. At least the coach should be able to provide some objective documentation indicating that an individual who fails to make the team is deficient in one or more areas or that other candidates possess greater skills and attributes.

Nevertheless, it still remains for the coach to make the final decision as to who will and who will not be on the team. Today's coach needs to be able to coherently and succinctly explain how such a decision was made. Today's coach needs to be ready to explain the process and the criteria by which the decision is made in terms of those would-be team members who are cut, that is, those who are not chosen for the team.

COACHING CONCEPT #259: **Most schools require a minimum number of days of full practices for tryouts to insure that all youngsters are given a fair and just opportunity to make the team.**

An example of a high school's effort to maintain some resemblance of consistency in terms of who coaches in that school should go about holding tryouts and selecting individuals to become members of a team/squad can be seen in the handout provided below and given to coaches by the then athletic director, in this case, Doug Wescott, the former AD at Brockport High School (New York).

Choosing a Squad

The following procedures are to be followed by all coaches:

1. All candidates should be given a minimum of threes full practices.
2. Each coach should discuss tryout procedures to be used with the Director of Athletics before the start of your season.
3. Each coach should discuss the tryout procedures with the candidates. The discussion should include the following:
   a. Minimum and maximum number of players that will be kept on the team.
   b. What objective tests (criteria) will be used.
   c. What subjective rating procedures (criteria) will be used.
   d. Selection dates.
   e. How candidates will be notified if they have made the team.
4. Coaches should not post the names of who has made the team or who has been released (not made the team).
5. All coaches should discuss with each player why the candidate did not make the squad/team.
6. Rosters:
   a. All coaches must submit a team roster to the Director of Athletics the day your team has been selected. The athletic department tea, roster form will be given to all coaches in their Coaching Packet. Additional forms are available at the Director of Athletics office.
   b. Team Roster forms should be turned in within 24 hours after your team has been selected.

Examples of Subjective and Objective Criteria

What are objective and subjective criteria? Criteria in the selection process consist of standards, measures or yardsticks by which a would-be athlete is judged to possess those skills necessary to be a member of the team. Objective criteria are those marks, traits or standards that are easily and definitely measurable and are less subject to interpretation or variance. Examples of objective criteria might include:

1. How much weight can the candidate bench press?
2. How fast can the individual run the 440? The 100 meters?
3. How high a vertical leap can the person achieve?
4. How many free throws (or field goals) can the person make out of 100 attempts in comparison with other would-be team members?
5. How tall or heavy is the individual?
6. How quick is the individual according to standardized tests?
7. How far can the individual throw the baseball or softball?
8. What is the batting average of the candidate during preseason tryouts?
9. How far can the student throw the shot put in 5 attempts in comparison with the other candidates for the squad?
10. How many times can the student serve the volleyball (or tennis ball) into the service court out of 15 tries?

Subjective criteria, on the other hand, are those determinants or factors that are a result of personal interpretation and judgment, based upon experience, feelings and perception as well as informal training and formal education. An example of a single subjective criterion might be how a coach views an individual athlete's commitment for the sport.

Other subjective criteria can include, but not be limited to, the following:

1. How an individual plays with other specific team members.
2. How well the person reacts under pressure in a game-like situation.
3. The potential for growth or improvement in the future.
4. The individual's desire for excellence in that sport.
5. How likely the candidate is to adhere to the team rules.
6. Whether the student can be motivated or is self motivated.
7. Whether or not the individual is a trouble maker.
8. Whether or not the would-be team member is likely to remain academically eligible to compete.

9. How well the athlete can adjust to the style of play required by the coach.

10. How well the person fills the current needs of the team in terms of skills and physical attributes.

Use of Sociograms in Assessing Athletic Team members

Some coaches, in an attempt to find out how their athletes view each other, utilize sociograms to find out about the interpersonal relationships of the team members. A sociogram or sociometrix diagram represents the pattern(s) of relationships between individuals within a group. This pattern of relationships is typically represented or expressed in terms of which individuals other members of the group tend to associate with or to interact with.

Evaluating Four Areas of Competency for Team Selection (and Retention)

Essentially, there are four areas that coaches typically use to screen those individuals trying out for an athletic team. These include the (1) person's physical size and maturity, the (2) essential physical attributes possessed by the individual, the

The quickness of a successful run (athlete).

(3) candidate's actual athletic skills, and the (4) heart and desire (mental, psychological and social attributes) demonstrated by the youngster. See chapter seven for additional information on desirable characteristics of athletes.

There are various qualities that coaches might look for in their athletes, figure 9.8. Although different coaches might consider other qualities as important, the author consider these four categories to be the most essential for athletes competing on his teams. The possession of these qualities by youngsters enables the coach to have a sound foundation upon which to start the season.

Physical Size, Physical Presence and Maturity

Physical size, height and weight, is often used to paint a picture of the overall potential contributions that the individual youngster might make for the program. For example, a 9th grade student who is somewhat awkward, has never really played basketball, but who stands 6'10" in height, might well get the attention (over another youngster who stands only 5 1/2 feet) of the basketball coach who sees potential in the person's height alone in this sport.

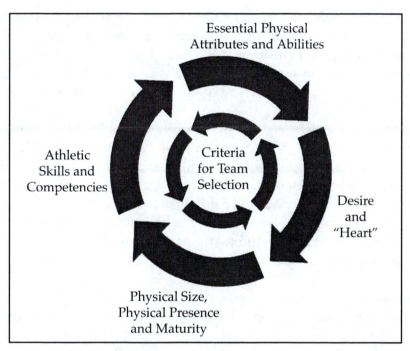

FIGURE 9.8—Factors Commonly Taken Into Account When Choosing Team Members

Essential Physical Attributes and Abilities

There are a whole host of tests that can be used to determine the current status of a would-be athlete's strength, agility, flexibility, endurance, jumping ability, quickness, speed, etc. Coaches may use these objective measurements to provide them with some insight into the physical attributes and general physical fitness of the wanna-be athlete. Coaches can organize physical exercises and drills for the candidate who is then timed or measured (evaluated) in comparison with other candidates for the team and against norms of other individuals who had previously experienced success in the sport.

The use of these types of physical tests provides some objectivity into the evaluation and team selection process. In the sport of football an objective measurement or criteria might include, among other factors, the amount of weight a candidate can lift in any number of specific exercises. Other sports might use the running of a specific distance within a specific amount of time.

Athletic Skills and Competencies

And, of course, how well a candidate for the team actually can perform the essential individual and team skills in practice and in competitive situations (under fire) will have a significant effect upon the final decision of the coach. For example, an individual might possess great physical skills in terms of strength, agility, endurance, quickness and be a great physical specimen—but still not be capable of making the team.

There is more to athletic success than merely possessing basic physical qualities and characteristics. There is the matter of skill, and the potential for developing and/or enhancing the present level of skill possessed by the individual. A high school senior desiring to make the ice hockey team who possesses limited or no skating skills will most likely not make the varsity team.

Thus, coaches want to see how well would-be team members do in terms of performing the actual skills involved in the sport, both on an individual basis and in a team setting, both in a non-competitive setting and in a very competitive, tense, setting.

In the sport of cross country, candidates might be evaluated in terms of how fast and well they can cover a specific distance against competition, the other youngsters trying out for the team. In swimming, one of the criteria might be the amount of time it takes to cover a specific distance, either a short sprint or over a longer distance. In tennis, one of the criteria might include the number of times a server can hit the ball into the serving area on the court out of 20 attempts. In basketball, it might be the number of field goals or free throws made out of a specified number attempted. In softball, it might be the number of strikes a pitcher can get over the plate with and without a batter in the batter's box.

Of course requiring athletes to physically perform by playing the sport itself places the coach in a position to use both objective and subjective criteria. For example, a basketball coach can watch how the candidates actually play in a scrimmage or practice competition and can make a subjective evaluation as to the skill level and potential for each individual on the court. Additionally, the coach can also look at the statistics after the scrimmage or game and look at objective measurements in terms of field goal percentage, free throw percentage, rebounds, steals, turnovers, assists, and total points, playing time, etc.

COACHING CONCEPT #260: True athletes have heart as well as superior physical skill and attributes.

Desire and Heart

Observing youngsters perform, individually and as a member of a group, whether in drill situations, in scrimmages, or under game conditions can often provide the experienced coach with a fairly accurate insight into an individual's current level of competency as well as the individual's potential. In everything that the coach has a candidate perform, it is important for the coach to examine more than just the physical aspects, the physical attributes, the physical skills.

Successful, experienced and wise mentors also seek to evaluate the so-called intangible aspect of a would-be athlete involving the person's desire and heart. For in reality, possessing natural sport skills does not guarantee competency as a sport performer. Having the blessings of size and weight does not guarantee success as an athlete. And, it takes more than merely being strong, agile, quick, etc., to ensure success as an athlete. It even takes more than the combination of all of these. It takes heart. It takes desire. It takes internal motivation and fortitude.

Coaches should seek out those individuals who possess the mental and psychological temperament to excel as an athlete both in the practice scene and in the more glorious (and risky) atmosphere of actual game competition. Coaches need to take into consideration the social aspect when determining who will make the team and who will not.

Thus, coaches would do well to look at the social, the interpersonal relationship skills possessed by candidates. Can a youngster get along with others? Is an individual, or can the person become, unselfish and a team player? Can the candidate put the good of the team above the welfare of the individual? Will this person be willing to make the necessary sacrifices and commitment necessary for the modern day athlete—at that particular level of competition? Although there are instruments that purport to aid the coach in making these judgments, frequently coaches use their own subjective judgment based upon their training and experience in coming to appropriate conclusions.

In the final analysis, the athletic team is like a miniature society with many of the same demands and challenges that exist in a society as a whole. Athletes need to be capable and willing to work as a member of a group, this miniature society, under the leadership of the head coach.

Selective Classification (Moving Youngsters up a Level in Competition)

In many schools, coaches and athletic directors are faced with the situation in which they have one or more youngsters at the middle school or junior high school level who are exceptionally skilled/talented, mature and highly motivated—and who might be good enough to move up and compete/play at the varsity level. In many states there are well established screening procedures in place to help determine (qualify) whether or not the youngster is capable (physically, emotionally, socially) of handling the increased pressure situation present in playing at a much higher level of competition. After all, there are perils whenever one attempts to determine whether a "12 or 13 year-old is prepared to be on a team with 18 year olds and face the rigors of high school competition" (Moving Middle Schoolers Down, 2005, p. 13).

COACHING CONCEPT #261: **The screening process used in evaluating whether youngsters are ready to move up in terms of a higher level of competition can be challenging, time consuming and risky.**

Conducting or Structuring Tryouts

In dealing with the selection process itself, coaches are often faced with the challenge of, on the one hand, providing an adequate and fair opportunity for would-be athletes to try out for the team. On the other hand, these same coaches are operating under a time restraint in terms of possessing a limited number of practice days prior to the first actual competition.

COACHING CONCEPT #262: **Coaches must not waste too much time in selecting their team—sufficient time must be made available to prepare team members for actual competition.**

Thus, these coaches must weigh the rights of the would-be candidates, those trying out for the team, against the rights of the team members (whoever they may be) to have adequate preparation (both conditioning and instruction) prior to the start of the season. In many cases this necessitates a rather limited amount of time devoted to actual tryouts for many athletic teams—both on the high school and college levels.

Tryouts can be organized and structured in many different ways. Some coaches mandate that anyone who wishes to even try out for the team must have previously undergone a strenuous and rigorous conditioning program. For example, some football coaches require that all candidates take part in an out-of-season (informal) weight training program. In this case, the school's weight room is made available from January through early August and the wanna-be athletes are encouraged (required) to take part in a twice/thrice weekly workout program (possibly with attendance being taken by the captain(s) or other team leaders).

In other instances, coaches require that would-be athletes participate in other sports in order to earn the right to even try out for their particular sport. For example, a basketball coach might require that all candidates for the basketball team must participate in the fall cross country program. Or, the varsity football coach might require that all would-be candidates be members of the previous spring's track and field program (if they were in school at that time).

And, in still other instances, coaches will require that would-be candidates demonstrate on the first day of practice that they are capable of achieving some type of physical performance at a minimum level of competency. For example, a football coach might require candidates to lift so many pounds in a variety of different lifts. Or, the volleyball coach might require an athlete to demonstrate proficiency in serving. Or, the cross country coach might require that all candidates, on the first day of tryouts, run 5 miles within a specific time.

The importance of athletes (at all levels) reporting in shape to the first day of practice/tryouts can be seen in the quote by Scott Berchtold, Vice President of the Buffalo Bills, who said: "It used to be camp was a time for the team to get away and get guys in shape. Nowadays, the most important thing we do is still getting the team ready, but guys have to come to camp in shape" (Roth, 2000, p. 1-D). The same concept holds true for amateur sports, if not more so.

Eliminating the Wanna-bes From Early Contention as Team Members

Those individuals who are unable or unwilling to meet these requirements are excluded from further efforts to try out for the team. These individuals have eliminated themselves from further consideration by failing to meet preconditions which make them eligible to even try out for a team.

COACHING CONCEPT #263: **Establishing preconditions for eligibility to even try out for a team eliminates those faint of heart, the unmotivated and the groupies.**

Some coaches subscribe to the philosophy that by establishing such requirements they weed out those wanna-bes who lack the dedication and the physical skills necessary to become a member of the team. Only those students who are very dedicated, confident and willing to pay the price will take the time and expend the effort (joining another team, working out in the weight room for 4-5 months, conditioning themselves to perform a specific, measurable physical feat) to meet such preconditions in order to earn the right to even try out for a team.

Of course, this type of approach—establishing stringent preconditions for would-be candidates—will not work if there are not sufficient numbers of candidates wishing to try out for a particular squad. In that case, the coach might well want to consider not having any preconditions to trying out for the team. Why put obstacles in the way of people deciding to try out at the last moment, especially when the team is desperate for candidates.

COACHING CONCEPT #264:   Never give special considerations to prima donnas when selecting a team—to do so causes a coach to lose credibility.

One caution should be observed when establishing preconditions for tryouts. There may be times when the star of the team might become reluctant to pay the price by meeting these established preconditions. The so-called star athlete might well reason that being a returning star, perhaps even being the most valuable player, that there is no need to go through all of the preseason or out-of-season work. This individual might anticipate that the coach would certainly not prevent such a star athlete from joining the team. Nevertheless, in this instance, the coach must be prepared to follow through and render the decision (penalty) that had been announced, regardless of who had failed to meet these preconditions. If the star athlete knows that the coach means business, then the athlete will usually conform. If not, the coach is fortunate that the true personality of this spoiled but talented athlete (brat) came to light when it did because the coach will not be wasting time with such a prima donna.

No special considerations, exceptions or special dispensations should be given to a star player (acting like a prima donna) merely because the individual is a talented athlete. To do so can cause the coach great harm in terms of a loss of credibility. Thus, it is imperative that the coach emphasize to all returning athletes and those who wish to try out for the first time next year that the preconditions will be strictly enforced, *with no exceptions*. Then, the coach must follow through and not make exceptions unless these exceptions are established and communicated well in advance.

COACHING CONCEPT #265:   Exceptions to the precondition requirements for tryouts should be articulated well in advance and communicated with all appropriate individuals and constituencies.

One such exception would be the arrival of a candidate for a team who is a new student to the school. This youngster would not have knowledge of a particular precondition in order to try out for the team in the fall. For example, a new high school junior just moved into the district in early August. If the head football coach had a policy that all would-be candidates must have worked out in the weight room during the off-season, an exception might well be made for this new student. This is because this newly arrived student did not have the benefit of knowing about the requirement prior to arriving in the community in early August. However, exceptions must be based on real reasons, not stretches of the coach's imagination.

Should Non-Starting Seniors Be Retained on the Team?

The decision whether or not to keep seniors on a team, whether in college or in high school, is frequently a controversial one—especially if these seniors had been part of the program since they were freshman. Some coaches (and most parents, especially at the high school level) feel that seniors, who have been with the program since their freshman year, deserve the right to be on the varsity team just because they are seniors. Some would even argue they deserve to play.

This so-called *right*, according to some, would have been earned by these seniors because of their prior involvement in the sport. Thus, so goes this line of reasoning, those seniors who have played the sport at that school (freshman, sophomore or varsity levels) in previous years deserve the right to be a member of the team as seniors merely because of their longevity. Some would argue that seniors certainly deserve the right to be on the varsity team before sophomores are elevated to the team because the latter still have three years left in school to compete.

Some coaches feel that seniors who had previously played the sport throughout their careers at that school at least deserve to make the team during the senior year—even if they are not starters. Other coaches have the concept that unless seniors are going to assume (by earning) a substantial role as starters during their last year in school, they have no special claim to even a spot on the team. These latter coaches will not keep a senior unless they are a starter, period.

To be a successful athlete one must often overcome significant obstables.

Strategies for Announcing Who Made the Team Following Try-outs

---

COACHING CONCEPT #266: Plan carefully how you will announce who has made the team and who did not.

Once a coach has made a decision whether or not an individual has made the team, there is a question of how this information is to be communicated to the youngster. There are several different things to consider in doing so. First, there is the matter of expediency. Time is often of the essence. As a result, coaches often face a real challenge in that they don't have a lot of time to spend in communicating with large numbers of youngsters who have failed to make the team. Second, there is the matter of the feelings of the individuals. Third, there is the question of exactly what should be shared with the individual in addition to the fact that the person has or has not made the squad.

> **COACHING CONCEPT #267: Never embarrass an athlete in announcing who made the team—always provide an avenue for the youngster to save face.**

Some coaches merely take the tack of posting a list of names of those who have failed to make the squad on a bulletin board. Or, a list of names of those who have made the team is posted on the bulletin board. Although these are quick methods of disseminating the information in terms of who made the team and who did not, this does little in terms of soothing the feelings, the disappointment and sadness of those who failed to make the squad.

When there are very large numbers of candidates, the posting of names may be the only viable alternative. It is suggested however, that if a list of names is posted, that it be the list of those *who had made the team.* In this way, those who have not been chosen will not have their names publicly displayed in a negative atmosphere (having failed to make the squad). It is important never to embarrass an athlete. Negative news such as not making the team should be shared in such a fashion that the youngster is able to save face and retain one's dignity.

> **COACHING CONCEPT #268: If time permits—coaches should share privately with those who failed to make the team the reasons behind the decision.**

Other coaches have elected to meet with each individual candidate and personally inform the individual as to whether or not the person has made the squad. Scheduling a meeting with those who made the team creates an opportunity to give a so-called pep talk to those members of the team, to indicate their strengths and areas which require further work, and to share with each of them what is expected of them individually and as a team.

Meeting with those persons who did not make the team is an effort to take into account the feelings of the candidates. Such an effort also prevents publicly embarrassing those who have failed to meet the team. That is, the meeting creates an opportunity for the coach to personally, and privately, share with each youngster the reason(s) why the individual did not make the team. Coaches can also provide suggestions in terms of what area(s) the individual should work on in the future should the would-be athlete desire to try again next season. Of course, this last option is only viable for those students who will be returning to that school the following year.

In a few instances, candidates who have been unsuccessful in their bid for a place on the team might well make excellent helpers in terms of statisticians, equipment managers, or all-around helpers for the coaching staff, if approached properly by the coach. However, it takes an exceptionally dedicated and committed youngster to go from a potential team member to a support role for the same team. But there are those who can make such a transition—with pride and competency.

COACHING CONCEPT #269: When sharing negative news to unsuccessful candidates provide some positive messages as well, thus providing support to the individual.

During this private meeting between the head coach and the unsuccessful aspirant, it is helpful if positive feedback (reinforcement) can be given to the student in addition to the information that the person did not make the team. Sandwiching the negative message between positive comments (proficient in conditioning; good in performing the drills; excellent effort) allows the individual to retain or even enhance positive self-esteem and respect. Taking time to spend the effort to spare the feelings of those who took the time to try out for the team can have positive ramifications. For example, parents and others in the community quickly become aware of the humanistic method used by the coach in delivering the message.

Yet another strategy that has been used successfully at both the high school and college level is to post the names of those individuals who have made the team, in an inconspicuous place (inside the team's locker room), while indicating that individuals who did not make the team but *who would like to meet privately* with the head coach should make an appointment within a specific time frame. This gives to those candidates who desire an opportunity to meet the coach the chance to do so. It also does not force such a meeting upon those who would just as soon forego such an experience.

The important concepts involved in choosing team members is to do so in an expedient fashion, be successful in selecting the best qualified candidates in terms of both physical skills and psychological make-up, all the while being fair to all concerned *and* being supportive of those who failed to make the team. If a coach can accomplish these four objectives the team (and coaching staff) is off to a very good start for the upcoming season.

Strategies for Removing Team Members from the Squad

One might think or expect that once individuals have been selected for a team at the beginning of the season, that the roster is firmed up and that this part of the personnel aspect of the team would be completed. However, as we will see, this is not always the case. In some instances, if not many, further personnel decisions are warranted made as the season progresses.

> **COACHING CONCEPT #270: Athletic participation is a privilege—not a right.**

There is always the possibility of a situation arising in which athletes will, *by their actions or inactions,* warrant disciplinary action. Such disciplinary action might consist of their being temporarily removed from the active-duty roster. It must be remembered that athletic participation is indeed a privilege, earned by the individual. Athletic participation is not a divine right. Individuals do not have the automatic right to be on a team; they have to earn it by demonstrating competencies in terms of physical skills, understanding and knowledge, appropriate attitudes, adherence to rules and expectations, etc. And they have to keep on earning that right each and every day throughout the season.

> **COACHING CONCEPT #271: When it comes to team membership—the good of the team takes precedence over the good of the individual.**

Athletic teams are composed up of athletes and their coaches. Athletic teams are just that, teams, groups of individuals working together for a common cause, a communal purpose. In this sense the good, the interest, of the whole (team) supersedes the welfare of the individual (athlete). This concept is exemplified in the slogan or saying that has been posted in thousands and thousands of coaches' offices and locker rooms over the years *There is no I in team.* While individualism is respected, team cohesion is essential for eventual success. An individual's wishes or desires must frequently be subordinated or subservient to those of the team. Coaches must emphasize to their athletes that the team concept necessitates individual sacrifices for the benefit and welfare of the team.

In the event of a very serious transgression or series of infractions, an individual team member may be permanently eliminated from the squad. Or, in those instances in which the improper behavior of the athletes is not as serious, the consequences might be less severe and the ban from participation might involve only a limited amount of time.

COACHING CONCEPT #272: **In terms of negative behavior of team members—retain those athletes who hurt only themselves, remove those athletes who injure (hinder the progress of) the team.**

Dismissing an athlete from the team or prohibiting the individual from playing for a specific number of contests are examples of severe punishment. The consequences for the individual athlete, parents and family members as well as the team itself can be many, varied and significant. Coaches need to exercise great care and caution prior to making such an important decision.

Many coaches subscribe to the philosophy that one should retain an athlete on the team, even if the individual becomes a pain in the neck as long as the athlete really hinders only himself or herself. However, when the individual's behavior and actions become so unsettling that the team itself becomes affected, then it is time for the coach to seriously consider removing the source of the disturbance, to remove the person from the team, for the good of the team and perhaps for the good of the individual.

In those instances in which the athlete is removed from the squad, it is imperative that the student be adequately warned. For example, it is unacceptable for the coach to bark out: "Missy, you have been late for the last time. You are hereby kicked off the team." In this case, regardless of the number of times poor Missy may have previously been late, she deserves to be forewarned of such a serious consequence as being booted off the squad for good. If the coach wanted to wield this type of punishment, then the coach should have informed, warned, the athlete that the next time she was late she would be off the team. Accordingly, Missy would then have been adequately forewarned of the outcome of her behavior and could make her decisions accordingly.

COACHING CONCEPT #273: **When administering severe punishment such as removal from the team—athletes have the right to have been forewarned of such drastic consequences.**

Wise, experienced and humanistic coaches follow the practice of forewarning their athletes of the severe negative consequences resulting from specific behavior or patterns of behavior. Specifically, it is strongly recommended that coaches share with their athletes that specific actions or inactions will result in severe and even drastic measures (such as removal from the team or suspension from the squad). In these cases the athletes need to be forewarned as to the seriousness of the consequences. Then, the youngsters can make a conscious decision in terms of their actions and inactions and can be expected to bear the consequences of same.

But, the important concept is that individuals have the right to know not only what is generally expected of them as athletes, but also what will happen to them if specific expectations are not met. In those instances, when harsh or severe punishment is to be the result, athletes (and parents as well as school officials) need to know exactly what is expected and what is to be the penalty for non-compliance.

COACHING CONCEPT #274: **Never surprise your athletic director—always keep your boss informed of your intended actions in controversial situations.**

Kicking a person off of a team has the potential for being a very controversial situation. In such situations, it would behoove the coach to keep the athletic director and other appropriate administrators apprised of the situation. In short, sometimes it is smart to run through your intended plan of action with your athletic director to be sure that there are no hidden agendas or problems lurking in the background of which you are unaware. Naturally, the coach must adhere to the established policies and procedures dealing with the removal of a current athlete from a team.

If there is a potential problem with removing a current member of the team from the squad, it is better to be forewarned by the athletic director ahead of time than to find out about it after the coach had told the athlete to leave. If you inform you athletic director of your intentions and receive the go-ahead—should you end up sitting on the end of the proverbial limb, your athletic director will be sitting right there alongside you. It is easier to survive controversies when you have the full backing and support of your athletic director.

COACHING CONCEPT #275: **When removing an athlete from the team—the athlete deserves access to an appeal process.**

Student-athletes always deserve the right to appeal dire consequences such as being removed from a team of which they are currently a member. Being removed from a squad because of specific behavior such as violating established team or school rules and regulations, or failure to live up to specific behavioral expectations necessitates that there be due process provided for the individual. Due process involves a thorough fact finding examination of the situation, through an appeal process, arbitrated frequently by disinterested parties (not by the coach) to insure that the actions taken in the specific case are warranted, fair, and appropriate.

COACHING CONCEPT #276:   Athletes need to be protected from capricious and arbitrary actions of coaches.

Athletes, as individuals, need to be protected from the arbitrary and capricious actions of a coach. Coaches are not perfect nor are they expected to be. Coaches are human—with the strengths and frailties of human beings. Coaches can exercise poor judgment. They can be unfair. They can make mistakes. They can make poor decisions and render questionable verdicts. They can carry grudges. They can be biased and prejudiced. They can be unthinking and uncaring. Individuals, as members of the team, need to be protected from instances in which their rights as athletes and as human beings are violated. Thus, an appeal process must be in place.

Notifying Individual Athletes That They Are Removed From the Squad

When an athlete is to be notified that the person is no longer a member of the team, it is wise to share this information in privacy or semi-privacy. Some coaches will meet individually with the athlete in question and inform the person as to the reasons why such a decision has had to been made. For many coaches, privacy is preferred because of a desire to protect the athlete from further embarrassment.

However, many coaches prefer to embrace this confrontational type of meeting only with a witness, either an assistant coach, an athletic administrator or other staff members, or even the principal. The idea here is to have a witness in the event that the meeting turns out not to be as cordial or productive as desired. This is especially true if there is any expectation that the athlete will become belligerent, argumentative or violent. Similarly, such a tactic is warranted if there is anticipation that what will take place at this meeting will be subject to interpretation, in terms of public relations within the community, in an appeal process, or perhaps even in a court of law.

BEING A GOOD PRACTICE COACH

Coaches need to develop skills in organizing and conducting practices. Practices must be well organized. Various coaching/teaching and practice activities need to be prioritized and presented. Practice time must be wisely spent. Individual attention for individual athletes is an essential element in any good practice session. High individual and team motivation is also most important. A variety of activities is also important in terms of motivation. Understanding the *why* of what is taking place on behalf of the athletes themselves is similarly very important for their motivation and confidence levels.

> **COACHING CONCEPT #277:** A *good coach* can be a very good PRACTICE COACH or a very good GAME COACH—a *great coach* is one who is a very good PRACTICE COACH and a very good GAME COACH.

There are many reasons why practices are so important. Coaches should recognize that there are a number of very important roles that practices can play in the success or failure of a team and its players. Practices are where the athletes are able to develop skills and understandings which must be learned and mastered in terms of the cognitive, affective and psychomotor domains.

For example, it is in practice that the athletes develop the physical and psychological conditioning necessary to be competitive in game or contest situations. It is in practice that the athletes learn to work with their peers and their coaches. It is in practice that the athletes acquire and learn specific skills. It is during practice that the knowledge of the game, the rules, the techniques and tactics are learned and improved upon. It is in practice that errors are detected, reduced or eliminated. And, it is in the practice setting that correct activities and actions, proper techniques and sound tactics, are perfected to a high degree of competency and skill and made into habits for use in actual competition.

> **COACHING CONCEPT #278:** Practice is private and the purpose is to prepare—game competition is public and is for real.

Practices are where coaches and teams prepare for very public competition against other teams, opponents, who are also trying to excel, TO WIN THE GAME. It is the responsibility of the coaching staff to teach, reinforce, motivate, encourage, and thereby prepare their charges to be ready to meet such opponents in actual competition. It is in competition, out there on the firing line, where not only is the score kept for real but the game is played in the public eye for all to discern and evaluate. Practice is private and for preparation. Game competition is public and is for real.

If preparation for competition is the key to success in actual competition, it is clear that practice sessions, the planning and implementation of practices for athletic teams, is absolutely a critical element in the overall success of any team. Much of the success that is experienced by the athletes (and therefore by the coaching staff) can be traced directly to their practice experiences. Without a sound practice regimen individual athletes (and teams) do not usually develop into exceptionally skilled participants or successful teams enjoying extraordinary success in actual competition.

Coaches must remain focused at all times.

BEING A GOOD GAME (BENCH) COACH

Another element of actual teaching and coaching involves those activities that take place in actual competition, in games, in contests. The decision making ability of the coach, in the heat of battle, is often critical in the eventual success of the team. Such decisions must be made not only in terms of strategies and tactics but also in terms of personnel. Additionally, coaches need to be able to react to tactics and strategies employed by opponents—both those tactics and strategies that were anticipated and those which were not anticipated. Dealing successfully and forcefully with the unexpected, the unusual, is a highly important competency for any coach.

COACHING CONCEPT #279:   Game coaching is similar to playing a game of chess.

Coaching in game situations, in actual competition, has often been likened to playing a chess game. One needs to carefully plan one's moves while anticipating—often two, three or even four moves in the future—both the opponent's likely reactions and one's own counter-moves.

Practice sessions in a sport enables the team and the coaching staff to prepare for what is anticipated in actual competition at a later date. However, in the game itself, decisions must be made *now, in the present*. In game competition there is precious little time to think about, deliberate and weigh all of the options and counter-options in terms of possible actions and the consequences of acting or failing to act.

There are so many variables that exist in a heated (contested) game that it is not possible to always anticipate all of the possible scenarios that can arise in every game. As a result, it is a highly desirable ability, trait or skill for a coach to be able to react to, analyze, interpret and come to a correct or appropriate decision—in the heat of the battle regarding a course of action that will favor one's own team, that will give one's players and team an advantage over the opponents.

There is a very real difference between the practice setting and the game situation for athletes. There is also a significant contrast between coaching in a practice environment and coaching out there on the so-called firing line of actual competition, in front of the crowd in a pressure pack situation. The game situation is the culminating activity following weeks, months and perhaps even years of planning, strategy, work, dedication, sacrifice and the overcoming of numerous obstacles and challenges. Game situations are all too frequently what separate the successful coaches from those who are not as successful.

COACHING CONCEPT #280: Being a competent game coach means being able to adjust, adapt and make appropriate decisions—in the heat of battle.

Being a good game coach also means making timely and judicious decisions with a minimum amount of time available (sometimes literally seconds)—all in the heat of battle. Being a good game coach necessitates being able to change one's strategy, to improvise, to adapt, and to react to both anticipated and unanticipated events and happenings. It means making quick but nevertheless correct or appropriate judgments. It means being able to take advantage of one's experience and intuition. It means being able to assess and evaluate information and data and then having the confidence to carry out these decisions. It means being able to assess one's own players and the opposing players in terms of their performance, their short-comings, and their strengths. And, being a good game coach means having the ability to motivate one's players to similarly adapt to varying circumstances in a fluid game situation *and* to accept the coach's decisions knowing that such judgments are appropriate and expedient for that situation. Becoming a good game coach requires experience and deliberate work in these areas of coaching.

REFERENCES

Athletics Notes. (1990, November 28). *The Chronicle of Higher Education.* p. A-38.

Brady, E. (1993a, November 8). Black athletes dream of pros but value school. *USA Today* p. 1-A.

Brady, E. (1993b, November 8). Survey: Sports foster social unity. *USA Today,* p. 2-C.

Brittain, T. (2006, October/November). Winning them over. *Athletic Management, XVIII*(6), 636-7.

College Athletic Clips. (October, 2007). Retrieved from: http://www.college athleticsclips.com/s/375/index.aspx?sid=375&gid=1&pgid=15&cid=292&new sid=945

Fielitz, L. (2000). Using the Internet for athletic recruiting. *Journal of Physical Education, Recreation and Dance, 71*(2), 13-15.

Holcomb, T. (2007, May 19). Only the (relatively) few become college athletes. *Atlanta Journal-Constitution.* Retrieved from: www.ajc.com/highschool/content/sports/highschool/stories/2007/05/19/0520spthsscholarship.html

Manos, K. (2001, April/May). Want to join us? *Athletic Management, XIII*(3), 13, 15, 17.

Moving middle schoolers down. (2005, February/March). *Athletic Management, XVII*(2), 13.

Myers, J. (1991, December 18). Reaching pros a tough trek. *USA Today,* p. 4-C.

NBA Stardom, (1998, February 20-22). *USA Weekend/Democrat and Chronicle,* p. 5.

Read, D. (2001, March). Offseason: Not offered. *Directing Athletics, 4*(1), 13-17.

Roth, L. (2000, April 2). Bills camp changes for better at Fisher. *Democrat & Chronicle,* p. 1-D.

Simons, J. (1997, March 24). Improbable dreams. *U.S. News & World Report,* pp. 45-57.

SportScan—Coaching careers short & part time. (1988). *American Coach,* Champaign, Illinois: Human Kinetics, p. 1.

Stier, W. (1974, January). Everything the athlete always wanted to know about selecting a college but was afraid to ask. *Scholastic Coach,* pp. 80-81, 94.

Stier, Jr., W.F. (1986, March). Competencies in amateur/youth coaching. Resources in Education (RIE). ERIC Document Reproduction Service No. ED263-060.

Stier, Jr., W.F. (1986, Spring). Athletic administration: Athletic administrators expect qualities, competencies in coaches. *Interscholastic Athletic Administration,* p. 7.

Name: _____

Student ID #:_____

EXERCISES FOR CHAPTER 9

A. Explain how advance planning can help expedite a coach's efforts? Be specific. Provide examples.

_____

_____

_____

_____

_____

_____

B. What are some of the differences and similarities between recruitment at the junior/senior high school level, the college level and in youth sports?

_____

_____

_____

_____

_____

C. How would you go about attempting to increase the retention rate of your team members?

_____

_____

_____

_____

_____

D.   How would you go about cutting candidates from your team? What criteria would you suggest using for your specific sport(s)? What objective and subjective criteria might be appropriate to use in your sport(s)?

E.   How would you notify the unsuccessful and the successful candidates who tried out for your team? Why? Justify your position.

F.   If parents complained to you about why their youngsters are not getting sufficient playing time, how would your respond? Why?

G. What is your position regarding keeping (and playing) seniors on the team just because they are seniors?

H. What differentiates a successful practice coach from a successful game coach?

I. How would you construct initial practices during which would-be athletes would try out for your high school team? Be specific. Provide a rationale for your choice(s).

J. If you had tryouts for your team, would you establish any preconditions that would-be athletes must satisfy in order to be eligible to try out for the team? Why or why not? If so, be specific in terms of preconditions. What are advantages or disadvantages of such preconditions?

_____

_____

_____

_____

_____

_____

_____

_____

RESEARCH QUESTONS FOR CHAPTER 9

1. Interview both volunteer coaches and paid coaches at any level and determine the differences, if any, in terms of the duties, obligations, satisfactions and workload, etc., between the two types of coaches.

_____

_____

_____

_____

_____

_____

_____

_____

2. Go to a library or use other sources and read about sociograms as well as various physical or psychological tests that might be used to determine whether or not a candidate might be suitable for athletic competition on an athletic team at the interscholastic or collegiate team. Summarize your readings, being careful to include sociograms and explain their possible use in sports.

   _____

   _____

   _____

   _____

   _____

3. Survey current high school coaches and junior high school coaches in an effort to determine *how* other coaches conduct tryouts for their teams.

   _____

   _____

   _____

   _____

   _____

   _____

4. Interview a non-varsity coach of a team sport to determine how they go about recruiting future/potential athletes to their teams—from within the school itself and from the community (very young future/potential participants).

   _____

   _____

   _____

   _____

   _____

5. Approach several coaches of different sports (team and individual sports) to determine if they use written coaching (teaching) plans in terms of advance planning for their individual practices and explain their reasons for either creating and using such written plans/notes or not using them.

Chapter 10

Components of Successful Practice Sessions

The joy of victory.

STRATEGIES FOR COACHING IN PRACTICE

As previously stated coaches must be competent in conducting practices for their charges. It is during these practices, from the first day of practice to the last, that athletes may be introduced to the knowledge and the physical skills that must be mastered for actual game competition. It is during practices that athletes are provided opportunities to develop and improve their sport skills. The method by which practices are planned, are structured, are used, will go a long way in determining the effectiveness of the coach and the level of skill of the athletes, individually and collectively.

It cannot be emphasized too strongly that coaches must be skilled in planning, conducting, evaluating and adjusting their practice sessions. Regardless of the level of competition, coaches must be concerned about the readiness and the potential of their athletes in terms of the physical, psychological, social, and knowledge aspects of the sport.

Dan Gable, who won 10 NCAA national championships as coach of the Iowa Hawkeyes' wrestling team, said: "In every practice session, you have to emphasize the fundamental areas, drill on them, and see that the athletes feel self-satisfaction after every practice" (Manos, 2005, p. 36). Coaches should spend most of their time and effort in practices, in preparing their charges for competition, mentally, physically, and emotionally.

Properly planned practices provide athletes with opportunities to actually learn more about themselves, their teammates, their coaches, and their sport. Properly structured practices provide opportunities for team members to improve their skill level, their physical, social and mental capabilities in a particular sport. Properly conducted practices facilitate youngsters being able to expand upon their own potential as athletes and to refine their performance skills.

COACHING CONCEPT #281:   **Coaches should plan their practices for the entire season in advance—at least in general terms.**

Planning practices mean more than merely thinking about what needs to be accomplished tomorrow. It means much more. Planning practices involves sitting down and scheduling, in broad terms, *everything* that needs to be covered during the pre-season period of time, during the in-season, and during the post season (see chapter 9). Practice content needs to be delineated for each of these three time periods.

COACHING CONCEPT #282:   **No practice plan is foolproof—coaches must be able and willing to make adjustments in today's and tomorrow's practice plans.**

Of course, no coach can sit down in advance of the pre-season practice time and decide with 100% certainty what the team (and individual athletes) will be doing during every minute of every single practice session during the entire season. This is not a realistic expectation. Neither is it reasonable nor feasible. Greater specificity will come as each specific practice session approaches. And exceptions may be necessary almost on a daily basis. Changes and exceptions to the practice schedules, including the weekly and the daily practice schedules, will be made in light of what transpired in the previous practice. Changes are inevitable. Changes are not something negative. Rather, it is a wise and prudent coach who is able to adapt and change tomorrow's (and the next day's) practice plans to compensate for something that occurs unexpectedly today.

For example, a baseball coach in high school had planned to spend only 15 minutes introducing his athletes to a defense against the double steal. However, after the time period had elapsed it was evident that the athletes had not understood the strategy. They had failed to learn the physical skills (at least to the level expected by the coach) involved in defending against the double steal. As a result, the coach might very well change tomorrow's practice schedule to include an additional 10 or 15 minutes devoted to this crucial defensive strategy. Or, the coach might spend an additional 10-15 minutes today on this area and then choose to eliminate some other activities from the current practice plans. Adjustments are necessary. This is to be expected.

COACHING CONCEPT #283:   Coaches should have a reason for everything they do or plan in a practice session.

The planning of practices during the pre-season, in-season, post season time periods needs to be further broken down into monthly practice schedules, weekly practice schedules, and daily practice schedules. *Everything*, yes, *everything*, that the coaches anticipate covering in practice during these three time segments should be planned for in detail, in writing. Coaches need to anticipate the needs of the team and individual team members and then organize, plan and implement appropriate practice sessions. The goal is to prepare the athletes, individually and collectively, for upcoming competition.

Planning Practices by Thinking Backwards

One way to plan for practices is to work backwards. That is, the head coach (with help from assistants, if any) sets specific objectives of what the athletes must achieve during each of these three time periods and then plans backwards and plans when the athletes will work on those objectives. The coaching staff has the responsibility of determining what the athletes and the team should be capable of understanding, knowing and mastering. They must be able to answer these types of questions. How will youngsters learn specific skills necessary to be competitive? When? What physical characteristics or abilities should they possess? What knowledge, skills and experiences should be introduced (and when) to the athletes within the pre-season period, the in-season period and the post season period? What must be learned (and at what level of competency) by the athletes during each time period? What specific skills are to be mastered by individual athletes by the time actual competition begins? How much time should be spent on any single aspect of the offense, the defense, the conditioning, the special plays, etc., during the pre-season, the in-season and the post season period of competition? When should the team and specific individuals spend time doing what? With whom? Under what conditions?

COACHING CONCEPT #284:   **Don't re-invent the wheel—use what has worked in the past or what works for others unless there is a compelling reason to do otherwise.**

There is no need to re-invent the wheel when it comes to planning practices. If something has worked for you in the past, use it again. If something has been successful for others in the past, there is nothing wrong in seeing if the same technique, tactic or strategy might work for your team. The key is to find out what works and stick with it. Too many inexperienced coaches tend to vacillate from one strategy to another, from one style of play to another, to one method of conducting practice to another—always searching for that perfect answer. Such frequent changes tend to create confusion among the players as well as the coaching staff. Stability and consistency are advantages. Change only when there is a good reason to do so.

The author once knew of a football coach who was so indecisive that he was forever changing things, constantly tinkering with the offensive and defensive systems. It seemed that every time the team lost (which was quite often), the coach would come in the office Monday morning with so many *new plays or variations* that the players and even the coaching staff had great difficulty in learning any single offensive or defensive system. As a result, the team was less than successful for the duration of the time that that coach was at that particular school.

COACHING CONCEPT #285:   **Objectives and goals of practices should be realistic, attainable and measurable.**

Coaches need to decide what their athletes should be doing from the very first day of practice until the conclusion of the competitive season. Then, it behooves the staff to identify the various learning experiences and teaching techniques and tactics to be used at various times of the season and decide how and when these teaching/coaching experiences will comprise the practice hours available each and every day of practice.

COACHING CONCEPT #286:   **Beware of 2 o'clock wonders (Pseudo Stars) in practice.**

In athletic parlance, the 2 o'clock wonder or pseudo star is the team member who exhibits great skills and competencies during the 2 o'clock practices when competing with one's teammates, when there is no pressure, when the crowds are absent, when it is only practice. However, this same would-be elite performer chokes big-time when it comes to duplicating this same level of elite performance when it actually comes time to participate in actual competition. All coaches have come across such individuals. It is not their fault. It is just that there is a big difference between competing in a practice session and actually performing when it really counts, in a game situation, in front of a crowd, for big stakes, etc.

COACHING CONCEPT #287: **Be in attendance at all practices, start to finish—don't let assistants (on a continual basis) conduct practices and to run the show in your absence.**

Coaches are in charge of practices. They plan and implement practice plans. They must be in attendance at every practice. They must also be on time and be actively involved in all practices. This is sometimes difficult for part-time coaches who hold full time jobs elsewhere and must travel to the site of the athletic practice. Sometimes head coaches arrive late for practices and allow their assistant(s) to conduct and run the practice session until the head coach is on the scene. Although this might be acceptable on a rare occasion, such a practice on a continual basis is just poor coaching and poor practice. The role of an assistant is not to substitute for the head coach in this fashion. There are some tasks that should not be delegated by the head coach to others. The head coach should set the example for punctuality. The head coach must lead by example. If the head coach cannot get to the site until 4 p.m. then practice should not start until 4 p.m.

PLANNING FOR THE PRE-SEASON PRACTICES

During the pre-season practices, **one** of the major objectives is to evaluate the candidates for the team and to select those who will be part of the squad. A **second** objective during this time period is to insure that the athletes are in sufficient physical condition to engage in actual competition. Assuming that the athletes had arrived at the first official practice period in reasonably good physical shape, the pre-season time segment can be used to improve upon and increase the conditioning level of the athletes.

Having the athletes arrive on the first day of practice in excellent physical condition enables coaches to spend more time on the actual teaching of knowledge and skills and the refinement of these skills needed for successful competition. Too many coaches are forced to spend far too much valuable time in practice working the athletes into physical shape to compete. Pre-season practice time is rather short for many sports. Coaches need to use every precious minute of their practice sessions teaching and reinforcing the skills and knowledge of the sport. Coaches should not be wasting time attempting to get out-of-shape would-be athletes into acceptable physical condition. Granted that conditioning activities are necessary during practices, but such activities should be used in a supplemental fashion to build upon and to sustain the level of conditioning that the individual athletes possesses when they report for practice.

COACHING CONCEPT #288:   **Athletes should report to the first day of practice in excellent physical shape—pre-season practices are too valuable to merely be spent getting athletes into shape.**

A **third** major objective of pre-season practices is to provide to each squad member the appropriate knowledge and information (strategies and tactics) necessary for the success of the team. A **fourth** major objective of the pre-season is for the coaches to know their athletes as individuals and for the youngsters to better know their coaches. A **fifth** major objective is to have each athlete develop those individual and team physical skills and competencies required for success in a particular competitive sport. And, the **sixth** major objective of pre-season practice sessions is to blend all of the individuals into a cohesive whole, capable of working together as a true team, comprised of skilled, experienced and motivated athletes.

In short, the pre-season practice schedule must be so designed by the coaching staff that the athletes are able to learn, at least at the minimum competency level, all that they need to know and perform *in order to be reasonably competitive in the initial athletic contest.* Of course, an athletic team or individual athletes will not be capable of mastering in the pre-season everything the coaches would like for them to learn at the highest level of performance. Athletes are expected to improve throughout the season as they are introduced to and learn additional skills and knowledge. However, athletes also need to be ready to compete on the first day that the regular season competition begins. It is up to the head coach to be sure that one's athletes have been adequately prepped in terms of meeting their first opponents.

COACHING CONCEPT #289:   **Don't prejudge or pigeonhole athletes in terms of their performance—give them the benefit of the doubt and give them a chance to demonstrate competency.**

Sometimes coaches are surprised when their athletes return to school in the fall and find that the youngsters have improved, sometimes significantly, from their performance level the previous season. These coaches shouldn't be surprised at all. Athletes can be expected to improve over a period of time. Coaches need to be wary of anticipating that an athlete will be like the individual was the last time the coach saw the youngster. The basketball coach who has not really been in contact with a player on a daily basis since the season ended the previous February or March can often be pleasantly surprised the following October when the player steps on the court once again.

In some instances, the basketball coach may have erroneously pigeonholed or predetermined that a particular athlete will probably perform at a level similar to that achieved the previous school year. However, just taking into account the passage of time, not to mention the possibility of hard work and additional sport experience during the off-season, it is entirely possible (and most likely highly probable) that this athlete has significantly improved in terms of sport skills and physical capabilities and potential.

Thus, coaches should not be limited by their preconceived ideas of what an athlete can and cannot do based on what the athlete could do in the past. Instead, make a new, a fresh assessment in terms of what the individual athlete is capable of achieving based on current data, as a result of current evaluation.

Likewise, coaches should expect, not be surprised, when their athletes improve their level of skill, their conditioning capability and their physical stature during the season itself. If the coach is doing a good job, the youngster should improve as an athlete. If the athletes are working hard, they should improve their level of performance. After all, that is why the coach is there, to teach the individual athlete how to be a better performer and to develop greater physical skills, increase one's knowledge of the sport and to enhance physical, psychological and social attributes or characteristics.

Sharing Practice Plans with Athletes

COACHING CONCEPT #290: Athletes must have confidence in their coaches —it is a responsibility of the coach to build and develop such confidence among the athletes.

One of the ways that coaches can help build the confidence that athletes must have of the coaching staff is to conduct meaningful, well organized and structured practices. Preparing the athletes for actual competition is a very serious responsibility and a very important task. It is not something that can be left up to chance.

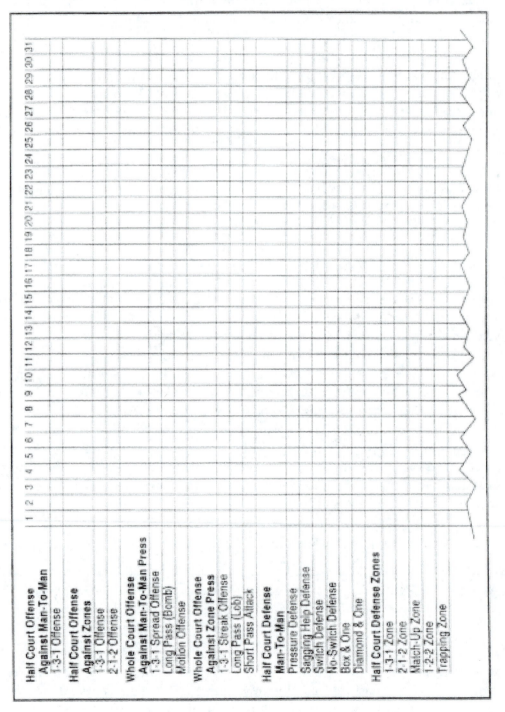

Half Court Offense
Against Man-To-Man
  1-3-1 Offense

Half Court Offense
Against Zones
  1-3-1 Offense
  2-1-2 Offense

Whole Court Offense
Against Man-To-Man Press
  1-3-1 Spread Offense
  Long Pass (Bomb)
  Motion Offense

Whole Court Offense
Against Zone Press
  1-3-1 Streak Offense
  Long Pass (Lob)
  Short Pass Attack

Half Court Defense
  Man-To-Man
  Pressure Defense
  Sagging Help Defense
  Switch Defense
  No-Switch Defense
  Box & One
  Diamond & One

Half Court Defense Zones
  1-3-1 Zone
  2-1-2 Zone
  Match-Up Zone
  1-2-2 Zone
  Trapping Zone

FIGURE 10.1a—Daily Practice Schedule for Varsity Basketball—Preseason

	1	2	3	4	5	6	7	8	9	10	11	12	13	14	15	16	17	18	19	20	21	22	23	24	25	26	27	28	29	30	31
Whole Court Defense																															
Man-To-Man Press																															
Switching Press																															
Trapping Press																															
"Token" Press																															
Whole Court Defense																															
Zone Press																															
1-2-1-1 Press																															
2-2-1 Press																															
1-3-1 Press																															
"Token" Press																															
Drills - Offensive																															
Alley-Opp Drill																															
Screening Drill																															
Cutting Drill																															
Passing Drill																															
Shoot and Tip Drill																															
Passing Drill																															
Pre-Game Warm-Up Drill																															
Drills - Defensive																															
Rebounding Drill																															
Block-Out Drill																															
Side Drill																															
Break-Out Drill																															
Step-Out Drill																															
Conditioning Drills																															
Sprint-Stop Drill																															
Zig-Zag Ball Drill																															
Flexibility Drill																															
Jumping Drill																															
Agility Drill																															
Pass-Shoot Drill																															
Shot Rebound Drill																															
Go-Go Drill																															
Warm-up Shoot-Around																															

FIGURE 10.1b—Daily Practice Schedule for Varsity Basketball—Preseason

	1	2	3	4	5	6	7	8	9	10	11	12	13	14	15	16	17	18	19	20	21	22	23	24	25	26	27	28	29	30	31
Shooting Drills																															
Round Robin Drill																															
Drill Spot Shooting Drill																															
Pivot Drill																															
Perimeter Drill																															
Corner Drill																															
21-Drill																															
Shoot and Rebound Drill																															
Screen and Shoot																															
Dribble and Shoot																															
Free Throw Drill																															
Competitive F-T Drill																															
Blind Fold F-T Drill																															
Scrimmage Time																															
Whole Court Scrimmage																															
Half-Court Scrimmage																															
Special Plays																															
Out-of-Bounds, Offense																															
Under Basket																															
From Sideline																															
From Endline																															
Out-of-Bounds, Defense																															
Under Basket - Zone																															
Under Basket - M/M																															
From Sideline																															
From Endline																															
Last Second Off. Plays																															
Against Zones																															
Against Man-to-Man																															
3-Seconds Left																															
10-Seconds Left																															
Defending Last Second Plays																															
3-Seconds Left-Alert Defense																															
10-Seconds Left-Zone																															
10-Seconds Left-M/M																															

FIGURE 10.1c—Daily Practice Schedule for Varsity Basketball—Preseason

It is one thing to adequately plan logical and appropriate practice sessions that take into account individual athletes' physical, mental and psychological needs and abilities, whether such practices are during pre-season, in-season or post season. It is yet another to plan practices that also help to instill confidence among the athletes in the competency of their coaches.

COACHING CONCEPT #291: **Athletes who possess confidence in the decisions of their coaches have a greater likelihood of improving their own performance.**

This is an important concept, that of having the athletes understand that their coaches are experienced, skilled and competent and that the coaches know what they are doing. Coaches need to instill in their charges the awareness that their mentors are competent and knowledgeable as coaches. Figures 10.1a-c are examples of charts *(activity poster boards)* detailing practice plans for the sport of basketball during a thirty-one-day pre-season practice season.

Activity Poster Boards

This type of chart, if used correctly, will go a long way to not only help the coaching staff organize and structure upcoming practices but will also help build confidence in the athletes themselves. A not inconsequential benefit from the use of this tactic is that the head coach's superiors, both athletic and central administrators, who see evidence of this type of advance planning and scheduling can come away with a positive impression of the coaches (especially the head coach). These administrators, as well as others who have the opportunity to view the posters displayed in the practice facility, will come away with the impression that the coaching staff is competent and knowledgeable, both in terms of content and in terms of planning appropriate activities to use in teaching the athletes what is necessary for competition.

The practice schedules for each day of the entire pre-season time period are printed on several large poster boards. Two sets of these boards are created. One set is placed in the team's locker room. The other is placed on a bulletin board in the practice gymnasium. Each set of identical poster boards is created and displayed for easy reference by the team members and coaches. The posters illustrate how the coaches are planning on using each day of practice to insure that that which needs to be practiced indeed takes place.

Along the left side of the chart, running from the top of the poster to the bottom, are offensive techniques, defensive techniques, various drills, conditioning activities, special plays, etc., that will be taught to and practiced by the team during the pre-season practice time period. Along the top of the posters, from left to right, are the sequential dates of each of the scheduled practice days. Drawing intersecting horizontal and vertical lines creates a criss-cross pattern as shown. Inside each box is placed the approximate amount of time (in minutes) to be spent on that particular day adjacent to the activity listed along the left side of the poster.

Naturally, not all of the possible drills or practice activities will be attempted on a single day. Rather, the goal is to insure that at the end of all of the pre-season practice sessions the athletes can readily see that they have indeed spent a significant amount of time on *all* of the skills, drills and strategies that are necessary to be adequately prepared to enter competition against the first opponent.

The mere fact that the athletes can observe how organized the coaches are goes a long way towards building confidence in the athletes. Couple this with the fact that athletes are also able to recognize that they have spent sufficient time learning and mastering (at least to some degree) those essential skills and competencies necessary to enter competition—and it can easily be seen that the athletes can develop a great deal of confidence not only in their coaches but in their own abilities to meet and conquer the competition. On the other hand, there is nothing that destroys the confidence of a team, as a group or individually, than for the team to go through the pre-season practices only to be surprised in the first few games by facing a tactic or a strategy for which they had not been prepared.

Pre-season Daily Practice Schedule—Via the Activity Poster Boards

The use of the *Activity Poster Boards* should not be used in lieu of detailed daily, weekly and even monthly practice plans. Rather, they should be viewed as an additional teaching and public relations tool at the coach's disposal. They are a device that can help the coach become a better coach, as well as a means of developing a sense of confidence among athletes and others in the coaching and organizational skills of the coaching staff.

Daily Practice Plans

A daily practice schedule can consist of nothing more than a written list of activities to be performed by the coaching staff and the athletes on a particular day. Many coaches also specify how much time to spend on each activity during the practice session. Other coaches preplan each activity in terms of scheduling an exact time to start and end each activity. These coaches preplan how every minute of that day's practice session will be spent by athletes and coaches, from the beginning to the conclusion of practice. There are two key concepts concerning the daily practice plans. First, such plans are created in advance. And, second, these practice plans serve as a

Daily Practice Schedule

Date: _____ **Site:** _____

Time:	**Activity**
3:15	Flexibility Warm-Up Activities
_____	_____
_____	_____
_____	_____
_____	_____
_____	_____
_____	_____
_____	_____
_____	_____
_____	_____
_____	_____
_____	_____
_____	_____
_____	_____
_____	_____
_____	_____
_____	_____
_____	_____
Notes:	_____
_____	_____

FIGURE 10.2—A Daily Practice Plan

road map for both coaches and athletes in terms of what activities should take place, where, and when, during every single minute of the practice.

COACHING CONCEPT #292:   **After each practice, ask yourself what could have been done differently to have improved that practice—then make plans for necessary adjustments in the future.**

Figure 10.2 is an example of a daily practice form. On the front side of the sheet is room to place the date and the actual practice site (some teams have more than one site at which to conduct practices). Along the left side of the page is room to insert the specific time when an activity is to begin. The actual activity is listed to the right of the time and may contain as much detail as the coach desires. The objective is to remind the coach that a specific practice activity is to take place at a particular time.

At the bottom of the front page is an area for the coach to scribble any important notes either during the actual practice or afterwards. Additional information or comments can also be placed on the bottom of this sheet and on the reverse side. For example, an incident with an athlete who misbehaved or who broke a training rule might be noted here. Or, additional comments (positive and negative) regarding the day's practice activities, progress of or difficulties with individual athletes, or notations regarding future practice activities might be included.

Finally, the reverse side of this daily practice sheet is also used to record the circumstances surrounding any accidents that occurred during the practice session. Of course, in the event of an accident, the coach should also complete the school's or organization's standard accident form and obtain written statements from witnesses.

COACHING CONCEPT #293:   **In the event of an accident—after caring for the injured party, be sure and complete the accident forms and secure written statements from all witnesses.**

Securing Accurate Witness Statements for All Accidents

In a severe accident at the State University of New York, Brockport, a volleyball player injured herself following the conclusion of a game. Specifically, the young athlete was in such a hurry to get a drink of water that she stepped off to the side of the court and ran beneath the supporting guide wire that held up one of the posts that stabilized the net. In so doing, she was partially scalped at the front of her head—the scalp was literally laid back away from the skull. After the injured athlete was cared for, the head coach secured signed statements from the available witnesses per the established policy of the athletic department.

COACHING CONCEPT #294:   **Not all witnesses to accidents possess perfect or even accurate recall—double check all written statements from witnesses for accuracy and completeness.**

However, the athletic director, in examining all of the signed statements of the witnesses, found a serious discrepancy in one case. One of the witnesses wrote that the accident happened during the competition when the athlete tried to lunge for the ball as it went out of play and subsequently struck her head on the metal guide wire. All of the other witnesses had described, in writing, what had actually taken place. However, this one witness to the same accident just happened to see it differently. Or, this individual's perception was completely different from all other witnesses as well as the injured athlete. The amount of time that passed from the accident and the writing and signing of the witness forms was less than 30 minutes. Witnesses to accidents do not always see reality. It is absolutely essential that the individual securing the written statement of any witness check to see whether the statement does, in fact, coincide with reality.

Making Changes in the Planned Practices

As stated before practice schedules (daily, weekly, monthly) should always remain subject to change. They must be flexible due to the very nature of the athletic practice sessions and the unpredictable nature of athletes. It may take longer to teach a skill to a team or individual participants. Events with upcoming opponents may dictate that a coach change a strategy, a tactic or place greater emphasis on a specific aspect of the game. The coach may make a command decision in light of how the athletes are performing and elect to do something other than what had been planned. The point is that if changes are indeed made in a given practice session, other changes may also be necessary to implement during the rest of the week or even in subsequent weeks.

Weekly Practice Plans

Many coaches also construct weekly practice plans in advance. Figure 10.3 depicts such a weekly schedule. Use of a weekly schedule is done in an effort to guide athletes over a longer period of time. Usually the weekly practice plan does not involve the amount of detail that a daily plan would possess. The weekly

Monday	Tuesday	Wednesday	Thursday	Friday

FIGURE 10.3—A Weekly Practice Plan

schedule generally contains, at a minimum, a list of those activities that the coaches anticipate using within a particular day's practice. This might include conditioning activities, drills, scrimmage opportunities, introduction of new tactics or strategies, individual work with athletes, group activities, refinement of previously taught skills, etc. Later, when each individual daily plan is formulated for the actual days in that particular week, the coaching staff will be able to provide more detail information, more specificity, in terms of exactly when the various activities will take place, with whom, and for what period of time.

Monthly Practice Schedules

Some coaches also create a general outline of intended practices for a much longer period of time period, such as a month. Some even do so for the entire season that year. In so doing, they attempt to paint a general picture of what they would like, what they hope, to accomplish during this longer period of time. Of course, when dealing with such a significant window of time there is less specificity or details in terms of what is to be covered than in the weekly practice sessions or in the daily practice plan. In short, what a coach anticipates or plans to do and to accomplish during a 30-day period in the future is not necessarily an exact prediction of what will actually take place during each of those 30 days. But such expectations are very helpful in guiding the coaching staff in organizing and planning for the weekly activities and the daily practices. Again, the monthly or season long practice plan serves as a general road map for the staff.

Thus, it is up to each coach to establish a general, broad outline of how practices will be organized and run from a global perspective, that is, when looking at the monthly (or season long) practice schedule. From that general outline, weekly practice schedules can then be determined. And, from these weekly schedules, coaches are then able to determine specifically what will take place during each available minute on any particular day of practice during the week.

Naturally, care must be exercised by the coaches not to be too ridged and uncompromising with their practice plans, even their daily plans. The monthly practice plans, the weekly plans and the daily plans are just that— plans, anticipated courses of action. The wise, experienced and highly skilled coach is able to make exceptions, is able to make a decision to change a previously made plan to adjust to the current situation. These all important decisions by coaches frequently need to be made in the heat of the battle of the actual practices. Coaches need to be capable of making such decisions in reaction to what takes place in practice, with short notice, just as they will be required to make similar split second decisions as coaches in actual game competition.

Excellent individual athleticism is essential in team and individual sports.

PLANNING FOR THE IN-SEASON PRACTICES

Once the actual competitive portion of the season begins, the coaching staff is faced with a whole different challenge in terms of coaching their athletes. It is at this point that the athletes are actually competing with other teams or individuals out there on the firing line. During this period of time, it is essential that coaches continue to refine the skill levels of their charges and to maintain, and even improve, their level of conditioning. Additionally, in many sports, coaches are able to introduce additional information, additional knowledge for the athletes to assimilate. In many sports, there are additional skills, strategies and tactics that can be introduced

COACHING CONCEPT #295: Planning practices during the competitive portion of the season depends on how well the team is performing and who the upcoming opponents are.

to the players and the team once actual competition begins. And, of course, there are always the efforts by the coaches to prepare their athletes and teams to meet a very specific opponent or opponents.

In many sports, like football, soccer, wrestling, cross country, tennis, basketball, and others, the athletes and coaches are able to plan their strategies in light of the perceived strengths and weaknesses of upcoming opponents. Thus, these teams might have their practices adjusted in terms of who the upcoming opponent(s) will be that week. Additionally, practices during the actual in-season part of the sport season will be determined by how well the team and individual athletes performed in previous competition. This is one area where the skill of the coach is truly put to the test, that is, recognizing what the athletes and the team need to work on to improve their overall competency level, their specific sport skill level, their motivational level, and their ability to work together as a team.

Conditioning and Strength Training During In-season

During the competitive portion of the season, athletes will still need to spend time on general and specific conditioning. They need to maintain and increase their strength, their endurance, their speed, their quickness, their jumping ability, their reaction time, etc. They will also need to spend time on relearning or overlearning specific skills. They will need to refine and improve specific skills. They will need to improve their level of competency in playing their sport in actual (real) competition, in front of crowds. And, they will need to be introduced to new knowledge, new skills, new strategies and tactics.

Learning and refining skills as well as maintaining and improving physical and mental capabilities in one's sport are major objectives during the competitive portion of the sport season. It is during this part of the total season that the ability of coaches are put to the sternest test. This is where coaches must be able to evaluate their own athletes, the abilities of opposing athletes, and to come to appropriate and timely decisions in terms of what one's own team, one's own athletes should be doing during practices. This ability to react to what is happening in games and in practices and to make the appropriate decision in terms of planning and organizing one's own practice sessions is what distinguishes a great coach from a mediocre one.

PLANNING FOR THE POST SEASON PRACTICES

During the post season, teams and athletes are in a sudden death type of situation. For example, on the high school level, if the football team is involved in the sectional, regional or state competition, the team remains in contention for the ultimate prize, the championship, only so long as it continues to win. The college ice hockey team that is selected for post season competition remains eligible to compete as long as it remains undefeated. One loss and the season abruptly ends for that team.

Post season competition is for all the marbles. Post season competition is for the star in the sky, that is, the championship. Whether the championship is at the youth sport level with midget football or little league baseball, at the high school level with the state championship, or the collegiate level with a national championship at stake, post season competition is unique. In post season competition, there is only one winner. Other teams which are fortunate enough to qualify or be invited to such competition will be summarily eliminated if they stumble and are beaten by a better and/or luckier opponent.

COACHING CONCEPT #296: **In post season competition, coaches would do well to stay with what they have been successful doing and with the athletes who brought the team to this point.**

Thus, the practices that coaches plan and organize for this time period are significantly different than those structured for the pre-season and for most of the in-season practices. During the post season competition, time and emphasis is spent on refining both the individual and team skills and abilities. Although sometimes *new* things are added to a team's or an individual's repertoire, this is not usually the case.

Rather, many coaches tend to stay with the style of play that proved to be successful in getting them this far. It is rare for a coach to throw out a style of play in favor of a completely different style just because they are involved in post season competition. It is rare for a coach to plan on teaching the athletes completely new ways to perform their sport skills. There is usually just insufficient time to have athletes learn a great deal of *new* information, *new* knowledge, *and new* skills. However, this does not mean that an innovative coach will not take advantage of the opportunity to institute different wrinkles in some aspects of their game. For example, a different twist in some tactic or strategy that the team (or individual) is already familiar with during the regular season is frequently instituted in post season to keep the squad from being too predictable and thus giving opponents an unnecessary advantage.

Thus, in post season competition, in planning and structuring the practices during this time period, emphasis should be placed on two major areas. First, to refine and to improve those areas that the individual athletes and the team have already mastered and in which they have demonstrated proficiency during the season. Second, to take into account the specific strengths and weaknesses of the next opponent(s) in the post season competition to exploit weaknesses and to attempt to lessen the impact of each opponent's strengths, ability, skill and competency.

COMPONENTS OF A PRACTICE SESSION

Every practice session usually has several common components regardless of the level of competition or the nature of the sport itself. These components or elements of a practice form the framework for the practice itself. Inside this framework, coaches design their own unique combination of activities which go to make up the total practice session.

The framework of a daily practice session generally consists of the following:

1. Warm-up activities.
2. Conditioning activities.
3. Introduction of new information, knowledge and skills to be learned.
4. Reinforcement of previously taught skills and knowledge.
5. Use of individual and group drills.
6. Use of scrimmages or game-like competition.
7. Cool-down or concluding activities.
8. Interpersonal-interaction visitation time between coaches and players.
9. Implementation of risk management tactics.

Some practice sessions might well include all nine areas listed above. Others might involve only 4 or 5 of these elements. It is up to the individual head coach in every sport, at every level of competition, to decide which of these elements will actually be used in any given day's practice plans as well as what exactly will take place within each of these broad categories.

WARM-UP ACTIVITIES

What type of warm-up activities are the athletes going to engage in prior to the start of the actual guts of the practice? Will the warm-up activities consist of mere stationery exercises or will jogging and running also be a part of the warm-up effort? What about flexibility exercises or stretching maneuvers? What type of flexibility or stretching exercises (specifically) will the athletes participate in prior to engaging in more strenuous physical efforts as well as at the conclusion of such activity?

Will all of the athletes do the exact same warm-up exercises, in cadence, at the direction of the coach(es)? Or, will the athletes be permitted to decide for themselves, individually, which warm-up exercises they will perform (following prior expert instruction concerning warm-ups from the coaches)? How long will the warm-up period last? Will sport skills be used as part of the warm-up process (shooting baskets in basketball; throwing the softball or baseball, kicking the soccer ball)? These are just some of the questions that each head coach must decide upon when planning and designing a practice session.

Of course, every coach and athlete understands the necessity of having adequate warm-up and stretching exercises at all practices and games. The challenge is in determining the type of specific activities, when they are to be used, for what duration and in what manner. Coaches should be aware of the three types of stretching that are used to increase the flexibility of athletes. The first is *static stretching*, the most common type of stretching, in which an individual holds a stretched position for between 15-30 seconds, all the while passively placing the muscles and connected tissues at their greatest length, all without pain. The second type of stretching is *ballistic stretching,* which involves repeating a bouncing movement for a short period if time. This action forces an increase in the range of motion. The third type is referred to as *proprioceptive neuromuscular facilitation (PNF) stretching.* This action sees alternating contracting and relaxation of alternating muscles in an effort to increase range of motion (Karp, 2000).

Taking Individual Differences into Account Doing Warm-up Exercises

Individual differences of athletes can be taken into account by allowing each athlete to utilize warm-up activities that suit that particular youngster. There is no overriding need to have all of the athletes warm-up using the identical exercises, all performed in cadence, just like army recruits during basic training. Once the athletes have been taught the fundamentals or basics of warming up for practice, there is no reason why each athlete cannot make the decision as to what specific warm-up activities will constitute that athlete's warm-up routine. In fact, such freedom given to the athlete might well help motivate the individual to accomplish more during this time period than if the coach was standing overhead barking out instructions as to what exercise is to be performed, when to do it and how many times it will be done, etc.

Allowing athletes to choose from a range of appropriate warm-up activities enables them to take into consideration their own preferences, their own experiences, attributes, skills, abilities, fitness levels, endurance and stamina, present mood, etc., in constructing their own warm-up routine. Besides, if three or five different warm-up drills or exercises will get the job done, what is lost if the coach gives the ability to choose one or more of these drills to individual athletes? Nothing is lost and there is potential for much to be gained since the youngsters made the choice and have confidence in what they are doing.

CONDITIONING ACTIVITIES

While a detailed examination of various conditioning programs is outside the purview of this book, it is nevertheless appropriate to provide a cursory glimpse into some of the various methods, tactics and techniques used by coaches to get their youngsters into acceptable levels of physical condition, depending upon the specific sport being played.

There are literally thousands of books and pamphlets and many more articles written about conditioning programs for athletics. Some of the publications are sport specific while others are more generic in nature. Some deal with only the physical exercises that make up a significant portion of any conditioning program for athletic teams. Others, however, concentrate on the nutritional aspects of conditioning. "If you look at helping an athlete to perform to the best of his or her ability, then the fuel is a really critical component of that equation. It's very difficult to do one without the other" (Berry, 2000, p. 35). Coaches need to be knowledgeable in the area of nutrition so that they can instruct and motivate their athletes in the proper way to eat and drink. They also need to be excellent role models in this area.

Nutritional knowledge (and nutritional decisions) by athletes is important not only in terms of pre-game meals but equally important on a daily basis throughout the entire season, as well as the entire calendar year. "What athletes eat in the hours and day leading up to a big game may determine whether they have the energy to win" (Bonci, 2000, p. 28). And, when one thinks of nutrition, one must also include adequate amounts of water in addition to the proper amount and types of foods.

Just as there are numerous publications dealing with ways to physically and psychologically condition one's team and athletes, there are many different methods and strategies that can be used to help athletes achieve optimum or near optimum conditioning levels, as well as performance levels. It is important for the coach to be aware of the potential for significant benefits emanating from both the proper use of various physical exercises and appropriate and sound nutritional choices by athletes. The challenge for coaches is to secure a basic understanding of sound nutritional practices and physical conditioning activities (not to mention the psychological training) that might be appropriate for their specific sport(s).

Generic and Sport Specific Conditioning Activities

Conditioning exercises can be thought of as being sport generic and/or sport specific. Sport generic means that a conditioning exercise or activity can be beneficial regardless of the type of sport in which one participates. Sport specific denotes activities or exercises that specifically aid in the mastery of a particular sport or sports (Wakeham, 2001). In recent years, there has been increased emphasis placed upon cross training for competitive athletes in order to help them keep motivated as they continue to refine their physical skills and increase their fitness levels (Dilts and Frankel, 1992).

Since there are numerous conditioning activities that might be utilized for a wide variety of sports and sporting activities, readers should utilize this chapter as a beginning, a starting point, and then continue to study and read about training and conditioning methods for the sport or sports they intend to coach. It is up to each coach to develop a sophisticated level of knowledge, understanding and appreciation of various training and conditioning techniques and strategies. For, without adequate conditioning, all the skill in the world will not produce success on the so-called playing field. Athletic performance is dependent upon the performer's level of agility, flexibility, strength, endurance, maneuverability, jumping ability, speed, etc.

Types of Conditioning Activities

Of all of the conditioning activities, perhaps the mere act of running itself is the most important and fundamental method of achieving overall conditioning for the athlete. Running has always been a reliable method of developing physical fitness among athletes. Long distance, middle distance and sprint training can be used by coaches as means to the end of getting their charges into a high level of physical condition. Speed-power training is now common place among athletic teams (Paul-etto, 1993) as are forms of circuit training.

Training Principles

Generally speaking, one can think of training in four distinct terms or principles. These fundamental principles can be considered as general guidelines that support the development of training programs. These principles are (1) overload, (2) specificity, (3) reversibility, and (4) individuality

The principal of overload indicates that the training regimen should include what is considered an increase or greater stress or load on the body than what would normally be experienced in order to produce improvement in performance/training. To gain in terms of endurance as well as in strength one needs to overload the muscular system. The result is the muscle group reacts by adapting and thus one must provide a progressive overload of resistance (training) for continued improvement. In terms of resistance training, Bryant, Franklin, & Peterson (2001) state that overload can be obtained through one or more of the following: (1) increasing resistance or weight, (2) increasing the repetitions, (3) increasing the sets, and/or (4) decreasing the rest period between sets or exercises.

> **COACHING CONCEPT #297:   Overloading a muscle group involves change,
> with an increase of resistance against the
> muscle(s).**

The principle of specificity deals with adapting training programs that are specific to the type of training as well as to the volume and intensity of the activity and exercise performed. The third principle, that of reversibility implies that the gains achieved through training will be reversed when and if training is stopped, interrupted for a length of time, or reduced too severely and quickly. Finally, the principle of individuality implies that each person is an individual and individual differences should be taken into consideration when creating and implementing specific training programs (Lim, 1999, p. 7).

Aerobic and Anaerobic Conditioning Activities

There are numerous types of training activities that comprise the physical conditioning programs for athletes in various sports. In general, conditioning can be classified as anaerobic and aerobic in nature. Aerobic exercises are those activities that involve continuous work for a prolonged period of time. Aerobic capacity has been thought of as the major index of general endurance or physical fitness. "Anaerobic power is the ability to work in excess of the body's capacity to take oxygen into the tissues, resulting in an oxygen debt" (Stone and Kroll, 1986, p. 6).

Aerobic exercises are typified by the continuous running over a long period of time. An anaerobic physical activity involves an athlete going all out for a brief period of time, such as when an offensive lineman in football attempts to move the defensive opponent off of the line of scrimmage in order to open a hole for the half-back to make a big gain.

Free Weights and the Use of Machines

The use of free weights in strength training or the use of various machines —those manufactured by Nautilus, StairMaster, Universal, NordicTrack, Cybex, and a whole host of others—have become a mainstay in most athletic teams' training repertoire. Similarly, the use of isometric, isotonic and isokinetic contractions and exercises can play a large role in facilitating the strength development of one's athletes. The use of free weights allows the individual athlete to focus on the athlete's sport specific objectives while, at the same time, providing for an increase in the person's kinesthetic awareness and overall stability. The use of machines allows the individual athlete to move a predetermined amount of resistance through a predetermined path (range) of motion all the while reducing the possibility of injury.

However, with both free weights and machines there is still the need to involve a system of stretching to maximize benefits of training (Westcott & Loud, 2000).

COACHING CONCEPT #298: **Coaches should not neglect the need for stretching regardless of the type of training they have their athletes perform—proper stretching is the key to adequate training and conditioning.**

Many colleges and universities now have hired strength and conditioning coaches to help their athletes develop their bodies to the fullest through a concentrated regimen involving specific exercises. In fact, every Division I institution has a full time strength and conditioning coach, according to Charles Stiggins, Executive Director of the Collegiate Strength and Conditioning Coaches Association (Funk, 2005).

Even high schools have gotten into the act of strength training for their athletes by becoming more skilled and competent themselves in the area of training their charges within the arena of strength and conditioning. In addition, some secondary coaches have sought the advice and counsel of experts who work at the college level in an effort to help their athletes. And, other secondary schools have seen their athletes themselves engage personal trainers to help them increase strength and improve the level of conditioning.

There are three specific resources that coaches can go to in an effort to learn more about strength and conditioning. The first of these is www.nsc-lift.org and is the site of the National Strength and Conditioning Association (NSCA) which certifies strength and conditioning specialists and provides research and resources. This organization also has high school and college special interest groups. The second resource is www.cscca. org which is the site for the Collegiate Strength and Conditioning

Athletes must work hard during and out of season to achieve excellence.

Coaches Association (CSCCa). This group got its start in 2000. The web site provides information on how to maximize athletic performance as well as the latest news on collegiate strength training. The third site is www.AthleticSearch.com/about.htlm which belongs to the journal *Training & Conditioning* and offers many helpful articles in each issue on strength and conditioning and it also contains an archive of its articles for the reader (Fund, 2005).

Questions Coaches Must Answer
Regarding Conditioning for Their Teams

Questions which each coach must be prepared to ask and answer in light of one's own team include: What is the purpose of the conditioning activities? Are such activities to be used to get the athletes into competitive shape? Are they being implemented to retain the current level of fitness and conditioning? Will conditioning activities remain the same throughout the entire season? Will conditioning significantly change once the team or individuals begin actual competition within the in-season phase of the sport? What type of conditioning activities would be suitable for a given athletic team, at a specific age level, at a particular point during the entire season? When during a typical daily practice session should conditioning activities be implemented? Should they be used in the beginning, in the middle, or at the end of the practice period? Will weight training be involved, and if so, to what extent and when during the season? How much emphasis will be placed upon aerobic and anaerobic exercises? Exactly what conditioning activities will be used for your specific sport?

The answer to these and other questions regarding the type of physical conditioning exercises and activities will differ in light of the objectives being sought. And, of course, the objective(s) themselves might well differ at different times during the multi-month season.

INTRODUCTION OF NEW INFORMATION, KNOWLEDGE AND SKILLS TO BE LEARNED

> **COACHING CONCEPT #299:** Coaching is teaching—to be a successful coach, one must be a successful teacher of skills, knowledge and concepts.

An athletic practice session is similar to any regular classroom or science lab. One of the few differences is that the athlete is a member of a team by choice, most of the time. However, the learning principles remain the same as for the classroom. Coaches need to truly teach their athletes the knowledge, the strategies and tactics, and the physical skills required for success in their competitive sport. Competent coaches need to follow the same principles of good teaching that competent instructors use in the regular classroom.

COACHING CONCEPT #300:   Fundamentals are the key to athletic success—fundamentals should be emphasized until they become a habit.

Coaches need to be able to reinforce learning on behalf of the athlete. They need to be competent in discerning errors in performances. They need to be capable of giving constructive feedback to the athlete. They need to be able to adequately motivate individual learners. And, they need to be able to build on the previous knowledge and skill of their athletes. They need to train their athletes in the fundamentals of the sport so that these fundamentals become second nature, until these fundamentals become a habit.

Coaches need to decide when their athletes are ready to be introduced to new information, new knowledge and new skills. When during the season will it be appropriate to introduce something new? When during a daily practice session should new concepts or knowledge be introduced? Is it wise to have a vigorous, physically demanding practice for 90 minutes and then attempt to teach one's charges something new—when they are mentally, physically and psychologically exhausted? Of course not. Yet, coaches commit almost as great an error when they fail to take into consideration the mental and physical state of their athletes before introducing new material, new skills to them.

Today, athletes are expected to perform community service.

COACHING CONCEPT #301:   Since God created coaches with two ears, two eyes, and one mouth—they should do more watching, more listening and much less talking when coaching (teaching).

Typically, inexperienced, and sometimes experienced, coaches talk too much during practice. Of course coaches need to speak. However, they also need to shut up and observe their athletes practice skills. They need to ask questions and then listen. They need to insure that the youngsters spend adequate time actually practicing those skills and maneuvers that have been presented to them.

An example of a poor coaching (teaching) technique is the coach who has the athletes warm-up for some 20 minutes. At that point in time, the coach calls over all the athletes and has them sit for almost 15-20 minutes. During this time period, the coach proceeds to go into great detail describing a new offense to be learned during that same practice. Whereupon the ill-prepared coach has the athletes get up (they naturally are no longer warmed-up but are stiff and cold) and has them run through a competitive drill activity involving part of the new offense. It would have been better had the coach not taken up so much time talking about the new offense. It would have been better if the coach had allowed the athletes to warm-up properly following a much briefer explanation of part of the new offense. The point is simple: too much time is spent listening to the coach and not enough time is spent by the athletes actually learning and performing essential skills.

Athletes learn their skills and strategic maneuvers by doing them, by physically performing as well as by thinking about and making judgments concerning what must be accomplished. Thus, coaches need to limit their own verbiage in practice thereby allowing the athletes to perform, to physically work on their skills.

COACHING CONCEPT #302: **It is not how much information the coach gives to an athlete—but rather the quality of that information and the manner in which it is disseminated.**

Too much talk by the coach and the athletes waste valuable time. Too much talk and the athletes are unable to perform their skills. Coaches need to walk silently and carry a big stick when it comes time to speak in a practice session. Coaches need to save their comments in order to provide corrective feedback to the athletes, in as few words as possible. Time in any practice is valuable and should not be wasted. Also, athletes should not be confused with long, drawn out explanations that are difficult to follow, comprehend and implement. Coaches need to be able to cut to the chase, to the point, so that the youngsters will immediately know whether or not they are performing a particular skill correctly and, more importantly, will know how to make appropriate corrections.

COACHING CONCEPT #303: **Have young athletes generalize rather than specialize in a sport—too early specialization may hinder their progress in the future.**

"Specialization and year-round play are putting active kids at increased risk of crippling injury" (Gorman, 2006, p. 61). Too early specialization in one sport to the exclusion of others can often lead to burnout for the youngster. Junior high and youth sports coaches should be involved in teaching fundamentals and should not be concerned with *winning*. Athletes at this level should be exposed to a broad array of athletic opportunities both in terms of the number of sports and the actual positions played in each. To have a youngster specialize in one sport or in one specific position at too early an age does not take into account the fact that this same individual might have excelled in other sports or in other positions if given the opportunity.

Using Metaphors, Similes and Analogies for Coaching Instruction

Metaphors have been successfully utilized in a variety of instructional settings throughout history. The metaphor, as a teaching tool, can be very effective in coaching sports for all ages. A metaphor is "A way of speaking in which one thing is expressed in terms of another, whereby this bringing together throws new light on the character of what is being described" (Gordon, 1978, p. 28). "Metaphors have performance-enhancing properties" (Gassner, 1999, p. 33). In simple terms, the coach can verbally present stories, statements or examples in an effort to paint a picture or image or illustration in the mind of the athlete, a picture that will create a fuller understanding of that act or performance to be learned. Metaphors, similes and analogies can involve examples or stories that help bring a learner from a present level of understanding and performance to a new (higher) level of comprehension and skill level.

REINFORCEMENT OF PREVIOUSLY TAUGHT SKILLS AND KNOWLEDGE

> **COACHING CONCEPT #304:** Athletes master physical skills through repetitive practice—practice, practice and more practice is the essence of reinforcing previously taught skills and knowledge.

Coaches need to be sure that athletes have sufficient time to practice that which they are attempting to learn, to master—both mentally and physically. Athletes need to have opportunities to reinforce what they have been taught. Athletes need to overlearn certain skills so that these skills become habits, many of which will be automatic. To facilitate this overlearning, coaches need to provide sufficient opportunities for the athletes to actually practice the skills correctly. Repetition in the learning of physical skills is a must.

Does the high school quarterback think about his footwork when dropping back into the pocket before releasing the ball to the intended receiver? Does the volleyball setter think about foot placement and hand placement before setting the ball to a teammate? Does the baseball player consciously think about all of the technical components of sliding into second base before doing so in the heat of a contest? The answers to all of these questions is no, not really.

These and many other movements are automatic on behalf of the athlete once these skills have been mastered. But, to become automatic responses, the athlete must have opportunities to repeatedly perform these skills in a variety of situations. The athletes need to reinforce their learning of these skills through actual performance of the skills and maneuvers. Thus, athletes must overlearn specific skills and knowledge until they become automatic, without conscious thought.

> **COACHING CONCEPT #305:** **Athletes usually improve on that which they practice—it is hard to improve upon a physical skill unless one works at it.**

Coaches need to recognize that athletes can improve only when they actually work on improving themselves in specific ways. Practice can involve both physical practice as well as mental practice. Athletes need to think about that which they must learn and perfect. They need to physically work in order to develop and refine skills needed in their sport. Coaches should not expect that athletes can significantly enhance their level of skill by doing nothing. This doesn't mean that skill improvement is automatic just because an individual practices the skill. The practice(s) must be suitable, timely, appropriate and, frequently, specific.

> **COACHING CONCEPT #306:** **Be aware of the so-called Hawthorne Effect—athletes frequently improve when they are aware that they are being required to practice specific skills and techniques.**

It sometimes doesn't matter exactly how one works on a specific skill or competency—only that one actually does work at it. Take free throws in basketball, for example. There must be scores of different ways to practice and teach free throws to athletes. It is difficult to single out one *best* method of learning and/or practicing the skills comprising the free throw shot. However, the mere fact that coaches have their athletes practice shooting free throws (in any number of different ways) will often be sufficient to have the athletes improve in this all important skill. In this example, the mere fact that emphasis (and time, effort, etc.) is being placed on a particular skill is sufficient to result in significant improvement in that skill.

USE OF INDIVIDUAL AND GROUP DRILLS

All coaches use drills of some sort or another. The use of drills in the learning process is a technique whereby athletes practice part of the total skill needed in actual competition. The use of drills reinforce learning. The use of drills, involving repetitive acts, enables the athlete to overlearn the physical skill. When a skill becomes almost second nature, it is said to be overlearned. As a result, the individual can perform the skill at an acceptable level at other times, in practices and game situations. This is because the skill becomes a habit or a reaction and can be performed almost without thinking. The athlete has internalized the act within; it has become a part of the individual. The skill can hence be performed consistently at a considerably high level.

In teaching repetitive skills, it is wise to have the athletes develop a specific pre-performance routine that they feel comfortable with and that they go through each time they attempt a repetitive skill. For example, the shooting of free throws in the sport of basketball. Or, the softball player getting ready in the batter's box for the anticipated pitch. The routine itself—whatever it happens to be—helps make the athlete feel comfortable and at ease. As a result, the individual becomes more competent in performing this familiar routine and the repetitive skill.

Breaking Down a Skill into its Component Parts

Breaking down the total skill, an offensive series for example, into its component parts and then having athletes practice these parts is what is referred to as breakdown drills. Today, coaches need to be able to break down the large aspects of a sport into smaller, more manageable pieces. Then these smaller pieces need to be mastered by the athletes in practices in such a manner that these components are overlearned so that they become habits.

Since shooting field goals is a highly desirable skill in the sport of basketball, it is common to see athletes practicing the skill of field goal shooting both in individual type drills and in team drills. An example of an individual field goal drill is to have an athlete shoot a specific number of field goals at designated spots on the court within a specific time limit while keeping track of made baskets. A team drill involving field goals might be one in which two groups of athletes, divided into two competing team, would spot shoot (without defense) at specific spots on the floor (at the same spots where the players would be freed up for a shot when the regular offense is executed). The team with the best percentage of field goals and/or the greatest number of made baskets would be declared the winner.

Most drills are characterized as breakdown type drills. That is, the drills call for the athlete to perform a part of the skills, maneuvers and tactics in practice. In baseball, for example, the pick-off play between the pitcher and first-base player can be made into a drill. Hitting drills with a mechanical pitcher involves only the skill of hitting by the players. Some drills can be implemented because of their value in improving or enhancing the athletes' physical conditioning. Other drills are used because they help in the actual learning of the total skill. Other drills are beneficial because they help the athlete improve upon previously taught skills and knowledge. Some drills are used because the players enjoy them and they help motivate the athletes.

COACHING CONCEPT #307: Make practices as close to reality as possible (transfer of learning).

The objective when using any drill in practice is to make the learning or practice situation as close to the real thing (game situation) as possible. Doing so enables the individual athlete to perform better when actually placed in the real life game situation or environment. The more familiar and experienced the athlete is in performing the skills required in the game during the practice sessions, the greater the likelihood of a positive transfer of learning from the practice session to the game itself.

In some situations, this means creating the same atmosphere. For example, practicing in the actual game facility, wearing game uniforms, with a crowd yelling from the stands and/or music being played in the background. In another situation, it might mean creating a pressure-packed situation in which the individual athlete must actually perform at a specified skill level while under some strain or tension or experiencing some urgency to execute the physical skill(s) successfully. For example, having the athletes divide into two groups and compete with each other in performing a specific skill.

Thus, providing for game-like practice opportunities in practices is always highly recommended. This can be done for individual athletes on an individual basis. It can also be done for the team as a whole or for groups of athletes as they perform any number of individual or group skills or tactics.

An Example of an Individual Game-Like Drill in Practice

In the sport of basketball, one would not usually have youngsters shoot 100 free throws during practice and consider the tactic similar to a game situation. This is because no athlete would ever shoot 100 free throws at a single time in any game. However, if an athlete shot 1, 2 or 3 free throws at a time and then had to move off the line and then return later to shoot an additional 1, 2 or 3 free throws, this would more closely approximate the situation found in a game.

However, adding some competitive factor into this free throw shooting would make it even closer to the game situation by creating some pressure or competition for the athletes to experience. To create an even closer approximation between practice and game situations, the coach might have the athletes run a specific distance after shooting no more than three free throws and then having the individuals return to the free throw line where they would have to attempt one, two or three throws while they are recovering from the physical exertion of just having completed a strenuous run.

This more closely approximates the actual game situation in which a basketball player goes to the free throw line after having run up and down the court playing offense and defense. Usually a basketball player, in an actual game, attempts free throws following some strenuous physical activity, usually involving running, jumping, etc. This is why many coaches, during practice, will have athletes refine and improve their free throw shooting by having them shoot free throws only after they have exerted or extended themselves physically. That is the condition they will find themselves shooting free throws during a game.

COACHING CONCEPT #308: Do not combine conditioning drills with skill acquisition drills—to do so, hinders mastery of skills.

Drills can be categorized as conditioning drills as well as skill acquisition drills or as skill refinement drills. In conditioning drills, the goal is to have the athletes enhance their physical conditioning, their stamina, their endurance, speed, etc. Skill acquisition drills are utilized to help the individual learn a new skill or an advanced skill. And, skill refinement drills, as the name suggests, are used to help the athletes refine an already learned skill, maneuver, tactic or strategy.

However, to mix conditioning drills with skill acquisition drills is incongruent with the purpose of each. Conditioning exercises should *not* be coupled with a physical skill that is new to the athletes and remains yet unlearned or unmastered. When an athlete begins to learn a skill, the individual should not be tired, physically, mentally or psychologically. When learning a new skill or attempting to master the skill, one should be concentrating on the skill itself rather than attempting to simultaneously enhance one's physical conditioning. To do otherwise is to be counterproductive.

> **COACHING CONCEPT #309:**   When conducting practices — attempt to kill two or three —birds with one stone in terms of time management.

However, in other aspects of the practice scene it is often wise to attempt to kill two or more birds with one stone. When planning some drills, coaches would do well to attempt to accomplish two or more things simultaneously. This effort can be beneficial as the practice time becomes more productive; therefore more can be accomplished in less time. For example, the use of suicide drills as part of a conditioning effort can be combined with athletes practicing *skills already mastered,* such as dribbling and passing (basketball) or kicking and passing (soccer) the ball while running through the up and down patterns of the traditional suicide drill. The ultimate objective is for the athletes to view the combination of suicide drills and dribbling drills, not as punishment but as a means to increase conditioning and simultaneously practice and even enhance skills already learned. This strategy can be highly motivating for the athletes.

USE OF SCRIMMAGES OR GAME-LIKE COMPETITION

> **COACHING CONCEPT #310:**   Utilize game-like scrimmages, especially with older athletes—younger athletes should use drills more than scrimmages.

The use of *practice scrimmages* is an ideal way to create a situation similar to that found in actual game situations. Scrimmages can be held by having athletes from the same team divide into opposing squads and compete against each other during practice. Or, an outside team might be secured to attend a practice where they scrimmage against the host squad, or a J.V. team might scrimmage the varsity players.

When team scores and individual statistics, as well as time on the clock, are kept by the coaching staff, the practice situation moves closer to the real thing. When the team's players have an opportunity to compete against other athletes, even in a practice scrimmage or contest, they gain valuable experience due to the game-like conditions.

The older the athlete, the more beneficial scrimmages can be due to the nature and characteristics of the athlete in question. With young athletes, coaches would do well to sparingly utilize scrimmages and concentrate on basic drills in the teaching of fundamental skills and maneuvers. Young athletes have not yet developed the level of skill performance which would enable them to benefit from extended use of scrimmage situations. Of course, some exposure to scrimmage experiences is needed for all athletes and teams lest they be completely unfamiliar with the game situation when faced with it for the first time in actual competition. Game-like scrimmages, with officials, help familiarize athletes with the atmosphere and conditions they will face in actual competition.

Of course, the actual conduct of and make-up of any practice session is a highly personalized matter with each head coach. For some, practice would not be a practice without a predominance of various kinds of drills with very little, if any, involvement of scrimmages. For other coaches, game like situations, scrimmages, are the only way to go and much of their typical practice session is devoted to this type of activity.

COACHING CONCEPT #311: **The use of scrimmages in practice facilitates motivation on behalf of the athletes—it is fun and enables them to demonstrate what they have learned.**

Athletes always need to be motivated. Some are more easily motivated than others. Thus, coaches are always looking for ways to keep the attention level and motivation level high for their charges. While the use of drills can sometimes be viewed by athletes as boring, dull and plain hard work, they frequently have an entirely different perspective when it comes to scrimmaging in practice.

In fact, scrimmages are fun. Scrimmages are so like actual game situations that scrimmages are frequently not looked upon as work at all. Rather, they become the fun part of the practices when the athletes get to do what they joined the team to do in the first place, that is, to actually compete against others and to demonstrate their level of achievement, accomplishment and performance. As a result, many coaches use scrimmages as a reward mechanism as well as a teaching tool. This is yet another example of killing two birds with one stone, providing a motivating experience as well as a learning experience for the athletes.

COACHING CONCEPT #312: **Provide opportunities for athletes to experience success in practices, especially game-like scrimmages.**

Athletes, at all ages, should experience success in practices. The self-concept of each athlete should be a very real concern of the coach. As a result, youngsters should be provided with opportunities to experience success during practices. No, this does not mean that every athlete has total success during every practice. Nor does it imply that athletes should not experience challenges as well as defeats or failures. On the contrary, athletes need to be challenged. They need to experience failure. However, they also need to experience success. They need to know that they are making some type of progress. They need to understand that there was *something* that they did during the practice that was of value, that was of worth. Perhaps they demonstrated above average effort and determination. Perhaps they performed one specific skill or tactic or maneuver correctly. Perhaps they had made some improvement in a particular skill. The point is that athletes need to experience success during their practices. They sure don't need to feel a hopelessness or think of themselves as failures in terms of their effort, their performance or their future.

COACHING CONCEPT #313:   Use analogies or examples when explaining difficult concepts or skills—examples help crystallize the picture in the athlete's mind.

Sometimes it is difficult for athletes to understand what it is the coach is trying to teach. Sometimes it is hard to conceptualize the parts and the whole of the skill to be learned and mastered. Sometimes it seems like the athlete has a mental block in terms of comprehending what it is that must be learned or how to actually perform a specific skill.

In this situation, coaches should attempt to provide examples or analogies for the youngsters. Merely using bland instructions, however straight forward they might be, may not be sufficient for some athletes. Provide verbal examples. Provide verbal pictures. Provide verbal illustrations. Provide comparisons. Enable the athlete to begin to learn something new by providing a verbal reference point from which the athlete can build upon.

COACHING CONCEPT #314:   Use audio-visual aids in teaching and coaching athletes.

Another important practice when it comes to facilitating the athlete's learning is for the coaching staff to take advantage of all of the modern day audio-visual aids that are now available. Films, video-tapes, film-strips, photographs, slides, records, audio-tapes, etc., are available and should be taken advantage of by coaches. Coaches should be willing to use any audio-visual tool in the teaching (coaching) process that will enhance or facilitate the mastery of the knowledge and physical skill involved in the sport in question.

COOL-DOWN OR CONCLUDING ACTIVITIES

Just as warm-up activities are essential for any successful practice session, so too are adequate cool-down maneuvers (Fact Sheet, 1991). The body, after it has been strenuously exercised, should not just be immediately shut down. Like a thorough-bred horse after a race, the athlete, regardless of age, needs time to gradually cool-down physically. This can be accomplished by simply gradually reducing the level of physical activity in which the athlete is involved. Or, cool-down efforts can consist of deliberate activities (exercises) designed to allow the body to gradually adjust to less intense physical exertion.

Examples of cool-down activities might include athletes engaging in light running or jogging, which in turn can lead to brisk walking. Performing drills or other physical activities at three-fourths or half speed can be effective in cooling down. Also, performing light stretching or flexibility exercises can be an excellent concluding activity for the cool down efforts of athletes.

INTERPERSONAL-INTERACTION VISITATION TIME BETWEEN COACHES AND PLAYERS

Almost every practice session should provide opportunities where athletes and their coaches can interact on a personal as well as a professional basis. This means that after the hard work which is involved in most practice sessions, there should be adequate time and opportunity for athletes and coaches to have a dialogue, to communicate with each other on a less intense, less formal, basis. It is also an excellent time for reflection and evaluation of that day's practice session by both athletes and coaches. During the formal time for practices, time is of the essence and usually there is not time for small talk or chic-chat. However, following the conclusion of the regular practice there should be a less formal opportunity for athletes and coaches to communicate with each other without the undue strain or pressure frequently created in a formal practice session.

Maybe this interaction could take place near the end of the practice session, perhaps during the cool-down portion of the practice. Or, perhaps the opportunity for such dialogue could take place after the official end of practice and before the time when the youngsters head for the showers. Or, after the athletes are through showering and dressing and before they head home. The point is that there is a need for a dialogue opportunity to exist between coaches and their charges near the end or immediately after the conclusion of the formal practice session. There can be great give-and-take and much can be shared, between the athletes and the coaches, in these informal get-togethers. It is during these informal conversations, lasting from a mere few seconds to many minutes, that coaches are frequently able to learn more about their athletes than they would ever have had the opportunity to learn in a hundred official practices.

COACHING CONCEPT #315:   Coaches should not be afraid to be themselves—to let their hair down in informal settings with athletes.

These end-of-practice conversations can also serve yet another purpose. That is, they can provide an opportunity for athletes to see coaches in a more human perspective, in a less threatening posture. During practices, it is often all business and nothing but business for coaches. However, following practices, when things and individuals are calmer, cool and collected, people tend to be more themselves and more relaxed. They let their hair down and are more themselves. Both youngsters and coaches tend to open up and reveal more of themselves which can be a positive consequence for both the individuals and for the team itself.

IMPLEMENTATION OF RISK MANAGEMENT TACTICS

COACHING CONCEPT #316:   An ounce of prevention is worth a pound of cure.

Expert medical care is a "must" to protect the athlete and the school.

Coaches should be concerned with risk management when they plan and implement their practice sessions. No coach wants to be sued for negligence. No coach wants to be responsible for an injury to a student. The concept of risk management revolves around the concept of *preventing the likelihood of injuries* to athletes. It is always easier to prevent than to react to such a terrible catastrophe. That is why coaches and athletic directors use variations of *informed consent forms* and *waiver forms*. The informed consent form ". . . is a major tool in meeting your duty to warn participants and it may be your best protection against a lawsuit" (Borkowski, 2000). And, today, "Courts in an increasing number of States are enforcing liability waivers signed by parents on behalf of minors" (Cotton, 2005, p. 71).

Coaches should be constantly on the alert that they perform their duties and fulfill their responsibilities in a proper manner. Coaches must not be negligent in their duties. Coaches serve as a substitute for the parents of their athletes and as such have certain responsibilities and obligations towards their charges. To be deemed negligent, in the legal sense, there must be the failure to perform one's duties up to the standard expected of a prudent individual under similar circumstances.

COACHING CONCEPT #317:   Coaches are judged in light of their competent peers in the determination of negligence.

The standard of care required of coaches in their role as mentors of athletes is that standard which would be expected of similarly trained, educated, experienced, professionals in similar circumstances and settings. This judgment in light of one's peers is an important concept. Ignorance is frequently not an acceptable excuse because the coach, by the very nature of having accepted the coaching position, should have known what to do and what not to do.

How does one become legally liable for being negligent? What does one have *to do* or *not do* in order to be deemed negligent in the eyes of the law? In essence, there are four criteria that determines liability. First, the coach must owe a *duty* to the person who is injured to provide a safe environment. Second, the coach must have done something (commission) or must not have done something (omission) that breached that duty to the athlete. Third, what the coach did or failed to do must have been the proximate cause of the injury to the athlete. And, fourth, there must have actually been injury or damage to someone.

COACHING CONCEPT #318:   Athletes and their parents must be warned, in writing, as to the potential (real) dangers/consequences of sport participation even if the individual performs as instructed (informed consent).

Common Reasons for Negligence in Athletics

There are seven major areas of concern that coaches should constantly be on the alert for in terms of preventing injuries to their athletes. The following areas have been the most common sources of negligence being lodged against coaches.

1.   Lack of proper supervision for athletes.
2.   Use of defective equipment and supplies.

3. Improper instruction and/or directions.

4. The existence of hazardous conditions of buildings, facilities and/or grounds.

5. Poor or improper selection of activities that athletes are required to perform or engage in.

6. Teaching or coaching an unapproved activity or technique.

7. Inappropriate coaching decisions (e.g., improper treatment of an injured athlete; playing athletes who should not play).

COACHING CONCEPT #319:   Athletes who are injured must be evaluated to determine whether they are capable of returning to practice or competition.

Principles of Supervision (Coalition of Americans to Protect Sports)

There are eleven general principles of supervision presented by the *Coalition of Americans to Protect Sports*. These include:

1. BE THERE—Don't let your athletes warm-up unsupervised! Accidents can and do happen in practices as well as games.

2. KNOW THE ACTIVITY YOU ARE SUPERVISING—A skilled swimming coach should not supervise field hockey practice if he/she is not familiar with that sport.

3. FORESEE POTENTIAL PROBLEMS—Understand the potential risks of the activity and meet your obligations to them. A boys' lacrosse coach, for example, should make sure the helmets are certified.

4. UNDERSTAND THE NUMBERS—Coach-to-player ratios are variable depending upon age, activity, experience and level of risk. Foresight, training and common sense determine the appropriate level of supervision. The higher the risk of an activity, the higher the required level of supervision. If you have any doubts, increase the supervision.

5. CHECK THE ACTIVITY—Is it an appropriate activity that can be supervised?

6. INSPECT THE EQUIPMENT BEFORE USING IT—Do you have enough? Is it appropriate for your athletes?

7. REVIEW SAFETY RULES WITH YOUR ATHLETES BEFORE THE PRACTICE OR GAME BEGINS—Warn the players about what can happen if they do not follow these rules.

8. KNOW YOUR PLAYERS—Know their strengths and weakness. Don't place a player in a position that increases his or her potential for injury.

9. BE A STRONG SUPERVISOR—Make sure everyone knows you are present in control, and available, and that you care about them. If your athletes know you care about them, they will be less apt to question your supervision—and that increases safety.

10. QUESTION THE SITE OF THE ACTIVITY—Is it appropriate and free of potential hazards?

11. USE SIGNS—Warning and information signs can hammer home your safety messages. But please do not rely on signs alone to prevent accidents.

Athletes will be injured. Some will be injured more seriously than others. Whenever an athlete has received an injury, it is always wise to consider four basic factors before deciding whether or not to reinstate the athlete into a practice or a game situation. First, is there still severe pain? Pain is a warning sign and athletes with significant pain should not be involved in practices or competition. Second, is the youngster's range of motion affected? Limited range of motion is a warning sign that should cause the coach to hesitate before putting the athlete in a practice or game situation. Third, to what degree is the individual's strength affected? Loss of significant strength should deter the athlete from returning to practice. And, fourth, to what extent has the level of performance of the athlete been affected? If the performance is limited, then the youngster should remain away from practice or competition unless cleared by appropriate medical personnel.

COACHING CONCEPT #320:   Don't place the importance of a contest over the welfare of an athlete.

Whenever an athlete is injured, coaches are faced with a challenge, especially when the individual in question is a superior performer. While the coach is anxious to have the youngster return to the starting lineup, the decision to do so must be balanced with the potential for further injury to the individual if prematurely returned to practice or competition. With the ever present pressure being placed on coaches and teams to excel in the win column, it is not unusual to find coaches being torn in this area of their decision making responsibilities. In short, coaches want their star athletes back in service as soon as possible, if not sooner.

This is where controversy can arise. Coaches who push athletes, consciously or unconsciously, to return to action prior to when they should return, face dire consequences should the individual sustain further damage as a consequence. This is why it is an absolute must for coaches to relinquish to the physician, the physician assistant or the NATA trainer, the decision as to whether or not the athlete is able to return for competition or practice following injury or illness. In no case should the coach have the responsibility for this ultimate decision, regardless of how important the athlete is to the team or the significance of the upcoming athletic contest. It is the responsibility of the appropriate medical personnel to make that decision, not the coach.

Eating Disorders

Today, coaches need to be aware of eating disorders that affect many athletes. It is estimated that in the United States there are 10 millions females and a million males with some form of an eating disorder. Coaches need to take note that more than 90 percent of these individuals are females between the ages of 12 and 25 (Popke, 2006). It is important that coaches take a proactive posture when dealing with eating disorders, in terms of (1) the education of one's athletes as to the dangers of eating disorders, (2) the recognition of the problem, and (3) seeing that affected athletes receive necessary, appropriate and timely support and assistance (especially from the youngster's family).

REFERENCES

Berry, L. (2000, April/May). Today's special: Nutrition. *Athletic Management, XII*(3), 35-38, 40-41.

Bonci, L. (2000, May/June). Event eating. *Training & Conditioning, X*(4), 27—28, 30.

Borkowski, R. (2000, June/July). Fair warning. *Athletic Management, 12*(4). 20.

Bryant, C., Franklin, B., & Peterson, J. (2001). Resistance training 101. *Fitness Management, 17*(7), 34, 35, 38, 40

Cotton, D. (2005, March). Are you safe? *Athletic Business, 29*(3), 66-69, 71-72.,

Dilts, J. and Frankel, E. (1992, Spring). Cross training. *Training & Conditioning, 22*(2), 4-8.

Fact sheet—Guidelines. (1991). National Youth Sports Foundation for the Prevention of Athletic Injuries, Inc. Needham: Massachusetts, p, 1.

Funk, A. (2005, June/July). Strengthening your staff. *Athletic Management, XVII*(4), 61-65.

Gassner, G. (1999). Using Metaphors for High-Performance Teaching and Coaching. *Journal of Physical Education, Recreation, and Dance, 70*(7), 33-335.

Gorden, D. (1978). *Therapeutic Metaphors.* Cupertino, CA: Meta.

Gorman, C. (2006, September 18). To an athlete, aching young. *Time,* pp. 60-62.

Karp, J. (2000, April), Flexibility for fitness. *Fitness Management, 16*(5), 52-54.

Lim, J. (1999, Summer). Training principles. *Sport Supplement, 7*(3), 7.

Manos, K. (2005, February). The five W's of successful practices. *Coach and Athletic Director,* pp. 36-38.

Pauletto, B. (1993). Speed-Power training—Part 1: The forgotten edge. *Scholastic Coach. 63*(1), 30, 31.

Popke, M. (2006). Diminishing returns. *Athletic business, 30*(12), 34-40.

Stone, W. J. & Kroll, W. A. (1986). *Sports conditioning and weight training—Programs for athletic competition.* Boston: Allyn and Bacon, Inc.

Wakeham, T. (2001, April). Training for the game. *Training & Conditioning,* XI(3), 41-47.

Westcott, W., & Loud, R. (2000, June). Stretching for strength. *Athletic Management, 16*(7), 44-46.

Name: _____

Student ID #:_____

EXERCISES FOR CHAPTER 10

A. Describe some circumstances that might force a coach to made significant adjustments in one's practice schedule, provide specific examples.

B. Work out (on a separate sheet of paper) a complete daily (and detailed practice schedule for a week in a sport in which you intend to coach. Include all activities for each day, including times. Also identify the time during the season which the practice schedule is to take place.

C. As a coach of an individual or team sport, make out a list (on a separate sheet of paper) of *all* activities that you would have a team (as well as other individuals) go through during the pre-season practice span of time, on and off the proverbial playing field/court.

D. Comprise a list of so-called *Ten Commandments* outlining the ten most important (in your opinion) things that need to be done by a good practice coach.

1. _____

2. _____

3. _____

4. _____

5. _____

6. _____

7. _____

8. _____

9. _____

10. _____

√ E.   Describe at least five things that good practice coaches should not do in their practices.

1. _____

2. _____

3. _____

4. _____

5. _____

√ F.   Describe the steps you would take as a head coach to insure that your players would not suffer accidental injuries during practices and/or games.

_____

_____

_____

_____

_____

_____

RESEARCH QUESTONS FOR CHAPTER 10

1. Survey a team sport coach and an individual sport coach. Ask them what their philosophies are regarding conducting both pre-season and in-season practices.

   ----

2. Ask a coach of a team or individual sport what steps that coach has taken or is taking to address the problem/challenge of eating disorders.

   ----

3. Ask a varsity coach how practices are organized during pre-season, in-season and post season relative to conditioning activities for the athletes. That is, what does the coach do differently (or similarly) during these time periods to help insure that athletes get/keep in condition? Provide evidence of what the coach does (condition wise) during these time periods.

   ----

4. Find out from a coach of a team sport (flagship sport) how that coach goes about insuring that youngsters trying out for the team are in reasonably good physical shape (physical conditioning) when the potential athletes come to the first day of tryouts.

    _____

    _____

    _____

    _____

    _____

    _____

    _____

5. Interview an athletic director of a high school and find out the procedures that the athletic department follows in terms of coaches keeping records and coaches reacting to accidents and/or injuries to athletes during practices and games. Be specific and provide copies of forms that are used and any policy statements used by the school/athletic department.

    _____

    _____

    _____

    _____

    _____

    _____

    _____

Chapter 11

Effective Coaching Decisions

Everyone loves an afternoon at the ball park.

COACHING CONCEPT #321: One cannot do the same thing over and over again and yet expect different results.

STRATEGIC DECISIONS FOR PRACTICE SESSIONS

When thinking about what should take place within any future practice session, coaches are faced with making some very important decisions, decisions that might be different under varying circumstances and different situations. These decisions, based on careful and thoughtful strategic planning, fall within several important areas or categories and are made in light of the:

1. People involved
2. Time available

3. Established policies, procedures, practices and priorities
4. Needs as well as the abilities and potential of the athletes
5. Capabilities and preferences of the coaching staff
6. Availability of facilities, equipment and supplies
7. Caliber of future opponents
8. Selection of prior practice activities

These decisions that coaches must make involve the determination of *what* activities will comprise each practice. A decision must be made in terms of *when* different activities will take place, that is, what activities will take place first, second, third, and so on. A decision must be made in terms of *how much* time will be spent on each particular activity. A decision must be made as to *which athletes will be involved*. And, decisions must be made as to *which coaches,* if there is more than one, will be involved in which activities.

There are as many ways to conduct a practice as there are coaches. No two practices are alike. Individual athletes are different. Teams as a whole are different. Coaches are different. Circumstances in which the team, the athletes and the coaches operate are different. The time of the season may be different. The upcoming opponent will be different. However, there are some general guidelines and suggestions which govern the decision making process of all coaches, regardless of the sport they coach. These suggestions or guidelines, if followed, can be of significant assistance to the coach in structuring practices throughout the pre-season, in-season and the post season.

**COACHING CONCEPT #322: Proper planning prevents the proverbial poor
performance—both in terms of coaching and in
terms of athletic performance.**

CONDUCTING MEANINGFUL PRACTICE SESSIONS

Practice time is determined and regulated by determining what types of activities the athletes will be performing, the amount of time each of these activities will take and the spacing or priority of these learning activities within the defined practice session.

Distributed and Massed Practice Sessions

When the work or learning activities assigned to the athletes are separated or interrupted by a rest period or some other type of alternative activity (comments from the coaching staff, for example), it is said to be a distributed practice session. In this type of situation, the coach will provide opportunities for down time in terms of strenuous physical activity so that there is a break or division from one work period to another work period within the same practice session. This provision is especially beneficial to the athletes when they are involved in the beginning or early learning stages of skills or tactics when the emphasis is being placed upon the correct technique, style or form.

Massed practice sessions, on the other hand, involve little time for rest periods or down time during the individual practice sessions. Massed practices are advisable when the coach desires to provide opportunities for the athletes to refine skills already introduced. Massed practices involve less frequent interruptions and only occasional comments from the coach, while providing ample opportunities for practice and repetition of previously learned skills. Thus, conditioning and the use of scrimmages can be significant components or outcomes of massed practice sessions.

COACHING CONCEPT #323: Organize practices so that they are productive and interesting.

One of the problems with athletic practices is that they can become boring. It is difficult enough for the athletes to be involved in a 2-hour (or longer) practice that requires them to do hard work, but when the entire experience is an additional ordeal because the session is also boring or uninteresting—coaches have a real problem on their hands. Thus, it behooves coaches to attempt to make the practices interesting, yes, even fun. It goes without saying that the practice sessions must also be productive. However, being productive and being interesting are not mutually exclusive. Practices can be both and athletes deserve, at the very least, an honest effort on behalf of their coaches to make them so.

COACHING CONCEPT #324: Mediocrity breeds mediocrity—mediocre expectations usually generate mediocre results.

Practices must also be challenging. Athletes are not looking for easy practices. They are not seeking to spend their time in a recreation type setting. Rather, they need to be pushed, they need to be challenged, and they need to have high expectations. Mediocrity breeds mediocrity. If a coach has mediocre expectations or hopes for individual athletes or the team the likelihood of the athletes producing at the mediocre level is very high.

COACHING CONCEPT #325   Set meaningful and lofty goals—but be sure that goals are realistic, reasonable, challenging and obtainable.

Just as high expectations are recommended, it is also important to be sure that whatever goals and objectives are set that they be realistic and obtainable. It does absolutely no good, and in many instances can be a real hindrance, for the coach to have such lofty goals or aspirations for individuals or the entire team that the goals are totally unrealistic and, in fact, rather foolish. Goals are important, yes. High expectations and standards are desirable, yes. However, the goals, the expectations and the standards set for the team and for oneself must be realistic and achievable. To do otherwise is courting disaster because the individual or the team will always end up in failure. And continued failure can be a futile breeding ground for additional failure. Whereas success tends to breed success, continued failure tends to breed failure and disillusionment.

COACHING CONCEPT #326   In establishing team and individual goals and objectives, concentrate on small and immediate goals—realization of such goals can serve as a motivating factor.

Another important factor to remember about goals is to make many of them small rather than global and place them in the immediate time frame rather than far in the future. A youth sport basketball player might want to have as a goal winning the NBA championship while starting for the Chicago Bulls, but this is a distant goal both in terms of time and in terms of skill. There is nothing wrong with this global goal, but it is necessary for this youngster to also have and concentrate on more reasonable (small), immediate, and obtainable goals.

For example, the youngster should, with the coach's help, establish goals such as to make 5 out of 10 free throws in practice tomorrow. Or, to be able to increase one's vertical jump by a half-inch during the next month. Or, being able to reduce the number of violations in the next game or practice. Thus, when these small, more readily obtainable goals are realized, the athlete (regardless of the age of the individual) will be motivated to continue to work and strive towards new and loftier goals. In summary, the goals should be neither too low (too easily realized) or too high (almost impossible to achieve).

> **COACHING CONCEPT #327**   **Practice does not make perfect—but perfect, planned, purposeful, and proper practice makes perfect.**

Practice, by and in itself, is not enough to insure that athletes are able to learn the skills necessary to successfully compete in their sport(s). Having athletes practice is not sufficient. Having athletes doing the right things at the right time with the right people in practice is the key. Anyone can plan a poor practice. It takes a competent coach to plan an appropriate, proper practice, one at which athletes continue to learn new skills and knowledge as well as enhancing those previously learned. What this means is that the activities making up the daily practice routine must be appropriate and suitable for both the athletes and for the skills and knowledge to be learned. The goal of any coach is to execute a suitable, an appropriate (perfect), and a purposeful practice in which athletes are able to take advantage of the planned activities to enhance their mastery of the sport and its various components. Practice does not make perfect, but perfect, planned, purposeful, and proper practice makes perfect (Mackay, 1988, Stier, 1988).

> **COACHING CONCEPT #328:**   **Emphasize in practice those things that will have a significant positive impact or effect on the team's success.**

Everything that takes place within a practice session should benefit the athletes and the team in some respect. Coaches need to be careful lest they have athletes perform activities or be engaged in tasks that have no direct bearing upon the team's or individuals' ultimate success in that sport. This doesn't mean that everything that occurs in a practice must be related to the physical performance of a skill. For example, some tasks and activities might be associated with the social, psychological and mental aspect of the sport.

> **COACHING CONCEPT #329:**   **Coaches need to maintain statistics and records in practices in order to develop a realistic picture of the capabilities of individuals and the team as a whole.**

All coaches recognize how important it is to keep accurate records and statistics during games and competitive events. However, it is equally important, if not more so, to retain some records and statistics from practices. This is because important decisions for both future practices and contests can be determined on the basis of available hard data that can be generated from practices. Both team and individual statistics should be kept. With such records, the coach is able to determine progress, if any, of both players and the team itself. It is also easier to detect problem areas with the availability of hard data rather than relying exclusively on one's feelings or hunches.

The exact nature of these records and statistics will vary, naturally, depending upon the nature of the sport being coached. However, it is important to remember that these records can represent not only the athletes' performances in scrimmages during the practice but also their efforts in drills and other repetitive performances of specific drills. The availability of statistics, hard data, about each athlete can significantly aid the coach in coming to decisions about the specific role that each individual athlete might play within the greater scheme of things, including who should play what position and who should be starters and who should come off the proverbial bench.

COACHING CONCEPT #330: Don't become buddy-buddy with athletes—
coaches don't have to be liked to command respect.

Perhaps one of the biggest challenges, especially for younger coaches, is to be able to deal with one's athletes in a professional manner without becoming buddy-buddy with selected athletes. Almost every person has an innate desire to be respected, to be liked, to be accepted. Coaches need to be respected but must not become one of the kids. Frequently, the coach walks the tightrope between being a buddy-buddy on the one hand and being too aloof, too far removed and uncaring, on the other hand.

Young coaches might be involved with athletes who are only a few years younger than they are themselves. Such a situation can place a coach in a unique and sometimes uncomfortable position. Great care must be taken by the coach so that there will be no hint of impropriety on behalf of the coach. For example, driving athletes home, especially those of the opposite sex, following games or practices should be avoided lest the wrong impression be given to others, including the athletes.

EDWARD THORNDIKE'S LEARNING LAWS

Edward Thorndike formulated three learning laws that are applicable to the coaching scene. These are the law of *exercise* (repetition), the law of *effect*, and the law of *readiness*. The law of *exercise* deals with the fact that practice (repetition) is important and the more that repetition is experienced the greater is the likelihood for learning a particular skill. The concept that *practice makes perfect* is important, but more important is the understanding that perfect practice makes perfect. That is, practice must be meaningful in that sport practice must be similar to that which is to be experienced in an actual game or contest situation/environment. In addition, practice must be such that the individual is aware of what the person is doing correctly as well as incorrectly.

For coaches, the law of *effect* refers to the type of reaction athletes have to a given situation (stimulus) or experience. If an athlete has a positive experience in learning a skill then that individual is more likely to continue to strive to learn that skill. A positive reaction to a situation or experience tends to reinforce the desire to repeat that experience. Conversely, if a youngster has a negative experience, that individual will tend to avoid the circumstances and environment that generated the negative reaction or feelings. In teaching sport skills coaches need to attempt to provide situations and an environment in which the learning environment has a positive effect upon the individual athlete—leading the athlete to desire to continue the effort at mastering the skill(s) in question.

The law of *readiness* has implications for a coach in that an athlete will not be able to adequately learn unless that individual is truly ready to learn (mentally, physically, socially, etc.). One cannot teach a youngster who is five years old to correctly shoot a jump shot in basketball or to run over the hurdles in preparation for a track meet. Coaches need to be very careful that their athletes are truly ready and capable of learning that which is to be mastered.

STYLES OF TEACHING OR COACHING PHYSICAL SKILLS TO MALE AND FEMALE ATHLETES

The command style, in which the coach simply dictates (without question or challenge) what is to be done in practice, when it is to be done, by whom, and at what level of performance, has been the prevalent style of choice for decades. Although this style is still very much in vogue, there are emerging some changes or variances in this traditional method of coaching among farsighted coaches in recent years. This is especially true with those coaches of women athletes and the coaches of youth sports and junior high sports.

Coaching Male and/or Female Athletes

Should coaches be careful to coach female athletes differently than male athletes? Should female athletes be expected to act and react differently in practice and in games than male athletes? Are females more emotional than males within the competitive athletic environment? Must females be handled with kid gloves by coaches, especially male coaches? What should coaches of females be on the alert for in conducting practices and coaching in game situations? Is there any definitive differences in what a coach should do, has to do, when coaching females that is not necessary when coaching males?

Yes, there are some differences involved in the coaching of male and female athletes. However, for many coaches, there are more similarities than there are differences (Cohen, 1992). Just as there are individual differences among male athletes, there are individual differences among female athletes. Some male athletes need to be pushed, challenged and even yelled at to have them work to their potential. For other male athletes, such coaching behavior is a turn-off and only hinders or impedes learning and mastery of skills. However, some female athletes also need to be pushed, challenged and even yelled as if they are to excel. And for some female athletes, this type of behavior would be abhorrent to say the least. In short, it is dangerous to single out any single characteristic or need for female athletes and to paint all females with the same brush. Females are not the weaker sex who needs to be pampered and coddled to in either the practice setting or in game situations. Suffice it to say that coaches of females and males should pay attention to determining the existing skill level of their athletes and attempt to meet their individual needs—all the while taking into consideration the individuality of each athlete and the circumstances which exist at the time.

In short, coaches need to find out what makes a person interested in and capable of learning and then take advantage of that factor(s) in facilitating learning by the individual. Each athlete is truly unique. What motivates some athletes will not do so for others. In some cases, what motivates one individual to learn and improve might hinder learning in another. Some athletes can be yelled at by coaches while others clam up and retreat into their own little shell. In the latter situation, learning and mastery of physical skills can be severely impaired (hampered), if not significantly curtailed, as a result of improper or inadequate motivation. Coaches need to treat each athlete as a unique individual, with individual needs, wants, abilities, strengths, weaknesses and goals.

Does the Sex of the Coach Make a Difference?

Stier (1988, p. 13), an experienced college/university/high school athletic director and department chairperson, offers some interesting thoughts regarding the sex of the coach in response to the above question when he stated:

> "The primary criterion for the selection of any coach should be the
> The competency level of the individual—male or female—who
> aspires to a coaching position. However, there is the matter of a
> role model to consider. Many individuals, both inside and outside
> the profession, believe it is important for women athletes to have

meaningful exposure to qualified women who can serve as role models. The possibility that female athletes might be coached exclusively or almost exclusively by men throughout their careers is unacceptable to many of us—both as parents of female athletes and as professionals in the field.

" . . . from the standpoint of many athletes, it is not a matter of which sex the coach happens to be but rather, what competence level the individual coach possesses. From this perspective, the sex of the coach does not matter . . . . But, from the standpoint of many professionals in the field, especially woman seeking coaching positions, it is deemed highly desirable, if not essential, that the women athletes have a significant number of experiences with female coaches who can serve as meaningful role models. In this case, the sex of the coach does indeed matter."

Cross Gender Coaching

Coaching the opposite sex (cross gender coaching) does present some unique challenges for the coach to overcome. A female coach might be coaching males or a male coach might be in charge of a female team. It is important to remain cognizant of the fact that coaching the opposite sex does involve a careful examination of the what, where, why, when and how of coaching activities. Besides the obvious concern about not being able to go into the athletes' locker room while they are changing before or after a game, coaching the opposite sex also requires that the coach be extra sensitive to perceptions held by others—athletes, parents, school officials and the general public.

Nothing of value comes easy— it takes hard work, sacrifice and dedication.

What might be perfectly acceptable for a male coach to do with a male athlete (for example, slapping the athlete on the buttocks as the youngster is being substituted into a game) is absolutely unacceptable to do with a female athlete. Ditto with a female coach and a male athlete. Although most cross gender coaching is being performed by male coaches, that is, male coaches are coaching female teams and female athletes; this is not to say that women coaches are not assuming responsibilities for coaching of male athletes. It is just that there are many more male coaches coaching females than female coaches coaching male athletes—at least for the present.

There are a whole host of questions that the coach who serves as the mentor for the opposite sex must ask oneself, some of which are provided below. Many of the answers will depend upon the sport situation (circumstances and level) in which the coach finds oneself.

1. Are there any differences between coaching males and females in terms of?
    a. Conditioning.
    b. Motivating.
    c. Communicating.
    d. Evaluating.
    e. Strategy development.
    f. Traveling arrangements (including hotel and eating accommodations).
    g. Risks undertaken by the coach as a direct result of assuming the coaching position.
2. Should there be an assistant coach who is of the same sex as the athletes?
3. How to deal with the sharing of confidences by student-athletes with the coach who is of the opposite sex?
4. How to deal with discussions pertaining to the menstrual cycle among female athletes?
5. How female athletes make male coaches aware that their periods may be affecting their physical performance?
6. Does a woman's period affect her sport performance? How does the male coach react and handle the situation?
7. What specific or special challenges should the young (21-35 year old) coach face working with 18-year old athletes of the opposite sex?
8. Should a coach ever meet with a student (privately, in a room with the door closed) alone? What about keeping the door open? What about the door having a glass pane in it?
9. How should the coach deal with specific injuries—groin, chest areas, etc.?
10. Should a coach treat (physically, mentally, psychologically) male and female athletes identically or differently just because of their sex?
11. Can coaches touch their athletes in any way? What about hugging?
12. What are the implications of so-called innocent (and not-so innocent) flirting by the athlete, by the coach?
13. Are attitudes towards winning/losing and towards commitment similar or different in terms of female and male teams (when coached by same sex coach or opposite sex coach)?
14. Are there innocent words or gestures that might contain hidden meanings?

15. What comprises sexist language, attitude, etc., displayed by a coach? By athletes?

16. How does the coach deal with the dressing room situation?

17. What about taping the athletes—where and when should such taping be done? By whom?

18. What are the parents' attitudes towards the male coach of the female team? Or, the female coach of a male team? What about the attitude of the athletes? The attitude of the school administration?

19. Do male or female coaches subject themselves to more exposure, pressure or danger of a lawsuit as a result of coaching the opposite sex?

20. Would female athletes prefer a male or female coach? Why? Would male athletes prefer a male or female coach? Why?

21. Should there be special travel arrangements made with athletes of the opposite sex?

CHARACTERISTICS OF PRODUCTIVE PRACTICES

Productive practices (activities) are often distinguished by five essential characteristics (Siedentop, 1991). These include:

1. They are *pertinent*—practice activities are indeed appropriate and suitable for the individual athletes' abilities, age, interests, and experiences.

2. They are *purposeful*—practice activities directly relate to the skills and tactics to be learned.

3. They are *progressive*—skills are introduced from the simple to the complex and are ordered in such a fashion as to lead to meaningful and timely learning.

4. They are *paced*—learners have sufficient space between the challenge of learning one skill or series of skills and being introduced to new skills.

5. They are *participatory* in nature—the coach involves as many athletes as possible in the learning of the skills.

PRESENTATION OF SKILLS WITHIN PRACTICES— COACHING METHODS

There are a variety of methods of presenting skills to be learned to athletes. Two of the methods of teaching physical skills in practices are the whole method and the whole-part-whole method of teaching/coaching.

Whole Method of Teaching/Coaching

In this method of teaching a physical skill, the coach introduces the entire skill or the whole movement pattern to be learned. Naturally, the types of skills that can best be learned through the whole method of instruction are those skills that are not overly complicated to begin with. It is the more simplistic physical skills, patterns or maneuvers that can be learned by athletes through this method. Athletes can easily duplicate the performance of simple tactics, maneuvers or skills if the coach is able to paint an accurate and clear picture of that which is to be learned.

The whole method of teaching or coaching revolves around the ability of the learner to see, grasp and understand the total physical activity at one time, and then to be able to begin to perform this skill from that basis. This gestalt viewing of the skill, this grasp of the total performance activity or movement pattern, is based upon one's ability to comprehend the act from viewing it in its entirety. The whole picture of the skill may be presented by a personal demonstration by the coach, a demonstration by an accomplished athlete, or through an audio-visual means such as a film, a video tape or even a still picture.

Whole-Part-Whole Method of Teaching/Coaching

Complex skills, tactics and maneuvers usually require that the coach break down that which is to be learned into its component parts and present each of the major parts or components to be learned separately. Thus, concentration on only portions or segments of the total skill is necessary in many complex physical movement activities *prior to* having athletes attempt to combine these related patterns into a whole. This is why coaches devise breakdown drills so that the youngsters can practice the component parts of the whole before putting the parts together into a complete movement pattern, maneuver or skill.

COACHING CONCEPT #331: In teaching complex skills, use the whole-part-whole method of coaching.

Thus, in the whole-part-whole method, youngsters are initially presented with a glimpse or view of the total physical movement pattern or maneuver. A verbal explanation, followed by a demonstration, provides a look at the complete, correct skill to be learned. Players are then introduced to various portions or aspects of the total pattern to be practiced as isolated skills or activities. Finally, these isolated physical activities, patterns or skills are combined to make up the complete physical act. The movement from isolated parts of the whole to the complete physical act does not come automatically, or sometimes easily. Coaches must work very hard to provide the bridge between the performance of the individual parts and the successful performance of the complete act or movement pattern.

Johnny Wooden, arguably the best basketball coach in the history of the sport with ten NCAA national championships in twelve years (seven in a row) from 1963-64 through 74-75 was very successful in using the whole-part-whole method of coaching. He broke down those complicated skills and maneuvers just like he did in teaching math. His coaching and practice sessions revolved around his explaining what was to be learned, demonstrating the skill or activity, having the athletes practice the skills or tactics (repetition, repetition and more repetition), providing correction to individual athletes, and providing additional practice opportunities (more repetition) under the watchful eyes of the coaching staff (Wolff, 1989).

In summary, the key concept of the whole-part-whole method is to initially introduce the skill in its entirety, then break down the skill or pattern into component parts and have athletes practice those parts or segments (repetition), and then attempt to bring the parts together into the complete pattern or skill and provide more opportunities for repetition. Of course, correct performance in executing the components or isolated parts of the whole is essential.

ENHANCING ATHLETIC IMPROVEMENT IN PRACTICES

COACHING CONCEPT #332: Athletes' improvement can be significantly enhanced because of a variety of factors—maturity, practice, game experience, and good instruction/coaching.

Coaches should anticipate that their athletes will indeed get better, will improve in their sport because of a variety of factors, including:

1. Maturity process—as time passes and athletes get older and develop physically (mature) their capacity and potential for improvement increases.

2. Appropriate practice opportunities—active participation in drills and game-like situations (scrimmages) can enable athletes to refine those skills necessary for actual competition.

3. Game experience—playing on the firing line provides excellent opportunities for athletes to improve upon the mental, psychological and physical aspects of their game.

4. Good instruction/coaching—athletes with knowledgeable and experienced coaches who are skilled instructors can make quantum leaps in their own level of proficiency.

As stated in an earlier chapter, it is essential that coaches keep an open mind when making assessments of their athletes in terms of their current skill level and their future proficiency in the sport. Coaches need to be careful lest they fail to anticipate that an individual will improve, as the season progresses and from one season to another. Athletes, if they work at it and have competent coaching/instruction, should improve from the beginning of the season to the end of the season. Athletes, if they earnestly work at their sport and on their own physical conditioning during the off-season, should improve from one season to the next. When athletes return to the first days of pre-season practice, following weeks and months of off-season down-time, coaches need to start with a blank slate (no pre-judgments) regarding both the skill level and potential of each athlete.

COACHING CONCEPT #333: **Athletes tend to learn more when they work in a wholesome, supportive atmosphere—when the learning experience is enjoyable and productive for the individual athlete.**

Athletes naturally learn better when the learning experience is positive rather than negative. When an athlete enjoys being at practice, the athlete will probably learn more than if practice is the pits in the eyes of the youth. If the athlete feels good (takes pride) about mastering a specific skill, the likelihood of this individual learning additional skills is enhanced. This is especially important when dealing with younger athletes, but is also applicable at every age level.

Yes, there have been and are currently examples of successful coaches who coach via fear and intimidation. Could many of these same coaches also be successful if they did not use fear and intimidation? Could many of these mentors even be more successful? Many would say yes—to both questions. If an individual athlete experiences failure after failure in an effort to learn a skill and is made to feel inferior in the process, the learning potential can be significantly restricted. If individual athletes operate under the atmosphere of fear, their learning curve can be significantly hindered, not to mention their motivation for the sport may be diminished.

Thus, it is absolutely imperative that coaches do everything in their power to make sure that each individual athlete, generally speaking, has a positive experience in the practice sessions. Success breeds success. The athlete needs to be told that the individual is of worth, is making progress, and will experience success in the future. This does not mean that errors are not pointed out. However, an athlete can be shown an error in a positive and constructive manner, with the result being a renewed effort to correct or eliminate same.

COACHING CONCEPT #334: Find out the skill level and existing knowledge of each individual athlete and the team as a whole—then teach from that level.

Always be sure to check the present level of skill performance of athletes before attempting to teach them something new. Take the swimming coach who was involved in a youth team. The coach started out by having the youngsters ease into the shallow end of the pool, blowing bubbles and doing some flutter kicks. A short time later, one of the youngster's parents came to the pool and observed what was taking place. Whereupon the mother asked her child to go to the deep end, dive off the 3-meter board and swim the length of the pool using four different strokes—and the youngster did exactly that, to the astonishment of the coach.

COACHING CONCEPT #335: Treat each athlete as an individual—physically, mentally, socially and psychologically.

There are two important points in this story. First, coaches need to know where the youngsters are currently at in terms of their skill level. Only then can the coach successfully build upon the skill level and understanding of the athlete in the teaching of more advanced skills. Second, coaches need to treat each athlete as an individual. Each individual athlete may differ significantly from others in terms of physical skill level, experience, potential for learning and their current motivational level.

COACHING CONCEPT #336: When coaching/teaching physical skills—build upon the skill level and understanding by moving from the simple to the complex.

Once a coach has ascertained the skill level of individual athletes, it is possible to teach and coach more advanced skills. However, in doing so, it is necessary to move from the simple to the more complex skills and understandings. Just as a building must have a firm foundation, so too must an athlete have a sound mastery of the fundamentals (simple) before attempting to be adept in more advanced (complex) skills and knowledge.

Athletes will learn best when they have an adequate base in terms of physical, social and mental maturity coupled with a sound foundation of physical skills already mastered. It is hard to teach an individual an elite skill if the person does not have the foundation on which to build the more advanced skill. A youngster in 6th grade should first learn the basketball fundamentals involving the lay-up and set shot rather than be introduced to techniques involved in shooting the three point jumper. This seems obvious, but would-be coaches violate this basic principle all the time.

Using a Rubric to Help Assess Current Team Members

Many coaches search out tools in the form of a matrix or rubric to help them in the evaluation and assessment process for their athletes. This is true in terms of subjective as well as objective criteria. One such example of a rubric, template or matrix that had been used by a high school basketball coach is presented in Appendix D.

This rubric or matrix is constructed so that the names of the individual athletes are inserted along the left side, from top to bottom. Along the top, from left to right, are different criteria or standards on which individual athletes are evaluated. Such an evaluation can be done by the coaching staff each week or every two weeks in an effort to accomplish two major goals. First, to help the coaches arrive at some type of determination, on a particular date, insofar as to how each athlete rates on a scale of 1-10 in terms of each of the 15 different skills, abilities or traits.

**COACHING CONCEPT #337: Never embarrass youngsters when evaluating
                                             them during tryouts or during the regular season.**

Second, this technique allows each athlete to find out (feedback) how that individual rates on the rubric as well as how one ranks in terms of other members of the squad, especially those athletes competing for the same playing or starting position on the squad. One must be very careful not to embarrass any individual athlete when using this form or a variation of it. Thus, it is suggested that instead of posting the form at the end of a week for the athletes to view with the names of each youngster listed, that each student is given a confidential number and that these numbers (instead of names) are placed on the form.

Coaches should give a copy of the completed form containing the scores (but not the names) of all of the youngsters to each youngster at the end of a certain period of time (weekly or bi-weekly). Each youngster receiving a copy of the form has only his or her name on that particular copy of the filled-in form so that one can identify one's own scores in comparison to others. Coaches should not post the form on some bulletin board for everyone to see.

This form leads to a better understanding on behalf of the coaching staff of exactly how each youngster ranks in terms of each standard and in terms of other youngsters being evaluated. It also helps the youngsters understand where they stand in the eyes of the coaching staff. In those instances there are more than one coach involved, any differences in scoring for any athletes can serve as an excellent discussion point to find out why there are differences of opinion among the staff.

THE MENTAL ASPECT [MENTAL SKILLS TRAINING] OF COACHING

COACHING CONCEPT #338: Use mental practice to enhance the learning experience of one's athletes.

One does not learn only by physically practicing skills and movement patterns. Rather, one can also significantly enhance one's learning skills and mastery of a sport by taking advantage of the mental aspect of training. Such training is referred to as psychological skills training. The advantages of psychological (or mental) skills training can be summarized as:

1. It can be practiced anywhere.
2. It is time efficient.
3. It is neither physically demanding nor fatiguing.
4. The mind frequently cannot tell the difference between reality and day dreaming (imagery).
5. It can be effective and successful.
6. It can be motivating for the participant.

COACHING CONCEPT #339: Relaxation plus imagery plus concentration equals the potential for better performance.

"More and more coaches and administrators are realizing that maximizing success means training and not just their athletes' physical skills, but their minds as well

. . . . Mental training anticipates the mental challenges of actual competition—what we call the mental moments . . . . It helps the athlete develop and rehearse proper responses to those moments" said Craig Wrisberg, professor of sports psychology and mental training consultant at the University of Tennessee, (Smith, 2005, p. 26). The goal of mental skills training is to enhance learning and physical performance through by helping athletes to be more aware of what they can do to help themselves mentally, emotionally, physically, and behaviorally (Voight, 2005).

Using such techniques as visualization, mental rehearsal, imagery, focusing strategy as well as a variety of mental exercises—coaches work on overcoming insecurity, a lack of confidence on behalf of individual athletes and the team as a whole in an effort to prepare them for the mental challenges and burdens created by actual game/contest competition,

Athletes can help themselves improve by mentally viewing themselves as being successful in performing the sport. Specifically, basketball players can mentally picture themselves shooting successful free throw after successful free throw or jumping high near the rim to garner the ever elusive rebound. The football player can visualize himself throwing the pass and having it caught for a big gain. The softball player can visualize herself throwing strike after strike and mowing the opponent's batters down one after another. Have athletes take advantage of imagery, the mental conceptualization of performing a physical act or skill in an effective, efficient and successful manner.

COACHING CONCEPT #340: The key to psychological skills training is practice and time spent on task.

There has been much written in recent years in the area of psychological skills training programs. Whole books on this relatively new approach have been published in the past few decades. The mind is truly a wondrous thing. The mind can play a major role in the mastery of physical activities or in one's failure to master them. Of course, imagery is not guaranteed to work. Nothing is.

Practice is a most important factor in motor imagery guidelines. Mental training involves practice and the ability to focus, to spend time on task. The ability of an individual to relax, to concentrate, to visualize, to conceptualize can be taught to individual athletes. It takes time, effort

The satisfaction of having played well is rewarding enough for one's efforts.

and consistent practice to learn how to take advantage of the mental and psychological dimensions of the athlete's makeup so as to achieve better performance.

Although reading books or professional journal articles on mental training or sport psychology does not make one a sport psychologist or mental training expert, it is nevertheless strongly recommended that the reader pursue a variety of sources (books, journals, experts in the field of sport psychology) in an effort to become more familiar with all of the ramifications of this relatively new dimension of athletic coaching and training.

INTRODUCTION OF NEW SKILLS AND KNOWLEDGE— READINESS OF ATHLETES

COACHING CONCEPT #341: Don't introduce a new skill when the athletes are tired or when the end of practice is near.

A common mistake coaches make in practice is to attempt to introduce the learning of new knowledge or physical skills when the athletes are tired from working hard in practice. This typically happens when the new material is introduced during the last part of the practice session. When athletes have already spent 75% of the practice period working very hard, both physically and mentally, it is unwise to then attempt to introduce new material for them to absorb.

Teaching new and/or intricate skills and strategies following strenuous physical exertion is counter productive. When mentally tired and physically exhausted, no one is ready to attempt to master new knowledge or new skills. New material should be reserved for when the youngsters are relatively fresh, both physically and mentally, when they are more likely to be able to retain and master that which is new.

COACHING CONCEPT #342: Athletes learn best only when they are ready to learn—coaches must plan practices in light of the age, capabilities and experiences of the athletes.

Athletes learn best when they are ready and capable of learning. Whether an athlete is ready to learn depends upon the physical maturity and skill level of the individual as well as the current mental and physical state of the individual. Make sure each athlete is ready to learn that which is to be taught. Some athletes might be too young, physically, mentally or socially to master specific skills or strategies or tactics. A youngster who is only five years old is obviously not capable of learning how to shoot a jump shot or spike a volleyball. Such a child is not ready to learn these skills, either physically or mentally. Even some secondary school athletes may not be ready to learn what the coach wishes them to master either because they are not physically ready (capable) to learn or are not mentally or psychologically ready (prepared) to do so.

Since readiness refers to the capability for learning, coaches would do well to pay particular attention to what they ask their players to learn. Similarly, coaches need to be careful when they introduce new knowledge and skills to the youngsters. Far too frequently, inexperienced or untrained coaches will attempt to teach too much too soon to too many athletes.

COACHING CONCEPT #343: Athletes should practice essential skills until the performance of these skills become second nature, a habit.

LENGTH OF INDIVIDUAL PRACTICE SESSIONS — EFFECTIVE TIME MANAGEMENT

Some coaches subscribe to the philosophy that more is better. Not so. All too frequently, practice sessions are too long, too dragged out and too time consuming. How much is too much? How long should practices really be? There is no one answer for these types of questions. Coaches should use their best judgment in light of a number of variables. For example, the length of practices depend upon:

1. The age level of the athletes (their attention span)
2. The level of the athletes' conditioning
3. The sport itself
4. The available facilities and equipment
5. The available staff
6. The activities that will take place during the practice
7. When the next competition is scheduled
8. The type of weather (outdoor sports) the practice will take place in
9. The time of season—whether it is during pre-season, early in the season, during the mid-part or near the end of the competitive season

---

COACHING CONCEPT #344: Being a good practice coach involves doing the right things (being effective) and doing things right (being efficient) in practice.

Coaches must balance the need to be effective with the necessity of also being efficient. Coaching decisions (both in practices and games) are made in terms of what will work, what will help the team or individual athletes reach desirable objectives and goals. However, these coaching decisions must be made in light of what is practical and what is efficient. There are many things that can be done in practices that might be considered effective but are not very efficient. Time is almost always of the essence in terms of practices. One of the big problems facing coaches is to be time efficient and people efficient when they plan and conduct their team practices.

The key is to be both effective and also efficient so that the greatest accomplishment or achievement can be realized, individually and collectively, within the minimum amount of time allocated to the athletic practices. The trend is to attempt to reduce the amount of time spent in athletic practices, not to extend them. This means that more and more pressure is being placed upon coaches to get as much, if not more, accomplished within a shorter practice time.

COACHING CONCEPT #345: Practices don't have to be overly complicated—keep it short, simple and succinct (KISSS).

Practices are organized to either teach an athlete something or to have the athlete expand, perfect or refine that which he has already been taught. Practices don't have to be complicated. They do need to be properly organized, structured and executed. It is better to have a very simple practice session and to have the athletes do that which they need to do to improve or learn new skills than to attempt to over complicate matters and have confusing, long and boring practices. Keeping verbal instructions and conversations succinct aids in keeping practices performance oriented rather than conversation or verbiage oriented. Less talking means more opportunities for physical practice to take place.

Another tactic that has helped expedite practices is to have a student manager keep the clock in practice. That is, give to the student manager the daily practice schedule with the allocated times and instruct the manager to run the clock and to remind the coaches when a specific learning activity should be stopped and the next scheduled activity initiated. Of course, the coach might want to deviate from the written daily practice schedule, but the presence of the practice time keeper will help remind the coach to keep things on track and to move the practice along.

COACHING CONCEPT #346: There is no definitive evidence indicating that long practices are better—rather, shorter practices, may be the order of the day.

For many sports at the high school and college level, two hours (give or take 15 minutes) of actual practice time seems to suffice. However, there are still many (too many) coaches who feel that practices at this level must consume three hours or more. This is just not true. There is no evidence indicating that longer practices are equated with superior athletic accomplishments and achievements.

For some sports, especially early in the pre-season part of the season, coaches prefer to use two shorter practices a day for a specific number of days. This is done in order to break up the monotony of strenuous practices and also to provide the athletes with an opportunity to rest and replenish their mental and physical energies before they begin the second practice for that day. Typically, practices become shorter as the end of the season approaches. This is done to avoid burning out or boring athletes.

COACHING CONCEPT #347: Long, drawn-out practices are often symptomatic of a disorganized practice schedule and/or a disorganized coach.

Problems with Long Practices

Coaches can get as much accomplished, and sometimes more, in a shorter practice session if every minute is structured and the athletes as well as the coaches use the available time to their best advantage. There are two essential problems or challenges associated with long, drawn out practices. The first problem is that athletes become tired and lose motivation as the practice time is drawn out, and as a result they have shorter attention spans and have a difficult time really learning or refining their skills. After a while, it becomes a matter of diminishing returns. The second problem revolves around the safety issue. Specifically, when athletes are forced to practice strenuously for a long period of time, they not only become tired but are more susceptible to injuries, both serious and not so serious.

Thus, when looking at the matter of length of practice sessions, the coach must take into account what can reasonably be accomplished by the athletes (and the coaching staff) without reduction in attention, motivation, learning capability and safety. The objective is to have manageable practices, practices that are effective and efficient. Student-athletes have many other responsibilities facing them at the conclusion of their practices, not the least of which is to study for their classes. Coaches self-destruct when they demand so much time of their athletes in practices that the youngsters cannot adequately function in the classroom or have difficulty studying for classes as a result of being exhausted and/or not having sufficient time to devote to the academic aspect of their lives.

COACHING CONCEPT #348: **Practices should involve constant and meaningful activity—unless there is a good reason for down time.**

Most coaches could have shorter practices and yet still cover all of the things they want to cover in the practice if so much time would not be wasted doing absolutely nothing. This so-called down time is the bane of every coach. This down time is valuable time just going to waste because either the coaches are not doing anything significant or the athletes are not actively involved in learning, mastering or reinforcing the skills necessary for their particular sport. Most coaches have about the same amount of time to spend in practice; the key is how that time is spent. Is it wasted? Is it put to effective and efficient use? Some coaches just seem to accomplish much more than other coaches in the same period of time. Practice time is a precious commodity. Athletes should always be kept busy, doing something meaningful, physically and/or mentally.

COACHING CONCEPT #349: **The worse bane for any coach in practice is the wasting of precious, valuable time.**

As a result, many coaches have taken the position that their athletes are to be constantly on the move, constantly doing something that will facilitate the learning and mastery of the mental and physical aspects of their sport. No, this doesn't mean that everyone has to be running around like chickens with their heads cut off. However, it does mean that there is literally no standing around—except when such lack of activity is required because (1) the coach is speaking, lecturing or otherwise attempting to obtain the undivided attention of the athlete(s), or (2) the athlete is to observe something or someone else during the practice session. However, under no circumstances are athletes just standing or milling around waiting for something to happen. If this occurs, it is the fault of the coaching staff more so than the athletes for allowing this type of foolishness to take place. Organized properly, with careful foresight, practices can take up far less time than most team practices now consume—regardless of the level of competition.

HINDRANCES OF LEARNING—LEARNING PLATEAUS

Coaches should expect that individual players, and even whole teams, will experience learning plateaus in their efforts to master physical skills and movement patterns. This is normal and should be anticipated by both coaches and athletes. What is a learning plateau? The learning plateau ". . . is a temporary stagnation or slight decline in performance or training" (Gambetta, 1999, p, 19). It is when athletes are not able to improve upon their performance, either in terms of physical or mental performance. Individuals can continue to work diligently and yet there seemingly is little, if any, progress. The results can be frustrating and disappointing to the youngsters as well as the coaching staff.

> **COACHING CONCEPT #350: Expect learning plateaus on behalf of athletes when learning physical skills—the mastery of skills and the grasp of knowledge varies among individuals and by individuals.**

During those times when athletes are experiencing the frustration of a learning plateau, it is important that the athletes and the coaches do not lose heart or immediately jump to an erroneous conclusion that the youngsters are not working hard enough or that something is wrong with the way the coaches are teaching or dealing with the athletes.

> **COACHING CONCEPT #351: One overcomes a learning plateau by remaining patient, committed and focused.**

Sometimes a different approach by the coaches or the athletes to working on the skill or movement pattern can help youngsters break out of the rut, and can help athletes move to the next level in terms of performance. On the other hand, it may merely take a period of time for the athletes to move to that next performance level, while at the same time continuing to work very hard and remaining very focused on the task or tasks at hand. It is imperative that youngsters not be discouraged. If it was easy, anyone could become an elite performer in sport, and we all know that that is not the case. The key to overcoming a learning plateau is to remain patient, committed and focused.

KEEPING THINGS IN PROSPECTIVE —
POSITIVE PRACTICE STRATEGIES

> **COACHING CONCEPT #352: Pay attention to details—both in practices and in games.**

Details mean a lot, both in practices and in games. Coaches should not overlook anything in the preparation of practice sessions and actual competition. A coach, who is caught unprepared, regardless of how serious the matter is, gives the impression of incompetence to players and to others. Failure to pay attention to details often distracts the athletes and the coaching staff from the more important matters at hand, that is, what is to take place in practice and in the game.

This paying attention to details can pertain to almost anything. It can involve a coach forgetting something important about the transportation plans for the game. As a result, the team and coaches are stood up waiting until the bus or van finally arrives. In the meanwhile, and as a direct result, the players and coaches can become irritable and can lose focus on what is most important, the upcoming game. Or, the coach can overlook something for practice and is unable to conduct practice as previously planned. Thus, alternative actions must be implemented and the smooth sailing of the practice session is interrupted as is the focus of those at practice.

Little things do mean a lot. In fact, little things mean *everything* because it is the details that form the basis for eventual success. Coaches must be cognizant of the importance and impact that seemingly small details can have upon the overall success of the program and the team.

COACHING CONCEPT #353:   Teach or reinforce something to one's athletes every practice—allow them to attempt to perfect previously learned skills during almost every practice.

It is important that athletes have a sense of accomplishment. This is important in practices as well as in actual contests. Thus, it behooves the coaching staff to attempt to teach *something* to the youngsters during every practice. In simple terms, each athlete should have an opportunity to learn something, whether that something is completely new or merely an expansion of that which was previously taught.

A second key concept is to provide ample opportunities for athletes to practice previously introduced skills. Only infrequently will athletes learn and master a skill or tactic in one practice session. Athletes need to *overlearn* many skills and maneuvers and this requires practice, repetitive practice over a long period of time for complete mastery. Thus practice opportunities must be provided so that athletes can enhance, can improve, their performance levels in critical areas. It is equally important to point out to athletes that they are being provided opportunities to do just that—to improve upon those skills, techniques and maneuvers that had been taught or introduced at an earlier time.

COACHING CONCEPT #354: Tell athletes how to do what you want them to do—don't assume they already know.

Never assume that athletes know what you want them to do. Be sure and explain, in detail, exactly what you want them to do and how you want it to be done. This is especially important when working with inexperienced athletes or when introducing new skills to be learned. Having athletes attempt to perform difficult skills, especially those that have not yet been mastered, creates the potential that the youngsters will do them incorrectly. This can result in a complete disaster.

Be specific in giving directions. Be specific in explaining what you want done. Be specific in explaining how you want it done. Be specific in indicating when and where the athletes are to perform. Even in those instances in which the coach gives the athletes great leeway in making individual choices and decisions, one must be specific and give clear directions and guidance. Don't assume that the athletes know what you want them to do or expect of them unless you provide specificity in your communication and take time to clearly enunciate your expectations.

COACHING CONCEPT #355: Being fair to athletes does not mean they all are treated exactly alike—rather, each should be treated appropriately while taking into account individual differences and extenuating circumstances.

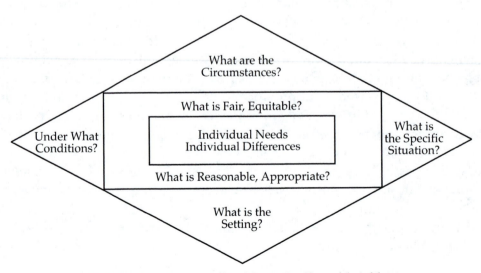

FIGURE 11.1—Factors to Consider In Dealing with Athletes

Don't confuse appropriateness with strict equality. Coaches do not have to treat each athlete exactly alike. No two athletes are identically alike. What is demanded of coaches is to treat their charges fairly and equitably. What is expected of coaches is to deal with their players on an individual basis, while taking into account the individual needs and abilities of each athlete. The key concepts in dealing with athletes are fairness and appropriateness, coupled with understanding and recognition of individual needs and circumstances, figure 11.1.

MOTIVATING ATHLETES —
PSYCHOLOGICAL CONDITIONING FOR ATHLETICS

It is the responsibility, the duty, of each coach to help the individual athlete develop to the athlete's potential and an integral part of this process involves the ability of the coach to motivate the youngster to action over a period of time (Hansen, Gilbert & Hamel, 2003). The major role of motivation in sports is to facilitate the acquiring of knowledge and the mastery of skills and human performance. One motivates to help one perform better, to learn more, to be more skillful and competent. Another aspect of sport motivation hinges around keeping the enthusiasm alive within the individual involved in the sport. Meaningful learning and performance without enthusiasm is too frequently wanting and deficient.

There are two perspectives of sport motivation that should be recognized and addressed. First, there is the whole question of motivating one's athletes. Second, there is the matter of the motivation of coaches themselves. Both need to be examined. Far too often the impact of motivation (or the lack thereof) in terms of coaching is overlooked or neglected. The basis of all learning is in having a motivated and receptive learner combined with a motivated and receptive teacher or coach. Ideally, there is a need for both.

COACHING CONCEPT #356: Youngsters bring different degrees of competitiveness and motivation to their sport—coaches must recognize this and take advantage of it.

No two athletes are the same. Each individual brings to the sport scene different experiences, different perspectives, different abilities, different desires and levels of motivation. It is the responsibility of the coach to recognize these differences between athletes and treat them as individuals in terms of motivation and the teaching of skills and knowledge. This is one of the most challenging aspects of being a coach. But, it is also one of the most necessary.

> **COACHING CONCEPT #357:** To conduct a meaningful and beneficial practice, coaches should know the needs and potential of their athletes—and be capable of motivating them to proper action.

Coaches must be skillful in discerning the needs of their charges in the practice setting. They must be capable of motivating their athletes in practice. They must be willing to work with the youngsters in developing the fundamentals skills, the conditioning and the more sophisticated sport skills in light of each athlete's current capabilities and potential. In short, successful coaches are those mentors who are able to structure practices in such a manner that meaningful and appropriate learning as well as overlearning takes place. It is much more of a challenge to motivate athletes for practices or, heavens forbid, out-of-season conditioning, etc. It is far easier to motivate youngsters for the actual game or contest.

> **COACHING CONCEPT #358:** Successful coaching is successful teaching and successful teaching is successful motivating—for athletes to learn and excel, they must be motivated.

Reaching high to excell.

A wise and experienced teacher/coach once indicated that half of the battle of teaching and coaching is being a good motivator. That is, having the athlete really want to learn, to want to work—and be willing to sacrifice and make the commitment to do what it takes to increase one's level of performance. Part of the motivation equation is enabling each learner (athlete) to experience success in light of his or her needs, abilities and potential. Successful coaches know this and recognize each person's unique individuality when it comes to each youngster's ability to master that which is to be taught. Coaches can significantly affect the learning curve, the ability to learn, of their players either positively or negatively by what they do and/or do not do as teachers.

The Unmotivated Athlete

COACHING CONCEPT #359: **Don't be surprised when athletes are self-centered—the unselfish, self-motivated athlete is a rare gem to be admired.**

However, one must be realistic. Not all youngsters can be motivated to be a model athlete. One must be pragmatic. We live in a *me, me* society. Most athletes, at least when they begin their involvement in sports as youngsters, are self-centered. Some remain so throughout their athletic career. Such an attitude often reveals itself in game situations but can exist in practices as well.

It is the responsibility of the coach to help the athlete learn the true meaning of teamwork, unselfishness, sacrifice and commitment as an athlete and as a human being. But coaches should not be surprised to find that youngsters, at all ages, are selfish, egotistical, me centered. Some individuals can grow out of it. Others can consciously work to avoid this pitfall. However, there will be some individuals who may remain in the *me, me* mode and provide a real challenge for the coach and other team members. Coaches should anticipate such occurrences and work to prevent, eliminate or reduce the negative consequences of such behaviors. The key is understanding that such behavior is to be expected from some would-be athletes and being able to adequately handle the situation.

COACHING CONCEPT #360: **Beware of those athletes who desire immediate gratification and aren't willing to pay the price to excel.**

Selfishness can also be expressed in the desire for immediate gratification on behalf of the athletes. That is, individuals don't want to make the sacrifices that are often required in order to achieve an important goal or objective. It is like the famous pianist who was approached following a successful recital by an individual who gushed: "Oh, how wonderfully you played this evening. If only I could play like that. I would give anything to play like you do." The pianist, who might have been slightly irritated, replied: "No, you would not. You would not give anything to play like I do because if you really wanted to play at my level you could. All you would have had to do is to practice 5-6 hours a day for 25-30 years. Then you could play as I do today because that is what I have had to do. What you really mean to say is that you would like to play as I do without having to do all of the work, without having to pay the price and make the sacrifices."

Unwilling to Pay the Price for Excellence

Athletes are similar to this aficionado. They would like to achieve great things. They desire excellence. But, they are all too frequently reluctant to pay the price, to be unselfish, to be committed, to do what it takes to reach such heights and to realize such goals. The desire for immediate gratification is too great for many would-be athletes. They want to excel in the sport without having paid the price. It is the responsibility of the coach to educate athletes as to the necessity of expending the necessary amount of hard work for the potential of sizable rewards, both internal and external.

Intrinsic and Extrinsic Motivation

Motivation may be thought of as being intrinsic or extrinsic. *Intrinsic* motivation refers to being self-motivated, to being motivated because of an inner drive to achieve, to realize a specific goal or goals based on the satisfaction and gratification that accompanies such an achievement. Intrinsic rewards are more mental than tangible. Such motivation does not depend upon something extrinsic to (outside of) the activity itself but is intertwined with the performance of the sport or activity. Winning and the enjoyment that comes with winning, as well as the satisfaction that comes with doing one's best, are examples of intrinsic motivation.

Extrinsic athletic motivation is that which comes outside of the sport experience. For example, motivating an athlete on the basis of being able to earn a letter jacket as the result of lettering in a sport, or earning a ring in commemoration of winning a championship, or getting one's name in the paper. In each of these three instances, it is the securing of something outside the sport performance (jacket, ring or news clipping) that is the prime motivating factor rather than the performance (and resulting satisfaction) of the activity itself.

Gimmicks in Motivation—Fluff versus Substance

The use of so-called gimmicks such as the use of motivational signs or sayings, the posting of newspaper clippings (one's own and those of other teams) on the team bulletin board, the awarding of special weekly awards or honors to those athletes who have performed superbly during practice or a game, are all examples of extrinsic rewards that some would say are gimmicks. Nevertheless, the general rule of thumb in coaching circles is that such gimmicks, such tactics, are acceptable and appropriate when used sparingly, judiciously and in good taste. However, for a coach to rely on such tactics as the mainstay of one's motivational efforts will find them to be ineffective as it can be a case of too much of a good thing or too much fluff and not enough substance.

COACHING CONCEPT #361: Be careful what you say to the press—don't provide opponents with ammunition they can use against you.

A special warning should be made regarding the news media. Coaches and athletes alike must be careful lest they inadvertently say something that might appear in print or travel over the air waves which can be used against them by serving as a motivating factor for the opposition. Coaches and athletes should refrain from making utterances that can come back and haunt them. Keep such rhetoric to yourself and away from the press. It is not uncommon for coaches to pin up clippings that describe what upcoming opponents have said about future games as a motivating tool for their own players. Play the game on the playing field and not in the newspapers. Don't provide motivational ammunition to your opponents.

Too Much Motivation—The Fallacy of Keying Up Athletes Sky High

---

COACHING CONCEPT #362: Don't over-do the motivation thing—keying up the athletes to be sky high can be counter-productive.

Is there such a thing as motivating one's athletes too much? Is there a danger of getting one's athletes at too high of an emotional peak? Yes, definitely. Too many coaches believe that they can keep their charges on an emotional high throughout the season or for a significant length of time. Wrong. Dead wrong. Quite the contrary actually. There are several problems with this type of thinking.

First, not everyone can be motivated in the same way or to the same degree. Nor will individuals stay motivated for the same amount of time. Motivation must be viewed as both an individual process as well as a team process. Motivating athletes on an individual basis enables the coaches to take personal differences into account. Team members respond to different motivational techniques in different ways. Thus, in attempting to motivate a team, via an inspirational or motivational half-time talk (a Knute Rockne imitation), some of the athletes might already be sky high or too highly motivated, others might be operating just within the comfort zone at that point in time, while the remaining might indeed be in need of a jolt to get them going. However, following the hypothetical half-time narration, perhaps the majority of the youngsters are now too highly motivated, too high emotionally. The result is that their performance is negatively affected while only a portion of the squad is now at an appropriate stimulated level as a result of the stirring monologue. It takes great care and experience to successfully motivate athletes as a team, as a whole.

Second, the effect of motivation, especially motivation that seeks extreme arousal on behalf of athletes for a specific event, such as a big game against an arch rival, is usually only short-lived. Thus, what frequently happens following the big game is that the team does not maintain that same intensity and there is the possibility of a psychological and physical let down, a decrease in performance. Whenever there is a mountain, there is also a valley. When athletes peak in terms of motivation, there is a very real danger that the quality of subsequent performances may suffer.

This can be seen over and over again when a team performs superbly against an arch rival only to stumble the very next game against a far less talented team. Extremely high motivational levels cannot be sustained over a long period of time. Thus, many coaches attempt to have their athletes perform and operate at more of an even keel lest they experience this roller coaster ride of extreme motivation. Besides, the normal thrill and excitement that accompanies the so-called big game should be sufficient to motivate most athletes.

Specific Motivating Tactics and Techniques

Motivation is involved in overcoming hurdles and obstacles. It is about helping the athlete go over, under, around or through difficulties that might impede the individual's progress in mastering and performing the physical movement, skill or technique. There are many things coaches can do to help motivate athletes each and every day. There is no need to wait until a specific or special day to carry out a Knute Rockne style of address. Motivation can be, and should be, ongoing and constant. It can involve a word, a look, an act. It can be as simple as a nod of approval or saying good try. It can encompass the use of motivational slogans or sayings in the locker room, the posting of news clippings, the keeping of records and statistics, the giving of awards (tangible and intangible), etc. Some additional motivating tactics and techniques are provided below.

1. Provide a change of pace in practice—is the spice of life. Watch for activities that are monotonous for the athletes—and change.
2. Include activities that the athletes enjoy and look forward to.
3. When dealing with athletes, make a distinction between the athlete and the individual's performance.
4. Provide appropriate approval and/or assessment for the athlete after both successful and unsuccessful performances.
5. Show a genuine interest in each athlete, both personally and athletically.
6. Chart progress of individual athletes in specific skills.
7. Work with athletes on realistic individual and team goals.
8. Emphasize that athletes compete against themselves as well as others.
9. Stress not winning but doing one's best (work to potential).

10. Never blame individual athletes for losing a contest.
11. Show confidence in the athlete by giving responsibilities, on and off the playing field; build up the athlete's confidence.
12 provide athletes with challenges to overcome and goals to strive for.

Motivation of Athletes—The Carrot or the Stick Approach

COACHING CONCEPT #363: One gets more with sugar than vinegar when it comes to motivating athletes.

How does one motivate athletes? Should one hold a carrot out to the athlete as a goal or objective, such as the joy and pride that accompanies a hard-earned victory or a physical goal realized? Should one use the so-called stick in attempting to encourage the athlete to do better? In this case, the stick is some negative factor or punishment that the athlete wants to avoid. Negative motivation is essentially built around fear—fear of the coach, fear of what will happen (punishment) in the future, fear of failure.

It is important to realize that motivation is, at its best, an imperfect science. Many coaches would call motivation more of an art than a science (Deci, 1985). According to some coaches, athletes should be motivated, prodded and pushed because of the fear of punishment, the desire to avoid that which is unpleasant. Some coaches subscribe to the philosophy that fear of losing or failing to do one's best is a strong motivating factor. Other coaches strongly advocate just the opposite and suggest that motivation is best when it is based on the positive, on an attraction to something desirable, something sought after, rather than being based on avoidance, such as fear, dread and apprehension. And many coaches use both positive and negative motivation (carrot and the stick) in their coaching efforts.

Motivation and Fear and Punishment

COACHING CONCEPT #364: Don't usually motivate through fear or via the negative.

The basis of athletic motivation centers on goals—either goals that the individual athlete seeks to avoid (fear, punishment) or those goals that the individual desires to obtain (positive rewards or benefits) (Martin & Lumsden, 1987). There are literally thousands of examples of both positive and negative motivation when it comes to sports. It is the responsibility of all coaches to decide for themselves the type of motivation that will be most appropriate in light of their personalities, experience, current setting or circumstances and the type of athletes they are coaching. It is important to remember the old adage, however, that one catches more flies with sugar than vinegar. It is also important for coaches to remember that not all modern day athletes respond to motivational strategies and techniques like athletes did in the past or in the manner in which the coaches did when they were athletes.

Generally speaking, punishment has little value when utilized *as a learning tool* (Bolles, 1977). Although the fear of punishment might motivate individuals to work hard or harder, punishment or the likelihood of punishment does not really aid the athletes in terms of their ability to actually improve upon skills and human movement (Warren, 1983).

Fear—an Obstacle to Learning

Fear is emotionally draining and all too frequently can be a block to the learning curve. Athletes should not be preoccupied with fear. Fear is a negative motivational technique that can be merely restrictive to some, while totally destructive to others. Fear can be a cause of over-anxiousness, which in turn impedes performance, both mentally and physically.

COACHING CONCEPT #365: Athletes who fear making mistakes will not be appropriately assertive in competition.

Instead of being overly concerned with avoiding failure or earning punishment, athletes should be concentrating on the positive aspects of their performance and work ethic. Being afraid of incurring the wrath of the coaching staff can make some athletes too tentative, so tentative that they are afraid to take calculated risks. And calculated risks are what athletic competition is all about. When athletes are afraid of making mistakes, they become hesitant. Athletes need to be risk takers and assertive in practice and in competition. Mistakes will happen, and the whole world will not come to an end because of them.

Motivation and the Coaching Staff

COACHING CONCEPT #366: Coaches must motivate themselves.

Coaches must be highly committed, motivated and enthusiastic about the sport. They must successfully convey this feeling to their charges if the athletes are to be motivated. It is difficult to be a highly motivated and committed athlete when one's own coach or coaches convey or portray a less than enthusiastic image. Enthusiasm and motivation are contagious. As a result, coaches need to display that honest enthusiasm and motivation in everything they do, but especially in their dealings with individual athletes and the team as a whole.

Part of the process of remaining motivated as a coach is to take time to reflect upon all of the positive things that emanate from one's coaching experience. Coaches need to take time to recognize all of the good, all of the positive consequences that are the result of their hard work and high level of competency. Realizing the impact that they have upon youngsters, in a wide range of categories, can in itself be highly motivating and rewarding to the coach. Yes, coaching is hard work. But coaching also has many rewards. One of these rewards is knowing that, as a coach, one has had a positive impact upon another person's (the athlete's) life and achievements, not only in the present time frame but throughout the athlete's life.

COACHING CONCEPT #367: Coaches must remain the eternal optimist.

It is also important for coaches to realize that not everything they do will turn up roses. There will be many problems, challenges and stumbles along the way as a coach. However, keep things in their proper perspective. Remember that such problems and challenges are to be expected. As each day comes to a close, it would behoove coaches to take time to reflect upon the many successes, both big and small, that they have experienced that day, as well as the challenges that might have come up. Always looking at the negative can be draining and discouraging for anyone. Coaches need to concentrate on the positive, on the upbeat, and remain the optimist.

HANDLING MISTAKES BY ATHLETES

A very good reason why coaches should spend more time observing and less time talking is to be able to discern when athletes are making errors. This is especially important when the individual athlete is in the process of learning a new skill, strategy, tactic or maneuver. The goal of practicing a physical skill is to have the skill become a habit, an automatic response on behalf of the athlete. If the athlete learns a particular skill incorrectly, because the coach has failed to point out the error, it becomes more difficult to change the habit because it has become routine for the athlete; it has become ingrained in the repertoire of the individual.

An example of this can be seen in the case of a 7th grade basketball player, who is right handed, and is allowed to shoot a lay-up from the left side of the basket with the right hand. The correct technique is for the athlete, regardless of being either right or left handed, to shoot the lay-up with the left hand with the left leg being extended off of the floor. If this individual is allowed to practice, to learn and to perfect the right handed lay-up from the left side, it will be extremely difficult to change to the left hand when the student is a sophomore or junior in high school. Habits are hard to break. Physical habits are doubly difficult to change.

Even practicing a skill incorrectly for a few minutes can have severe, negative consequences. Thus, it is imperative that coaches pay close attention to their athletes when they initially perform physical skills lest they do so incorrectly and begin to perfect errors, errors that are difficult and time consuming to compensate for or to attempt to correct.

COACHING CONCEPT #368: Use the power of positive reinforcement in teaching and coaching athletes.

Don't concentrate on the negative all of the time. Athletes will make mistakes (even coaches do sometimes, really!!!). When athletes err, make sure they know what they did that was wrong and the consequences resulting from the mistake. Instead of dwelling on the blunder or omission, concentrate on how to correct the faux pas so that it is not repeated, especially in a game situation. There is a big difference between issuing an embarrassing reprimand and pointing out an error made by an athlete.

COACHING CONCEPT #369: Be descriptive when correcting mistakes—don't be judgmental.

When correcting athletes, be sure to do so in a positive, supportive manner. Coaches need to explain in descriptive rather than judgmental language what the mistake was, what caused it, and the steps necessary to correct it. This is so that the athlete knows what the error is, how to correct it, and what will be the positive consequence(s) of performing the skill correctly. Finally, be sure and keep the correction non-personal; the coach should never be *personally* upset or angry with the athlete because of mistakes—even if such actions were the consequence of deliberate malfeasance or because of a lack of trying or effort. Coaches must maintain a professional attitude and presence at all times. The fact remains, the athlete must not be allowed to practice mistakes lest such mistakes become perfected and become habits.

COACHING CONCEPT #370: Use the double sandwich approach when pointing out mistakes and making corrections.

In pointing out a mistake and having the individual athlete make appropriate corrections and adjustments, it is imperative that you, as a coach, not dwell excessively on the mistake itself or you will risk establishing an atmosphere of *fear of failure*. Rather, provide *corrective instruction* and *assessment* for the athlete who is performing a skill, a drill or a routine. The emphasis must remain on the positive, on the learning aspect of the performance. One way to accomplish this is to utilize what is called the double sandwich approach, figure 11.2.

The double sandwich approach consists of providing *two* constructive remarks or comments prior to *and* following constructive suggestions as to how to correct the mistakes. This wrap-around technique helps makes the athletes feel better about themselves and helps motivate them to work even harder to improve their performance. In other words, the athletes' self-image and respect are retained, the motivation level is kept relatively high, and the youngsters are made aware of how to correct the mistakes that were made without an undue emphasis on fear of making other mistakes. Too often athletes are fearful of making mistakes, fearful of being aggressive in terms of their decisions and actions for fear of being admonished and

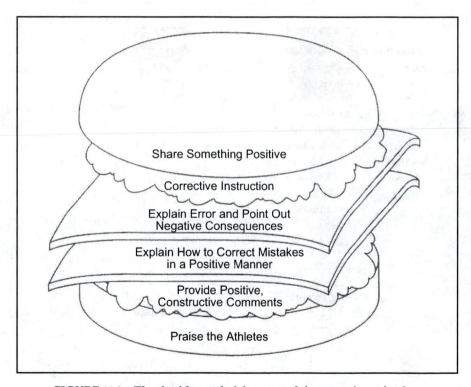

FIGURE 11.2—The double sandwich approach in correcting mistakes

embarrassed by the coach (and others) should a mistake result. The double sandwich approach is described below. The goal is to have athletes identify their mistakes within a positive, wholesome environment or atmosphere, and be able to make appropriate adjustments and timely corrections so that the mistakes will not occur again.

1.   Share *something positive,* if possible, about what the athlete did or attempted to do (effort), etc.
2.   Provide *corrective instruction,* point out specifically *what* they did incorrectly.
3.   Tell *why* it was wrong and the *negative consequences* that can result.
4.   Explain *how* to correct the mistake(s) in an *encouraging* and *positive manner*—not punitive. Emphasize the positive.
5.   *Emphasize* not the mistake but rather *the positive result(s)* from making the corrections or adjustments in the performance and provide *positive, constructive comments* and *encouragement.*
6.   *Praise the athlete* (immediate reinforcement) when the skill is performed correctly.

COACHING CONCEPT #371: An error doesn't become a mistake unless you repeat it—unless you fail to make adjustments and correct it.

Stretching one's ability or reaching for the sky.

It is important that both coaches and athletes realize that it is perfectly permissible to make errors in practices and even in games. It is more important to be able to correct the error so that it is not repeated. Thus, one should not be fearful of making errors as long as the experience itself is a learning experience and that correct actions result from it. When athletes are initially introduced to a skill, the likelihood of athletes picking up the skill immediately and performing it perfectly is very small. Most likely, the players will experiment with that which is to be learned and will practice the skill or maneuver, making some errors, correcting the errors, practicing the activity correctly, and refining its performance over a period of time. Expect that athletes will make errors when learning any physical skill. Just be sure that they learn how to correct their errors so that they can learn to perform the activity correctly.

HAVING ATHLETES MAKE CORRECTIONS

> **COACHING CONCEPT #372: Feedback is an essential coaching tool—it assists both coaches and athletes.**

Athletes deserve to know where they stand in the eyes of the coach. The giving of such information is called feedback. Positive feedback can reinforce learning (Tutko, 1993). Feedback can take the form of providing information to athletes in terms of (1) *specific* learning of skills, and (2) how the athletes are doing in *general*, in comparison with other members of the squad.

In terms of specific learning of skills, athletes deserve to know what they are doing correctly and incorrectly in all phases of their performance, in practices, in competition and away from the sport. This type of feedback is essential for all athletes at all levels. Knowing where one stands in the eyes of the coach enables the individual athlete to know what to work on and what is currently acceptable and what is not.

Qualify feedback consists of the following:

1. Provide sufficient and accurate feedback to the athlete.
2. Don't overload the athlete with 1001 messages, with too much information.
3. Feedback is not synonymous with negative criticism.
4. Don't go overboard by praising every little thing—overdoing it lessens its impact in the future (it doesn't mean as much).
5. Feedback should be restricted to the performance itself (not personal).

Types of Feedback

There are commonly three types of feedback. First, evaluation which is designed to provide information as to *how well* the athlete performed the skill. For example, "You executed a superb jump shot, Barbara." In this instance, the athlete was apprised of the fact that her performance met with the coach's approval and expectation. Second, evaluation can be *corrective* in nature. That is, the coach can provide information to the athlete in terms of what needs to be corrected or changed in order for the skill or performance to be appropriate or enhanced. For example, "Willy, your feet were too close together when you swung the bat." Finally, there is the third form of feedback, that feedback which is *neutral in nature* and merely provides the athlete with information pertinent to the performance. For example, "Reba, your time for the race was 4 minutes and 56 seconds."

All three forms of feedback can help provide the athlete with an accurate picture of one's performance. Such feedback can provide an informative snapshot to the athlete in terms of how the performance is being viewed by others, and in some instances, can also provide insight as to how to improve the performance.

Importance of Feedback in Motivating Athletes and Preventing/Correcting Mistakes

> **COACHING CONCEPT #373: Always attempt to prevent an athlete from practicing an incorrect skill or technique—a learned error is difficult to correct (and impedes learning).**

It has been pointed out earlier that practicing an incorrect skill or maneuver is catastrophic for any athlete. No one would willingly learn an incorrect skill or continue with a performance that is wrong. However, there are many instances in which athletes do indeed continue to practice a specific skill incorrectly. This is simply because, in most cases, they have not been notified of their error and they are not in a position to diagnose the mistake themselves. Thus, it is imperative that coaches take all precautions to prevent such a disaster from occurring in their practices. Calvin Murphy, basketball Hall of Famer, suggests that practice is not productive unless the youngsters possess the right fundamentals and mechanics and that athletes practicing incorrect skills or habits is worse than not even practicing (To hit your best shot, 1993, February 16).

How can a coach prevent significant errors from being practiced by athletes? First of all, the coach must be able to provide immediate feedback to the athlete as soon as the athlete is attempting to perform a newly introduced skill or maneuver. This can be done by viewing each athlete individually as the skill is executed. Or, it can be accomplished in a group setting by the coach viewing a number of athletes or the entire squad as they go through the specific skill or movement pattern. Also, coaches can implement what is referred to as reciprocal coaching. This is a simple technique in which the coach groups athletes in pairs or even small groups of three or four individuals. The coach then instructs each of the athletes as to how to evaluate their peers when they individually perform a specific skill or activity.

In this manner, the coach is able to have numerous athletes serve as peer evaluators, providing critiques to other athletes as they attempt to practice correct techniques and tactics. The key to the success of this reciprocal coaching style is being able to teach individual athletes what to look for in determining whether or not other athletes are correctly performing a skill. An additional benefit of this style of coaching and teaching is that if an athlete can conceptualize and identify the correct and incorrect performance of a skill or activity in a teammate, it is frequently easier for the athlete serving as the evaluator to perform the same skill or activity. This is because the evaluating athlete is able to understand, conceptualize and identify the correct method of performing the activity.

USE OF AUDIO-VISUAL AIDS AND WRITTEN MATERIALS

The use of films and video tapes has had a long history of being used to help coaches in their teaching and coaching efforts. "Sport coaches have long recognized the benefits of video analysis . . . . These days, video analysis has gone digital. The click of a mouse provides instant access to requested scenes" (Gambetta, 2001, p. 27).

The ultimate objective is to help clarify the information and knowledge you are attempting to share via means of pictures and video aids. This can be facilitated by having the athletes being given opportunities to view the correct way of performing a skill or tactic as well as to recognize errors in performance. This, is turn, can be made possible by showing video tapes or films depicting the correct performance of a skill or tactic whether the performance is of an individual or of a team. Many coaches utilize video of their athletes performing correctly or expertly so that these tapes can be used to demonstrate the proper method of executing a skill or routine to other players at a different time.

COACHING CONCEPT #374: **When teaching/coaching—use as many different senses as possible (visual, auditory, touch, smell, taste) to facilitate learning.**

Coaches would do well to consider the option of video taping parts of practices and contests and using such tapes as instructional tools in the teaching of skills, concepts, tactics and strategies to current athletes and future teams. Today, "high school, college, and professional coaches, in a variety of sports all over the world, regularly use videotaped performances and practices to assess, demonstrate to, and motivate their players" (Seifried, 2005, p. 36). Developing and refining video instructional tapes as teaching tapes have been found by many coaches to be a powerful tool to show to individual athletes and teams for the purpose of illustrating how a particular skill, movement or action should be done. Similarly, coaches can also use video tape of their athletes in practices and contests to point out errors or areas of performance which might be improved.

Similarly, the use of overhead transparencies as well as a portable chalk board can be a boon to the coach's efforts to illustrate more complex plays, strategies and tactics. There will be many times when the coach will need to illustrate a point or maneuver, and being able to draw or illustrate the concept can significantly assist the athlete is mastering that which is to be learned.

COACHING CONCEPT #375: Create team handbooks/notebooks—and use them as teaching tools.

Finally, the traditional coaching playbook or handbook can be very beneficial for some coaches. The coaching handbook can contain information regarding the philosophy of the coaching staff, expectations of the athletes, team rules and regulations, operational information regarding home and away contests, as well as very specific information regarding the offensive and defensive strategies and tactics to be used in practice and in game situations. The advantages of such a sport handbook are three-fold. First, such a handbook forces the coach to crystallize one's thinking and philosophy in terms of the sport and to put in writing one's philosophy, etc. The coach is forced to think things through in respect to what is to be expected of the athletes. The second advantage is that the sport handbook can really aid in the learning of the offensive and defensive maneuvers of team sports, in the performance of the skills involved in the sport, and can set the tone in terms of the philosophy and the expectations of the athletes. Naturally, parents of the athletes would have an opportunity to view their youngsters' sport handbook or playbook. The third advantage of creating and using such a playbook is the positive image or reputation that the coach can derive from its use from the school administration, the parents, and the general public. If the playbook or handbook is professionally written, printed and bound—the mere existence of the playbook can be a boon in terms of the positive public relations fallout for the coach.

CONCLUDING PRACTICES

COACHING CONCEPT #376: Always end a practice on a positive note—never send youngsters home with a sour taste in their mouths (about themselves, about the coaches or about the program).

Always, always, end a practice on a positive note. This refers to the team as a whole and each individual athlete. Never have the athletes leave practice thinking negative thoughts about themselves, about you the coach, or about the program itself. That negative feeling and atmosphere all too often is carried by the athletes and can begin to eat at their insides and can affect their future motivation and performance, both at practices and in actual competition.

All too frequently, coaches will attempt to discipline athletes by kicking them out of practice or making them hit the showers before the rest of the players conclude their practice session. This is not a wise move. Athletes who depart on a sour note can carry that negative feeling with them until the next practice session. This negativism can, in fact, have an adverse effect upon the next practice and upon an individual athlete's subsequent performance(s). Why would a coach want an athlete or a whole team to leave a practice session in a negative and dejected mood? What positive consequences will come from such a situation? Few, if any.

However, there is ample evidence that some coaches do just that, they end a practice session on a down note, on a negative theme. Some indicate that they do so in order to motivate their athletes, a form of negative, fear or punitive motivation. And yet, some of these same coaches still manage to win. Does that mean that other coaches or would-be coaches should emulate their actions? No, not at all. Perhaps those same coaches who coach that way might experience greater success, on and off the competitive playing field, if they avoided operating through the medium of fear or negativism. Thus, it is important that young, beginning coaches not copy or emulate this type of negative coaching just because some coaches who happen to be successful in the won/loss column exhibit this type of behavior.

Instead, the coach should strive to make sure that every athlete leaves the practice session following some positive individual (or group) achievement. The coach should verbally emphasize the achievements of individual athletes (privately or publicly) as well as the accomplishments of the team as a whole. Of course, the coach will also want to point out what still needs to be worked on. But the major objective is to emphasize the positive aspects of the just concluded practice (hopefully there is some positive aspect that can be highlighted).

This is done to help the individual develop a strong, positive self-concept and to help motivate the individual. Athletes should depart a practice looking back at their accomplishments and achievements, not their failures. They should be anxiously looking forward to the next practice where they will again have an opportunity to learn something, to master something, to refine something, to demonstrate competency in *something*.

PREPARING THE TEAM FOR COMPETITION— STRATEGIC DECISIONS

There are many decisions that a coach must make every single day. However, some of the most important decisions to be made revolve around those that affect the so-called game day or actual competition. These decisions are critical because they affect the outcome of the actual competition against one's opponents. Many of these decisions are made well in advance of the actual day of the contest while others are made the day of the game or event, but before the competition begins, while still others are made during the course of the competition itself. And, of course, there are those decisions to be made following the end of the contest, when the team has emerged either victorious or having been defeated, or in some sports, having been tied by the opposing team.

> **COACHING CONCEPT #377: Coaches need to pay attention to the execution of what an athlete does—rather than merely on whether or not the attempt was successful.**

Sometimes there is a significant difference between what or how an athlete performs a skill and the actual result of that performance. For example, a base runner might have successfully stolen home even though the 3rd base coach had not called for the steal. Or, a basketball player might have successfully driven to the basket for just one more score even after the coach had instructed the team to run out the clock. Or, a quarterback might have successfully thrown a pass for a touchdown right through three unseen defenders who, only through luck, did not intercept the ball and run for an uncontested touchdown.

What do all three of the above examples have in common? Well, to begin with, each has the athlete being successful in terms of the *end result*. That is, the performance of each of the athletes resulted in success in terms of a base being stolen, a made field goal and a touchdown being made. However, each of these examples also involved a significant error or mistake. Should coaches really be primarily concerned with end results or is the form or process equally or even more important?

The answer is that the end result does not excuse errors in performance, in judgment or in execution. The point that the particular act was successful or that the contest ended in a victory should be immaterial in terms of evaluating the overall performance of the players and the team. There can be many instances in which the performance of the athletes (as well as the coach) can be substandard and yet the team might be victorious over the opposition (who also could have performed poorly). The important thing for coaches to remain focused on is the actual performance of the athletes. Did the individual athletes and the team as a whole perform adequately, regardless of the eventual outcome of the contest?

COACHING CONCEPT #378: Following a victory, coaches should critically analyze the performances of athletes (and themselves) as if the competition had resulted in defeat—don't let a victory distort the actual performance level of one's team.

A final example to emphasize the point. In a game of basketball, both teams might come down to the wire with only seconds to play and the score is tied. One team finally scores and emerges the victor while the other team becomes the vanquished. The winning coach and athletes are all smiles and feel happy and confident in their hard fought victory. The losing coach and athletes are dejected and are critical of their performance that ended in a defeat. *However,* the winning coach and athletes should not be so concerned with the end result but with the quality and level of play they exhibited throughout the game, regardless of the eventual outcome in the won/loss column. One lucky field goal near the end of the game does not eliminate or cover-up all of the lackluster performances displayed in that game. Yet, that is exactly what some coaches seem to do after a victory. They focus on the end result, the victory, and forget all of the individual and team performances within that game. Ditto for the coach of the losing team.

Thus, a coach should not view a contest differently just because the game ended in a win or a loss. The wise coach views the performance of the team and each individual participant (athletes and coaches) with a critical eye in terms of what was successful and what needs further work. Coaches who, following a victory, look at the team's performance through rose colored glasses and only see the victory itself are only fooling themselves and can, in fact, hinder the overall progress of the team and the athletes.

COACHING CONCEPT #379: No one knows athletes like the coach—the coach sees each individual in the best of times and the worst of times.

Athletes are very close to the coach and vice versa. In many coaching situations there is no one who knows the athlete as well as the coach. That is because the coach has the opportunities to see the individual athlete in a wide range of circumstances, both positive and negative, both enjoyable and painful, both difficult and easy. Probably no one else, not even the parents, are able to see the individual athlete perform and act in such a wide range of different circumstances and settings, some more challenging than others. Yet, there will always be those individuals, non-coaches, who think that they know the athletes better than anyone and know just how these athletes should be used in the greater athletic scheme of things. How tragic, both for the individuals holding such an erroneous opinion and, in some instances, for the athletes as well.

The author once had an adult fan come up to him following a contest commenting on how wonderful and dedicated a certain athlete must be. This fan was able to discern how super-duper the athlete was due to the energy and enthusiasm with which the youngster performed in the pre-game warm-up exercises. The author regretfully, but diplomatically, pointed out that the fan only gets to see this athlete during the pregame warm-ups. The coach, on the other hand, sees the athlete every day in practice, under challenging and varying circumstances.

It would also had been possible to point out to the fan that perhaps the reason why the youngster was so energetic during the warm-ups was because he wanted to impress his girl friend sitting in the stands. Additionally, there was not a lot of pressure on this athlete when all he had to do was to shoot uncontested lay-ups and short field goals before the game even started.

This story has an important moral to it for all coaches. No one usually knows individual athletes like the coach does because of the close working relationship of the coach/athlete. The coach and the athlete see each other and work with each other in the best of times and in the worst of times. Yet, there will always be Monday morning quarterbacks and fans who feel that they know more about your players than you, the coach. Such is life. Coaches need to live with this reality while attempting to educate fans and the general public.

Determining the Starting Lineup

Determining who will start and who will not is a challenging and difficult job for any coach. Yet, this decision is a critical one. So, too, is the decision as to which athlete or athletes will best fill the role of a substitute, that is, coming cold off the bench, to assume an immediate playing position in the heat of battle.

> **COACHING CONCEPT #380: It is the responsibility, the prerogative of the coach to determine who will play, when, and at what position.**

As stated previously in an earlier chapter, it is the inherent right of the head coach to pick the members of the team. Similarly, it is up to the head coach, and no one else, to make the final decision as to who will play and who will sit the bench.

And it is the responsibility of the coach to also determine what position each player will assume. Naturally, coaches will seek feedback from assistant coaches (if any). And, coaches will seek to use factual information, hard data, to come to a defensible conclusion in terms of who will start, etc. But, the buck stops at the desk of the head coach, period.

Being a head coach and shouldering the responsibility of determining who will start, who will play and what role each athlete will assume is just one of the tough burdens of a head coach. However, this responsibility comes with the territory. This is one decision that the head coach cannot really delegate to anyone else. Regardless of the recommendations received, the ultimate decision, and the ultimate responsibility (blame or accolades), is the head coach's alone.

COACHING CONCEPT #381: **Coaches need to keep statistics and records of individual and team performances in games—on-the-spot decisions can be facilitated by viewing hard data.**

Keeping statistics of individual and team performances in games can provide a partial picture or snapshot of how well the athletes are currently performing. It is important for a coach to maintain some type of statistics in every sport. In some sports, statistics play a more prominent role than in other sports, merely by the very nature of the sport itself. Many important coaching decisions can be made on the basis of such information, such hard data.

One word of warning when it comes to keeping records and statistics. The information collected must be accurate and consistent. Using data to provide a pattern of behavior or performance is very important. However, if the data is flawed or biased, is not accurately depicting what takes place in the competitive scene, it is useless. Such information is not only useless; it is dangerous and can impede the decision making process as well as hinder the team's progress. Thus, coaches must take adequate steps to insure that whoever keeps statistics does so in a careful and flawless manner. It is recommended that adults, trained in keeping such records, be used as bench statisticians so that the coach can be assured of accurate and timely data. Don't rely on athletes sitting on the bench to keep unofficial game statistics. You are just asking for trouble and flawed data.

COACHING CONCEPT #382: **Don't emphasize the amount of playing time individual athletes get—stress teamwork rather than individual achievement.**

One statistic which the author strongly recommends not publicizing to the players or to the public is the actual playing time of athletes in those team sports where playing time is a factor. Publicizing statistics regarding playing time can hurt moral in the long run. It is too easy for youngsters to target in on their own playing time and, if they feel that they are not getting sufficient playing time, to become disgruntled team members.

If coaches really feel that they need this type of information so that they can base some decisions regarding individual athletes, it is still possible to keep such statistics but yet not disseminate the information to the athletes, their parents and the general public. Playing time can be divisive if not used in a constructive fashion. In general, making available the playing time of each athlete to everyone does not seem productive in the long run. In other words, more negative than positive consequences usually result. Again, this comes back to the topic of selfishness among athletes. Coaches should promote the team concept rather than the *me-me* concept. Publicizing the statistic on playing time is likely to emphasize the *me-me* or I perspective. And, as stated before, there should be no *I* in team.

Determining Playing Time

COACHING CONCEPT #383: Coaches need to use both subjective and objective judgment in arriving at who will start and who will play the role of a substitute.

In making any important decision, it is necessary to rely on both subjective and/or objective data. Hence, there is nothing wrong with a coach making a decision based upon that coach's experience or that coach's feelings about what an athlete can and cannot do in actual competition. Yes, it is helpful to be able to look at concrete data, statistics, and then to come to a conclusion. However, statistics do not tell the entire story. There is still a need for the coach to rely upon one's experience, one's feelings, one's interpretation of events and circumstances, in arriving at many decisions, including the decisions as to who will start, when players will play, and who will assume what positions or roles within the team.

Similarly, making decisions regarding the substituting of players in team competition is often done on the basis of the coach's feelings, the coach's interpretation of what is happening in the actual contest, and the coach's reading of which athlete might be able to be more successful at that particular point in time, within the competitive environment that exists in the game at that exact moment.

It is not possible to break down or attribute every coaching decision to mere statistics. If it was, there would be no need for experienced coaches. Rather, it takes competent mentors to successfully interpret the present situation, based upon one's experience, knowledge as well as feelings and gut reactions—and then to make appropriate decisions in light of the available circumstances facing the team at that moment.

COACHING CONCEPT #384: **Coaches should be aware of the synergistic effect of playing the right combination of athletes at any one time.**

Some athletes perform better or play at a higher plane when matched or paired with other athletes. The synergism that can result when the right combination is obtained on the playing field can frequently be seen in competitive team sports. It is a case of chemistry being created when individual players are placed together. In such an instance, the whole is far greater than the sum of its parts. In the case of team sports such as basketball, field hockey or soccer, getting just the right combination of players on the floor or field at one time can produce a highly competent, competitive unit that performs at a higher level than is possible through the use of any other combination of players on that team.

COACHING CONCEPT #385: **Athletes should earn the right to start on the basis of their performance in practices and in actual competition.**

Athletes need to actually demonstrate their competency and skill level in order to earn the right to play or to start a game. This demonstration of skill can take place in two areas. First, the athlete can use practice sessions to demonstrate to the coach (es) that the individual can indeed perform the skills and maneuvers at an acceptable level. Second, the athlete can use playing time (if given the opportunity) in a game or contest to demonstrate what the individual is capable of doing in actual competition. In effect, coaches need to provide to athletes the opportunity to earn their right to play (or start) in competition by demonstrating their superior performance of skills in practices *and* in actual games.

Catch-22 Situation—Earning the Right to be a Starter

There is one trap that some coaches fall into, however, when it comes time to making a decision regarding a player's playing time. That is, the youngsters are told that they must prove themselves by performing well in game situations and then these same athletes are never given an opportunity to do that. That is, they are never placed in a real competitive game setting where the coach can see how the players

**Positioning oneself
for the ball and the score.**

will react under actual game pressure. In this situation, those athletes who are not starting or not getting a lot of playing time are caught in a catch-22 situation. They can't get a starting berth or significant playing time until they demonstrate that they can play in a pressure situation in a real game. And, they can't get the opportunity to play in a pressure situation, in an actual contest, because the coach doesn't have confidence in their ability to handle such pressure and that is because the coach has never seen the athletes successfully handle such game pressure. This type of catch-22 situation can become a vicious circle for the athlete.

Thus, in this type of situation, there must be opportunities for athletes to earn a starting berth or significant playing time *by demonstrating their skills during practice sessions*. This may require the coach to create, in practices, game-like situations in which athletes can experience realistic game pressure and competition. Scrimmages can often serve as a proving ground for would-be starters. And, coaches must be more willing to substitute and play these future or would-be starters more frequently in actual game situations. Coaches must be risk-takers.

COACHING CONCEPT #386: Never keep a senior on the team unless that individual will be a starter OR is willing and capable of serving, as a non-starter, as an excellent role model and motivator for the other players.

Being a senior on a team and not being a starter can be a real challenge for many athletes. Whether it is ego or what, the problem remains that it takes a special type of dedicated, unselfish individual to play a role of a non-starter as a senior. Many a coach has experienced dire consequences from keeping a senior on a team who is not going to be a starter. Dissension among such seniors is common. So, too, is the creation of negative role models, individuals who not only do not serve as leaders but deliberately create roadblocks for the coach and the other athletes to overcome.

In this light, it is suggested that coaches not keep a non-starting senior on the squad unless it is clear to the coach, and the senior, that the role of such an individual is to serve as a model, a true leader, one who can motivate the younger players by one's own example of dedication, hard work, sacrifice, and teamwork—even though the senior is not a starter. If the non-starting senior is capable *and* willing to assume this role, then keeping the individual on the squad is justified and worthwhile. For the younger players can look to the non-playing or non-starting senior and marvel at that person's commitment and effort for the welfare of the team.

Suffice to say there is always potential for a senior to become disgruntled in being assigned a secondary role on the team, that is, as a non-starter. This is especially true if the athlete had previously assumed a starting role as a junior or even as a sophomore. It does take a special person, as a senior, to graciously play a supportive role on a team and yet still serve as a motivating factor for other players. The risk of a non-starting senior becoming a malcontent is very real and coaches need to be on the guard lest they become saddled with such a burden. One rotten apple can indeed spoil the entire barrel, especially if the apple happens to be a senior, or worse yet, several seniors.

> **COACHING CONCEPT #387: Seniors deserve a right to start and play only if they are substantially superior to juniors and sophomores—coaches need to look to the future.**

This is a controversial position for any coach to take. However, it is one that faces every high school varsity coach as well as every college or university varsity coach. What does one do with seniors on the team in terms of playing time? Does the senior, especially in high school, deserve to be a starter just by the nature of being a senior and having stayed with the program for four years? Or, should the coach play the best athlete regardless of what year in school the player is in? If the senior is equal to a junior athlete or an underclassperson, should the senior get the nod to start and play?

Such a decision is a very personal one for head coaches. And the eventual disposition of this challenge will depend upon many factors and circumstances in which the coach and the team members find themselves. The situation is a little different for high school coaches than for college coaches. In high school, the argument goes like this: "Athletes who are seniors have been a part of the program for the previous three years and don't deserve to sit the pine as seniors. They deserve to have their chance to represent the school since they have put in their time." The argument against this line of thinking is that: "Participation on a team is not earned by mere longevity but, rather, on the basis of skill and the ability to contribute to the team." On the college level, where there is even greater emphasis, usually, placed upon winning and being competitive, there is less pressure to play or start seniors as long as the team is otherwise successful, that is, the team is victorious in competition.

In general, however, the author suggests that the best athletes—at both the high school and college levels—should start and play. Now, the definition of the best athletes might differ from coach to coach and from situation to situation. However, generally speaking, those individuals who are the best athletes, those who are able to contribute the most to the overall goals of the team, deserve the right to play and to start. If the best athletes, however this is defined, happen to be juniors, sophomores or even freshman, then these athletes should play, should start, over the less skilled athletes on the team. Of course, the coach is then left with the challenge of how to handle those athletes (and their parents and friends) who are seniors or juniors and who are playing behind younger athletes. No one ever said coaching was easy.

Making Intelligent Decisions in Actual Game Situations—
Being a Good Game Coach

COACHING CONCEPT #388: Successful coaches make smart strategic moves in the heat of battle, in actual competition.

Making appropriate and timely decisions in the heat of battle, in actual competition, is the mark of a competent and experienced coach. During contests, when there are a myriad of things to be aware of, it is extremely difficult for the coach to be able to interpret and process all of the input that can go to make up a coach's decision. Thus, it is important for a coach to concentrate on being capable and willing to make quick but yet appropriate, and hopefully, correct decisions. It is the game decisions (being a good bench coach) that really separate the superior coaches from the would-be successful mentors.

It is one thing to be a good practice coach. In practice, there is almost always more time to make decisions. In practice, there is usually not the hurried or pressure packed atmosphere that commonly exists in the real world of athletic competition. However, in actual games or contests, it is a different matter. In actual competition, time is of the essence. Being a competent game coach means making split second decisions, decisions that are a result of experience and interpretation (the art of coaching) as much as relying upon mere data or statistics.

COACHING CONCEPT #389: Coaches should not shoot themselves in the foot by committing stupid mistakes—think (of the consequences) before you act.

There are enough problems facing coaches today without shooting themselves in the foot by doing really stupid things, especially in game situations when such mistakes are readily seen by one and all. For example, an inexperienced high school basketball coach once had a 29 point lead on an opponent late in the first half. Thinking that the other players should get an opportunity to get some playing time, the coach liberally substituted other players. The only problem was that the other team did not likewise substitute but kept in their starters. Soon, too soon, the big lead was slowly eaten away. Then the smaller lead began to rapidly disappear. Then the starters were quickly returned to the game with only a very small lead. However, at that point in time, the starters were cold from sitting on the bench for over a quarter and a half. As a result, the opponents quickly caught up and even took the lead for a brief time. In the end, however, the team that initially had the big lead managed to hold on for dear life and emerged victorious, in overtime.

After the game, the coach was lambasted from all quarters, by parents, by fans, by members of the booster club, by the general public, by the news media and even by the athletic director. In fact, one of the parents indicated to the coach, as the coach was leaving the building that night, that had the team lost through such a stupid move, the coach should have been packing the next day. Remember, there are some things that are just stupid and which should not be done, period. Be forewarned; don't shoot yourself in the foot. In hindsight, the coach should not have taken out all of the starters at one time. Keeping one, two, or even three starters in the game while substituting for the remaining positions might have perhaps prevented this near catastrophe from occurring.

An Example of Shooting Oneself in the Foot

Coaches should act like knowledgeable mentors. Coaches should present themselves as professionals and make appropriate and intelligent decisions. They need to make the right decisions during the game. Take the example of the college football coach who failed to do just that. At a home game, with some 25 seconds left in the first half, and his team down by 2 touchdowns, the ball was positioned on his team's own 25-yard line. Fourth down was coming up and the team possessed a total gain of minus 3-yards for the half. Under these circumstances the football coach shot himself in the foot with both barrels and called for a long pass play.

The pass was intercepted and run back to the 15 yard line. On the next play, the opposing team passed the ball into the end zone for the third touchdown of the first half.

When the coach was asked the reason for the pass call by the athletic director the next day, the football coach replied: "There was only 25 seconds left, I thought we could get a long pass completed and move the ball the 75 yards for a touchdown. Then we would have only been down by 7 points rather than 14. Besides, I figured that even if the pass was intercepted, that the opponents would not be able to score in the limited amount of time that was left."

Such illogical, flawed thinking is what gets coaches into hot water. That was a poor coaching decision. It was a terrible coaching decision and everyone in the stands knew it. It showed a lack of understanding of the game of football and caused the competency of the head coach to be questioned.

Shooting oneself in the foot, as this college mentor did, does absolutely nothing to endear the coach to the players, the parents, the fans, or to the sport administration. The conclusion is obvious. Don't shoot yourself in the foot by making obvious mistakes for everyone to see. Don't make stupid mistakes. Think before you act. Coaches who make obviously absurd mistakes in judgment do not find themselves coaching for very long.

COACHING CONCEPT #390: Never embarrass an athlete during a game.

When athletes commit a turnover or mistake in a game, they are usually immediately aware of the error. Yet, how many times have we seen supposedly intelligent coaches scream and yell, rank and rave, at their charges because the individual made a mistake. It is almost as if the coach is trying to convince the crowd that the mistake was not the coach's, that the coach did not teach the youngster to do such a stupid thing, and that the whole responsibility should be burdened by the athlete. As a result, coaches continue to yell and berate their players for every little mistake made.

The result is that athletes are embarrassed by their coaches. Worse yet, they are shamed in public, in front of their friends, their classmates, their peers, and their parents and family members. And, the athletes have to stand there (at least the vast majority of them do) and continue to take this verbal abuse by their coaches. How tragic. How stupid.

There is never a valid reason to embarrass your athletes, especially in public. There is just not a good or acceptable justification for doing so. It does not facilitate communication with the athlete. It does not build confidence in the athlete. It does not help the learning process. What it probably does do is make the coach feel better. But, what a price to pay. Treat each of your athletes with the dignity and the respect that you would like to be treated or that you would expect your own child to be treated.

COACHING CONCEPT #391: Never publicly blame individual athletes for a loss.

Blaming athletes or a team for a loss, especially publicly, is just counter productive. No single athlete ever causes the loss of the game. That is because no athletic contest is ever played without numerous mistakes and errors being committed by athletes, coaches and officials alike. Thus, when a coach singles out one athlete and places the burden of defeat on that person's shoulders, the coach is really saying that everyone else associated with the contest performed in a perfect manner and that this one individual, or this one act or failure to act resulted in the loss, the defeat, the humiliation. Hogwash. Coaches should know better and they certainly should act differently.

Criticizing an athlete or the team publicly is just foolhardy. This also involves the humiliation of one's players, individually and/or as a team. There is just no reason to do so. If criticism must be pointed out, then make it constructive criticism on an individual basis or on a team basis, within the confines of the locker room or the practice facility. But, don't hang out one's dirty laundry for all to see. Don't publicly assign the blame for a loss upon any one individual unless it is upon yourself. Coaches need to remember that "there is no such thing as *off the record* when dealing with the media" (Steinbach, 2005, p. 26) and act accordingly, especially when dealing with or talking about athletes and parents.

KNOWING THE RULES OF THE SPORT

> **COACHING CONCEPT #392: The coach must know the rules of the sport—and the athletes must demonstrate knowledge of the rules as well.**

It goes without saying that coaches should know the rules of the sport that they coach. In fact, they should be experts in the rules. However, this is far from the case with most coaches, regardless of the level at which they coach. In reality, coaches should be competent officials in the sport(s) they coach. They should actually study and sit for the examination that is used to qualify individuals as officials in that particular sport. Coaches who are knowledgeable in the rules and who are qualified officials themselves not only have a better understanding of the sport itself, but an added insight into the role and challenges of the officials—information that can be of benefit in one's coaching efforts.

Similarly, the athletes need to know the rules of the game that they are playing. Taking time to teach the athletes the rules can certainly result in a better chance for victory. Of course, this is to be expected of any team and a coach should not get any extra brownie points for simply doing what is expected of a coach, that is, teaching the players the rules of the game.

However, perhaps a more important aspect to remember is when the athletes or the coach demonstrates a lack of knowledge of the rules and regulations. It is when such a faux pas occurs (not knowing the rules of the game or misinterpreting them) that the coach is really exposed as being not as competent as expected. Don't be an idiot and embarrass yourself by not knowing the rules. Nothing makes a coach look worse—in the eyes of the players, the athletic administration and the general public—than not knowing the rules of the sport one has been hired to coach.

> **COACHING CONCEPT #393: Never run up the score against an opponent—coaches have long memories and the worm does indeed turn.**

Coaches would do well to exhibit the high standards of sportsmanship. For example, running up the score against a hapless opponent is ill advised for several reasons. First of all, it is poor sportsmanship. Second, the worm usually turns sometime in the future and such inappropriate actions will be returned ten fold. Third, such action can create a negative reputation among one's coaching peers and there might well be retaliation from any number of other teams. No one looks good in a lopsided scoring frenzy—neither the winning team nor the losing squad. Coaches need to earn the respect of their peers. This is accomplished by acting in a professional manner and treating others with respect and honesty. It involves never embarrassing a peer and not taking an unfair advantage of someone's misfortune.

> **COACHING CONCEPT #394: Coaches must be humble in victory and gracious in defeat.**

No one likes an arrogant person. Everyone detests an arrogant coach. Coaches need to be mindful that how they are perceived by others is all important in establishing an image and reputation as a person and as a coach. Whether winning or losing as a coach, be humble and gracious. Never present oneself as a know-it-all or as an egotistical fanatic. While some coaches who are highly successful might be able to get away with such antics while they are winning, it is nevertheless never really acceptable. And, heaven forbid that the team/coach should experience a drop in the success ratio in the future. When that time comes, the offending coach soon finds out whose one's friends really are (if there are any). When the arrogant or egotistical coach, who is sometimes tolerated because of a highly successful team or teams, becomes less successful, the sharks seem to come out of nowhere for the kill.

When you are successful as a coach, be humble. When you are involved in a defeat, accept it not with polite resignation but with a strong desire to do better in the future, without offering excuses upon excuses for failure.

REFERENCES

Bolles, R. C. (1977). Theory of motivation. Scranton, PA: Harper & Row Publishers.

Cohen, A. (1992, December). Standard Time. *Athletic Business, 16*(12), 23-26, 28.

Deci, E.L. (1985). *Intrinsic motivation.* New York: *Plenum Press Company.*

Gambetta, V. (1999). Breaking through plateaus. *Training & Conditioning, IX*(8). 19-23.

Gambetta, V. (2001). The digital difference. *Training & Conditioning, XI*(9). 27-32.

Hansen, B., Gilbert, W., & Hamel, T. (2003). Successful coaches' views on motivation and motivational strategies. *Journal of Physical Education, Recreation and Dance, 74*(8), 45-48.

Mackay, H. (1988). *How to swim with the sharks without being eaten alive.* Ivy Books, New York: Ballatine Books.

Martin, G. L. & Lunsden, J.A. (1987). *Coaching: An effective behavioral approach.* St. Louis: Times Mirror/Mosby.

Seifried, C. (2005). Using video athletic contests within Mosston's teaching methods. *Journal of Physical Education, Recreation and Dance, 76*(5), 36-38.

Siedentop, D. (1991). *Developing teaching skills in physical education* (3rd ed.). Mountain View, California: Mayfield Publishing Company.

Steinbach, P. (2005, September). On the record. *Athletic Business,* p. 26.

Smith, L. (2005, April/May). Mind over matter. *Athletic Management, XVII*(3), 24—26, 28-31

Stier, W. F., Jr. (1988, September). Does the sex of the coach really matter? *Journal of Physical Education, Recreation and Dance, 69*(9), 13.

Stier, W. F. Jr., (1988). The pragmatic versus the philosophical approach to coaching sport—The assessment of the athletic experience by athletes. *Proceedings of the United States Olympic Academy XII, June 15-18, 1988.* Penn State University Park Campus, pp. 199-206.

To hit your best shot, hit the gym. (1993, February 16). *USA Today,* p. 2-C.

Tutko, T. (1993, Summer). The underachiever. *Sports Psychology,* 8(4), 1-4.

Voight, M. (2005). Integrating mental-skills training into everyday coaching. *Journal of Physical Education, Recreation and Dance, 76*(3), 38-47.

Warren, W. E. (1989). *Coaching and winning.* Englewood Cliffs, New Jersey: Parker Publisher Company.

Wolff, A. (1989, March 20-26). The coach and his champion. *Sports Illustrated*, pp. 94-98, 100, 104-106, 111.

Name: _____

Student ID #: _____

EXERCISES FOR CHAPTER 11

A. Select short, intermediate and long range goals for a specific high school player in a sport of your choice. List goals under each of these categories and justify your choice of such goals.

B. How would you go about motivating athletes in a team sport? Be specific. Establish a situation in which you, as the coach, are involved with a typical group of high school or youth sport youngsters and explain your motivational tactics and strategies. Also, what would be different, if anything, if the sport was an individual team sport such as track & field, cross country, or swimming?

C. Why should or shouldn't athletes on the bench be involved in keeping needed game statistics (not official records) for the coach? Explain your position and, if your viewpoint is that they should not keep such statistics, how would you go about getting the statistics recorded during all games?

_____

_____

_____

_____

_____

_____

D. What is your current thinking about how to handle the senior athlete on your soccer team who is not as good as some juniors and sophomores? How would you deal with the senior? Would you keep the individual on team?

_____

_____

_____

_____

_____

_____

E. How could you make practices enjoyable for athletes? Be specific.

_____

_____

_____

_____

_____

_____

RESEARCH QUESTONS FOR CHAPTER 11

1. Interview a coach who coaches a team of opposite sex athletes and find out the challenges posed by coaching the opposite sex and what step the coach takes to insure a productive learning experience for the athletes.

   ----

2. Ask a coach of a team or individual sport how the coach recognizes when an athlete has improved and when improvement is not forthcoming and what the coach does to help the athlete who is not improving as expected.

   ----

3. Survey several coaches and find out their practice or philosophy regarding the length of practices (time wise) during the preseason, in-season and post season time frames and the rationale for their position.

   ----

4. Interview a coach of a flagship varsity sport and find out what type of statistics and records are used for the individual athletes and for the team as a whole.

----

5. Survey coaches of team sports and find out their opinions as to their self-assessment of their skills as a bench coach and as a game coach and why the coaches think of themselves as they do.

Chapter 12

Problem Solving Strategies for Coaches

**Press row overlooking an athletic contest—
an important aspect of any sport competition.**

As stated in chapter five, one of the important responsibilities of coaches is to be able deal with problems. In fact, almost everything a coach does can be thought of as dealing with some type of problem or challenge. Many of thee problems are relatively minor and/or routine, involving everyday obligations and responsibilities, events or activities. Developing a series of practice plans for the upcoming week is an example of overcoming a routine problem or challenge. Similarly, choosing which players will start a particular game is another example of problem solving as is deciding which player to substitute out of as well as into an actual contest.

> **COACHING CONCEPT #395:**   **Problems, of differing severity, occur in the sport world— that is just the nature of the profession.**

However, there are other difficulties, problems or challenges which will confront the coach (at every level of amateur competition) which are of a more series nature. These may have the potential for far more serious consequences, implications or impact upon the coach and the coach's sports program. Whether the problems or difficulties faced by the coach are relatively routine and minor or unusual and more serious one essential element remains the same and that is the fact that the coach must be able to make appropriate and timely decisions.

> **COACHING CONCEPT #396:**   **Problem solving involves making appropriate and timely decisions.**

A coach's life is really composed of a series of decision making situations in which the individual is confronted with a challenge or a situation and the coach is forced, due to the nature of coaching, to arrive at a suitable decision. It is this decision making responsibility which is so important for the eventual success of the individual coach.

PREVENTING PROBLEMS

Before dealing with how problems can be adequately dealt with it should be pointed out that coaches should be concerned with preventing problems from cropping up in the first place. A problem prevented is a situation which does not have to be dealt with by a coach.

> **COACHING CONCEPT #397:**   **A key to problem solving is prevention and the key to prevention is anticipation.**

How does one prevent problems? By conducting oneself as a professional coach would be expected to do. By anticipating problems a coach is often able to take precautionary action so that the causes of the problem are non-existent. By anticipating possible problems developing the coach can make decisions and take actions which will prevent such problems from ever arising in the first place.

However, the coach must be capable of both anticipating a possible problem(s) *and* doing something about the situation so that the problem(s) does not become reality. It does no good to anticipate that some of the athletes might become involved in underage drinking or in drugs without the coach making some advance decisions and then taking some precautionary action to help prevent such a situation from becoming reality.

When it comes to preventing problems the adage *the proof is in the pudding* is most appropriate. Anticipating problems without doing something to prevent their occurrence doesn't count. Rather, it is being able to anticipate problems and difficulties and then to do something which will prevent these problems from happening that is at the crux of problem solving. When problems do crop up, when difficulties do arise, when challenges must be faced (as will invariably happen) it is up to the coach to then assume a different mode, that of problem solver.

STEPS INVOLVED IN DEALING WITH PROBLEMS AND CHALLENGES

COACHING CONCEPT # 398:   One has to become aware of a problem before one
                             can attempt to deal with the problem.

There are five basic steps involved in the problem solving process. The *first* is to be able to be aware of the problem and to recognize the situation as a potential problem for the coach, the athlete, or the sports program. Without this recognition of the existence of a problem there can be no attempt to resolve the situation. All too often coaches fail to recognize the early signs of a problematic situation until it is too late and what might have initially been a minor problem mushrooms into a major difficulty with significant repercussions, consequences and implications for all concerned.

The *second* step of problem is to become aware of all of the pertinent and accurate facts (circumstances) surrounding the problem situation. Without adequate information the coach is usually unable (or finds it to be extremely more difficult) to arrive at an appropriate plan of attack to resolve the problem. This collection of information relates to hard data (facts, irrefutable information, pictures, tapes, records, etc.) as well as soft data (opinions, thoughts, hearsay, etc.). The goal at this point in the problem solving effort is to gather as much information and facts (data) as possible so that the coach is fully aware of the extenuating circumstances as they affect the current problematic situation.

COACHING CONCEPT #399:   Problems left unattended has the tendency to
                            grow into bigger and more difficult problems.

Actually arriving at a suitable (and well thought out) plan of attack in terms of dealing with the problem is the *third* step in problem solving. It is at this point that the coach needs to arrive at a reasonable plan of how the problem might be dealt with, that is, resolved or solved.

COACHING CONCEPT #400:   **Coaches should deal with difficulties and problems when they are cool, calm and collected.**

However, it is absolutely essential that the coach remain cool, calm and collected when considering all of the various options open relative to addressing the problem. It does no good at all; in fact it is far too often a significant impediment to wise decision making and appropriate action to be too emotionally involved in the situation. One should be professionally detached in the decision making process. One should be emotionally neutral when considering various options. To do otherwise would place the coach in jeopardy of making a poor decision based on an emotional response. Professionals aren't supposed to do that. Reason and careful thinking should permeate the planning process of the successful athletic problem solver. The plan of action should be based on solid facts and sound reasoning, not hampered by emotional entanglements.

The *fourth* step involves the implementation of this plan. Someone actually has to do something—or deliberately choose to do nothing. Usually it is the coach who must initiate action or a series of actions which will hopefully result in an acceptable (in the eyes of most of the people involved) resolution of the problem, difficulty or conflict.

COACHING CONCEPT #401:   **Usually problem solving requires some type of deliberate action on behalf of the coach.**

Problems Consume Valuable Resources

When one is involved in addressing a particularly serious or distressing problem it is important to recognize that not only must the problem be addressed but the coach's regular obligations and duties must also be met. One cannot simply forget about one's other responsibilities and drop everything to handle the BIG PROBLEM. If the problem occurs during the season the coach must still be involved in performing those tasks and fulfilling those responsibilities of a coach during the season—plus addressing the problem situation.

Whenever there is a problem to be addressed it is also important to realize that a specific number of resources must be directed at the problem. These resources can involve money, time, personnel, facilities, equipment, etc. Additionally, the amount of time, effort and money spent in the problem solving arena should be appropriate to the seriousness of the problem. One shouldn't attempt to kill a fly with a sledgehammer. Yet, on the other hand, one shouldn't attempt to sink a battle ship with a BB gun either. Choosing the appropriate tools from one's arsenal is an important decision for the coach.

Coaches should use positive reinforcement to motivate athletes.

Being Distracted by Problems

One of the challenges faced by a coach when dealing with significant, serious problems is that one becomes distracted by the problem and the efforts expended to deal with the problem. This should not be the case. Of course the coach will pay attention to the problem. Of course the coach will spend time dealing with the problem. Of course the coach will be thinking about the problem, quite a bit. But, the problem should not become such a distraction that the coach is unable to function at an adequate level in terms of the other aspects of the coach's job description. Successful coaches are able to do both—handle the troublesome problem and continue to do one's job satisfactorily. Being able to establish priorities, to plan and to organize one's personal and professional life are essential if the coach is to be able to handle all of the pressures brought about by a serious problem in addition to the normal pressures brought about by one's job as a coach of a competitive team.

COACHING CONCEPT #402:   Hindsight is a valuable tool—Use it when problem solving

---

The *fifth* and final step in problem solving involves taking the time and making the effort to evaluate the degree of success (or failure) of one's problem solving efforts. Once the problem has been dealt with or is no longer a significant threat, the coach (as well as others) should sit down and review the entire situation. This involves asking oneself what was successful and what was not quite so success in terms of what the coach had done (decisions and actions) in light of the problem or difficulty. Hindsight is a great and valuable tool. It should be used to help the coach develop an understanding of what worked and what didn't work so well in the past so that the coach will be able to make better decisions and take more appropriate actions in future problematic situations.

COACHING CONCEPT #403:   A coach becomes a better problem solver with in handling a wide variety of problems.

It is through careful scrutiny of one's past actions that a coach can truly learn from the often times traumatic and fatiguing experience of dealing with a so-called serious problem or challenge. And there will be many serious problems confronting the average coach regardless of the level of competition. Even if the problem solving experience has been negative in the sense that the situation was not handled well and/or the fallout from the problem created more difficulties, the fact that the coach critically assesses one's own performance can lead to a better coach, better prepared and armed with greater experience with which to tackle the next challenge—for there will be further challenges, both small and large, both serious and the not so serious. It is also wise to attempt to learn from the problem solving efforts of others as well so that one can add that information and insight to one's arsenal of problem solving knowledge.

TIMING OF PROBLEM SOLVING TACTICS

When faced with a significant problem there is often a very specific window of opportunity within which specific decisions and/or actions must be taken if the problem is to be effectively and efficiently addressed. It is this window of opportunity that the coach must be cognizant of. This time frame will vary, of course, in each situation. It is up to the coach to ascertain the time frame for appropriate decision making and actions.

COACHING CONCEPT #404:   Time is often of the essence when it comes to problem solving in sports.

The coach needs to be aware that just as it is inappropriate to jump right into the problem situation and make decision and render judgments *too soon*—it is likewise unacceptable to wait too long before making a move to resolve or solve the problematic or challenging situation.

REDUCING THE IMPACT OR FALLOUT OF THE PROBLEM SITUATION

A major concern of any coach when faced with a significant problem is how to minimize the negative fallout or consequences of the problem. This is important for the coach and the sports program as well as for the sponsoring organization, whether it be a school or a community sports organization. Negative fallout from a problem emanating from a coach or a specific team can have serious, if not disastrous, consequences for the entire sports program. This is because the coach and the team members represent not only themselves and the team but also represent the school or the sponsoring entity itself.

> **COACHING CONCEPT #405:** **Fallout from the problem can be much more severe than the problem itself.**

Thus, it behooves the coach, the problem solver, to attempt to minimize the damage which the initial problem might have on the team, the coach's own reputation and on the school or sponsors of the sports team. Frequently this can be accomplished by dealing (the process) with the problem in a forthright and honest fashion. It can also be accomplished by dealing with the problem in an acceptable time frame. And, finally, it can be accomplished by arriving at an acceptable conclusion or decision (end result), one which is viewed as fair and appropriate.

THE VALUE OF THE ATHLETIC DEPARTMENT'S POLICY HANDBOOK

One of the key tools available to every coach in terms of problem solving is the athletic department's policy handbook. In this document are a variety of policies, procedures, practices, priorities and a statement of philosophy. Coaches should utilize this handbook in terms of preventing many of the problems that they might otherwise encounter. They should also utilize this handbook—and the policies, procedures and practices outlined within it—when a problem surfaces since many policies

> **COACHING CONCEPT #406:** **The athletic department handbook and the individual sport handbook can be effective tools in both preventing problems and in dealing with problems.**

and procedures will exist which will guide the coach in terms of the proper actions to take and the time table for such actions.

Similarly, the coach's own sport handbook might well contain important documentation in terms of the coach's expectations of athletes, the team rules and regulations, the various types of disciplinary actions which might be invoked for specific transgressions, the criteria for team membership and individual athletic awards (including lettering in the sport), etc. The creation of a suitable team handbook (as well as the athletic department's policy handbook) can go a long way towards preventing problems in the first place as well as providing a blueprint for the coach (and others) to follow should a serious problem poke its ugly head into the life of the coach. See appendix E for an example of a school's policy regarding athletes earning awards (i.e., varsity letter awards).

Problem Solving Is a People Job

Problem solving (prevention) is a *people* job. This means that most of the problems which coaches face are related to people, to what people think, and to what people do and to what people don't do. If one is not skilled in dealing with people, problem solving will be truly a challenge, for many an insurmountable challenge.

COACHING CONCEPT #407:   **If you are not a people person it will be that much more difficult to be a successful coach and a successful problem solver.**

Six Sources of Problems

There are six major sources of problems and challenges which face athletic programs (and therefore involving coaches) at all levels of competition (Stier, 2004). These include:

Facilities must be maintained in tip-top shape to create a positive image and to prevent injuries.

1. Athletes
2. Athletic Coaches
3. Other individuals, faculty, administrators, boosters, fans and others
4. Policies, procedures and practices within the organization
5. Controversial issues
6. Special situations

Of the above six categories of problems, five are directly related to people, while the sixth deals with policies, procedures and practices which have been established by people. Obviously, people are at the heart of the problem solving arena not only as potential sources of problems but in terms of whom the coach must work with in an effort to solve or resolve the difficulty within an appropriate time frame.

Some Problems Can Have Significant and Severe Negative Impact upon a Coach and Upon the Coach's Career

Some problems or problematic situations just must be prevented or avoided at all costs—lest their existence be the end of an individual's employment at one's current place of employment (as a result of firing or non-rehiring) or worse yet, the end of one's coaching career. Some of these most serious problematic situations are associated with physical/mental abuse of others, excessive drinking, drug abuse, inappropriate behavior of a sexual nature, the existence of hazing, cheating and unethical actions, sexual harassment, physical violence, as well as any number of felonious acts,

---

COACHING CONCEPT #408: Because a coach is typically held to a higher standard of behavior due to holding the post of *coach*, it is imperative that the coach avoids and prevents inappropriate behavior and scandalous situations—by oneself, by one's staff members and by one's athletes.

The Actions of the Coach Can Have Significant Impact On Potential Problems

The way the coach is perceived by others is important, as already explained in this book. This perception of the coach as viewed by others is important not only in terms of whether a problem may arise in the first place, but is important in the problem solving/resolving process itself. Thus, it is important that coaches watch what they do, what they say, the reactions of others, and the motivations of others.

COACHING CONCEPT #409: The process of solving a particular problem should be viewed as fair and appropriate and the end result is also fair and appropriate in light of all of the facts and circumstances.

**Staying focused on the task at hand
is imperative for athletic success.**

Coaches also need to be sure that their everyday coaching decisions and actions (and inactions) are fair, just, honest and appropriate—and are viewed by others to be the same. Coaches need to treat people with respect and to observe the GOLDEN RULE—treat others like you would like to be treated. The same can be said of coaches' efforts to solve or resolve problems. They need to be viewed as honest, impartial, just, and fair in rendering decisions. They need to be viewed as having no conflict of interest and of having the student-athletes' interests at heart.

Problems Take a Measure of the Individual

The potential for problems exist and will always exist for coaches. Problems will occur and coaches must be prepared to deal with them. In a very real sense, one should be thankful for problems as their existence necessitates that the sport organization seek someone who is sufficiently qualified, educated, experienced and motivated as to be able to deal with a variety of small and big problematic situations. If there were no major problems there were be no real need for someone as competent and skilled as you will be.

COACHING CONCEPT #410:   **Be thankful for problems as their existence helps justify the need for someone as qualified, educated, experienced and motivated as you.**

PROBLEMATIC SITUATIONS TO RESOLVE

Future coaches need to be prepared to handle problems in a calm, cool and collected (3-Cs) manner. Preferably, mentors should be in a position to prevent many problems that can face them. However, there are other problematic situations that might not be able to be prevented and, in that event, coaches need to have the skill, patience, experience and maturity to resolve the problem or problematic situation with as little negative fallout as possible.

Part of the answer to being better prepared to deal with problems is to anticipate such problems as well as to have some practice in tackling potential problems and offering a coherent and feasible course of action. Following is a partial list (167) of problem situations that coaches might face.

PARTIAL LIST (167) OF PROBLEMATIC SITUATIONS FACING THE COACH

1. Behavior of athletes
2. Drugs and alcohol
3. Grades, academic achievement
4. Money
5. Picking team members
6. Playing athletes
7. Communicating with athletes
8. Disciplining (punishment) athletes
9. Gender inequity
10. Title IX
11. Working with assistants
12. Working for a head coach
13. Conducting tryouts—selecting appropriate candidates for the team
14. Choosing a starting lineup
15. Substituting during a contest
16. Removing a player from a team
17. Sexual harassment
18. Physical harassment
19. Coaches' burnout
20. Working with an interfering athletic administrator
21. Working with an administrator who doesn't understand athletics
22. Academic standards
23. Ethical decisions
24. Academic eligibility
25. Fundraising, promotions, marketing
26. Remaining current in one's field(s), both sports and teaching
27. Paper work overload
28. Appropriate record keeping
29. Risk management—legal liability
30. Parental interference

31. Working with the media
32. Obtaining volunteers to help with the team
33. Training and motivating statisticians
34. Training and motivating managers
35. Budgetary challenges
36. Travel arrangements
37. Expectations of athletes, of parents
38. Securing a job
39. Stress management
40. Juggling too many responsibilities
41. teaching/coaching conflict
42. Pass to play
43. Pay to play
44. Violence in sports, violence in school/outside sports
45. Orientation of assistants and volunteers/helpers
46. Developing a team handbook
47. Using audio visual aids in practice and games
48. Inventory control
49. Ordering equipment and supplies
50. Facility maintenance and preparation
51. Belonging to professional organizations
52. Attending professional conferences and workshops
53. Pressure to win, win and win BIG
54. Cross gender coaching
55. Team pregnancy
56. Time management
57. Sports medicine challenges
58. Motivating athletes
59. Family (spouse) conflicts
60. Lack of adequate compensation and long hours
61. Lack of adequate number of would-be athletes trying out for a team
62. Mandatory study halls for athletes
63. Tutors for athletes
64. Allowing athletes to miss class for contests
65. Lack of assistants and/or other help
66. Washing and caring of uniforms

67. Upgrading facilities
68. Refurbishing selected equipment and supplies
69. Certifying equipment and supplies as safe
70. Proper fitting of equipment and supplies with athletes
71. Actions taken in light of an injury or accident
72. Working with the medical personnel (physician, physician assistant, nurse, trainer, physical therapist)
73. Affirmative action
74. Officials
75. Establishing priorities, keeping on task
76. Student recruitment for one's own team
77. Helping one's student-athletes secure opportunities to compete at the next level
78. Conditioning and training methods
79. Use of weights in training
80. Out-of-season training/conditioning/practices
81. In-season training
82. Being a risk taker
83. Crowd control
84. Year-round sport involvement
85. Being a role model
86. Scheduling problems
87. Image enhancing activities
88. Honoring current athletes
89. Honoring former athletes
90. Cost containment in one's sport
91. Proposition 48
92. In-service education program
93. Code(s) of conduct [fans, athletes, coaches, staff]
94. Being evaluated (by one's superiors, athletes, parents, community members, etc.)
95. Defending one's sport from the threat of elimination
96. Locker room supervision
97. Job security
98. Working in a farm system versus an independent system
99. Eating disorders

100. Coaching the son/daughter of an influential person (or one's boss)
101. Hazing
102. Working with boosters and athletic support groups (ASGs)
103. College recruiters
104. Dress Codes
105. Scouting plans
106. Dealing with representatives of the news media
107. Student conduct in and out of school, in and out of the classroom
108. Dress code
109. Providing due process for students
110. Facing lawsuits brought by student-athletes and/or parents
111. Being organized as a coach
112. Team meals for athletes/teams
113. Developing practice plans
114. Determining starters for an athletic contests
115. Picking specific student-athletes for specific roles (positions) within team sports
118. Working with the school band
119. Working with the school cheerleaders
120. Specialization versus generalization of athletes
121. Trash Talk
122. Moving junior high athletes to the varsity level (selective classification)
123. Determining travel squad size
124. Travel plans for teams
125. Being a mentor to coaches as well as athletes
126. Seniors who do not start or play a lot
127. Dealing with the chain of command
128. Crisis management problems
129. Awards for athletes—letter criteria
130. Awards banquet for teams
131. Off-season weight programs
132. Risk taking as a coach
133. Multi-Tasking
134. The use of computers in coaching efforts
135. Developing and maintaining a web page for one's sports
136. Speaking before groups

137. Conducting open forums for parents and community members
138. Teacher-coach role conflict
139. Alumni
140. The faculty lounge
131. Preseason plans and activities
132. In-season activities
133. Post season activities
134. Out-of-season activities
135. Working with the elite athlete
136. Unmotivated athletes
137. Prima-donna athletes
138. Too large a group of students trying out for a team
139. Insufficient number of students trying out for a team
140. Athletes quitting the team
141. Unreasonable expectations of athletes
142. Unreasonable expectations of parents
143. Dealing with the wanna-be athlete(s)
144. Cheating in sports of school
145. Two o'clock wonder
146. Selecting captains
147. Health medical reports
148. Injury reports/records
149. Moving up the career ladder
150. Being viewed as a competent coach
151. Workload
152. Making decisions in contests
153. Being a part-time coach
154. Males wanting to play on female teams
155. Facebook
156. MySpace
157. YouTube
158. Staff meetings
159. Teachers who don't support athletics
160. AIDS and other diseases
161. Rehabilitation of injuries
162. Athletes returning to practice or competition too soon after illness/injury

163. Lack of medical personnel/attention
164. Preconditions for tryouts
165. Planning and conducting practices
166. Lack of institutional control
167. The old-boys or old-girls network

REFERENCES

Stier, W.F., Jr. (2004), *Athletic Administration—Successful Decision Making, Risk Taking and Problem Solving*. Boston, MA: American Press.

Name: _____

Student ID #:_____

EXERCISES FOR CHAPTER 12

A. In your opinion, what will be three of your most pressing problems as a coach? Be specific and provide examples.

_____

_____

_____

_____

_____

B. What might you do to prevent problems relating to your efforts in selecting members of your team as well as picking a so-called starting lineup?

_____

_____

_____

_____

_____

C. Discuss the statement: *Coaches should literally drop everything they are doing or thinking about and immediately handle the serious problem.*

_____

_____

_____

_____

_____

D. Discuss the statement: *A coach who has a lot of problems must not be a very good coach because competent coaches have few, if any, really serious problems.*

E. Provide an example in which a problem confronting a coach turns into an even bigger problem due to the fact that the coach did not act in an expedient fashion when addressing the problem.

F. Identify specific content areas within an *athletic department's handbook* **and** a coach's *coaching handbook* which might contain information which could play a role in either preventing a problem or in dealing with the aftermath of a problem. Be specific.

RESEARCH QUESTONS FOR CHAPTER 12

1. Survey one or more junior varsity coaches and find out what are the top five problems facing them.

    ----

2. Ask a varsity coach what are the top problems facing the individual as a coach.

    ----

3. Interview an athletic director and find out from the AD's perspective the top problems he/she feels that coaches face in their day-to-day work.

    ----

4. Through a review of literature briefly outline the difficulties that hazing activities by athletes create for coaches today and the steps that coaches should take to prevent hazing activities.

_____

_____

_____

_____

_____

_____

_____

_____

_____

_____

5. Interview a coach and solicit ideas or suggestions regarding how to avoid problems with other people (especially other coaches and school personnel) while on the job as a coach.

_____

_____

_____

_____

_____

_____

_____

_____

_____

_____

Chapter 13

Excellent facilities are needed for all sports.

HOW TO GO ABOUT GETTING A COACHING JOB

There are two related questions that are in the mind of every future or would-be coach when planning one's career. The first question is: How does one make oneself marketable (attractive) to a potential employer? The second is: How does one go about actually getting a job as a coach? Going about obtaining a coaching position depends, to a certain extent, upon the type of position desired. For example, an individual seeking a position as a part-time youth coach will have a different challenge than the person who desires a full time teaching and coaching job at the high school level. And the person wanting to be able to be a full time coach at the college or university level will have a still different challenge to overcome. Nevertheless, there are some factors that remain the same regardless of the level at which the prospective coach seeks employment.

INTERSCHOLASTIC AND COLLEGIATE
QUALIFICATIONS FOR COACHING

Regardless of the level at which the person desires to coach, it is essential that the candidate be aware of any state regulations regarding minimal qualifications for coaches. This is important on the secondary level since a number of the 50 states do have some type of minimum qualifications that coaches at this level must satisfy. Sisley and Wiese (1987) published a summary of all existing state requirements for coaches at the junior and senior high school level. There are no state requirements as such to become a youth sport coach or a coach at a college or a university. In fact, there are no state, regional or national qualifications to meet in order to become a college coach. Colleges and universities are autonomous in this regard and can and do establish their own minimal requirements.

That is why you will frequently see many, many NCAA Division I institutions that advertise for coaches (especially for the so-called flagship or major sports) require only minimal requirements in terms of education, that is, possession of merely a baccalaureate degree. On the other hand, the vast majority of small to medium colleges and universities that belong to the NCAA Division III or the NAIA national governing bodies include in their advertisements that the minimum educational requirement for head coaching candidates is the master's degree. And, many such institutions are now indicating that the doctorate degree is the preferred degree. Perhaps this is true because many of the coaches at this level are also involved in teaching within the college or university.

COACHING CONCEPT #411: Securing a coaching position does not happen by chance—one has to work at securing a job through a planned, well-thought out process or strategy.

In order to be successful in one's job hunt, it is necessary for four things to happen. First, the person must know how to go about becoming aware of coaching vacancies. A person cannot apply and be hired if one does not become aware that the job is even open. Many times jobs are vacant and the word is not disseminated widely at all. Not every coaching position is advertised state-wide much less regionally or nationally. Second, the person seeking a coaching job must be able to present an attractive application package including impressive references (or confidential credential file). One needs to set oneself up as a unique and/or better qualified than other candidates for the position. With some 100 applicants for any single coaching job, your application must jump to the top of the pile in order to be considered.

Third, the candidate must be a good match for the position. This means that the candidate must have appropriate skills, competencies and experiences that are needed in the particular position. And *fourth,* the would-be coach must be skilled in the interview process itself in order to convince the hiring authority that there is an excellent match between the person being interviewed and the coaching vacancy. Not only must the would-be coach have competencies and experiences that will help the athletic program meet its needs, objectives and goals—but the applicant must be able to sell oneself, must be able to convince the school or athletic authorities of that fact, figure 13.1.

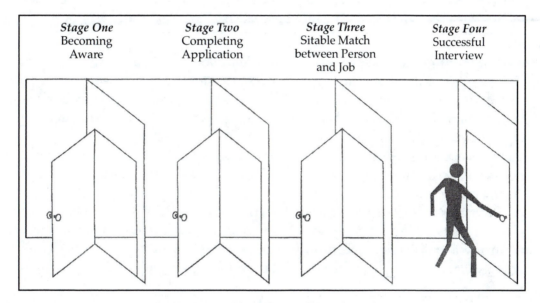

FIGURE 13.1—The Process of Securing a Job

FINDING OUT ABOUT COACHING VACANCIES

Not all coaching jobs are extensively advertised. In fact, many jobs are filled without any advertisement at all. And, yes, contrary to law some jobs are publicly advertised but the *powers to be* have already decided ahead of time that a particular individual will be given the job. The advertising for the job is sometimes (unfortunately) done only to meet legal or local requirements. These so-called phantom searches, as they have become known as, are unfair, unethical and illegal. Nevertheless, they do occur.

Witness some of the job advertisements included within such national publications as *The Chronicle of Higher Education* in which head coaching positions at some

NCAA Division I institution are advertised. Included with the advertisements are specific cut-off dates for receipt of applications. And, low and behold, even before the final date of the advertised receipt of applications, there is sometimes a press conference or a news release announcing the name of the new coach chosen at that particular university. Although this type of tomfoolery is not legal and is discriminatory, it nevertheless does happen. Fortunately, it seems to be occurring less frequently than in the past. This type of action is especially discriminatory against minorities and members of the protected class (women).

COACHING CONCEPT #412: You can't secure a coaching job if you don't know about the vacancy and make an application.

You can't get a coaching job if you don't know about it. So how does one go about finding out about coaching vacancies? Would-be coaches need to make a concerted effort to find out about current and potential vacancies for which they might be qualified. This means checking one's college placement office and securing listings of coaching positions that are placed there by schools and other organizations seeking coaches. It means checking the job vacancy bulletin boards at local colleges, both in the placement office as well as in the offices of the physical education departments and the athletic departments. It means visiting local schools in the area to check for possible job listings that may be posted on various bulletin boards for their entire school system. It also means writing and/or phoning potential employers and inquiring about present and future vacancies all the while making them aware of your availability as well as your areas of expertise and prior athletic experiences.

COACHING CONCEPT #413: To broaden one's knowledge of coaching vacancies—obtain vacancy notices that are sent to other colleges and universities (other than one's own).

A technique that has proven to be successful for some coaching hopefuls is to obtain the vacancy notices from other colleges and universities. This can be accomplished by asking your friends and acquaintances, brothers and sisters, to subscribe to their own institutions for the listings of coaching vacancies and then sharing these lists with you. This way you can significantly expand your exposure to coaching openings throughout the state as well as the nation, especially if these other institutions are located in different parts of the country. Of course, if you are also seeking a teaching post along with a coaching position, you should obtain lists of both teaching and coaching posts from the placement office of other colleges and universities.

Coaching hopefuls should check the local newspapers for openings as many youth sport organizations and public schools often place advertisements for job vacancies in the want ad sections. Even local colleges sometimes place such ads, especially for part-time positions. And, one can visit the local library and glean through newspapers (want-ads) from other parts of the country. Writing and/or calling schools and sport entities can result in being told of vacancies or anticipated vacancies. Don't hesitate to ask for an application for a coaching (and teaching) position when you call. Many elementary and secondary schools will allow you to fill out the school's formal application that will be kept on file by the school for a specific period of time. Remember, always type the information on the application.

Finally, networking with acquaintances, professional colleagues, friends and family members and making these individuals aware of your job search can pay big dividends in finding out about possible vacancies. The objective is to make your availability known to others. Let schools and athletic directors know of your interest in securing a coaching or a coaching and teaching position at that particular school or in that school system. Read newspapers to see which coaches are making professional or career moves. If you are taking a coaching class or attending a workshop, let others know of the type of position you are seeking.

There are numerous publications that also can provide information regarding job vacancies within the coaching arena. Some of these publications include:

1. *The NCAA news.*
2. *Journal of Physical Education, Recreation and Dance (JOPERD).*
3. *The Chronicle of Higher Education.*
4. *Update* (a publication of the American Alliance of Health, Physical Education, Recreation and Dance).

COACHING CONCEPT #414: Don't hesitate to write letters—ask if there is a job vacancy.

In addition, today the WWW offers tremendous opportunities to find out about possible vacancies. Many candidates utilize the Internet to search out the web sites of schools and school districts to determine if there might be a vacancy or anticipated vacancy for a position for which the person might be qualified. The Internet also has sites specifically existing to disseminate information about possible vacancies in specific areas. Some examples include:

1. http://www.hoopjobs.com — basketball vacancies
2. http://www.pigskinjobs.com — football vacancies
3. http://www.athleticdirectorjobs.com — athletic director vacancies

4. http://www.unemployedcoaches.com — coaches' vacancies
5. http://ww3.sportsline.com/u/sportscareers/index.html — electronic classifieds

The Shot-Gun Approach to Job Prospecting

Contacting schools and school systems on a cold call basis is certainly not new but one that can be extremely effective. A college teacher/coach was known some years ago to have typed a personal letter to each and every college in the United States which had less than 6000 students. This coach wrote to some 1800 institutions by typing 15 letters each day for some 120 days. At the end of four months this individual had two firm job offers. Neither job vacancy was ever advertised outside of the institutions themselves.

COACHING CONCEPT #415: **Many of the efforts expended by coaching candidates are wasted—but no one can anticipate or predict with complete accuracy which efforts will have meaningful results.**

The press row activities can greatly enhance the sport experience for spectators and boosters.

Of course it took approximately 1800 letters in order to end up with two firm job offers but at least the individual had a job. It certainly would have been easier if the candidate knew ahead of time which schools had openings and which did not. Unfortunately, the candidate did not know ahead of time which schools would be having suitable vacancies. Similarly, it would have been easier if the candidate knew which schools would have actually offered contracts. Only two letters would have had to be written. Of course, there was no way for the person to know this information. As a result, the would-be teacher/coach had to use the so-called shot-gun approach and actually communicated with some 1800 different institutions over a four month period. However, the consequence of all of this work was a contract firmly in hand and a job beginning in the following fall.

The Rifle Approach to Job Prospecting

The rifle approach simply refers to making an application for very specific, advertised vacancies. This means that the potential candidate has somehow secured information relative to a coaching vacancy that currently exists. Consequently, the would-be coach prepares and sends an individual (cover) letter of application which might include a separate résumé and names of references. This type of job application is dependent upon first finding out about a particular job opening. As a result, this type of application (cover) letter should speak directly to the vacancy itself and address how the candidate meets the advertised minimum qualifications.

PRESENTING AN ATTRACTIVE APPLICATION PACKAGE

An appropriate and impressive application package is an absolute must. There are usually many, many applicants for each coaching position. Those individuals who review the large stacks of applications and who have the responsibility for determining who will be interviewed for the job must be impressed with a candidate's application and recommendations. This is due to the fact that all too frequently this is all the information and data that the screeners and members of the individual search committee have in front of them to base their decisions as to whom to invite for an interview.

Typically, the application package for full time employment (coaching and teaching) at the secondary level consists of a (cover) letter of application of interest, completion of the school's application and submission of recommendations or a list (with phone numbers) of references. However, many colleges, especially four year institutions, do not require the completion of a formal application form but will process a candidate's application consisting of a letter of application, a résumé and either a list of references (with phone numbers) or recommendations sent directly to the school from those individuals writing the recommendations.

The biggest difference in the application package when applying at secondary schools and at colleges or universities is that secondary schools often require that their own employment applications be filled out in their entirety, in addition to the letter of application and résumé that might be sent. Colleges infrequently use formal application forms although some do. And, junior and community colleges tend to imitate the secondary schools in requiring the completion of their own, individual, application forms.

However, applying for *part-time* coaching positions at the secondary level usually involves only a letter of application, a résumé and a list of recommendations sent on behalf of the applicant. When a school uses an actual application form for a part-time coaching position, it is frequently a much shortened or abbreviated version.

COMPLETING THE SCHOOL'S APPLICATION FORM

When an institution or school system requires that their application form be completed it is just that, a requirement. Without the form being completed, the applicant will usually not be considered a candidate. This is especially frustrating for those candidates who are making applications at multiple schools since it takes time and effort to neatly complete the multi-page applications in their entirety. Nevertheless, these forms must be completed in a timely fashion and submitted according to the established deadlines. These application forms must be filled out completely and neatly. Remember, the application form represents you to the search committee.

Similarly, when a school indicates a specific date by which the completed application package must be submitted, that date is non-negotiable. If one of an applicant's recommendations is not received by that date or if some other part of the complete application is missing, the school is obligated not to consider that individual as an applicant. That is why more and more schools are deliberately choosing not to specify an exact date by which all application materials *must* be received. Rather, the schools are indicating in their advertisements applications and accompanying materials will be received until the position is filled. In this fashion, the school can still legally and ethically consider individuals who submit applications (and documentation) right up to the moment that the job vacancy is actually filled.

The Letter of Application

The letter of application should be typed (no errors, no white-outs and no strike-overs) on good quality bond paper. The letter should be grammatically correct and speak to the point of your qualifications for the position you are seeking. Being able to succinctly highlight (without bragging) your positive attributes, experiences and skills is a great asset. Senne (2002) explains that the typical cover letter is broken down into three sections, an introductory section, the body or main message section, and the conclusion or closing section.

COACHING CONCEPT #416: If you include you e-mail address in a résumé be sure it is a professionally sounding address— nothing cutesy or objectionable; and the same goes for your telephone answering machine as well as the name and contents of your personal web site.

The letter should indicate why you are writing the letter. Are you writing in response to an advertisement announcing a coaching vacancy? Are you writing in answer to an inquiry made of you by someone at the school? Is the letter being sent to find out whether or not a coaching position is currently available or anticipated to be available in the future? Or, is the letter being written because you wish to make the school aware of your interest in the event that something opens up in the future? Regardless of the exact purpose, you should attempt, in a single page letter, to convey your strengths, your experiences and skills, (accompanied by a one-page résumé). You are attempting to present a snapshot of what and who you are and why you have chosen to apply for the position.

The Résumé

The résumé should provide an accurate snapshot of yourself. "A . . . résumé should be, above all, an honest account of one's accomplishments" (Overton, 2005, p. 89). The résumé is a one-page, or more rarely a two-page, document which highlights your education, your experiences, and your achievements and accomplishments. It can include the names of three or four references with addresses and phone numbers. Remember to always obtain permission to use a person as a reference—ahead of time. There are many excellent books and booklets in bookstores and school libraries that illustrate acceptable ways to present yourself via the résumé. Similarly, college and university career and placement offices have materials as well as professional staff who can be very helpful in providing assistance in your construction of an effective and informative résumé.

It is vital to be completely honest (no falsehoods or exaggerations) in your résumé (or bio or vita) when applying for a position. To do otherwise is an open invitation for complete disaster. Take the case of George O'Leary, who was hired (December, 2001) by the University of Notre Dame as its head football coach, and who subsequently resigned after only five days due to the fact that false information was included in his biography. "In light of some high profile coaches losing their jobs because of inaccuracies in their bios, even the smallest discrepancies are now being called into question" (New Ideas, 2002, p. 6). Similarly, the use of names of individuals as references means that you have received permission to use their names as references. Larry Keating, Senior Associate Athletic Director is quoted as saying: "Checking references is an obvious and important part of the hiring process" (Smith, 2005, p. 26).

COACHING CONCEPT #417: Check to confirm the accuracy of your records held by the schools from which you earned your degree(s).

It is also important to double check your records held by the schools from which you earned your degree(s). There is always the danger that the school(s) might erroneously report that you did not earn a degree when in fact you had—with the possible result being that you might be thought to have lied on your résumé or bio. Take the very sad example of Tom Collen who was a victim of his alma mater's reporting error which cost him dearly, which cost him his job and a $1 million dollar-plus coaching contract.

Tom left his job at Colorado State where he was a highly successful women's basketball coach, to take a $1 million dollar-plus post (with a 5–year contract) at Vanderbilt, However, one day later he was forced out after his alma mater (University of Miami, Ohio) incorrectly released information that he did not earn two master's degrees from that institution as coach Collen claimed on his résumé. It took around a month for the University of Miami (Ohio) finally admitted its mistake and that coach Collen had earned two master's degree, (Patrick, 2003).

Establishing the Confidential, Credential File— Closed Versus Open Files

There are two types of credential or reference files maintained by colleges and universities for their students and alumni/ae. In terms of federal law there are open and closed files. These are files that hold recommendations on behalf of a candidate. Those files that are open contain recommendations and references for a candidate that may be viewed by the candidate.

Individuals who maintain closed reference or recommendation files have waived their legal right to see their own recommendations. Naturally, closed files are of much greater value than the so-called open files due to the obvious fact that no one in their right mind would knowingly have negative recommendations sent on their behalf to a prospective employer. In fact, many employers today won't even take time to read the open files because of this very fact. It is akin to asking one's mother to write a glowing, positive, supportive recommendation for oneself. It doesn't mean anything, least of all to the prospective employer.

In fact, even the closed files kept at various career and development offices at different colleges and universities have become somewhat suspect of late. Employers recognize that candidates will always be able to find someone who will provide a glowing recommendation or reference. Thus, these types of reference files are of limited value in some instances. However, this does not mean that one should not maintain such a file, preferably a closed file.

Phone Calls Made to References by Schools

More and more employers are taking the route of making personal phone calls *from the list of names provided by applicants*. Other employers have taken the tack of requesting permission from the individual candidates *to contact any additional person or group* in an effort to obtain information and insight (via phone as well as through the written word) into the candidate's worthiness and suitability for the position.

There is an increasing effort towards the securing of information and opinions by phone. This calling of references is in addition to or in lieu of reviewing the so-called standard letters of recommendations provided (1) directly by the individual applicants (having made copies of *to whom it may concern* recommendations received from the persons who wrote the references), or (2) by various colleges' placement offices (on an open or closed basis), or (3) personally by those individuals who are providing the actual recommendations.

By calling individuals willing to provide recommendations on behalf of applicants, prospective employers attempt to garner more accurate and more appropriate insight into the employability and suitability of the candidates. Some prospective employers feel that those who provide references and recommendations are frequently more likely to provide honest and forthright comments when asked personally (via phone). This is because many people feel more comfortable giving verbal recommendations due to the ever increasing possibility of being sued by a candidate who fails to obtain a position because of a negative recommendation or comment. Another major advantage of contacting phone references is that the person seeking the recommendations is able to individualize the conversation and can structure the questions in light of specific information provided by the person giving the reference.

Obtaining Impressive References

It pays to plan in advance in terms of who you will ask to give recommendations on your behalf. It is also important to know the type of recommendation you are requesting from any individual. Some individuals might be asked to provide confidential recommendations that are placed as part of your closed credential file. Other individuals might be asked to write recommendations (To Whom It May Concern) that are given directly to you so that you can copy and distribute same to prospective employers along with your initial letter of application. Still other individuals might be approached and asked to write (or to make a phone call)—sometime in the future, from time to time—personal, individual recommendations when such are asked for by you. And, finally, there might be individuals who agree to have their names included as part of your reference list from which a prospective employer might elect to call for specific information.

> **COACHING CONCEPT #418: Take care when soliciting recommendations and references—lest they not be totally supportive and positive.**

Nothing is worse than having a letter of recommendation or a personal phone call contain negative information. If the candidate is unable to secure positive recommendations, what does this say about the candidate? In point of fact, seemingly everyone has glowing, positive, super-duper, wonderful, supportive recommendations. Perhaps letters of recommendations do not do that much to actually convince employers to hire a specific individual but they can be quite significant in terms of turning off prospective employers and eliminating a person from further consideration. Candidates have been eliminated from further consideration based on what the letters of recommendations (or phone calls) *do or do not* reveal or include.

Participation in sports involves risk taking and initiative.

When seeking a recommendation from a coach, a teacher, a colleague, a business person, be assertive enough to ask the individual if he or she would be willing to provide you with a positive recommendation that speaks directly to your qualifications, training, experiences as well as your potential to perform the job for which you have made application. Also, be willing to provide the people you are asking to write a recommendation some written documentation attesting to your qualifications, training, experiences and potential to do the job. In other words, help the person by providing some information that can be used to formulate a positive recommendation on your behalf. A negative reference or one that is less than glowing can be worse than no reference at all. In fact, it can be disastrous, a death keel.

> **COACHING CONCEPT #419: Seek recommendations from individuals whose opinions are valued and whose professional status is recognized.**

The rule of thumb when it comes to obtaining references is to secure recommendations from the most important people you can, those individuals possessing the most clout, the best reputation, and exerting the greatest influence, etc., with the people who are doing the interviewing and hiring. The more influential the person is who is writing or phoning the recommendation on your behalf—the better. This is where contacts and prior experiences come into the picture.

MATCHING THE CANDIDATE
WITH THE APPROPRIATE COACHING POSITION

There has to be a real and legitimate match between the qualities possessed by the candidate and the needs of the school or the coaching job itself. Every coaching position has needs that must be filled by the individual assuming the role of coach. Different coaching jobs require different skills by coaches. Candidates need to have a realistic perspective of the needs and limitations of the position and whether or not they possess the talent, skills and experiences that will put them in good stead to not only survive but be successful in any given coaching position.

If a specific coaching situation requires someone who is also an excellent fund-raiser and promoter, then an individual who feels uncomfortable in such a setting would be unwise in accepting the position. If the job of an assistant coach requires that the individual be capable of coaching a man-to-man defense (because the head coach only believes in this type of basketball defense), it would be singularly unwise for someone neither competent nor interested in man-to-man defense to apply and actually accept the post.

Realistic Expectations of What Can Be Achieved

One of the problems some coaches have, especially young coaches, is that they get so excited about the prospects of landing a big-time job that their judgment is impaired in terms of whether or not they can in fact be successful. All too frequently, inexperienced coaches will accept a job believing that they are more powerful than a locomotive, are able to leap over tall buildings in a single bound, are faster than a speeding bullet and are able to turn around any team or program into a highly successful winning phenomenon. However, after they are in the position for a while, they come to the brutal realization that there are some significant impediments to being successful or as successful as they had anticipated or had led people to expect. In fact, they begin to comprehend that there are some rather severe limitations and restrictions that exist that actually preclude such success.

COACHING CONCEPT #420: **Don't let the excitement of the job color your judgment in terms of your suitability for the position and the likelihood of success.**

Thus, coaches need to have a realistic perspective of what can actually be accomplished in any given coaching situation and in a specific length of time. What are the resources that are available that will facilitate success? What are the limitations and restrictions that might impede progress towards prosperity? Is it possible or feasible for the team or program to be as successful as the coach, the administrators and public wishes or expects? Far too often, coaches assume a post only to fail in their efforts. When faced with the consequences of such failure (threat of being fired or non-rehired, retirement, etc.), the coach cries that there were insufficient resources to get the job done. However, the response given by the school or athletic administrators is that the coach accepted the position with eyes open and knew, or should have known, what the situation was in terms of expectations, resources, limitations and the coach's own skills and talents. After all, the school administrators reason, if it was easy or if every resource imaginable was present, anyone could be successful. That is why the coach was hired in the first place, that is, to be successful with the available resources. Thus, coaches shouldn't cry foul when criticized for not meeting expectations when their own judgment was clouded by the excitement and thrill of the position.

COACHING CONCEPT #421: Can't make a silk purse out of a sow's ear—a successful coach must possess specific skills, abilities and potential for further growth.

Coaches need to be realistic about their skill level, their competencies as well as their personal and professional limitations and shortcomings. Coaches should not fool themselves into thinking that they can do everything and accomplish anything. Effort alone, although noteworthy, is not sufficient. It is necessary to actually possess specific skills, abilities and talent in order to be a successful coach over the long haul. A coach has to be competent. Results count. Effort alone does not. All of the window dressing and self-promotion in the world will not make a coach successful if the person does not possess skills and the potential for future growth and development as a coach. In short, you can't make a silk purse out of a sow's ear any more than you can make a successful coach out of someone who does not possess specific skills, talents and aptitudes or is lacking the potential for same.

Handling the Interview Session

Getting the job interview is a tremendous achievement. However, it is only the beginning. There is still a long gap between the interview experience and actually being hired. The interview serves three major purposes. First, it enables the school or sports administrators to determine the suitability of the candidate in a face-to-face meeting. Second, the interview experience allows the would-be coaches an opportunity to sell themselves to those conducting the interview. Third, it is also an excellent opportunity for the applicant to find out more about the school, the staff and the coaching position itself, including historical information. This includes general expectations of the program and of the new coach as well as available resources and any significant limitations or restrictions. Thus, *the interview is a two-way street allowing for communication to flow both ways*—to the applicant and to the interviewer representing the athletic program.

COACHING CONCEPT #422: **Do research about the position you are applying for before being interviewed—don't go cold-turkey.**

However, coaching candidates should never go into an interview session without having previously secured some basic or general knowledge about the school system and the coaching situation. Knowing something about the school and/or athletic program prior to coming to the interview session itself is simply very important. Demonstrating that the candidate has taken the time and expended the effort to at least secure rudimentary information and facts about the school and the sports program reveals much to the interviewers. Frequently, having access to such information enables the candidate to be able to offer concrete suggestions in terms of solving potential problems or challenges thus demonstrating that the candidate is capable of comprehending the needs and the potential of the local athletic scene. It also shows that the candidate is able to take the initiative by being able to proffer appropriate and timely suggestions or comments.

It is also important for the candidate to be aware of what to expect when taking part in a job interview session. To provide some insight into how athletic directors and schools plan for and organize such interview sessions, see appendix F. This appendix includes an interview format/structure, courtesy of Brockport High School (New York). Many schools attempt to organize or structure the interview session so that each candidate will be asked essentially the same questions or type of questions. This is done in an effort to ascertain whether the candidate is a good match for the school and the coaching position.

COACHING CANDIDATES NEED TO BE SKILLFUL IN INTERVIEWING FOR JOBS

During the interview session itself, it is imperative that the candidate convey in a professional manner (without being viewed as a braggart) the significance of one's previous experience, the level of competency as well as the potential for further professional growth. It is imperative that candidates emphasize their leadership experience and potential as well as their "followership" experience and potential in addition to the specific competency levels in various coaching and administrative skills. Similarly, being able to demonstrate one's willingness (through a pattern or history of similar activities) to learn new things and to meet new challenges is of great value. The short of it all is that candidates must be able to demonstrate that they have marketable and desirable skills, abilities, experiences and assets that will put them in good stead should they be given the vacant coaching position.

Being able to be a good and attentive listener is an important trait in any interview. Being able to effectively communicate—both verbally and through body language—is a decided advantage for any candidate. Showing a true interest in the position and illustrating how one's own experience and talents might be of specific assistance in solving current or potential programs within the athletic program is a decided plus. School and athletic administrators want to know how a candidate might meet the needs of the school and the athletic program. Candidates need to provide this type of information while conveying an image of professionalism and competency.

Presenting a Professional Image during the Interview

This image of professionalism denotes proper dress and appearance for the candidate. A male candidate would not go to an interview wearing cowboy boots (even in Texas) and an open collar shirt without a coat. A female candidate would not go to an interview session wearing sandals, Bermuda shorts and a halter top. Some things just are not done, period. The candidate should provide a professional physical appearance, one that would be appropriate if the candidate was meeting the board of education, or the school superintendent, or a president of a college or university.

COACHING CONCEPT #423: One only has one opportunity to make a first impression—first impressions are lasting impressions and are very difficult to change.

It is suggested that the applicant not attempt to negotiate for the job until the prospective employer has indicated that the applicant is wanted and an actual job offer is tendered. Broaching the subject of salary demands (or wishes), workload accommodations, etc., too early in the interview process only throws up a red flag to those interviewing the candidate. It is best to wait until the potential employer has indicated a sincere interest in you as a coach and has indicated that a contract would be offered before exploring further into the area of conditions of employment. At that point one can begin to negotiate in earnest with the employer. This is not to say, however, that candidates cannot inquire as to general conditions of employment.

Just don't negotiate until you know you are wanted and are the *one* to be offered a contract.

COACHING CONCEPT #424: Negotiate before you sign your contract—after you sign you are in no position to negotiate anything.

The time to negotiate regarding conditions of employment is before you sign the contract. Afterwards, it is too late. When representatives of the prospective employer make it known that it is you that they want—that is the time to begin negotiating for a reasonable employment package. You will most likely get more for yourself and for your program before you sign on the dotted line than afterwards. This is especially true in terms of salary.

Frequently the best way to get a raise for a coach/teacher is to make a move from one job to another or from one school to another. It is very difficult, unless the school has some sort of legitimate merit pay that adds significant amounts of money to one's base pay, to get any type of significant raise other than a cost of living raise plus a moderate across the board add-on to one's salary in a teaching/coaching situation.

NETWORKING

Networking is absolutely critical to your success as a coach, both before you secure a professional position and after you have been hired. Networking is the development of contacts who know of your work, your successes and your areas of competencies. You need to know many individuals. Conversely, you need to have many individuals know you as well as know of you. One of the reasons why networking is so important is because those individuals with whom you maintain close contact with and who have respect for you can help you secure information about job vacancies. Another very important reason is that these same individuals can help provide to others a positive recommendation on your behalf. This is especially important if these individuals are themselves people of influence in our society and/or within the athletic world. The time to start developing one's professional and personal network of colleagues and centers of influence is *now*. And, networking can be a never-ending process lasting throughout one's professional career and life. The objective is to develop long lasting and mutually beneficial personal and professional relationships (Turecamo, 1992).

What Networking Is Not

It is important to know what networking is not. It is not merely giving out one's business cards at a meeting or a dinner. It is not merely playing golf or tennis at the local club. It is not merely making a phone call on the spur of a moment to a stranger while dropping a mutual friend's name. These types of bush-league attempts at developing a so-called network of professional colleagues do more harm than good because such actions—in addition to being ineffectual—tend to irritate people and the result is simply counter productive.

COACHING CONCEPT #425: Remain in touch with your personal friends and professional colleagues because you never know when you may need them.

An important concept in networking is that it is an on-going process. You shouldn't suddenly become concerned with networking when you find yourself in need of a job. It is then too little, too late. You never outgrow the need to remain in touch with personal friends and professional colleagues. Never feel that you are too good or too far removed from your earlier contacts as you move up your career ladder. Far too often people who have reached great heights in terms of their professional careers, and who then forgot about their friends and those who have helped them climb the ladder of success, find themselves needing these same individuals on their way down the career ladder.

An Example of Maintaining the Integrity of One's Network

One coach who has developed an extensive network of friends and colleagues over the years has devised a concerted and conscious plan whereby the individual is able to maintain regular, periodic and meaningful contact with these same friends and colleagues. This coach has made the conscious decision that those individuals comprising the network will be communicated with at least twice a year by phone, by letter and/or in person.

Specifically, the coach actually makes 4-5 phone calls each working day throughout the year to individuals whom the coach normally would not be in communication with on a regular basis. In this way, with some 250 working days each calendar year, the coach is able to actually reach out and touch colleagues and friends via this type of voice communication some 1250 times. The phone conversations are not necessarily long, 3-6 minutes, some shorter and some longer. However, the coach is able to maintain a close relationship with others through this technique, a method that does not take an extraordinary amount of time or effort. The net result is that two-way communication efforts are made so that the professional and personal relationships between these individuals are thereby strengthened and enhanced.

Another coach maintains an extensive Christmas card list that is used to send Christmas greetings to those individuals within that coach's network. The Christmas cards contain appropriate handwritten postscripts as well as a one or two-page printed summary of what has happened to that particular coach and the coach's family during the proceeding year. This is yet another method of communicating with others and keeping one's name and presence alive in the minds of others.

Another coach uses a computer database to maintain records of birthdays, anniversaries and other important dates so that it is possible to send appropriate greetings and congratulations on the correct date. This coach also makes it a practice of writing *personal* letters of congratulations to peers, friends and colleagues when these individuals have earned recognition or specific achievements. Yet another coach uses the team newsletter as a communication vehicle by sending the newsletter to colleagues and friends on a monthly basis. Many of the newsletters are accompanied by a personal, handwritten note suitably scribbled.

All of the above are examples of individuals attempting to maintain contact with other professionals and colleagues. These individuals have made a conscious decision to deliberately communicate with others in an attempt to keep their contacts within the profession alive—keeping abreast of what others are doing and helping others to be knowledgeable about one's own activities and involvements.

COACHING CONCEPT #426: The key to finding a job is to network.

One of the essential steps coaching hopefuls should take in terms of enhancing their career paths is to develop a network of individuals with whom they can develop a professional and even a personal relationship. These individuals can be anyone and everyone. They can include coaches, former and current teachers, athletic administrators, principals, superintendents, and other school administrators and personnel, people in the community, current and former employers, etc. Almost anyone can be part of one's network of contacts that can prove helpful in assisting you in finding out about current and potential coaching vacancies *and* in providing meaningful recommendations on your behalf. This gathering of a network of contacts is an on-going process throughout an individual's career.

Establishing One's Own Network

Naturally, one should attempt to network within the coaching fraternity. However, don't stop there. Networking should also be done within the educational and business worlds. How does one go about developing such a network of colleagues and friends in the coaching profession, in education and in business?

One way to begin to establish one's own network is to get to know other people and vise versa. One should begin to attend coaching clinics and workshops while still in college in an attempt to meet other coaches and would-be coaches. Another technique is to make a deliberate attempt to introduce yourself and to meet coaches, athletic administrators and sports enthusiasts. This can be done by taking advantage of opportunities as they present themselves at athletic contests. Having mutual friends introduce you to other individuals who are in influential positions is yet another tactic in broadening your own contacts. Belonging to and playing an integral role in a school's booster club or athletic support group can help you meet other people and enable them to know who you are and what your capabilities and interests are in the area of sports and coaching.

COACHING CONCEPT #427: Don't be hesitant to volunteer your athletic services and time in an effort to network and to gain valuable and pertinent experience—no one starts at the top.

Volunteering one's time and services to work with and assist established coaches as well as athletic administrators can be very beneficial. This enables you to gain important experience and also enables others to develop an insight into you and your skills and competencies. These individuals, having worked with you or knowing of your interest, work and dedication, will be able to speak to these qualities with others. Would-be coaches can volunteer to help coach youth sport teams or they can volunteer to help coach at the local YMCA and YWCA organizations.

Since there are numerous summer sport camps located throughout each state, many located on college campuses, one might volunteer as a coach to help out. Becoming a certified official in several sports can open doors for developing contacts among coaches and sport administrators. Be willing to volunteer to help out in some capacity at your State Games if such competition is available in your particular state. The point is that you need to be involved in developing contacts with other individuals, especially in the area of sports and coaching. What you are trying to accomplish is to develop a list of influential individuals *within the coaching and athletic fraternity who YOU know and who know YOU.* These individuals within your so-called network of friends and professional colleagues and mentors might be in a position and be willing to help you in your search for a coaching position. These individuals can play a significant role in facilitating your career in sports. They can do this by helping you become aware of suitable coaching vacancies and by speaking positively in support of your candidacy for such coaching positions.

Evaluating One's Networking Efforts

To see what your sport or coaching network consists of today, take a piece of paper and draw two lines down the page from top to bottom as shown in figure 13.2. Use additional sheets if necessary. On the *left side* of the page, list those individuals in the coaching ranks or even in sports in general whom you know personally or have some contact with. In the *middle column* place the names of those individuals currently involved in coaching or the sports world who actually *know you*. These are sports people who, if asked if they recognize your name and would know what you do, could respond in the affirmative. In the *right hand column* place the names of those individuals involved in sports who, in your opinion, would feel comfortable in providing you with information about a coaching vacancy and/or with a recommendation for a specific coaching job.

The number of names you can place in each of the three columns will give you an immediate insight into the extent of your *current* professional network. The names reflect (1) your previous networking efforts (made consciously and unconsciously), (2) experiences you have had in the sports arena, (3) the impact you have had on others, as well as (4) your present knowledge of those who are local, regional or national sport leaders. The goal, of course, is to continually increase the number of individuals whom you can list in each of the three columns, but especially in the right hand column.

The left column should have the most names since this list is comprised of those individuals who are influential sport people whom you only need identify or with whom you have had some type of contact. Coaches and would-be coaches need to be knowledgeable in terms of who are the major role players and influential leaders in sport. The middle column will contain fewer names than the left column but more than the list on the right side of the page. For many college students who possess a desire to become a coach, the number of names in the middle and right columns may be very small indeed. However, despair not. Now is the time to begin to develop one's professional network of acquaintances and colleagues.

To expand the network list in the right hand column, you might include names of individuals who, although not actually involved in sports per se, are nevertheless influential in their own right in terms of their positions in their own professions. For example, the well-known and respected president of a large corporation in your city or state might not be directly involved in sports as such but that individual's recommendation or support on behalf of an individual coach might carry significant weight with those individuals making the decision as to whom to hire as a coach.

People I Know in the Coaching Profession	People in Sports Who Know Me or Know of Me	People in Sports Who Would Give Me a Professional Recommendation
1.	1.	1.
2.	2.	2.
3.	3.	3.
4.	4.	4.
5.	5.	5.
6.	6.	6.
7.	7.	7.
8.	8.	8.
9.	9.	9.
10.	10.	10.
11.	11.	11.
12.	12.	12.
13.	13.	13.
14.	14.	14.
15.	15.	15.
16.	16.	16.
17.	17.	17.
18.	18.	18.
19.	19.	19.
20.	20.	20.
21.	21.	21.
22.	22.	22.
23.	23.	23.
24.	24.	24.

Figure 13.2—Identifying One's Networking Contacts in Sports

COACHING CONCEPT #428: Today's friend or college classmate might become tomorrow's influential and well-known coach, athletic director or community leader.

It is important to remember that one's own peers can become excellent networking resources in the future. This is because your current friends, associates and peers—in the future—will advance in their own careers and will quite possibly hold important positions in a variety of prestigious settings, in sports, in education and in the business sectors. Thus, *making and keeping* meaningful contacts with your current friends and acquaintances are important steps in the development of an extensive network of contacts.

It is this effort of maintaining and nurturing meaningful personal and professional contacts that is so important in networking. One of the author's acquaintances during the high school years was a boyhood friend who also lived several houses down the street. Many long hours were spent playing basketball with this friend in the driveway of the author's home. Later, that high school friend, that teammate on numerous pick-up games in the neighborhood became the governor of that state, and later, a state senator. If the friendship had been closely maintained throughout all of those intervening years, the author, when applying for a coaching position, might have been in a position of having a very prestigious political figure (THE Governor, THE Senator) being willing to provide professional and personal recommendations on his behalf. Another example is former President Bill Clinton. When President Clinton formed his new cabinet in January of 1993, he chose Thomas Mack McLarty as his chief of staff. This individual had been the President's long-time friend (since kindergarten), a person who had maintained a close relationship and friendship with Bill Clinton throughout their adult lives. Mr. McLarty joined Bill Clinton in the inner circles of presidential politics because of his close personal and professional association with the President during all of these years.

Mentoring

Mentoring can be thought of as a form of networking although on a much closer and more personal basis. Mentors are those individuals who formally or informally take another person under their wings and serve as confidants, friends and advisers. The mentor is frequently in a position to assist a younger professional within an organization or along a specific career path by opening doors and providing opportunities for career advancement. This can be accomplished by providing recommendations as well as actual job opportunities, by providing support (moral and actual) and encouragement, by serving as a confidant and adviser, and by providing informal or formal tutoring and education for the person being mentored.

COACHING CONCEPT #429: Securing the services of a mentor to help and advise can be a significant boost to one's athletic career.

In essence, a mentor can be of immeasurable help by sharing advice gained through years of experience. The mentor is able to make recommendations on behalf of an individual to the mentor's numerous and extensive contacts. The mentor, being a person of significant influence and experience, can have a real impact upon the grooming of an individual for bigger and better things. The mentor can be instrumental in opening doors that would normally be closed to the person being mentored.

Head coaches frequently serve as mentors for younger coaches, especially their assistants, while grooming these young coaches for better positions, if not for their own post when it comes time for them to step down or to move to another position. Coaches should take advantage of those individuals who feel comfortable being mentors by seeking advice, information and knowledge from these more experienced and established leaders in our field. "Researchers have found that employees with informal mentors report greater career satisfaction, commitment, and mobility, as well as more positive attitudes than individuals without mentors" (Wilson, 2002, p. 37.

Securing (and Keeping) Employment as a Coach

Coaches need to recognize that the securing and the retaining of a coaching position, at any level, is sometimes as much a matter of politics as it is a matter of competency and ability. One needs to be realistic in this regard. One needs to be competent as a coach/teacher of sports, certainly. However, one should not underestimate the importance of also being politically astute. Coaches, by the very nature of their job, must recognize that they frequently operate within a political context, both in and outside of the school or coaching arena. As a result, it is imperative that they remain cognizant of the need for political expediency and are able to operate within the nebulous world of office politics, school politics, community politics as well as sport politics.

COACHING CONCEPT #430: Successfully securing a coaching job is frequently the result of being in the right place, with the right skills and experiences, at the right time, and knowing the right people.

Being competent is no guarantee that one will be selected as a coach. Being competent is usually a prerequisite for securing a suitable coaching position. Being minimally competent is usually only part of the equation. The other factors to be considered when it comes time to being selected or hired as the coach to fill a specific vacancy include, but are not limited to, the following: (1) being in the right place at the right time, (2) knowing the right (appropriate or influential) people, (3) having appropriate experience, (4) possessing the specific skills and competencies sought by those who are doing the hiring, and (5) presenting an appropriate image as a candidate.

Differences between Coaching at the High School Level and in College

---

COACHING CONCEPT #431: The greatest distinction between a quality high school coach and a quality college coach is in the level of skills of the athletes.

Quality coaches are quality coaches regardless of the level at which they work. Some people have the mistaken impression that to be a successful collegiate coach one must have superhuman powers, must possess extraordinary skills, and must be much superior in terms of knowledge of the sport and teaching skills than the successful high school coach. Not true. The biggest differences between a successful high school coach and the successful collegiate mentor is that one works at the high school level and the other is at the college level and that the skill level of athletes is greater at the collegiate level.

You might ask, aren't college coaches expected to be successful recruiters of student-athletes? The answer is, yes, of course. However, so too are high school coaches. Successful high school coaches must also be successfully engaged in recruitment (and retention) of student-athletes at their level. Are there differences between the recruitment (retention) processes associated with college athletics and those processes involved at the high school level? Yes, there are some differences. No, the differences are not so significant that the typical successful high school coach could not be successful as a recruiter on the college level. Thus, although the actual recruitment activities for the college coach are somewhat different from that experienced by the high school coach—coaches at both levels are necessarily involved in the recruitment wars.

Lets face it, the vast majority of successful high school coaches would do very well at the collegiate level *if* they were given the opportunity, the break, the chance, to actually coach at the college or university level. The typical successful high school coach is not inferior to the successful college mentor in any material way in terms of coaching knowledge or skill. Far from it. In fact, many high school coaches are probably better at teaching (coaching) the basic skills and fundamentals of various sports than many collegiate coaches. This is because there is a tendency at the higher skill level (college and university) to concentrate more on the recruiting aspects of being the coach and emphasize the game strategies while overlooking the fundamentals of the sport, the actual teaching of the sport skills.

High School Coaching Versus College Coaching

Coaches should not be discouraged that they are not able to secure a specific coaching position at a certain level. Many fine high school coaches would do just as well as coaches in the junior and senior college ranks should they be given the chance or opportunity. But, there are just so many coaching positions available at the four-year colleges and universities in this country. And, there are many more secondary and youth sport coaching opportunities to be filled. As a result, many individuals, both men and women, might desire to coach on the college level but will find that the opportunity may never present itself for such a move. This should not speak poorly for the unsuccessful college coaching applicant. Such is life.

COACHING CONCEPT #432: High school coaches should be careful about wishing to coach at the college level—the salary is not always worth the risk of minimal job security.

Far too often, future coaches have the mistaken impression that college and university coaches earn far more than they actually are paid in reality. Certainly, there are some outstanding coaches at NCAA Division I schools earning $300,000, $500,000, $900,000 and more in total annual compensation for their involvement as coaches of so-called flagship sports (basketball and football). However, these coaches are the exceptions. There are less than 300 institutions that actually compete in the so-called big-time level (NCAA Division I) of sports in this country. When one considers that there are of more than 2500-plus four-year colleges and universities in this country, it becomes crystal clear that the vast majority of coaches do not coach at the so-called major level. As a result, many head coaches as well as their assistant coaches are paid far, far less than the newspaper headline grabbing figures that attract the attention of the average reader.

Most high school teachers who also coach, and have done so for 15 -20 years, are earning the same, if not significantly more, than most college coaches with the same years of experience who coach at the NCAA Division III level. And, this is true probably at the division II level. In fact, this can also be said of many coaches of non-flagship sports at the NCAA Divisions I-AA and I-AAA level. Thus, high school coaches who have experienced success at the secondary level and decide to explore the possibility of moving up a step to college are frequently shocked *when they realize that they must take a sizable pay cut in addition to losing any job security they may have had as a high school coach and teacher.*

Even on the part-time coaching level, coaches at the secondary level frequently enjoy an equal or a higher salary than their part-time counterparts on the college or university level. Of course, there are always exceptions. However, for the most part, the average part-time college coach (especially at non-NCAA Division I institutions) is probably not paid significantly more than part-time coaches on the secondary level. Thus, individuals need to be careful when they start to examine the possibility of securing a coaching position at any level. These would-be coaches need to investigate all aspects of the position in coming to a realistic decision whether or not to accept the collegiate job with its advantages and disadvantages.

COACHING CONCEPT #433: Coaching major sports at the elite Division I level is a business and the risks are great.

Although many school administrators speak a great deal about how athletics, even at the big-time NCAA Division I athletic programs, are educational in nature, the reality of the situation does not support this rhetoric. NCAA Division I athletic programs, especially in the so-called major sports, are a business, a big business. The pressure to win in the visible or major sports is severe, on both the coaches, as well as the athletes.

The Hypocrisy of Big-Time Athletics

The then NCAA executive director Dick Schultz indicated in 1991 that he found some irony in the actions of Notre Dame and the University of Texas (Wieberg, 1992). At Notre Dame, former basketball coach Digger Phelps departed the university (some say under pressure or a cloud) in 1991 after taking the Irish basketball team to a total of 14 NCAA basketball tournaments in his 18 years at the helm of the Irish and graduating every one of his players. However, Notre Dame never won the national championship in the sport of basketball during his tenure. Meanwhile at the University of Texas, football coach Dave McWilliams was fired a year after he led the Longhorns to the Southwest Conference championship, thus earning the right to go to the Cotton Bowl. Both of these events occurred even though Notre Dame's former President, the Reverend Theodore Hesburgh, was co-chairman of the famous Knight Commission, and the president of Texas (William Cunningham) was serving at the time on the NCAA Presidents Commission.

A past president of the NCAA, Al Witte, faculty athletic representative at the University of Arkansas, was quoted as making the following statement after Jack

Crowe was fired as football coach at the university following a defeat at the hands of the lowly Citadel:

> "Coaches can have an excellent record on the academic performance of their athletes. They can be totally supportive of their players, not only in athletics but all other aspects of life. They can be caring people, fine human beings. But they often get fired for other reasons-and the most common reason is not winning. It's a reality not entirely consistent with rhetoric regarding academics and related issues" (Wieberg, 1992, p. 11-C).

School administrators frequently talk a good game in terms of the need for less pressure to be placed on winning while encouraging that more emphasis be placed on academic progress and conduct on and off the field or court. However, in reality, schools, by their actions rather than by mere rhetoric, still demand to have winners and will fire those coaches who do not win sufficiently, as evidenced by what continues to happen on the college level not only in 1992 but during the past several decades. The writing is on the wall, certainly at the NCAA Division I level; coaches had better win or the schools will find coaches who will win. The resulting pressure is significant and very, very real.

COACHING CONCEPT #434: Once successful as a coach—consider moving to a bigger and better job—the time to move is when you are successful.

Coaches frequently contemplate the possibility of moving to another coaching situation, preferably one that is better than their current job. Likewise, coaches are on the lookout—and naturally so—to better themselves and their position as coaches. An obvious fact needs to be stated here. It is a simple truism but one that needs to be restated firmly—the time to make a coaching move is when one is successful and does not have to have a new job. The worst time to look for a coaching job is when it is an absolute necessity that one secures such a new position.

Whenever coaches are successful, whenever coaches are sitting on the top of the world, that might be *the time* to begin to look to make a move. *One is most marketable when one has been successful*. Prospective employers are not looking for coaches who have had unsuccessful coaching experiences, period. Prospective employers are looking for coaches who have been successful in their own right at whatever positions they have previously held. They are looking for coaches who have had successful experiences as assistants or as head coaches. If the applicant has been serving as an assistant coach, it is extremely important that experience be successful. And, that makes perfect sense to most people. Who would want to hire someone—for a bigger, more important coaching post at a higher level—who had been unsuccessful or not as successful as the other candidates seeking the same position? Thus, the rule of thumb is simple. The time to look for a new position is when one has been successful in coaching activities, both on and off the playing field.

SECURING FULL-TIME EMPLOYMENT THAT INCLUDES COACHING RESPONSIBILITIES

Getting a full time employment situation, where one can coach, frequently involves a teaching and coaching situation on the high school level. The average teaching salaries (by state) in the United States are shown in Appendix G, retrieved 06-07-09, http://www.theapple.com/careers/articles/7514-teaching-salaries-2005-2006-2007-2008. Appendix H shows the actual average *beginning* teacher salaries for 2004-05 to 2006-07, Ranked by 2006-07 (American Federation of Teachers, AFL-CIO), retrieved 06-09-09, http://www.aft.org/salary/2007/download/AFT2007Salary Survey.pdf.

On the college level there is less likelihood of getting a coaching *and* teaching position other than in a smaller college program. However, there is sometimes the possibility of getting a college coaching post coupled with some other type of job responsibility (non-teaching) such as a residence hall assistant or director, as an admission's officer, as a student-personnel staff member, as a facility coordinator, or even as an assistant athletic director, etc.

SECURING PART-TIME COACHING EMPLOYMENT

One of the biggest problems associated with coaching is having sufficient time to do everything that the job demands. This is especially true for the part-time coach. This is true regardless of whether or not the job is that of a part-time youth coach, a part-time high school coach, or a part-time college or university mentor. Being free when one needs to be free in order to be able to coach, as well as perform other duties associated with the coaching responsibilities, is an ever present challenge.

The questions remain. How many people have full time jobs that allow them to have time to also become part-time coaches? How many employers allow their employees to take time from their full time jobs to fulfill home and away coaching responsibilities? If the answer is none to these questions, the would-be part-time coach remains the coaching hopeful but not the actual coach. However, there seems to be a trend in which more and more employers are willing to attempt to make some accommodations on behalf of selected employees to allow these individuals to assume a part-time coaching post.

Part of the reason why more companies and corporations are willing to make adjustments may be in the belief that such involvement is beneficial for the individual employee who is often able to be better motivated and rejuvenated by being involved in an attractive outside activity, that is, coaching. Also, some companies have indicated that such involvement, especially on the youth sport level, is a positive contribution for the community and for the children of the community. Thus, some companies may be willing to attempt to make accommodations that will allow their prized employees to assume such responsibilities as a community contribution as well as a motivating factor for their employee(s).

Problems Associated with Being a Part-Time Coach in a School

> **COACHING CONCEPT #435: Part-time coaches beware the school policy or union contract that requires that full-time teachers be given coaching jobs over part-time coaches.**

Some union agreements in junior and senior high schools have a stipulation that part-time coaches may be bumped (removed) by any full time teacher in the same school system who desires the part-time coaching position. This can be the case—and indeed, has happened—in a situation in which the part-time coach has just completed a state tournament finish with a team that has all the starters returning for the subsequent year. A full-time teacher within that system, with minimal coaching experience and competency, asked for that specific coaching position for the next year.

And, in this particular situation, the part-time coach was indeed not rehired for that job. Rather, the position was given to the full time school teacher who had expressed an interest in coaching the state tournament team the next year. In some school systems, such a switch is mandated by either school policy, practice or by union contract. Needless to say, this type of situation provides absolutely no job security or protection for the part-time coach. In fact, it encourages the replacement of highly successful part-time coaches by full time teachers in the school system who merely want to piggyback upon the successful work of the part-time coach.

The reason why this type of arrangement is tolerated, in fact is encouraged in some schools and school systems, is that administrators are desperate to secure coaches who are full time employees within the school system, or better yet, full time teachers in the same school as the sport is conducted. Thus, administrators would do almost anything that would facilitate a full time teacher being assigned as a coach, including bumping the successful part-time coach in favor of a full time teacher who was willing to coach, because of the advantages they believe full time teachers/coaches have over part-time coaches.

SECURING THAT FIRST REAL COACHING JOB

Just how important are good grades in college in terms of getting that first, post-college, coaching job? What about experience? What type of experience should the new graduates be able to point to in terms of making themselves attractive to prospective employers? First of all, grades are important. That is, good grades are important. The importance of obtaining a high grade point average (GPA) is more relevant when the individual is applying for that first full time job. After the person has worked for a year or two the importance of the undergraduate GPA diminishes in direct proportion to the number of years of experience and the type of experience the person is able to point to on the résumé.

In other words, good grades count for something when one is recently out of school because many new college graduates are not able to point to a wealth of meaningful experiences that are directly related to coaching. However, after the person has been involved as a full time employee, what really matters is how well, how effective, how efficient that person has been in satisfactorily completing the various job assignments and responsibilities. Good or excellent grades don't mean a darn for an individual who has been unsuccessful as an assistant coach and a teacher for a period of three years. What counts in the real world is how well this person has performed during the three years of full time employment.

COACHING CONCEPT #436: Good grades are important in securing that first full time job—but successful experience as a full-time employee is the determining factor in securing subsequent positions.

This is not to say that good grades are not important. They are. However, their importance is often exaggerated or magnified out of proportion to their real importance. Grades are important when an individual is seeking that *first* full time job because of the usual lack of a significant track record as a full time employee. And, face it, today, many students are able to present a good or very good grade point average from their college years. The challenge in securing that first job is to somehow set oneself apart from the vast number of one's peers (competitors) also seeking similar positions.

To become more marketable and more attractive to a potential employer than other applicants, to increase the likelihood of being hired by a school, the would-be coach needs to present, in addition to good grades, a wide range of meaningful experiences related to the coaching (teaching) arena. Such experiences might include volunteer work with youth teams, helping out at the state games held during the summer months, being on the staff of several coaching camps and clinics, attending various coaching workshops and clinics, playing on a varsity athletic team, volunteer work with Special Olympics, the State Games for the Physically Challenged, membership in several professional organizations, attendance at state (or regional or national) professional conferences and conventions, membership in honor societies, and membership in a college major club, etc.

Being a Leader and a Follower

What the future first year coach needs to present is an accurate snapshot or picture of oneself being both a leader and a follower, one who is dedicated, mature and willing to make sacrifices. The future coach is attempting to show that she or he has taken a keen professional interest in becoming a coach (and teacher or business person) *throughout the college years* and had exercised wise judgment in terms of prioritizing one's time and allocating resources while in college. The future coach should show that significant and meaningful experience had been gained within the sports scene and in other related areas that might help the person develop important skills and competencies. The coaching hopeful will attempt to show that one is dedicated and motivated to becoming a success by pointing to one's extraordinary efforts to gain meaningful experiences and develop worthwhile skills while still an undergraduate student.

> **COACHING CONCEPT #437: Most would-be coaches truly wish to be successful—far fewer are willing to sacrifice and do what it takes to actually earn that success.**

Almost all would-be coaches have an honest desire to be successful coaches. However, far too many of these individuals desire to achieve success without having to work diligently, patiently and consistently towards that goal. They desire success but with a minimum amount of effort and exertion. Thus, to set themselves apart from the vast majority of would-be coaches, the really dedicated future coaches must be willing to do those things that will help distinguish themselves from those who are not as highly dedicated and strongly motivated.

> **COACHING CONCEPT #438: Don't be too proud—be willing to start at the bottom, be willing to assume menial tasks.**

Individuals planning on becoming coaches need to recognize that they will be starting at the bottom of the profession. They may have been big shots in college, they may have been highly visible as star athletes on the university team. But, in real life, out there on the firing-line of coaching, they will be expected to begin at the bottom and start to work their way up the professional career ladder. In reality, nothing should be beneath a beginning coach in terms of professional activities. These new coaches can expect to be given mundane jobs and responsibilities until they can demonstrate that they are capable of successfully handling more important and challenging tasks and assignments. Don't expect to start at the top—one has to earn one's way there and the path to the top is through hard work, dedication, sacrifice and being willing to learn from one's experiences, both those that are satisfying and enjoyable and those that are boring and tiresome.

COACHING CONCEPT #439: Don't be parochial—be willing to move elsewhere (away from home) to get a job as a teacher/coach.

New graduates are often much too parochial in terms of their job prospects. Too many new graduates would like to find a coaching and teaching position within 50 miles of their home, preferably closer. This is simply not possible in many cases. The advice currently being given to those about to graduate from college is to throw a big net in terms of prospective employers. In order to be truly marketable, one must be willing to move away from the protective confines of one home and even away from one's home state. In

Camaraderie among the coach and athletes is a most valuable trait.

effect, in order to secure a teaching and coaching position, one must go to where there are vacancies. And if that is far from one's home—so be it.

SECURING SUBSEQUENT POSITIONS

Securing subsequent coaching positions at a level at which the individual has not coached can sometimes be most difficult. For example, an assistant coach who desires to become a head coach, a junior high school coach seeking to become a high school coach, a head coach in high school wishing to become a coach on the college level—all of these individuals seek to become what they have not yet been. How can an individual who has yet to have an opportunity to demonstrate success at a specific level secure that first position at the next or higher level?

Another Catch-22 Situation

It is like a person seeking a credit card for the first time. The individual, when asked about previous credit history and examples of credit debt paid off on time, responded that this was the first credit application to be filled out. The response from the company was that no credit card could be issued without a history of successfully paying off credit card debt. Thus, the individual was caught in a Catch-22 situation in which one cannot get a credit card without having shown a history of paying off a previously issued credit card. And this person is unable to show such a history without having been issued such a card in the first place.

So too, coaches face a similar situation when they seek a type of coaching position for which they have had no exact or similar experience. Making the move from assistant coach to head coach is a big step. Making the move from junior high school to high school coach is a big step. Making the move from high school coaching to college coaching is a big step. And, making the move from the NCAA Division III level of college coaching to the big-time, division I-A level is an even bigger step.

Examples of Discrimination

Women attempting to enter the coaching profession and advance through its ranks frequently run into similar hurdles and roadblocks. They are often turned down for head coaching positions of women sports or other coaching positions of importance because they lack the experience that many men possess. All too often, only coaches with previous head coaching experience or with extensive assistant coaching experience are seriously considered for many coaching positions. This eliminates many women from consideration because they have been unable to secure such positions because of this very posture taken by some sports administrators.

Thus, it is important that all coaches—men and women—who desire to move up the coaching ladder of success be cognizant that they must acquire and demonstrate the skills and abilities that are necessary and expected for success at the next level of coaching. It is also advisable for a coach to work, as an assistant, under the tutelage of a highly successful head coach. In that way, the assistant can learn from the head coach much as a student does from a teacher. Plus, the head coach can assume the role of a teaching mentor.

COACHING CONCEPT #440: Think twice about following a winner—if you win, it is because you had inherited a great team; if you lose it is your fault.

When applying for a head coaching position, many coaches want to be sure that they are securing a position where they can enjoy success and have the appropriate resources to be successful. In this vein, some coaches tend to shy away from positions that have been vacated by highly successful coaches unless it is clear that the level of success can be maintained.

Just as some coaches feel that the time to move to another position is when they have reached the pinnacle of success in a particular athletic situation, so too coaches are often reluctant to accept a coaching job where the team had just come off a phenomenal season or winning record. In other words, be careful about following a Johnny Wooden or an Adolph Rupp lest you fail to win like they did.

Understanding the School's Salary Scale for Teachers and Coaches

Coaches who hold full time teaching positions in secondary schools should understand salary schedules and how pay raises are figured for both teaching and coaching. Essentially teachers are paid on the basis of their experience *and* the degree held. Additionally, more and more school systems are looking at various types of so-called merit pay. Essentially, teachers who have more years of teaching experience are paid more than teachers with less experience. Similarly, a teacher with a baccalaureate degree will earn less than a teacher with a master's degree, assuming both have taught for the same number of years. A sample teaching salary schedule, figure 13.3 shows that a teacher with 5 years experience and a master's degree plus 15 graduate credits earns $34,000 for the academic year.

Figure 13.4 illustrates a hypothetical *coaching salary schedule* that reveals that a head coach in basketball on step 5, will earn $4500 for the season while the head softball or baseball coaches would receive $2850 on the 3rd step of the salary schedule.

On most teaching salary schedules as well as coaching salary schedules there is a cap beyond which a person cannot continue to advance to a higher salary. Beyond that particular level the teacher is limited to cost of living raises or across the board raises authorized by the school board. However, the teacher will not receive an automatic raise based merely on an ever-increasing number of years one has taught.

Restricting the Number of Years Credited for Outside Teaching Experience

Another factor that coaches and teachers need to remain cognizant of is the fact that most school systems restrict the number of years of outside teaching experience that a newly hired teacher can bring from another school system. For example, if a school system limited outside teaching experience to a total of 9 years and a prospective teacher/coach had had 15 year's experience as a teacher in another system—

STEP Years Experience	BA/BS	BA/BS + 15 Credits	BA/BS + 30 Credits	Masters	Masters + 15 Credits	Masters + 30 Credits	Masters + 45 Credits	Doctoral
1	30,000	30,500	31,000	31,500	32,000	32,500	33,000	33,500
2	30,500	31,000	31,500	32,000	32,500	33,000	33,500	34,000
3	31,000	31,500	32,000	32,500	33,000	33,500	34,000	34,500
4	31,500	32,000	32,500	33,000	33,500	34,000	34,500	35,000
5	32,000	32,500	33,000	33,500	34,000	34,500	35,000	35,500
6	32,500	33,000	33,500	34,000	34,500	35,000	35,500	36,000
7								
8								
9								
10								
11								
12								
13								
14								
15								
16								
17								
18								
19								
20								
21								
22								
23								
24								

Note: Maximum number of years credited for teaching outside of this district is nine years.

Salary increments increase with additional experience and higher degrees — to maximum of 24 years of experience.

FIGURE 13.3: An Illustration of a Salary Schedule for Teachers

Sport	Step 1	Step 2	Step 3	Step 4	Step 5	Step 6	Step 7	Step 8	Step 9	Step 10
Varsity Level Head Coaches										
V. Cross Country	2000	2150	2300	2450	2600	2750	2900	3150	3400	3450
V. Football	3000	3500	4000	4500	5000	5500	6000	6500	7000	7500
V. Basketball	2500	3000	3500	4000	4500	5000	5500	6000	6500	7000
V. Field Hockey	2200	2500	2800	3100	3400	3700	4000	4300	4600	4900
V. Base/Softball	2250	2550	2850	3150	3450	3750	4050	4350	4650	4950
Varsity Level Assistant Coaches										
Football					Etc.					
Basketball										
Gymnastics										
Lacrosse										
Modified Level Head Coaches										
Basketball					Etc.					
Swimming										
Base/Softball										
Track/Field										
Modified Level Assistant Coaches										
V. Base/Softball					Etc.					

FIGURE 13.4: A Hypothetical of a Salary Schedule for Coaches

that teacher/coach would be limited to being placed on the 10th tier of the salary schedule, that is, the teacher would have been granted a maximum of 9 year's credit, refer to figure 13.3.

> **COACHING CONCEPT #441:** Teachers/coaches who stay in the same school district for ten years will frequently find themselves stuck in that same system.

In essence, this transferring teacher/coach would have given up six steps on the salary schedule and most likely would have taken a significant salary reduction in moving to a new school system. As a result, teachers who have coached a large number of years all too often find themselves stuck in a particular school system. This is because such a move to another system would place them on a much lower tier on the new school's salary schedule due to the all too common restriction on the number of years of teaching experience that can be transferred/credited from one school system to another.

In light of this fact, many future coaches attempt to secure a teaching and coaching position in a rather large school district because they feel they have greater mobility and flexibility within the system itself because of the presence of numerous schools in the system. Having a job in a small system with one or two secondary schools limits one's mobility to those schools. If a coach desires to move to another system the individual is faced with moving early in one's career (before reaching the maximum transfer restriction) or taking a sizable pay cut if one moves later in one's career.

Exceptions to Being Stranded Within a School System as a Teacher/Coach

There are exceptions to every rule. And there is an exception to being stranded in a school system having taught there a large number of years. One exception revolves around coaches who move to a different system that has a significantly higher pay scale than the system from which the teacher/coach is leaving. Thus, coaches who move from a lower paying school system than their new system can sometimes find themselves in an equally good situation, if not a better position, *even if they are not granted credit for all the years that they have taught.*

This can be seen in a coach who has taught for 15 years and is near the top of the system's salary schedule, making some $34,000. Let us assume that the maximum number of tiers on the salary schedule at this particular school is 16. Upon moving to another system the coach finds that only 8 year's worth of prior teaching experience is credited on the new school's salary schedule. However, since the new school generally pays more to its teachers at the 9th level than the previous school pays to the teachers on the 15th level, the transferring teacher/coach actually will not lose any money by being placed back on the 9th tier. This is because the 9th tier on the new salary schedule calls for teachers to be paid $35,000, a greater salary than the previous school paid for 15 years (15th level) of teaching experience.

In fact, this person will receive significant benefits in the long run because of the potential for earning more money at each higher level at the new school. The top of the new school's salary schedule grants credit for a total of 22 years of teaching experience (in contrast to 16 at the old school). Since the new teacher/coach is now on the 9th tier, that individual has 13 more years to move up the schedule, earning more money each year. Without a doubt, the move in this instance has not hindered the coach but actually placed this individual in a much stronger position in terms of future earnings.

CLIMBING THE CAREER LADDER — TYPES OF COACHING POSITIONS TO CONSIDER

Would-be coaches have a wide range of positions to apply for in their quest for a suitable coaching position. Within the realm of education, coaching jobs can be pursued at any of the following levels and positions.

1. Junior High School

    Serving as an Assistant Coach
    Serving as a Junior Varsity Coach
    Serving as a Varsity Coach

2. Senior High School

    Serving as an Assistant Coach
    Serving as a Junior Varsity or Freshman Coach
    Serving as a Varsity Coach

3. Junior College

    Serving as an Assistant Coach
    Serving as a Junior Varsity Coach
    Serving as a Varsity Coach

4. College or University

    Serving as a Graduate Coaching Assistant
    Serving as an Assistant Coach
    Serving as a Junior Varsity or Freshman Coach
    Serving as a Varsity Coach

Graduate Assistantships

Coaching graduate assistantships are available at many colleges and universities, especially the Division I and II institutions. However, even NCAA Division III schools offer such coaching assistantships because they are the source of cheap, but nevertheless dedicated, highly motivated and skilled labor. These assistantships allow the individual student to earn a masters degree with a waiver of tuition while earning additional cash income—all in exchange for performing specific coaching duties.

The person who receives the coaching assistantship is able to derive three very real benefits from the experience. First, the person is able to earn some real money in addition to receiving free tuition for graduate classes. Second, the individual is able to earn the masters degree in a year or two. And, lastly, but most importantly, the individual is able to gain valuable coaching experience as the result of the coaching assistantship *and* is able to use the experience (plus the recommendations from the head coach) as real assets in gaining a subsequent coaching job following graduation. In today's world of higher education (physical education and athletics), one does not have to pay tuition for a master's degree with the abundance of graduate assistantships available in both physical education and in coaching.

Securing a graduate coaching assistantship is an excellent way to network and work your way into what may be a full time coaching position. However, as of fall 1992, there are now limitations that the NCAA has placed on Division I schools in terms of the number of assistants who can be hired in some sports and the amount of money the third assistant in basketball may be paid in any one year.

SERVING AS AN ASSISTANT COACH

COACHING CONCEPT #442: Be vigilant (wary) about staying too long in any coaching position—have a plan of attack.

There is a very real danger of staying as an assistant coach for too long a time period. Coaches who find themselves in a very comfortable teaching and coaching environment as an assistant coach might well find themselves stereotyped as an assistant type coach. The result can be disastrous. For example, a coach who has faithfully served as an assistant coach for 15 years might be suspect when seeking a head coaching position for the first time at age 37. Prospective employers might well ask the question as to why the assistant coach had not sought and secured a head coaching position long before now.

COACHING CONCEPT #443: **Be skeptical about accepting a head coaching job when one of the unsuccessful finalists will be your assistant.**

One of the key roles of any assistant coach is that of loyalty. Hence, when applying for a head coaching job, it is essential to take note of whether any of the other finalists will be your assistant should they not receive the position. On the other hand, if you are an assistant coach and put in your application at the same school for the head coaching post that becomes vacant do not be surprised when, if you don't get the job, the new head coach closely examines whether or not you should remain as an assistant. Head coaches desire, need and deserve loyal assistants. Sometimes assistant coaches who are unsuccessful candidates for the head position find it awkward, if not impossible, to then work for the new head coach. Likewise, sometimes new head coaches find it awkward to have an assistant working for them who had wanted the very job they now hold.

COACHING CONCEPT #444: **Assistant coaches who are unsuccessful candidates for the head coaching position may not be wanted as an assistant by the new head coach—especially on the college level.**

Many assistant coaches have opportunities to move up to the head coaching post when the head coach vacates the job. However, as stated above, there is some risk for the in-house assistant coach in becoming an active candidate for the head coaching position. Specifically, what happens if the assistant coach campaigns for the position and fails to secure the job? What if the head coaching position goes to someone else, someone who is coming in from the outside?

There are many persons who would not want an assistant coach working for them who had tried to get the head coaching post and now was in a position to be an assistant to the person who did land the position. There is the possibility that the head coach would not want someone as an assistant who had unsuccessfully applied for the head post. Thus, the risk for an assistant is that the assistant might not have a job even as an assistant in the situation where the new head coach has the final say over who the assistant(s) will be.

ENHANCING ONE'S MARKETABILITY AS A TEACHER (COACH)

> **COACHING CONCEPT #445: Being able to coach a sport(s) significantly enhances one's marketability as a junior or senior high school teacher (of any subject).**

To get a teaching job, any teaching job at the junior or senior high school level, one should be able to coach an athletic sport at that school or within the school system. *Simply put, being able to coach enhances one's attractiveness as a teacher regardless of the teaching discipline in which one is certified to teach.* Likewise, a physical education major graduating from college who desires to secure a high school teaching position without engaging in coaching is severely limiting one's chances in the job market. Students who will earn a teaching certificate in physical education must be ready to assume coaching duties if they are to remain marketable. Period.

In the real world, out there on the firing line, the vast majority of school administrators would not want to waste a physical education teaching slot on a non-coach. That is, they would not want a physical education teaching position to be taken up by someone who is not also coaching. Not only that, but in many schools (but certainly not all), the coaching slots of the flagship sports are reserved for the teachers of physical education. Thus, it is highly advisable for any new graduate attempting to secure a teaching position to be able to coach sports. It is almost mandatory for a physical education teacher to do so.

To further increase one's marketability as a teacher at the elementary and secondary level, *one should be able not only to be a qualified coach but should be able to coach more than one sport, preferably three sports, in three different seasons.* With these capabilities, the graduating teacher from college is far more attractive to principals and superintendents who are faced with the reality of filling a whole host of coaching slots at the junior and senior high levels.

ENHANCING ONE'S MARKETABILITY — BEING CERTIFIED TO TEACH IN TWO SUBJECT AREAS

Being a certified teacher in a subject other than or in addition to physical education can also greatly enhance one's job prospects. In reality, perhaps one of the worse things a person can do who wishes to teach and coach in a junior or senior high school is to major *only* in physical education. Now at first glance this may seem like heresy to the physical education profession but this statement is rooted in facts and supported by reality. Today, our junior and senior high schools have many more coaching positions than there are slots for physical education teachers.

There are only so many physical education teaching positions in any given elementary, junior high or senior high school. There are more athletic teams in any given school that require competent coaches than there are physical education teaching positions. In reality, the market for physical education teachers who do not want to coach is dismal, if not worse. The job market for all physical education teachers is very, very tight. It has been this way for decades and there is no relief in sight. In fact, the situation may get worse before it gets better.

However, if a would-be coach is being certified to teach physical education, it is highly recommended that the person become aquatic certified as well. This is because in some states, as high as twenty percent of the high schools possess swimming pools. Thus, the likelihood of a school hiring a physical education teacher (even one who could coach) who is not certified in aquatics is exceedingly small. Again it is a matter of marketability, of being able to meet the needs of the schools in which one is seeking employment.

> **COACHING CONCEPT #446: Most teams are coached by non-physical educators—there are many more sports in schools than there are physical educators.**

The time when physical education teachers could adequately cover a majority of the coaching positions in any medium to large junior or senior high school is long gone. In a high school with some 2000 students, grades 9 through 12, there might be as many as 25-30 different athletic teams for both boys and girls when one counts the freshmen squads up through the varsity teams. For these 25-30 teams, there might be an actual need for 40 or more different coaches, even assuming that some coaches would coach more than one sport. How many physical educators would be hired to teach physical education in this size high school? If 6 to 7 physical educators were needed for teaching responsibilities *and* were given coaching duties in addition—that would leave around 20 coaching positions still to be filled. Who would fill these vacancies? Certainly not physical education teachers because there would be no vacant teaching slots for them.

Some of the other 20 vacant coaching positions would be filled by teachers of other academic subjects, if there were any such individuals interested in adding coaching responsibilities to their teaching loads. And, the remaining coaching positions would be filled by outside applicants, those *off-the street* or *off-site* coaches, that is, the *rent-a-coaches* (paid) or the *walk-on coaches* (volunteers).

COACHING CONCEPT #447: Physical education teachers are not automatically qualified as coaches—in spite of what some would have you believe.

Satisfaction following a hard fought game.

In the far distant past in our schools most of the coaches were physical education teachers. However, the suggestion that colleges and universities should prepare additional physical education teachers to coach is foolhardy if not disastrous. There is no guarantee that a physical education teacher is a qualified or competent coach. There should be no presumption that a physical education teacher is a competent coach unless that individual undergoes specific training and educational experiences to prepare that person to be a coach (Stier, 1986).

AN EXAMPLE OF A TRULY MARKETABLE FIRST-YEAR HIGH SCHOOL TEACHER/COACH

Two young students had just graduated from a mid-western university, both with a major in physical education. The first student had a GPA of almost 3.8 (on a 4.0 scale) and wanted to be strictly a physical education teacher at the secondary level with no coaching responsibilities. The second graduate had a more modest 2.4 GPA and was also certified to teach physical education. However, in contrast to the first student, this graduate was willing and anxious to coach. And, in addition, this individual possessed dual certification in physical education and science as well as having certification as a NATA athletic trainer.

Who got jobs that spring when both students graduated? The first student who only wanted to teach physical education did not receive a job offer. The other student, certified in science, physical education and as a NATA athletic trainer, who was *willing* and *qualified* to coach several sports, received several bonafide job offers.

COACHING CONCEPT #448: Prospective employees must be able to meet the needs of the school or sponsoring agency if they are going to be hired.

Her hiring superintendent revealed (personal communication) that he had hired this Renaissance Person because the individual was so marketable, was capable of teaching two subject areas and was willing to coach three sports in three seasons while still serving as the school's NATA athletic trainer when time permitted. However, this student had a job—the other student did not get a teaching job that first year. The moral of this story is that one must do what is necessary to be marketable in the real world. One must be able to meet the needs of the individual who is hiring.

COACHING CONCEPT #449:　Don't accept a coaching position and then allow others to dictate how you coach the team.

Coaches need to be on the lookout for the situation where the athletic director or other administrator is likely to attempt to influence how the coach actually coaches. The individual who is hired to coach should coach, not be unduly influenced or be intimidated by one's boss in terms of being told how to do one's job. This is especially important when the athletic director has been a coach in the same sport that the new coach has been hired to coach. It is sometimes difficult for the athletic director, a former coach in sport X to step away from the coaching scene and allow the current coach to run the show without interference.

COACHING CONCEPT #450:　The image and reputation of an individual is often determined by how that individual leaves the coaching job as much as by what the person does as a coach.

An important concept that all coaches should remember is that their image or reputation as a professional coach is determined not only by what they are able to accomplish while a coach in a particular situation. They are also judged, and sometimes quite harshly, in light of how they depart from a particular post. For example, the coach who leaves a coaching position while under fire or pressure might be tempted to provide some parting shots at those tormentors before the coach actually leaves the scene. This might be accomplished by speaking in a negative or critical manner to the news media. It might be accomplished by backstabbing individuals or groups of individuals in conversations with others before the coach actually moves on to another position.

Be careful how you leave one position for another. There is no need to burn one's bridges behind you. You never know when you might need to travel that path once again in the future. Besides, coaches who pursue such negative actions are viewed as whiners or crybabies. Worse yet, they are viewed as unprofessional. Always depart a position in as positive a vein as possible, even if you have been fired outright. There is an old saying in coaching: *Never get into a fight with a skunk—even if you win, you lose*. On the contrary, leave the position by mending as many broken or dented fences as possible. Be professional.

SECURING A JOB IN COLLEGE COACHING (JUNIOR COLLEGES; SMALL, MEDIUM OR LARGE FOUR-YEAR INSTITUTIONS)

Securing a coaching position at the college level varies somewhat depending upon the type of school, the level of competition and the national governing body in which the school holds membership.

Coaches in NCAA Division I institutions are usually assigned only coaching duties directly related to the coaching of their sport(s). They normally are not required to teach in the classroom. However, as stated earlier, at NCAA II and NCAA III schools, there are many full time employees who have coaching duties and also hold a reduced teaching assignment in an academic department. This type of situation enables them to coach and teach in exchange for full time compensation. Or, coaches at these levels are able to assume staff positions in areas such as admissions or student affairs, thus being employed full time by the college or university. A letter written by an AD to the NCAA (appearing in the *NCAA News*) over 20 years ago in answer to an editorial printed in the *NCAA News* on the topic of securing a job as an athletic director at the NCAA Division I level is presented below. It is as appropriate today as the day it was written.

The Challenge of Getting That First Coaching Job in Division I

An editorial (next page) that appeared in the February 22, 1989 issue of The NCAA News (Stier, 1989) was written in response to a growing concern that Division I schools were being so exclusive in their searches for athletic employees (especially athletic administrators) that unless individuals had already been employed within a Division I school, the likelihood of their being selected would be rather remote. Although this editorial dealt for the most part with the position of athletic director at the Division I level, the principle is directly applicable to those in the coaching profession as well. The concept probably remains, to be a successful candidate for a Division I position, either in coaching or athletic administration, it is important to have had some type of prior experience at the Division I level. However, that brings up the question of how and when an individual will be given that *initial* opportunity to work at the Division I level so that the person will have experience at that level.

February 9, 1989

Editor
THE NCAA NEWS
Nall Avenue at 63rd Street
P.O. Box 1906
Mission, Kansas 66201

Dear Sir:

The letter from Mr. Richard Cosby which appeared in the January 25, 1989 issue of *THE NCAA NEWS* caught my eye and my interest. *I have a very simple response to his last question: "How can the smaller-college athletics director become a viable candidate for a position at the NCAA Division I institution?"* **The answer is** *not* **by attempting to jump directly from a smaller-college situation into the world of Division I.** It is too wide a chasm.

At one time, I thought that the days of the "good ol' boy/girl" network was disappearing to soon be a thing of the past. *Not so.* It is alive and prospering throughout the big-time athletic world. Witness the situation in which candidates are securing posts as athletic directors in Division I programs where the advertised minimum educational requirement is merely a baccalaureate degree. When one repeatedly reads in *THE NCAA NEWS* as well as *The Chronicle of Higher Education* that the minimum requirement for a Division I athletic director's position is the baccalaureate, one begins to wonder why the masters degree or even the doctorate, in some cases, are required or highly desirable at smaller colleges as well as on the high school level?

In looking at today's employment opportunities for athletic directors within Division I, it is clearly evident that there are three viable avenues open to an individual desiring to become an athletic director. The first, and probably the best, tactic to pursue is to work within a Division I level athletic program at the assistant or associate AD level for a number of years, gaining practical experience, and then attempting to secure an AD's post at the Division I level. A second all too familiar route to the AD's desk is by being a highly successful coach, also at the Division I level, and then being promoted to athletic director. A third avenue, which has become more popular in recent years, involves moving directly from the business world to the athletic director's office.

Nothing is inherently wrong with any of the above scenarios. It is just that individuals (men and women) who desire to become a Division I athletic director need to be cognizant that one of the most ineffective ways to get there is through formal education (i.e., doctorate degree) coupled with successful experience as an athletic director at a Division III or even II institution.

Search committees have a concern, and it can be a legitimate concern, about the candidate for the AD position who has never previously held significant administrative responsibilities within a division I institution. The members of such committees (rightly or wrongly) feel that there is just too great a difference between the athletic administration of a Division I program and the athletic administration at smaller colleges. Also, there is great pressure from the "good ol' boy/girl" network to secure the services of someone who already is a member of the inner sanctum fraternity.

And is it any different when it comes to hiring head coaches of the so-called flagship or major sports at the Division I level? How many successful small college coaches are hired directly into Division I head coaching positions in revenue producing sports such as ice hockey, football, basketball, etc.? Not many, I dare say.

One final thought. Isn't it ironic that with all of the apparent emphasis in higher education on administrative and management training and education that the vast majority of Division I athletic directors and the vast majority of *presidents at all colleges and universities* do not come from the ranks of professionals trained in **administration of higher education.** Division I athletic directors most frequently secure their positions via working from lesser posts within Division I. Presidents of colleges and universities frequently come from so-called academic departments, with doctorates in history, English, mathematics, political science, etc., **rather than possessing the doctorate in administration or management.** Athletic directors at Division I and Presidents at colleges and universities have minimal formal education at the doctoral level, in the area of administration and management of higher education.

Both Division I athletic directors and college/university Presidents seem to develop their expertise through actual experience (school of hard knocks) coupled with periodic administrative and management workshops and clinics attended subsequent to appointment to their respective posts. For athletic directors, such educational opportunities might be either the NCAA's or the NACDA's annual management workshops and seminars. For Presidents, it might be Harvard's Management Development Program (MDP) or its Institute for Educational Management (IEM).

So, to answer Mr. Cosby's question, the small college athletic director (male or female) desiring to eventually become a Division I athletic director should secure an entry level management level position at the Division I level and work one's way up from there. The road to the AD's position at the Division I level does not (usually) lead directly from the small college AD's office.

Sincerely,

William F. Stier, Jr., Ed. D.
Director of Intercollegiate Athletics
Professor of Physical Education and Sport
State University of New York
Brockport, New York 14420

Stier, Jr., W.F. (1989, February 22) [Letter to the Editor]. **Advice for would-be Division I ADs.**
The NCAA News, p. 4.

A Glimpse into Coaching at the Major Division I Level

A look into the typical male coach at the college or university level was conducted by John Loy (1981), professor and director of the University of Illinois graduate studies program in physical education. The profile revealed by this research indicated that the so-called typical male coach comes from a small town and a large family. His father was typically a blue-collar worker. The coach attended a small college or university and played (if not excelled) in *at least one varsity sport.* After earning the college degree, the future college coach takes a job at a small high school where the coach had several winning teams. Having experienced coaching success the individual moves on to a larger high school. Success continues at the bigger secondary school and leads to an *assistant* coaching job at an area college or university. Success in that position in turn leads to a *head* coaching job at another college campus.

The typical coach continues to be the average college or university coach, not the one cited in the paper for successive nationally ranked athletic teams. But he continues to be successful. As a result, he eventually obtains a similar head coaching position at a major institution of higher learning. Loy stated, ". . . our data on coaches reinforces the old 'rages to riches' tale of a man from a small town working class family who excels on the playing field and eventually becomes a head coach at a major college or university" (Loy, 1981, p. 59).

Cost Cutting Measures within NCAA Division I Institutions Can Affect Coaching Opportunities and Salaries

In 1992, the NCAA passed a controversial rule as a part of its cost cutting agenda that limits the use of graduate assistants. This regulation created what is referred to as a restricted-earnings coach. This is a member of the coaching staff who is limited to drawing from the institution a maximum of $12,000 during the season plus a maximum of $4,000 during the summer months from sports camps. Under these new guidelines, that took effect August 1, 1992, (and later rescinded) graduate assistant coaches were then designated as restricted-earnings coaches, along with part-time and volunteer assistant coaches (Democrat and Chronicle, 1992).

For example, in the sport of basketball, there was then a limit of three NCAA Division I assistants, one of whom could not earn more than $16,000 annually (Sports Illustrated, 1993, February; Wieberg, 1993, January 13). This meant that the opportunities to serve as assistant coaches or as graduate assistant coaches was being severely restricted. The fallout of all of this is that there were fewer job opportunities (and with severe restrictions on salary and earnings) at the Division I level.

Coaching at NCAA Division II Schools

Most people acknowledge that coaching a major sport at the NCAA Division I level is a pressure-packed situation, more reminiscent of a big business than an educational endeavor. What about at the other levels of competition within the NCAA? What is it like to be a coach of a sport at the Division II level?

First of all, it is important to remember that no blanket statement can be 100 percent accurate for every institution within any level of competition, whether it be the NCAA Divisions I, II, III, the NAIA, the NCCAA or the NJCAA. With that said, when one takes a peak at the division II picture, one can see that some member schools offer a full range of scholarships for all sports, the maximum allowable by the NCAA, while other schools provide scholarships for some sports and/or only a partial number of scholarships permitted by the NCAA.

And there are other Division II schools that provide no athletic scholarships at all. Yet, all of these schools vie for national championships with each other. Similarly, the responsibilities of coaches within this division may vary greatly. Some coaches, especially of so-called major sports, might have only coaching duties (and coaching related responsibilities such as recruiting and fundraising) assigned to them. Other coaches, at other schools or at the same institutions, might have teaching responsibilities or other tasks added to their coaching responsibilities.

COACHING CONCEPT #451: Coaching at the NCAA Division II level involves many of the same challenges as Division I—but with few of the benefits and advantages of Division I.

The Division II level of competition, with the possibility of offering athletically related financial assistance, has been likened to the NCAA Division I level of play in that these schools who compete in Division II have many, if not almost all, of the problems and challenges facing Division I institutions, but without very many of the benefits. The pressure to win, the pressure to recruit elite athletes, the pressure to keep athletes in school, the pressure to raise money, the pressure to survive—can exist at the Division II level. Yet, the benefits of winning for Division II mentors do not equate with those benefits that accrue to the big-time Division I coaches. Although this might be a harsh and seemingly biased statement by the author, it is the result of input from many coaches who compete within the NCAA Division II level of play.

Thus, coaches who are employed and coach within a NCAA Division II institution must face the reality of competing at the national level with opponents who are allowed to offer a full slate of athletic scholarships, even if they themselves are playing without such scholarships. These coaches must also be able to handle the increased pressure which often accompanies the availability of athletically related scholarships. This pressure includes an ever-increasing urgency to recruit talented, blue chip athletes and to garner a high ratio of victories over losses. Failure to do so will see a coach's job in jeopardy.

Coaching at Division III Schools

The NCAA Division III concept was implemented to alleviate some of the perceived problems with the scholarship divisions (I and II). Division III within the NCAA is the so-called no scholarship division. Schools that compete within Division III are not allowed to give a scholarship based on an individual's athletic ability or potential. However, in reality, there is extreme pressure for excellence within some schools that compete within the Division III ranks of the NCAA. In these schools there is indeed significant pressure to excel, to win, to earn championships and gain national recognition. However, for the most part, there is not pressure to the extent that exists within Division I or even within Division II. The emphasis within Division III schools remains, for the most part, on the academic objectives. Most coaches, who are full time employees of Division III colleges and universities, also hold teaching or other types of jobs.

Coaching at the Junior and Community College Level

Some junior colleges, just like some four year schools, elect to compete in the very competitive world of athletic scholarships. Other institutions elect to pursue the non-scholarship route to competition similar to that of Division III of the NCAA. One of the biggest challenges facing junior and community college coaches is that the athletes are only available for competition for a total of two years and then they lose their eligibility to compete at the JC ranks.

Thus, coaches face the perpetual problem of rapid turnover of talent within their teams and must be constantly on task in terms of recruiting another crop of incoming athletes who, in turn, will only be available for a maximum of two seasons of competition. Another challenge facing some JC coaches is that there may not be any dormitories available on their college campuses due to the nature or purpose of their particular schools (to primarily serve the needs of a specific nearby geographical location). As a result, recruitment of athletes from far distances may be hampered due to this lack of on-campus living facilities.

Yet another challenge facing junior and community college coaches, especially in the so-called major sports, is that their schools/teams might have to face opponents whose teams are made up of not only full-ride scholarship athletes but athletes who have been stacked or placed at the two-year school by a four year institution or athletic program. This stacking is done because an outstanding athlete might not be able to gain entrance to a big-time four-year school because of grades or other academic deficiency (such as a lack of specific high school courses). As a result, the Division I coach suggests and recommends that this blue chip athlete attend a specific junior college where the athlete will be exposed to excellent coaching and will be able to gain much needed playing experience participating in a style of play and level of competition that will help the athlete make the later transition to the big time, Division I institution. For the junior college coach who has an excellent relationship with Division I coaches, this type of understanding and cooperation can be a real boon. This is because the JC coach will receive a gift of talented athletes by way of being recommended by coaches at Division I schools.

A FINAL WORD ON BEING MARKETABLE AS A COACH

Being marketable as a coach, regardless of the level of competition, means that the individual possesses meaningful, successful experience and competencies. It means that the person is able to achieve results and reach objectives and goals that are deemed important by the potential employer, the school or the college. The matching of the skills and abilities of the coach with the needs of the institution is vital. A Division III school is looking for a different type of coach, in terms of philosophy, experience, skills, etc., than a typical division I (or even Division II) coach. It is important for the would-be coach to be aware of and recognize the differences between institutions and be comfortable in attempting to match oneself with a suitable employing institution.

> **COACHING CONCEPT #452:** **A degree and/or certification help open the door for employment as a coach—but it is experience, skills and competencies that determine the eventual success or failure of any coach.**

How a coach actually communicates this level of competency and skill is as important, perhaps, as actually possessing the competency and skill. Prospective employers (at any level) need to be convinced that there is a good match between what the school (the athletic and academic programs) needs and what the potential coach can provide in terms of coaching, teaching, recruiting, public relations, fundraising, interpersonal skills, etc. Towards this end, it is helpful for the would-be coach to develop a profile or portfolio of the coach's previous successful experiences, of one's achievements and accomplishments. In modern terms, this physical portfolio is called the 3-D résumé (Bigger than, April 1993).

Coaches need to use more than just the paper degree or coaching certification (if they possess such a credential) as proof of their skills and competencies. They need to document their experience and their level of competency. They need to do so in a professional manner. Thus, video tapes, coaching films, clippings, photographs (use of scrap books), documentation regarding levels of competition, special endorsements and commendations, etc., might all be utilized to help paint an accurate picture of the individual seeking a specific coaching post. The 3-D résumé is an excellent teaching tool to convince prospective employing institutions that the coach is the right person to fill the vacancy. The use of the 3-D résumé, reflecting success in terms of coaching experience and formal training coupled with excellent personal and professional recommendations from well respected mentors and associates, should at least make the candidate competitive in those job searches for which the individual is qualified to apply. After one secures a position, it is up to the individual to actually produce in light of the established expectations of the institution and the athletic administration.

REFERENCES

Loy, J. (1981, April). A look at a "typical" college coach. Coach & Athlete, p. 59.

Bigger than the SAT: Students build high academic profiles. (1993, April 9- 11). *USA Weekend*, p. 14.

Democrat and Chronicle. (1992, November 26). Rochester, New York, p. 3-E.

Dunn, T. P. & Dunn, S. L. (1992). The graduate assistant coach: A preliminary profile of an endangered species. *The Physical Educator, 49*(4), 189-193.

Henry, T. (1993, April 21). Disparity among teachers' salary keeps widening. *USA Today*, p. 11 -D.

New ideas on checking bios. (2002, April/May). *Athletic Management, XIV*(3), 6.

Overton, R. (2005, March). Protecting your resume and future. *wwwCOACHAD. COM*, PP. 89-91.

Patrick, D. (2003, March 5), Looking to get out of limbo. *USA Today*, p. 4-C.

Senne, T. (2002). Transition to teaching: Putting your best foot forward Part 1. *Journal of Physical Education, Recreation and Dance, 73*(1), 45-49, 53.

Sisley, B. L. & Wiese, D. M. (1987). Current status: Requirements for interscholastic coaches. *Journal of Physical Education, Recreation and Dance, 58*(2), 73-85.

Smith, L. (2005. February/March). Your next great coach. *Athletic Management, XVII*(2), 24, 26, 28, 30, 32, 34.

Sports Illustrated. (1993, February 1), p. 11.

Stier, Jr., W. F. (1989, February 22). [Letter to the Editor]. Advice for would-be division I ADs. *The NCAA News*, p. 4.

Turecamo, D. (1992, February). Does networking work? *Successful Meetings, 4*(2), 103-104.

Wieberg, S. (1992, December 2). Grades-vs.-wins issue raised. *USA Today*, p. 11-C.

Wieberg, S. (1993, January 13). Minority hiring shows improvement, says Schultz. *USA Today*, p. 10-C.

Wilson, S. (2002, June/July). What makes a mentor? *Athletic Management* 14(4, 37-41.

Name: _____

Student ID #: _____

EXERCISES FOR CHAPTER 13

1. Examine yourself closely to determine your current weaknesses and strengths in terms of being qualified in becoming a competent coach? Be specific.

   ----

2. What steps can you take immediately as well as in the next few months or years that might enhance your marketability as a future coach? Provide a time line in terms of specific tasks or goals you plan to work towards.

   ----

3. If you plan to be a teacher and a coach, what can you do to facilitate your being marketable as both a teacher and a coach?

    _____

    _____

    _____

    _____

    _____

    _____

    _____

    _____

4. What specific steps are you prepared to take to find out about coaching vacancies now and in the future?

    _____

    _____

    _____

    _____

    _____

    _____

    _____

    _____

5. Distinguish between the shot-gun approach and the rifle approach to job prospecting insofar as you are concerned.

    _____

    _____

    _____

    _____

    _____

6. List the names of ten individuals whom you would feel comfortable, today, in asking for a confidential recommendation on your behalf for a coaching position. If you are going to be a teacher, list the names of at least five additional persons who could provide you with positive recommendations.

----

7. Describe yourself (and your experiences and areas of competencies) as you would wish a prospective employer to view you. Then, describe yourself as you currently are in terms of experiences and areas of competencies.

----

8. List your five or ten strongest personal or professional traits—traits that might help make you a successful coach.

    _____

    _____

    _____

    _____

    _____

    _____

    _____

9. Describe your current network of personal and professional contacts. *Complete figure 13.2.* Are you satisfied in terms of your current network? What steps are you willing to take in the next 12-24 months to expand your network? Be specific and indicate when these steps would be taken.

    _____

    _____

    _____

    _____

    _____

    _____

    _____

10. List individuals who are or could become mentors for you.

    _____

    _____

    _____

    _____

    _____

    _____

11.   What level do you think you would like to coach as a beginning, first year coach? Why? What problems do you foresee in securing such a coaching position?

----

12.   Describe how you can enhance your marketability prior to graduation from college? What can you do during this time to facilitate your being hired as a coach (or as a teacher/coach)?

----

13.   Explain why a teacher/coach (an assistant coach) with 17 years of experience in a specific school system might find it a challenge to secure a head coaching position in another school system in a different state.

RESEARCH QUESTONS FOR CHAPTER 13

1. Interview an athletic director at a high school and find out the general steps the school follows to employ qualified coaches.

   _____

   _____

   _____

   _____

   _____

2. Survey near-by school districts and determine the salary schedules for full time teachers, full time teachers who coach, as well as part-time coaches. Provide a summary of salaries for first year full time teachers as well as part-time coaches of several sports.

   _____

   _____

   _____

   _____

   _____

3. Interview a varsity head coach of a flagship team sport and seek information as to *how* that coach attempts to get a competent assistant on his or her squad. How does that coach find out about competent potential assistants?

   _____

   _____

   _____

   _____

   _____

4. Interview a head coach who has assistants and explain that coach's thoughts about how assistants might go about preparing themselves for a head coaching post in the future *and* how the head coach might go about helping the assistant advance in the coaching profession.

    _____

    _____

    _____

    _____

    _____

    _____

    _____

5. Ask a head varsity coach how important references are for the candidate seeking a job as an assistant. How does the coach treat references for such candidates? Does the coach personally contact references of those candidates who are being seriously considered for the coaching post?

    _____

    _____

    _____

    _____

    _____

    _____

    _____

Appendix A

The National Standards for Sport Coaches (NSSC),[*]
2006, 2nd Edition[*]
ISBN 0-88314-908-7, 42 pages, paperback

Table of Contents

- Supporting Organizations for National Standards for Sport Coaches
- Introduction
- National Standards for Sport Coaches- Domains, Standards and Benchmarks
- The Three Levels of Coaching Education
- Topical Reference
- Resources for Coaching Education Programs
- Glossary
- NASPE Resources

The National Standards for Sport Coaches, 2nd edition, is a playbook for running a successful training program. It provides clear direction regarding the skills and knowledge every coach needs to have. From novice to highly skilled master coach, the National Standards work for all sports and at all competitive levels. If a program covers the information in this book, that program will prepare qualified coaches.

Reviewed and revised by experts from national governing bodies of sport. Over 100 organizations currently endorse the National Standards; including youth sport agencies, sport national governing bodies, school sport groups, and colleges and organizations. This straightforward guide identifies 8 domains and 40 standards of critical importance!

This publication is a MUST for:

➢ **Coaching Educators:** Provide quality training that will have a positive impact on your coaches¡⁻ performance.
➢ **Sport Administrators:** Establish benchmarks for hiring quality coaches for your program.
➢ **Coaches:** Develop a performance guide for professional growth and skill development.
➢ **Athletes:** Learn how a quality coach can optimize your sport experience.

The 8 Domains of Coaching Competencies

1. Philosophy and Ethics

---

[*] Retrieved: http://www.aahperd.org/naspe/template.cfm?template=domainsStandards.html

2. Safety and Injury Prevention
3. Physical Conditioning
4. Growth and Development
5. Teaching and Communication
6. Sport skills and Tactics
7. Organization and Administration
8. Evaluation

This publication identifies the skills and knowledge every coach needs to have and is organized into eight domains that describe significant coaching responsibilities.

Each of the 40 standards in this book is identified under a domain, presented with an explanation of its purpose and accompanied by benchmarks to provide concrete examples of actions and orientations that constitute coaching competence.

The benchmarks are performance guides which can be used in developing and assessing coaching competence, and can be applied to any sport or coaching program.

Purpose

The *National Standards for Sport Coaches* are intended to provide direction for administrators, coaches, athletes and the public regarding the skills and knowledge that coaches should possess.

Coaching educators can use this book to provide quality training that will have a positive impact on their coaches' performance. For sport administrators, this publication establishes benchmarks that can be used for hiring quality coaches. For coaches at every level, this publication is a performance guide for their own professional growth and skill development. The overriding premise in the development of this document; however, is that its contents be used to ensure the enjoyment, safety, and positive skill development of America's athletes.

8 Domains of Coaching Competencies and Sample Standards

Domain 1: Philosophy and Ethics is a new domain title that reflects the reorganization and prioritization of standards. Standards 1 through 4 clearly articulate the importance of an athlete-centered coaching philosophy and professional accountability for fair play by all. *Sample—see Standard 1*

Domain 2: Safety and Injury Prevention maintains the core standards of coach responsibility for providing safe conditions and appropriate actions when emergencies arise. It also addresses the need for coaches to know how to effectively participate as part of the sports medicine team. Standards 5 through 11 establish expectations for coaches to create and maintain a safe and healthy sport experience for all athletes. *Sample—see Standard 8*

Domain 3: Physical Conditioning is an updated and more behavioral description of coaching responsibilities in the areas of physiological training, nutrition education, and maintaining a drug-free environment. Standards 12 through 15 highlight the importance of using scientific principles in designing and implementing conditioning programs for natural performance gains. Specific attention is given to body composition and weight management issues as well as awareness of contraindicated activities and over-training concerns. The important role physical conditioning plays in preventing and recovering from injuries is also included. *Sample—see Standard 13*

Domain 4: Growth and Development maintains its original title and importance in the scope of coaching responsibilities. Standards 16 through 18 and related benchmarks more clearly identify developmental considerations in designing practice and competition to enhance the physical, social, and emotional growth of athletes. New to this area is the identification of the coach's role in creating an inclusive learning environment that leads all athletes to feel welcome and supported and to have experiences that foster leadership skills. *Sample—see Standard 18*

Domain 5: Teaching and Communication identifies standards for sound instructional strategies and interpersonal behavior of the coach. Responsibilities for creating a positive coaching style while maximizing learning and enjoyment are established in Standards 19 through 26. Emphasis is placed on individualizing instruction, empowering communication skills, and using good management techniques in designing practices. While effective instruction should enhance athlete motivation, additional attention is drawn to the critical influence coaching behavior plays in developing self-determined and satisfied athletes. Also new are benchmarks that make coaches aware of their role in mitigating bullying and harassment in the sport environment *Sample—see Standard 24*

Domain 6: Sport Skills and Tactics focuses on the need for coaches to have basic sport knowledge and be able to apply it to the competitive environment. Standards 27 through 29 focus on using basic sport skills and acceptance of prescribed rules in developing team and individual competitive tactics. Emphasis is placed on planning that is age appropriate, sequential, and progressive. Benchmarks highlight the coach's role in making tactical and personnel decisions during competition. Also includes definitive expectations for scouting and game analysis. *Sample—see Standard 29*

Domain 7: Organization and Administration identifies how the coach provides resources in the daily operation and management of the sport program. Standards 30 through 36 include risk management responsibilities as well as effective use of human and financial resources. Again, coaches play an important role in sharing administrative duties with any number of other stakeholders in maximizing the sport experience. *Sample—see Standard 31*

Domain 8: Evaluation is a new domain that captures the numerous assessment skills necessary to be an effective coach. Standards 37 through 40 identify the ongoing evaluation responsibilities of the coach in areas such as personnel selection, on-time reflection of practice effectiveness, progress toward individual athlete goals, game management, and program evaluation. Creating a meaningful evaluation process for self-reflection and professional growth is also included in this area. *Sample Standard 40*

Additional Coaching and Sport Resources Available from NASPE
http://www.aahperd.org/naspe/

- ✓ *National Standards for Sport Coaches*
- ✓ *Nutritional Supplements for Athletes*
- ✓ *Coaching Education: Designing Quality Programs*
- ✓ *Principles of Safety in Physical Education and Sport*
- ✓ *Liability and Safety in Physical Education and Sport*
- ✓ *Coaching Issues & Dilemmas: Character Building Through Sport Participation*

Standards and Benchmarks

Domain 1: Philosophy and Ethics
Standard 1: Develop and implement an athlete-centered coaching philosophy.

A well-developed coaching philosophy provides expectations for behaviors that reflect priorities and values of the coach. An appropriate coaching perspective focuses on maximizing the positive benefits of sport participation for each athlete.

Benchmarks
- Identify and communicate reasons for entering the coaching profession.
- Develop an athlete-centered coaching philosophy that aligns with the organizational mission and goals.
- Communicate the athlete-centered coaching philosophy in verbal and written form to athletes, parents/guardians, and program staff.
- Welcome all eligible athletes and implement strategies that encourage the participation of disadvantaged and disabled athletes.
- Manage athlete behavior consistent with an athlete-centered coaching philosophy.

Domain 2: Safety and Injury Prevention
Standard 8: Identify physical conditions that predispose athletes to injuries.

Athletes often join teams with pre-existing conditions or previous injuries that would preclude them from certain exercises or drills. The coach should be aware of such injuries and modify drills and exercises as appropriate.

Benchmarks
- Ensure that clearance for athletes to participate fully or partially in practices or contests is given by a parent, guardian, and/or medical professional.
- Recognize health status, body structure, and physical conditions that predispose athletes to common injuries specific to the sport.
- Be aware that an athlete's lack of sleep and/or emotional state could warrant a change in practice plans.

Domain 3: Physical Conditioning
Standard 13: Teach and encourage proper nutrition for optimal physical and mental performance and overall good health.

The coach must understand and teach appropriate nutrition and weight management practices. Counseling athletes about healthy eating is an important part of preparing athletes for sport performance. Proper nutrition and hydration are necessary to fuel the body.

Benchmarks

- Assist athletes in timing and selection of food options to fuel optimal energy production for practices and contests.
- Assist athletes in regulating safe levels of hydration.
- Provide accurate and timely information to athletes and parents/guardians about sound nutritional principles as part of training and preparation for competition.
- Provide accurate and timely information about body composition and healthy weight management.
- Be proactive in identifying potential eating disorders and referring athletes for appropriate professional assistance.

Domain 4: Growth and Development
Standard 18: Provide athletes with responsibility and leadership opportunities as they mature.

Sport provides an atmosphere for trial and error through practice and competition. Sport also allows opportunity for athletes to be challenged by additional responsibility. Through these opportunities, athletes learn how to deal with conflict, engage in problem solving, and seek positive resolutions. The coach should engage athletes in opportunities that nurture leadership and teamwork that can be learned on the field and exhibited in life.

Benchmarks

- Teach and encourage athletes to take responsibility for their actions in adhering to team rules.
- Design practices to allow for athlete input and self-evaluation.
- Communicate to athletes their responsibility in maintaining physical and mental readiness for athletic participation and preparation for competition.
- Encourage athletes to practice leadership skills and engage in problem solving.
- Provide athletes with different tools to manage conflict.
- Provide specific opportunities for athletes to mentor others

Domain 5: Teaching and Communication
Standard 24: Teach and incorporate mental skills to enhance performance and reduce sport anxiety.

Mental skill training assists the athlete in improving athletic performance. The variety of tools available allow the athlete to manage stress and direct their focus on their performance .

Benchmarks

- Demonstrate appropriate use of intrinsic and extrinsic rewards to enhance motivation and learning.
- Share with athletes effective stress management coping strategies.

- Utilize sound mental skills to build athlete self-confidence.
- Help athletes to develop a mental game plan that includes pre-game preparation, a contingency plan for errors during competition, and how to avoid competitive stress.
- Help athletes improve concentration by learning attention control strategies.

Domain 6: Sport Skills and Tactics
Standard 29: Use scouting methods for planning practices, game preparation, and game analysis

Preparing the athlete and/or team appropriately for competition is the responsibility of the coach. The coach should use appropriate scouting techniques that are in line with governing organizations and sport rules. Using resources available to evaluate opponents is a competitive advantage in preparing the athlete for competition.

Benchmarks
- Analyze opponent's personnel to organize team for competition.
- Create game plans by observation of opponent play, athlete statistical information, and previous competitive experience.
- Make adjustments in strategies for practice and competition by identifying patterns and styles of play of opponents.
- Develop scouting tools for collecting and organizing information about opponents.

Domain 7: Organization and Administration
Standard 31: Be involved in public relation activities for the sport program.

Public relations is the responsibility of the coach. Effective communication skills allow the coach to share the mission and values of the program and enlist support from the community. The coach must take every opportunity to be an advocate for the participants in the program.

Benchmarks
- Organize and conduct effective informational meetings before, during, and after the season.
- Communicate policies and ongoing program activities to athletes, staff, parents/guardians, administrators, and/or the public.
- Prepare athletes to be involved with public relation activities.
- Advocate the value of the sport program through positive communication with the media and others.

Domain 8: Evaluation
Standard 40: Utilize an objective and effective process for evaluation of self and staff.

The coach should assess the effectiveness of personnel that directly affect athlete and team performance. The evaluation should collect direct feedback from all program athletes and identify ways to improve techniques and coaching style. Self-evaluation is a critical source of information for professional growth and development.

Benchmarks
- Collect input from athletes, parents, guardians, coaches, and other stakeholders regarding athlete satisfaction, perception of season goals, and coaching performance.

- Conduct periodic self-reflections on coaching effectiveness.
- Seek feedback from experienced coaches to evaluate practice sessions, discuss observations, and implement needed change at regular intervals.
- Use formal written evaluations to assist in selecting and retaining program personnel.
- Be diplomatic when providing feedback on personnel evaluations or hiring decisions.

Appendix B

Extracurricular and Athletic Activities Code of Conduct
Bloomfield Central School District
Bloomfield, New York

Philosophy

At Bloomfield Central School extracurricular and athletic activities are an integral part of the educational experience. These programs are designed to promote greater desire in our student body and community to take an active role in our extracurricular and athletic activities as participants or spectators. Participation in extracurricular and athletic activities is a privilege that carries with it responsibilities to the school, the club or team, the student body and the Bloomfield community. Because participation is voluntary and is considered a privilege, student participants are expected to conduct themselves in a manner that represents the school, the club or team and the community in a positive and productive manner on and off school property, during and outside of participation times, during the season and the off-season.

This code outlines the conduct expectations for students who participate in extracurricular and athletic activities in addition to the Bloomfield Student Code of Conduct.

Definitions

Student Participant: This means any student enrolled in grades 6-12 at Bloomfield Middle/High School who participates in an extracurricular or athletic activity sponsored by the Bloomfield Central School District.

Extracurricular or Athletic Activity: This means any Bloomfield Central School District sponsored activity or sport that occurs beyond the scope of the school day for which grade is not given. This includes, but is not limited to clubs, performances, plays, sports tryouts, practices, games and contests. Extracurricular activities include, but are not limited to all sports, all clubs, school plays, Student Council, National Honor Society and Class Officers.

Code Coverage and Effective Dates: The provisions set forth by this code are in effect throughout the entire year, including weekends and holidays from the first day of fall sports to graduation.

General Provisions

Extracurricular Code of Conduct Acknowledgement Form: All students participating in extracurricular and athletic activities must have an Extracurricular Code of Conduct Acknowledgement Form signed by both the student participant and the parent/guardian on file in the athletic office prior to participation in any extracurricular or athletic activity.

Student Eligibility for Participation: All students participating in extracurricular or athletic activities will follow the academic and physical eligibility requirements as stipulated by the school board policies and building procedures.

Code of Conduct Provisions

Good Citizenship and Sportsmanship: Student participants will live by the laws of the country, state, county and town. Student participants will also follow the rules and policies of the Bloomfield Central School District and the athletic department as stated in the student agenda.

Consequences for Breaking the Good Citizenship and Sportsmanship Code of Conduct: Consequences, based on the nature, level of severity and the frequency of misconduct, can range from a warning, voluntary community service, one meeting or one game suspension to a year suspension as well as a suspension from attendance,

Tobacco, Alcohol and Drug Provisions:

Students participating in extracurricular and/or athletic activities are not allowed to use, be in the presence of, and/or engage in tobacco and alcohol and other drug activities, including performance-enhancing drugs. **("Alcohol and other drug activities" refers to sale, purchase, possession, consumption, being under the influence or in the presence of alcohol and/or other drugs on school grounds, at school functions, or at underage student activities off of school grounds.) ("In the presence of" is defined as going to and/or being at an underage student activity or function and not leaving immediately where illegal alcohol or drug activity occurs. This does not refer to family or religious events where alcohol is being served legally.)**

Consequences for Breaking the Tobacco, Alcohol and Drug Provisions:

All disciplinary action may carry over to subsequent activity time frame or regular sport season, i.e. a spring offense may result in a fall consequence. During the suspension period students will not be allowed to participate in clubs, performances, plays, sports tryouts, practices, games and contests.

FIRST OFFENSE
   A.) **Self-Report*:** If a student violates this code of conduct and self-reports to the advisor or coach, building administrator or athletic director, the student will be suspended for 10% of the activity time frame or regular sport season and will be assigned a drug and alcohol evaluation.

*Self-Report:** If a student participant initiates a meeting with the advisor or coach, building administrator or athletic director for the purpose of acknowledging involvement in a violation of the Bloomfield Central School District Extracurricular and Athletic Activities Code of Conduct. **The said acknowledgment must take place prior to the advisor or coach, building administrator or athletic director having knowledge of the incident.**

B.) **No Self-Report:** If a student violates this code of conduct, does not self-report and is found in violation, the student will be suspended for 20% of the activity time frame or regular sport season and may be assigned counseling**.

Counseling: In order to qualify for the counseling credit the student must receive a minimum of three approved counseling sessions through a referral by a school counselor or psychologist and provide written proof of participation within three weeks of the violation notification in order to continue in their extracurricular or athletic activity. Failure to receive this counseling within this time frame will result in suspension from these activities until the counseling requirement is fulfilled.

SECOND OFFENSE

If a student violates this code of conduct a second time and is found in violation the student will be suspended for 50% of the activity time frame or regular sport season and must undergo an individual evaluation and follow a prescribed intervention plan.

THIRD OFFENSE

Permanent suspension from participation in extracurricular and athletic activities. Students are eligible to apply for reinstatement through a superintendent's conference one year from the date of infraction.

DISCIPLINARY COMMUNICATION

1. A parent, student, teacher or administrator brings a concern to the coach, advisor or athletic director.
2. The advisor, coach or athletic director informs the Principal.
3. The Principal is then responsible for investigation, substantiation and communication around policy infraction. The athletic director will be involved in any parent/student meetings that take place concerning athletes. The meeting for the purposes of disciplinary action will afford the student and the parent the opportunity to discuss the proposed discipline with the individual authorized to impose the discipline. The student and or parent may appeal the disciplinary penalty to the superintendent within ten days. The superintendent shall render a decision within five days.

Athlete/Parent Contract Signature Agreement

I have read and fully understand my/our student participants and my/our responsibility regarding the Bloomfield Central School District Extracurricular and Athletic Activities Code of Conduct. I understand that he/she has a responsibility to abide by these rules and if he/she does not, disciplinary action will result. I agree to support the school in this effort.

Signed: _____   Date: _____
                    Parent or Guardian Signature

I have read the Bloomfield Central School District Extracurricular and Athletic Activities Code of Conduct. I promise to live by the Extracurricular and Athletic Activities Code of Conduct and understand that if I violate this contract, the result will be disciplinary actions as outlined.

Signed: _____   _____
                  Student Participant's Signature   Print Name

Date: _____

Signed: _____   _____
                         Coach's Signature   Print Name

Date: _____

Note: A copy of this contract will be field in the Athletic Office for twelve months from the day it is signed. The Extracurricular and Athletic Activities Code of Conduct is in effect during the entire school year from the start of the fall season until graduation. Student Participant's who do not have a contract on file will not be eligible to participate until this signed document is filed in the Athletic Office.

Appendix C-1

Finger Lakes Community College Intercollegiate Athletics Head Coach Evaluation Form (New York)

NAME: **DATE:**

SPORT:

Rating
Scale: 4   Outstanding
3   Commendable-Performance consistently above expectation
2   Competent-Work is being done in a professional manner
1   Conditional-Performance indicates effort must be made to improve.
0   Unsatisfactory-Performance is unacceptable
** A rating of 4 or 0 must include a brief explanation in the comments section.

PLAYER RELATIONS

1. ____   Communicates effectively with players.

2. ____   Appropriate use of motivational techniques.

3. ____   Sets high standards of conduct for himself/herself on and off the field.

4. ____   Sets high standards of conduct for athletes on and off the field.

Comments: _____

_____

ACADEMICS

Team GPA Fall _____

Spring _____ Overall _____

Graduation/Transfer Rate _____

1. ____   Makes student –athlete's education a priority

2. ____   Strives to keeps student-athlete class conflicts to a minimum.

3. ____   Communicates effectively (as needed) with Student /athletes' professors.

4. ____   Complies in a timely manner to all requests for information or action.

Comments: _____

_____

COMMUNITY SERVICE

1. Yes ___ No ___ Team participated in designated Athletics Department Community outreach initiative.

2. ____ Complies in a timely manner to all requests for information or action.

Comments: _____

_____

COMPLIANCE

1. Yes ___ No ____ Operated program with no major violations.

2. Yes ___ No ____ Secondary violations, if any, were reported in a timely manner.

3. Yes ___ No ___Attended all meetings. If no, how many were missed without prior

notice? _____.

4. Yes ___ No ___Follows NJCAA Recruiting Regulations.

5. ____ All necessary **Forms** completed in a timely manner.

6. ____ Complies in a timely manner to all requests for information or action.

Comments: _____

_____

BUSINESS AFFAIRS

1. ____ Operated within approved Budget.

2. ____ Submitted required documentation (i.e. PO requests, receipts, travel **forms)** in a timely manner.

3. ____ Submitted team travel itineraries on time.

4. ____ Participated in a positive manner during budget preparation process.

5. ____ Complies in a timely manner to all requests for information or action.

Comments: _____

_____

_____

FUND RAISING

1. ____ Participates in identifying potential Athletics Club donors.

2. ____ Participates in Athletics Department special events

3. ____ Complies in a timely manner to all requests for information or action.

Comments: _____

_____

PROFESSIONAL CONDUCT AND DEVELOPMENT

1. Yes ____ No ____ Followed all FLCC Athletics Department rules concerning personal conduct.

2. Yes ____ No ____ Participated in campus professional development opportunities.

3. Yes ____ No ____ Attended all departmental staff meetings.

4. ____ Complies in a timely manner to all requests for information or action.

5. ____ Maintains a good working relationship with relevant campus constituencies.

6. ____ Displays an enthusiastic and positive attitude toward the program, department and college.

7. ____ Confidentiality of college information. Displays loyalty to the program, department and college.

Comments: _____

_____

ATHLETICS COMPETITION

Final Results:
W _____ L _____ Conference Finish _____

Projected Goal: W _____ L _____ Conference Finish _____

Comments: _____

_____

_____

Recruiting Success:

Freshman _____ #Transfers _____

Squad Size (Start of year) _____

Squad Size (End of Academic Year) _____

OVERALL

POINTS ____ out of 92.

Comments:

I have discussed this evaluation this with the administrator identified below. I also acknowledge receiving a copy. I also understand that my signature does not indicate that I necessarily agree with the reviewer's statements.

Signed: _____ Date: _____ *Coach*

Signed: _____ Date: _____ *Athletic Director*

Appendix C-2

Albion Central School (New York)
Athletic Coach Performance Evaluation

Name: _____   School Year: _____

Sport: _____   Position: _____

U   = Unsatisfactory   Evidence indicates minimal/ineffective competency
B   = Basic   Evidence indicates sufficient but developing competency
Pro = Proficient   Evidence indicates effective competency
D   = Distinguished   Evidence indicates mastery of competency

DOMAIN 1:
PLANNING AND PREPARATION

_____ 1. Is familiar with the athletic policies of the Albion Central School District, N-O League, Section VI and N.Y.S.P.H.A.A.

_____ 2. Holds a pre-season meeting with students and also informs parents (through meetings or letters) of the philosophy of the program and of rules and regulations (schedules, practice times, attendance, criteria for earning a varsity letter or certificate, etc.).

_____ 3. Is responsible for the ACS athletic participation-parental consent forms to be accurately completed prior to submitting them to the nurse.

_____ 4. Plans, organizes and implements the teaching of fundamentals, strategy, rules and techniques.

DOMAIN 2:
ENVIRONMENT

A. Creating a Culture

_____ 5. Oversees the safety of the area in which the activities are conducted at times when athletes are present.

_____ 6. Promotes respect by example through appearance, manners, behavior, language and conduct during practices and contests.

_____ 7. Is prompt and consistent in meeting team for practices and contests.

_____ 8. Provides an atmosphere conducive to good sportsmanship and assists visiting teams, coaches and officials.

_____ 9. Properly supervises student-athletes.

657

B. Managing Procedures/Non-Instructional Duties

_____ 10. Secures medical clearance of squad candidates according to policies of ACS and N.Y.S.P.H.A.A. and S.E.D.

_____ 11. Submits list of candidates (tryout form) one week before the beginning date of the sports season to the Athletic Director for purpose of determining whether a student is eligible to compete in program.

_____ 12. Is responsible for the ACS athletic participation-parental consent forms to be accurately completed prior to submitting them to the nurse.

_____ 13. Submits roster to the Athletic Director in a timely fashion.

_____ 14. Issues equipment to players and maintains records of issued items.

_____ 15. Follows department policies for athletic transportation.

_____ 16. Maintains proper supplies, first aid kit and emergency cards at all times.

_____ 17. In cooperation with the school nurse, implements procedures for handling injuries and completing injury report forms for student health records and insurance purposes.

_____ 18. Promptly takes proper care of equipment, supplies and facilities.

_____ 19. Reports varsity game scores and other pertinent information to news media immediately following the game in accordance with District, League and Section policies.

_____ 20. Submits a list of collected, inventoried and stored equipment at end of season and completes end of season reports in a timely manner.

_____ 21. Makes recommendations concerning budget and equipment needs for the following season.

DOMAIN 3:
INSTRUCTION

_____ 22. Is available to counsel all participants in decision making relative to college choice, vocation or daily problems.

_____ 23. Head Coach: Instructs Assistants, J.V. and Jr. High coaches in technique, offensive and defensive systems.

_____ 24. J.V. Coach: Increases use of strategy, balances participation and winning.

_____ 25. Jr. High Coaches: Effective in teaching fundamentals and maximizes participation.

_____ 26. Plans, organizes and implements the teaching of fundamentals, strategy, rules and techniques.

_____ 27. Teaches and reinforces good health habits with athletes, including the establishment of sound training rules.

_____ 28. Teaches student-athletes to use only legitimate and ethical means in attempting to win a game.

DOMAIN 4:
PROFESSIONAL DEVELOPMENT/RESPONSIBILITIES

_____ 29. Maintains an interest in the student's academic performance.

_____ 30. Attends coaches' meetings, clinics, inservice programs.

_____ 31. Cooperates with Athletic Director, all other coaches/sponsors to upgrade total athletic program.

_____ 32. Cooperates with teaching staff, parents, members of the news media and other citizens to insure good public relations.

_____ 33. Holds a pre-season meeting with students and also informs parents (through meetings or letters) of the philosophy of the program and of rules and regulations (schedules, practice times, attendance, criteria for earning a varsity letter or certificate, etc.).

_____ 34. Evaluate total program and submit any recommendations for program improvement to Athletic Director.

COMMENTS/*EVIDENCE:

Athletic Director: _____ Date: _____

Building Principal: _____ Date: _____

COACH'S COMMENTS:

Coach's Signature: _____ Date: _____

*Evidence must be provided for areas evaluated at the Basic or Unsatisfactory levels.

Appendix C-3 Part 1

Assistant Coach Evaluation

Sport: _____   Head Coach: _____

Assistant Coach: _____   Position: _____

   1. Loyalty to head coach and system   _____ _____ _____
   2. Care of equipment   _____ _____ _____
   3. Knowledge of sport   _____ _____ _____
   4. Teaching ability   _____ _____ _____
   5. Ability to motivate   _____ _____ _____
   6, Rapport between coach and players   _____ _____ _____
   7. Intensity of interest in coaching this sport   _____ _____ _____
   8. Supervision of players in locker room/other areas   _____ _____ _____
   9. Rapport between coach and rest of coaching staff   _____ _____ _____
 10. Accepts duties given by head coach   _____ _____ _____
 11. General evaluation of this coach by:
     a. Head coach   _____ _____ _____
     b. Athletic administrator   _____ _____ _____

COMMENTS:

The coach's signature indicates that all phases of the appraisal have been conducted with the full knowledge of the coach.

Head coach's signature _____   Date: _____

Assistant coach's signature: _____   Date: _____

Athletic administrator's signature: _____   Date: _____

CIRCLE ONE:

Successful:	To be recommended for continued assignment
Needs Improvement	To be recommended for reassignment provided an understanding can be reached in areas where improvement is suggested
Unsatisfactory:	Not to be recommended for continued assignment

> White—Assistant Coach
> Canary—Superintendent's office
> Green—Head Coach
> Pink—Athletic Administrator
> Gold—Principal's Office

Coaching Observation Form

Date: _____

Coach _____ Position _____ Sport _____ Level _____

I. Teaching Personality

____ Self-control and poise

____ Appropriate sense of humor

____ Emotional stability

____ Vitality and good health

____ Enthusiasm in working with athletes

____ Appearance

____ Punctuality in attendance

____ Voice quality

____ Appropriate language

II. Professional Qualities

____ Has harmonious relationship with staff

____ Upholds department and school policies, rules and regulations

____ Follows prescribed practice plan

____ Has good relationship with parents

____ Follows goals and objectives for year

____ Submits written reports on time

____ Has good relationship with personnel from other schools

____ Keeps athletic administrator informed about sport

III. Team Management

____ Is prompt in meeting team

____ Supervises locker room before/after

____ Makes maximum use of time available

____ Demonstrates care of equipment/facilities

____ Uses good team discipline and control (respect, not fear)

____ Utilizes staff

____ Utilizes players

____ Commands respect by example in appearance, manners, behavior, language

IV. Coaching Performance

____ Has knowledge and expertise of sport

____ Has the ability to motivate athletes

____ Has the ability to give directions

____ Exhibits leadership on field/court

____ Provides individual/group instruction

____ Well versed in strategy

____ Practices are well planned

____ Has effective game organization

COMMENTS:

Athletic Administrator's Signature: _____

Appendix C3 Part 2

Head Coach Evaluation Form

_____
(Name of Coach   (Sport Assignment)   (Level & School)

General Comments about Season

_____

_____

1. Effective   2. Needs Improvement   3. Unsatisfactory   4. No Opportunity to Observe   5. Not Applicable   6. Refer to Comments

I PROFESSIONAL AND PERSONAL RELATIONSHIPS
1. Cooperates with the athletic administrator and faculty manager to submit participant lists, bus times, parent permission and physical cards, year-end reports, roster information and coaching plan prior to season. ____ ____
2. Follows policy in he athletic handbook and meets all criteria as outlined in job description. ____ ____
3. Provides training rules to team members in writing and follows due process procedures. ____ ____
4. Develops rapport with the athletic coaching staff ____ ____
5. Is appropriately dressed at the practice and game. ____ ____
6. Participates in in-service meetings and other activities to improve coaching performance. ____ ____
7. Develops sound public relations. Cooperates with newspapers, radio, television, booster club and interested spectators. ____ ____
8. Understands and follows rules and regulations set forth by all governing agencies: state association, Board of Education and league. ____ ____
9. Participates in parent's night, banquets, award nights, pep assemblies and letters to colleges regarding players. ____ ____
10. Maintains appropriate sideline conduct at games with respect to players, officials and other workers. ____ ____
11. Develops rapport with the teachers, coaches and administrators. ____ ____
12. Works cooperatively with junior high coaches in developing a coordinated program. ____ ____
13. Promotes all sports in the athletic program attempting to foster school spirit ____ ____
14. Cooperates and communicates with parents during the entire year. ____ ____
15. Works cooperatively with the athletic administrator. ____ ____

II. COACHING PERFORMANCE:
1. Develops respect by example in appearance, manners, behavior, language and conduct during a contest. ____ ____
2. Provides proper supervision and administration of locker and training room and on bus trips. ____ ____
3. Is well versed and knowledgeable in matters pertaining to the sport. ____ ____
4. Has individual and team discipline and control. ____ ____
5. Develops a well organized practice schedule which utilizes his/her staff and team to its maximum potential. ____ ____
6. Established the fundamental philosophy, skills and techniques to be taught by the staff. ____ ____
7. Holds periodic staff meetings, including junior high coaches to implement the above. ____ ____

8. Develops integrity within he coaching staff, fellow coaches and works to make better coaches. ____ ____
9. Is fair, understanding, tolerant, sympathetic and patient with team members ____ ____
10. Is innovative using new coaching techniques and ideas in addition to sound, already proven methods of coaching. ____ ____
11. Is prompt in meeting team for practices and games ____ ____
12. Shows an interest in athletes in off-season activities and classroom efforts ____ ____
13. Provides leadership and attitudes that produce positive efforts by participants. ____ ____
14. Knows the medical aspects of the position, including first aid, injury policies, working with team doctor and/or family physician ____ ____
15. Delegates authority with responsibility while remaining accountable for such delegations. ____ ____
16. Provides an atmosphere of cooperation in being receptive to suggestions and giving credit to those responsible for success. ____ ____
17. Uses all possible ethical means of motivation, emphasizes values of competitive athletics, acceptable personal behavior, decision-making and lasting values to each individual. ____ ____
18. Utilizes videotape along with providing instructions on proper care and use. ____ ____
19. Utilizes practice time for both individual and team development. ____ ____
20. Team performance consistent with quality of athletes available. ____ ____

III. RELATED COACHING RESPONSIBILITIES:
1. Is concerned about the care of equipment, including issue, collection inventory and storage. ____ ____
2. Is cooperative in developing non-league schedules and securing officials. ____ ____
3. Is cooperative in sharing facilities. ____ ____
4. Shows self-control and poise in areas related to coaching responsibilities. ____ ____
5. Displays enthusiasm and exhibits interest in coaching. ____ ____
6. Keeps athletic administrator informed about unusual events. ____ ____
7. Is cooperative in helping service clubs, booster club, recreation department and other organizations in their projects which in turn relate to the athletic program. ____ ____
8. Encourages all potential athletes to participate in sport programs. ____ ____
9. Follows proper procedure for purchase of equipment. ____ ____
10. Operates sport within the budget as submitted by the coach. ____ ____

SUMMARY   Date: _____   Season: _____

Number of years coaching in this assignment: _____
Number of years coaching in school district: _____

STRENGTHS:

JOB TARGETS:

COMMENTS:

_____   _____
(Evaluator's Signature and Position)   (Date)

_____   _____
(Head Coach's Signature   (Date)

CIRCLE ONE:

Successful: To be recommended for contract renewal

Needs   To be recommended for contract renewal
Improvement   provided an understanding can be reached
                   in areas where improvement is suggested

Unsatisfactory: To be recommended for non-renewal of contract

White—Head Coach
Canary—Superintendent's office
Pink—Athletic Administrator
Gold—Principal's Office

Appendix C-3 Part 3

Coach Self-Evaluation

Coach: _____ Sport _____ Date: _____

Rate yourself on the following items related to well-organized, effective coaching. Please indicate G (good), A (adequate), P (poor), D (deficient), or NA (not applicable) on the lines preceding each numbered item.

MAJOR PRE-SEASON RESPONSIBILITIES:

_____ 1. Medical clearance of squad candidates according to _____ Public Schools and _____ High School League regulations.

_____ 2. Alphabetized list of candidates, identified by grade and section, submitted approximately four weeks before the beginning date of the sports season to the athletic administrator for the purpose of obtaining information from the guidance department to assist in determining whether or not a student is eligible to compete in the interscholastic athletic program.

_____ 3. _____ High School League Participation-Parental Consent Forms accurately completed prior to submission to athletic administrator.

_____ 4. Insurance form completed and signed by a parent or guardian before candidate begins practice.

MAJOR RESPONSIBILITIES DURING SEASON:

_____ 1. Provides a rough draft of _____ High School League master eligibility list submitted to the athletic administrator in ample time for him to review, correct when necessary, and forward to a secretary to be typed and sent to _____ High School League office and each opponent on schedule one day prior to date of first game.

_____ 2. Issues of a _____ Interscholastic Athletic Regulations Handbook to squad members who are participants in sport for the first time, and reviews regulations with all squad members.

_____ 3. Supervision of squad members from time of arrival for a practice or competition until the conclusion of the activity.

_____ 4. Adherence to the regulations relative to towel service..

_____ 5. Care of equipment, supplies and school facilities.

_____ 6. Care of injuries and completion of injury report forms for student health records and insurance purposes.

_____ 7. Follows proper procedures to ensure that squad members are excused from school for athletic contests.

_____ 8. Adherence to regulations relative to overnight squad trips.

_____ 9. Personal pre-game preparations (transportation, equipment, facilities).

_____ 10. Appropriate personal conduct at games toward players, officials and spectators.

_____ 11. Reporting of varsity game scores and other pertinent information to all newspapers not represented at the contest as soon as feasible after a home game.

**MAJOR RESPONSIBILIIES AFTER SEASON
(SUBMIT TO ATHLETIC ADMINISTRATOR):**

_____ 1. Provide a list of squad members who completed the season (varsity letter winners, junior varsity certificate winners, special award recipients).

_____ 2. Season record—opponents and scores, any championships won and any outstanding achievements by a player such as mot points scored in a game, high scorer for season, etc.

_____ 3. Detailed list of players who failed to return issued school equipment.

_____ 4. Completed form for county health and physical education office which requires number of participants, record and information on injuries.

_____ 5. Inventory of equipment on hand—indicating condition.

_____ 6. Budget submitted for next season.

MISCELLANOUS ITEMS:

_____ 1. High ideals, good habits and desirable attitudes in person behavior.

_____ 2. Participation in coaching clinics and in-service programs. Studying films, magazines and books related to sport to aid in becoming a more effective coach.

_____ 3. Rapport with players.

_____ 4. Rapport with coaching staff.

_____ 5. Knowledge of game rules, fundamentals and strategy.

_____ 6. Ability to improve player performance.

_____ 7. Organizational ability.

_____ 8. Teaching student-athletes to use only legitimate and ethical means in attempting to win game.

_____ 9. Respect and concern for athletes, students, parents, colleagues and other citizens.

_____ 10. Cooperation with teaching staff, co-coaches, parents, newspapers, etc., to attain and maintain good public relations.

COMMENTS:

Signature of Coach: _____ Date: _____

Please return personally to athletic administrator for discussion of self-evaluation

I am in agreement with this self-evaluation, except as noted above.

Signature of Athletic Administrator: _____ Date: _____

Appendix C-4

Salamanca City Central School District (New York)
Coaching Staff Evaluation

Name: _____   Position: _____

> Please rate each behavioral characteristic by checking the appropriate box:
> 1 – Excellent   2 – Competent   3 – Needs Improvement   4 – Unsatisfactory   5 – N/A

1. Efficiency

	1	2	3	4	5
Uses the purchase order system properly	[ ]	[ ]	[ ]	[ ]	[ ]
Completes officials vouchers on time	[ ]	[ ]	[ ]	[ ]	[ ]
Inventories equipment annually	[ ]	[ ]	[ ]	[ ]	[ ]
Holds pre-season signups	[ ]	[ ]	[ ]	[ ]	[ ]
Gets names of potential athletes to nurse for physicals	[ ]	[ ]	[ ]	[ ]	[ ]
Has election criteria in place if athletic cuts apply	[ ]	[ ]	[ ]	[ ]	[ ]
Maintains accurate records/statistics for promoting and recognizing achievement	[ ]	[ ]	[ ]	[ ]	[ ]
Turns in typed rosters to Athletic Director at beginning of season and updates them at the end of season	[ ]	[ ]	[ ]	[ ]	[ ]
Holds annual awards ceremony for athletes	[ ]	[ ]	[ ]	[ ]	[ ]
Turns in accolades of team for Pow-Wow publication when requested by A.D.	[ ]	[ ]	[ ]	[ ]	[ ]
Turns in equipment an uniforms at end of season	[ ]	[ ]	[ ]	[ ]	[ ]

2. Work Habits

	1	2	3	4	5
Punctual	[ ]	[ ]	[ ]	[ ]	[ ]
Attendance	[ ]	[ ]	[ ]	[ ]	[ ]
Attitude	[ ]	[ ]	[ ]	[ ]	[ ]
Plans Well/Organized	[ ]	[ ]	[ ]	[ ]	[ ]
Represents our school district in a positive fashion	[ ]	[ ]	[ ]	[ ]	[ ]

3. Personal Relations

	1	2	3	4	5
Gets along with fellow coaches	[ ]	[ ]	[ ]	[ ]	[ ]
Gets along with immediate supervisor	[ ]	[ ]	[ ]	[ ]	[ ]
Attitude toward athletes	[ ]	[ ]	[ ]	[ ]	[ ]
Relationship with officials	[ ]	[ ]	[ ]	[ ]	[ ]
Personal appearance	[ ]	[ ]	[ ]	[ ]	[ ]

4. Initiative

	1	2	3	4	5
Accepts additional responsibility	[ ]	[ ]	[ ]	[ ]	[ ]
Uses good judgment	[ ]	[ ]	[ ]	[ ]	[ ]
Adapts/Accepts change	[ ]	[ ]	[ ]	[ ]	[ ]
Works with teachers in regards to academics and their athletes	[ ]	[ ]	[ ]	[ ]	[ ]

5. Community and Public Relations

Turns in the results to the press and high school office	[ ]	[ ]	[ ]	[ ]	[ ]

Turns in the results to the press and high school office [ ] [ ] [ ] [ ] [ ]
Works to promote the sport within the community [ ] [ ] [ ] [ ] [ ]
Communicates with the parents/guardians of athletes on a
    professional level when dealing with questions and/or
    problems [ ] [ ] [ ] [ ] [ ]
Works with the booster club to help raise money for the program [ ] [ ] [ ] [ ] [ ]

Evaluator's Comments:

Some Things I'd Like to See You Work On:

Supervisor: _____ Date: _____

I have read this evaluation and understand its content. I understand that I may attach a statement if desired.

Coach: _____ Date: _____

Appendix C-5a

Lyons Central School District
Athletic Department
Head Coach Evaluation Form

Name of Coach: _____ _____ Sport _____

Rating Scale: 1 weak → → → → → → → →3 average → → → → → → → → 5 strong

1. ___ Follows a clearly written Mission Statement regarding his/her athletic program.

2. ___ Provides opportunities for participation for all students who desire to participate.

3. ___ Goals are harmonious with the goals of the entire athletic program.

4. ___ Always considers the health and welfare of the athletes during practices and competitions.

5. ___ Maintains accurate and updated records on the documents (physical exam EMA, etc) turned in by student athletes and denies participation to those students who have neglected to turn in any single form.

6. ___ Attempts to improve the physical skills of the athletes.

7. ___ Attempts to improve the mental skills of the athletes.

8. ___ Attempts to improve the social skills of the athletes.

9. ___ Promotes an ethical approach to all contests and practices.

10. ___ Fosters sportsmanship in his/her athletic program.

11. ___ Does not conduct practices that disrupt the regular academic program of the school

12. ___ Designates the procedures that are to be followed regarding the distribution, care and collection of equipment.

13. ___ The coaching staff, under the direction of the head coach, supports and follows the decisions made by medical personnel regarding any athlete.

14. ___ Maintains regular and positive contact with parents.

15. ___ Maintains regular communication with the athletic director and/or principal

16. ___ Attends meetings consistently as called by the athletic director or principal.

17. ___ The entire coaching staff, under the direction of the head coach, maintains a cooperative and cordial relationship with administrators, faculty and other coaches.

18. ___ Maintains high standards of conduct for the entire coaching staff and student participants.

19. ___ The coaching staff, under the direction of the head coach, supports and follows the decisions made by officials.

20. ___ Designate the procedures that are to be followed regarding the supervision of athletes and the facilities.

21. ___ Promotes good citizenship and superior conduct in the student athletes.

22. ___ Communicates regularly and positively to all representatives of the media.

23. ___ Words effectively with the athletic director in establishing a budget.

24. ___ Follows all regulations, rules and policies as established by the national federation, state athletic association and local school board before, during and after the season.

Assistant Coach's Comments: _____

_____

_____

Athletic Director's Comments: _____

_____

_____

_____

_____   _____

  Signature of Athletic Director   Date

Coach's Comments: _____

_____

_____

_____   _____

  Signature of Coach   Date

_____   _____

  Signature of Principal   Date

Appendix C-56
Lyons Central School District
Coach's Evaluation

Name of Coach: _____

Assignment _____ **Level** _____ Date: _____

Rating Scale: NA=Not applicable   1=Improvement needed   2=Satisfactory   3=Good

Professional and Personal Relationships:

1.	Submits all lists, eligibility, equipment, needs and program information relative to sport to the athletic office.	NA	1	2	3
2.	Cooperates with maintenance personnel in care of sports area.	NA	1	2	3
3.	Rapport with other coaches and support staff.	NA	1	2	3
4.	Implements and accepts ALL athletic department decisions and policies	NA	1	2	3
5.	Carries out district policies relating to interscholastic athletics.	NA	1	2	3
6.	Sidelines conduct at games towards players, officials, fans etc.	NA	1	2	3
7.	Encourages students to participate in athletic programs.	NA	1	2	3
8.	Respects and supports other coaches and athletes during their season	NA	1	2	3
9.	Keeps athletic office informed of any and all problems that arise.	NA	1	2	3
10.	Keeps athletic office informed of the condition of practice and game fields.	NA	1	2	3
11.	Reports all injuries to the nurse and athletic training staff.	NA	1	2	3
12.	Conducts Chemical health Meeting with athletes.	NA	1	2	3
13.	Hands in preliminary, and final rosters on time.	NA	1	2	3
14.	Hands in officials rating cards on time.	NA	1	2	3

Coaching Performance:

1. Supervises athletes at ALL times (locker rooms, fields, and gymnasiums)   NA   1   2   3
2. Knowledge of: a) the sport
                     b) eligibility information
                     c) rules of the sport along with recent changes
                     d) section and state rules.   NA   1   2   3
3. Coach's expectations for student participation in sports (in writing).   NA   1   2   3
4. Arrives on time for meetings, practices and games.   NA   1   2   3
5. Remains current to new techniques and ideas along with established procedures for coaching. (clinics, workshops, etc.)   NA   1   2   3
6. Understands and demonstrates new techniques and ideas along with established practices for coaching.   NA   1   2   3
7. Does not let coaching interfere with classroom responsibilities.   NA   1   2   3
8. Demonstrates appropriate decision making skills.   NA   1   2   3
9. Encourages respect (verbal, physical, emotional and psychological for all the student/athletes.   NA   1   2   3
10. Tracks academic, attendance and discipline patterns of athletes.   NA   1   2   3
11. Evidence of pre-season planning and preparation.   NA   1   2   3
12. Maintains records and inventory of team equipment and supplies.   NA   1   2   3
13. Pursues opportunities for athletes beyond high school.   NA   1   2   3

671

14. Explains and understands and implements district and athletic program substance abuse policy.   NA   1   2   3

15. Encourages ALL athletes to develop:
         a) individually and as a team member
         b) intellectually   NA   1   2   3

16. Demonstrates quality leadership skills.   NA   1   2   3

Related Responsibilities:

1. Meets all deadlines.   NA   1   2   3

2. Turns in all related materials including year-end inventory, team rosters, outstanding uniforms list, and awards recommendations.   NA   1   2   3

3. Takes proper care of equipment, storage and issue.   NA   1   2   3

4. Request for supplies and equipment turned in to the athletic office.   NA   1   2   3

Additional Comments:

_____
_____
_____
_____
_____
_____

Coach's Comments:

_____
_____
_____
_____
_____
_____

Overall Performance in this Assignment:

Satisfactory	**Probationary**	**Unsatisfactory**
Recommended for continued assignment	Recommended for assignment provided an understanding can be reached in areas where improvement is suggested.	Not to be recommended for reassignment

_____   _____

Evaluator's Signature   Date   Coach's Signature   Date

Signature of coach is only to show that he/she has received this evaluation.

Appendix C-5c
Lyons Central School District
Interscholastic Coaching Evaluation

Coach' Name:
School Year:
Sport:
Level:

Key: C = Commendable   I = Improvement needed
          S = Satisfactory   NA = Not applicable

Note: Athletic Administrators are responsible for all coaching evaluations and will seek the input from varsity/head coaches for those coaches within their specific sport.

I. PROFESSIONAL AND PERSONAL RELATIONSHIP/COACHING PERFORMANCE;

		C	S	I	NA
A.	Displays appropriate behavior and embraces sportsmanship	☐ C	☐ S	☐ I	☐ NA
B.	Respects and supports other coaches and athletes	☐ C	☐ S	☐ I	☐ NA
C.	Is dressed appropriately at practices and games	☐ C	☐ S	☐ I	☐ NA
D.	Works cooperatively with Athletic Administrators and Athletic Office	☐ C	☐ S	☐ I	☐ NA
E.	Understands and follows rules and regulations of NYSPHSAA, Section V and Lyons Central School District.	☐ C	☐ S	☐ I	☐ NA
F.	Completes all end-of-the-season reports in a timely manner	☐ C	☐ S	☐ I	☐ NA
G.	Communicates budgetary needs and maintains current inventory (follows thru with A/D requests	☐ C	☐ S	☐ I	☐ NA
H.	Organizes daily practices	☐ C	☐ S	☐ I	☐ NA
I.	Cares for uniforms/equipment	☐ C	☐ S	☐ I	☐ NA
J.	Understands the needs of individual players	☐ C	☐ S	☐ I	☐ NA
K.	Submits Official Rating Cards in a timely manner	☐ C	☐ S	☐ I	☐ NA
L.	Accepts constructive feedback and is willing to change.	☐ C	☐ S	☐ I	☐ NA
M.	Demonstrates sound strategies during game situation	☐ C	☐ S	☐ I	☐ NA
N.	Exhibits good relationship with parents	☐ C	☐ S	☐ I	☐ NA
O.	Provides proper supervision and security of locker rooms and practice areas.	☐ C	☐ S	☐ I	☐ NA
P.	Maintains individual and team discipline and control	☐ C	☐ S	☐ I	☐ NA
Q.	Assists individual players and parents with recruiting efforts.	☐ C	☐ S	☐ I	☐ NA
R.	Understands and embraces the overall MS/HS mission and academic goals.	☐ C	☐ S	☐ I	☐ NA

II. PROFESSIONAL DEVELOPMENT

A. Attends coaching clinics and/or makes an attempt to increase knowledge and proficiency as a coach (i.e: sports caps, videos, professional, books, etc.)

☐ Yes ☐ No ☐ Sometimes

Comments:

B. Works with and/or assists with local sports organizations/programs

☐ Yes ☐ No ☐ Sometimes

Comments

B. Helps to develop assistant and/or lower level coaches within their sport.

☐ Yes ☐ No ☐ Sometimes

Comments:

D. Coaching Certification/Permanent:
- T.C.L. Completed ☐ Yes ☐ No ☐ NA
- Has been grandfathered ☐ Yes ☐ No ☐ NA
- Has completed all course work and is fully certified ☐ Yes ☐ No ☐ NA
- Needs to complete the following coaching courses:
  - ➢ Philosophy of Coaching ☐ Yes ☐ No
  - ➢ Techniques of Coaching ☐ Yes ☐ No
  - ➢ Health Sciences as it relates to coaching ☐ Yes ☐ No

E. Needs to update recertification
- First Aid (every 3 years) ☐ Yes ☐ No
- CPR/AED (annually) ☐ Yes ☐ No

F. Do you plan on returning next year? ☐ Yes ☐ No

COMMENTS:

☐ Satisfactory—will recommend for future assignment
☐ Probationary—will recommend with the agreement of:
  A. An agreement to work on areas that need improvement
  B. Providing a certified and qualified person does not put in for your position
☐ Unsatisfactory—will not be recommended for reassignment

SIGNATURES:

Coach: _____ Date: _____

Head Coach: _____ Date: _____

Athletic Administrator: _____ Date: _____

MS/HS Principal: _____ Date: _____

Appendix C-5d

Lyons Central School District
Athletic Department
Athlete's Coach Evaluation Form

Name of Athlete (optional): _____

Level (JV or V) _____ Sport: _____

Student athlete feedback regarding current athletic coach. The following statements represent aspects of the coach's job responsibilities. Please respond to these statements using the scale shown below.

Rating Scale: 3 = Exceeds expectations   2 = Meets Expectations   1 = Needs Improvement

MY COACH:

1. ___ Has knowledge and adheres to all athletic policies, the Code of Ethics and the. Academic Eligibility Policies of the District.
2. ___ Supervises athletes before, during and after all practice sessions and contests.
3. ___ Maintains appropriate discipline and works to increase morale and cooperation with the athletic program.
4. ___ Coaches individual participants in the skills necessary for achievement in the sport.
5. ___ Instructs and requires athletes to give proper care to all equipment.
6. ___ Establishes criteria for selection of team members and criteria for competition in his/her sport.
7. ___ Provides feedback to me concerning my performance.
8. ___ Has been consistent and fair in his/her dealings with me.
9. ___ Has supported and encouraged me in my role.
10. ___ Provides athletes and parents/guardians with practice and game schedules.
11. ___ Assists with development of goals and objectives for sport.
12. ___ Conducts himself/herself professionally at all times.
13. ___ Serves as a positive role model for students and other staff.
14. ___ Looks after me during the off-season as well as in season.
15. ___ Makes contact with college coaches
16. ___ Demonstrates enthusiasm for his/her job.
17. ___ Is clear with regards to his/her expectations of me.
18. ___ Goes beyond the call of duty (summer leagues, open gym, tournaments, etc.).

The part of the job my coach does particularly well: _____

_____

_____

_____

_____

_____

My coach could be more effective if: _____

_____

_____

_____

_____

_____

Other comments, concerns and suggestions: _____

_____

_____

_____

_____

_____

_____

_____

Appendix D

Individual and Team Basketball Rating Form

	Name of Athletes	1.	2.	3.	4.	5.	6.	7.	8.	9.	10.	11.	12.	13.	14.	15.	Average for team
RANK — *among centers*																	
RANK — *among forwards*																	
RANK — *among guards*																	
RANK — *AMONG TEAM MEMBERS*																	
TOTAL POINTS																	
Ability to prevent mistakes in critical situations																	
Knowledge/understanding of defensive Style																	
Knowledge/understanding of offensive Style																	
Attitude																	
Helpfulness to staff and team																	
Moral Value to Team																	
Sportsmanship and Decorum																	
Individual Defensive Play																	
Individual Offensive Play																	
Offensive team play																	
Defensive team play																	
Speed, Movement, Maneuverability																	
Effort, Output in Games and Practice																	
Observance of Training Rules																	
Physical Conditioning																	

RATING SCALE BASKETBALL
8-10 Excellent
6-7 Very Good
4-5 Adequate/Acceptable
1-3 Needs Improvement

Appendix E
Lafayette High School Athletic Requirements
For Earning a Varsity Letter

A. BASIC SCHOOL REQUIREMENTS FOR A VARSITY LETTER

- An athlete must participate in an athletic department community service project for each sports season in which they play a sport.
- An athlete must attend the sports banquet or they will not receive their certificate, letter or any other awards. The only exception is if the athlete is excused by the coach before the banquet date.
- An athlete must not miss any games or events because of participation in a non-school club, recreational, etc. activity.
- An athlete must display sportsmanship and conduct which exemplify the school to his or her opponent, spectators, teammates, and officials and must conform to practice and game rules/regulations as established by the school and the coach of that sport.
- An athlete must conform to all training rules established by the coach for that sport.
- The athlete must return all equipment issued to him or her to the satisfaction of the coach and/or athletic director.
- In the event of injury or other legitimate extenuating circumstances, letter winners will be made on the recommendation of the coach to the athletic director.
- Only one letter will be awarded to any athlete in attendance at Lafayette High School. When a letter is awarded to an athlete, the athlete will also receive a representative pin for that sport. Letter winners in more than one sport will be designated by a representative pin for that sport. Athletes who have earned a letter in a sport for more than one season will be given a service bar for each letter awarded.
- Once a letter has been awarded, the athlete may at his or her own expense purchase a letter jacket. The letter jackets will be purchased through Colonial Sports of Williamsburg—253-0277.
- Certificates will be given to all team members who participated for the full season.
- Pins will be given to team captains and co-captains.
- Super Ram certificates will be given to all senior athletes who participate in and complete the season in each of the three sports seasons of the year.
- Plaques will be given to all athletes who make a special select team, for example: First Team All-District, First and Second Team All-Region, First, Second, Third and Fourth Team All State.
- PRINCIPALS AWARD: Given to the outstanding male and female student/athlete of the senior class. This award will be chosen b the entire faculty and staff at Lafayette High School.

- GORDIE TUTMAN AWARD: Given to the outstanding senior athlete according to the guidelines established for the award. The winner of this award is chosen by all the Lafayette head coaches.

B. BASIC TEAM REQUIREMENTS FOR A VARSITY LETTER
- Played in 50% of all the quarters or halves played during the season for the following varsity sports: field hockey, football, basketball, soccer.
- Played and placed (when applicable) in at least one-half of all contests in the following varsity sports: golf, volleyball, tennis, wrestling, softball, basketball and cross country.
- Scored at least 20 points for their team during the year in the following varsity sports: swimming, indoor and outdoor track and gymnastics.

Points will be assigned for Lafayette Letter purposes as follows:

For single events:
    a. 7 points for a 1st place finish
    b. 6 points for a 2nd place finish
    c. 5 points for a 3rd place finish
    d. 4 points for a 4th place finish
    e. 3 points for a 5th place finish
    f. 2 points for a 6th place finish

Relay events—points for each participant in the event
    b. 4 points for a 1st place finish
    c. 3 points for a 2nd place finish
    d. 2 points for a 3rd place finish
    e. 1 point for a 4th place finish

- Cheerleaders must cheer at 90% of all contests in the following varsity sports: football, girls and boys basketball, and selected wresting meets.
- Mangers and trainers who have served the varsity for two or more sports seasons and attend three-fourths of all games and practices
- Any senior who has not met the award requirements, but has been a member in good standing for two or more years.
- The head coach may recommend awards in special cases to athletes who have not met the requirements.

Obtained from Dan Barner, Athletic Director at Lafayette High School,
Williamsburg-James City County Public Schools, Williamsburg, VA.

Appendix F

Organization of an Interview Session

Organization of an Effective Interview Session for Prospective Coaches
(Obtained from Doug Westcott, then AD at Brockport High School, NY)

I. **General Information**
   A. Introduction of candidate and screening committee members. Explanation of the responsibilities of committee members
   B. Format for the interview
      1. Designation of interviewing chairperson
      2. Timetable for interview: 20-35 minutes of questions from committee, 5-10 minutes of questions from candidates about position and responsibilities

II. **General Interview Techniques**
   A. Make the candidate comfortable. Use a quiet office or room where you will not be disturbed or interrupted. Have secretary hold all calls.
   B. Let the candidate talk. Listen attentively and acknowledge good points.
   C. Give direction to novice candidates who may have difficulty communicating
   D. Permit the candidate to ask you questions about the program goals, policies, etc.
   E. Tell the candidate exactly hoe you'll be communicating (letter, phone call, other). Tell the candidate that you'll be interviewing other candidates.

III. **Suggested Questions for Screening Committee**
   A. General Questions relating to one's background
      1. Review candidate's status for coaching and first aid
      2. Ask candidate for information on background education and experiences that have helped in the preparation to coach
         a. Experience as a player
         b. Experience as a coach
         c. Workshops, seminars, or camp participation
   B. Content questions relating to actual coaching of the sport, organization, and philosophy of sport
      1. What kind of relationship do you want with your players?
      2. What part will goal-setting play in your program, and will you share them with athletes?
      3. Use of positive and negative approaches to coaching

4. What is your philosophy on winning and losing?
    a. How many players on your team will see action in a close contest
    b. Do you see a need to explain to all players their role on a team?
5. What kind of expectations would you set for your players?
    a. Conduct
    b. Sportsmanship
    c. Accountability
    d. Appearance
6. What kind of image do you want your team to project? Yourself?
7. Describe how you might organize a typical practice
    a. How will you set the tone?
    b. How long will your practice be?
    c. Will you write plans for each practice?
8. How will you incorporate overall fitness and conditioning into your practice?
9. If coaching a female team, dhow will you treat the athlete in regard to
    a. Performance expectations
    b. Coach/player communication
10. How will you get a handle on feelings and concerns of individual team members?
11. What role would you play in the success of the athlete in the classroom?
12. What role will the assistant coaches have in your program?
    a. What will you do to define responsibilities?
    b. How honest will you be in the evaluation process?
    c. Would you recommend terminating an assistant coach who isn't supportive and doesn't carry out responsibilities?
C. Sport-specific questions to learn level of knowledge in offensive and defensive strategy and game preparation
    1. What would you do to prepare your team for a big competition?
    2. How would you motivated players to excel when the opponent is not competitive?
    3. How will you train athletes to react to specific game situations in practice?
    4. What role will execution of fundamental skills play in your practice sessions?
    5. Explain the use of a particular offensive or defensive scheme in relation to a specific game situation (question should deal with a sport-specific situation)
    6. How will you determined when a particular athlete or team has had enough physical exertion.
    7. What part will scrimmages play in your overall practice time?
    8. What would you do to promote your sport—during the season and out-of-season?
    9. What would you do to encourage students to participate in your sport?

IV. Special Questions

    A. How does the candidate handle these situations?

        1. Athlete who refuses to follow instruction or fails to perform to expectations due to lack of effort.

        2. Athlete who throws a tantrum every time a call goes against him/her or he/she makes a bad play.

        3. An athlete who is sulking because he/she is not playing.

        4. An athlete who wants to be excused every Monday to go to some other activity.

        5. An athlete "who knows more" than you.

        6. The athlete who comes an hour late to practice the day before the big game.

        7. An irate parent who confronts you right after the contest about their son/daughter not playing.

Appendix G
Average Teaching Salaries by State
2005-2006 and 2007-2008

State	2005-2006	2007-2008
Alabama	$40,347	$46,604
Alaska	$53,553	$56,758
Arizona	$44,672	$45,772
Arkansas	$42,748	$45,773
California	$59,825	$64,424
Colorado	$44,439	$47,248
Connecticut	$59,304	$61,976
Delaware	$54,264	$55,994
Dist. Columbia	$59,000	$60,628
Florida	$43,302	$46,930
Georgia	$48,300	$51,560
Hawaii	$49,292	$53,400
Idaho	$41,150	$45,099
Illinois	$58,686	$60,474
Indiana	$47,255	$48,508
Iowa	$41,083	$46,664
Kansas	$41,467	$45,136
Kentucky	$42,592	$47,207
Louisiana	$40,029	$46,964
Maine	$40,737	$43,397
Maryland	$54,333	$60,069
Massachusetts	$56,639	$60,471
Michigan	$54,739	$56,096
Minnesota	$48,489	$50,582
Mississippi	$40,576	$42,403
Missouri	$40,462	$43,206
Montana	$39,832	$42,874
Nebraska	$40,382	$42,885
Nevada	$44,426	$47,710
New Hampshire	$45,263	$47,609

New Jersey	$58,156	$61,277
New Mexico	$41,637	$45,112
New York	$57,354	$62,332
North Carolina	$43,922	$47,354
North Dakota	$37,764	$40,279
Ohio	$50,314	$53,410
Oklahoma	$38,772	$43,551
Oregon	$50,044	$51,811
Pennsylvania	$54,027	$55,833
Rhode Island	$54,730	$57,168
South Carolina	$43,011	$45,758
South Dakota	$34,709	$36,674
Tennessee	$42,537	$45,030
Texas	$41,744	$46,179
Utah	$40,007	$41,615
Vermont	$46,622	$46,593
Virginia	$43,823	$46,976
Washington	$46,326	$49,884
West Virginia	$38,284	$42,529
Wisconsin	$46,390	$49,051
Wyoming	$43,255	$53,074

http://www.theapple.com/careers/articles/7514-teaching-salaries-2005-2006-2007-2008

Source: NEA Research. Accessed 06-07-09

Appendix H

Average Beginning Teacher Salaries, 2004-05 to 2006-07, Ranked by State for 2006-07

Rank	State	2004-05 Beginning Teacher Salary	2005-06 Beginning Teacher Salary	Change 2004-05 to 2005-06	2006-07 Beginning Teacher Salary	Change 2005-06 to 2006-07
1	New Jersey	$41,403 a	$43,068	4.0%	$44,523	3.4%
2	Alaska	$38,657	$40,523	4.8%	$42,006	3.7%
3	Connecticut	$39,259	$39,898	1.6%	$41,497	4.0%
4	Maryland	$37,125	$38,649	4.1%	$40,849	5.7%
5	Wyoming	$30,097 a	$32,257	7.2%	$40,084	24.3%
6	Delaware	$37,648 a	$38,547	2.4%	$39,941 b	3.6%
7	New York	$37,321	$39,000	4.5%	$39,500 c	1.3%
8	Hawaii	$35,814 a	$37,317	4.2%	$39,361	5.5%
9	California	$35,760	$36,893	3.2%	$38,875	5.4%
10	Texas	$34,179 a	$34,891	2.1%	$38,522	10.4%
11	Illinois	$37,500	$40,130	7.0%	$38,363 b	−4.4%
12	Florida	$33,427	$34,517	3.3%	$37,600 b	8.9%
13	Pennsylvania	$34,978 a	$35,782	2.3%	$36,599	2.3%
14	Oklahoma	$31,732 a	$32,725	3.1%	$36,278 d, e	10.9%
15	Colorado	$32,464 a	$34,961	7.7%	$36,211	3.6%
16	Ohio	$33,671	$33,782	0.3%	$35,676	5.6%
17	Alabama	$31,364 a	$32,973	5.1%	$35,517	7.7%
18	Nevada	$33,737 a	$34,580	2.5%	$35,480	2.6%
19	Oregon	$33,704 a	$34,691	2.9%	$35,400 d, e	2.0%
20	Arizona	$30,404	$33,070	8.8%	$35,127	6.2%
21	Rhode Island	$33,815	$33,783	−0.1%	$34,838	3.1%
22	Louisiana	$31,283 a	$32,045	2.4%	$34,410 b	7.4%
23	Michigan	$35,557	n/a		$34,100	
24	Tennessee	$31,768 a	$31,939	0.5%	$33,459 b	4.8%
25	Minnesota	$31,656 a	$31,855	0.6%	$33,018	3.7%
26	Mississippi	$29,993 a	$32,173	7.3%	$32,141	−0.1%
27	New Mexico	$33,730	$31,315	−7.2%	$32,081	2.4%
28	Indiana	$30,844	$31,022	0.6%	$32,076	3.4%
29	Georgia	$29,552 f	$30,441	3.0%	$31,659 f	4.0%
30	Wisconsin	$25,222	$30,021	19.0%	$31,588	5.2%
31	North Carolina	$26,944	$28,906	3.4%	$31,478	8.9%
32	Washington	$30,120 a	$30,485	1.2%	$31,442	3.1%

33	South Carolina	$29,696 a	$30,556	2.9%	$31,336	2.6%
34	Kentucky	$29,256 a	$30,539	4.4%	$31,304	2.5%
35	Missouri	$29,276	$30,036	2.6%	$31,285	4.2%
36	West Virginia	$26,704	$28,090	5.2%	$30,626	9.0%
37	Arkansas	$28,784	$29,353	2.0%	$30,510	3.9%
38	Kansas	$27,840	$29,282	5.2%	$30,408	3.8%
39	Iowa	$27,284	$28,508	4.5%	$30,331	6.4%
40	New Hampshire	$28,297 a	$29,234	3.3%	$30,185	3.3%
41	Idaho	$27,500	$27,500	0.0%	$30,000	9.1%
42	Nebraska	$28,000 a	$27,517	−1.7%	$29,215	6.2%
43	Utah	$26,521	$27,437	3.5%	$28,653	4.4%
44	Maine	$26,643	$27,212	2.1%	$28,517	4.8%
45	Montana	$25,318	$26,022	2.8%	$27,134	4.3%
46	North Dakota	$24,872	$25,657	3.2%	$27,064	5.5%
47	South Dakota	$26,111	n/a[g]		$26,988	
	Massachusetts	$35,421	n/a[g]		n/a[g]	
	Vermont	$26,461	n/a[g]		n/a[g]	
	Virginia	$33,200	n/a[g]		n/a[g]	
	U.S. Average	**$32,158** h	**$33,227**	**3.3%**	**$35,284** h	**6.2%**

a. The 2004-05 beginning teacher salary numbers in some instances have been revised by state education agencies and therefore differ from the reporting in the AFT Survey and Analysis of Teacher Salary Trends 2005, thus altering the U.S. beginning average;

b. includes extra-duty pay;

c. median;

d. includes employer pick-up of employee pension contributions where applicable;

e. includes fringe benefits such as healthcare where applicable.

f. Georgia's state salary does not include district supplemental pay.

g. These states did not provide a response to the request for beginning teacher salaries.

h. The U.S. average for beginning teacher salary is a straight average of data received.

Source: American Federation of Teachers, annual survey of state departments of education. 2008, Page 24 / AFT Research and Information Services

http://www.aft.org/salary/2007/download/AFT2007SalarySurvey.pdf

Matthew Di Carlo, Associate, Research and Information Services
Nate Johnson, Assistant, Research and Information Services
with Pat Cochran, Staff, Research and Information Services

Retrieved 06-09-09

PHOTO CREDITS

Pages 1, 109, 216, 340, 439, 546, 559, 566, 579: Courtesy of Western Illinois University Visual Production Center

Page 3: Courtesy of Tampa Bay Rays.

Pages 13, 64, 262, 328, 334, 367, 383, 505, 534, 568, 590: Courtesy of the National Junior College Athletic Association (NJCAA)

Pages 42, 305: Courtesy of University of California, Santa Cruz, Sports Information. Photo by Dan Wood

Page 351: Courtesy of University of California, Santa Cruz, Sports Information.

Pages 15, 23, 88, 90, 111, 134, 139, 176, 179; 198, 212, 302, 326, 361, 374, 378, 417, 431, 465, 514: Courtesy of the College at Brockport, State University of New York, Photo by James Dusen.

Pages 59, 167, 170, 291, 409, 497, 611: Courtesy of University of Louisville Sports Information.

Pages 69, 114, 449: Courtesy of the National Association of Intercollegiate Athletics (NAIA).

Page 77: Courtesy of Vanderbilt University.

Pages 123, 155, 161, 319, 339: Courtesy of University of Nebraska at Omaha. Photo by Tim Fitzgerald.

Page 125: Courtesy of Rutgers University-Camden. Photo by Curt Hudson.

Page 191: Courtesy of Appalachian State University, Sports Information. Photo by Jonathan Williams.

Pages 401, 473: Courtesy of Appalachian State University, Sports Information.

Page 205: Courtesy of Cardinal Stritch College, Office of Sports Information.

Pages 222, 391, 584, 622: Courtesy of Texas Tech University Sports Information.

Pages 235, 424, 524, 563: Courtesy University of Arizona, Media Relations.

Page 247: Courtesy of Buffalo State College, State University of New York.

Pages 256, 288, 294, 357: Courtesy of the University of Southern California (USC).

Page 303: Courtesy of Azusa Pacific University, Sports Information. Photo by Gary Pine.

Page 486: Courtesy of Azusa Pacific University, Sports Information, Photo by Ken Williams.

Page 307: Courtesy of Air Cannons, Aurora, Colorado.

Pages 325, 475: Courtesy University of Tampa, Sports Information. Photo by Andy Meng.

INDEX